THE INSTITUTE FOR POLISH–JEWISH STUDIES

The Institute for Polish–Jewish Studies in Oxford and its sister organization, the American Association for Polish–Jewish Studies, which publish Polin, are learned societies which were established in 1984, following the First International Conference on Polish–Jewish Studies, held in Oxford. The Institute is an associate institute of the Oxford Centre for Hebrew and Jewish Studies, and the American Association is linked with the Department of Near Eastern and Judaic Studies at Brandeis University.

Both the Institute and the American Association aim to promote understanding of the Polish Jewish past. They have no building or library of their own and no paid staff; they achieve their aims by encouraging scholarly research and facilitating its publication, and by creating forums for people with a scholarly interest in Polish Jewish topics, both past and present.

To this end the Institute and the American Association help organize lectures and international conferences. Venues for these activities have included Brandeis University in Waltham, Massachusetts, the Hebrew University in Jerusalem, the Institute for the Study of Human Sciences in Vienna, King's College in London, the Jagiellonian University in Kraków, the Oxford Centre for Hebrew and Jewish Studies, the University of Łódź, University College London, and the Polish Cultural Centre and the Polish embassy in London. They have encouraged academic exchanges between Israel, Poland, the United States, and western Europe. In particular they seek to help train a new generation of scholars, in Poland and elsewhere, to study the culture and history of the Jews in Poland.

Each year since 1987 the Institute has published a volume of scholarly papers in the series *Polin: Studies in Polish Jewry* under the general editorship of Professor Antony Polonsky of Brandeis University. Since 1994 the series has been published on its behalf by the Littman Library of Jewish Civilization, and since 1998 the publication has been linked with the American Association as well. In March 2000 the entire series was honoured with a National Jewish Book Award from the Jewish Book Council in the United States. More than twenty other works on Polish Jewish topics have also been published with the Institute's assistance.

For further information on the Institute for Polish–Jewish Studies or the American Association for Polish–Jewish Studies, contact <polin@littman.co.uk>. For the website of the American Association for Polish–Jewish Studies, see <www.brandeis.edu/aapjs/>.

*This publication has been supported by
a donation in memory of*

DR GEORGE WEBBER
(1899–1982)

scholar, Hebraist, jurist

THE LITTMAN LIBRARY OF
JEWISH CIVILIZATION

Dedicated to the memory of
LOUIS THOMAS SIDNEY LITTMAN
*who founded the Littman Library for the love of God
and as an act of charity in memory of his father*
JOSEPH AARON LITTMAN
יהא זכרם ברוך

*'Get wisdom, get understanding:
Forsake her not and she shall preserve thee'*
PROV. 4: 5

*The Littman Library of Jewish Civilization is a registered UK charity
Registered charity no.* 1000784

POLIN
STUDIES IN POLISH JEWRY

VOLUME NINE

Poles, Jews, Socialists

The Failure of an Ideal

Edited by
ANTONY POLONSKY
ISRAEL BARTAL, GERSHON HUNDERT
MAGDALENA OPALSKI and JERZY TOMASZEWSKI

Published for
The Institute for Polish–Jewish Studies
and
The American Association for Polish–Jewish Studies

Oxford · Portland, Oregon
The Littman Library of Jewish Civilization

The Littman Library of Jewish Civilization
Chief Executive Officer: Ludo Craddock
Managing Editor: Connie Webber
PO Box 645, Oxford OX2 0UJ, UK
www.littman.co.uk

Published in the United States and Canada by
The Littman Library of Jewish Civilization
c/o ISBS, 920 N.E. 58th Avenue, Suite 300
Portland, Oregon 97213-3786

First published in hardback 1996
First published in paperback 2008
First digital on-demand edition 2008

© *Institute for Polish–Jewish Studies 1996, 2008*

All rights reserved.
No part of this publication may be reproduced,
stored in a retrieval system, or transmitted, in any form or by
any means, without the prior permission in writing of
The Littman Library of Jewish Civilization

The paperback edition of this book is sold subject to the condition that it
shall not, by way of trade or otherwise, be lent, re-sold, hired out or
otherwise circulated without the publisher's prior consent in any
form of binding or cover other than that in which it is published
and without a similar condition including this condition
being imposed on the subsequent purchaser

A catalogue record for this book is available from the British Library
ISSN 0268 1056

ISBN 978-1-904113-81-2

Publishing co-ordinator: Janet Moth
Copy-editing: John Waś
Proof-reading: Anna Zaranko
Index: Meg Davies
Design: Pete Russell, Faringdon, Oxon.
Printed in Great Britain by Lightning Source UK, Milton Keynes,
and in the United States by Lightning Source US, La Vergne, Tennessee

This book has been printed digitally and produced in a
standard specification in order to ensure its continuing availability.

*This volume is dedicated to
the memory of*

MARK PIPES
(1893–1973)

and

SOPHIA PIPES
(1902–1994)

Editors and Advisers

EDITORS

Monika Adamczyk-Garbowska, *Lublin*
Israel Bartal, *Jerusalem*
Antony Polonsky (Chair), *Waltham, Mass.*
Michael Steinlauf, *Philadelphia*
Jerzy Tomaszewski, *Warsaw*

EDITORIAL BOARD

Chimen Abramsky, *London*
David Assaf, *Tel Aviv*
Władysław T. Bartoszewski, *Warsaw*
Glenn Dynner, *Bronxville, NY*
David Engel, *New York*
David Fishman, *New York*
ChaeRan Freeze, *Waltham, Mass.*
Józef Gierowski, *Kraków*
Jacob Goldberg, *Jerusalem*
Yisrael Gutman, *Jerusalem*
Jerzy Kłoczowski, *Lublin*
Ezra Mendelsohn, *Jerusalem*
Joanna Michlic, *Stockton, NY*

Elchanan Reiner, *Tel Aviv*
Jehuda Reinharz, *Waltham, Mass.*
Moshe Rosman, *Tel Aviv*
Szymon Rudnicki, *Warsaw*
Henryk Samsonowicz, *Warsaw*
Robert Shapiro, *New York*
Adam Teller, *Haifa*
Daniel Tollet, *Paris*
Piotr S. Wandycz, *New Haven, Conn.*
Jonathan Webber, *Birmingham, UK*
Joshua Zimmerman, *New York*
Steven Zipperstein, *Stanford, Calif.*

ADVISORY BOARD

Władysław Bartoszewski, *Warsaw*
Jan Błoński, *Kraków*
Abraham Brumberg, *Washington*
Andrzej Chojnowski, *Warsaw*
Tadeusz Chrzanowski, *Kraków*
Andrzej Ciechanowiecki, *London*
Norman Davies, *London*
Victor Erlich, *New Haven, Conn.*
Frank Golczewski, *Hamburg*
Olga Goldberg, *Jerusalem*
Feliks Gross, *New York*
Czesław Hernas, *Wrocław*
Jerzy Jedlicki, *Warsaw*
Andrzej Kamiński, *London*

Hillel Levine, *Boston*
Lucjan Lewitter, *Cambridge, Mass.*
Stanisław Litak, *Lublin*
Heinz-Dietrich Löwe, *Heidelberg*
Emanuel Meltzer, *Tel Aviv*
Shlomo Netzer, *Tel Aviv*
Zbigniew Pełczyński, *Oxford*
Alexander Schenker, *New Haven, Conn.*
David Sorkin, *Madison, Wis.*
Edward Stankiewicz, *New Haven, Conn.*
Norman Stone, *Ankara*
Shmuel Werses, *Jerusalem*
Jacek Woźniakowski, *Lublin*
Piotr Wróbel, *Toronto*

Preface

THIS volume of *Polin* is the second to appear under the imprint of the Littman Library of Jewish Civilization in what we hope will be a long and fruitful partnership. *Polin* is sponsored by the Institute for Polish–Jewish Studies, an associate centre of the Oxford Centre for Hebrew and Jewish Studies, and by the American Association for Polish–Jewish Studies, which is linked with the Department of Near Eastern and Judaic Studies, Brandeis University. As with earlier issues, this volume could not have appeared without the untiring assistance of many individuals. In particular, we should like to express our gratitude to Professor Philip Alexander, President of the Oxford Hebrew Centre, and to the Chairman of its Publications Committee, Dr Jonathan Webber. We should also like to acknowledge the indispensable support of Professor Jehuda Reinharz, President of Brandeis University; Professor Jonathan Sarna, Chair, Department of Near Eastern and Judaic Studies, Brandeis University; and Mrs Irene Pipes, President, American Association for Polish–Jewish Studies. Like Volume VIII, this volume would never have appeared without the constant assistance and supervision of Connie Webber, managing editor of the Littman Library, Janet Moth, publishing co-ordinator, and the tireless copy-editing of John Waś. We also owe a debt to Anna Zaranko and Jolanta Kisler-Goldstein for keeping to a minimum the mistakes in the Polish language.

Plans for future volumes of *Polin* are well advanced. Volume X will have as its core a series of articles on the history of the Jews in the Polish–Lithuanian Commonwealth down to the partitions at the end of the eighteenth century. Its chief editor will be Gershon Hundert. Volume XI will be devoted to investigating the perspectives which sociology can provide on Polish–Jewish relations and the history of the Jews in Poland. We are also planning volumes on the varieties of the Jewish religious experience in Poland, on the triangular relationship of Poles, Jews, and Ukrainians in Galicia between 1772 and 1914, and on the Holocaust in the Polish lands. We welcome articles for these issues as well as for our section 'New Views'. We should also welcome any other suggestions or criticisms. In particular, we should be very grateful for assistance in extending our coverage to the areas of Ukraine, Belarus, and Lithuania, both in the period in which these countries were part of the Polish–Lithuanian Commonwealth and subsequently.

A.P.

Acknowledgements

This volume was published with the aid of a grant from Brandeis University. Richard Pipes's essay, 'Jews and the Russian Revolution', is reprinted by kind permission of Alfred A. Knopf Inc. from Richard Pipes, *Russia under the Bolshevik Regime* (New York, 1995), pp. 112–14.

POLIN

We did not know, but our fathers told us how the exiles of Israel came to the land of Polin (Poland).

When Israel saw how its sufferings were constantly renewed, oppressions increased, persecutions multiplied, and how the evil authorities piled decree on decree and followed expulsion with expulsion, so that there was no way to escape the enemies of Israel, they went out on the road and sought an answer from the paths of the wide world: which is the correct road to traverse to find rest for the soul? Then a piece of paper fell from heaven, and on it the words:

Go to Polaniya (Poland).

So they came to the land of Polin and they gave a mountain of gold to the king, and he received them with great honour. And God had mercy on them, so that they found favour from the king and the nobles. And the king gave them permission to reside in all the lands of his kingdom, to trade over its length and breadth, and to serve God according to the precepts of their religion. And the king protected them against every foe and enemy.

And Israel lived in Polin in tranquillity for a long time. They devoted themselves to trade and handicrafts. And God sent a blessing on them so that they were blessed in the land, and their name was exalted among the peoples. And they traded with the surrounding countries and they also struck coins with inscriptions in the holy language and the language of the country. These are the coins which have on them a lion rampant towards the right. And on the coins are the words 'Mieszko, King of Poland' or 'Mieszko, Król of Poland'. The Poles call their king 'Król'.

And those who seek for names say: 'This is why it is called Polin. For thus spoke Israel when they came to the land, "Here rest for the night [Po lin]." And this means that we shall rest here until we are all gathered into the Land of Israel.'

Since this is the tradition, we accept it as such.

S. Y. AGNON, 1916

POLIN
Studies in Polish Jewry

VOLUME 1 *Poles and Jews: Renewing the Dialogue* (1986)

VOLUME 2 *Jews and the Emerging Polish State* (1987)

VOLUME 3 *The Jews of Warsaw* (1988)

VOLUME 4 *Poles and Jews: Perceptions and Misperceptions* (1989)

VOLUME 5 *New Research, New Views* (1990)

VOLUME 6 *Jews in Łódź, 1820–1939* (1991)

VOLUME 7 *Jewish Life in Nazi-Occupied Warsaw* (1992)

From Shtetl to Socialism (1993): selected articles from volumes 1–7

VOLUME 8 *Jews in Independent Poland, 1918–1939* (1994)

VOLUME 9 *Jews, Poles, Socialists: The Failure of an Ideal* (1996)

VOLUME 10 *Jews in Early Modern Poland* (1997)

VOLUME 11 *Aspects and Experiences of Religion* (1998)

VOLUME 12 *Galicia: Jews, Poles, and Ukrainians, 1772–1918* (1999)

Index to Volumes 1–12 (2000)

VOLUME 13 *The Holocaust and its Aftermath* (2000)

VOLUME 14 *Jews in the Polish Borderlands* (2001)

VOLUME 15 *Jewish Religious Life, 1500–1900* (2002)

VOLUME 16 *Jewish Popular Culture and its Afterlife* (2003)

VOLUME 17 *The Shtetl: Myth and Reality* (2004)

VOLUME 18 *Jewish Women in Eastern Europe* (2005)

VOLUME 19 *Polish–Jewish Relations in North America* (2006)

VOLUME 20 *Making Holocaust Memory* (2008)

VOLUME 21 *1968: Forty Years After* (2009)

VOLUME 22 *Early Modern Poland: Borders and Boundaries* (2010)

VOLUME 23 *Jews in Kraków* (2011)

Contents

Note on Transliteration, Names, and Place Names	xiv
Abbreviations	xv
Introduction ANTONY POLONSKY	xvii

PART I

POLES, JEWS, SOCIALISTS: THE FAILURE OF AN IDEAL

Jewish Socialists in the Kingdom of Poland ALINA CAŁA	3
The Jewish Problem in Polish Socialist Thought MICHAŁ ŚLIWA	14
The Relation of the Polish Socialist Party: Proletariat to the Bund and the Jewish Question, 1900–1906 JANUSZ SUJECKI	32
The Jews, the Left, and the State Duma Elections in Warsaw in 1912: Selected Sources *translated by* STEPHEN D. CORRSIN	45
Jews and the Russian Revolution: A Note RICHARD PIPES	55
The Bund in Poland, 1935–1939 DANIEL BLATMAN	58
Łódź Remained Red: Elections to the City Council of 27 September 1936 BARBARA WACHOWSKA	83
The Jews of Vilna under Soviet Rule, 19 September–28 October 1939 DOV LEVIN	107
The Polish Underground and the Extermination of the Jews SHMUEL KRAKOWSKI	138

The Jewish Underground and the Polish Underground   148
TERESA PREKEROWA

The Pogrom in Kielce on 4 July 1946   158
STANISŁAW MEDUCKI

Antisemitism in Poland in 1956   170
PAWEŁ MACHCEWICZ

PART II
NEW VIEWS

Dov of Bolechów: A Diarist of the Council of Four Lands in the Eighteenth Century   187
ISRAEL BARTAL

A Peaceable Community at Work: The *Chevrah* of Nasielsk   192
ROSS KESSEL

Zionist Pioneering Youth Movements in Poland and their Attitude to Erets Israel during the Holocaust   195
DINA PORAT

Resistance through Education: Polish Zionist Youth Movements in Warsaw, 1939–1941   212
ERICA NADELHAFT

The Second Competition of Scholarly Works on Polish Jewish Themes   232
ALINA CAŁA

PART III
REVIEWS

REVIEW ESSAYS

History, Drama, and Healing: On the Television Play *A i B*, by Harvey Sarner   247
DAVID ENGEL

Inside, Outside: Interpreting Jewish Difference   255
SYLVIA BARACK FISHMAN

BOOK REVIEWS

Alfred Ebenbauer and Klaus Zatloukal (eds.), *Die Juden in ihrer mittelalterlichen Umwelt*   271
FRIEDRICH LOTTER

Rivka Schatz-Uffenheimer, *Hasidism as Mysticism* 274
LOUIS JACOBS

Jadwiga Maurer, '*Z matki obcej* . . .' 276
JOANNA ROSTROPOWICZ CLARK

Władysław T. Bartoszewski and Antony Polonsky (eds.), *The Jews in Warsaw* 280
PATRICIA HERLIHY

Maria Klańska, *Problemfeld Galizien in deutschsprachiger Prosa 1846–1914* 282
JOSEF SCHMIDT

Israel Oppenheim, *Tenuat Heḥaluts bePolin, 1929–1939* 284
MARK A. RAIDER

The Letters of Martin Buber, ed. Nahum N. Glatzer and Paul Mendes-Flohr 286
MICHAEL OPPENHEIM

Alexander Beider, *A Dictionary of Jewish Surnames from the Russian Empire* 289
PAUL WEXLER

Alice L. Eckardt (ed.), *Burning Memory* 295
JOHN S. CONWAY

Ruta Sakowska, *Ludzie z dzielnicy zamkniętej* 297
ALINA CAŁA

Iwona Irwin-Zarecka, *Neutralizing Memory* 299
ALINA CAŁA

Stanisław Meducki and Zenon Wrona (eds.), *Antyżydowskie wydarzenia kieleckie, 4 lipca 1946* 302
BOŻENA SZAYNOK

BIBLIOGRAPHY OF POLISH–JEWISH STUDIES, 1993 305
GERSHON HUNDERT

Notes on Contributors 319

Notes on Translators 322

Glossary 323

Index 329

Note on Transliteration, Names, and Place Names

IT has not been possible to achieve total consistency in the transliteration of Yiddish and Hebrew in this book, nor in the spelling of people's names. In the case of Hebrew, this is because both modern and traditional Ashkenazic styles of pronunciation were used in pre-war Poland, the latter moreover in a variety of regional and other dialectical forms; it was considered inappropriate and unhistorical to impose standardization. For Hebrew bibliographic references, however, a system of transcription has been used that aims at representing the pronunciation prescribed today for modern Hebrew to an English-speaking reader. For Yiddish, the transcription adopted follows the YIVO system—except for people's names, where the spellings they themselves used (which normally followed the Polish orthographic system) have been retained. Place names, in contrast, are spelt in the correct Polish way, even though Jews often used Yiddish names; this has been done so as to enable readers to find the places on maps and correlate information with Polish sources. In some cases, because borders have changed, we have given Lithuanian, Byelorussian, or Ukrainian forms of place names.

Abbreviations

AK	Armia Krajowa (Home Army), the principal underground resistance movement in Poland during the Second World War
BBWR	Bezpartyjny Blok Współpracy z Rządem (Non-Party Bloc for Co-operation with the Government), a political organization created after the coup of May 1926 to support the government of Marshal Piłsudski
CeKaBe	Centralne Towarzystwo Popierania Kredytu Bezprocentowego i Krzewienia Pracy Produktywnej wśród Ludności Żydowskiej w Polsce (Central Association for the Support of Interest-Free Credit and the Encouragement of Productive Work among the Jewish Community in Poland)
ChD	Chrześcijańska Demokracja (Christian Democracy)
ChZZ	Chrześcijańskie Zjednoczenie Zawodowe (Christian Trade Association)
CKR	Centralny Komitet Robotniczy (Central Workers' Committee)
DSAP	Deutsche Sozialistische Arbeitspartei (German Socialist Workers' Party)
FON	Fundusz Obrony Narodowej (Fund for National Defence)
JDC	Joint Distribution Committee
JNF	Jewish National Fund
KPP	Komunistyczna Partia Polski (Communist Party of Poland)
NKVD	Narodnii Komisariat Vnutriennykh Diel (People's Commissariat for Internal Affairs)
NPR	Narodowa Partia Robotnicza (National Workers' Party)
NSZ	Narodowe Siły Zbrojne (National Armed Forces)
ORT	Obshchestvo Razpostranienia Truda (Russian: Organization for Rehabilitation for Training)
OZON	Obóz Zjednoczenia Narodowego (Camp of National Unification)
PKW	Polski Komitet Wyborczy (Polish Electoral Committee)
POP	Podstawowa Organizacja Partyjna (Basic Party Cell)
PPR	Polska Partia Robotnicza (Polish Workers' Party)
PPS	Polska Partia Socjalistyczna (Polish Socialist Party)
PPSD	Polska Partia Socjalno-Demokratyczna Galicji i Śląska (Polish Social Democratic Party of Galicia and Silesia), the main Polish Socialist party in Galicia (Austrian Poland)
PSL	Polskie Stronnictwo Ludowe (Polish Peasant Party)
PZPR	Polska Zjednoczona Partia Robotnicza (Polish United Workers' Party)

RSDRP	Rosiiskaya Sotsial-Demokraticheskaya i Rabochaya Partia (Russian Social Democratic and Labour Party)
RSFSR	Rosiiskaya Sotsyalicheskaya Federalnaya Sovietskaya Republika (Russian Socialist Federal Soviet Republic), formal name for Russia in the Soviet period
SDKPil	Socjaldemokracja Królestwa Polskiego i Litwy (the Social Democracy of the Kingdom of Poland and Lithuania)
SL	Stronnictowo Ludowe (Peasant Party)
SRCh	Stowarzyszenie Robotników Chrześcijańskich (Association of Christian Workers)
TPD	Towarzystwo Przyjaciół Dzieci (Society of the Friends of Children)
Tsisho	Tsentrale Yidishe Shul-Organizatsie (Central Yiddish School Organization)
TSKŻ	Towarzystwo Społeczno-Kulturalne Żydów w Polsce (Social-Cultural Society of the Jews in Poland)
UB	Urząd Bezpieczeństwa (Office of Security)
WIZO	Womens' International Zionist Organization
WUBP	Wojewódzki Urząd Bezpieczeństwa Publicznego (Voivodship Office of Public Security)
YIVO	Yidisher Vissentshaftlikhe Organisatsie (Jewish Scholarly Organization)
ŻO PPS	Żydowska Organizacja PPS (Jewish Organization of the PPS)
ŻOB	Żydowska Organizacja Bojowa (Jewish Fighting Organization)
ŻPSD	Żydowska Partia Socjalno-Demokratyczna (Jewish Social Democratic Party)
ZSL	Zjednoczone Stronnictwo Ludowe (United Peasant Party)
ZZSP	Związek Zagraniczny Socjalistów Polskich (Union of Polish Socialists Abroad)

Introduction

ANTONY POLONSKY

> ... the less antisemitism will exist among Christians, the easier it will be to unite the social forces ... and the sooner a workers' solidarity will emerge: a solidarity of all who are exploited and wronged. Jew, Pole, Lithuanian, we are equally exploited ... we are all equally wronged by Moscow ... Let us encourage Jewish comrades whenever we meet them.
>
> JÓZEF PIŁSUDSKI,
> 'Kwestia Żydowska na Litwie', *Walka*
> (November 1903)

THIS pious hope, expressed by the man who was probably the dominant figure in Polish politics in the first half of the twentieth century and who was himself a Socialist at the beginning of his political career, when he wrote the article from which the quotation is taken, sums up the theme of this volume. A great deal of work has been done on the relationship between the Jews and the Socialist movement in the German-speaking lands. Works like Robert Wistrich's *Socialism and the Jews: The Dilemmas of Assimilation in Germany and Austria* (East Brunswick, NJ, 1982) and Jack Jacob's *On Socialists and 'The Jewish Question' after Marx* (New York, 1992) have illuminated questions such as the attitude of the Socialist movement and its principal ideologists towards the 'Jewish Question' and towards the development of political antisemitism and the reasons for the widespread support given by Jews in Germany and Austria-Hungary to Socialist parties in conditions in which this seemed to go against their economic interests.

Much less research has been undertaken into these problems in the Polish lands. In the period of Communist rule this was for a long time a taboo topic. When censorship began to relax, attention was concentrated on the vexed question of the role of the Jews in the Communist movement and in the Communist regime after 1944, particularly in its early years. This was also the main topic which interested *émigré* scholars. Some important work was done in the area including Paul Lendvai's *Antisemitism in Eastern Europe* (London, 1971), Michał Chęciński's *Poland: Communism, Nationalism, Anti-semitism* (New York, 1982), Jaff Schatz's *The Generation: The Rise and Fall of the Generation of Jewish Communists in Poland* (Berkeley, 1991), and particularly Krystyna Kersten's *Polacy, Żydzi, Komunizm* (Warsaw, 1991). These works have greatly illuminated this important problem, but they have often had an apologetic character, attempting either to explain Jewish support for Communism or to explain the persistence of antisemitism in Poland by this alleged Jewish support for Communism.

In fact, the question of the impact of Jewish issues on the Socialist movement in the Polish lands is considerably more complex than is suggested by attempts to analyse the nature and character of the myths and facts which surround the concept of Żydokomuna (Judaeo-Communism). In this volume we have attempted to deal with the multi-sided nature of the problem. Much more research remains to be done, and it has been above all our intention to suggest the areas which would repay more investigation. In the first place, there is the question of why Socialism, whether in its reformist or in its revolutionary forms, was attractive to so many Jews. This is discussed in the articles by Alina Cała, Daniel Blatman, and Barbara Wachowska, whose analysis of the victory of the combined forces of the left in the municipal elections of 1936 in Łódź not only illustrates the possibilities and problems inherent in co-operation between Polish and Jewish Socialist organizations, but also shows how middle-class Jews could be persuaded to vote for the Polish Socialist Party (PPS) in order to defeat the antisemitic right. Similar issues are raised by the documents on the election to the Russian Duma in October 1912 edited by Stephen Corrsin. A number of different factors seem to be involved in the Jewish attraction to Socialism. In the first place, it seemed to offer a road to integration into the larger society at a time when the liberal emancipationist principle of transforming the Jews from a religious and historical community, linked by a common culture and way of life which transcended national boundaries, into Englishmen, Frenchmen, or Poles of the Hebrew faith seemed no longer to be a viable alternative, at least in east central Europe. This was well articulated in general terms by the German pioneer sociologist and social democratic activist Robert Michels. He explained the prominence of Jews in socialist movements

> by the peculiar position which the Jews have occupied and in many respects still occupy. The legal emancipation of the Jews has not been followed by their social and moral emancipation . . . Even when they are rich the Jews constitute . . . a category of persons excluded from the social advantages which the prevailing political, economic, and intellectual systems ensure for the corresponding portion of the Gentile population . . . For all these reasons, the Jewish intelligence is apt to find a shorter road to socialism than the Gentile.[1]

Ezra Mendelsohn has described what this meant in the conditions of east central Europe: 'if these intellectuals were no longer able to identify with the old Jewish culture nor free to become assimilated into Russian life, they could at least identify with "the people", the peasant, or the proletariat'.[2]

---

[1] Robert Michels, *Political Parties* (New York, 1959), 259–60.
[2] Ezra Mendelsohn, *Class Struggles in the Pale* (Cambridge, 1970), 29.

Then, many Jews may have been attracted to the Socialist idea, seeing it consciously or unconsciously as a secularized version of the age-old Jewish Messianic longing. This has been convincingly argued by Will Herberg in his article 'Socialism, Zionism and the Messianic Passion',[3] where he claims that the Messianic impulse, transformed through secularization, emerges from only one element in traditional Judaism to become the dominant passion motivating many Jewish Socialists (and also Zionists). This issue is alluded to in a number of articles in this volume, most notably those by Alina Cała and Daniel Blatman, but it would be worthy of further research.

Finally, in the Polish lands many Jews were driven to the Socialist movement by the deep poverty of the Jewish proletariat. This is strikingly described by a former Jewish Communist activist, Wacław Kuchar (whose memoirs we were unable to print in this volume because of lack of space). Describing the life of his family in Łódź just before and after the First World War, where his father was a handloom weaver, he wrote:

The ceiling of the room was very low and there was no running water, toilet, or electricity, not to mention other necessities . . . Every bucket of water had to be carried through the long back yard up to the fourth floor. Every bucket filled with garbage or excrement had to be carried down from the fourth floor to the sewer. Seven of us lived in this room . . . my father worked as a contractor . . . From daybreak in the summer, and by the light of an oil lamp late in the evening in the wintertime, spindles with colourful threads on the big handloom beat out the measures of a weaver's life of resignation and helplessness. . . .

Contractors were exploited: they had no insurance and they lived and worked without work regulations. My father's work was tied to the seasons. During the summer months he wove heavy wool scarves with fringes for the following winter, and during the winter months, lighter scarves for the next summer . . . The average working day for a contractor was twelve to fourteen hours, and in the peak of the season everyone wanted to weave as much as possible, so after only a few hours of sleep my father was again at the loom . . . When he returned home with money he always bought some treat on his way . . . On Fridays he would buy fish for Saturday. It wasn't a carp or a pike, it was a small fish, cheap and full of bones, yet the tradition was maintained . . . On weekdays, in my childhood, dinner always consisted of one course: a thick soup when we had some money, and a thin one when there was hardly any work. Even if we had enough to buy some meat, it was boiled in the soup; each of us got a little piece on a plate so we could feel full longer.

Secondly, there is the question of the attitude of the various Socialist groupings to the 'Jewish Question' and to the development of antisemitism. This is a complex of issues which has been thoroughly investigated in the German-speaking lands, and as a result we have a much clearer idea of the views of the leading Socialist ideologists, starting from Marx himself, concerning Jewish issues. Much more remains to be done on the Polish lands, and the articles by Michał Śliwa, Janusz Sujecki and Paweł Machcewicz suggest some fruitful lines of

---

[3] *Midstream*, 2/3 (Summer 1956), 68.

approach. Daniel Blatman and Barbara Wachowska both describe how the question of the correct way to deal with antisemitism created serious problems for Socialist activists, concerned both to defeat a reactionary and anti-socialist ideology and to retain the support of their rank and file, among whom hostility to the Jews as a group was often widespread.

Thirdly, there is the character of the specifically Jewish Socialist groups which developed in the Polish lands, especially the General Jewish Workers' Alliance (the Bund) and the various Labour Zionist groups such as Po'alei Tsion. Much has been written on the history of the Bund before the First World War, but there is much less on the period between the two world wars, when the party evolved towards a social-democratic position and began to develop a not always firm alliance with the Polish Socialist Party. In the late 1930s the growth of antisemitism and the apparent bankruptcy of the political positions of the other Jewish parties gained for the Bund a mass following on the 'Jewish street'. These developments are described in the article of Daniel Blatman, author of an important doctoral thesis on the Bund and its allies in England and the United States in the years between 1939 and 1947.

Finally, there is the question of the effect which Jewish support for Socialist groupings had on Polish–Jewish relations. This is a somewhat wider issue than the problems raised by the vexed question of the role of the Jews in the Communist movement in Poland and the establishment and consolidation of Communist rule there. From the first emergence of Socialist groups in the Polish lands, there were strong differences of views among them about how to achieve the Socialist millennium. Whereas Józef Piłsudski believed—as expressed in the quotation at the head of this Introduction—that the interests of Jewish Socialists and of the Jews in general were best served by supporting the struggle for Polish independence, the Bund was interested in a general Socialist transformation of the Russian Empire, which would also make possible the achievement of Jewish civic and possibly national rights. According to the Bund's 1897 programme, 'A general union of all Jewish Socialists will have as its goal not only the struggle for general Russian political demands; it will also have the special task of defending the specific interests of the Jewish workers, carrying on the struggle for their civic rights, and, above all, combating the discriminatory anti-Jewish laws.' Those Jews who were involved in the Russian revolutionary movement or in its Polish offshoots like the Socjaldemokracja Królestwa Polskiego i Litwy (SDKPiL: the Social Democracy of the Kingdom of Poland and Lithuania) were even less interested in the goal of Polish independence. It was Lenin himself who wrote in 1913 that 'those Jewish Marxists who, in international Marxist organizations amalgamate with the Russian, Lithuanian, Ukrainian, etc. workers, contributing their might (in Russian and in Yiddish) to the creation of the international culture of the working-class movement, such Jews, despite the separatism of the Bund, continue the best traditions of the Jews, fighting the slogan of "national culture".'⁴ These issues are examined by Alina Cała, Janusz Sujecki, and Michał Śliwa. Professor Śliwa also looks at the way these issues were transformed by the achievement of Polish independence in the aftermath of the First World War, as do Daniel Blatman and Barbara Wachowska.

The role of the Jews in the Communist movement is discussed by Richard Pipes, who investigates the question of Jews in the Bolshevik Party, and by Dov Levin, who shows that the attitude of Jews to the establishment of Soviet power in Vilna in September 1939 is considerably more complex than is sometimes suggested. In an important exchange, Shmuel Krakowski and Teresa Prekerowa dispute the extent to which the attitude of the Polish underground movements, above all the Armia Krajowa (AK: Home Army), towards the Nazi anti-Jewish genocide and the Jewish resistance movement was conditioned by the belief that a significant part of the Jewish underground was sympathetic to Communism. Aspects of the Jewish question in the immediate postwar period and in the upheaval of 1956 which led to the end of Stalinism in Poland are examined by Stanisław Meducki and Paweł Machcewicz.

We are conscious of how much more work remains to be done, and we hope that this volume will stimulate some of this research, particularly since the new political conditions mean that archives which were long inaccessible are now fully open.

In particular, we should have liked to have more material on the role of Communists of Jewish origin in the interwar period and on the attempts of the Bund to create a Socialist Jewish culture. Local studies of the various Jewish Socialist groupings would also add significantly to our understanding of the political geography of Poland and of its Jewish community.

This volume also has a section of articles dealing with new views ranging over the whole of the Polish Jewish past. In addition, we include two review essays, and again have a full review section. One innovation is our bibliography of Polish Jewish Studies for the year 1993, edited by Gershon Hundert, a feature which we hope to include in all future volumes. We welcome suggestions for what should be included in this bibliography as well as for articles and themes for future volumes.

⁴ V. I. Lenin, *Critical Remarks on the National Question, 1913*, (Moscow, 1954), 27.

PART I

Poles, Jews, Socialists
The Failure of an Ideal

Jewish Socialists in the Kingdom of Poland

ALINA CAŁA

SOCIALISM at the end of the nineteenth century owed much to the assimilated Jewish intelligentsia. Their presence was noted in all Socialist organizations, parties, spin-offs and factions in the Russian Empire, across the three partitions of Poland, and in Europe. Among the political prisoners sentenced to Siberia by the Tsar between 1878 and 1880, about 4 per cent were Jewish Socialists.[1] They played the leading role in Russian social democracy, and were activists in all the revolutionary organizations of Russia, Lithuania, and Poland. With great fervour they produced underground press material and smuggled it across the border, worked among the Polish, Lithuanian, and Russian workers, and, dressed as peasants, agitated in the villages of the Empire. They were not, however, very interested in the problems of their own group. They saw the emancipation of the Jewish masses as dependent upon the emancipation of the entire proletariat. They perceived the 'dumb, backward' Jewish masses much as this group was regarded by assimilation activists, seeing in them solely 'insignificant gesheftists and profiteers'.[2]

In the Vilna circle of *narodnik*s, the companions of Józef Piłsudski were Aron Zundelewicz, Izaak Kaminer, Aron Samuel Lieberman, Abe Finkelstein, Leon Jogiches, Charles Rapoport, J. Martov-Tsederbaum, Yosif Mill, and Arkady Kremer (subsequently founder of the Bund), as well as Izaak Dembo, who was later implicated in plans to assassinate the Tsar and the Prussian Emperor.[3] It was in Vilna that Zofia Sandberg, sisters Rachel and Fanny Puzyreński, Ewa Gordon, and sisters Ester and Elżbieta Gordon[4]—later activists in the organization Proletariat—began their activist careers.

---

[1] *Literatura Partii 'Narodnoy Voli'* (St Petersburg, 1905), 356, cited in *Katorga i Zsyłka*, 38 (1928), 29–56.
[2] L. Deich, cited in L. Greenberg, *The Jews in Russia* (2 vols.; New York, 1976), i. 148.
[3] A. Tartakower, 'Ruch proletariatu żydowskiego w dobie przedwojennej', in I. Schiper (ed.), *Żydzi w Polsce Odrodzonej* (2 vols.; Warsaw, 1936), i. 535–6.
[4] A. Tsherikover, 'Der unhoyb fun yiddisher socialistisher bavegung', in *Historisher Shriftn* (Warsaw, 1929), vol. i; L. Baumgarten, 'Rewolucjoniści Żydzi w pierwszych polskich kółkach socjalistycznych i w Wielkim Proletariacie', *Biuletyn ŻIH* 47–8 (1963), 3–28; L. Baumgarten, 'Pierwsze kółko żydowskiej młodzieży rewolucyjnej w Warszawie', *Biuletyn ŻIH* 63 (1967), 65–88.

Things progressed to the point where a conspiratorial circle was active even in the Vilna Rabbinical School. One of its partisans was Aron Samuel Lieberman (1844–80). The grandson of the rabbi of Łuna (Grodno province) and son of a *maskil* and Hebrew publicist, in 1874 he began to work in Zundelewicz's group within Narodnaya Volya [The People's Will]. Barely a year later, threatened with prosecution, he escaped across the border. In London he associated himself with Piotr Lavrov's *narodnik* publication *Vperiod* [Forward]. Lavrov, in an effort to reconcile revolution with tradition, had discerned threads of Socialism in the beginnings of Christianity as well as in the institution of *obshchina*, an archaic form of landownership still maintained among Russian peasants into the nineteenth century.[5] Copying Lavrov's tortuous historical-philosophical ideas, Lieberman referred to the inheritance of the Old Testament:

> For us Jews Socialism is not strange, *obshchina* is our way of life. Revolution is our tradition; Communism is a principle of our Torah and its decrees, finding its expression in the dictates and rules of the Bible about land, in the laws regarding '*shmitah* and *yovel*' establishing that land may not be sold to anyone for eternity, and in the precepts about equality and brotherhood. Our ancient social structure was anarchy; our mutual connections form the Internationale. In the spirit of our people were raised the great prophets of the current era: Marx, Lassalle, and others.[6]

In 1876 Lieberman created the Agudat Hasotsialistim Haivriyim BeLondon (Jewish Socialist Union in London). The constitution was written in an anarchical tone, which was even more evident in its call, in Hebrew, 'to the intelligent Jewish youth'. The institution of government, monarchic or republican, was described by Lieberman as one of the sources of social evil, the cause of domination by one nation over another.[7]

Lieberman contributed to the founding in Berlin of the Jewish Section of the International League of Socialist-Revolutionaries; he also organized meetings attended by his old compatriots: Zundelewicz, G. Górewicz, M. Aronson, and W. Jochelson. They resolved to publish a Hebrew-language legal publication called *Ha'emet* [The truth]. The editorial staff, composed of I. Kaminer, C. Szereszewski, M. Winczewski, and the poet L. Cukierman, adopted the *Vperiod*

---

[5] *Obshchina*, connected with a three-field rural division, was based upon periodic division among the families living in a given village of the acreage of tilled land there. In case of insufficient fertilization, the three-field system protected the land against impoverishment; it was divided into three and only one part was cultivated, the rest being left fallow. Every so often the tilled portion was abandoned and the fallow plot worked again. The village supervised the division and assigned each family a field to work. Normally, the land in its entirety counted as communal property, belonging to the village and not to individual inhabitants. This form of ownership was known throughout Slavic regions; however, it survived longest in Russia as an element of the villein system.

[6] A. Lieberman, in *Vperiod*, 35 (1875), cited in H. Piasecki, 'Aron Lieberman (1844–1880): Pionier ruchu socjalistycznego wśród Żydów', *Biuletyn ŻIH* 2/102 (1977), 19.

[7] Ibid. 23.

programme. Although this initiative was criticized by nearly all Hebrew periodicals, some *maskilim* sympathized with it. The publisher of *Hatsefirah* [Dawn], Chaim Zelig Słonimski, wrote in a letter to Lieberman: 'I am happy to see the appearance of this periodical and foresee much success for it, if there are no external barriers.'[8] Słonimski had Tsarist censorship in mind. Barriers, however, appeared from the least likely quarter. Piotr Lavrov, who tolerated Lieberman's reflections on the subject of Communistic elements in Judaic ancient history when these were printed in *Vperiod*, assumed a critical attitude towards similar expositions in the pages of *Ha'emet*, describing the periodical as 'national-liberal'. He accused the publishers of anarchistic deviation and protested against publication of the periodical. This resulted in its suspension after only three issues.

Lieberman was a somewhat troublesome activist for Socialists. His views did not fit into any of the ideological canons. 'Within him fought two spirits: that of a Hebrew *maskil* and that of a radical cosmopolitan,' in Tsherikover's words.[9] Further contradictions could be found in his personality. In advocating nihilism with a Jewish character, he sometimes used forms of argument which foreshadowed those which the Zionists were soon to create. At one of the meetings of the Jewish Socialist Union he spoke against a proposal to call a meeting on the holy day of Tishah be'Av, justifying his protest with the words: 'This day, Tishah be'Av, is the day on which we lost our freedom, and for over eighteen centuries, to this very day, our nation has observed a period of mourning for that freedom. This should mean enough to us for the meeting to be postponed.'[10]

Although Lieberman was violently antireligious, in the second issue of *Ha'emet* he assured his readers that he did not plan to fight Hasidism. He praised the youth studying in *yeshivot*, appreciating their value as the Jewish intelligentsia, from among whom 'come the best writers'.[11] Such a high evaluation of traditional schooling was something extremely rare among contemporary Jewish thinkers.

Lieberman's fervour and uncompromising views even inhibited organizations which arose from his own initiative. In 1876 his attacks on religion in a speech at the foundation rally for a labour union of Jewish workers in London led to fights between believing and non-believing workers, and this produced a great scandal. Lieberman was forced to resign from the Jewish Socialist Union, which was in fact soon dissolved. Ousted by Lavrov from his job in the printshop of *Vperiod*, he lost his sole source of livelihood. A lack of due care in the organization of the smuggling of Socialist literature to Russia in 1878 led to his arrest. Documents and lists which were found on his person gave ground for two trials, in Austria and in Prussia. Still worse, they led to the arrest of some of his confederates in Königsberg and Berlin. After serving a short sentence, and excluded from all

---

[8] Ibid. 27 (documents of the Vienna Lieberman archives).
[9] Tsherikover, 'Der unhoyb', 94.
[10] Ibid. 54 (protocol from the meeting of the Jewish Socialist Union in London, 22 June 1876).
[11] Piasecki, *Aron Lieberman*, 25.

activism, he emigrated to the United States, where he committed suicide in 1880.

Lieberman's unsuccessful attempts to 'translate' into Hebrew the historiography of Lavrov were directed more at the Jewish intelligentsia than to ordinary people. In trying to gain influence over the youth studying in *yeshivot*, his aim was to raise a cadre of activists among them. Similar principles directed Morys Winchewski when he edited *Asefat chakhamim* [Assembly of the wise], a Hebrew-language Socialist periodical which succeeded *Ha'emet*. This publication was as short-lived as Lieberman's initiative.

In contrast to the ample participation of assimilated intelligentsia in the first Socialist organizations, the Jewish proletariat remained largely unaffected until the 1890s. After the arrests which led to the break-up of the organization Proletariat in 1885, Socialist circles active in Warsaw—including Maria Bohuszewiczówna's group, whose members included, among others, Szyfra Szawel, Fanny Sztajn, and Sara Trop (formerly connected with the Vilna Socialists)—had no connection with workers. As police investigations showed, the only representative of the common people involved in the case was the servant of the arrested Szyfra Szawel.

One of the first female activists who attempted to undertake political action among the Jewish proletariat was Rozalia Felsenhardt. She was born in 1864 into an assimilated family of the Warsaw intelligentsia connected with Polish independence circles. Her father Natan, a surgeon's assistant by trade, took part in patriotic demonstrations in Warsaw in the years 1861–3. Such a pro-Polish family background was not exceptional in the Warsaw Jewish intelligentsia, who were connected with the Polish community through ties of family and friendship. Feliks Kon, Rozalia's fiancé, left for Russia to join the Bolsheviks, then took part in the aggression against Poland, and later became a loyal member of Stalin's government,[12] but he was raised in a tradition of Polish patriotism which is recalled in his Russian-language memoirs.[13]

Already as a high-school student Rozalia Felsenhardt had taken part in Socialist circles associated with Maria Bohuszewiczówna's group. In 1882, after finishing high school and obtaining a teaching certificate, she became active in the Red Cross Society, an organization connected with Proletariat which brought aid to political prisoners and their families. While working at a private boarding school

[12] Feliks Kon was a member of Proletariat from 1883; two years later he was sentenced to ten years' hard labour. He returned to Poland in 1905 and joined the Polska Partia Socjalistyczna (PPS: Polish Socialist Party), whose leader was Józef Piłsudski; in 1907 Kon led a faction, standing as the leader of the party's left wing. After a period of forced emigration he came to Russia in 1917 and joined the Bolshevik Party. Together with Feliks Dzierżyński and Julian Marchlewski, he was a member of the Temporary Revolutionary Committee formed on the home front of Budionny's army in Białystok during the Polish–Bolshevik war in 1920, thus becoming an enemy of the army led by his former colleague, Piłsudski. Under Stalin he held a high position in the Ministry of Education as well as in the Radio Committee of the USSR. He died in Moscow in 1941.

[13] F. Kon, *Pod sztandarem rewolucji* (Warsaw, 1959), 13–14.

for wealthy Jewish girls, where she organized secret classes for the students, she also gave free lessons at an elementary school for girls run by the Jewish community. Here she tried to encourage Socialist agitation among the parents of the pupils, the majority of whom belonged to the lower, proletariat classes.

In about 1883 Rozalia became a member of Proletariat (the date is difficult to establish because she had already worked with the organization earlier). When its leaders were arrested (among them Feliks Kon, her fiancé), responsibility for action fell to the girls who remained free, and who managed fairly well under the leadership of Bohuszewiczówna. Rozalia was given the task of organizing agitation among the Jewish workers and apprentices. She helped to collect money for prisoners and their families, and arranged contacts with them. This activity was interrupted by new arrests, and she was herself detained, spending the last year of her life in Pavilion 10 of the Citadel, a political prison and place of torture for many revolutionaries and freedom fighters. Sentenced to the relatively lenient term of five years' imprisonment in 1887, she died *en route* to Siberia. The cause of her death was typhus and the wounds she suffered defending herself against an attempt at rape by a guard.[14]

Participation in the Socialist movement was often one means of achieving social integration. Revolutionary work made entrance into the society of the majority population easy through contacts with Polish comrades. Ideological involvement made it possible to skip certain phases of the assimilation process, which would often start with acculturation and move on rapidly to full amalgamation. This was the case with many Socialists originating from Orthodox circles. However, at the period which is of interest here, the end of the nineteenth century, the phenomenon was rarely conspicuous: few workers took part in the movement, and almost nothing was known of the environment from which they came. The majority of activists came from wealthy families which were already assimilated, and usually became politically active in high school or during their studies. What impelled them towards Socialism was a feeling of frustration which they experienced both as members of the intelligentsia and as representatives of a disadvantaged minority. The humiliation which educated persons encountered at a time of relative 'overproduction' of the intellectual classes was common both to the socially progressing Jews and to the Polish intelligentsia.[15] Educated and aspiring to Polish culture, Jews were discriminated against by the Tsarist laws, while they suffered from a very strong sense of rejection by Polish society. Their world-view, laying more stress on class than on ethnic divisions, helped them to escape problems of identification arising from assimilation and social advancement. Access to revolutionary parties directed their cultural aspirations

[14] D. Wawrzykowska-Wierciochowa, 'Rozalia Felsenhardtówna (1864–1887): Mało znana działaczka Wielkiego Proletariatu', *Biuletyn ŻIH* 2 (1966), 108.

[15] J. Jedlicki, *Jakiej cywilizacji Polacy potrzebują: Studia z dziejów idei i wyobraźni XIX wieku* (Warsaw, 1988).

towards avant-garde groups leading unconventional lives. All this differentiated these young people from the assimilation activists who propagated an ethos of the 'honest man' in harmony with his surroundings, and constituted the greatest point of difference between them and the 'Gypsy spirit' honoured by the ideologically close Polish Positivists. The Socialist youth made social rebellion a part of their lives. They drew from it such powerful inspiration that it allowed them to survive prison, torture, exile, and humiliation. In this spirit of exhilaration they went to their deaths and killed their enemies.

Jewish Socialists were rejected by their own society. If a fascination with ideology went hand in hand with rebellion against traditional customs, while their aspirations were turned towards the ruling culture (mostly Russian in Russia, Lithuania, and Belarus, Polish in the Kingdom of Poland, and Polish and German in the Austrian partition), then it was the community of *non*-Jewish labourers which they most desired to influence. This could have been one of the reasons for a general lack of activity among the Jewish working class. The life of Rosa Luxemburg (1870–1919) may serve as a paradigm of such choices in life and activity. Born in Zamość, the cradle of Polish Haskalah, she completed high school in Warsaw and undertook work with the Second Proletariat. Threatened with arrest, she left for Zurich, where she studied economics, and in 1898 she obtained her doctoral degree on the basis of a dissertation entitled *Die industrielle Entwicklung Polens* [The industrial development of Poland]. She was the co-creator and ideologue of the Socjaldemokracja Królestwa Polskiego i Litwy (SDKPiL: the Social Democracy of the Kingdom of Poland and Lithuania), publisher and editor of *Sprawa robotnicza* [The workers' cause], an activist of the German Social Democrats and leader of the movement's left wing, and finally creator of the German Communist Party and the Spartacus League. She wrote in Polish, Russian, German, and French. Nowhere, however, did she leave any trace of interest in the Jewish problem. In the corpus of intimate letters written to Leon Jogiches, her companion of many years,[16] the word 'Jew' appears only once. Occasionally—very rarely—a Yiddish saying appears, indicating that she knew that language at least in spoken form. Like all Socialists she was a non-believer, but she observed Christmas and Easter in a secular, albeit quasi-Christian, form.[17]

A great influence on the views of Rosa Luxemburg was Leon Jogiches, better known in Poland by his pen-name, Jan Tyszka. He was born in Vilna in 1867 into a family which was fairly well-to-do and assimilated. His mother's name was Zofia and her father's was Paul. His siblings were also given non-Jewish names: Paweł, Osip, and Emilia. Jogiches began his revolutionary activism in the mid-1880s, joining forces with the Vilna group Narodnaya Volya. The significant role

[16] R. Luksemburg, *Listy do L. Jogiches-Tyszki*, ed. F. Tych (Warsaw, 1968).
[17] R. Luksemburg, *Listy z więzienia*, ed. F. Tych (Warsaw, 1982), 248.

he played in the Russian, Polish, and German revolutionary movements caused many of his comrades to set aside the less attractive characteristics of his personality. According to Charles Rapoport, he was snobbish, uncommunicative, exaggeratedly conspiratorial, and sarcastic and venomous in his humour, but at the same time wise, stubborn, obstinate, and possessed of a strong will.[18] Luba Akselrod described him as a 'romantic and aesthete of the revolution', obsessed by the unorthodox lifestyle of Socialists, in love with the 'movement', not just the goal of its activity. She wrote of him:

> Taking an active part in the work of the Vilna organization, Jogiches stood at the same time as if on the sidelines. He did not personally associate himself with any one of his comrades, and treated them with a certain disdain, whence his nickname 'Jupiter' . . . like every romantic, he liked mystery and conspiracy for their own sake.[19]

That exaggerated sense of conspiracy turned out to be helpful to him. The group Narodnaya Volya, of which he was a member, plotted to assassinate the Tsar. When the police uncovered the preparations for the attack, Lenin's brother received the death sentence, Bronisław Piłsudski was sentenced to fifteen years' hard labour,[20] and Bronisław's brother Józef was condemned to five years of exile—but Jogiches was freed owing to lack of evidence. His sole punishment was a mandatory draft into the army, from which he deserted; in 1890 he escaped to Switzerland and undertook studies there. In Zurich he met Rosa Luxemburg and entered into a relationship with her which lasted for many years.

The beautiful and passionate letters of Rosa acquaint us only indirectly with the personality of Jogiches. He was not an easy person. While the complicated personality of Rosa Luxemburg mingled great sensitivity and feminine softness with a strong will, bravery, and intellectualism, the trait most evident in the personality of Jogiches was his almost psychopathic passion for conspiracy, so exaggerated that it came to dominate even his private life. He had a great influence on the views of Rosa Luxemburg, directing her career and conduct, and yet played throughout the part of an *éminence grise*. While exerting a powerful influence on her, he nevertheless wished to remain in her shadow.

Like Rosa Luxemburg, Jogiches devoted little attention to the Jewish problem. In 1894 he wrote an article on the subject, included in the January issue of *Sprawa robotnicza*. There he discusses four speeches which he had given in 'one of the Russian cities' (i.e. Vilna) to groups of Jewish workers celebrating May Day (1892). He notes the significant fact that only one of the speeches was given in

---

[18] F. Tych, foreword, in Luksemburg, *Listy do L. Jogiches*, p. xxiii.
[19] In Tych, ibid., p. xxiv.
[20] He took advantage of his stay in Siberia to conduct pioneering ethnographic research into Siberian peoples, such as the Ajnas.

Yiddish, the other three being in Russian. Though fewer than a hundred Jewish workers listened to this Socialist presentation, the group still occasioned astonishment. They were still regarded as 'new comrades', by no means the normal object of the endeavours to capture the spirit of the proletariat: 'This fact, that the ideas of social democracy have penetrated even the Jewish proletariat, gives clear witness to how fertile in the Russian empire is the ground for Socialist agitation.'[21] The word 'even' is indicative of the distance from which he addressed the Jewish question. He invites the reader to gauge the spirit of the Jewish proletariat only in terms of how far they resembled the Russian proletariat in the extent of their sympathetic response to the work of Socialist agitators, who themselves were pleasantly surprised to encounter an appreciative audience among the Jewish community. It would be interesting to know if it was just such a vision that Leon Jogiches had before his eyes, segregated after all as he was from the hard reality of the Tsarist empire.

In the meantime, interesting things were taking place in Vilna. From 1887 onwards a revolutionary circle existed there which described itself as the 'Jewish social democrats'. Arkady Kremer was active in it, among others, and the membership included a few labourers. In a report of 1900 directed to the Internationale, Martov-Tsederbaum and Kremer characterized their activities in this manner:

> The first Jewish intellectuals who undertook propaganda among Jewish labourers did not have in mind the creation of a separate Jewish workers' movement. Assigned to the Pale of Settlement, and not having any possibility of devoting energy to the Russian workers' movement, they were forced to work among Jews so as to have some way of satisfying their desire for revolutionary activity. The Jewish workers' movement has secondary meaning for them; their faith resides primarily in the Russian labourer, in whom they place all their hopes and from whom they expect also the emancipation of the Jewish proletariat . . . Their propaganda is carried out in the Russian language.[22]

At the end of the 1880s and beginning of the 1890s more similar groups arose; they were active in various cities of the Pale of Settlement and also in Warsaw. Education was undertaken on a self-help basis. Jewish workers taught themselves reading, writing, arithmetic, the natural sciences, and Socialism in the Polish or Russian language, depending on the area in which the circle was active. Socialist 'enlightenment' implied acculturation; what is more, the workers on the receiving end of this process accepted it as the one road to intellectual advance.

The 1890s forced Socialists towards an interest in the Jewish problem. Internal changes in Jewish society contributed to this. Relationships in the small-craft workshops had changed. Patriarchal-religious relationships between workers and

---

[21] J. Tyszka [Leon Jogiches], 'Nowi towarzysze', *Sprawa robotnicza* (Jan. 1894), cited in H. Buszek and F. Tych, *Socjaldemokracja Królestwa Polskiego i Litwy* (2 vols.; Warsaw, 1957), 147.

[22] K. Frumkin, 'Der Bund un zayne gegner', *Tsukunft*, 2 (1903), 281.

their patrons began to disintegrate. Owners no longer produced directly for the consumer: the development of mass transportation resulted in greater participation by middlemen and traders. Apprentices had fewer chances to become independent and open their own workshops. It became ever more apparent that they were becoming a hired proletariat. Labour organizations which had been established earlier began to disappear. Instead of the *chevrot* (pre-industrial guilds), workers' provident funds began to be founded. These changes were accompanied by a rise in the popularity of Socialist ideas in this community. The participation of Jewish workers in the May Day celebrations in Vilna in 1892 surprised the Socialist activists, creating something of a sensation.

In 1893 Arkady Kremer published a brochure *Ob agitatsii* [On agitation]. It had a significant influence, as much on the character of revolutionary activity in Russia as on the change in the Socialists' position towards the Jewish question. The author gave pointers on how to organize mass agitation. He suggested that greater attention be devoted to the problems of workers, less to theoretical debates conducted at secret meetings. He called for the formulation of propaganda appropriate to the intellectual level and interests of the proletariat. To bring these simple principles into life it was essential to write for the workers in their own language; Kremer himself faced the problem of creating a literature which would reach the Jewish workers. Difficulties with language appeared. Few of the assimilated activists knew Yiddish; the majority entertained a prejudice, typical of the assimilated community, against that language. Even the closest companions of Kremer protested at his suggestions. One of the members of the Vilna group, the engraver Abraham Gordon, argued that the worker should first acquire knowledge and only later fight for improvement in economic conditions. Such knowledge he could acquire only in small, self-taught circles, and since there was a lack of literature in his native tongue, he could learn only in Russian. For that reason, protested Gordon, agitation in Yiddish was not desirable: it deprived workers of the sole reason they had for acquiring knowledge.[23]

The creation of an organizationally separate Jewish Socialism was not connected with the clear consciousness of nationalistic goals, but resulted from the need for mass agitation in the mother tongue. A body of this character was the Żydowska Organizacja Polskiej Partii Socjalistycznej [Jewish Organization of the Polish Socialist Party], founded in Warsaw in 1893, as well as the Żydowski Związek Robotniczy w Warszawie or Yidisher Arbayter Farband in Varshe (Jewish Labour Union in Warsaw), founded by Yosif-John Mill.[24] In 1897 the same motives directed Kremer and Mill when, together with thirteen comrades, they founded in Vilna a party named Algemayner Yidisher Arbeterbund in Rusland un Poyln (General Jewish Labour Union in Russia and Poland), or

[23] K. S. Pinson, 'Arkady Kremer, Vladimir Medem and the Ideology of the Jewish Bund', in A. Duber and M. Ben-Horim (eds.), *Emancipation and Counter-emancipation* (New York, 1974), 297.

[24] H. Piasecki, *Żydowska Organizacja PPS* (Warsaw, 1978), 23.

Bund. This organization united the activities of the Socialist circles of Vilna, Vitebsk, Mińsk, Białystok, and Warsaw. In contrast with its predecessors, the Bund demanded the organizational separation of Jews. It wanted to encompass in its activity the whole Jewish proletariat residing in the Pale of Settlement. It declared its co-operation with Russian as well as Polish Socialism, and its members continued to participate in the revolutionary movements of both those nations. They joined a group of organizers of the Social Democratic Party of Russia, founded in 1898.

Although the Paris Convention of Socialists in 1892 formulated the principle of equality of all nations, both the PPS and the SDKPiL were somewhat vacillating in their application of the doctrine to Jews. Social democrats accepted the premiss of a struggle to emancipate nations, above all as a counterbalance to the influences of the nationalistic right. Their primary concern, however, was class struggle. They believed wholeheartedly that in a Socialist system national problems would cease to be important:

> At least one can imagine that in a Socialist society millions of people, feeling at heart a tribal community, might want to live together in one territory; and with mutual understanding such resettlement could occur. Yet one may doubt whether the Jews 'will want to want'. Blood ties are a strong factor, but stronger than these are the cultural tie with the people among whom one lives and the tie with the country with whose natural environment a person has bonded. That is why it is very unlikely that, in such circumstances, a tendency towards separatism could arise.[25]

The changes in the relationship of Polish revolutionary parties with the Bund gave rise to the astonishing successes of that party among the Jewish proletariat, particularly during the 1905 revolution. In December 1905 *Kurier codzienny* [Daily courier], the then legal organ of the PPS, included an article by H. Walecki (Maksymilian Horowitz) entitled 'W sprawie żydowskiej [Regarding the Jewish matter]'. Walecki formulated a programme for solving the Jewish problem. He demanded the repeal of discriminatory laws as well as the cultural equality of Jewish people. He supported the right to linguistic freedom, allowing the use of the Yiddish language or Hebrew in private and public life, and particularly in courts, administration, and education. He called for the government to finance education in both those languages, and to eschew any form of coercion in this sphere. The author did not tackle the question of whether the Jews constitute a nation, but he recognized their right to cultural autonomy.[26] The mouthpiece of the Jewish organization within the PPS, *Der arbeter* [The worker], published a translation of this article.[27] This did not mean, however, full acceptance of the

---

[25] J. Marchlewski, *Antysemityzm a robotnicy* (Kraków, 1913), 96.
[26] H. Walecki, 'W sprawie żydowskiej', *Kurier codzienny*, 2 (1905).
[27] *Der arbeter*, 12 (15 Dec. 1905).

Bund. Its influences were to be minimalized, and to this end the leaders of the PPS gave greater support and organizational aid to the Jewish organization within the PPS. Such a political position *vis-à-vis* the Bund was characteristic not only of Józef Piłsudski (who agreed to co-operate with the Bund in Lithuania), but was to a greater degree a feature of the assimilated activists—Jews such as Feliks Perl, Józef Kwiatek, and F. Sachs.

The joint struggle, shared responsibility, and solidarity which were necessary in the conduct of conspiratorial work had to result in the formation of strong group ties. Socialists—Poles, Russians, and Jews—learnt together, acted together, and shared goals, and together in chains they went to Siberia. But there is a striking absence of mixed relationships (marital or other) in the community of the first Socialists. The first breach of this code (and a considerable misalliance) was the couple Stanisław Mendelson, one of the leaders of the PPS in Galicia, and Maria Zaleska-Jankowska, descendant of a great landowning family. Scandalously, she began her relationship with Mendelson while married to her first husband, abandoning her home and children.

For the assimilated Jewish youth, access to Socialism was one way of finding a political answer to the questions which the events of history raised in the Jewish mind. Revolt pushed aside and made less important many of the problems which the process of this group's emancipation at a time of official discrimination had called forth. Many of their peers engaged themselves in Jewish nationalist movements. Zionism and Socialism developed side by side. In contrast, the Socialists desired the most comprehensive opening up of all societies. In the Utopia of a worldwide brotherhood of the oppressed they saw a solution to their own, Jewish pains. These were two, very different, replies to the same troubling question.

The Jewish Problem in Polish Socialist Thought

MICHAŁ ŚLIWA

By the Jewish problem, strictly speaking, we understand a mutual internal relationship between Christian societies and the Jews who live among them. It is a matter of the differentiation of Jews from the rest of society in traditional, social, and, in general, cultural terms; it is a matter of the current and future lifestyles of Jews in the midst of non-Jewish nations.[1]

It was in this way that Józef Kwiatek, a prominent activist of the Polska Partia Socjalistyczna (PPS: Polish Socialist Party), defined the concept of the Jewish problem in a brochure entitled *Kwestia żydowska* [The Jewish problem]; it was issued in October 1904 as the 28th edition of the monthly, *Latarnia* [Lantern], published by the Polska Partia Socjalno-Demokratyczna Galicji i Śląska (PPSD: Polish Social Democratic Party of Galicia and Silesia). This definition was commonly accepted by Polish Socialists and Social Democrats. They were in general agreement concerning the genesis and existence of the Jewish problem within Polish territory and how it differed from the question of the socio-economic and cultural status of Jews in other countries, although some of the publicists and ideologists of the Polish workers' movement, not always sharing the social democratic orientation—such as Socjaldemokracja Królestwa Polskiego i Litwy (SDKPiL: the Social Democracy of the Kingdom of Poland and Lithuania)—emphasized above all the economic circumstances of the Jewish problem. What divided Socialist thinkers, however, was the variety of approaches to the solution of the problem, although all foresaw its disappearance along with the liquidation of unjust social relations. Some postulated assimilation as the one means of resolving it, others spoke out for full equality of Jewish people in every area of social life, and others again saw the solution in the realization of the idea of national-cultural autonomy, or within the framework of some similar form of national self-government.

The climax of disagreement among Polish Socialists over the Jewish matter took place in the first and fourth decades of the twentieth century. In the first period various concepts and viewpoints were worked out in an attempt to address the

[1] T. Wileński [J. Kwiatek], *Kwestia żydowska* (Kraków, 1904), 3.

many new issues which arose at the turn of the last century as a result of the sociopolitical processes taking place in Jewish society in Poland. In the later period, though socio-economic conditions in Poland were by then wholly different, the previously formulated concepts and solutions enjoyed a continuing currency. This did not mean, of course, that Socialists failed to discuss Jewish problems at other times. Jewish matters had always absorbed their attention from the earliest days of the movement, as may be seen, for example, in the works of the precursors of modern Socialism dating from the first half of the nineteenth century; and this extended through to the 1940s, as several publicists and activists of the PPS reflected on the barbarization of human society and the Jewish Holocaust. But in the two decades singled out above Socialists evolved the most mature programmes and attitudes within their political philosophy, in the course of extraordinarily lively and creative intellectual discussions and disagreements.

It was primarily Socialists from the Russian and Austrian partitions who were concerned with the Jewish question: the small numbers of Jews under the Prussian partition, and their Germanization, meant that the question scarcely arose in that area. The Russian and Austrian Socialists always considered the question within the wider context of doctrinal explorations of Socialism, and therefore above all in connection with the theory of nation and nationalism, the concept of change in social relationships, and the vision of a new social order. They also analysed the matter against the background of the socio-political processes taking place in Jewish and Polish society. They saw the genesis and development of the problem as closely connected with the birth of a new social system, capitalism. It is thus no coincidence that such great attention was devoted to the Jewish question at the turn of the century. At that time the assimilation movement among Jews had broken down, even as, with ever increasing strength, they manifested their national-cultural aspirations. They took up the slogans of the right to work, to be educated, and to enjoy equal status. The First World Congress of Zionists took place in 1897. In October of that year the General Jewish Workers' Union, popularly known as the Bund, formed itself, covering the territory of Russia and the Congress Kingdom. Eight years later a similar workers' organization was established in Galicia, the Żydowska Partia Socjalno-Demokratyczna (ŻPSD: Jewish Social Democratic Party), which acceded to the Bund in 1920.

Apart from the rise in national-cultural aspirations of the Jews, fundamental changes were taking place in the social stratification of the Jewish people as a result of pauperization and proletarianization, among other things. These changes led to rather sharp socio-political divisions and to the evolution of two modern Jewish movements, comprising the nationalists and the workers.[2] Their

[2] For the formation and development of the latter see e.g. H. Piasecki, *Żydowska Organizacja PPS 1893–1907* (Wrocław, 1978); id., *Sekcja Żydowska PPSD i Żydowska Partia Socjalno-Demokratyczna 1892–1919–20* (Wrocław, 1982); G. Aronson *et al.* (eds.), *Di geshikhte fun Bund* (4 vols.; New York, 1960–72); J. Holzer, *Mozaika polityczna drugiej Rzeczypospolitej* (Warsaw, 1974), 277.

aims were not usually in line with those of Polish socio-political movements of a similar character, nor with the interests of Polish society as a whole. Against a background of economic rivalry between Poles and Jews, antisemitism began to arise, leading to pogroms against the Jewish people. Clear contrasts ensued between the process of shaping a modern Polish society in the industrial age and the awakening of national-social aspirations of Jews. All this was happening under conditions of dependence upon foreign governments, which again had a bearing on the Polish–Jewish relationships. For example, the Tsarist regime, in discriminating against Jews in various sectors of public life, forced their resettlement within the borders of the Congress Kingdom, so that they became the unwitting tool of Russification in the Polish community—the so-called Litvak Jew problem. Furthermore, Jewish workers' parties distanced themselves from the Polish Socialist movement, particularly from its independence-irredentist tendencies, and searched for their own place in the overall structures of national Social Democracy.

Polish socialists were faced with especially difficult problems. They often had to reconcile contradictory interests and aims, because on the one hand they appeared as representatives of the social-national Polish aspirations of the working class, while on the other they were seen as promoters of universal values, which excluded any dependence whatsoever on social-national structures. It was inevitable that some would accuse them of philosemitism and national apostasy, while others charged them with nationalism and misappropriating the ideals of international proletariat solidarity.

The Marxist concept of nation and nationalism weighed heavily in the Socialists' deliberations on the question of nationality and their search for an optimal arrangement of Polish–Jewish relations. The interpretation of the idea of a nation formulated by Marx, which stemmed from a tradition of the Enlightenment and owed much to Hegel, exerted a particular influence; a nation was conceived of as a historical-geographic and cultural community ('historical nation'), while the naturalistic concept of nation as a tribal-linguistic community ('ahistorical nation') was also accepted.[3] According to this classification, Jews, as an 'ahistorical nation', did not have any opportunity to create their own nation state, and their only chance was—as Karl Marx contended in *The Jewish Question* (1843)—full assimilation within the framework of a new social system—socialism.[4] This view was later expanded by numerous commentators on Marx, among them Karol Kautsky, who argued that a nation which is a linguistic community

---

[3] On the ambiguous and general character of the Marxist theory of nationalism and the question of nation see e.g. A. Walicki, 'Marks i Engels o sprawie polskiej; Koncepcja narodu i ujęcie kwestii narodowej', *Z pola walki*, 2 (1980), 3–25; J. J. Wiatr, *Naród i państwo: Socjologiczne problemy kwestii narodowej* (Warsaw, 1969), 26; M. Bębenek, *Teoria narodu i kwestia narodowa u Kazimierza Kelles-Krauza (na tle refleksji marksistowskiej 1848–1905)* (Kraków, 1987), 11; G. Haupt, M. Lowy, and C. Wein, *Les Marxistes et la question nationale 1848–1914* (Paris, 1974), 22.

[4] See K. Marx, 'W kwestii żydowskiej', ed. F. Mehring (London, 1896), 12.

may exist permanently only within the borders of its own national territory, where it constitutes a majority of the inhabitants. In the present case, then, Jews had ceased to be a nation and should therefore fully adjust to their scattered condition and assimilate themselves to the culture of the dominating nation.[5]

Polish Socialists were aware of the weight and meaning of the Jewish question for the future of Polish society and for their socio-political movement, and were equally conscious that Marx's categories were of limited value for an analysis of the nation-forming processes which were taking place at the turn of the century. Even before the formation of the PPS, in the summer of 1892, Feliks Perl, replying to a request by Stanisław Mendelson that he should write a preface to the planned Polish edition of Karl Marx's treatise (cited above), explained that the text was already outdated and that any introduction should characterize the general attitude of Socialists and of Poland to the Jewish matter, and describe contemporary attempts to resolve the question, the state of the Socialist movement among Jews, and the problems of antisemitism and Zionism. He advised its publication by the Biblioteka Społeczno-Polityczna [Socio-Political Library]; in fact it was not published until four years later, with a preface not by Perl but by Franz Mehring, a German Social Democrat. The edition was funded by the Związek Zagraniczny Socjalistów Polskich (ZZSP: Union of Polish Socialists Abroad).[6]

The aim of Polish Socialists in describing their position *vis-à-vis* the Jewish problem was largely to win over the Jewish working classes. Great weight was attached to this from the first moment of Józef Piłsudski's participation in the PPS. In the pages of *Robotnik* [The worker] and *Przedświt* [Dawn] he expressed the hope that, in spite of the tendency of the Litvaks towards Russification, a significant part of the Jewish population, especially the lower classes, would react against the discriminatory politics of the Tsarist regime, and entrust their political future to the Socialist programme of the PPS. Piłsudski also furnished aid to Jewish Socialists in Vilna and helped them make contact with the editors of *Der arbeter* [The worker], the Jewish organ of the PPSD (see below).[7] He tried with his colleagues to incorporate groups of Jewish Socialists from the Russian partition into the activities of the PPS, and to include Jewish workers in the activities of the Polish proletariat, such as May Day demonstrations, strikes, and anti-Tsarist protests. It is not surprising, then, that the PPS leadership took a negative view of the formation of an autonomous organization of Jewish workers, the Bund. It perceived the Bund as an agent of the Jewish bourgeoisie, and

---

[5] These views were presented in, for example, the first treatise in Marxist literature devoted to the theory of nation, Kautsky's *Die moderne Nationalität* (n.p., 1887) translated into Polish as *Narodowość i jej początki* (Warsaw, 1891); cf. M. Walldenberg, *Wzlot i upadek Karola Kautsky'ego: Studium z historii myśli społecznej i politycznej* (Kraków, 1972), 578.

[6] See further M. Śliwa, *Feliks Perl: Biografia* (Warsaw, 1988), 34–5.

[7] Cf. H. Piasecki, *Żydowska Organizacja*, 16.

correlated Bundist separatism with Polish antisemitism.[8] The creation of the Bund also encouraged the ZZSP to commence printing of the Yiddish newspaper *Der arbeter*. This came out at irregular intervals from December 1898 in the face of great obstacles, chief among which was the lack of knowledge of the Yiddish language on the part of the publicists and activists of the PPS (whose large Jewish membership tended to be from the intelligentsia of Polonized communities, often with a richly patriotic tradition, where Yiddish was not spoken). Thus, for example, the editor of *Przedświt*, Leon Wasilewski, had to learn the language specially so that he could edit *Der arbeter*. He was helped by a Jewish woman from Słonim who, in contrast, knew little Polish—Teresa Reznikowska, later Feliks Perl's wife.[9]

Relations between the Bund and the PPS became inflamed after the Fourth Convention of the Bund in 1901, which accepted, following the example of Austrian Social Democracy, a programme of national-cultural autonomy worked out by its theorist on matters of nationalism, Otto Bauer. In addition, delegates at the convention advocated a united federation of all Social Democratic organizations in the Russian Empire, and a guaranteed monopoly for the Bund over the organization of the Jewish proletariat. The leadership of the PPS perceived this as a sign of the strengthening of Jewish nationalism, separatism, and pro-Russian centralism aimed against the Polish Socialist movement and adversely affecting the Polish question. The Sixth PPS Convention, which took place in June 1902 in Lublin, assumed a broader attitude to this problem. It condemned the Bund's politics and instigated opposition to it as an 'organization harmful on account of its programme and its relationship to the political solidarity of working people in Poland and on farms'.[10] With reference to the resolution of the Jewish question, it repeated the old position of the PPS that

> the aim of achieving a democratic and independent republic suits the interest of Jewish workers, not only as workers but also as Jews. For a republic will ensure for Jews complete equality as citizens and will allow them free development and the exertion of a satisfactory influence on public affairs ... in our country, which is at the same time their country.[11]

At the same time the convention declared that it would not decide the question of whether Jews constituted a nation, nor whether they satisfied the conditions for separate development, because in the contemporary situation these matters no

---

[8] See e.g. 'W kwestii żydowskiej', *Robotnik*, 26 (2 Feb. 1898), 1; 'Sprawa żydowskiego proletariatu', *Przedświt*, 4 (1898), 12.

[9] L. Wasilewski, 'Polska londyńska emigracja na progu XIX i XX wieku', *Niepodległość*, 1 (1929), 256; 'Ze wspomnień, 2. 1899–1904', *Z pola walki*, 4 (1974), 213.

[10] CA KC PZPR (Centralne Archiwum Komitetu Centralnego Polskiej Zjednoczonej Partii Robotniczej' (presently in the Archive of Modern Documents in Warsaw), call no. 305/III, i/2. 42; 'Szósty Zjazd PPS', *Robotnik*, 46 (1902), 3.

[11] CA KC PZPR, call no. 305/III, i/2. 43.

longer had any practical meaning. It also took a decision to form the Żydowska Organizacja PPS (ŻO PPS: Jewish Organization of the PPS), which was to ease the way for Polish Socialists to reach the Jewish proletariat and create a counterbalance to the Bund.

The Bund leadership reacted critically to the resolution of the Polish Socialist convention regarding the Jewish matter, contending that the Jewish proletariat and Socialists could not count on 'the mercy of the Polish people', because rights granted to Jews in this way instead of being won by them would remain rights 'only on paper, and at any moment could be taken away with the same ease with which they were granted'.[12] The Bund added that it was organizing Jewish workers not only within the territory of the Congress Kingdom but also throughout the Russian Empire—about which the PPS seemed to have forgotten—and for that purpose a national, uniform, and independent Jewish Socialist party was indispensable. Thus, there were continual controversies between the PPS and the Bund.

Some Polish Socialists of Jewish descent who were members of ŻO PPS adopted a conciliatory stance towards the Bund, and drew attention to significant concessions towards the Jewish people in the area of language and culture. In the meantime a group of older PPS activists who derived from the long-Polonized Jewish intelligentsia, such as Feliks Perl—with Piłsudski at their head and with strong party encouragement—advocated assimilation of the Jewish people and fought the effect of the Bund on the Jewish proletariat. This move was beset by arguments and tactical problems within the PPS concerning matters of independence, revolution, and war, as well as the relationship to Russian Social Democracy and the SDKPiL, which for once co-operated with the Bund and supported it as a counterbalance against the PPS. No wonder then that, after the wrangles within the PPS, the ŻO PPS merged in 1907, not with the PPS Frakcja Rewolucyjna (PPS Revolution Faction), headed by Piłsudski, but with PPS-Lewica (PPS Left), which gathered Socialists of a more radical line, more interested in collaboration between Russian, Polish, and Jewish Social Democrats.

Socialists within the Austrian partition were faced with similar problems. The Jewish question had already been discussed at the First Convention of the Galicijska Partia Socjalno-Demokratyczna (Galician Social Democratic Party) of 31 January, 1892. Ignacy Daszyński's programmatic paper dealt with the question. He pointed out that the differing views on how to resolve it—e.g. assimilation or the emigration of Jews—were of relevance to Socialists because they had to do with the Jewish working classes. He reminded those present of the position taken by the Second International Congress in Brussels in 1891—that Socialists cannot be either philosemites or antisemites, but should discern within the Jewish

---

[12] See *Polska Partia Socjalistyczna o żydowskim ruchu robotniczym* (London, 1903), 9 (published by the General Jewish Workers' Alliance in Lithuania, Poland, and Russia—the Bund); *Walka Polskiej Partii Socjalistycznej z 'Bundem'* (London, 1898) (published by the Bund).

people the same class divisions and conflicts between the bourgeoisie and the proletariat that were in evidence elsewhere. The delegates were in agreement with the conclusion of his speech:

Let us treat Jews as any other nation, let us give them the same rights. The first goal of Socialism is to throw a spark of the class struggle among Jews, to unite with the Jewish proletariat, and to bring into its consciousness the principle that its interests are associated with those of the proletariats of other nations.[13]

It was decided to issue a publication in the Yiddish language, in order to encourage agitation for the cause.

The unequivocal recognition by the convention of Jews as a nation, equal in rights with others, a move which flew in the face of traditional Marxist and Social Democratic tradition, failed to satisfy the national-cultural aspirations of a section of the Jewish activists. In July 1892 they announced in Galicia that they were forming the Żydowska Partia Robotnicza (Jewish Workers' Party), with *Arbeter shtime* [The workers' voice] as its mouthpiece. However, the party failed to develop independently and joined up with the Galician Social Democratic Party; accordingly, the following year that organization began to publish the Yiddish-language *Der arbeter*, realizing in this way the decision of its first convention.[14]

The idea of inaugurating a separate and independent Jewish Social Democratic party in Galicia, however, still preoccupied the local Socialists. For that reason Jan Kozakiewicz, the leading activist of the Galician Social Democratic Party, set forth a formal proposition concerning this matter at the party's congress in Przemyśl in 1897, where it changed its name to Polska Partia Socjalno-Demokratyczna Galicji i Śląska (PPSD Galicia and Silesia). But this was thrown out on a vote as a result of a counteraction by two activists of Jewish descent, Herman Diamand and Emil Haecker. Another opponent of Kozakiewicz's proposal, Herman Lieberman—also of Jewish descent—even explained his objection by stating that Jews were not a nation and that the Jewish proletariat was not striving for a separate organization. PPSD activists of Jewish descent were afraid not only of the political consequences of Jewish separatism in the Socialist movement itself, but also of the danger of increasing antisemitism and its association with antisocialist action. This was expressed by Diamand in a letter to his wife written during the Jewish pogroms in Western Galicia in 1897:

The fierce fight with Socialism here takes on an antisemitic mask, making my work difficult. I have happened upon a moment when 'patriotic' Socialists subjugate themselves to 'Slavophilism' so that it is difficult to accomplish anything by means of lucid argumentation. It is possible, when Daszyński arrives, that he will be able to help,

---

[13] CA KC PZPR, call no 1854; 'I Zjazd Galicyjskiej Partii Socjalno-Demokratycznej', *Naprzód*, 4 (15 Feb. 1892), 1–3; I. 'Daszyński, *Pamiętniki* (2 vols.; Kraków, 1925), i. 76.

[14] See further W. Najdus, *Polska Partia Socjalno-Demokratyczna Galicji i Śląska 1890–1919* (Warsaw, 1983), 167.

because I as a Jew cannot achieve any success at all against this most recent humbug.[15]

So it was no wonder that Jewish activists who had always resolutely fought antisemitism found strong support in the PPSD and contributed to a rise in the party's membership from the ranks of the Jewish community, especially the intelligentsia. Concurrently, by working closely with Poles inside a single Social Democratic movement, they weakened nationalistic tendencies and Zionist aims among Jews.[16]

However, the aim of Jewish Socialists in Galicia—to create an independent and national Jewish movement—turned out to be stronger than the principle of solidarity between Polish and Jewish workers and the declared tactical programme of the PPSD leadership concerning the affairs and aspirations of Jewish workers and Socialists. And thus, as mentioned above, in June 1905 the ŻPSD was founded, with the aim of achieving national-cultural autonomy for Jewish people; eventually, in 1920, it united with the Bund. In 1906 an autonomous Sekcja Żydowska (Jewish Section) was called into being within the framework of the PPSD, with the task of leading Social Democratic agitation among the Jewish proletariat. In 1907 it was transformed into the Żydowska Socjalna-Demokracja Galicji (ŻSDG: the Jewish Social Democracy of Galicia), though still part of the PPSD. After four years of independent activity, however, it merged with the ŻPSD. This decision was accepted by the PPSD leadership, including Ignacy Daszyński, because, as he explained at the conference ratifying the change, it resulted from the character of Polish–Jewish relations, which were founded on two premisses: 'The Jewish masses are isolated from Polish society, and constitute a minority in the country. So on the one hand they demand a separate organization for the Jewish proletariat, and on the other we have a Jewish minority which should fight for its rights in the country.'[17] Taking leave of his Jewish colleagues, he reminded them that the most important thing was practical co-operation. 'As proof that we will never allow the limiting of your rights I cite a fact from our past. Jews make up 11 per cent of the population of this country, 5 per cent of the organization, and at rallies always 40 per cent—and we never had anything against that.'[18]

The process of merging Jewish Social Democratic organizations in Galicia certainly accelerated the recognition in 1908 by an international language conference held at Czernowitz of Yiddish as the language of the Jewish nation and, two years later at the forum of the Vienna Government Council, an undertaking by the

---

[15] H. Diamand, *Pamiętnik Hermana Diamanda zebrany z wyjątków listów do żony* (Kraków, 1932), 35.
[16] Cf. e.g. the criticism of Zionism by E. Haecker, 'Über den Zionismus', *Neue Zeit*, 2 (1895), 759–60.
[17] 'Kongres Zjednoczenia', *Der Sozialdemokrat*, 41 (13 Oct. 1911), 1–2.
[18] Cited in H. Piasecki, *Sekcja Żydowska PPSD*, 259.

leadership of the Austrian Social Democracy to further the realization of national-cultural autonomy for Jews.

Jewish Socialists from both the Austrian and the Russian partitions were not content with the conciliatory but essentially compromising position of the PPS and PPSD with regard to the Jewish question. Against the background of a clear acceleration in the first years of the twentieth century of the processes which shaped modern nations and the formation within them of strong nationalistic tendencies, the voices of Polish Socialists, trying to analyse Polish–Jewish relations in an objective manner and not lose the perspective of co-operation among the working class of both ethnic groups, fell on deaf ears. The most theoretically mature position with regard to the Jewish question was presented in the pages of the Kraków *Krytyka* [Critique] in 1904 by the distinguished PPS intellectual Kazimierz Kelles-Krauz. His aim was to answer commonly asked questions 'Are Jews a nation and is Yiddish their national language?' Analysing the emergence of nations in his own day, he reached the conclusion that:

Jews are becoming a nation . . . the Jewish nationality is being created under the influence of the same factors which strengthened and called to life or sparked the French, German, Italian, and Slavic nationality, all the way through the Serbian–Lusatian rebirth. At any rate, the influence of the most important of these factors is certain—that great current of history whose starting-point is the French Revolution and which led to the democratization of culture, facilitating the people's access to the acquired wealth of civilization, their continual mastering of that wealth, and its further development by the human masses.[19]

In contrast to the previous Marxist stance regarding the national question, Kelles-Krauz emphasized the significance of the nineteenth-century process of the democratization of culture and the involvement of broad sectors of society in the building of new nations. He also noted that in the formation of Jewish nationality the principal factors were not economic, but were rather phenomena from the cultural sphere, such as the popularization of democratic ideals, the raising of the cultural level of the Jewish masses, a growth in humanistic and social aspirations, the development of Yiddish, etc. He predicted that in future Yiddish, the language of the people and based on an Old German dialect, would be transformed, like the Byelorussian and Ukrainian languages, into a national language of culture. But Kelles-Krauz acknowledged the difficulty of accurate prediction at a time when two powerful processes were starting to align: the aim of the rebirth of the Jewish nation and its Polonization when faced with the apparent superiority of Polish culture over the Jewish. He therefore concluded that the mission of the Socialist movement within both nations should be the exhibition of a unity of social and political interests between Poles and Jews. Thus, he rated highly the political stand of the PPS *vis-à-vis* the

---

[19] M. Luśnia [K. Kelles-Krauz], 'W kwestii narodowości żydowskiej', *Krytyka*, 1 (1904), 59, repr. K. Kelles-Krauz, *Pisma wybrane* (2 vols.; Warsaw, 1962), ii. 318–41.

Jewish question, as expressed at the party's Sixth Convention (see above)—that Poland was a country of working-class Jews and that Jews had as much reason to feel at ease in Poland as Poles themselves. He therefore suggested that the concept of equal rights of citizens be expanded to encompass the right to possess one's own nationality and to recognize the Jewish nationality 'to the extent that Jews themselves adopt it' as well as the disposition of mutual relations on the basis of brotherhood.

Józef Kwiatek expressed himself in similar vein in the essay *Kwestia żydowska*, cited at the start of this paper. He too linked development of the Jewish problem with nineteenth-century democratic changes in all areas of social life. He also identified the economic, religious, and nationalistic sources and forms of antisemitism, as well as its antisocialist function: the ruling classes wanted to use it to turn the attention of the proletariat from the true source of their slavery, capitalistic exploitation. He concluded:

Not with empty chatter about the superiority of assimilation over cultural difference or vice versa, but with the idea of the necessary co-operation of the working classes which constitute the great majority of the nation, Socialism draws closer to resolving the Jewish problem . . . let every Socialist, if he be a Jew, fight Zionism in word and deed, and if a Christian, counteract antisemitism through agitation and by his own example.[20]

Bolesław Limanowski, the Nestor of Polish Socialism, also took a stand on the Jewish question, frankly declaring that 'If Jews have a feeling of national community, then we will not succeed in persuading them that they are not a nation.'[21] Before the split in the PPS an avid supporter of equality for Jews in Polish society was Maksymilian Horwitz. Comparing the cultural (traditional-moral) and political-legal senses of the concept of nationality, he asserted that Jews constituted a nation solely in the former designation of the term, and that this should guarantee them the right to use the Yiddish language in schools, courts, and government offices, and recognition of their claim to a national culture of their own.[22] His position was accepted by the PPS Left after the split, the organization whose

---

[20] T. Wileński [J. Kwiatek], *Kwestia żydowska*, 34. It should be noted that in reaction to the rising wave of antisemitism after the collapse of the 1905 revolution, Socialists, like Social Democrats, published many articles exploring the true essence of antisemitism and defending the Jewish working classes; see e.g. *Antysemityzm* (Warsaw, 1906), published by the PPS; Kmicic [M. Bielecki], *Przesądy antysemickie w świetle cyfr i faktów (Przyczynek do kwestii żydowskiej)* (Vilna, 1909); J. Marchlewski, *Antysemityzm a robotnicy* (Chicago, 1913); S. Sempołowska, *Żydzi w Polsce* (Warsaw, 1906); L. Wasilewski, *Kwestia żydowska na ziemiach dawnej Rzeczypospolitej* (Lwów, 1913); *Zarys stosunków galicyjskich* (Warsaw, 1906).

[21] B. Limanowski, 'Naród, państwo, międzynarodowość', *Krytyka*, 1 (1908), 336.

[22] See M. Horwitz, 'Stosunek PPS do kwestii żydowskiej', *Kurier codzienny*, 2 (6 Dec. 1905), 3; id., *Przyczynek do programu PPS* (Warsaw, 1906); id., *W kwestii żydowskiej* (Kraków, 1907); id., 'Kwestia żydowska wśród robotników', *Kuźnia*, 24 (29 Nov. 1913), 788–94:; the last three were reprinted in H. Walecki [M. Horwitz], *Wybór pism* (2 vols.; Warsaw, 1967), i. 111–36, 137–233, 427–36. See also Tarski [I. Rechmiewski], 'Kwestia żydowska wśród robotników', *Kuźnia*, 21 (18 Oct. 1913), 788–94.

membership included, for various reasons—among them its attitude towards an independent Poland and the Russian revolutionary movement—nearly all the previously mentioned advocates of the concept of mutual support in Polish–Jewish relations.

However, as indicated earlier, this concept did not appease the aspirations of Jewish Socialists, and it stood in contradiction to the growing demands for emancipation among Jews, and to contemporary trends towards nationalism. By way of reaction there emerged an independent Jewish Socialist theory and movement, whose theoretical foundations were most fully presented by Henryk Grossman, the primary spokesman for the ŻPSD and, in the interwar period, a Communist activist. He set out his views in the form of a polemic against the views of Kelles-Krauz. Fundamental to his reasoning was the premiss that Jews were a nation, formed in the course of a long historical process. The Jewish question, at heart, involved only the proletariat and could be reduced to 'the choice of the fastest means to achieve the goal of placing power in the hands of the proletariat'.[23] The shaping of the Jewish nation had been harmed and inhibited by the Polonization (assimilation) to which the Jewish intelligentsia had succumbed. The Jewish proletariat, however, constituting a significant part of the Galician population, remained a separate, independent, and unassimilated group, possessed of a reborn national consciousness. That was why it was important to set it on an equal footing with the proletariat of other nations of the Austro-Hungarian Empire, so that

> the revolutionary movement of the Jewish proletariat would destroy each day, by thousands of proofs, the nonsense of Polonization, and not rest until the myth of the ghetto and separatism, so undeserved by the proletariat, would disappear—until all of these unquiet ghosts disappear, leaving behind no more than a myth of this myth.[24]

A specific construct of the concept of nation-proletariat runs throughout Grossman's deliberations: this was something widespread at that time among the radicalizing Social Democrats. It simultaneously expressed the social-national aspirations of the Jewish proletariat, built up pride and a feeling of dignity, and strengthened the proletariat in its conviction of the role it was destined to fulfil in the process of liquidating the capitalist system and in the national renaissance of the Jews.

The move to the PPS Left by those who wished to resolve the Jewish question in Poland by recognizing Jews as a separate, independent nation and by according them complete equality with Poles clearly diminished the interest of the PPS Revolution Faction in the Jewish question and lent strength to the promoters of

[23] H. Grossman, *Proletariat wobec kwestii żydowskiej: Z powodu niedyskutowanej dyskusji w 'Krytyce'* (Kraków, 1905), 18.   [24] Ibid. 37.

a traditional, dogmatic political viewpoint. This was expressed above all by the leading party theorist, Feliks Perl. He rebuked all the supporters of national-cultural autonomy for Jews as a manifestation of 'naïve and arrogant nationalism', criticizing their unfamiliarity with contemporary legal, economic, and sociological issues. Above all, he reproached them for forgetting that the basis of all economic-political relations is territory. That was why the demand for non-territorial autonomy would infringe upon the interests of territorial nations (e.g. Poles, Lithuanians, Ukrainians), would surrender them to the centralist politics of the Russian government, and would inhibit the development of their own national culture since either Russian would become the officially recognized language or else all languages would be given equal status, leading to a chaotic situation. Besides, Perl contended, the project for a national-cultural autonomy was rooted in the false premiss that the Jews constituted a nation: this was and would remain untrue because they did not control a tangible national territory—an essential factor in the constitution and integration of a social group. Even if one were to accept Bauer's characterization of the Jews as a nation,[25] one would have to understand that their type of nationhood was a relic from medieval times (witness detachment of their economic occupations and their racial-religious isolation): they were in essence, as Kautsky convincingly claimed, a caste. Then did they have a future? Only one of full assimilation 'with a territorial nation', replied Perl, because

both in their material struggle for existence and in their endeavour to achieve a higher spiritual culture Jews must use the language of the majority, and claim for themselves its intellectual property. They should work to multiply this wealth, and contribute to its growth and excellence. Jewish jargon will never serve the cultural needs of a higher level—it is only a temporary tool, an elementary guide to culture for the unenlightened masses. Together with the growth of culture, above all with the establishment of normal political relations, the language of the country's majority must take on an ever increasing meaning in the lives of the Jewish masses.[26]

In the contemporary situation, Perl argued, cultural-national autonomy for Jews was a pipedream, and dissemination of the idea harmful because Jewish national pursuits were intrinsically contradictory to Polish national aspirations.

Identical arguments against a national-cultural autonomy for Jews were then advanced by Wasilewski, the PPS expert on national issues and editor of *Przedświt*, who suggested assimilation along the lines of Jewish integration in

---

[25] O. Bauer presented his theory of nation as a cultural community in *Die Nationalitätenfrage und die Sozialdemokratie* (Vienna, 1907), translated into Polish and published in an abridged version as *Zagadnienie narodowości* (Warsaw, 1908).

[26] Res [F. Perl], 'W sprawie autonomii narodowej Żydów', *Przedświt*, 11 (1908), 7.

western European countries as the one way to resolve the problem.[27] A similar viewpoint was expressed by Polish Social Democrats, who saw the final resolution of the problem within the framework of a loosely defined international Socialist community,[28] though they had always fought against the main promoter of national-cultural autonomy for Jews, the Bund. It is thus unsurprising that the party programme passed at the Tenth Congress of the PPS (First Congress of the PPS Revolutionary Faction) in Vienna in 1907 did not take a stand on the Jewish question, speaking in general terms of legal equality and socio-political freedom for all citizens in the future independent Polish democratic republic, regardless of sex, race, nationality, or religion.[29]

The policy established at that time for the resolution of the Jewish matter became a standard doctrine in the Polish Socialist movement for the next thirty years, until the proceedings of the Twenty-fourth PPS Congress in February 1937. But after Poland regained her independence the Jewish problem had persisted—indeed, it had even grown to some extent in the 1930s. That is why it continued to attract the attention of Polish Socialists. They viewed the matter in the context of the need to ensure the security of the Polish government and consolidate independence, while simultaneously allowing Jews normal conditions for growth and winning over their Socialist and democratic factions in the struggle for Socialism in Poland. This last task was no easy one, because co-operation of the PPS with Jewish Socialists (with the Bund and Po'alei Tsion) was impeded by significant ideological and tactical divergences and differences in their positions with regard to nationalism.

The slogan of autonomy was also taken up by other Jewish parties, coupled with a campaign for religious autonomy. These aspirations were partially met by proposals for regulating the Jewish problem in Poland on the basis of national-cultural autonomy, advanced by leftist Socialist groups such as PPS Opozycja (Opposition) and the Niezależna Socjalistyczna Partia Pracy (Independent Socialist Labour Party), Kazimierz Domosławski's group. But the majority of Polish Socialists within the PPS were against such ideas. They argued that the introduction of non-territorial autonomy would weaken the unity of the country, strengthen separatism, hinder the process of assimilation, and separate the Jewish people from Polish culture, the culture of the group forming the majority in the country. They were therefore also strongly opposed to the postulates of this autonomy as advocated by Jewish groups in Poland in accordance with the so-called Minority Statute passed at the Peace Conference in Paris in 1919. During

---

[27] Wasilewski, *Kwestia żydowska*, 26 ff.

[28] Cf. e.g. Marchlewski, *Antysemityzm a robotnicy* 89 ff.; A. Warski, 'Antysemityzm w praktyce', *Młot*, 15 (12 Nov. 1910); 'W sprawie żydowskiej', *Nasza sprawa*, 4 (4 Mar. 1911), 12–15.

[29] Cf. *Program Polskiej Partii Socjalistycznej* (Warsaw, 1907), 11; A. Wroński [W. Jodko-Narkiewicz], *Objaśnienie programu Polskiej Partii Socjalistycznej* (Kraków, 1913), 120 ff.; *Di juden in pojlen* (n.p., n.d.), published by the Jewish PPS.

a constitutional debate in the Sejm Mieczysław Niedziałkowski, an expert on constitutional law and distinguished PPS activist, speaking against a motion by the Związek Posłów Narodowości Żydowskiej (Union of Delegates of Jewish Nationality) in support of this type of autonomy, stated: 'We are ready to grant all rights to cultural and political development to particular factions of minority groups scattered throughout the whole country, but we must necessarily preserve the general, fundamental principle that the Polish government is exclusively Polish.'[30]

At the same time Polish Socialists opposed any link between national and religious autonomy, and indeed the very concept of autonomy for minority groups. They based their refusal of these rights for the Jewish people on their perception that Jews were not a separate nation, were dispersed, and could not claim a language of their own: Jewish 'jargon' was not recognized anywhere, and could not be considered a national or religious trait of Jews. The best way to regulate the Jewish question in Poland would be full legal equality with the Polish population and inclusion of Jews in the governmental and national work of the country. This could only be achieved through the elimination of social injustice as a whole.[31]

Thus, after ratification of the constitution of March 1921 the majority of Polish Socialists felt that the principle of equal rights for all citizens adopted therein also met the demands of the Jewish minority. The PPS was one of only a few Polish groups which placed such great stress on the full realization of that principle. It invested a great deal of energy in the struggle against any and all forms of nationalistic pressure, such as cultural, economic, or administrative discrimination and the violation of constitutional provisions guaranteeing national minorities equal rights in society. It linked the minority problem closely with the development of the international situation and the role of Poland in the arrangement of political power in Europe. In its programmes, declarations, and testimonies the PPS stated that the principle behind its policy with regard to the so-called dispersed minorities, including Jews, was guaranteed freedom of cultural-social development and of other distinctive national traits. This principle was introduced into the party's programme concerning nationalism passed at its Nineteenth Congress in January 1924,[32] and formed part of the

---

[30] Sprawozdanie Stenograficzne Sejmu Ustawodawczego (SSSU; Shorthand reports of the Sejm), position 185 (13 Nov. 1920), ch. 35.

[31] I discuss the views of Polish Socialists concerning the Jewish question in my 'Kwestia narodowościowa w publicystyce i programach socjalistów polskich w okresie Drugiej Rzeczypospolitej', *Dzieje najnowsze*, 1–2 (1983), 107–27.

[32] *Robotnik*, 4 (4 Jan. 1924), 1–2; cf *Sprawozdanie CKW na XX Kongres PPS w Warszawie* (Warsaw, 1925), 6–7; M. Pszczółkowski [L. Wasilewski], *Polska dla Polaków czy Polska dla wszystkich obywateli polskich? (Sprawa mniejszości narodowych w Polsce)* (Warsaw, 1924); id., *Sprawa kresów i mniejszości narodowych w Polsce* (Warsaw, 1925).

congressional resolution of the Socialist Workers' International, which included the issue of nationalism at its Second Congress in August 1925, in Marseilles.[33]

After Piłsudski's coup of May 1926 the PPS took an increasing interest in the Jewish question and in the Jewish Socialist movement as a potential ideological and political ally. The matter of national-cultural autonomy for the Jewish people was discussed in the pages of *Robotnik* as one of the most sensitive problems in Polish–Jewish relations. It was conceded that Jews did in fact constitute a nation because they possessed their own national consciousness. The Jewish problem should be investigated in terms of class and government—from a democratic rather than an anti- or philosemitic position. The problem would not be solved by the emigration of Jews to Palestine, because not everyone would want to go there, and in any case Palestine would not be able to absorb them all.[34] Jewish Socialist programmes were popularized and Jewish Socialists were given access to the pages of PPS periodicals. The PPS advocated close co-operation with Jewish Socialists and, eventually, the creation of a single united Socialist party which would fight antisemitism.

But it was only in the light of the struggle against Fascism in Europe and authoritarian regimes in Poland that Polish Socialists radically changed their feelings concerning the Jewish minority. One of the social repercussions of the great economic depression was the heightening of nationalistic antagonisms, and especially Polish–Jewish tensions. Representatives of almost all Polish classes levelled various accusations against the Jewish people; these passions were fanned by Polish nationalistic groups and the politics of the Sanacja regime. Socialists mounted a defence against the growing wave of nationalism and antisemitism. They contended that these were not manifestations of natural human behaviour, because hatred for other people is not an inborn characteristic. Antisemitism, in their view, flourished in situations of perceived social injustice, and was encouraged by constant and planned action on the part of the ruling class, which saw in the development of nationalism and antisemitism a bulwark against the development of Socialism. The victory of Socialism and progress in all areas of social life would enable the resolution of problems of nationalism, including the Jewish question. They wished to enjoy permanent co-operation with Jewish Socialists on the basis of a joint socio-political and national programme. This was established at a conference of Jewish, German, and Ukrainian Socialists and labour unions on 3 May 1936. In an appeal directed to the whole Socialist left in Poland it was declared:

The conference calls upon the whole of the working class, without regard to national differences, to engage in solid and energetic opposition to nationalism and antisemitism, and

---

[33] *Zweiter Kongreß der Sozialistischen Arbeiter-Internationale in Marseille, 22. bis 27. August 1925* (Berlin, n.d.), 364.

[34] See e.g. R. Dąbrowski, 'Jeszcze o kwestii żydowskiej', *Robotnik*, 261 (23 Sept. 1927), 3.

in a joint brotherly fight of the exploited against the exploiters of all nations. Only a united front of working people of all nations against all manifestations of inequality and national and social oppression can fulfil the great mission of the complete liberation of the people.[35]

The PPS itself, in a programmatic document composed by Niedziałkowski and passed at the party's Twenty-fourth Congress of February 1937 in Radom, accepted that the theoretical basis for its new position on nationalism would be the Bauer concept of nation as a 'cultural community', a concept which played and continues to play an immense role. That is why it accepted in principle a policy of nationalism in the future Polish Socialistic republic in regard to the so-called dispersed minorities (including the Jews), as the foundation of their national-cultural autonomy.[36]

Yet after nearly fifty years of dispute, the recognition by the PPS of the principle of non-territorial autonomy still did not satisfy some Polish Socialists. Thus, the editor of *Robotnik*, Jan M. Borski, engaged in a polemic against the new national programme of the PPS,[37] and instead supported the emigration of Jews from Poland as the appropriate means of solving the Jewish problem. He contended that this was not at all a reactionary and antisemitic policy because, in general terms, emigration, correctly organized and planned, from countries which were over-industrialized to those which were underpopulated was destined to become an important phenomenon in the future. On the other hand, the growth of Socialism in Poland would not automatically resolve the Jewish question: this would continue to exist independently of any antisemitic agitation. This view was grounded in the fact that Jews constituted a relatively numerous and separate people in Poland, not connected by any 'spiritual or emotional ties' with the country in which they had settled. They were not antagonistic towards Poland, but neither did they recognize the country as their own motherland. Under conditions obtaining in Poland they were unable to transform themselves into a modern nation because there was very little opportunity for social or geographic mobility, while, in the midst of the Polish population, they would always be, in terms of race, religion, language, and tradition, a distinct ethnic group, isolated from Polish life. Borski therefore envisaged that a small segment of the Jewish community, deeply tied to Polish culture, would remain in the country, while the

---

[35] *Program ludu pracującego: Postulaty polityczne i gospodarcze* (Warsaw, 1936), 6–7; cf. A. Czarski [Z. Zaremba], 'Uzgodnienie poglądów i taktyki', *Światło*, 5 (1936), 7–11; *Program dobrobytu: Ruch robotniczy Polski wobec zagadnień gospodarczych* (Warsaw, 1937).

[36] *Program PPS, uchwalony na XXIV Kongresie w Radomiu* (Warsaw, 1937), 11.

[37] The author indicates that his criticism was directed at W. Alter, the Bund leader, though in essence he was attacking the new nationalism programme of the PPS; see J. M. Borski, *Sprawa żydowska a socjalizm; Polemika z Bundem* (Warsaw, 1937). Discussions among Socialists concerning the Jewish question and antisemitism were treated more extensively by the present author in *Polska myśl socjalistyczna (1918–1948)* (Wrocław, 1988), 156–61.

majority would emigrate to Palestine or to some other locale of permanent or temporary colonization. He added that support for emigration was to be found in some Jewish parties and in the majority of Polish opinion, while international factors lent weight to the proposal, which should not be equated with 'expulsion' of Jews from Poland. Anti-Jewish feeling was being exacerbated by the Bund's idea of cultural-national autonomy. Some Polish Socialists accepted the notion of emigration and felt that the earlier it occurred, the sooner would reactionary antisemitic arguments fall silent.

Zygmunt Zaremba, a leading PPS activist, took issue with Borski,[38] doubting whether emigration would provide a solution to the Jewish problem in Poland. It was only poverty that provided an incentive to emigration. Jews themselves, for the most part, were not interested in abandoning the country to which they were so closely connected, at a time when a feeling of patriotism was developing in them. As the cultural level of society improved, national differences would decrease and the various nationalities would live together in harmony. The elimination of national antagonisms would occur as part and parcel of a reform in economic relations. Emigration was no longer a viable means of resolving an economic crisis. Polish Socialism, imbued with a tradition of fighting for national freedom, respected individual nations, and desired to make of the Jewish population a creative and useful group for the country and society. The introduction of a Socialist economic system would eliminate the phenomenon of Jewish isolation and remove the economic basis of antisemitism. The settling of the Jewish question on the economic level would be accompanied by the cultural development of Jewish society. For that reason the PPS, as part of its programme, embraced the slogan of national-cultural autonomy.

At the foundation of this debate by Polish Socialists concerning the means to resolve the Jewish problem lay a variety of interpretations of the concept of nationhood and of the tendencies of national development and national consciousness. This had been a constant feature in the controversy regarding the Jewish question since the 1890s. Advocates of the Marxist concept of nation as a historical-territorial community ruled out the principle of national-cultural autonomy as a means for settling the Jewish question. On the other hand, those who understood nationhood in terms of a cultural community recognized non-territorial autonomy as the natural way to organize the Jewish minority in Poland. For almost half a century the negative view taken by the majority of Polish Socialists towards such autonomy had been reinforced by the fact that its programme was accepted by Jewish Socialists distancing themselves, for various reasons, from the Polish Socialist movement and seeking a level of co-operation with the Russian and German workers' movements. In addition, Polish Socialists, raised in the tradition of Polish romanticism, were convinced of the superiority of

---

[38] Z. Zaremba, 'Różnice czy błędy', *Światło*, 4–5 (1937), 18–22.

Polish culture and its great powers of absorption with regard to the cultures of minority groups. They believed that under a democratic Poland each nationality would be guaranteed proper conditions for social and cultural-national development. In their view concerning the Jewish minority they did not, however, rely on any concept of the Polish state, but referred to universal, humanistic, and democratic values, and in this way hoped to satisfy the needs and aspirations of that minority. In Polish society they fought actively against all forms of nationalism and antisemitism, and worked to disclose the sources of the wrongs and humiliation inflicted upon Jews. Even in the course of the barbarization of human culture in the 1930s, they assumed that Jewish national-cultural development could occur within the Polish nation following achievement of legal-political nonterritorial autonomy.

The Relation of the Polish Socialist Party: Proletariat to the Bund and the Jewish Question, 1900–1906

JANUSZ SUJECKI

POLSKA PARTIA SOCJALISTYCZNA: PROLETARIAT (PPS Proletariat—Polish Socialist Party: Proletariat) was founded in July 1900 by the Secessionists, a group of PPS activists who separated from the foreign section of the Lwów branch of the party in May 1900. The Secessionists, led by Ludwik Kulczycki (1866–1941), were openly critical of the structure of the parent organization, as well as the way it formulated its political objectives and the means it proposed to fight the oppressive Tsarist state. PPS Proletariat, active until 1908 and sometimes referred to as Proletariat III, was most influential during the revolution of 1905–7. Even then, however, it was the weakest Socialist party in the Congress Kingdom of Poland. Its members published a number of articles that dealt with the General Jewish Workers' Alliance in Lithuania, the Bund in Poland and Russia, and what was known as the 'Jewish question'.

Here we shall consider how the views expressed by the leadership of PPS Proletariat relate to the political objectives of the Bund, its status, and the impact it had on the Socialist labour movement within the Congress Kingdom of Poland in the Tsarist Empire. Alongside many statements on the Bund itself, the press of the PPS Proletariat was responsible for formulating the party's position on the Jewish question in general, which was perceived as a combination of political, economic, and social factors that made up the fabric of the Jewish community in the Congress Kingdom and the Russian Empire (especially as these related to Jewish labourers and tradesmen). The political position of PPS Proletariat on the Bund and the Jewish question is contrasted with the views held by the Polska Partia Socjalistyczna (PPS: Polish Socialist Party) and the Socjaldemokracja Królestwa Polskiego i Litwy (SDKPiL: the Social Democracy of the Kingdom of Poland and Lithuania), as well as with those expressed by the Rosiiskaya Sotsial-Demokraticheskaya i Rabochaya Partia (RSDRP: Russian Social Democratic and Workers' Party).

The period covered in this study begins with 1900, the year in which the Jewish Socialist workers' movement was first referred to in *Proletariat*, and ends with 1906, when the last essay on this subject appeared in *Proletariusz* [The proletarian]. The present paper is principally based on the source material in the three press organs of the party: *Proletariat* (1900–14), *Do boju* [To battle] (1904–15), and *Proletariusz* (1905–19). The memoirs of some of the party activists, although published much later, were also used.

The leader of PPS Proletariat, Kulczycki, was also its main ideologue and publicist, and wrote most of the pertinent essays. His personal outlook concerning the Bund and the Jewish question can be safely identified with that of the party itself. The other contributors are anonymous, and their views are overtly derivative from their leader's. The relationship of PPS Proletariat to the Bund and the Jewish question has merited only passing references in Polish and Soviet historiography (Bernard Mark, Walentyna Najdus, and Inessa Yazborovskaya, Rosaliya Yermolayeva, Aleksandr Manusievitch).[1] Moreover, official Soviet sources are overtly biased in their presentation of the Bund, depicting it as a viciously 'nationalist and opportunist' organization. Rather than presenting an honest analysis of that movement, Soviet historians quoted indiscriminately from Lenin's articles in *Iskra* [The spark]. None of the authors engaged in any in-depth investigation of the origins and specifics of the Bund's activities, and they completely avoided the issue of national identity that was just beginning to take shape among Jewish tradesmen and labourers.[2] A similar tendency also pervaded the Polish studies, which affected the general perception of PPS Proletariat itself; all instances of its support for the Bund were viewed unfavourably.[3] The relationship between the Bund and PPS Proletariat is also marginally dealt with in volume ii of the Yiddish history of the former, published in New York in the early 1960s.[4]

In May 1900 eleven party activists, including Ludwik Kulczycki, left the foreign section of the Lwów branch of PPS. These Secessionists signed a statement announcing their decision and the reasons behind it. This did not cover the specifics of the party's stance concerning the Jewish question or the Bund, although it did point out that 'the leadership of the PPS, because of its lack of political acumen and arbitrariness of conduct, estranged a great many people sympathetic to the cause'.[5]

[1] B. Mark, 'Proletariat żydowski w przededniu rewolucji 1905 r.', *Biuletyn Żydowskiego Instytutu Historycznego*, 13–14 (1955), 70–1; W. Najdus, *SDKPiL a SDPRR 1893–1907* (Wrocław, Warsaw, Kraków, and Gdańsk, 1973), 228–9; I. S. Yazborovskaya, *Idieynoye razvitiye polskovo rievolutsionnovo rabotchevo dvizeniya* (Moscow, 1973), 147; R. A. Yermolayeva and A. J. Manusievitch, *Lenin i polskoye rabotchiye dvizheniye* (Moscow, 1971), 65, 78.
[2] See *Historia Komunistycznej Partii Związku Radzieckiego*, i (Warsaw, 1968), 299, 330–1.
[3] See Mark, 'Proletariat żydowski', 70–1.
[4] G. Aronson et al. (eds.), *Di geshikhte fun Bund*, ii/1 (New York, 1962).
[5] 'Do CKR PPS', Archiwum Akt Nowych—Oddział VI [AAN—O.VI], microfilm no. 1440/8.

Kulczycki, in a letter of 18 May 1900 advising Kazimierz Kelles-Krauz of his departure from the party's ranks, stated quite explicitly that 'the loss of the Jewish movement in the country to the formal patronage of the Bund can only be blamed on the leadership of PPS itself'.[6] That Kulczycki took up this particular issue in the context of his break with PPS was not so much because of his personal involvement or that of his fellow Secessionists; it was rather a convenient argument for his critique of the style of the party's leadership.

The founding of PPS Proletariat, bitterly opposed to PPS, was welcomed with interest by the Bund, not primarily for the political concepts it espoused but because the Bund was seeking a prospective ally in its political struggle with PPS.[7] In April 1901 the Fourth Congress of the Bund carried a motion to establish friendly relations with PPS Proletariat—'as with any other revolutionary socialist organization', irrespective of differences 'in their approach to certain tactical problems' (i.e. the role of terrorist tactics in the political struggle).[8]

PPS Proletariat, for its part, set its sights on the Bund only a few months after its political birth. *Proletariat* was very critical of PPS's opposition to the Bund, which it had consistently characterized as a 'chauvinistically Jewish movement' or branded as 'anti-Polish and politically convenient for the Russian regime'.[9] The publicists grouped in *Proletariat* emphasized the substantial power-base of the Bund, its influence, and its considerable success both in organizing the Jewish proletariat into a political body and in rendering assistance in its struggle. The Bund's publishing achievements also earned some praise.

The resolution of the Sixth Congress of PPS (June 1902) calling for establishment of a special committee for Jewish affairs to be formally overseen by the Centralny Komitet Robotniczy (CKR: Central Workers' Committee) was promptly dismissed by *Proletariat* as 'bizarre and without any real significance' in relation to the Bund's overwhelming following among the Jewish labourers.[10] Kulczycki described PPS's opposition to the Bund as 'one of its gravest political errors'. He also argued (by the same token revising his own earlier stance)[11] that the resolution passed by the Fourth Congress of PPS was completely unjustified,

See also J. Targalski, 'Geneza Polskiej Partii Socjalistycznej Proletariat', *Z pola walki*, 2–3 (1973), 63.

[6] Letter from L. Kulczycki to M. Lusnia [K. Kelles-Krauz], Lwów, 18 May 1900, AAN—O.VI, microfilm, no. 1190/4. See also J. Targalski, 'Geneza Polskiej Partii Socjalistycznej Proletariat', *Z pola walki*, 2–3 (1973) 39–79.

[7] See 'Luźne notatki', *Przedświt*, 11 (1900), 40; L. Wasilewski, 'Ze wspomnień' (1899–1904)', pt. 2, ed. J. Myśliński and W. Władyka in *Z pola walki*, 4/68 (1974), 218–27.

[8] *Di geshikhte fun Bund*, i (New York, 1960).

[9] 'Żydowski ruch robotniczy w Polsce, na Litwie i w Rosji', *Proletariat*, 4–5 (1901), 3–4 at 3.

[10] Ibid.; 'Podwójna buchalteria . . . w polityce', *Proletariat*, 9 (1902), 36.

[11] Kulczycki, during his detention in the Kresty prison in St Petersburg in spring 1898, wrote a short essay entitled 'A Voice on the Jewish Question', in which he subscribed to the views formulated at the Fourth Congress of PPS in its resolution on the founding of the Bund. See L. Kulczycki, 'Głos w sprawie żydowskiej', AAN—O.VI, microfilm no. 1190/4.

as 'no Socialist party from one nation can or should impose on any party of another nation'. PPS Proletariat's own position towards the Bund was correct from the very start, according to Kulczycki. It granted the Bund full recognition as a separate political entity, unlike PPS, which opposed the Bund in the name of Polish centralism.[12]

The recognition of the Bund as a separate political entity uniting the Jewish proletariat was a cornerstone of PPS Proletariat policy. The leader of PPS Proletariat presented arguments in favour of this view which were in fact the same as those of the Bund. Kulczycki did not believe that the Bund would give sanction to the Yiddish language and thus hinder the process of assimilation. He realized, however, that the actual use of this language for propaganda purposes might bring massive Jewish support for the Socialist cause. 'From the standpoint of national interest,' argued Kulczycki, 'the existence of a separate Jewish organization is also well justified, because every nationality should be granted the right of self-determination.'[13]

In the period 1901–5 PPS Proletariat defined its position on the Jewish question. The Jews were clearly perceived as a separate nationality, as can be seen in the essay 'The Jewish Labour Movement in Poland, Lithuania, and Russia', published in *Proletariat* in 1901.[14] Duly recognizing the resolutions passed by the Fourth Congress of the Bund and using the term 'nationhood' in relation to Jews, PPS Proletariat invoked the inherent right of every nation to self-determination. 'We Poles have no right to pass judgement on whether the Jews should see themselves as Poles or as a separate Jewish nation; it is up to them, and the Fourth Congress of the Bund representing the masses of Jewish labourers is competent enough for us in this matter', declared *Proletariat*'s columnists in 1902.[15]

Kulczycki developed this idea still further in 1904–5, stating that PPS Proletariat was quite happy to leave this issue entirely to the Jews to decide. 'If a certain group of people see themselves in terms of a separate nation . . . then this in itself constitutes a sufficient criterion to acknowledge that it indeed is one'; PPS Proletariat recognized as a nation 'any group of people that possessed a sense of national identity'.[16]

PPS Proletariat remained neutral on the much-publicized issue of Jewish

---

[12] M. Mazowiecki [L. Kulczycki], *Historia ruchu socjalistycznego w zaborze rosyjskim* (Kraków, 1903), 349–50, 387.

[13] 'Żydowski ruch robotniczy'. It is worth noting that PPS Proletariat was opposed to the founding of an independent organization of the Jewish working class in Galicia. Kulczycki argued that both social and political conditions in that region were conducive to a close co-operation between the Polish and Jewish proletariat within a single party. See 'Samodzielność organizacyjna a Żydzi', *Proletariat*, 12 (1903), 31–3.   [14] See n. 9 above.

[15] 'Z powodu Czwartego Zjazdu Żydowskiego Związku Robotniczego na Litwie i Polsce i Rosji', *Proletariat*, 6 (1902), 9.

[16] 'II Zjazd Rosyjskiej Socjalno-Demokratycznej Partii Robotniczej (dokończenie)', *Proletariat*, 17 (1904), 13–14; 'Co dać może nasz program proletariatowi żydowskiemu', *Do Boju*, 7 (1905), 32.

assimilation in the Polish community, but was in principle opposed to any compulsory acceleration of this process. It agreed with the Bund's view, which 'did not prejudice the prospective outcome of this debate', as Kulczycki pointed out. He envisaged the process of Jewish assimilation both in the Congress Kingdom and in Lithuania as a rather lengthy one.[17]

By recognizing the Jews as a separate nation, PPS Proletariat granted their language equality with those of other national minorities. In its 1906 manifesto it declared that whenever a particular minority (including Jews) constituted 15 per cent or more of the local population, it should automatically be guaranteed the right to official use of its own language.[18]

In 1903 PPS Proletariat also adopted a position concerning the Lithuanian Jews, who were accused of manifesting 'Russophile attitudes'. Kulczycki dismissed the charges, explaining that Lithuanian Jewry had never been under strong Polish influence. The process of Russification, introduced in Lithuania shortly after the failure of the January Rising of 1863, was a contributory factor, argued Kulczycki. The attraction of the flourishing Russian culture, 'to which foreign elements simply gravitated', also contributed to its dominance. He did not, however, rule out the possibility of Polonization of the Lithuanian Jews if Polish culture proved to be more virile and richer than their own.[19]

The political essays published by PPS Proletariat do not offer any analyses of the orgins of antisemitism in certain parts of Polish society. They do, however, consider the issue of Jewish pogroms (in essays from 1905-6) as a social phenomenon incited and managed by the Tsarist authorities and intended 'to deflect the revolutionary spirit within the society towards a bitter strife between its elements, instead of concentrating on mounting an open challenge to Tsarist rule'.[20] PPS Proletariat was involved in a host of propaganda activities aimed at the Polish peasantry and the working class to demonstrate the deviousness of this campaign to incite violence. It was also to encourage the Jews to set up their own self-defence groups. Following the pogrom in Białystok in 1906, the front page of the twelfth issue of *Proletariusz* was bordered in black in protest against the carnage.[21]

The political programme of PPS Proletariat from 1902 defined the concept of nation as 'a group of people possessing a distinctly individual cultural tradition, its own language, a nucleus of national literature, etc. This concept does not extend to those peoples and tribes who do not manifest their own culture and do not have a sense of national identity': 'Program Polskiej Partii Socjalistycznej—Proletariat (1902)', in *Polskie programy socjalistyczne 1878–1918*, collected, with a historical commentary, by F. Tych (Warsaw, 1975), 434.

[17] 'Bibliografia: Przegląd Socjaldemokratyczny. Nr. 1, 2 i 3: Autonomia narodowa nieterytorjalna', *Proletariat*, 10 (1902), 25–00 at 30; 'Co dać może nasz program', 31; Mazowiecki [Kulczycki], *Historia ruchu socjalistycznego*, 463–4.
[18] 'Program Polskiej Partii Socjalistycznej—Proletariat (1908)', in *Polskie programy*, 454.
[19] Mazowiecki [Kulczycki], *Historia ruchu socjalistycznego*, 402–3.
[20] 'Pogromy', *Proletariusz*, 1 (1905), 4.
[21] Ibid.; 'Odezwy', *Do Boju*, 7 (1905), 70–3; *Proletariusz*, 12 (1906), 1.

PPS Proletariat was the only political party to advocate perception of the Jews as a separate nation, and to take the view that the problem of eventual assimilation should be allowed to run its own course. The leadership of PPS refused to acknowledge a separate Jewish national identity and was endeavouring to facilitate assimilation, ignoring any manifestations of a separate national character among Jewish labourers; the Jewish organization of the PPS belonged to the assimilationist wing of the party. Only in the light of the revolutionary experiences of 1905–7 did PPS change its position on the issue of a Jewish national identity, language, and culture. In 1906 it postulated that the Jewish community be granted the right to use the vernacular in its own schools, and eventually also recognized a separate Jewish national character as a unique cultural heritage.[22]

In the ranks of SDKPiL, Stanisław Trusiewicz was closest to Kulczycki's views. At the Third Congress of SDKPiL in 1901 Trusiewicz's point of view was not popular, the vast majority of the delegates sharing the opinion of Olga Badiorova who argued that 'the Jews are not a separate nation and do not possess their own cultural heritage'.[23] It was deemed necessary to point out in the resolution passed by this congress that the party did not endorse the views put forward by the Bund, though for purely tactical purposes the Bund was granted formal recognition as an 'independent, fraternal organization'.[24] SDKPiL took an assimilationist approach to the Jewish question.

A similar approach was espoused by the RSDRP. It was particularly evident among the supporters of *Iskra* and in the contemporary political writings of Lenin. Showing a clearly biased approach to the Jewish question, Lenin cited Kautsky's 'fundamental traits' of nationhood—language and territory—and then used these as the essential criteria, which effectively prejudiced the outcome in the case of the Jewish question. To uphold the concept of a separate Jewish nation was seen by Lenin as an attempt to propagate a 'false and Zionistic' idea, which was reactionary from the political standpoint and 'contrary to the interests of the Jewish proletariat'. In due course this interpretation was to be replaced by accusations of nationalism against the Bund.[25] There was a strong conviction in the ranks of the Second International that the nationalist aspirations of the Jewish labourers were without basis, which made the support of PPS Proletariat

[22] H. Piasecki, *Żydowska Organizacja PPS 1893–1907* (Wrocław, Warsaw, Kraków, and Gdańsk, 1978), 182–4, 235–9, 263–5; *Di geshikhte fun Bund*, i. 317–18; ii/1. 130–6.
[23] 'Uchwały III Zjazdu SDKPiL', 28–9 Sept. 1901 (Warsaw), in *SDKPiL, Materiały i dokumenty*, i. *1893–1903*, pt. 2 (Warsaw, 1962), No. 71, pp. 226–7. [24] *Di geshikhte fun Bund*, i. 319.
[25] W. I. Lenin, 'Pozycja Bundu w partii', *Dzieła*, vii (Warsaw, 1953), 92–4; see also *Di geshikhte fun Bund*, ii/2. (Płoce, n.d.), 529. It would be difficult to agree with the view of Jerzy J. Wiatr, who regards Lenin's stance on the Jewish question as supportive of 'natural assimilation'. This would be tantamount to saying that the growing sense of national identity never in fact existed among the Jewish labourers, and consequently that the leaders of the Bund were acting in opposition to predominant trends in the Jewish community, trying to stem its 'natural' drive towards assimilation. See J. J. Wiatr, 'Naród i państwo', *Socjologiczne problemy kwestii narodowej* (Warsaw, 1973), 76–8.

for the Bund and its approach to the Jewish question very unusual at the beginning of the twentieth century.

PPS Proletariat openly criticized the views expressed in *Iskra*, although it accepted the Leninist approach to nationhood—something which the Bund found 'inconsistent'.[26] 'In our opinion', argued one of *Proletariat*'s writers in 1904, 'we are not being inconsistent in our approach, as the fundamental difference between us and *Iskra* is that it does not recognize the Jews as a separate nation, and consequently withholds from it all other characteristics of nationhood. We, on the other hand, leave this issue to be resolved by the Jews themselves... It is therefore perfectly consistent to espouse [*Iskra*'s] approach to the very concept of nationhood while rejecting its specific views on the Jewish question at large.[27]

The differences in their approaches to the Jewish question were not the only reason for PPS Proletariat to engage in a polemic with *Iskra*. PPS Proletariat, unlike Lenin, strongly advocated the federalist model of a national party, which it believed to be quite consistent with active support of the Bund's view. It did not dispute *Iskra*'s concept of 'uniform and resilient action co-ordinated by a central leadership',[28] although it differed on the proposed means of implementing it. PPS Proletariat believed this uniformity would be best achieved by a national federation of different national groups co-ordinated centrally by a committee of representatives from the Socialist parties of all the different nationalities. Such a model would not jeopardize unity; it would promote political initiatives and offer 'freedom of action' not only to the Bund but also to all other parties. It was perceived as 'the only feasible combination of revolutionary powers within Tsarist Russia, both before and after the revolution'.[29]

PPS Proletariat fully endorsed the resolution passed by the Fifth Congress of the Bund (1903) on its organizational activities in southern Russia. 'The assumption of the Bund's leadership of the Jewish movement in the southern area of the Russian Empire is seen by us as a positive development that would be, contrary to the opinions voiced by *Iskra*, instrumental in building political awareness among the local Jewish community and would also enrich its cultural environment', declared *Proletariat* in 1903.[30]

PPS Proletariat defended the Bund against accusations of chauvinism and nationalism. The Bund's own contribution to the suppression of Zionist tendencies was given prominence by the political writers of PPS Proletariat and was

---

[26] 'Iz rievolutsionnovo dvizheniya na Ukrainach', *Viestnik Bunda*, 1–2 (1904), 20.

[27] 'II Zjazd Rosyjskiej', *Proletariat*, 17 (1904), 13–14; see also 'Sprawozdanie z konferencji Pol. Par. Soc. Proletariat' (Oct. 1903) in *Do Boju*, 2 (1904), 12–13.

[28] 'Samodzielność', 30. See also W. I. Lenin, 'Czy proletariatowi żydowskiemu potrzebna jest "samodzielna partia polityczna"', *Iskra*, 3 (1904), in *Dzieła* vi (Warsaw, 1952), 341.

[29] Mazowiecki [Kulczycki], *Historia ruchu socjalistycznego*, 387.

[30] 'Samodzielność', 31.

hailed as a true example of opposition to the viciously nationalistic trends.[31] Its relation to the Bund and the Bund's position on the Jewish question was far from homogeneous, however. Kulczycki approved of the Bund's position on organizational matters and fully endorsed the fundamentals of its political programme, consistently publicizing and offering his own theoretical explications in support. In 1904 he published articles in *Głos Bundu* [Voice of the Bund], *Viestnik Bundu* [Herald of the Bund], and *Der yiddisher arbeter* [The Jewish worker] presenting PPS Proletariat as sympathetic to the Bund and pointing out the sections in both parties' manifestos that showed how closely related they were on many issues.[32]

Kulczycki's views were also shared by Kazimierz Pruszkowski (whose pseudonym was 'Orczyk'), one of the most prominent party activists and the organizer of the party's printing shop in Geneva. Bolesław Drobner, on the other hand, a member of the Central Committee of PPS Proletariat and a party activist since 1902, represented the assimilationist wing.[33] Another member of the leadership, Kazimierz Jeziorowski, accused Kulczycki many years later of 'advocating close collaboration with the Bund', which he considered to be a serious error.[34] The differences of opinion amongst the activists of PPS Proletariat were not reflected in the party press. They may not even have been addressed at the party conference in October 1903, nor at its congress in late December 1905.

Kulczycki gave prominence to his assessment of the Bund's position on the issue of Polish independence. As early as 1901 he acknowledged that the Bund never opposed an independent Poland or the right of the Poles to a sovereign state. On the other hand, the Bund was openly critical of PPS, which called for national independence while rejecting all other political aspirations. 'That is why', declared Kulczycki, 'the way we bring forward the issue of national independence and political freedom has not made any enemies in the ranks of the Jewish organization so far.'[35]

The significant similarity in the approach of both parties to the issue of Polish independence was that they did not rule out the possibility of an independent Polish state in specific political circumstances. PPS Proletariat put it forward only tentatively, and the Bund did not include it in its programme at all, considering the issue of national independence irrelevant to the current political struggle of the proletariat.[36] Kulczycki was of the opinion that even though the Bund stopped short of calling for the national independence of Poland, it was,

[31] See 'Drugi Zjazd Rosyjskiej Socjal-Demokratycznej Partii Robotniczej', *Proletariat*, 15–16 (1904), 13; 'Działalność Bundu w ostatnim roku', *Do Boju*, 4 (1904), 15–16.
[32] *Di geshikhte fun Bund*, i. 262–3; Mazowiecki [Kulczycki], 'Listy polskie z zaboru rosyjskiego', *Głos Bundu*, 2 (1904), 11–17; ibid. 3 (1904), 20–7; Mazovietski [Kulczycki], 'Pis′ma iz Russkoi Pol′shi', *Viestnik Bunda*, 4 (1904), 16–19.
[33] B. Drobner, *Bezustanna walka: Wspomnienia 1883–1916*, i. (Warsaw, 1962), 155–6, 176–7.
[34] K. Jeziorowski, *Wspomnienia z lat 1886–1924* (Siedlce, 1934), 79.
[35] 'Żydowski ruch robotniczy', 4.
[36] Ibid.; *Di geshikhte fun Bund*, ii/2. 254–5.

nevertheless, a desirable ally. From the purely pragmatic standpoint, it still served the cause of national independence by opposing the Tsarist state, the main adversary of Polish national aspirations. Still, in 1903 Kulczycki declared that 'it is quite unreasonable to bear any grudge towards the Jewish party for not calling for the overthrow of the Tsarist regime. Why should the Jews desire to establish closer ties with the Polish nation and culture than with the Russian, for instance?'[37]

In 1905 he changed his view, advocating the revival of an independent Poland as being in the interests of the Jewish proletariat of the Congress Kingdom. 'An independent Poland would guarantee a great many benefits . . . to the Jewish proletariat, providing for better constitutional laws than in Russia. The Jewish proletariat could thus become amenable to the possibility of breaking away from Russia.'[38] While propagating the party political programme in 1905, he also tried to demonstrate that the tentatively postulated Polish independence could appeal to the Jewish working class as well.

In 1902 PPS Proletariat, following the Fourth Congress of the Bund in 1901, expressed itself in favour of Jewish national and cultural autonomy. This stance showed the influence of programmatic concepts from the Austrian Social Democrats. The concept of non-territorial nationhood put forward by the Bund drew violent criticism from the supporters of *Iskra*, who alleged that the Bund had set its sights on much wider aims than even the Bund itself ever originally contemplated. The 'non-territorial autonomy' was supposedly extended to self-governing and administrative functions, whereas the Bund, as stated in the report from its Fourth Congress, had merely 'national and cultural objectives in mind'.[39]

The reaction of SKDPiL in 1902 was similar: non-territorial autonomy was freely interpreted in *Przegląd Socjaldemokratyczny* [The Social Democratic review], but in a way that was incongruous with the intentions of the Bund. The concept was subsequently criticized on the grounds that 'even the Bund itself will never be able to prove how such a thing [non-territorial autonomy] could possibly be implemented'.[40]

In the course of his polemic with *Przegląd Socjaldemokratyczny*, Kulczycki endorsed the Bund's position on the issue and endeavoured to make this concept even more explicit. He perceived it as complementary to a territorial one, indispensable in the case of countries of mixed population, and necessary when 'it is not possible to define precisely the territory populated by a particular national minority'. He advocated that a specific mechanism be set up to facilitate transition to a model of non-territorial autonomy in a constitutional Russia.

[37] Mazowiecki [Kulczycki], *Historia ruchu socjalistycznego*, 349–50.
[38] 'Co dać może nasz program', 34–5.
[39] *Di geshikhte fun Bund*, i. 186, 314–15.
[40] 'W kwestii żydowskiej', *Przegląd Socjaldemokratyczny*, 3 (1902), 21–5.

When bodies of different levels of local government are debating the allocation of funds for education and various cultural establishments . . . these funds could be subdivided among the diverse national groups in proportion to their numerical strength, delegating the authority to use the monies to the representatives of each group in those institutions. This way each national minority inhabiting a 'mixed territory' might not need to have its own territorial institutions, making use of the common resources for their own ends.[41]

Attempting to specify the concept of non-territorial national autonomy, Kulczycki postulated that every national minority, including the Jews, that was dispersed throughout the land be granted the right to possess its own legislative body—'a parliament made up of the representatives of this particular minority. Such a parliament would have the power to levy taxes on all those who declared themselves members of this group. The funds so raised would then be assigned to various national institutions: institutes of higher education, museums, repositories of art, etc.'[42]

In Kulczycki's opinion, the parliament could also control the vast body of national and cultural matters as well as some of an economic nature, provided that it would not infringe the country's constitution. Kulczycki also advocated the creation of a higher chamber of the prospective national parliament in which each national minority would be represented by an equal number of deputies. Its prerogative would be to 'guard the interest of the small minorities against infringement by large ones', without hampering the legislative process itself or hindering 'the joint action of the proletariat of the diverse national minorities inhabiting the country'.[43]

The Jewish national assembly and Jewish representation in the higher chamber of the parliament were seen as potentially 'beneficial to the development of a national culture without isolating them from the central parliament or the provincial parliament [of the Congress Kingdom] in matters of state and country'.[44] Kulczycki envisaged national non-territorial autonomy within an autonomous territorial system of the state, assuming that the courts and other state institutions would be common to all the constituent national minorities. He granted the Jewish proletariat the right to enjoy 'all the privileges' for which they were eligible as a national minority while emphasizing that 'the general policy of the group must be consistent with the interests of the country's proletariat as a whole'.[45]

Pointing out the 'great merit' of the Bund, which put forward the postulate of non-territorial autonomy, Kulczycki was hoping that the Bund would eventually

---

[41] 'Biblografia . . . Autonomia narodowa nieterytoryalna', 29.
[42] Ibid.   [43] Ibid. 29–30.
[44] L. Kulczycki, *Sprawozdanie z działalności Polskiej Partii Socjalistycznej Proletariat od połowy 1900 do początku 1908 r.* (n.p., 1908), 56–7.
[45] 'Co dać może nasz program', 33–5.

present its own interpretation of the concept.⁴⁶ He argued that a wide autonomy for the constituent parts of the whole country, combined with the adoption of the federalist model (the transformation of Russia into a democratic federal republic comprising several smaller republics—including the Congress Kingdom—totally autonomous in their respective internal policies), would appeal to the Jewish proletariat because 'it would thus stand a far better chance of winning substantial gains in the Polish or Lithuanian local parliament, where it would boast proportionally a much larger representation than it would ever be eligible for in the central Russian parliament'.⁴⁷

Like the Bund, PPS Proletariat advocated a federalist model for a national party and endorsed the Bund's position on the Jewish question, but it also pointed to the issues dividing them. These mainly concerned the tactics to be adopted in the struggle for political freedom. The Bund, unlike PPS Proletariat, was adamantly opposed to the use of terrorism, even when restricted to self-defence or as a tool in the political struggle. The publicists of PPS Proletariat considered this to be 'the only weak element of the Jewish movement in the Tsarist state', a movement that in their opinion did not have 'an appropriate revolutionary tactic'.

In 1902 *Proletariat* criticized the resolution passed at the Fourth Congress of the Bund recommending that acts of police brutality be countered by filing formal complaints against the perpetrators, organizing public protests, and open condemnation of such incidents in the party press. The columnists of PPS Proletariat called on the Bund to allow terrorism as a tactical means in order to adopt 'a more revolutionary approach'.⁴⁸ According to the supporters of *Proletariat*, the Bund put far too much emphasis on industrial action as a method of pursuing the political struggle. They advised restraint in this respect, but were in favour of the Bund's methods of organizing public protests and demonstrations.⁴⁹

Additional differences between the Bund and PPS Proletariat came to light in 1905–7. The Bund demanded that an All-Russian constitutional assembly be set up, yet decided against a separate Warsaw constitutional assembly.⁵⁰ The publicists of PPS Proletariat regarded the call for two separate assemblies within one country as utter nonsense; they were in favour of setting up a parliament in Warsaw in 1905 (a provisional parliament that would only put forward projects for legislation and would eventually be transformed into a parliament vested with

---

⁴⁶ In Dec. 1904 the Central Committee of the Bund demanded Jewish national autonomy and defined the concept. In Nov. 1905, at its Sixth Congress, the Bund formulated the national programme, narrowing its view of cultural-national autonomy. See 'Biblografia . . . Autonomia narodowa nieterytoryalna', 30; *Di geshikhte fun Bund*, i. 311, ii/1. 90, 253–4.

⁴⁷ 'Jakiej chcemy autonomii?', *Do Boju*, 6 (1904), 6.

⁴⁸ 'Z powodu Czwartego Zjazdu', *Proletariat*, 6 (1902), 7–10. ⁴⁹ Ibid. 7–8.

⁵⁰ 'Z powodu uchwały VII Zjazdu PPS o Zgromadzeniach konstytucyjnych', *Głos Bundu*, 4 (1905), 5–7; *Di geshikhte fun Bund*, ii/1. 254–5.

full legislative powers). The Bund was accused of failing to take a position on such a vital issue.[51] Kulczycki too expressed the view that the Bund should unequivocally proclaim itself in favour of transforming Russia into a democratic federal republic.[52]

In early 1906 PPS Proletariat began a campaign to set up a council of workers' delegates in the Congress Kingdom of Poland to co-ordinate the activities of Socialist parties and eventually their unification. The Bund (like PPS and SDKPiL) opposed this on the grounds, Kulczycki suggested, that it might loosen the ties of Bund members in the Congress Kingdom with those operating in Lithuania and Russia.[53]

Neither tactical nor political differences in the struggle against the Tsarist Empire affected the much-publicized sympathetic relationship of PPS Proletariat to the Bund and the fundamentals of its programme. In the party press and its publications, the Bund was called 'the most competent and the sole'[54] representative of the Jewish labourers and was considered 'a desirable and powerful ally' in the revolutionary struggle.

In the period 1900–6, the press and publications of PPS Proletariat published five articles and eleven extensive paragraphs dealing with the Bund and the Jewish question. In this period PPS Proletariat consistently defended the Bund's position as a separate and independent organization of the Jewish proletariat, supporting its call for national cultural autonomy for the Jewish community and advocating, together with the Bund, a federalist model of an All-Russian party. Kulczycki and the other publicists pointed to the large following and considerable political success of the Bund, and defended it against the accusations of nationalism.

PPS Proletariat regard the Jewish question as a predominantly nationalist issue, only occasionally addressing its social and economic aspects. As Władysław Wic once observed, the concept of non-territorial national autonomy postulated by Kulczycki 'was introduced on the Polish scene as an original one, irrespective of the postulates formulated by the Austrian Social Democrats at the Congress in Berne ... and is ... a certain contribution in the theoretical and practical aspects of the nationalist issue.'[55]

PPS Proletariat regarded the Jews as a separate nation and supported equality

[51] 'Co dać może nasz program', 36. [52] Ibid. 31–2.
[53] [L. Kulczycki], *Sprawozdanie z działalności Polskiej Partii Socjalistycznej—Proletariat* [from mid-1900 to 1908] (n.p., 1908), 136.
[54] 'Samodzielność', 29; Mazowiecki [Kulczycki], *Historia ruchu socjalistycznego*, 463–4. The phrase 'most competent and sole' [representative] did not mean that the Bund was accorded a monopoly on the representation of Jewish labourers; rather, it reflected the Bund's position as an organization. See 'Z działalności naszej organizacji', in *Z teorii i praktyki socjalizmu u nas i gdzie indziej* (WÓW, 1905), 179.
[55] W. Wic, 'Problematyka narodowa w poglądach Ludwika Kulczyckiego (1887–1908)', in *W kręgu twórców myśli politycznej: Zbiór studiów* (Wrocław, Warsaw, Kraków, and Gdańsk, 1983), 61.

of status for the Yiddish language with the languages of other national minorities. It remained neutral, like the Bund, on the issue of Jewish assimilation, opposing compulsory assimilation as well as hampering any spontaneous drive to bring it about.

The position of PPS Proletariat concerning the Bund and its programme differed considerably from those of PPS, SDKPiL, and RSDRP. It was also far from the preponderant view among the members of the Second International. As emphasized in the first volume of *Di geshikhte fun Bund*,

> the demand for national rights for Jews was never granted recognition by the non-Jewish parties of the Empire. . . . The Bund's position on the nationalist issue was met with resistance by almost all Socialist tendencies currently existing within the Russian Empire . . . Even those who recognized the right of the other national minorities to non-territorial/national-cultural autonomy could not extend recognition to the Jews, because in their view the Jews would thus be condemned to total denationalization.[56]

The relations between the Bund and PPS Proletariat were very friendly, although as a potential ally PPS Proletariat had limitations because of its lack of power. It is rather difficult to determine to what extent PPS Proletariat support for the Bund was merely tactical. Most of the publications supporting the Bund appeared in 1904, probably owing as much to rising interest in its political programme in the aftermath of the Second Congress of RSDRP as to the severance of relations with SDKPiL in mid-1903. The break may have prompted isolated supporters of PPS Proletariat (still in conflict with PPS) to intensify contacts with the Bund. In the second half of 1905 the publications relating to the Jewish question aimed at winning the support of at least some sections of the Jewish community to strengthen the position of PPS Proletariat. By 1906 those publications no longer mentioned the issue. This disappearance coincided with the campaign to set up a council of workers' delegates in the Congress Kingdom of Poland, which Kulczycki and his followers believed would rescue the fading political authority of the party and give it a new lease of life.[57]

---

[56] *Di geshikhte fun Bund*, i. 312, 320.

[57] We do not know a great deal about the methods employed by PPS Proletariat to win over the Jewish labourers. There are certain references in the party press to the publication of some leaflets in the Yiddish language and also to the 'jargon' issue of *Proletariusz* (of which no copy survives). The political activity of the Jewish organization of the PPS and its following also merits a separate investigation. See [L. Kulczycki], 'Sprawozdanie', 179–80; 'Z kraju: Warszawa w maju 1904', *Proletariat*, 15–16 (1904), 57; 'Z działalności naszej organizacji', *Proletariusz*, 30 (1907), 4.

The Jews, the Left, and the State Duma Elections in Warsaw in 1912: Selected Sources

Translated by
STEPHEN D. CORRSIN

INTRODUCTION

THE election to the fourth Russian State Duma, in the autumn of 1912, represented a critical break in the history of Polish–Jewish relations in Warsaw. For the first time the Jewish voters had a potential majority; more importantly, they managed, for the most part, to remain united. By contrast, the Polish voters split between two nationalist lists, one headed by the National Democratic leader Roman Dmowski, the other by a member of the National Democratic 'Secession', Jan Kucharzewski, who was supported by many anti-Dmowski Poles.

Socialist groups in the city, on the other hand, were weak and badly split; the major ones were the Jewish Bund, Polsko Partia Socjalistyczna-Lewica (PPS-Lewica: Polish Socialist Party Left), and the Socjaldemokracja Królestwa Polskiego i Litwy (SDKPiL: Social Democracy of the Kingdom of Poland and Lithuania). Yet, when the time came to choose a Duma delegate in November, the Jewish electors turned to the Socialists as the only Polish elements active in the campaign which accepted, in their platforms, the idea of equal rights for Jews. The Jewish electors (mostly businessmen) resolved to cast their votes for a Polish Socialist in spite of their own misgivings and in the face of threats from practically all Polish nationalist and liberal elements; this turned out to be Eugeniusz Jagiełło, a metal-turner and political nonentity from the PPS Left, whom the party had put forward because none of its leaders met the legal requirements. The main result of this was a furious anti-Jewish boycott supported by many parts of Polish society, under the slogan *Swój do swego po swoje*, which roughly means, 'Stick to your own'.

This was the only occasion on which a Polish Socialist of any sort ever got into the Russian State Duma, but the Socialist parties do not seem to have been very pleased with their success. The Social Democrats claimed that Socialist parties should not be accepting bourgeois votes in such a fashion, and the PPS Left seems to have been at least embarrassed by the outcome.

Here are translated recollections and comments on these events from the memoirs of a Polish Jewish journalist, Bernard Singer,[1] who witnessed the events as a young resident of Warsaw, and from contemporary Russian police reports describing Jewish political meetings and summarizing the scanty facts available on the city's new Socialist delegate to the State Duma.

THE YIDDISH PRESS

(*by* BERNARD SINGER)

At the start of 1912 two Yiddish newspapers published in Warsaw gained greater and greater influence; their print-runs grew. This was not the result of a taste for politics.

For the shop-owners, who were exporting goods to Russia or importing various things from the West, political news was no longer a matter of indifference. The owners of the larger shops read Polish and Russian newspapers, and even the *Berliner Tageblatt* [Berlin daily]. For the new, smaller merchants, these were incomprehensible languages. But events in Russia, whether famine in some areas, or strikes, affected their decisions about where it would be worthwhile to send a travelling salesman, or from where they might expect to have bills returned unpaid. People heard the news from St Petersburg with alarm, or read with consternation the speeches of the 'Black Hundred' delegates in the Third Duma. Their influence grew as the wave of strikes increased.

The spirit of competition, which ruled in trade, also dominated the newspapers. Every reader was fought over. They tried to wrest readers from their competitors by serializing gutter novels, or by *feuilletons*. News was plagiarized from rivals. *Haynt* [Today] gave prizes in the form of a group trip to Palestine. Its competitor *Moment* promised plots in Palestine. They scrambled for leading writers and popular journalists. Older readers were outraged by vulgar passages. The editor of the *Haynt* would say to his employees: 'A reader, like a pig, eats everything, and likes the taste of shit.' In a popular, often vulgar, style, surveys of foreign news were given, and *feuilletons* were sprinkled with exempla from the Talmud. Thus the Jews, who had emerged not long before from the *yeshivah*, who had listened to politics in the *shul* or *mikvah*, were ushered into the political arena.

The Jewish dailies did not scorn the high-school graduate, the autodidact, the reader of Polish and Russian newspapers. It was necessary to consider the respect

---

[1] *Moje nalewki* (Warsaw, 1959), 161–9, corresponding to the following two sections, 'The Yiddish Press' and 'The Elections and the Boycott'. Singer became a popular writer for the Polish-language Jewish paper *Nasz przegląd*, [Our review] in interwar Warsaw; he escaped to England during the Second World War, where he remained.

of the newly won reader for serious learning. On Fridays the paper was transformed into a magazine. On the second page an article discussed the high values of Jewish ethics, on the third an erotic serial was printed, on the fourth there was an article about Spinoza, and on the fifth a scandal or brutal attack on a competing newspaper.

Polish affairs were not mentioned. The Yiddish journalists mostly came from Lithuania, and it was felt that anyone who went to the Polish theatre or read Polish books would look for reviews in the Polish newspapers.[2]

In 1911, in Kiev, a Christian child was murdered. The Russian 'Black Hundred' press reported that it had been a ritual murder. This news was generally disregarded at first. Even when word came from the prosecutor's office that a Jew, Beilis, had been charged, people scoffed at the news. The Jewish press showed a strange optimism; it drew encouragement from the attitudes of the liberal newspapers and from the reports in the foreign press. Soon it was learnt that the Tsarist government had decided to arrange a show trial, directed against all of Jewish society. The Jewish newspapers sent a number of correspondents to Kiev, since it was impossible to rely on the tendentious local or foreign dispatches of the government's St Petersburg Telegraphic Agency.

At this time I was invited to visit *Haynt* by one of the newspapermen; its editorial offices were at 8 Chłodna Street. When I entered the building on the ground floor—it was in the morning—I was stunned by the shouting. In the first room several newspapermen were working, or rather, they were yelling back and forth. A synagogue cantor was bargaining over a review with the music critic, while a music lover, noisily outraged over a contemptuous treatment of Wagner, waited his turn. In the other room my friend sat with bundles of German and French newspapers. I could not understand how he worked; the whole time he was arguing with another newspaperman, who was cutting clippings from American Yiddish newspapers.

After a while the chief editor of the newspaper, Jackan, entered the room; he looked knowingly at my friend, and turned to me. 'They say that you are educated, a Pole.' After these words he took me to his office. It took me a long time to get used to his Yiddish accent. Jackan informed me that he really did not need me, but he wished to have me on the staff in order to forestall a competing newspaper. He had a proposition. He had recently made a deal with Wojciech Korfanty to get news from Germany and France, in Polish, through him. Korfanty had a newspaper business in Silesia and used the Wolf, Reuter, and

---

[2] On the Yiddish press in Warsaw see Moshe Grosman, '*Haynt*: Ershter period, 1908–1915', and Mendl Mozes, 'Der Moment', *Fun noentn ovar*, 2 (1957), 3–67, 241–69; Marian Fuks, *Prasa żydowska w Warszawie, 1821–1939* (Warsaw, 1979); and an extensive review of Fuks, correcting errors and noting additional sources, by Chone Shmeruk, 'A Pioneering Study of the Warsaw Jewish Press', *Soviet Jewish Affairs*, 11/3 (1981), 35–53. General comments on *Haynt* and the election appear in Y. Davidsohn, 'Der *Haynt* un Yagello', *Haynt yubilei-bukh, 1908–1928* (Warsaw, 1928), 12–13.

Havas telegraphic agencies. Jackan proposed that I translate these reports into Yiddish. He was not discouraged when I answered that I did not know Yiddish well enough. None of the newspaper's reporters could write well. A special member of the staff reworked the manuscripts. Jackan handed me an article by one of the reporters; I was barely able to decipher a report of a meeting of the National Democratic 'Fronde' about the coming elections to the Duma. Jackan did not understand a word of my explanation about the significance of the Fronde.[3] For him, National Democracy was a band of antisemites, and its shadings did not have the least significance. He tossed the reporter's note into the waste-basket. He was not interested in the elections, since it was obvious to him that, one way or another, Dmowski would be elected.

Jackan was not put off by my refusal; he often asked me to come again, treating me as a naïve fellow who was ready to keep him informed about Polish matters for free.

THE ELECTIONS AND THE BOYCOTT

(*by* BERNARD SINGER)

The Jewish delegates who played a decisive role in the election of the delegate from Warsaw to the fourth Duma did not come from the ranks of leading politicians, or people of great character. They were mostly merchants and factory owners who did not want to get into trouble with anyone. Moreover, they were horrified at the events in Russia. The last stage of the Beilis case had been announced. Father Pranaitis and Professor Sikorski were ready to speak as experts against the man accused of ritual murder. Both these men, it was known, had received large sums from the Ministry of Internal Affairs. It was clear that if the jurors convicted Beilis of ritual murder, then pogroms would begin, the very next day, and these could spread to Warsaw. Boys on the street were already shouting 'Beilis!' at bearded Jews. Thus, there was no talk of a Jewish delegate from Warsaw.

A way out was found after meetings and agreements. Apart from the delegates of the National Democrats and the Secession, with Kucharzewski as the candidate, there existed in Warsaw a workers' curia which had ten or eleven represen-

---

[3] By 'Fronde' Singer is referring to the National Democratic 'Secession', which broke away from National Democracy proper between the third (1907) and fourth (1912) state Duma elections, because of dislike of Roman Dmowski personally and of his policy of conciliating the Russian government. In the fourth election its candidate, the historian Jan Kucharzewski, was supported by a coalition of anti-Dmowski Polish nationalists, who called themselves the 'National Concentration'. See Stephen D. Corrsin, *Warsaw before the First World War: Poles and Jews in the Third City of the Russian Empire, 1880–1914* (Boulder, Colo., 1989), 78–106, and 'Polish–Jewish Relations before the First World War: The Case of the State Duma Elections in Warsaw', *Gal-Ed: On the History of the Jews in Poland*, 11 (1989), 31–53.

tatives, mostly members of the SDKPiL and the PPS Left.[4] None of them had any chance of being elected.

I do not know who came up with the idea of making an agreement between the Jews and the workers' curia; I remember only that from the beginning it shocked the editorial offices of the Yiddish newspapers. The Jewish delegates themselves were horrified when, at one meeting, an agreement with the workers' curia was proposed. It was not so long ago that there had been strikes in factories belonging to certain Jewish delegates. An uprising linked, according to rumours, by a pact with the PPS Left was like a red rag to *Haynt*.

Once, in the courtyard of *Haynt*, I noticed a well-known Zionist, the merchant Podliszewski, heatedly talking with a tall, thin, somewhat stooped man. They spoke in Yiddish: Podliszewski quickly, his interlocutor slowly, choosing words with difficulty. A few minutes later Podliszewski was in the editorial offices. It turned out that he had been speaking with the lawyer Bronisław Grosser. He spoke about him like an antisemite distinguishing one Jew from the entire mass of Jewish society: 'Grosser's a Bundist, but a decent person.' Grosser had informed Podliszewski that the PPS Left had agreed that the Jewish delegates would vote for their candidate, but the Social Democrats did not intend to make a deal with the Jewish bourgeoisie. Much later, in independent Poland, I found out from Grosser's wife, the secretary of the Communist fraction in the Sejm, that Wacław Wróblewski of the PPS Left had taken part in the discussions.

On the day when the delegates were convened to elect the deputy, I was standing, in the morning hours, in Theatre Square in front of the city hall, together with several dozen people who were waiting, as I was, for the results of the voting. It was late autumn, 1912. Rain was falling.

A Jewish delegate who was late got out of a cab; he was the owner of a commercial office and a steel-pen factory. He lingered at the building's entrance and was glad to start a conversation with me, although I knew him only fleetingly, from visits to the offices of *Haynt*. To him, the workers' curia was a collection of thugs. He did not know the candidate, but he could not understand why a party which contained educated people had nominated a metal-turner.[5] He was upset that, behind the backs of the delegates, decent Jewish merchants and factory

---

[4] Two delegates represented Warsaw in the State Duma. Voting was indirect: the voters chose electoral curiae which then selected the delegates from their own ranks. In 1912 one delegate (Sergei Alekseev, of the Union of the Russian People) was chosen by a separate Russian curia and the other by the combined electors of the non-Russian, chiefly Polish and Jewish, general and workers' curiae. Eligible voters in the general curia consisted of resident adult men who were owners of real estate or businesses; were supervisors or managers in business, paying taxes on 'personal industrial occupations'; paid taxes on large apartments, or at least rented apartments 'in their own names'; or were members of certain groups of government pensioners. The general curia was thus upper- and middle-class in composition. Adult male workers in large factories and railway workshops chose only 3 electors to sit with the general curia's 80.

[5] Jan Tomicki, 'Jagiełło Eugeniusz', *Polski słownik biograficzny*, x. 313–14, gives a brief biography of this obscure figure.

owners had been pushed into negotiations with the Bund. He expressed the conviction that it would do harm to the Jews in Russia. I wanted to ask him why, in this case, he had agreed to vote for a representative of the Socialists, but he anticipated me, declaring that he hoped that everything would change at the last moment. He asked if I had heard anything about Mendelson,[6] whether he was the son of a former banker in Warsaw. He spoke about him with anger. Stooped and grumbling, he entered the city hall.

The election procedures took quite a while. It kept getting colder; there were only a few of us left in front of the building. Suddenly there was a shout inside the city hall. I saw the Secession elector and friend of the Jews, the noted surgeon Ignacy Baranowski, who was still shouting and waving, and brandishing his cane. I understood easily from his shouts that thanks only to the Jewish electors a representative of the left had got into the Duma. The Jews, silently, not looking around, with lowered heads, came down the steps. The expressions on their faces would have suited the Day of Atonement.

The news of the election result ran quickly through the city; two hours later the first windows had been broken in the Jewish stores on Elektoralna Street. Next day the Endek newspapers proclaimed with horror that the Jewish candidate Jagiełło, a member of the PPS Left, had got into the Duma. The Endecja launched a campoign of boycotting the Jews, and a few days after the elections its leader, Roman Dmowski, established the *Gazeta codzienna dwa grosze* [Twopenny daily gazette],[7] which was aimed at spreading the economic and social boycott. On all pages of the *Dwugroszówka* (as it was known) appeared the provocative slogan *Swój do swego po swoje*. The paper unmasked Jewish shops which had Polish names, and called for a boycott of Jewish doctors and lawyers—even though these were doctors and lawyers who condemned the action of the Jewish electoral delegates, and had called for Kucharzewski's election. The boycott had no effect on the Jewish delegates, who were dependent on the Russian market.

In the Jewish newspapers reports appeared that Paderewski had hurried to provide immediate assistance for the *Dwugroszówka*, a charge which he categorically and repeatedly denied. Natanson, owner of a paper factory, did not deny that he had provided credit for the first purchase of rotary paper.

The boycott quickly spread from Warsaw to the provinces. Łódź alone remained unscathed—there the Jews had chosen their own deputy, Dr Bomash. The Jewish section of Warsaw, which had become involved in politics only recently, fell into a state of paralysis. Walks into the Polish section gradually

---

[6] On Stanisław Mendelson see below.

[7] Actually *Gazeta poranna* [Morning gazette], not *codzienna*. On the boycott campaign that followed see Samuel Hirszhorn, *Historia Ż'dów w Polsce od sejmu czteroletniego do wojny europejskiej (1788–1914)* (Warsaw, 1921), 309–33; and Frank Golczewski, *Polnisch-judische Beziehungen: Eine Studie zur Geschichte des Antisemitismus in Osteuropa* (Wiesbaden, 1981), 106–20.

ceased. Music-lovers stopped going to the Philharmonic, except for Bach and Beethoven. There was a nasty incident at one of the concerts, a performance of Beethoven under the direction of the well-known Warsaw conductor Birnbaum, a Jew by descent. After the applause, the conductor, in accordance with the usual custom, extended his hand to Oziminski, the first violinist; his hand hung in the air. The Jewish public abandoned the Philharmonic. Gradually it also gave up the theatre.

Worried, famous Poles who lived in Russia began to travel to Warsaw. General Babianski came, then Aleksander Lednicki, Professor Leon Petrazycki, and finally Professor Baudouin de Courtenay. The last gave a lecture in the Towarzystwo Naukowe [Learned Society], and outraged his listeners with comments about the herd mentality, and about taking revenge against the weak.[8] Only *Nowa gazeta* [The new gazette] managed to include a short summary of the lecture. But it was in hot water: the Polish bourgeoisie boycotted Kempner, the editor, as a Jew, and the Jewish bourgeoisie was angry at him because he did not publish Jewish complaints and kept his distance from the nationalistic Jews.

Only the Realists' paper, *Kurier polski* [Polish courier], edited by Ludwik Straszewicz, opposed the boycott campaign. The journalist Ludomir Grendyszynski published articles opposing Dmowski.

The decision was made among the Jewish bourgeoisie to establish a newspaper in the Polish language. But there were not many Jewish newspapermen who wrote in Polish, and it was hard to find an editor. At last one was located: Stanisław Mendelson, one of the founders of Proletariat and a friend of Ludwik Warynski, one of the prisoners at the Kraków trial. He had earlier emigrated to London, where he kept in contact with Friedrich Engels, and at last, revising his views towards the end of his life, became an ideologue of Zionism. With this past, it was very hard for him to manage the new paper, entitled *Przegląd codzienny* [Daily review]. He himself wrote on international themes, and tried to keep a circumspect tone in polemics with the Warsaw press.

One day I managed, with difficulty, to get in to see the chief editor. My visit did not turn out very well. The bent, weary, grey-haired gentleman received me politely but coldly. He handed back my first *feuilletons*, and with this broke off the conversation. I was not interested in his opinion about my writing, but in the person who had played a part in the struggles of Proletariat. After five minutes of conversation he grew milder, but bitterness was evident in his words. I left, disillusioned by my conversation with him. Later, I often felt the same disappointment when I met living legends.

The boycott spread. Dmowski won among the Polish bourgeoisie. Nationalism won on the Jewish street. I tried to make contact with the workers' organizations. I went to *Wiedza* [Knowledge] on Żelazna Street, but I quickly learnt there that

---

[8] Published as Jan Baudouin de Courtenay, *W 'kwestji żydowskiej'* (Warsaw, 1913).

SDKPiL and PPS Left were secret organizations, and it was possible to reach them only by knowing someone. The strongly growing sense of being observed won out over the desire to act, and I gave up my attempts to make contact.

I was sentenced to return to the ghetto. Walking in Łazienki Park, I was hit with a stick from behind. From then on, I went beyond Nalewki only unwillingly. But I was drawn to the public library, and the bookshops, and the historical buildings. The price of a master-key was, however, too high. I decided to try for permission to live in Russia. I was only waiting for the verdict in the Beilis case.

EXCERPTS FROM THE WARSAW OBERPOLITSEIMEISTER'S FILES[9]

1. *Report to the Oberpolitseimeister, from the Ministry of Internal Affairs official (N. Akaemov?) for special assignments with the Warsaw Oberpolitseimeister, no. 44, 18 September/1 October 1912*[10]

This report is of a meeting of Jewish voters held 17/30 September and chaired by Dr S. Goldflam. There were 150 present, 'Jews belonging to various political orientations'. Nahum Sokolow spoke first:

He indicated that up to this time, in the Duma, there had not been a single Jewish deputy from the Polish Kingdom, even though a large share of its population consists of Jews. At the present time the Jews have the possibility of electing their own deputies in Warsaw and Łódź. But, in view of the agitation in certain Polish circles, they have agreed to limit themselves to the single deputy from Łódź, yielding to a Polish deputy in Warsaw, even though this seems to be a very strange pretension on the part of the Poles—that they must elect a Pole from Warsaw. It seems that the Poles think that Warsaw's deputy is not the same sort of deputy as those from other cities, but in some way is the head of the deputies from the Polish Kingdom. Yielding to this Polish whim, the Jews have agreed to the election of a Pole from Warsaw; but they have to stipulate unconditionally that this Pole cannot be an enemy of equal rights for Jews. If the Poles would not agree to this con-

---

[9] In the Archiwum m. st. Warszawy, Zarząd oberpolicmajstra warszawskiego, file 21. The 'high chief of police' of Warsaw reported directly to St Petersburg, and having extensive powers beyond those of an ordinary police chief, was in many ways the most important civilian official in the city.

[10] Fos. 78–9 (the earlier date refers to the Julian calendar, still in use at that time in the Russian Empire). Most Jewish names are transliterated here from Russian into English, using the Library of Congress tables, except for a few very well-known figures. The term 'conservative Jews' refers to traditional Orthodox and Hasidic Jews. The 'left bloc' consisted of the Bund and the PPS Left (formally the 'Socialist Electoral Alliance'); the SDKPiL, then undergoing a schism, ran a separate campaign. In the general curia the Jewish list won 8 of the 15 precincts and 46 electors, with 40% of the 23,000 votes cast; the Concentration won 5 precincts and 23 electors, with 30% of the votes; and the National Democrats won 2 precincts and 11 electors, with 27%. Kucharzewski was among the winning electors, so he still had a chance of gaining the Duma seat; Dmowski had lost and was therefore out of the running. Of the three workers' electors, two were Social Democrats and the third was Jagiełło himself, from the PPS Left.

dition, Sokolow proposed that a Jewish deputy be elected. In conclusion, he indicated that all Jewish groups, it seemed, agreed with the views he had expressed, unless one were to believe the rumour that some of the so-called Jewish conservatives were prepared to support Polish pretensions out of fear that the Poles would otherwise harm the Jews in commerce. But, Sokolow said, Jewish honour is dearer than commercial considerations.

The same point of view was supported by the lawyers Handelman and Grosser, though the latter felt that if the Poles were to reject equal rights, one should join the left bloc. The secretary of the Jewish communal administration, Zaideman, seconding the opinion expressed by Sokolow, pointed out that Kucharzewski, the candidate of the bloc of the opponents of National Democracy, was in essence just like Dmowski, and should therefore not be voted for.

Pfefer, one of the assimilated Jews, announced that he would prefer to vote even for a workers' candidate, so long as it wasn't a Polish antisemite. The next speaker, Dushevskii, supported Grosser's proposal that it was necessary to vote for the left bloc. Then the resolutions proposed by Sokolow and Grosser were put to a vote; Sokolow's resolution was passed with five dissenting, and Grosser's was rejected, though with seventeen votes in favour. (All assimilated Jews voted for this resolution.) The assimilated Jew Likhtenberg proposed an addendum to Sokolow's formulation, that the Jews demand recognition of their 'equal civil rights and that in the event of failure of negotiations with the Poles, the Jews wish to elect a Jew, though not a nationalist.'

The addendum was rejected. The report's author notes that discussions were in Polish.

2. *Report no. 51, in the same hand (N. Akaemov?), 28 September/11 October 1912*[11]

This report is of a meeting of Jewish voters held on 27 September/10 October 1912, organized by I. Davidson (Y. Davidsohn) and Geshel (Heschel) Farbshtein and chaired by the contractor Novinskii. Thirty people attended from various districts. The lawyer Zaideman spoke first, stating that he could not support Kucharzewski,

who is trying to limit their rights. Even among the assimilated Jews the idea is gaining strength that Kucharzewski cannot be supported by Jewish votes. In view of this, the majority of the assimilated Jews have decided, it seems, to abstain completely from the elections, and only a small group headed by Natanson is trying to carry out its promise to deliver Jewish votes, counting on drawing a part of the so-called conservative Jews to its side.

The resolutions passed at this meeting were:

1. to ask all synagogue leaders to make an announcement to the Jews on the Sabbath about the necessity of appearing at the electoral commissions and getting the electoral lists there;
2. to announce as quickly as possible a list of electors who are opponents of the candidacies of Kucharzewski and Dmowski;

[11] Fos. 149–50.

3. to nominate candidates for electors;

4. to ask the Jewish press to announce that the lists of electors will be made public as soon as possible.

3. *Report from the Ministry of Internal Affairs, Warsaw Oberpolitseimeister, no. 11379, 29 October/11 November 1912, sent to the Warsaw Provincial Administration*[12]

The report concerns Eugeniusz Jagiełło, elected on 28 October/8 November 1912 from the general and workers' curiae of Warsaw to the fourth State Duma.

Eugeniusz Jagiełło [Evgenii Iosifovich Iagello], 39 years old, of the Roman Catholic faith, a permanent resident of the city of Warsaw (bourgeois—*meshchanin*), bachelor, studied in a private four-class school, metal-turner, works at the Borman and Szwede metal-working factory on Srebrna Street, earning 70–100 roubles per month. Lives alone, renting for 8 roubles per month a room on the fourth floor with a separate entrance. Has never displayed any interest in party activity in the past. Has never fallen foul of the courts or legal system, enjoys no influence among the workers, has not taken part in a single workers' demonstration, and, possessing no firm political convictions, has hardly occupied any definite position in leftist political organizations. Only recently, in the period of the electoral campaign, has the fact that he belongs to the Social Democratic Party of Poland and Lithuania become apparent. His election can be explained, to a significant degree, by the party-political struggle between the Christian and Jewish parts of the population, as a result of which an accidental candidate appeared, who in fact does not satisfy a single one of the political parties. Appearing in the ranks of the electors, Jagiełło was the only Christian who was not an antisemite. The electors were guided by the fear of arousing indignation and the violent taking of revenge, up to possible pogroms, were a Jew to be elected, and although there were more Jewish electors than Christians, they decided not to elect a Jew as a member of the Duma. And as they did not wish to elect an antisemite, they gave their votes to the worker Jagiełło. Jagiełło's worker comrades, including those who belong to leftist nationalist parties and the majority of the Christian population, responded with indignation to this election; they call him the 'Jewish deputy' and have been threatening him, which frightened him to such a degree that he was in hiding for the last days before the election, did not sleep in his own apartment, and is now trying to obtain a passport to go abroad. Jagiełło knows Russian poorly and cannot be counted among these workers blessed with exceptional intelligence. In appearance, small and ill-favoured.

---

[12] This report misidentifies Jagiełło as a member of the SDKPiL, which indicates how obscure he was. He was, however, admitted to the Social Democratic faction in the Duma, with Menshevik support, over Bolshevik objections (Corrsin, *Warsaw*, p. 103). One PPS Left member recalled: 'We accepted with great reserve the accidental election of Jagiełło as the delegate from Warsaw.... The fact that the Socialists from the SDKPiL and the PPS Left had not achieved unity for the elections was for us the basic matter, harmful and contrary to the postulates of unity. The question of the antisemitic uproar which had arisen during the elections was something secondary' (Roman Jabłonowski, *Wspomnienia 1905–1928* (Warsaw, 1962), 138–9). Substantial material on the PPS Left in this election can be found in *PPS-Lewica, 1906–1918: Materiały i dokumenty*, ii (Warsaw, 1962).

Jews and the Russian Revolution: A Note

RICHARD PIPES

ONE of the most disastrous consequences of the Russian Revolution was the identification of Jews with Communism. It was partly caused by the sudden appearance of Jews in positions and in places where they had never been seen before. The perception was reinforced and given a spurious theoretical underpinning by the so-called *Protocols of the Elders of Zion*, a forgery which in the years immediately following the Revolution gained great popularity in Russia and elsewhere, notably Germany. The book accused Jews of seeking, through various devious means, to conquer and subjugate Gentile society. After 1918 Communism was widely interpreted as one of the devices world Jewry used to achieve its purported aims.

In view of the role this accusation had in paving the way for the mass destruction of European Jewry, the question of Jewish involvement in Bolshevism is of more than academic interest: for it was the allegation that 'international Jewry' invented Communism as an instrument with which to destroy Christian (or 'Aryan') civilization that provided the ideological and psychological foundation of the Nazi 'final solution'. Fantastic disinformation spread by Russian extremists alleged that all the leaders of the Soviet state were Jews. Many foreigners involved in Russian affairs came to share this belief. Thus, Major-General H. C. Holman, the head of the British military mission to Denikin, told a Jewish delegation that of thirty-six Moscow commissars only Lenin was a Russian, the rest being Jews. An American general serving in Russia was convinced that the notorious Chekists M. I. Latsis and Ia. Kh. Peters, who happened to be Latvians, were Jewish as well.[1] Sir Eyre Crowe, a senior official in the British Foreign Office, responding to Chaim Weizmann's memorandum protesting against the pogroms, observed 'that what may appear to Mr. Weizmann to be outrages against Jews, may in the eyes of the Ukrainians be retaliation against the horrors committed by the

---

This note is an excerpt from the author's *Russia under the Bolshevik Regime* (New York, 1994), 112–14. Reprinted with the permission of Alfred A. Knopf.

[1] I. B. Shekhtman, *Pogromy Dobrovol'cheskoi Armii na Ukraine* (Berlin, 1932), 298–9.

Bolsheviks who are all organized and directed by the Jews'.[2] For some Russian Whites, anyone who did not wholeheartedly support their cause, whether Russian or Western, including President Wilson and Lloyd George, was automatically presumed to be a Jew.

What are the facts? Jews undeniably played in the Bolshevik Party and the early Soviet apparatus a role disproportionate to their share of the population. The number of Jews active in Communism in Russia and abroad was striking: in Hungary, for example, they furnished 95 per cent of the leading figures in Bela Kun's dictatorship.[3] They were also disproportionately represented among Communists in Germany and Austria during the revolutionary upheavals there in 1918–23, and in the apparatus of the Communist International. But then Jews are a very active people, prominent in many fields of endeavour. If they were conspicuous in Communist circles, they were no less so in capitalist ones (according to Werner Sombart, they invented capitalism), not to speak of the performing arts, literature, and science. Although they constitute less than 0.3 per cent of the world's population, in the first seventy years when these awards have been given out (1901–70) Jews have won 24 per cent of the Nobel Prizes in Physiology and Medicine and 20 per cent of those in Physics. According to Mussolini, four of the seven founders of the Fascist Party were Jews; initially, Jews constituted a higher percentage of Fascist Party members than any other Italian group.[4] Hitler said that they were among the early financial supporters of the Nazi movement.[5]

Nor must it be deduced from the prominence of Jews in the Communist government that Russian Jewry was pro-Communist. The Jews in Communist ranks—the Trotskys, Zinovievs, Kamenevs, Sverdlovs, Radeks—did not speak for the Jews, because they had broken with them long before the Revolution. They represented no one but themselves. It must never be forgotten that during the Revolution and civil war the Bolshevik Party was very much a minority party, a self-selected body of the elect, whose membership did not reflect the politics of the population: Lenin admitted that the Communists were a drop of water in the

---

[2] Richard H. Ullman, *Britain and the Russian Civil War* (Princeton, NJ, 1968), 219 n. This view was prevalent in British governmental circles, especially the Foreign Office. Among British statesmen, Winston Churchill alone seems to have understood the monstrous nature of the pogroms and to have urged Denikin to put a stop to them: Winston Churchill, *The World Crisis: The Aftermath* (London, 1929), 255; Ullman, *Britain*, 218–19.

[3] I. Iu. Levin in *Rossiia i Evrei*, i (Berlin, 1924), 126.

[4] Zeev Sternhell, *The Birth of Fascist Ideology* (Princeton, NJ, 1994), 5. Prof. Sternhell kindly advised me that this information derives from Renzo de Felice, *Storia degli ebrei italiani sotto il fascismo* (Turin, 1972), 75, and Philip V. Cannistraro, *Historical Dictionary of Fascist Italy* (Westport, Conn., 1982), 406. The two sources indicate that in 1938 22.5% of Italian Jews were members of the Fascist Party, as against 6.12% of the Italian population as a whole.

[5] Domenico Settembrini, in George R. Urban (ed.), *Eurocommunism* (London, 1978), 159; Hermann Rauschning, *Hitler Speaks* (London, 1939), 234.

nation's sea.⁶ In other words, while not a few Communists were Jews, few Jews were Communists. When Russian Jewry had the opportunity to express its political preferences, as it did in 1917, it voted not for the Bolsheviks but either for the Zionists or for the parties of democratic Socialism.⁷ The results of the elections to the Constituent Assembly indicate that Bolshevik support came not from the region of Jewish concentration, the old Pale of Settlement, but from the armed forces and the cities of Great Russia which had hardly any Jews.⁸ The census of the Communist Party conducted in 1922 showed that only 959 Jewish members had joined before 1917.⁹ It was only half in jest that the Chief Rabbi of Moscow, Jacob Mazeh, on hearing Trotsky deny he was a Jew and refuse to help his people, commented that it was the Trotskys who made the revolutions and the Bronsteins who paid the bills.¹⁰

In the course of the civil war the Jewish community, caught in the Red–White conflict, increasingly sided with the Communist regime: this, however, it did not from preference but from the instinct of self-preservation. When the White armies entered the Ukraine in the summer of 1919 Jews welcomed them, for they had suffered grievously under the Bolshevik rule—if not as Jews then as 'bourgeois'.¹¹ They became quickly disenchanted with White policies which tolerated pogroms and excluded Jews from the administration. After experiencing White rule, Ukrainian Jewry turned anti-White and looked to the Red Army as protectors. Thus a vicious circle was set in motion: Jews were accused of being pro-Bolshevik and persecuted, which had the effect of turning them pro-Bolshevik for the sake of survival; this shift of allegiance served to justify further persecutions.

⁶ V. I. Lenin, *Polnoe sobranie sochinenii*, 5th edn. (Moscow, 1958–65), xlv. 98.

⁷ 'When the Bolsheviks took power, Zionism was unquestionably the dominant movement in Russian Jewish life: Nora Levin, *The Jews in the Soviet Union since 1917*, i (New York and London, 1988), 87. At the All-Russian Jewish Congress in 1917 Zionist candidates won 60% of the vote: Zvi Gitelman, *Jewish Nationality and Soviet Politics* (Princeton, NJ, 1972), 79.

⁸ In the provinces in which the worst pogroms occurred the pro-Bolshevik vote was minuscule: in Wołyń 4.4%, in Kiev 4.0%, in Poltava 5.6%. Only in Ekaterinoslav did the Bolsheviks gain 17.9%, but even this was far below their national average of 24.0%, obtained mainly in the northern, Great Russian, areas: A. M. Spirin, *Klassy i partii v grazhdanskoi voine v Rossii* (Moscow, 1968), 416–19.

⁹ I. P. Trainin, *SSSR i natsional'naia problema* (Moscow, 1924), 26–7. It may further be noted that Jews were disproportionately represented among Tsarist police spies: Jonathan Daly, 'The Watchful State' (diss. Harvard, 1992), 144.

¹⁰ Baruch Knei-Paz, *The Social and Political Thought of Leon Trotsky* (Oxford, 1978), 546 n.

¹¹ N. I. Shtif, *Pogromy na Ukrainie* (Berlin, 1922), 5–6.

The Bund in Poland, 1935–1939

DANIEL BLATMAN

IDEOLOGICAL DECISIONS AND POLITICAL STRUGGLES

THE months of April and May 1935 were turning-points in the history of the Jewish community in Poland between the two world wars. At that time two events occurred that marked the beginning of the change. In April 1935 Poland received a new constitution, one that legitimized the existing autocratic regime by transferring broad powers of government from the Sejm to the president. The new constitution made the rights of citizenship for all citizens conditional on fufilment of their obligations to the state. In May 1935 Józef Piłsudski, who had led Poland through a critical period, died. His demise cleared the way for the rise of Fascist and explicitly antisemitic elements. The new constitution and Piłsudski's death were unfavourable portents for the civil and legal status of Polish Jewry, their sources of livelihood, and their relationships within Polish society. These events also influenced political forces within the Jewish community.[1]

Even before the Nazis came to Poland there were segments of Polish society that regarded the Jews, who were a large, vibrant community, as an unwanted population that was not and could not be an organic part of the Polish nation. Extremist and moderate political elements from the government camp as well as the opposition Socialists and Endeks believed that mass emigration of the Jews from Poland was the most desirable solution to the Jewish question. In a country beset with severe economic and governmental problems, as well as political and social tensions, the Jewish problem became a focus for public discussion, whose effects were felt even outside Poland. In these insecure times Jews struggled for their daily bread in an economy large segments of which had been closed to them even before the second half of the 1930s. They defended themselves against violent attacks in the streets and searched for countries that would open their gates to the large numbers of Jews who wanted to emigrate. The Jewish political parties and movements took part in the struggle for existence and proposed various courses of action.[2]

---

[1] On these critical months and their significance with regard to Polish Jewry see E. Meltzer, *Ma'avak medini bemalkodet: Yehudei Polin 1935–1939* (Tel Aviv, 1982), 39–43. On the post-Piłsudski government see E. D. Wynot, Jr., *Polish Politics in Transition* (Athens, Ga., 1974).

[2] For a summary of the ideology, framework, and social foundation of the Jewish parties in Poland

By the second half of 1933 the Jewish Workers' Party, the Bund (Algemayner Yidisher Arbeter Bund in Poyln),³ came to the end of a process of crystallization, reorganization, and ideological change that had begun in the early 1930s. As a result of these changes the Bund was able to play a central role in the political struggle of that decade.

In preparation for the fifth Bund convention in Poland, held in June 1930 in Łódź, members of the movement held a meeting to clarify the Bund's position and decide whether the party would participate in the Second Socialist International.⁴ This was a central issue for the movement in the first decade of its existence in independent Poland. Two factions were active in the Bund at this time. One, led by Chaim Rafaelowicz (Meir Wasser) and Yosef Leszczyński (Y. Chmurner), claimed that affiliation with the International would make it impossible for the Bund to participate in the Soviet-led Comintern; the movement would become a reformist Socialist party like the Social Democratic parties in Britain and Germany and the Polska Partia Socjalistyczna (PPS: Polish Socialist Party). The second faction, headed by Viktor Alter, Henryk Erlich, and long-time activists such as Yekutiel Portnoy (Noah) and Vladimir Kosowski, had lost faith in the Soviet Union, primarily because of Stalin's regime, and regarded affiliation with the Second International as a step towards becoming an important element in the revolutionary wing of European Socialism. Adherents of this faction believed that participation in the Second International would strengthen the Bund's international position, as well as promote an image of the movement as a national workers' party that was concerned with more than the interests of the Jewish proletariat alone.⁵ At its fifth convention the Bund decided to join the

between the two world wars, and especially in the 1930s, see C. S. Heller, *On the Edge of Destruction* (New York, 1977), 173–293; J. Marcus, *Social and Political History of the Jews in Poland, 1919–1939* (Berlin, 1983), 261–91.

³ The name of the movement that was founded in Vilna in Oct. 1897 was 'The General Union of Workers in Russia, Lithuania, and Poland—the Bund'. With the liquidation of the movement in Russia after the Bolshevik Revolution and the transfer of its activities to Poland the name was changed. The main sources on the history of the Bund during the Russian period are M. Mishkiński, *Reshit tenuat hapo'alim hayehudit beRusiyah: Megamot yesod* (Tel Aviv, 1981); J. Frankel, *Prophecy and Politics: Socialism, Nationalism and the Russian Jews, 1862–1917* (New York, 1981), 171–257; A. Gelbard, *Besearat hayamim: haBund harusi be'itot mahapekhah* (Tel Aviv, 1987); Henry J. Tobias, *The Jewish Bund in Russia from its Origins to 1905* (Stanford, Calif., 1972); also the collections of articles edited by Y. Sh. Hertz, *Di geshikhte fun Bund* (5 vols.; New York, 1960–81), which include articles on the movement in Russia and Poland.

⁴ At the end of April and the beginning of May 1930, in preparation for the party convention, a fierce argument between the supporters of participation and those opposed was published in the pages of the party newspaper *Naye Folkstsaytung* [*NF*]. See Y. Sh. Hertz, 'Der Bund in umfahengikn poyln 1926–1932'; also Hertz, *Geshikhte*, v. 64–9.

⁵ On the ideological differences within the Bund in the 1920s see E. Novogrodski, 'HaBund bein shetei milhamot ha'olam', in *Entsiklopediah shel galuyot: Warsaw B.* (Jerusalem, 1959), 74–9; B. K. Johnpoll, *The Politics of Futility: The Jewish Workers' Bund of Poland 1917–1943* (New York, 1976), 82–156.

International, and in 1931 a delegation from the movement participated in the Second International in Vienna.[6]

Viktor Alter, as principal leader of the change in the Bund's image, was one of the central figures in shaping the movement's ideological and political direction during the second half of the 1930s. Alter's Socialist beliefs changed during the years 1933–5, and this change influenced both the Bund and the Jewish Professional Unions in Poland, of which he was the leader. Alter believed there were two paths the working class in Europe could take to improve its social and professional status. The first was to join a revolution of the type exemplified by the Bolsheviks, a path that would lead to improvement in the economic and professional status of the working class, along with loss of any hope of political influence or power within the ruling bureaucracy. The second path involved emulating the Socialist parties in the Scandinavian countries, which tried to improve the rights of workers in a democratic way through participation in political and economic decisions. Although these parties had not yet succeeded in repairing all the evils of the capitalist system, Alter felt it was an interesting attempt and ought to be the direction the Bund should take.[7] He supported participation in the Second International but rejected the idea of a union with the PPS. In his eyes the PPS was not revolutionary, but was based on nationalism and conservativism. Alter believed the Bund's role should be that of a Jewish Socialist party within the European Socialist camp, especially within the Polish left. At the same time, he called for creation of a joint force made up of the revolutionary parties of all the nationalities living in Poland. He considered this struggle, in which the Komunistyczna Partia Polski (KPP: Polish Communist Party) also participated, to be pragmatic rather than ideological, and viewed its purpose as a political battle against the nationalist reaction which had gained strength in Poland during those years.[8]

The internal polemics in the Bund at this period were alien to the majority of the Jewish workers and artisans who formed the bulk of the party's potential supporters. There was, however, a clear connection between the Bund's new ideological direction and the continuous rise in the movement's strength at that

---

[6] Those who opposed the direction taken by the party leadership, headed by Erlich and Alter, continued as an opposition faction that criticized the new direction and argued with the leadership in the pages of the party newspaper. In 1935 Rafaelowicz (Wasser) declared that Stalin should not be seen as a dictator because, in a Socialist country ruled by the proletariat, there could be no dictator other than that proletariat. Wasser regarded the Socialist International as a body that lacked the ability to take action, whose weakness was uncovered at the time of the liquidation of the Socialist Party in Germany after Hitler assumed power, and when it failed to counteract the absorption of the Socialist parties by others in Austria, Lithuania, and Spain: Chaim Rafaelowicz, 'Undzere halukei dayes', *NF* (27 Jan. 1935).

[7] V. Alter, 'Unzer virshaflekher program', *NF* (22 Nov. 1935).

[8] Id., 'Far an aktiver aynhayt-politik', *NF* (6 Jan. 1935); see the thorough summary of Alter's ideas and their influence on the Polish left in A. Jaeschke, 'Myśl polityczna Wiktora Altera z latach 1933–1935', in *Z Pola Walki*, 1/21 (1988), 46–64.

time. From the moment it joined the Second Socialist International, the Bund became the only Jewish party to participate in an international political framework, one to which the strong parties of Britain and France also belonged. In the light of the continually deteriorating situation of Polish Jews and their feeling that they were left to confront a hostile country and regime on their own, this gave the Bund an important advantage over other Jewish parties. It was a time when all hope for help from the Jewish and non-Jewish worlds outside Poland had almost disappeared.

In the town of Korytnica in Wołyń province Hechaluts, a pioneering Zionist movement, had ten members from a population of some 350 Jews. The successes of Fascism in Germany, Italy, and Spain, along with events in Poland, led this group to believe that their struggle as Jews was part and parcel of the world struggle by progressive forces against reactionary elements. In the Bundist *Folkstsaytung* [People's newspaper] they called for action by the Bund and the Polish left. They left the Hechaluts movement and founded a Bund cell in Korytnica.[9] This was characteristic of what was happening in many of the other small cities, where the Bund was able to found cells of members and supporters.[10]

With the death of Piłsudski in May 1935, the Bund realized that a new period in the history of Poland and Polish Jewry had begun. There was now nothing to prevent the mounting influence of antisemitic elements within the Sanacja. The party formed an alliance with the National Democratic Party (Narodowa Demokracja-Endecja), since both groups viewed the solution to the Jewish problem in Poland in a similar light.[11] In 1936 the Bund led the political camp that defended the basic rights of the Jewish minority in Poland. The strike declared by the Bund and the Jewish professional unions on 17 March 1936 in response to the pogrom in Przytyk, the elections to the municipality in Łódź in September 1936, the decision to take part once again in the Jewish communal elections, the party's position on the decree concerning ritual slaughter, and the attempt to hold a Jewish proletarian congress to express opposition to antisemitism—all these demonstrate the Bund's changed direction.

The pogrom in Przytyk on 9 March 1936, in which clashes resulted in the deaths of two Jews and a Pole and injuries to more than twenty, was a traumatic event for Polish Jewry, even though this was just one incident in a wave of anti-Jewish violence that had started at the beginning of 1933.[12] A number of factors combined to make this pogrom a prominent symbol of the physical vulnerability of Polish Jewry. One of these was the precise preparation and planning of the attack, which

---

[9] Letter by members to *Folkstsaytung*: *NF* (10 Mar. 1935).

[10] In Feb. 1935, at the Eighth Bund Congress in Poland, the central committee announced that the number of registered members was 12,000. This was an increase of some 4,500 over the 7,590 paid-up members registered in 1929: see *NF* (16 Feb. 1935). Erlich determined that the efforts of the party in 1936 should lead to the establishment of fifty branches and new groups throughout Poland: H. Erlich, 'Di naye shlag oyfgabe', *NF* (24 July 1935).

[11] *NF* (18 June 1935).   [12] See Meltzer, *Ma'avak medini*, 78–82.

was backed by political antisemites from the Endecja. The Bund leadership was shaken, not by the actual violence—there had been attacks on Jews in June 1935 in Grodno and in November in Odzibol—but rather by the indifference of the Polish Senate. Some representatives succumbed to Endecja propaganda claiming that the events in Przytyk were additional proof that the Jewish problem could only be solved through emigration.[13] The decision to proclaim a half-day protest strike on 17 March 1936 was an important test for the Bund.

For the first time the party led a Jewish-nationalist event that was in opposition to strong political forces and the beliefs of many Poles. Although the Bund did not plan to carry out a nationalist action, the fact that the PPS did not participate in the strike (although Polish workers did take part as individuals),[14] while other Jewish parties such as Po'alei Tsion Left and Right and Agudas Yisroel did support the Bund's initiative, gave the strike a decidedly national tinge.

There is also evidence of a new national-Jewish consciousness in the Bund's renewed participation in the Jewish communities (*kehillot*). For years the party leadership regarded the communities as archaic clerical institutions that had nothing in common with the needs of the proletariat. These communities were responsible for overseeing religious services and supporting education (which was generally religious), and were ruled by members of Agudas Yisroel, the Hasidic courts, Jewish businessmen, and the middle class. The Bund now decided to take part in elections to the Jewish communities. In this instance the decision-making process was unusual: in July 1936 the Bund's central committee declared that the Bund would not contest the elections. Henryk Erlich published an article sharply criticizing the Polish head of government, F. Sławoj Składkowski, who had proclaimed a policy of 'Economic boycott—yes! But no violence' that supported the boycott against the Jews and aimed to expel them from Polish economic life. The hypocrisy of the Polish government was clear, Erlich declared: on the one hand it encouraged the boycott and discrimination against the Jews, and did not try to prevent violence of the sort that had occurred in Przytyk and Mińsk Mazowiecki,[15] while on the other it granted the Jews the right to hold elections to the Jewish communities. The Bund, Erlich stated, rejected these 'favours', and would not participate in the elections.[16] This decision was opposed by the lower echelons of the movement, who put pressure on the leadership to reverse their decision. On 18 July 1936 a twenty-four-member delegation appeared before the party's central committee and demanded that the Bund participate in the community elections, and on 29 July the central committee reversed its

---

[13] *NF* (15 Mar. 1936).

[14] In Łódź, for example, many Polish workers took part in the strike, even against the factories they worked in. Y. Sh. Hertz, *Di geshikhte fun bund in lodz* (New York, 1958), 388.

[15] In Mińsk Mazowiecki violence against Jews took place in June 1936, at the time of the trial of those accused of participating in the events in Przytyk.

[16] H. Erlich, 'Moykhl di privilegi', *NF* (10 July 1936).

decision.¹⁷ Viktor Alter and Maurycy Orzech, founder of the Union of Socialist Artisans and one of the more important publicists of the party, justified participation in the elections: the Bund's decision, they wrote, was motivated by an effort to use the communities as weapons in the struggle against antisemitism and turn them into institutions concerned with the needs of the Jewish proletariat. Alter admitted, however, that the decision was also the result of pressure from activists at a lower level.¹⁸

The decision to participate in the elections, in which the Bund achieved important successes with the Jewish voters, reflected the new social composition of the movement. From the beginning of 1936 until the elections in Warsaw in September of that year, some 3,000 new members and sixty-two clubhouses and branches throughout Poland were added to the Bund.¹⁹ The success of the strike on 17 March enhanced the party's prestige in the eyes of many Jews, who joined the movement not because of its leftist political bent, but because it was a way to express opposition to the circumstances of Jewish life in Poland. The party encouraged Jews from the lower classes to join, even if they did not have the same ideological outlook. In Warsaw, for example, there was a special clubhouse for Orthodox Jews and supporters of the Bund.²⁰ These new activists, especially in the provincial towns, did not want to be excluded from the communities' sphere of influence, since they were important elements in Jewish life, and so they forced the movement's leadership to change its decision. The party thus became more involved in matters of a specifically Jewish nature.²¹

At the end of September 1936 municipal elections were held in Łódź. These were especially important: although only local, they raised issues of national significance such as the call by the Endeks to rescind the civil rights of Jewish inhabitants of Poland, besides reconsidering the Bund's relationship to centrist and leftist opposition parties. It was thought that the Bund would participate as part of a political bloc with the PPS in order to obtain a Socialist majority in the municipality. From the Bund's perspective, however, the PPS was not a revolu-

---

¹⁷ *NF* (30 July 1936).
¹⁸ V. Alter, 'Der bund geyt tsu di kehile-valn', *NF* (1 Aug. 1936); M. Orzech, 'Klasn-kamf in di kehiles', Ibid. (5 Sept. 1936).
¹⁹ Ibid. (19 June 1936).   ²⁰ 'Mit khasidishn bren . . .', *NF* (5 Jan. 1938).
²¹ In the elections to the communities that were held in 97 cities and towns (excluding Warsaw), the Bund received approximately 8.8% of the votes. In Warsaw, where its success was greater, 15 Bund representatives were elected out of a total of 50 community members; 5 Bund representatives were elected to the *kehillah* leadership. For an analysis of election results, see Meltzer, *Ma'avak medini*, 121–3. In Warsaw some 11,000 voted for the Bund. That same year there were 2,500 registered members in Warsaw: H. Erlich, 'Nakhn zig', *NF* (11 Sept. 1936). Although the Bund regarded this as a great success, the number of those who voted for the party in the Warsaw community elections was smaller than the number of those who had supported it in the Sejm elections of 1930, which the Bund had participated in. At that time 13,331 Jews voted for the Bund in Warsaw. A. Hafftka. 'Życie Parlamentarne Żydów w Polsce Odrodzonej', in *Żydzi w Polsce Odrodzonej*, ii (Warsaw, 1933), 304.

tionary party: rather, it was a Socialist-reformist party with an explicitly nationalist foundation that sought economic and social reforms to the capitalist system. Within the Bund, PPS proposals were compared to the reforms of the New Deal in the United States.[22] At the same time, the PPS was one of the few parties (excluding the Socialist parties of other national minorities with limited influence on Polish politics)[23] to support equal rights for all citizens and oppose the anti-semitism of the government and the extreme right. In these elections the PPS did not agree to establish a political bloc with the Bund. The reason given was that each party would be better able to exploit the full potential of its supporters by remaining separate. The PPS was afraid that association with the Jewish Bund would alienate the Polish workers. The Bund, which despite ideological differences had wanted to establish a joint list with the PPS and the German Social Democratic Party in Łódź, found itself in a fierce struggle with the PPS for the votes of the Jewish worker. A pamphlet aimed at this group published in Łódź in September 1936 declared:

We know that all other movements are not unified . . . The Bund is the representative of the interests of the Jewish working class. Why now, at the time of municipal elections, does the PPS turn to the Jewish worker and demand his vote? Why does it not establish a joint bloc with the Bund in order to unite the Socialist powers? The Bund wants to participate in a joint camp of this sort, but it is the PPS that opposes it. They are afraid that if they join together with the Bund, they will be attacked by the Endeks, who will say that this is a Jewish list and the Polish worker will not want to vote for a list of this sort . . . If the Jewish workers vote for the PPS, there will not even be one representative of the Jewish working class in the Łódź municipality. There will be representatives from the Jewish businessmen and bourgeoisie, but not one Jewish worker. This will be a double victory—for Jewish and Polish reactionary forces alike.[24]

Despite the fierce struggle for Jewish workers' votes, the Bund and Po'alei Tsion Left, whose candidates were on the Jewish workers' union list, achieved modest success—more than 23,000 Jews voted for them. The PPS received some 95,000 votes. It was clear that many Jews had supported the Polish party to keep

---

[22] P.L., 'Farvos davke in bund?', *NF* (19 Jan. 1936); the reformist trends in the PPS were crystallized after the twenty-third party congress in Feb. 1934. At the same time the party formulated its views on the creation of a unified anti-Fascist front that would include non-Socialist elements and all opposed to the autocratic government of a Fascist nature that had emerged in Poland. On this subject there were differences of opinion between the PPS and the Bund: see J. Holzer, *Mozaika polityczna Drugiej Rzeczypospolitej* (Warsaw, 1974), 481–510.

[23] In the elections to the Łódź municipality the Bund attempted to establish a joint bloc with the German Socialists. Despite their basic support for such a bloc, the latter would not agree to participate without the PPS. PPS opposition to a joint bloc with the Bund led the Deutsche Sozialistische Arbeitspartei (DSAP: German Social Democratic Workers' Party) to join the PPS, which included candidates of German origin in its list: Hertz, *Der bund in lodz*, 397–8.

[24] *Tsu dem yidishn arbetndikn folk fun lodz! Mir viln hobn far aykh a din torah!*, in Bund Archives [BA] of the History of the Jewish Labour Movement, New York, MG-2/330; cf: 'Farvos zenen tsvey sotsialistishe listes in lodz?', *NF* (20 Sept. 1936).

the Endeks from obtaining a majority in the municipality.[25] The electoral success, which had been achieved under difficult conditions, came as a great surprise to the Bund and, together with the good showing in the Jewish communities, there was a growing sense that the party was becoming a central political power among Polish Jewry. The Bund had more confidence in its ability to attract the votes of Jewish workers, and in the municipal elections of 1938 and 1939 the Bund put forth its own list on almost every occasion.

At this time the party was especially active in the struggle against antisemitism and anti-Jewish violence. In the disturbances of 1935–6 the central party committee organized battalions of guards, led by Bernard Goldstein, which protected party demonstrations and rallies. These groups were sent to different places to keep antisemitic agitators from attacking and harming Jews. The battalions were made up of Jewish workers, often unemployed, and members of the underworld, who received a hot meal at the workers' kitchen in return for their services. Towards the end of the 1930s the Bundist youth movement Tsukunft established defence groups as well. Those groups, which were influenced by the Austrian Schutzbund and the volunteer brigades of the Spanish Civil War, were intended to emulate the revolutionary and Socialist fighters. The Bundist defence organizations prevented many instances of violence, made their presence known in places such as Mińsk Mazowiecki and Brześć, where violence against Jews had occurred, and ensured the peace at Bundist rallies at the time of the Łódź elections.[26] They were not able to protect Jews or their property, however, because these were responsibilities of the Polish authorities.

In February 1937, with the establishment of Obóz Zjednoczenia Narodowego (OZON: the United National Camp), led by Adam Koc, and with the acceptance of the thirteen points regarding the Jews in May 1938, the government camp became overtly antisemitic. The radicalization in approach to the Jewish problem in Poland found expression in several political movements, not only the antisemitic ones. The first party to adopt the Endek position, encouraging Jews in Poland to emigrate, was the Stronnictwo Ludowe (SL: Peasants' Party). Opposed to the ruling Sanacja, this group was formed in March 1931 from three peasant parties. Led by Piast, the SL believed that Jews could not be organically integrated into the Polish nation. What was worse, SL supporters also believed that Jews constituted most of the middle class in the national economy and thus prevented the development of a true Polish middle class. At its convention in

---

[25] Compared with the number of votes they received in the 1930 elections to the Sejm, the success of the Bund and Po'alei Tsion Left is evident: then there were 7,155 votes for the Bund in Łódź and 2,381 for Po'alei Tsion Left; see Hafftka, 'Życie Parlamentarne'.

[26] For a detailed and often tendentious description of the activities of the Bund's defence organizations see B. Goldstein, *Tsvantsik yor in varshever bund* (New York, 1960), 200–318; A. Rowe, 'Jewish Self Defense: A Response to Violence', in J. A. Fishman (ed.), *Studies on Polish Jewry, 1919–1939* (New York, 1974), 107–49.

December 1935 SL rejected violence against Jews and supported equal rights for all citizens, but declared that the Jewish problem in Poland must be solved through the organized emigration of Jews to Palestine.[27] In 1937 certain elements within the PPS also accepted this view, although it was not officially included in the party platform. These factions saw organized emigration to Palestine as carrying with it the prospect for Jews to establish a free and just society with firm economic foundations and Socialist values. Further, they claimed it was better that the Socialists, not the capitalists, should take care of the emigration of the Jews, since the latter had only a financial interest in the affair. Jan Borski, a PPS activist who published a pamphlet on this subject, attacked the Bund for its narrow outlook on emigration. Borski declared that by stubbornly refusing to see it as an honourable way of solving the Jewish problem in Poland, the Bund guaranteed the Jews 'a future stretching to the horizons of Kock and Kałuszyn'.[28]

For the Bund, the position that a political movement adopted on emigration was central—whether the movement was Jewish or Polish.[29] From the Bund's perspective, the encouragement of emigration was a hindrance to the acceptance of Jews as equal to other Polish citizens. The party believed that, just as a solution to the problems of the Ukrainian and Byelorussian minorities was not sought through emigration, so the solution to the Jewish problem was not to be found in emigration. There was a fierce argument among the Bund, the PPS, and the Zionist parties on this subject. Conflicts with the PPS, which was the only party with wide public influence that had demonstrated sensitivity to attacks on Jews, were particularly harsh. The Bund primarily took issue with the position that Jews exerted an unfavourable influence on the Polish economy. Alter reasoned that Jewish emigration would worsen the Polish economy rather than improve it. It was not the fault of the Jews that they had been forced into non-productive economic activities, Alter declared, but of Polish society, which limited them to the fringes of economic activity. Only equal rights would improve the situation of the Jews while also aiding the Polish economy, which would be able to take advantage of the talents and efforts of the Jews.[30]

Alter's claims were not directed at the antisemitic Endek party or the SL, as these believed that the cultural differences between Jews and Poles were

---

[27] J. Cang, 'The Opposition Parties in Poland and their Attitude towards the Jewish Problem', *Jewish Social Studies*, 1 (1939), 248–9.

[28] J. W. Borski, *Sprawa Żydowska a Socjalizm: Polemika z Bundem* (Warsaw, 1937), 17–20. See the analysis of the problem of Jewish emigration at this time in Marcus, *History*, 387–410.

[29] Only the small Stronnictwo Demokratyczne (SD: Polish Democratic Party) agreed with the Bund on the subject of emigration. This party, founded in 1937 by a group of Polish intelligentsia headed by Mieczysław Michałowicz, opposed nationalist extremism and attacked the manifestations of nationalism in Poland at that time. It opposed all attacks on Jewish civil rights.

[30] V. Alter, *Antysemityzm gospodarczy w świetle cyfr* (Warsaw, 1937); see also Alter's statements following the publication of J. Borski's pamphlet in B. Bronsztejn, *Ludność Żydowska w Polsce w okresie międzywojennym: Studium statystyczne* (Wrocław, 1963), 107–8.

unbridgeable, but rather towards the Polish left, which seemed more rational about Jews, supporting emigration for economic and utilitarian reasons. Neither Alter nor the other Bundist leaders could accept the idea of emigration as a solution to the Jewish question. They refused to see that during those years strong nationalist sentiments were prevalent in the PPS. Although the PPS opposed antisemitism, it none the less viewed Poland as a nation in which it would be difficult for 3.5 million Jews to find a place. A turning-point for the PPS was the party convention in February 1937, at which it was decided not to ask the Communists to join in the struggle against OZON and the right. This was in contrast to the Bund, which supported the creation of a broad proletarian front against Fascism. Instead, PPS joined with the more conservative SL. At the same time, several leaders of the leftist wing, Norbert Barlicki, Stanisław Dubois, and Sofia (Wanda) Wasilewska, were pushed out of the party's central committee.[31]

While it was quarrelling with the PPS over these issues, the Bund was also in the midst of a conflict with the Zionists, which frequently led to harsh accusations and bitterness. In October 1935, on the occasion of the thirty-eighth anniversary of the founding of the Bund, Henryk Erlich wrote in the *Folkstsaytung*:

The fate of Zionism is intimately connected with the fate of Fascism and antisemitism, against which the Jewish working class must wage a life-and-death struggle. Zionism rejects and negates the role of the diaspora and the existence of the masses in the diaspora . . . Therefore there is nothing but uncompromising struggle between the Bund and Zionism.[32]

In its propaganda against Zionism, the Bund repeatedly claimed that the Zionists' emphasis on Palestine as the home of the Jewish masses legitimized Polish antisemitic demands to force the Jews out of Poland. In response to Jabotinsky's slogan of 'evacuation', the Bund declared that emigration was a general problem in Poland.[33] Many people, not just Jews, wanted to emigrate, Erlich claimed. Presenting emigration as a strictly Jewish problem strengthened antisemitism and did not help those Jews who remained in Poland, whether by choice or through lack of other alternatives.

[31] J. Holzer, *PPS Szkic Dziejów* (Warsaw, 1977), 153–4.
[32] H. Erlich, 'Der Bund', *NF* (20 Oct. 1935).
[33] Id., 'Men muz zey lernen derekh-erets!', *NF* (16 Oct. 1936); according to Viktor Alter, the Bund did not reject emigration completely, but rather rejected the ideology of emigration, which Bundists called 'emigrationism'; they did not reject the idea of Jewish settlement in Palestine, but opposed 'Palestinism'; V. Alter, 'Dos is bundism', *NF* (29 May 1938); workers' unions directed by the Bund ran an office to give aid to emigrants (Arbeter Emigratsie Byuro), which helped members of the unions who wished to emigrate. Y. Sh. Hertz determined that this office helped tens of thousands of members of the professional unions emigrate from 1924 to 1939: Hertz, *Der bund in umfahengikn in poyln*, 101–6. In 1938 there appeared every few days in *Folkstsaytung* a column titled 'Emigratsie yedies' in which details regarding the possibility of emigration to various countries, especially Australia, Argentina, Mexico, and the United States, were given.

It is difficult to differentiate between the Bund's pragmatic rejection of Zionism and emigration to Palestine and its ideological rejection of political Jewish nationalism. There were certainly practical reasons for the Bund's view: Palestine could not absorb millions of immigrants into its economy, and was thus unsuitable for mass immigration; the danger to Jews from Arab attacks was as great as the threat posed by antisemites in Poland; and the diaspora would not be ended even if hundreds of thousands of Jews were to emigrate to Palestine. Jews should build a life for themselves in the diaspora based on co-operation and unity with the country they lived in, with hopes for a democratic regime in Poland.[34] In response to the Peel Commission's suggestion to partition Palestine and establish a Jewish state, Erlich wrote:

What type of Jewish state would this be? The Bund has no enthusiasm for these British imperialist exercises or any attempt to found a Jewish state. Is there anything in this that is new for the millions of Jews in Poland and other countries? Would this country not create additional difficulties for the Jewish masses in their struggle for life and existence? On top of the continuity struggle has been added the declaration regarding the establishment of a Jewish state. The area of Palestine is approximately equal to that of the province of Warsaw. Only a small portion of this would be allocated to the Jews. Where will the millions go? What place exists for them there? In the Jewish state there are 300,000 Jews and approximately the same number of Arabs. The immigration of millions more to the Jewish state is not possible. The Zionists say that in future the Jewish country will probably grow. What does this mean? Is this acceptable to the Arabs? This state will only lead to one thing—the antisemites in Europe will say: 'They have a country—go there!' The historic mission of the Bund is to keep the Jewish masses from following this national mysticism that does not solve a thing. The Jewish masses do not need these British gifts.[35]

From 1937 to 1938 Erlich and Alter shaped the Bund's attempts to give direction to the activities of the Jewish community in Poland, and especially to those whom party terminology called 'the Jewish masses', the proletariat and members of the poorer classes in Poland. Its basic principles were as follows.

1. Antisemitism and the political forces influencing it in Poland are part and parcel of European Fascism and reactionary forces, forces that preach racial hatred of national minorities, liberal forces, and the supporters of Socialism. We must

---

[34] See e.g. Arieh, 'Elf toyzent yidn arayn keyn palestine in yor 1937', *NF* (5 Feb. 1938); the author of this article claimed that even the quota of 12,000 certificates for 1937 would not be filled, despite the money that the Zionist movement had collected for the settlers in Palestine, because Palestine, in the writer's opinion, was not a country the Jews were interested in emigrating to, nor would it be in the future; see also H. Erlich, 'Meshuge?', *NF* (30 Mar. 1938), an article which attacked Yitzhak Grünbaum and Arthur Ruppin for encouraging Jews to emigrate to Erets Israel. Erlich claimed that Grünbaum, who left Poland, had no right to come and tell the Jews that it was 'better to receive a club on the head in Palestine than to be stabbed with a knife on the streets of Warsaw'.

[35] H. Erlich, 'Di englishe matone', *NF* (9 July 1937).

struggle against them in any way possible through co-operation with the proletarian forces in Poland and other countries. Only a Socialist victory in Poland and elsewhere in a Europe suffering under reactionary regimes (Italy, Germany, Spain, Romania) will lead to the annihilation of antisemitism.

2. The antisemites claim that the Jews are a national minority that influences Polish society and economy adversely. It is true that the Jews are not a productive force and their occupations, for the most part, are those characteristic of the lower middle class, but this is a result of antisemitism and discrimination. When discrimination against the Jews stops, they will contribute to the country's economy and their abnormal situation will be set right.

3. Zionism as a national movement is reactionary in its nature and goals. Through its emigration propaganda, Zionism legitimizes the demands of Polish antisemites that the Jews be expelled from Poland and forced to emigrate to Palestine, a parcel of land that cannot support the immigration of millions of Jews and which is inhabited by an Arab population that opposes this immigration. Even Socialist Zionists have betrayed the fundamentals of Socialism by not understanding that it is not possible to build a socially just society while negating the national rights of the Arab inhabitants and forcing them from their land.

4. Since the majority of Polish Jewry will remain in Poland, the Bund must continue to develop Jewish education and culture by means of Jewish institu-tions and the Yiddish language. The party must try to attain Jewish cultural autonomy, for which it has been struggling since the beginning, in spite of government obstacles.[36]

From 1936 to 1938 the Bund and other Jewish parties tried to establish a broad framework for co-operative action. It was the Bund that first attempted to hold a congress of the Jewish proletariat to oppose antisemitism. Viktor Alter, who scheduled this event for April 1936 (it was to be postponed several times by the government), hoped for the participation of the Jewish workers' unions, the Bund, and Po'alei Tsion Left. Alter did not expect that the PPS would agree to participate in such a congress, but hoped that it would be a first step to a union of the Jewish proletarian forces in the war against antisemitism and the fight for

---

[36] V. Alter, *Tsu der yidn-frage in poyln* (Warsaw, 1937); in July 1938 Erlich published a two-part article in response to the criticism directed at the Bund by the historian Simon Dubnow in the pages of *Folkstsaytung*: 'Vegn der izolatsie fun bund', *NF* (29 July 1938). Dubnow claimed that the Bund had abandoned the Jewish people (*klal yisrael*), and only by giving up its policy of assimilation and co-operating with the rest of the democratic forces within Jewish society would it be able to develop a leadership respected by the Jewish community. In his reply Erlich rejected the possibility of co-operation between the Bund and the Zionists. See H. Erlich, 'Tsi iz der tsionism a bafrayendike demokratishe bavegung?', *NF* (29, 31 July 1938); also the response of Erlich to M. Kleinbaum (Sneh), which declared that the Bund's attacks on Zionism would only lead to a weakening of the Jewish hold on Palestine: H. Erlich, 'Tsionism un antisemitism', *NF* (23 Oct. 1938).

Jewish rights.[37] In June 1936, in reaction to the formation of OZON and the antisemitism of the government, Jewish delegates in the Sejm and Polish Senate formed a temporary political bloc that was to be the basis for a political framework representing the entire Jewish community in Poland. At the beginning of 1938, prior to the general Jewish congress in Poland, Zionist activists broadened their sphere of activity, aided by members of the World Jewish Congress such as Moshe Kleinbaum (Sneh), Noah Prilutski, Anshel Reis, Arieh Tartakover, and others.[38]

The congresses were never held and the attempts to bridge the differences between the Bund and the other Jewish political organizations were ineffective, except for Po'alei Tsion Left. While the Bund rejected Jewish national unity and promoted class unity, the Zionist leadership believed that Jewish nationalism was the critical element, especially in view of what was happening in Poland. Even Viktor Alter, however, had a difficult time explaining why he called for a congress of the Jewish proletariat rather than the general proletariat. Apologetically, he explained that although it was not then possible, in the future a congress of workers would be held that would include all proletarian forces opposed to antisemitism in Poland. His hope was that the passionate struggle against antisemitism would also affect the Polish Socialist camp. As to the general Jewish congress being planned, Alter claimed:

Our congress is aimed at those Jews who live from their work and who believe in the future of Socialism. The second congress . . . is connected with capitalism and arranged by capitalist bodies. This must be made clear to the Jewish masses who will choose the people they wish to associate with: Socialists or capitalists, a general Jewish congress or a congress of workers. The Jewish masses must answer unequivocally.[39]

Although the party leadership took a firm stance on ideological matters, the members understood that the main function of the Bund was not to create a unified workers' camp in Poland or to solve the problems of European Socialism, but rather to concentrate on the problems of the Jews. In 1937 and 1938 the opposition parties to the left of OZON demonstrated less and less willingness to focus on the defence of Jewish rights. The PPS grew closer to the SL, and both agreed with the other opposition parties in believing that the internal problems of Poland

---

[37] Statement of the central committee of the Bund on 15 May 1936 calling on all the organizations connected with the Bund to elect representatives to the congress, YIVO Archives, Poland (1939–1945)/6.4; manifesto of the organizing committee of the congress published in a special bulletin during the months of preparation, *Arbayter kongres tsum kamf mitn antisemitism* (24 May 1936).

[38] The delegation (Tymczasowa Reprezentacja Żydostwa Polskiego) included representatives of the Zionist parties (except for the General Zionists A and the parties of the Zionist left) and representatives of Agudas Yisrael, as well as other Jewish organizations. On this subject see Meltzer, *Ma'avak medini*, 261–73.

[39] V. Alter, 'Der kongres tsum kamf mitn antisemitism', *NF* (3 Apr. 1936); cf. id., 'Der tsionistisher kongres', *NF* (7 Jan. 1938).

took precedence over the Jewish problem. In 1938 the PPS demanded that the Bund and the Polish unions hold separate demonstrations on 1 May.[40]

Opposition to co-operation with Jewish capitalists and the clerical parties, as the Bund defined them, did not prevent the party from supporting Agudas Yisroel in its struggle against government attempts to limit ritual slaughter in February and March 1936. The party organ claimed that its support was based on a defence of the interests of Jewish butchers and workers; in other words, it was part of the class struggle. In the community elections, too, the Bund understood the sentiments of its supporters who wanted representation in community leadership. Similarly, the party leadership now understood the importance of supplying kosher meat to the Jewish masses. In June 1936 the Bund joined the strike initiated by the General Zionists, Po'alei Tsion Right, and Mizrachi following the sentences given at Przytyk. In this case the party also justified participation in the strike as part of the struggle against antisemitism and opposition to the politics of the Jewish bourgeoisie. This duality continued to exist within the Bund until the outbreak of the war: on the one hand the party rejected the idea of co-operation based on Jewish nationalism, arguing fiercely with the Zionists, and on the other hand the Bund was becoming increasingly involved in the problems of Jewish existence and attempts to ease the situation of the broad segments of Jewish society that had been distanced from work, education, and services.

THE EFFORT TO IMPROVE THE STANDARD OF LIVING AND EDUCATION OF THE JEWISH WORKER

Large sums of money were needed to help the poorer elements in Jewish society, whose economic situation was worsening through government policies. The Bund and its affiliated organizations had no such funds, for the party had been in difficult economic straits since the mid-1930s. This was especially true for the Yiddish education network Tsisho (Tsentrale Yidishe Shul Organizatsie) run by the Bund, as well as for the Central Association of Jewish Trade Unions (Tsentral-rat fun di Profesionele Klasn—Fareynen). The Jewish workers' organizations in the United States and the Joint Distribution Committee (JDC), an American and Jewish charitable body, were virtually the sole financial support for the Bund.

The connections between the Bund in eastern Europe and the Jewish workers' unions in the United States had been formed at the end of the nineteenth and the beginning of the twentieth centuries. In 1900 the first branch of the Bund opened in the United States. By 1904 there were forty branches organized centrally, but with differences that reflected those among party activists in Poland and Russia.

---

[40] J. Żarnowski, 'Polityka kierownictwa PPS w przededniu II wojny światowej', *Przegląd historyczny*, 52 (1961), 502–9.

Supporters of the Bund in America had adapted to the reality of life in a new country by distancing themselves from one of the ideas central to the Bund in eastern Europe, the realization of cultural autonomy within a multinational state. Although American pluralism and the system of government did not accord with traditional Bundist ideology, members of the movement continued to be involved in Yiddish culture and education in the United States, supported the Jewish workers' movement in Poland financially, and organized professional Jewish unions, the largest and most important of which was the Yidisher Arbayter Komitet (Jewish Labour Committee), founded in the mid-1930s.[41] Between the two world wars the Jewish workers' unions became increasingly distanced from the ideology of the Bund in Poland but preserved a close connection with the party and its organizations, especially the Yiddish schools and workers' committees.

The connection between the Bund and the JDC was more complex. The traditional policies of the JDC were to refrain from giving direct subsidies to political parties for their activities. The JDC in Poland in the mid-1930s maintained a network of popular lending societies (CeKaBe) to grant small interest-free individual loans (of about 90 zloty).[42] Between 1936 and 1938 the number of such loans increased from 167,000 to roughly 221,000. During the years of economic discrimination they were an important source of aid, saving many Jewish families from hunger.

The Bund rejected the JDC's methods in Poland completely, believing that the financial problems of the Jews stemmed from economic discrimination. The way to improve the situation was through political struggle and not philanthropic activity. The JDC would be better advised, declared Henryk Erlich, to give its money to organizations and institutions that had the power to address the true problems of Polish Jewry, even if they were connected to political parties and movements. The Bund adamantly refused to participate in a general Jewish umbrella organization that would distribute the JDC's financial aid, and demanded that it transfer its subsidies to the Bund. David-Leyb Neimark, a journalist and member of the Bund, told Dr Bernard Kahn, head of the European office of the Joint Committee in Paris, and his aide, Dr David Shweitzer, during their visit to Warsaw in March 1935 that the JDC was unjustly dividing the money between the Jews of Erets Israel and those of the diaspora.[43]

[41] N. Levin, 'The Influence of the Bund on the Jewish Socialist Movement in America', *Gratz College Annual of Jewish Studies*, 5 (1976), 53–60.

[42] CeKaBe: Centralne Towarzystwo Popierania Kredytu Bezprocentowego i Krzewienia Pracy Produktywnej wśród Ludności Żydowskiej w Polsce. On the activities of this organization and the amount of the loans see Y. Bauer, *My Brother's Keeper* (Philadelphia, 1974), 199–200.

[43] See the report in *NF* (14 Mar. 1935) on the press conferences held by Kahn and Shweitzer during their visit to Warsaw, as well as the editorial by Erlich on the same day, 'Tsu der prese-konferents fun joint'. According to the Joint Committee's information, the organization had transferred some $16m to Poland between 1920 and 1938. From 1914 to 1938 the JDC Committee transferred

The Bund was concerned about its network of Yiddish schools (Tsisho). Yosef Leszczyński, head of the Tsisho network, said that many schools might have to close because of Polish government policies that placed heavy financial demands on the schools, forcing them to spend money they could not afford. In 1934 nineteen Tsisho institutions were shut down (some were evening schools and professional courses), and at the beginning of 1935 another seven schools faced imminent closure. At the same time there were many more applications from Jewish students ejected from the general Polish education system because of the antisemitism of teachers and students. The Tsisho schools could not accommodate them.[44]

Po'alei Tsion Left and supporters of Yiddish education joined the Bund in administering the Tsisho network. This provided a secular education that emphasized the Bund's and Po'alei Tsion's left-wing Socialist ideology. In 1938 most of the members of the public council running the Yiddish education network were from the Bund.[45] Two Bund activists headed this group: Chaim-Shlomo Kazhdan, the director of Tsisho, and Shlomo Mendelson, secretary, who was also a member of the party central committee. The Vladimir Medem Sanatorium in Międzeszyn, near Warsaw, was a unique educational institution associated with Tsisho but managed independently by educators who were also Bund members. It was a sanatorium for children with incipient tuberculosis, run by Shlomo Giliński. The children resided there for several months, receiving education and medical care. There was a special relationship between the pupils and the institution's employees that allowed the children significant fredom to control their lives and surroundings. But in the mid-1930s the sanatorium fell on difficult financial times, and by 1935 it was able to care for only 614 children (compared with the 800 it had accepted the previous year).[46] That year the institution and the Bund had a difficult time raising sufficient funds to support the

approximately $9m to aid the Jews in Erets Israel, a larger sum than that sent to Germany or Romania: figures listed in 'Aid to Jews Overseas', *Report on the Activities of the American Jewish Joint Distribution Committee for the Year 1938* (New York, 1939), 55–6. Neimark said to Kahn that the money for the Jews should be distributed according to the number of Jews in each country. In Palestine there were only some 300,000 Jews compared to the millions needing aid in Europe.

[44] From a report sent by Y. Leszczyński to the JDC in Nov. 1934 on the situation of Jewish education in Poland and the Tsisho network, JDC Archives (New York), file 828; the crisis hit Tsisho in 1937–8, at a time when the government demanded that the network pay 900,000 zloty to renovate old school buildings and build new ones. The Joint Committee contributed 150,000 zloty for this purpose: S. Mendelson to the Joint Committee leadership in Warsaw, 16 Sept. 1938, BA M-12/12. See Mendelson to the JDC in New York, 10 Jan. 1939, JDC Archives, file 828; S. Mendelson to Y. Pat and E. Novogrudski, 19 July 1939, BA M-12/26.

[45] On the Jewish education system in Poland between the two world wars, and especially on Tsisho, see M. S. Kazhdan, *Di geshikhte fun yidishen shulvezn in umophengikn poyln* (Mexico City, 1947), and also S. Rusenhak, 'Al ma'arekhet hahinukh hayehudi bePolin bein shtei milḥamot ha'olam', *Beit Israel bePolin*, ii (Jerusalem, 1953), 142–55.

[46] From a report sent by the management of the Medem Sanatorium to the Tsisho Planning Commission on 26 Mar. 1936, BA M-12/30.

sanatorium, in part because the JDC's decreased income led to a decline in aid. From 1937 on, the amount of aid allocated by the JDC to the Medem Sanatorium increased, although it was still not sufficient for the institution's needs.[47]

The Bund leadership strongly criticized the JDC for its unwillingness to fund party organizations; the Bund did not understand how limited the JDC's funds had become by the mid-1930s and how thinly it had to stretch its resources over the many areas it was involved in. Moreover, the JDC feared that too close association with the opposition Socialist parties would affect its work in Poland adversely.[48] None the less, Mendelson and his friends in Tsisho were right when they criticized the JDC for not funding education programmes that increased productivity among Polish Jewry. Central activists such as Abraham Kahn and Dr Bernard Kahn from the JDC Joint Committee on Poland and Eastern Europe joined in this criticism.[49]

The connections between the Bund and the JDC were exclusively financial ones, while those between the party and the Jewish workers' organizations in the United States were ideological as well. In the 1930s such co-operation was based on similar viewpoints and important financial considerations. Although cooperation had existed since the beginning of the century, its nature changed by the end of the 1930s, when Bund activists from Poland arrived in the United States and comprised an important part of the Jewish Labour Committee. Among the first to arrive were Benjamin Tabaczyński and Yaakov Pat, journalists and men of culture, who emigrated to the United States in 1938 and became active in the Jewish Workers' Committee and other public committees designed to help the Bund and the Yiddish education system. The departure of Henryk Erlich at the end of 1937 for a tour of the United States led to a turning point in the relationship between the party and the American activists. The party understood the importance of these connections with the Jewish workers' movement in America.

---

[47] Correspondence between S. Giliński and the JDC in Sept. and Oct. 1935, and a memo sent by S. Giliński and Yosef Brumberg to the JDC following their arrival in the United States in 1941, concerning financial aid to the sanatorium, JDC, Archives, file 841; in 1935 the JDC transferred $6,306 to the sanatorium. In 1939 the amount reached $11,518: JDC Archives, file 841b. The Bund decided to undertake a special campaign to raise 50,000 zloty from supporters: see request from Emanuel Novogrudski, secretary of the central committee of the Bund, to the leadership of YIVO in Vilna in Nov. 1936, YIVO Archives, Territorial Collection, Warsaw 10; also *NF* (4 Nov. 1936).

[48] At a meeting in June 1939 with the Polish consul in New York JDC activist Edwin Goldwasser was told that the Polish government opposed the involvement of Bundists in the work of the Joint Committee. That same month Isaac Giterman, head of the JDC in Warsaw, was invited to visit the chief of the Warsaw police for a discussion. Giterman saw this as a sign of government dissatisfaction with the connections between Maurycy Orzech, a member of the Bund's Central Committee, and Morris Tropper, manager of the European office of the JDC in Paris. The two proposed a compromise that would make broad participation by the Bund in the JDC's work in Poland possible: see memo of Giterman to the JDC in New York, 17 July 1939, JDC Archives, file 795.

[49] On the argument regarding the financing of educational activity see 'Memoir of A. Kahn', 4 July 1939, ibid.

A year later Emanuel Novogrudski, one of the long-time activists in Poland and secretary of the central committee, was sent to New York to establish political representation there. Party leaders did not seek to broaden activities in the United States or to found groups of the type established in other European countries. They understood that the American political system had no place for a separate Jewish party, so movement activists in the United States concentrated on collecting money for the party and its organizations in Poland.[50]

The activities of Bundists within the Jewish workers' unions in the United States frequently caused friction between them and supporters of Po'alei Tsion within these organizations. The Jewish Labour Committee and its general secretary, Adolf Held, who was also a member of the JDC leadership, did not want to be identified with a particular party in Poland. They felt themselves to be members of American Jewry and transferred money to Poland through the JDC. Held explained to Yekutiel (Noah) Portnoy in 1937 that the Jewish Labour Committee would find it difficult to transfer money directly to subsidize Bundist political activity. It was able to support educational endeavours or the activities of the Jewish workers' unions on behalf of the Jewish working class, but not explicitly political activity. Held suggested that the Bund send a representative to the United States to work separately among supporters of the movement. This suggestion contributed to the decision to send Novogrudski to the United States.[51]

Besides Tsisho, the Tsentralrat fun Yidishe Proffaraynen (Central Association of Jewish Trade Unions) was also an important organization directed by the Bund. It united various groups of workers and artisans, most of whom were from the Jewish working class. Beginning in the 1920s, in the face of discrimination against Jews in the workforce, especially through government monopolies, the association stressed that Jews had an equal right to work.[52] In 1935 the number of workers who were members of the unions increased. That same year 22,577 workers were registered in the professional unions. At the sixth congress of the unions, held in 1937, 254 delegates participated, representing some 72,000 Jewish workers, including 29,155 members of unions led by the Bund. In 1938, at the seventh congress, there were 98,810 members, including 43,500 workers from unions controlled by the Bund.[53] A factor contributing to

---

[50] In Mar. 1937 a committee to support Jewish schools in Poland, headed by Chaim Zhitlovski, was established. Nominated as members were the main activists of the Jewish Workers' Committee, including Adolf Held, David Dubiński, David Meir, Berl Vladek, and others: pamphlets and memos of the committee, BA M-12/26, M-12/8A. Yaakov Pat, who arrived from Poland, directed the committee's activities.

[51] A. Held to Y. Portnoy, 27 May 1937, BA M-12/12.

[52] E. Novogrudski, 'Kamf far rekht oyf arbet', in Hertz, *Geshikhte*, v. 147–8.

[53] Documents of the secretariat of the central council of Jewish professional unions in Warsaw from Apr. 1937 and 1939, BA MG-9/226; *Sprawy narodowościowe*, xi/1–2, 3 (Warsaw, 1937), 123, 313; S. (Arthur) Zygelbojm, 'Di yidishe profesionele bavegung in poyln', *Zygelbojm bukh* (New York, 1947), 85–103.

the increase was the liquidation of the Polish Communist Party, most of whose Jewish members joined the Bundist unions.

Viktor Alter, general secretary of the association, estimated that some 300,000 Jews took advantage of the association's welfare services, and he requested 150,000 zloty from the JDC in the name of the poor masses.[54] The council needed this amount to finance special welfare programmes that it set up at the end of 1938 and in early 1939 to help Jewish deportees from Zbąszyń and Socialist refugees who fled to Katowice from Czechoslovakia. This aid was distributed by a special committee, the Robotniczy Komitet Pomocy Uchodzcom z Niemiec (Workers' Committee for Aid to Refugees from Germany), established by the Association of Jewish Trade Unions and members of the PPS. The association also formulated a programme to obtain modern transportation for the meat marketers in Warsaw and asked to found a lending society for its members.[55]

The JDC allocated $3,000 to finance these activities, but made all future help conditional on agreement between the Bund and the special Central Committee, which would centralize the work of the JDC in Poland; the latter was at that time still in the process of formation. Nahman (Natan) Shafran, one of the heads of the special-aid committee for refugees (two others who worked with him in the secretariat were Shlomo Mendelson and Shlomo Giliński), explained the activists' anger over the JDC's policies:

Up to now we have not received any answer from the JDC to the report we sent on 20 March [1939] . . . Since then the JDC has neither granted any subsidies nor even responded to our plea. This is a disgrace, because according to the information in our hands, the workers in America transfer money for refugees through the JDC . . . This is not a matter of money alone. It is impossible to comprehend that the Joint Committee, which raises large sums of money these days to aid the refugees, is ignoring our activities.[56]

The Jewish Labour Committee and the public committees established in the United States to support the activities of the Bund and its organizations did send money to Poland in those days, but the amounts were smaller than expected by the movement's leadership. The exact sum is difficult to determine because the money was sent by different organizations, often without precise records. Some funds were sent by private donors to their school or town of origin, or to a branch

---

[54] V. Alter and S. Shveber to the JDC leadership in Paris, undated, BA MG-9/222; memo of D. Shweitzer regarding connections between the JDC and the Jewish workers' unions, 6 June 1939, JDC Archives, file 818.

[55] A number of memos were sent in 1939 to the activists of the Jewish Labour Committee and the leadership of the JDC in New York on the activities of the association and its financial needs; see Secretariat of the Workers' Committee to Yaakov Pat, 22 Feb. 1939, BA MG-9/215; V. Alter to A. Held, 30 Mar. 1939, BA MG-9/218.

[56] N. Shafran to E. Novogrudski, 11 May 1939, BA MG-1/53.

of the youth movement in a particular city.[57] It is possible that the total amount was some 10–15 per cent above the documented totals.

In the period between January 1934 and July 1939 Bund supporters in the United States transferred $83,727.83 and 37,892.13 zloty ($7,378.42 at 5 zloty to the dollar) to the party and its institutions in Poland. The total was $91,306.25 (including small sums sent from South America and western Europe). The lion's share—$63,622.71—was for Tsisho institutions and the Medem Sanatorium. From the end of 1938 until July 1939 $10,418.42 was sent to the Committee to Aid Refugees, a respectable sum considering how recently the committee had been formed. In that same period, for example, the JDC sent only $3,000 to the workers' unions. A total of $17,265.12 was sent by American supporters of the Bund for party use. In addition, members in New York sent $1,170 for the party newspaper, *Naye Folkstsaytung*.[58]

Three main conclusions can be drawn about the Bund's system of collecting money in the United States.

1. The presence of party members from Poland in the United States had a decisive influence on the party's ability to collect funds. This is evident from the campaign run by Kazhdan to collect money for Tsisho in 1934–5, and from the substantial increase in funds sent to Poland beginning in 1938, when Pat, Novogrudski, and Tabczyński arrived in New York. The talent of these Bund activists worried members of the JDC, who feared that competition for Jewish donations would develop and that other organizations would follow the Bund's lead. In June 1939 Bernard Kahn met with Novogrudski, who promised that the Bund would campaign only among its traditional groups of supporters, the workers' unions and supporters of Yiddish education.[59]

2. Despite the fact that much of this money was donated by supporters of the party, the funds were primarily used for educational purposes and social welfare. Most of the money sent for party needs (some $9,000 out of $17,000) was collected by Novogrudski, who was the only one of the activitists in New York with a specific role in the Bund and a background of political activism in Poland. This money was mostly donated in 1938–9, the year the Bund reached the peak of its strength and political influence in Poland.

---

[57] Various Tsisho schools, such as those in Pinsk, Świeczyn, Tuzisk, Częstochowa, Łódź, and Rovno, turned to emigrants from their respective cities to collect small amounts of money and transfer the donations to Poland. See B. Lewin to the Tsisho management in Warsaw, 1 and 22 June 1937, BA M-12/12, M-12/29; letter of S. C. Kazhdan to Y. Pat, 24 Apr. 1937, BA M-12/31A and 22 June 1938, BA M-12/29.

[58] For the statistics on the transfer of money from the Jewish Labour Committee and the Jewish workers' organizations in the United States to the Bund in Poland in 1934–9 see BA M-12/22, M-12/8A, M-12/26, M-12/28, M-12/31, MG-1/53, MG-9/215, MG-18/23, MG-18/24; on the transfer of money from the JDC to the workers' unions of the Bund in 1939 see report of M. Tropper to J. Hyman, secretary of the JDC, 10 June 1939, JDC Archives, file 794.

[59] Memo of B. Kahin on his meeting with E. Novogrudski, 30 June 1939, JDC Archives, file 841.

3. The absence of donations to the Bund youth movements, Tsukunft for 16- to 21-year-olds and Skif (Sotsialistisher Kinder Farband) for children between 10 and 15, is evident. At the end of the 1930s these youth movements had approximately 20,000 members,[60] and the leaders, Yosef Lifszyc, Ludwig Hodes, and Lucjan Blit, tried hard to collect money on their behalf. It appears that the small amounts that the party received for the youth movements were designated for the youth organizations' educational activities. It must be remembered that Tsukunft and Skif were integral parts of the party, and their activities had a party-oriented educational nature, unlike those of Hechaluts, which were part of an autonomous framework. This fact made it easier for the JDC and the Jewish Labour Committee to support the activities of Hechaluts, while it prevented the transfer of money to the Bund youth organizations.[61]

THE TEST OF PUBLIC SUPPORT: THE MUNICIPAL ELECTIONS, 1938–1939

The municipal elections held in Poland at the end of 1938 and the beginning of 1939 were the most important test of public support for the Bund. The party had not taken part in any national elections since 1930, because it, along with the Polish left, decided not to participate after the elections to the Sejm in 1935.[62] At the last elections the Bund took part in the party received approximately 71,000 votes—not enough to send a representative to the Polish house of representatives.[63] Support for the movement by the Jewish public increased in the mid-1930s. This was clearly expressed in the elections to the Jewish communities in 1936, and was strengthened by the elections to the community council in Białystok in December 1937. In these the Bund received eight seats, while Agudas Yisroel and Po'alei Tsion received three each; the General Zionists received only two. In addition, readership of the *Folkstsaytung* increased: in 1929

---

[60] Marcus, *History*, 281; in 1936 3,000 new members joined Tsukunft: *Sprawy narodowościowe*, x/3 (Warsaw, 1936), 288–9; in the summer of 1938 Skif ran 21 summer camps in which some 2,500 children participated. In the summer of 1939 there were 35 summer camps for 5,000 children: memo of the leaders of Skif to the Jewish Labour Committee, 29 Apr. 1939, BA MG-9/243; summary of the Bund youth movements and their activities in Poland: Hertz, *Der bund in poyln*, 107–34.

[61] On the support of the JDC for the training farms of the youth movements see Bauer, *My Brother's Keeper*, 165, 191, 202; the leaders of Skif requested that Y. Pat try to persuade the heads of the JDC and A. Held to send money for their educational activities. Pat answered that there was opposition to this because the Bund youth movements were part of a political framework: Y. Pat to the secretariat of Skif, 9 Feb. 1939, BA MG-1/53.

[62] Johnpoll, *Politics of Futility*, 155–6, 167–8.

[63] From an accounting by the party central committee for the fourth general congress of the Bund held in Warsaw in Jan. 1929, AB, MG-2/442.

the newspaper sold some 10,000 copies daily, by the mid-1930s it was selling around 18,000. (In the years 1937–8 sales of the newspaper declined to approximately 14,000 copies daily; but all Jewish dailies experienced a similar decline at that time.)[64] The Bund had approximately 7,000 registered paid-up members in 1935; by 1939 there were 20,000.[65] The party did not consider these achievements symbols of political success because it felt that such success would come only through a strong showing in general elections. According to Erlich, Jewish support for the Bund was much greater than its showing in the community elections. Many Jews tended to vote for traditional lists in those elections because they were seen as an internal Jewish matter. In general municipal elections, however, the Jews would vote along political and class lines, and the Bund could have more success.[66] The boycott of national elections to the Sejm increased the significance of the municipal ones to the parties of the left.

In December 1938 municipal elections were held in Warsaw, Łódź, Kraków, Poznań, and 492 other cities and towns. This electoral period, which lasted until May 1939, brought great success for the Bund. The party made significant gains in Warsaw and Łódź and in 1939 in Vilna, Lublin, and Białystok. Joseph Marcus estimated that in seven major cities, with a total population of approximately 840,000 Jews (Warsaw, Łódź, Lublin, Vilna, Białystok, Kraków, and Lwów), some 40 per cent of the Jewish voters voted for the Bund. In the twenty-six cities with Jewish populations of less than 10,000 approximately 20 per cent of the Jewish residents voted for the Bund, and some 45 per cent for the Zionist lists. All in all, Marcus estimated, the breakdown was as follows: Bund 38 per cent, Zionist lists 36 per cent, middle-class groups and Agudas Yisroel 23 per cent, others 3 per cent.[67] The party's preparations for these elections and the fact that it was able to obtain representatives in 102 cities and towns in Poland are noteworthy.[68] From these results it appears that the Bund had become a powerful political force among Polish Jewry at this time. From a small party that had received only 71,000 votes in the Sejm elections of 1930, the Bund had become a mass movement supported by a broad segment of the Polish Jewish community (in 1938 the Bund received 42,724 votes in Warsaw alone).

Interpretation of the election results differed. Yitzhak Grünbaum, a staunch

---

[64] M. Steinlauf, 'The Polish-Jewish Daily Press', *Polin*, ii (1987), 224–7; see also A. Paczkowski, *Prasa codzienna warszawy w latach 1918–1919* (Warsaw, 1983), 243–4. Researchers evaluated the distribution of the various Jewish dailies in those years very differently. M. Fuks, a scholar of the Jewish press in Poland between the two world wars, estimated the distribution of newspapers to be twice as great as the numbers quoted by the Polish Ministry of the Interior. He put distribution of the *Folkstsaytung* in 1932–8 at approximately 18,000 per day, compared to Steinlauf's figure of 16,500, which was based on statistics compiled by the Polish police and Ministry of the Interior. It appears that Fuks's estimates are exaggerated and were based on imprecise information furnished by the newspapers themselves.   [65] Marcus, *History*, 125.
[66] H. Erlich, 'Białystok' [editorial], *NF* (2 Dec. 1937).   [67] Marcus, *History*, 468–9.
[68] According to the estimate of E. Sherer in 'Vol-sakh hakolen', *NF* (28 July 1939).

opponent of the Bund and one of the more vilified leaders of the Zionist movement in the pages of the *Folkstsaytung*, claimed that the Bund's success was not evidence that the Jewish masses supported Bundist ideology. Their vote for the Bund, in Grünbaum's opinion, was a protest vote against the antisemitism of the Polish government. However, Grünbaum did admit that in the conditions that existed in Poland in those days only a party such as the Bund, whose actions were exclusively directed towards helping the Jewish community in Poland, could provide the necessary means to fight for the rights of Polish Jewry.[69] There were other factors contributing to the Bund's success: for example, the inability of the Zionist parties to find solutions to the problems of those wanting to emigrate to Erets Israel and the Jewish voters' criticism of the 'emigrationist' propaganda that kept Polish society from seriously considering the Jewish question. The historian Emanuel Meltzer declared that the Bund was strengthened only in those places where it was already strong, especially in Congress Poland; it did not increase its power in Galicia, Wołyń, or Zagłębie.[70]

The Bund interpreted the results differently. The general view was that it had become the main political force in the Polish Jewish community. The old-time Bundist leaders, headed by Henryk Erlich, evaluated the movement's achievements at the end of the 1930s more realistically, however. In 1937 Erlich stated that not all of those who voted for the Bund, nor all of the readers of the *Folkstsaytung*, were ideological supporters of the movement.[71] He saw the increase in the Bund's strength as a reflection of the growing feeling among various segments of the Jewish public that the only path open to Polish Jewry was the struggle for equal political and social rights. There was nothing wrong with a love for Erets Israel, Erlich stated, but the Jewish public understood that its feelings for the biblical homeland could not determine political action in a country that was, in the long run, its country.[72] Younger leaders regarded the electoral success of 1938–9 as evidence of mass support for Bundism and, as Emanuel Sherer claimed, proof that the Jews preferred to vote for the Bund rather than the PPS. If they wanted to stop the forces of reaction and protest against the antisemitic policies of government, he declared, they would do better to strengthen the Polish left.[73]

Factors beyond the election results entered into the changes that took place in the power relationships among the Jewish parties in this period. It is true that the Bund was strengthened primarily in Congress Poland, an area in which its influence had previously been recognized, but support for the Bund had also grown in areas where it had been weak in the 1920s. This was true of the two large concentrations of Jews in Zagłębie: Będzin and Sosnowiec. In the elections to local

---

[69] Y. Grünbaum, 'Aliyato shel haBund', in *Milḥamot yehudei Polaniah, 1918–1940* (Tel Aviv, 1941), 427–9.
[70] Meltzer, *Maa'vak medini*, 288. [71] H. Erlich, 'Ver zenen mir?', *NF* (26 Sept. 1937).
[72] Id., 'Sakh hakolen', *NF* (23 Dec. 1938). [73] E. Shrer, 'Vol-sakh hakolen', *NF* (28 July 1939).

government in Zagłębie in 1928 some 3.6 per cent of Jewish voters supported the Bund in Będzin, and some 8.6 per cent in Sosnowiec. In 1939, in the municipal elections, 7.1 per cent voted for the Bund in Będzin and 22.2 per cent in Sosnowiec.[74] In Tarnów, the second largest area of Jewish concentration in western Galicia, the Bund received 4,100 votes in the elections of March 1938, compared with 2,900 for the national Jewish bloc that opposed it.[75] The elections of 1938–9 were the beginning of growing support for the Bund among the Jewish community, even in areas where the party had traditionally been weak. Erlich correctly attributed this to the situation of Polish Jewry at the end of the 1930s; in other words, the Jewish public's vote for the Bund was based on pragmatic, and not ideological, considerations.

CONCLUSION

Pragmatism was one of the identifying marks of Jewish voting patterns in Poland and of fluctuations in the strength of the Jewish parties between the two world wars. These voting patterns were primarily influenced by the situation in Poland. In periods of crisis and distress, as always, there was a tendency to vote for Jewish candidates who opposed the government. In the early 1920s, for example, in the wave of antisemitism and anti-Jewish violence of the first years of Polish independence, Grünbaum and the Minorities' Bloc succeeded in forcing the Polish government to recognize the national rights of the Jewish minority. At the end of the 1930s the Bund played a similar role: the party tried to obtain the status of a national group for the Jews with cultural autonomy, freedom, and equality. The 'Socialist option', which was foreign to the majority of Jews in Poland, was given a different interpretation by Marxist theorists in the Bund from the one entertained by the Jewish masses. In this way we can understand the success of a party whose principles were Marxist but many of whose supporters were religious in one form or another. The Bund was a Marxist party that fought for the right to Jewish ritual slaughter, founded special clubs for its Orthodox supporters, administered Jewish communities, and was concerned with ritual baths, cemeteries, and the selection of local rabbis.

Joseph Marcus defined the Bund's course in Poland between the two world wars as one of 'splendid isolation'.[76] Bernard K. Johnpoll, who wrote about the same period, concluded that from the beginning the party was destined to fail. Its failure, Johnpoll believed, rested on the Bund's inability to become part of an alternative government; it did not unite with either the PPS or the Communists, and guarded its separateness, refusing to join even with other Jewish parties. As

---

[74] Statistics in W. Jaworski, 'Żydowskie partie polityczne w Zagłębiu Dąbrowskim w okresie międzywojennym w świetle akt archiwalnych', *Biuletyn Żydowskiego Instytutu Historycznego*, 3–4 (1988), 98–9.

[75] 'Der groyser sotsialistisher zig', *NF* (10 Mar. 1939).   [76] Marcus, *History*, 282.

the product of a party whose principal goal was to influence the composition of the government, the policies of the Bund were doomed to failure from the beginning.[77] The Bund's inability to influence the Polish government has no bearing on how well it succeeded in Polish Jewish society at that time. No single Jewish party or bloc of parties had the ability to influence the government in Poland. False hopes of this type were raised a number of times: by the establishment of the Zjednoczony Komitet Mniejszości Narodowych (United Committee of National Minorities), which contested the Sejm elections in 1922 as the Minorities' Bloc, or by the 1925 agreement (*ugoda*) with the Polish government.[78] Both these experiments ended in failure and disappointment.

In the 1930s the Bund succeeded in building a framework for co-operation (although it was sometimes only partial) with the PPS, a strong political element whose power increased greatly in those years. Although the PPS hesitated to co-operate with the Bund before 1937, the need for an alliance among all democratic political forces to fight against Polish Fascism caused it to change its attitude. The Bund opposed such a co-operative democratic alliance in principle, however, because it rejected the notion of co-operation with non-proletarian elements. The PPS had not changed its position on the Bund's proposed solution to the Jewish question.[79] Nevertheless, the Bund's ability to raise funds was useful: it had close connections with Jewish workers' organizations overseas, which transferred significant sums of money to its educational institutions, workers' organizations' and cultural and welfare projects. The Bund's 'splendid isolation' was its inability to co-operate with other Jewish parties. This caused the party difficulties in its struggle to improve the situation of the Jews in Poland, who faced rising government antisemitism. Although the Bund forced this political isolation upon itself, the party kept its deep roots in Jewish affairs, even though involvement in such matters did not always go hand in hand with the party's declared ideology. The party was ready to accept the task of leading the Jewish people in Poland. Its mistake was its desire to do this alone.

---

[77] Johnpoll, *Politics of Futility*, 259–68.

[78] On the Minorities' Bloc see M. Landau, 'Gush hamiyutim (1922)—makhshir behirot o etgar medini?', *Gal-Ed*, 4–5 (1978), 365–96; also S. Netzer, *Ma'avak yehudei Polin al zekhuyoteihem ha'ezrahiyot vehale'umiyot, 1918–1928* (Tel Aviv, 1980–1), 290–7. On the *ugoda* (agreement) see S. Landau, *Miyut yehudi lohem* (Jerusalem, 1986–7), 209–23, 237–43; and E. Mendelsohn, *Zionism in Poland: The Formative Years, 1915–1926* (Hanover, NH, 1981), 300–37.

[79] For a summary and evaluation of the relationship between the Bund and the PPS in the late 1930s see A. Brumberg, 'The Bund and the Polish Socialist Party in the Late 1930s', in Y. Gutman, E. Mendelsohn, J. Reinharz, and C. Shmeruk (eds.), *The Jews of Poland between Two World Wars* (Hanover, NH, 1989), 75–94.

Łódź Remained Red: Elections to the City Council of 27 September 1936

BARBARA WACHOWSKA

IN Łódź, Poland's second-largest city and main textile centre, city council elections were held on 27 September 1936. It was the fifth municipal election held in Poland since the nation had regained its independence, although it was only the second under the statute establishing a partial change in the municipal government's political system (passed on 23 March 1933). The first election under this statute took place on 27 May 1934. It represented the triumph of the Polish National camp, which earned 98,461 votes out of 219,638 cast. This gave the nationalists 39 of the 72 city council seats. Even the victors were surprised at the scale of their success: National Party support had increased sixteenfold since the parliamentary election of 1930.[1] In fact, the party had not prepared a full list of councillors.

This municipal election resulted in a painful defeat for leftist workers. The Polska Partia Socjalystyczna (PPS: Polish Socialist Party), in alliance with the Bund and the Deutsche Sozialistische Arbeitspartei (DSAP: German Social Democratic Workers' Party), secured only 27,352 votes, which gave them just seven seats on the city council. The Communists (listed thirteenth on the ballot sheet), whose candidates won 19,203 votes, failed to secure a single city council seat after the authorities had declared their list invalid.[2] The electoral results alarmed labour circles and the Polish left, especially because this poor showing had occurred in the very city in which the Socialists had been brought to power six years earlier by the elections of 9 May 1927. It was they who grieved most over the election.[3]

The election fixed for 27 September 1936 had thus aroused general interest in Poland. Everyone waited to see how the Łódź electorate would behave; the vacillation of the Łódź electorate was of interest not only to contemporaries but also

---

[1] M. Nartownowicz-Kot, 'Oblicze polityczne samorządu miejskiego Lodzi w latach 1919–1939', *Rocznik Łódzki*, 31 (1982), 118.

[2] B. Wachowska, 'Między wojnami', in '*W dymach czarnych budzi się Łódź*': *Z dziejów łódzkiego ruchu robotniczego 1882–1948* (Łódź, 1985), 298–9.

[3] J. Karbowiak, 'Wspomnienia z wyborów łódzkich 1936 r.', *PPS wspomnienia z lat 1918–1939*, i (Warsaw, 1987), 364

to scholars over the years.[4] Notwithstanding, few studies have appeared concerning the city council or the 1936 election,[5] although the latter, as a significant event of the 1930s, has been alluded to in general histories, monographs, and regional studies.[6]

What made the municipal elections in Łódź even more the subject of tense anticipation was the fact that the voters had given municipal authority to the National Democrats in May 1934. Yet on 8 September 1935 the parliamentary election had been boycotted to a greater extent than in the rest of the country. Only 33 per cent of those eligible voted, and of these only 31 per cent were valid (107,562 of 347,631 eligible voters).[7] Łódź residents thus clearly demonstrated their disapproval of the rightist Sanacja regime, the ruling government of Poland at the time.

The elections were supposed to have taken place earlier. By law, the authorities were required to fix an election date within six months after the city council had been dissolved. This had taken place on 2 July 1935 by the decision of the Minister of Internal Affairs, who deemed the Łódź city council unable to carry out its duties and appointed Colonel Wacław Gałązka as presidential commissioner.[8]

This was not the most favourable period for the municipal authorities. Boycotting the parliamentary elections was not the only way in which the Łódź electorate expressed its disapproval of the imposed constitution and the new electoral law. Waves of mass demonstrations struck the entire country: the unemployed demonstrated, workers went on strike, the peasantry revolted, and the intelligentsia became more and more radical. Łódź actively participated in this process, especially in the period 2–17 March 1936, when the city became the centre of a general textile workers' strike as well as sit-ins. According to official statistics, there were 222 sit-ins in Łódź province in that year.[9]

Although the authorities may have wished to, it was impossible to put off elections any longer—it had been almost a year since the city council had been

[4] J. Borkowski, 'Samorządowe wybory miejskie 1933–1934', Z pola walki, 3 (1976).
[5] P. Korzec, ' "Czerwona" łódzka rada miejska w latach 1936–1937', in Paweł Korzec (ed.), Studia i materiały do dziejów Lodzi i okręgyw łódzkiego (Łódź, 1962), 207–54.
[6] J. Kowalski, KPP 1935–1938, Studium historyczne (Warsaw, 1975), 307–8; H. Brodowska, 'Realizacja idei jednolitego frontu w ruchu ludowym na terenie województwa łódzkiego w latach 1935–1938', in Wkład Ziemi Łódzkiej w rozwój państwa polskiego (Łódź, 1967), 97; B. Wachowska, 'Zarys portrety politycznego elektoratu żydowskiego Łodzi międzywojennej w świetle parlamentarnych i samorządowych kampanii wyborczych 1918–1938', in W. Puś (ed.), Dzieje Żydów w Łodzi 1820–1944 wybrane problemy; L. Meissner, Niemieckie organizacje antyfaszystowskie w Polsce 1933–1939 (Warsaw, 1973), 197–9; B Krzywobłocka, Chadecje 1918–1937 (Warsaw, 1974), 368; H. Przybylski, Front Morges w okresie II Rzeczpospolitej (Warsaw, 1972), 113–16.
[7] Mały rocznik statystyczny 1935 (Łódź, 1937), 181.
[8] Kurier Łódzki [KŁ] 3/178 (15 July 1935), 190.
[9] See B. Wachowska, Z dziejów jednolitego frontu w łódzkim okręgu przemysłowym (Łódź, 1973), 355.

dissolved. Thus, the Łódź voivode Aleksander Hauke-Nowak was obliged to announce on 29 June 1936 that the next elections would take place on 27 September. The statute that greatly limited the autonomy of municipal government and diminished voting rights had been passed on 23 March 1933 in spite of protests. As a result, the minimum voting age was set at twenty-four, whereas it had previously been twenty-one. In addition, no one under thirty could run for office (this limit had been previously set at twenty-five). The new statute also required a candidate to have a good command of spoken and written Polish. To enforce the language requirement, an examination for candidates to the city council was introduced, a practice that opened up the possibility of corruption. The new rules divided city communes into electoral districts, in order to limit the likelihood of opposition groups gaining a majority. The redistricting was executed by the general administrative authorities, who assigned a certain number of city council seats (not fewer than three) to each district based on the last census. In practice this meant that the authorities' decisions were almost impossible to change. The voting itself took place in precincts that were created within the new districts.

The laws governing pre-electoral meetings, although they hindered the activities of some political groups, were somewhat more liberal. Only meetings held outdoors required advance notification to the administrative authorities, who had the power to ban them. Indoor meetings did not require permission. If a meeting was open to the public, the security police could appoint their own representatives to dissolve it 'in cases authorized by the law'.

The electoral rules for municipal government, although not fully democratic, allowed for freer political expression than the electoral law passed by the Sejm and Senate in 1935. Opposition groups had thus refrained from boycotting the legislation. Since the national parliament did not truly reflect public opinion, the new statute governing municipal elections was perceived as a means to allow the expression of views, at least as far as local government was concerned. That is why the whole nation watched the events in Łódź with so much interest.

The election was also significant because the city's population, an important component of which was the heavy concentration of factory workers, was made up of diverse religions and nationalities. On 1 January 1936 there were 638,857 inhabitants of the city. Women formed the majority, numbering 348,239 as opposed to 290,618 men—120 women to every 100 men. This proportion had increased from the previous general census on 9 December 1931, which showed 117.3 women to 100 men within the smaller population of 604,629 inhabitants. The census also showed that the city's population consisted of 340,179 Catholics (56.3 per cent), 202,497 Jews (33.5 per cent), 56,159 Protestants (9.3 per cent), and 5,526 people of other religions (0.9 per cent). The statistics of religious affiliation did not entirely correspond with those for nationality, the criterion for determining which was 'mother tongue'. Polish was the mother tongue of 356,987 people (59 per cent), while 191,720 indicated Yiddish or Hebrew (31.7 per cent) as their main language, 53,562 German (8.9 per cent), and 1,828 a variety of other languages (0.3 per cent).[10] While Poles, Jews, Germans, and a few other groups voted in the elections, nationality, religion, and mother tongue were not noted in any electoral statistics.

In the end, the main significance of the Łódź elections was that they occurred when political power in Poland was undergoing a transformation. On the one hand, the left was increasing its strength, while on other the Polish National camp was becoming more aggressive. Along with these, the second most powerful rightist group, the ruling Sanacja party, was in the process of disintegration, while the other centrist political groupings were being gradually marginalized. All of these tendencies were expressed in the Łódź elections.

The first tensions were caused by the appointment of a Main Electoral Commission. Otton Veseille, district court vice-president in Łódź, was appointed chairman of this body, with district court judge Eugeniusz Wiśniewski as his deputy. The provincial governor appointed Dr Marian Stanisław Gąsiorowski, director of the hospital, and Tadeusz Bełdowski, director of the Scheibler and Grohman factories, as members of the commission. Karol Bajer, director of the Industrial Trade Chamber, and a lawyer, Antoni Obuchowicz, who were recommended by the city president, were also members. There were no representatives from labour on the Main Electoral Commission, nor were there any among the group of alternates, which included Modest Słoniewski, a public notary, later replaced by Dr Tadeusz Mogilnicki. Also included was Karol Algajer, a senator, and the officials Jan Mileski and Albin Grabowski.[11] The District Commission of Trade Unions protested against the composition of the Main Electoral Commission, but neither the voivode, to whom the protest was sent, nor any other arm of state authority reacted to the complaint.[12]

Further conflicts arose when the Minister of Internal Affairs fixed the electoral calendar. The projected date was superficially a reasonable one, as it allowed twenty days to check the list of electors and submit appeals to the district commissions, although it did not give enough time to the electoral committees, who were given only six days to submit a list of candidates to the Main Electoral

---

[10] *Mały rocznik statystyczny miasta Łodzi 1936* (Łódź, 1938), 12–15.

[11] It was similar in the district electoral commissions led by Franciszek Waszkiewicz (district I), Szymon Tułecki (II), Miron Lewandowski (III), Wiktor Chudziński (IV), Jan Holcgreber (V), Jan Ćwikliński (VI), Marian Zdrojewski (VII), Henryk Ochedalski (VIII), Antoni Remiszewski (IX), and Wacław Wojewódzki (X). See Archiwum Państwowe w Łodzi [APL], Akta m. Łodzi [AmL], file 1221/11, 507; Zarządzenie wojewody, *Dziennik Zarządu m. Łodzi [DzZmŁ]*, 8 (15 Aug. 1936), 514; *KL* 209 (1 Aug. 1936), 5. In order to make the technical preparations for the election and supervise compilation of the electoral register, the city president appointed an electoral department on 30 June. Municipal government Director Mieczysław Kalinowski became the department's chairman and Adam Wysocki, head of the Census Bureau, became his assistant: *DzZmŁ* 7 (15 July 1936), 520.

[12] Korzec, 'Czerwona', 224.

Commission and at the same time remove defects and mistakes pointed out by the commission. The lists had to be approved or declared invalid ten days before the election. If a list was declared invalid, no chance was given to an electoral committee to make any changes to it, and this led to the disintegration of some committees and the liquidation of their lists. Finally, the Main Electoral Commission announced the lists and published posters with instructions on how to vote barely a week before election day.[13]

City council candidates had to submit a declaration that expressed their intent to run and willingness to serve if elected. The list of candidates had to be signed by 300 electors of a given district. An elector was given the chance of retracting his signature, which opened up another level of pressure from the administrative authorities and impeded the electoral campaign. The Main Electoral Commission's order that candidates were required to pass an oral and written Polish language examination was perceived as more than a mere annoyance. On 15 September, the Main Electoral Commission called in fifteen people for examination; in protest, four candidates from the Jewish lists failed to appear. Of the remaining eleven, barely four 'were able to demonstrate knowledge of Polish to the degree required by the ordinance'. The candidates who did not attend, as well as those who had failed the examination, were removed from the lists.[14] The date of the examination coincided with that set for the final ratification of lists, after which it was impossible to nominate new candidates. Moreover, the way in which the Main Electoral Commission interpreted and executed the edict provoked controversy; many representatives felt that the sole aim of the language examination had been to eliminate unsympathetic candidates rather than test their knowledge of Polish.

Candidates were allowed to run from only one district, which is why each district submitted separate lists. The number of candidates on a list could not exceed three times the number of seats in a given district. Although each of the lists was given a number, the same grouping was sometimes assigned a different number in different districts.

The city was divided into ten districts and 203 precincts. The districts were given the names of major quarters of the city:

District I: Bałuty Wschód
II Helenów, the S. Staszica (3 May) park
III Widzew
IV Scheibler district
V Chojny
VI Karole Rokicie
VII Polesie Konstantynowskie, Koziny

[13] *DzZmŁ* 8 (15 Aug. 1936), 591; *KŁ* 179 (2 July 1936), 4.
[14] *KŁ* 251 (13 Sept. 1936), 4; ibid. 254 (16 Sept. 1936), 5.

VIII   Bałuty Zachód
IX   Old City district
X   Central City district

Some 72 city councillors were to be chosen: 9 from the 23 precincts in district I, 5 from the 15 precincts in district II, 6 from the 17 precincts in district III, 6 from the 16 precincts in district IV, 8 from the 22 precincts in district V, 4 from the 10 precincts in district VI, 8 from the 24 precincts in district VII, 8 from the 22 precincts in district VIII, 7 from the 23 precincts in district IX, and 11 from the 31 precincts in district X.[15]

The electoral confrontation heralded a new period of intensive organizational and political preparations by the various parties. They observed and assessed their opponents, searched for allies, and consolidated party ranks. This all took place in an atmosphere of sharp conflict stimulated by the complicated reality of that time. The elections were a special challenge for leftist workers. Both Communists and Socialists were aware of this, and both concluded that the bitter defeat of 1934 could be avoided only by united action in a unified front.[16] That was not easy. The Communists and Socialists mistrusted one another; there was a history of reluctance, injury, and fear. Overcoming these feelings was difficult, and, considering the essential differences on the question of unified action—differences that had existed for generations and continued to exist between the Komunistyczna Partia Polski (KPP: Polish Communist Party) and the PPS—a unified front seemed hopeless. Overcoming differences and building trust required a willingness to compromise and an emphasis on what both movements had in common. Although efforts to form a united front between the two were very often in jeopardy, a common ground was slowly developed.

In the beginning, the KPP thought about creating a broad front that would include leftist and centrist workers' organizations. The project of organizing party circles began in June 1936, when the KPP's national secretariat received word of the authorities' decision to announce city council elections for Łódź. KPP leaders planned to create a front with such local organizations as the National Workers' Party (NPR), the Christian Democratic Party (Chadecja), cultural-educational societies, intellectual societies like the teachers' union, the tenants' unions, middle-class circles, and the unions of artisans. Of course, this would be based on an alliance with Polish (PPS), Jewish (Bund), and German (DSAP) Socialists.[17]

After a more extensive evaluation of the situation, the KPP decided that a united front was not feasible, and abandoned the idea. As a result, local party organizations in districts, precincts, and quarters focused on co-operating only with

---

[15] *DzZmŁ* 8 (15 Aug. 1936), 589; *KL* 209 (1 Aug. 1936), 5.
[16] Karbowiak, *Wspomnienia*, 364.
[17] Korzec, 'Czerwona', 211; Kowalski, 'KPP', 308.

Socialists. This co-operation was facilitated by a common presence in trade unions and joint efforts to promote workers' demands. The experience of the general textile strike of March 1936 turned out to be especially valuable, because the peaceful co-operation of Socialists and Communists contributed to significant increases in membership and raised KPP authority and influence in workers' circles within Łódź factories.[18]

The PPS viewed the elections with equal seriousness: the Chief Council, district organizations, and party headquarters in Łódź campaigned vigorously. For Socialists, the election results were important in determining the scope of PPS influence in the city, and as a gauge of the general interest outside of Łódź. The PPS wanted to regain authority and importance in an area in which it had previously been the dominant force. At the same time, PPS leaders were aware that the party could not win widespread electoral support on its own, nor were alliances with Jewish and German Socialists sufficient—such an alliance in May 1934 had unexpectedly ended in defeat. Moreover, the PPS knew that the KPP was very influential among the Łódź workers. Election results from 8 October 1927 showed the need to join forces with the KPP. If authorities did not annul the Communist list—No. 5 (the Bloc of Workers' Unity)—which boasted 42,111 votes, then the Socialists would have to share power in the city with the Communists, who had secured fourteen seats. If the Communist list were to stand, some people estimated it might carry 50,000–60,000 votes. Indeed, this is what happened in the parliamentary elections of 4 March 1928: list No. 37, the Workers' Union, gained 49,230 votes and brought two deputies into the Sejm, Władysław Bitner and Paweł Rosiak.

The favourable electoral showing by the KPP was repeated on 16 November 1930, when in spite of harassment, terror, and repression from Sanacja, the Communist list, No. 22 (Jedność Robotniczo-Chłopska, the Workers' Peasants' Union), won 53,694 votes, and Chil Rosenberg and Władysław Danecki became Sejm deputies. Even in May 1934, which was an unusually difficult period for the left, the Communists again demonstrated their power, despite the fact that votes for their list (No. 13) were no more than a gesture, the list having been invalidated.[19] The growing Communist support brought home to the PPS the need for an agreement with them. For their part, the Communists wanted such an agreement because separate lists might lead to nullification of their list. Thus, both sides agreed that defeating the right and winning the election could only be achieved together.

The party rank and file were also aware of the need to combine forces, and voiced this at several gatherings. One policeman reported on a meeting that had taken place in Chojny on 4 July 1936 attended by some 200 people. Jan Haneman delivered a lecture 'on the present political situation'. He appealed to participants

[18] Wachowska, *Z dziejów jednolitego frontu*, 315–19.
[19] Wachowska, 'Między wojnami', 259, 261, 285, 299.

'to go to the elections as one front, and then we will secure a victory'. Other speakers also urged participants to act in unity. Chaja Zand recalled the demonstration of 1 May 1936 which had been organized by Socialists and Communists. 'It was so strong that even the police had to sit quietly.' She appealed to the audience to give all their votes to 'working-class' candidates, assuring them that if 'we vote as a unified front, then we are bound to win'. None of those present opposed unified action.[20] This meeting represented a broad spectrum of workers.

Each side viewed the alliance differently, however. The only shared point of view was that support for the bloc should be based on class trade unions. There were important differences concerning the political scope. The Communists wanted a common list of all Socialist parties that would include the PPS, the Bund, the DSAP and, of course, the KPP. They also wanted representatives from those parties to be on the list of candidates for the city council. The PPS declared its solidarity with the Jewish workers, although they knew that this would alienate the Polish workers who had been influenced by the antisemitic propaganda of the Polish national right. The push towards solidarity led the PPS to collaborate with the Jewish Socialists and co-operate with the future city council, even though they presented separate lists. PPS leaders believed that separate lists would attract voters whose national sentiment might have otherwise made them reluctant to vote PPS. The experience of 1934 had taught them that a common PPS–Bund list would end up in defeat because many Polish voters would look on it as Jewish.

The Bund wanted to co-operate with Polish and German Socialists, although they too were aware that many Jewish voters, like the Polish voters of 1934, would reject a list of 'Working Socialist Unity and Class Trade Unions' as a Polish list. In the end, Jewish Socialists presented a separate list because, as a contemporary activist argued, 'they wanted to gain Jewish supporters, who would not be inclined to vote for Polish candidates, given the antisemitic incidents'.[21] This seemed a convincing line of thought.

Inter-party relations were directly linked to the politics of an electoral alliance, which found expression in the name given to the list of candidates. Different points of view began to surface between Communists and Socialists. The latter were represented in negotiations by Antoni Szczerkowski, Edmund Chodyński, and Henryk Wachowicz. Szczerkowski, the long-time council chairman of the textile workers' trade union, played an important role. Under his leadership a session of the District Council Commission of Trade Unions took place on 18 July. Samuel Milman represented Jewish trade-union members, while Emil Zerbe represented the Germans. The electoral list proposed by the PPS Okręgowy Komitet Robotniczy (District Committee of Workers, local branch of Polska Partia Socjalistyczna) was presented under the title 'The PPS and Trade

[20] APŁ., Starostwo Powiatowe Łódzkie, teczka 38, kart 14, Meldunek sytuacyjny No. 140.
[21] Ibid., ZW, No. inw. 413, Wspomnienie E. Ajnenkiela, 4.

Unions'. While the trade-union members accepted the name as well as the inclusion of German Socialist representatives on the list, the Jewish Socialists ended up presenting a separate list.[22]

The Communists initially opposed this name, the strongest objection being articulated by the national secretariat of the KPP. Leaders of the Łódź organization of the KPP, however, were less surprised at the inclusion of 'PPS' in the name. This fact, and the desire to oppose pressure by the national leadership, turned out to be important factors in building a unified electoral bloc. Local activists found it necessary to focus on the most important issues rather than criticize PPS propositions. This pragmatic approach somewhat appeased the bitter feelings that had continuously come to the fore. The position of Communist interlocutors convinced both the 'young' faction, found in the OKR, and the 'old' faction, which attached excessive importance to the name of the list. That is why the agreement to accept it was finally secured. Eugeniusz Ajenkiel recalls that in this way 'the creation of a united front in the electoral struggle was achieved by small concessions'.[23]

A single Łódź Electoral Committee was created after the positions were agreed. It consisted of eighteen people: nine PPS representatives and nine trade-union members. Among the latter were five Communist activists. M. Zdziechowski became one of two vice-chairmen. District and precinct committees were created soon afterwards, as were separate committees in the larger factories. The Communists formed a majority on many committees, particularly the precinct ones. This aroused some concern in the PPS, which feared that the KPP would have a distinct advantage. To dispel these fears, the KPP agreed to increase the number of Socialist representatives on precinct committees in exchange for more representation in the general Łódź electoral structure.[24] Both parties agreed to this.

The General Łódź Electoral Committee for the PPS and Trade Unions list was formed at the end of July. The committee announced a public meeting to proclaim its formation and the beginning of a pre-electoral campaign on 1 September. Security authorities, however, forbade the meeting;[25] this was one of the ways in which the authorities repressed leftist workers.

The consolidation and intensification of the left wing were accompanied by a process of continual weakening of the centre in Łódź, despite countermeasures by various centrist groups. The Stowarzyszenie Robotników Chrześcijańskich (SRCh: Association of Christian Workers) passed a resolution on 29 June affirming its desire to join the Chrześcijańskie Zjednoczenie Zawodowe (ChZZ: Christian Trade Association) during pre-electoral activities, to which the ChZZ

---

[22] KŁ 196 (19 July 1936), 4.
[23] APL, ZW, No. inw. 413, Wspomnienie E. Ajnenkiela, 4.
[24] Kowalski, 'KPP', 305.
[25] KŁ 208 (31 July 1936), 4; ibid. 209 (1 Aug. 1936), 5.

agreed. A meeting of SRCh and ChZZ council members from different divisions took place on 9 July, when representatives chose the administrative body for the electoral committee, appointed a propaganda and financial commission, and called for all Polish Christian workers' organizations to unite for the election. These ideas were formulated by Adam Cyrański, Antoni Harasz, Feliks Kieszkowski, Stanisław Jeżierski, and Anna Tomczyk.[26]

The Union of Young Catholic 'Revivalists', the Catholic Cultural-Education Association, and representatives of Chrześcijańska Demokracja and the Narodowa Partia Robotnicza-Prawica (NPR Right: National Workers' Party) were willing to join and began to discuss formation of a Great Christian Bloc, invoking the principles 'expressed during the meeting in Morges' (known as the Morges Front in Łódź).[27]

Consolidation of forces was also proposed by the Narodowe Stronnictwo Pracy (National Party of Labour, previously called the National Workers' Party Left). Engaged in this effort was Ludwik Waszkiewicz, one of the party's main founders and a long-time deputy.[28] The NPR Right reacted to the call for co-operation by sending its representative, F. Kwieciński, to take part in common meetings. The Zjednoczenie Zawodowe Polskie (Union of Polish Trades), led by Stefan Kulczyński, also began to be more active. The Union wanted to present its own list, but the leaders of Związki Zawodowe 'Praca' (Trade Unions 'Work') proposed that they enter the elections together. The District Council of Trade Unions 'Work' passed a formal resolution on 21 July calling for an electoral bloc with the Union of Polish Trades and the National Party of Labour. This council proposed the creation of a 'National Workers' Electoral Committee'.[29]

The NPR Right, searching for contacts with the Union of Polish Trades and the National Party of Labour, formed an electoral committee together with the Association of the Working Youth 'Union' in mid-July and proclaimed that it would present lists in all districts. At the end of July initiatives for agreement began to appear from all these electoral committees. After much discussion, representatives from the Trade Unions 'Work', the Christian Trade Association, the National Party of Labour, the NPR, Chadecja, the Stowarzyszenie Robotników Chrześcijan (Association of Christian Workers), and the Narodowy Związek Robotniczy-Kilińczycy (National Workers' Union), closely linked with the Narodowa Partia Robotnicza, met on 4 September. (Jan Kiliński, a shoemaker by profession, was a hero of the Kościuszko uprising of 1794.) They decided to create a unified electoral committee to present a common list in all districts.[30]

The participation in the alliance of the weak Christian Democrats and the

---

[26] *KŁ* 178 (1 July 1936), 4; 182 (5 July 1936), 5; 187 (10 July 1936), 4.
[27] Ibid. 199 (22 July 1936), 5.
[28] A. Andrusiewicz, 'Stronnictwo Pracy 1937–1950', in *Ze studiów nad dziejami najnowszymi chadecji w Polsce* (Warsaw, 1988), 15, 50.
[29] *Gazeta polska* [*GP*], 203 (22 July 1936), 10.   [30] *KŁ* 214 (6 Aug. 1936), 4.

unpopular pro-Sanacja groups in Łódź did not bode well for the elections. Following the example of the NPR and its satellites, other organizations with the same pro-government orientation began to enter the electoral bloc. One of these was the Unia Związków Zawodowych Pracowników Umysłowych (Association of Trade Unions of White-Collar Workers), which, after unsuccessful attempts to form its own electoral committee, decided not to join a bloc but to give its members the option of choosing 'those candidates who would guarantee the appropriate attitude to the problem of municipal government'.[31] At this time, one faction of the White-Collar Trade Union association announced its decision to join the newly formed bloc, and changed its name to Narodowo-Chrześcijański Front Robotniczy (the National Christian Workers' Front).

The Związek Nauczycielstwa Polskiego (Union of Polish Teachers) acted similarly, stressing that it was a 'strictly apolitical vocational organization' that would not support any list. Members were told 'to vote for those candidates who care deeply about education and schooling issues'.[32] It also encouraged union members to cast their votes for the list supported by the intellectuals.

In addition, local sections of organizations such as the Związek Legionistów Polskich (Union of Polish Legionaries), the Polska Organizacja Wojskowa (Polish Military Organization), the Polski Związek Obrońców Ojczyzny (Polish Union of Defenders of the Fatherland), the Związek Rezerwistów (Union of Reservists), as well as the Komitet Wyborczy Zblokowanych Organizacji Kobiecych (Electoral Committee of the Unified Organization of Women), which heretofore had been in the Non-Party Bloc for Co-operation with the Government, now allied themselves with the National Christian Workers' Front.[33]

Pro-Sanacja currents in the National Christian Workers' Front, however, began to gather strength, which caused conflict within Chadecja. Soon a dissident group arose that opposed Stanisław Mruk, who had accepted the Front's political platform. The dissidents presented a letter to the board requesting that it take a stance on this issue. Although chairman Władysław Tempka recommended that the Łódź Chadecja join with the NPR Right and the Hallerczyk Union, he did not prevail. Both the Hallerczyk Union and the Związek Młodzieży Katolickiej Łódzkiej Akcji Katolickiej (Union of Young Catholics of the Łódź Catholic Action) were absent from the meeting called by Chadecja on 23 July to create such a bloc.[34]

Followers of Mruk, supported by Ludwik Waszkiewicz and Józef Socha from the Trade Unions 'Work', announced to the pro-Sanacja partisans that they would lead the National Christian Workers' Front towards co-operation with Sanacja. On the other hand, sections of the Chadecja organization in Łódź were influenced by the aggressively nationalistic Stronnictwo Narodowe (National Party), and promoted support for its position. All in all, this caused a campaign

[31] Ibid. 233 (26 Aug. 1936), 5. [32] Ibid. 255 (17 Sept. 1936), 4.
[33] Korzec, 'Czerwona', 215. [34] Krzywobłocka, *Chadecje*, 368, 370, 373.

replete with contradictions and compromising statements, one that discredited the candidates and lowered their value in the eyes of the electorate.[35]

Outside the bloc was the 'Christian Committee of Unified Łódź Voters working for the Nation, the State, and Autonomy', founded by Władysław Kuryluk, Józef Mandecki, and Edward Potęga. In spite of its pro-Sanacja orientation and promises to join the National Christian Workers' Front, it maintained a separate organization and gained additional support from three trade unions representing the post, telegraph, and telephone workers.[36]

The Związek Rzemieślników Chrześcijań (Union of Christian Artisans), the board of Christian guilds, members and activists of the Izba Rzemieślnicza (Artisan Chamber) along with the chairman, as well as a group of intellectuals and the Chadecja-oriented middle class, comprised a separate electoral committee with its own list of candidates. Initially the plan was 'to join with one of the parties in a platform similar to that of the Christian artisan parties'.[37] A commission was formed with Stanisław Kopczyński, Andrzej Lewandowski, Jan Janowski, and Adolf Vize, which began working towards co-operation. In the end, however, they created their own 'Citizens' Economic Committee' and proposed their own candidates.[38]

Organizational confusion, differences between the electoral programmes of the groups aiming to create this bloc, the beginnings of the disintegration of Chadecja, and the exposure of the slogan 'struggle of the Catholic-national elements against Communist radicalism' helped to ensure that the Łódź electors gave this bloc only minimal support. They did not listen to assurances that it had acted against 'the inclusion of Fascist and Communist dictatorial tendencies'.[39] The presentation in the Łódź daily press of the National Christian Workers' Front as one of three large electoral blocs[40]—which was a misrepresentation of the true structure of political power in the city—did not deceive the electorate. The PPS organ, Łodzianin, pointedly described this bloc as 'a political department store'.[41]

Sanacja had its own electoral committees in Łódź, even though it strongly sup-

---

[35] Przybylski, Front Morges, 113, 114, 116.
[36] KŁ 196 (19 July 1936), 4–7; ibid. 202 (25 July 1936); 213 (5 Aug. 1936); 230 (23 Aug. 1936).
[37] Ibid. 210 (2 Aug. 1936), 5. [38] Ibid. 201 (24 July 1936), 5; 247 (9 Sept. 1936), 7.
[39] Przybylski, Front Morges, 114. [40] KŁ 237 (30 Aug. 1936), 5.
[41] On 4 Sept. 1936 the paper Łodzianin wrote that 'the National Workers' Party publishes proclamations against the government, the Sanacja, while legionaries and members of the Polish Military Organization support the government. The paper Praca [Work] fights againsts Socialists, the Association of Trade Unions, and Chadecja, and is antisemitic and reactionary. At the same time as the legionaries and members of the Polish Military Organization are becoming more radical, the Christian Trade Unions fight with the National Democratic Party, craftsmen flirt with the National Democrats, workers' unions act against industrialists, and the Christian Association of Merchants and Industrialists with Mr Fiedler at its head articulates slogans in support of private businesses. In other words, Mr Waszkiewicz has established a political department store': quoted in H. Przybylski, Chrześcijańska Demokracja i Narodowa Partia Robotnicza w latach 1926–1937 (Warsaw, 1980), 319–20.

ported the National Christian Workers' Front. It should be added, however, that the National Workers' Party, one of the Front's partners, attacked 'the system that weighed on Polish life like a terrible nightmare, oppressing and demoralizing it, and creating havoc', while the Chadecja press wrote that Sanacja 'smells of dead bodies'. It failed to gain popularity in Łódź, which in any case had not been an area of traditional support for Chadecja. The weaknesses of Sanacja caused it to resort to repression when confronted by the 'unemployed and hungry who only desire work and bread'. Amid dismissals of senators and the confiscation of government newspapers, conflicts in government circles were perceived as evidence of disintegration of the ruling camp. Moreover, the dissolution of the Bezpartyjny Blok Współpracy z Rządem (BBWR: Non-Party Bloc for Co-operation with the Government) deprived the government camp of formal unified representation, revealing the scale of internal fragmentation. Some left-wing workers even said that 'Sanacja fell on its head and only occasionally got up'.[42]

The rightist Sanacja camp that governed the country was experiencing difficult times: it could not form a single electoral committee in Łódź under the open government policy and did not present an official list. Sanacja hid within three different electoral blocs, still trying to gain allies in the leftist camp. The first of these electoral committees was the Association of Trade Unions, whose district council proposed on 13 August the creation of 'an electoral bloc exclusively from workers' organizations and employees, based on the entire state and defending the class interests of the workers'.[43] This was addressed to Trade Unions 'Work', the Christian Trade Association, the Polskie Zjednoczenie Zawodowe (Polish Trade Association), and the PPS and Class Trade Unions. These organizations declined to participate in the initiative, and the Socialists and Communists, in a resolution rejecting the proposition, recalled that the Association of Trade Unions was brought to life by Sanacja to disrupt the working-class movement and had played a disruptive role in the struggle of the proletariat in Łódź.[44]

Acting in the name of the District Council of the Association of Trade Unions, chairman Jan Barczewski and secretary I. Lewicki held a meeting on 23 August with the Union's administrators and formed its own electoral committee, led by Zygmunt Leśniczak. Only a small group from the Union of White-Collar Workers joined.[45]

The second electoral committee was formed by organizations from the dissolved BBWR. It consisted of associations of soldiers, artisans, civil servants, workers, women, and other social groups. Forty associations comprised the com-

---

[42] APŁ, SPŁ, t. 38, Komenda Powiatowa Policji Państwowej, meldunek sytuacyjny No. 140, p. 44.
[43] KŁ 230 (23 Aug. 1936), 7.
[44] S. Ajzner, *Związek Związków Zawodowych 1931–1939* (Warsaw, 1979), 287.
[45] KŁ 231 (24 Aug. 1936), 2; ibid. 233 (26 Aug. 1936), 5; 235 (28 Aug. 1936), 5.

mittee when it was announced in the press, and this number increased to 45 and then 52. Although the initial feeling was that these bodies were pro-government, they went to the election 'with apolitical slogans of economic development for the good of the city' and tried to recruit both left- and right-wing elements. In the course of the pre-electoral campaign the committee became more openly political, which led its constituent groups to be presented as 'wavering between the PPS and Endecja'.

Sejm deputies Marian Wadowski and Michał Wymysłowski, who were well-known Sanacja activists in Łódź, and Karol Argajer, Adjutant Council member for the Provisional President of Łódź, were political leaders of these groups. Eugenia Godlewska led the Stowarzyszenie Kobiece (Association of Women) in this bloc. Although initially presented as the United Electoral Committee of Labour for the State and City, on 4 August the group decided to take the name Polish Electoral Committee.[46]

Finally, Sanacja decided to appeal to electors from the PPS list of the former Revolutionary Faction, which was known as a 'committee of fighters for independence'. Stressing separateness and autonomy, Sanacja sought council candidates among people who had been honoured with the Cross of Independence, which they regarded as a most reliable guarantee of social approval. The first name on this list was Stefan Półciennik.[47]

As to the Association of Trade Unions, left-wing supporters of Sanacja even opposed the government for its reluctance to support candidates it had proposed, despite strong pressure.[48] Besides, the Polish Electoral Committee was regarded as a government mouthpiece, while the PPS arm of the former Revolutionary Faction was presented as the only legitimate inheritor of the tradition of struggle for national independence and as the guardian of Polish sovereignty.

Neither the centre nor the ruling Sanacja was a real threat to the left. This came from the National Party, which had been very strong and influential for many years in Łódź. It focused its entire effort on opposition to the left and treated the anti-Jewish campaign as part of this fight. Jędrzej Giertych wrote that 'there are two political camps in Poland: the National camp and the People's Front camp, whose core is the Communist Party and whose engine and most valuable cadres are Jews (including bourgeois Jews). Everything between these two camps has disintegrated.'[49]

In its struggle with the left, the national camp was ready to co-operate with the police. It brought to Łódź the most able agitators from other centres. Vice-President Karol Wierczak represented the administrative board of the party and came to Łódź twice a week. Money flowed into the national camp. Members of

[46] *KŁ* 182 (5 July 1936), 5; 189 (12 July 1936), 15; 194 (17 July 1936), 4; 206 (29 July 1936), 5; 213 (5 Aug. 1936), 4; 228 (21 Aug. 1936), 4.
[47] Ibid. 228 (21 Aug. 1936), 4; 237 (30 Aug. 1936), 5.   [48] Ajzner, *Związek*, 287.
[49] J. Giertych, *Po wyborach w Łodzi: Obserwacje i wnioski* (Warsaw, 1936), 12.

the National Party's fighting bands provoked conflicts with leftist workers and Jews, and its attitude was described by J. Giertych as: 'If there was to be a fight, the National Party would rather beat up than be beaten.'[50]

The National Party at that time was undergoing a transformation in membership. There were more and more youthful supporters, many from the Camp of Great Poland that had dissolved on 28 March 1933, and there were also more from the Obóz Narodowo-Radykalny (ONR: National Radical Camp) which from 4 July 1934 had begun to gain an advantage. The National Party in Łódź was clearly under the control of the youth, with Kazimierz Kowalski at its head, chosen as Łódź vice-president by the former city council on 20 December 1934. The second vice-president was Zygmunt Podgórski. Former town councillors Leon Grzegorzak, Wacław Kapczyński, Aleksander Stolarek, and Stanisław Bugaj also showed an interest in municipal government. Kazimierz Kowalski was supported in the National Party's district board by Zbigniew Michalak, Wacław Bursiewicz, Ewaryst Zwierzewicz, Franciszek Szwajdler, and Henryk Szulc.[51]

The electoral committee of the National Camp undertook a very aggressive campaign, focusing on burning social issues in Łódź. Unemployment remained high among both factory workers and artisans. Lack of employment opportunities and fear of job loss made for increasing radicalization. It was easy to blame Jews for this situation, especially with so many Jewish factory owners in the city—the majority of factories were owned by Jews, even if they were small and unprofitable. The 1931 census reveals that 77 per cent of Poles were proletarians, while for Germans the figure was 79 per cent and for Jews 36 per cent. In contrast, 77.4 per cent of textile factories were in Jewish hands, 14.9 per cent were owned by Germans, and Poles owned only 7 per cent. Of the thirty-two factories employing over 500 workers, none was Polish-owned: Germans owned twenty of them and Jews six. Jews were also prominent in trade (about 60 per cent) and crafts (about 55–65 per cent). The situation was similar in the white-collar professions, especially among those working in privately owned businesses (in the textile industry about 42.1 per cent) and in the liberal professions (about 50–60 per cent).[52] That is why calls for discrimination against Jews so that unemployed Poles would have work were attractive.

Workers in Łódź were most strongly represented in the National Party, and this made it different from other organizations in the country. Thirty-six per cent of the National Party's members were from the lower middle class, with an especially high participation of merchants and some craftsmen such as tailors, shoemakers, and carpenters. There were even representatives from the liberal

---

[50] K. Kamiński, 'Skład społeczny Stronnictwa Narodowego w Łodzi w latach *1936–1930*', *Rocznik Łódzki*, 37 (1987), 289–90.
[51] Quoted in Sz. Rudnicki, *Obóz Narodowo Radykalny, Geneza i działalność* (Warsaw, 1985), 290.
[52] K. Kamiński, 'Łódzka organizacja Stronnictwa Narodowego w "Obozie Narodowym" (1934–1936)', *Rocznik Łódzki*, 39 (1989), 148–9.

professions, such as lawyers.[53] In a proletarian and debilitated city like Łódź, attitudes were easily polarized along national lines, creating an ideal environment for the antisemitic propaganda of the National Party. Voters were receptive to such slogans as 'expropriate the Jewish manufacturers' and 'Judaeo-communism—the closing down of churches'.[54] This propaganda brought together the Polish national camp and groups of German voters enchanted by Fascism. It was not accidental that the lawyer Kurt Aleksander Klikar, known for his Fascist sympathies, was chosen by the City Council from the list of this bloc.[55] Efforts of the national camp to turn the elections into a plebiscite 'for or against Jews', a fact noticed by the security police, as well as efforts to ignite street brawls with the camp's opponents, were viewed with increasing alarm by those who were attacked.[56]

The political élites of the Jewish electorate initially formed five electoral committees, but because one list was declared void in the final phase of the campaign, only four of the lists were valid. These included the Electoral Committee of the Bund and Class Trade Unions of Jewish Workers, the United Jewish Electoral Bloc, the Electoral Committee of the Unified Zionist Bloc, and the Unified Jewish Front of the Górna and Chojna Districts. The Main Electoral Committee opposed Mojsze Herszkowicz, who represented the Po'alei Tsion Right Bloc (which also represented Po'alei Tsion Left, the activists), because he had not taken the Polish language examination.[57] Although the committee demanded that Herszkowicz be replaced, the plenipotentiary of the list opposed the committee, and the Po'alei Tsion Right Bloc list was declared void because it had 'not removed the mistakes pointed out by the head of the Main Electoral Committee'.[58]

The Unified Jewish Front of the Górna and Chojna Districts that included factions of Po'alei Tsion Right and middle-class parties did not play an important role either. Because an electoral alliance was made between political forces in Łódź with different party platforms, the alliance needed at least one mandate in the southern part of the town, where there were very few Jews. The effort to gain such support was unsuccessful.

Middle-class Jewish representatives preserved the earlier electoral blocs. The Unified Zionist Bloc included the General Zionist Organization, Mizrachi, the Union of State Zionists, Hitachdut, and economic and trade groups, which consisted of six of the ten organizations of the Union of Petty Merchants, the Merchants' Union, and WIZO (the Women's International Zionist Organization). Long-time Sejm member Dr Jerzy Rozenblatt managed the electoral campaign of the Zionist Bloc. Szaja Rozenberg, Zygmunt Ellenberg, and

---

[53] K. Kamiński, *Skład społeczny*, 292–3.   [54] Kowalski, 'KPP', 308.
[55] *KL* 267 (29 Sept. 1936), 5.
[56] APŁ, Urząd Wojewódzki Łódzki [UWŁ], sygn. 2507n, Sprawozdania miesięczne [SM] for Sept. 1936, 3–4.   [57] *KL* 255 (17 Sept. 1936), 4.   [58] *DzZmŁ* 10 (15 Oct. 1936) 697.

Gerszon Lichtensztajn were also active.⁵⁹ The goal was to win over voters and go beyond the success of 1934 to extend their sphere of influence even further.

At the end of July the United Jewish Social-Economic Front was founded. Representatives of the National Textile Industry Union, the Association of Łódź Merchants, the Association of Textile Industry Manufacturers, and a few retail unions declared that they were joining the new front. As a result of further dialogue and numerous meetings, an agreement was reached with organized political groups, such as Agudas Yisroel, the Folkists, the Zionist-Revisionists, the general Zionists, the Bezpartyjni Żydzi Religijni (Independent Religious Jews, of the Aleksandrów *tsadik*), Po'alei Agudas Yisroel (Orthodox workers), and assimilationists. The bloc was formed on 25 August, in the intense atmosphere of a political campaign, and went to the election as the Unified Jewish Electoral Bloc.⁶⁰

Since members of the United Jewish Electoral Bloc had little in common, it was not clear whether it would survive as a unit. The ordinance requiring each organization in the bloc to campaign for its own candidates ended up ensuring the group's survival. The most active parties in the pre-electoral campaign were the Folkists and Zionist-Revisionists. The leaders of the bloc were Juliusz Lewsztajn, Lajbuś Rozenberg, Mendel Balberzycki, Feszel Liberman, and Benjamin Russ. Sejm deputy Lejb Mincberg withdrew from the bloc after being attacked by the opposition in the Agudah, which accused him of entering into an agreement with 'atheists' and assimilationists.

The most dynamic leftist Jewish bloc was the one formed by the Bundists. Initially it tried to renew the 1934 alliance, when it acted together with the PPS and the DSAP. The Bundists discussed such an alliance with representatives of the KPP as well, and tried to convince W. Zdziechowski of its benefits, arguing that it was supported by the radical 'Jewish street'. But when it became clear that two Socialist lists were to be created, the Bund turned to Po'alei Tsion Left, even though it had initially fought this alliance. Both sides admitted that they would improve their electoral results only by acting together. Negotiations were long and difficult. Although the press often reported that the agreement had been finalized, the negotiations, which started in July, lasted almost to the end of August.⁶¹ Resistance was overcome through the efforts of Victor Alter and Henryk Erlich, the main parties' leaders, who came to Łódź to mobilize all members.⁶² It is in this way that the bloc of 'Bund and Class Trade Unions of Jewish Workers' was formed.

In addition to these two parties, the bloc contained the Council of Trade

---

⁵⁹ APL, UWL, file 2507n, Sm Aug., p. 6; Sept., p. 6.
⁶⁰ Wachowska, *Zarys portretu politycznego elektoratu żydowskiego*, 275.
⁶¹ *KL* 198 (21 July 1936), 6; ibid. 214 (6 Aug. 1936), 4; 217 (9 Aug. 1936), 4; 228 (21 Aug 1936), 4; 230 (23 Aug. 1936), 7; 241 (3 Sept. 1936), 6.
⁶² APŁ, UWŁ, file 2507n, Sm Aug. 7; Sept. 8.

Unions, trade organizations, the 'Kultur-Amt' (Cultural office), and cultural associations ('Kultur-Liga'). The Bund was especially active, organizing a staff of 1,000 agitators and on election day bringing approximately 150 members of Bundist self-defence groups to Łódź from its organizations outside of the area. It mobilized workers, youth, women, and craftsmen. Using a voluntary levy on all members and sympathizers, it collected sufficient funds for campaign expenses. Samuel Milman, Szlama Nutkiewicz, Chaiim Lejb Poznański, and Lew Holenderski held numerous meetings with voters. Po'alei Tsion, on the other hand, was less active.

Germans in Łódź also demonstrated significant interest in the election. Socialists of internationalist leanings with a long tradition of co-operation with the PPS were also present in this alliance. A strong advocate was Emil Zerbe, who was supported by Edward Ganzke and Karol Serwatka. They also attempted to use the campaign to recruit Sozialistischer Jugendbund, a youth organization whose leader at that time was Alfred Seidler.[63]

The pro-government German Cultural-Economic Union did not build its own bloc, preferring to give its members and sympathizers a free hand in the election, although it was suggested that they vote for the German lists presented by the Deutscher Volksverband in Polen (German People's Union) and the Jung Deutscher Verband (Young German Union). It had been initially rumoured that both parties would participate together in the elections, but the negotiations to unite the two were unsuccessful. Each organization created a separate electoral committee and presented its own lists of candidates.[64]

Such was the arrangement of the main political forces in Łódź struggling for city council seats. In spite of efforts at consolidation, the situation was unusually complicated. There was increased conflict and tension, a largely divided electorate, and a polarization of attitudes on the eve of the elections.

Twenty-two electoral committees were created, which presented lists of candidates: fifteen Polish, five Jewish, and two German. The Christian Committee of United Łódź Electors dissolved itself, but the Polish Front of the Unemployed, the Radical-Democratic Electoral Committee, and the National-Christian Labour Front were dissolved by the Main Electoral Committee. The Front of the Unemployed was dissolved 'because it changed the name of its list after voters' signatures had been collected', while the others were dissolved as 'fictitious'.[65] The list of Po'alei Tsion Right was also declared void.

Thus seventeen committees went to the elections: eleven Polish, four Jewish, and two German. They presented 92 lists of candidates, of which 87 were approved: 51 Polish, 19 Jewish, and 17 German. This included 632 people, of whom 37 were not accepted by the Main Electoral Committee. So in the end 72

---

[63] Meissner, *Niemieckie organizacje antyfaszystowskie*, 197, 198, 199.
[64] *KŁ* 214 (6 Aug. 1936), 4.
[65] *KŁ* 9 (30 Aug; 3 Sept. 1936); *KŁ* 217: 4; *KŁ* 237: 5–6.

councillors were chosen from the 595 candidates.⁶⁶ Although the electoral battle itself is beyond the scope of this study, it must be stressed that the struggle was not waged over party platforms. All the important political forces focused on the same social problems: work for the unemployed, care for the poor, extending health services, building more schools, an effective system of universal primary-school teaching, the improvement of the city's sanitary conditions, a just division of taxes, full democratization of government, etc. What differentiated the parties was the amount of attention they gave to particular issues and the way they formulated their platforms.

Political differences were none the less strong, and the national parties clearly expressed national hatreds and religious discrimination, which had been aggravated by the pre-electoral atmosphere. The sizeable organizational effort of each committee was accompanied by persecution and repression, mainly by government authorities towards leftist workers. Government actions were aimed at weakening the left as much as possible by searching the apartments of Socialists, arresting Communists, imprisoning them, sending people to the Bereza Kartuska concentration camp, setting trial dates during the pre-electoral period to promote wide publicity by the press,⁶⁷ suspending activities by organizations such as the Union of Primary School Teachers, and closing down the meeting-places of associations like the Związek Zawodowy Pracowników Handlowych (Trade Union of Businessmen).⁶⁸

On the other hand, terrorist actions directed by Nationalist armed bands using canes, sticks, gas-pipes, iron rods, and stones led to public brawls and fights, which made the streets of Łódź dangerous. Police arrested and imprisoned eighty-four members of the National Party for creating the disturbances.⁶⁹

In spite of these disturbances, election day proceeded peacefully. Participation was high: from the electorate of 344,304, 256,218 (74.4 per cent) ballots were cast. The large turnout in the Łódź election was significant, particularly when compared with that for the parliamentary elections the previous year. The greatest turnout occurred in district VIII, Bałuty Zachodnie, where 77.9 per cent voted. The lowest was in district X, Central City, with 71.6 per cent.⁷⁰

The voters gave the victory to the left. Polish and Jewish Socialist lists together gained 118,640 votes, or 46.3 per cent of the total cast (see Table 1). The election results clearly showed that of the sixteen electoral blocs taken into consideration by official statistics, only six were of importance among the Łódź electorate: two leftist and three rightist lists, as well as the main German list, the German People's Union. The first was the Polish united front, the lists of the PPS and Class Trade Unions, and a similar Jewish list of the Bund and class trade

---

⁶⁶ *DzZmŁ* 10 (15 Oct. 1936), 697.   ⁶⁷ *GP* 361 (29 Dec. 1936), 4.
⁶⁸ APT, ZW, No. inw. 483, Wspomnienie E. Ajnenkiela, 5–7.
⁶⁹ APL, UWŁ, file 2507n, Sm Sept. 1936, 32.
⁷⁰ *Mały rocznik statystyczny miasta Łodzi*, 154.

Table 1 Results of Elections to Łódź City Council (27 September 1936)

List	Votes cast	Mandates
PPS and Class Trade Unions	94,955	34
National Camp	77,831	27
Bund and Class Trade Unions of Jewish Workers	23,685	6
United Jewish Electoral Bloc	14,935	3
German People's Union	13,059	0
National-Christian Workers' Front	11,464	0
United Zionist Bloc	10,599	2
Young Germans' Party	3,211	0
Association of Trade Unions	2,309	0
Association of Christian Estate Owners of the Łódź Suburbs	1,450	0
Widzew Independent Electoral Committee	760	0
Citizens' Economic Committee	715	0
PPS-former Revolutionary Faction	693	0
United Jewish Front of the Góra and Chojny Districts	250	0
Polish Electoral Committee	165	0
Independent Electoral Committee, Blue and White Collar Workers of the Chojny District	137	0
TOTAL	256,218	72

Source: *Mały rocznik statystyczny miasta Łódź, 1936* (Łódź, 1938), 115.

unions. Rightists were represented by the National Party on the Polish side and two middle-class Jewish parties. Thus voters eliminated the ruling Sanacja from the contest for seats in the city council and distanced themselves from both centrist and German lists.

Nationally, the electorate was not limited to the three Jewish, two German, and the Polish lists. The PPS and Class Trade Unions list gained votes from German workers as well because it included German names. What is more, the list gained support from radical groups of Jewish workers voting for Communist candidates. Mieczysław Niedziałkowski noted this when he analysed the Łódź election. He examined districts with a large Jewish population in which unskilled workers, lower middle-class, and white-collar workers also supported the list of the unified front.[71] The majority of these votes were cast for the Communists.

This is evidenced in the Widzew, Chojny, Zachodnie Bałuty, and Old City districts, largely inhabited by Jews, where more Communist than Socialist candidates obtained seats. Yet in the Karolew–Rokita district, where there were very few Jews and no Jewish list competed for city council seats, Socialists gained two and one Communist became deputy councillor.[72]

It is difficult to separate votes won by Communists from the 94,955 valid votes

[71] Wachowska, *Zarys portretu politycznego*, 277.
[72] APŁ, AmŁ, t. 118/11529–38, Protokóły i zestawienia okręgów wyborczych.

for the PPS and Class Trade Unions. Some estimate that about 30,000 had been cast for the Communists.[73] Others regard this figure as too low, since in the 1930 parliamentary election the KPP in Łódź had gained 53,694 votes.[74] The latter figure is probably more reliable, since a comparison with the 1936 elections reveals that the group of thirty-four candidates who gained seats at that time included more Communists than Socialists (eighteen to sixteen). After all, this is what the PPS feared would happen: its leaders, according to police reports, were concerned at the large number of votes the Communists had won.

The internal disputes were not so important in the wider context of Łódź political forces. It was clear that the left could succeed within the system when Polish, Jewish, and German Socialists co-operated with the Communists.[75] The results were understood by party and trade-union activists as an expression of the 'regained trust of the working class'. This mobilization of the entire Socialist camp, they argued, restored to Łódź the lost title of 'red city'.[76]

The victory of leftists did not mean the defeat of the national camp, however, even though the nationalist vote had declined by 20,530 since the 1934 election. Despite this, the position of the National Party in Łódź was still strong. The alliance of Communists and Socialists that beat the National Party into second place was weak: it obtained only 17,124 more votes than the nationalists. If the leftist alliance had disintegrated, the National Party would have again won through to become the largest faction in the municipal government.

In some districts the nationalists did prevail over the Socialists. They had a significant lead in Bałuty Wschodnie and a smaller but decisive lead in Widzew and the Scheibler districts; they were far behind the leftists only in the Chojny, Old City, and Central City districts. Nationalists and leftists received an almost equal number of votes in the other districts[77]—and those were votes cast by workers, the unemployed, craftsmen, and the intelligentsia.

The narrowness of the defeat is the reason why National Party leaders received the election results calmly, as if they had anticipated their losses, and treated the defeat as spurious. They affirmed that the election only temporarily delayed a trend that would eventually put the national camp in power. But scholars describe this setback as 'a cold shower' for the nationalists.[78] Predictions of a struggle between the nationalist camp and the people's front turned out to be accurate, causing the National Party to look on the people's front as its most significant enemy and direct all its energy towards the struggle with the leftists. It

[73] J. Żarnowski, *Polska Partia Socjalistyczna w latach 1935–1939* (Warsaw, 1965), 150.
[74] Kowalski, 'KPP', 307.
[75] A. Ajnenkiel, *Polska po przewrocie majowym: Zarys dziejów politycznych Polski 1926–1939* (Warsaw, 1980), 512.
[76] W. Zatke, 'Wspomnienie z działalności łódzkiej organizacji PPS', in *PPS: Wspomnienia z lat 1918–1939*, ii (Warsaw, 1987), 1210.
[77] *Mały rocznik statystyczny miasta Łodzi 1936*, 154.
[78] Rudnicki, *Obóz Narodowo Radykalny* 290.

also led to a less contentious stance against the government, which in the case of the Łódź organization had characterized pre-electoral activities.[79] The fact that workers turned their sympathies towards the leftists not only deprived Polish nationalists of a victory, but also led to the defeat of the Sanacja camp. From the three lists of the Association of Trade Unions, PPS-former Revolutionary Faction, and Polski Komitet Wyborczy (PKW: Polish Electoral Committee) Sanacja barely managed to gain 3,167 Polish votes, or 1.7 per cent. Thus, in Poland's second-largest city, Sanacja failed to win a single seat. What was striking was that the Association of Trade Unions collected only 2,309 votes for its list, far less than the number of trade-union members in the territory of Łódź included in the association: the textile trade union alone, for example, had 9,000 members in 1935.[80] Was the electoral behaviour of trade-union members a response to attacks by the Association of Trade Unions on the PPS and Class Trade Unions, which accused them of bringing 'Communist and Jewish teenagers in a common procession to the streets' on 1 May 1936?[81] The ruling Sanacja retired from the Łódź political scene.

The elections revealed even deeper changes in the political geography of the industrial city. Centrist parties such as Chadecja and the NPR, which campaigned together in the elections under the name of the National Christian Workers' Front and were once strong in Łódź, were also defeated. This list did not win enough votes to gain a single seat in any of the ten districts. Losses were sustained not only by those governing circles that had consistently supported the bloc, but also by the Front Morges, which had allied itself with pro-Sanacja elements. That is why, after the defeat of its party, the Christian Democratic press complained about 'wasting' many Polish votes, which had been 'channelled into the wrong river'.[82]

The results of the municipal government elections in Łódź reflected changes that had taken place in Polish political geography, and provoked general interest and a flurry of commentaries throughout Poland. M. Niedziałkowski said that Łódź was a spotlight, a clear 'light of orientation'. For the Communist Julian Leński the results had enormous significance for Poland because they revealed the power relations. He declared that 'working-class Łódź should become an example for all working people'.[83]

So the new city council had forty leftists and thirty-two rightists. Among the former were Polish, German, and Jewish Socialists and Communists. For the first time in the history of interwar Łódź the Communists were represented in its municipal government. Among the rightists were twenty-seven councillors from the Polish national camp and five from the Jewish middle class.

[79] Kamiński, *Łódzka organizacja Stronnictwa*, 167.   [80] Ajzner, *Związek*, 289.
[81] J. Borkowski, 'O Związku Związków Zawodowych, Piłsudczykach i Zełowcach— polemicznie', *Rocznik Łódzki*, 32 (1982), 190, 192.   [82] Przybylski, *Front Morges*, 115–16.
[83] J. Leński, *O front ludowy w Polsce 1934–1937: Publicystyka* (Warsaw, 1956), 238–9.

The city council consisted of fifty-seven Poles, eleven Jews, and four Germans. It was characteristic that all the Jewish councillors were chosen from their own lists, while the German lists did not obtain a single seat. Germans entered the city council from Polish lists: three from PPS and Class Trade Unions and one from the national camp. The composition of the city council was almost entirely male. The only two female members were chosen from PPS and Class Trade Unions lists—the Socialist Maria Jaworska and the Communist Anna Lewinson.

The age structure was to a large degree determined by the municipal government statute setting the minimum age at thirty. The largest number of city council members (forty-one) were aged between thirty and forty. There were sixteen members between forty-one and fifty, ten between fifty-one and sixty, and five over sixty. The oldest members were the Communist Franciszek Wojkowski, the Socialist Rafa Kempner, and, from the national camp, Aleksander Knor, Jan Pawlicki, and Antoni Czernik. The youngest were the Communists Mieczysław Zdziechowski and Edward Mużdżyński, Zurech Sztrauch from the Zionist bloc, and Izaak Lewin from the United Jewish Electoral Bloc.[84]

With regard to the occupational structure, workers were the largest single group, numbering twenty-four. Next came the bureaucrats (twenty), and then representatives of the free professions (twelve). The rest comprised one teacher, three merchants, two industrialists, three craftsmen, one landlord, one factory manager, one laboratory assistant, and one assistant rabbi.[85]

Rightists, including both the ruling Sanacja party and the National Party opposition, were unwilling to participate in the activities of the new city council because Communists were present among the leftist majority. This gave rise to the rightist anti-election protest delaying validation of the results. The protest was led by the national camp of district IV and the Zionist Bloc from district IX,[86] and caused a postponement of the first meeting of the city council until 17 December 1936. Although both national camp council members and the Ministry of Internal Affairs, which was against the proposed make-up of the city council executive, tried to impede the adoption of rules for its creation and membership, these were decided during the city council's first meeting, which chose Norbert Barlicki as president and Bolesław Dratwa, Artur Szewczyk, and Adam Walczak as vice-presidents, all PPS members.

The city council adopted the principle of proportional representation for choosing councillors. Members selected from the Socialist bloc were Bronisław Kruczkowki, Antoni Napieralski, Józef Niedzielski, Czesław Piotrowski, and Szmul Milman, while from the National Camp Jan Dembiński, Leon Grzegorzak, and Konstanty Patora were chosen. The Ministry of Internal Affairs rejected the council's selection particularly because of its opposition to N.

---

[84] *DzZmŁ* 10 (15 Oct. 1936), 698–702.
[85] APL, AmL, Wydział Prezydialny, file 11 551, Akta osobiste radnych, 11.
[86] *GP* 280 (7 Oct. 1936), 12; *KŁ* 276 (8 Oct. 1936), 5.

Barlicki, who was supported by Communists.[87] When on 25 February 1937 the city council had again chosen Barlicki as president, the ministry sent a note of rejection on 9 March, but the council refused to ask Barlicki to step down, claiming it had acted in the name of 120,000 voters. The ministry responded by dissolving the city council on 31 March 1937.

The city council held its last closed meeting on 8 April, when it passed a unanimous resolution to contest the decision of the Ministry of Internal Affairs by taking it to the Supreme Administrative Tribunal.[88] As expected, the ministry's decision was upheld. The Sanacja regime did not intend to tolerate a 'red' council in which it did not have a single representative. When the last city council election in Łódź before the outbreak of the war took place on 18 December 1938, the leftists again won. That is why the public said that Łódź remained red.

[87] J. Tomicki, *Norbert Barlicki 1880–1941* (Warsaw, 1968), 361; *GP* 43 (12 Feb. 1937), 4.
[88] APŁ, AmŁ, file 12 735, city council protocols from 8 Apr. 1937, 7.

The Jews of Vilna under Soviet Rule, 19 September–28 October 1939

DOV LEVIN

IN the abundant historical writings dealing with the Vilna Jewish community, no mention is made of the brief six-week Soviet occupation of the city between 19 September 1939 and 28 October 1939. This may be attributed to various factors:

1. the frequent changes of regime (between 1914 and 1944 the administration in Vilna changed hands thirty times; in five of these instances the Red Army was involved);
2. the clearly temporary nature of this occupation from the outset;
3. the lack of contemporary written documentation, as the military regime banned the press and left little in the way of official papers;
4. the overshadowing of this brief episode by subsequent socio-political events that led to the tragic demise of the Vilna Jewish community.

Although, not surprisingly, the few survivors of the Vilna Jewish community have no clear recollection of this occupation, initial analysis of the available material reveals that this forty-day period was historically significant in its own right. We may observe that despite its brevity, the Soviet occupation of Vilna provided a preview of the general Jewish reaction to the Sovietization of eastern Poland, from Białystok in the north to Lwów in the south, as well as an illustration of tensions between Jews and the local population, which erupted upon Soviet withdrawal. During the Second World War, Vilna became a major ideological and communications centre for Polish Jewry, and the repeated changes in its regimes directly affected the fate of tens of thousands of Polish Jews.

BACKGROUND

Vilna, the capital of Lithuania, was annexed to Poland in October 1920 and remained severed from Lithuania until 1938. Vilna Jews met their Lithuanian relatives once a year, on the Ninth of Av, in cemeteries near the border. Jews

This paper originally appeared in Hebrew in *Gal'ed*, 3 (1976), 213–44. It is dedicated to Leyzer Ran, a citizen of 'Jerusalem of Lithuania'.

comprised a significant proportion of the city's population prior to the Second World War: of its approximately 200,000 residents, 45 per cent were Poles, 37 per cent Jews, 10 per cent Lithuanians, 5 per cent Byelorussians, 2 per cent Russians, and 1 per cent Tartars, Karaites, and others.

With the outbreak of the Second World War on 1 September 1939, Vilna experienced several bombing raids, but in comparison with other Polish cities suffered only slight damage. Despite the fact that the war provided a prime opportunity for Lithuanian seizure of the Vilna region, which it had never officially relinquished, this small state chose to maintain its strict neutrality,[1] as did the neighbouring Baltic States, Latvia and Estonia.

On 17 September Soviet forces occupied eastern Poland to the River Bug, in accordance with the Ribbentrop–Molotov agreement, while German forces were engaged in a blitzkrieg from the west.[2] Among the areas seized by the Red Army with minimal Polish resistance was Vilna, which had been left for all practical purposes with no government. Upon its entry into the city on 19 September, the Red Army immediately instituted a temporary military regime. Only minimal steps, including the formation of a 'Workers' Guard',[3] were taken towards public civilian organization in Vilna; apparently the Soviets intended a rapid replacement of the military regime with a civilian administration that would ratify Vilna's annexation to the Byelorussian Soviet Republic. But this course was interrupted pending the results of Soviet–Lithuanian negotiations regarding the region's future. Although plans to hold general elections for a General Assembly of West Belarus were announced on 6 October in the adjacent areas of eastern Poland, in Vilna all such political activity was suspended. On 10 October a full agreement was reached between the parties. In exchange for Soviet bases in Lithuania to house 20,000 Red Army troops, the Vilna region was to be turned over to Lithuania.[4]

Scheduled to go into effect a week later, the agreement's implementation was delayed. In the interim, the Soviets moved machinery, goods, and even entire factories to Soviet territory, including, for example, the Elektrit radio factory, whose workers emigrated voluntarily (though not without incentives). In Vilna itself

---

[1] This despite diplomatic pressure by Nazi Germany on Lithuania to attack Poland. See *Documents on German Foreign Policy*, series D, relations, vii (Washington and London, 1956), 404, 411, 423

[2] See esp. the secret codicil to the agreement signed on 23 Aug. 1939, in R. J. Sontag (ed.), *Nazi–Soviet Relations, 1939–1941* (Washington, DC, 1948), 76–8. When Soviet occupation of eastern Poland became a reality, the parties agreed to correct the codicil in order to ensure Soviet dominion over Lithuania. For the amended text see ibid. 107.

[3] Russian 'Rabochaya Gvardiya'. Workers' Guards were established in all Soviet-annexed areas, where they functioned as a civil militia. Members were drawn mainly from the ranks of former Communist activists and leftist trade unionists. In some locations the term 'Red Guard' was used.

[4] *Vneshnaya politika SSSR*, Sbornik dokumentov, iv (Moscow, 1946), 456–7. Cf. *Hatsofeh* (12 Oct. 1939), 3.

conditions deteriorated: shortages, overcrowding, hunger, and disease were on the increase as the Soviet regime ignored the steadily increasing flood of refugees from other regions of Poland (although some individuals were expelled from the city—mostly political prisoners). Moreover, neither the imposition of a curfew nor the regime's 'iron hand' prevented criminal elements, released in the course of the change of regimes, from engaging in looting.

In neighbouring Lithuania fund-raising campaigns were being carried out for Vilna's starving residents. Governmental and public agencies prepared supplies of food, medicines, and other goods intended for distribution to Vilna's civilian population with the Lithuanian takeover. After several delays Moscow finally gave the Lithuanian forces the green light on 27 October 1939,[5] and Lithuanian army columns proceeded towards Vilna the next day. Concurrently, in accordance with the agreement reached earlier, the Red Army units began their evacuation of Vilna and its environs for their Lithuanian bases. This movement took two to three days and was completed by 30 October.

With the Soviet–Lithuanian changeover, riots broke out in Vilna that rapidly assumed the nature of violent anti-Jewish pogroms. Not only did the Lithuanian security forces fail to suppress these disturbances, but some of their units participated in attacks on Jewish bystanders. Only forceful intervention by Jewish public representatives in Lithuania and Vilna, coupled with threats to appeal to the nearby Red Army for assistance, induced the Lithuanian forces to restore order to Vilna.

Vilna maintained its status as the capital of independent Lithuania for only a brief nine-month period, until Lithuania's official annexation to the USSR on 3 August 1940.

THE BOMBING

Saturday, 16 September 1939
Today fear stole into my heart. I woke at dawn and slept no more. Some intangible unfathomable feeling strongly reverberated in the inner chambers of my mind. I could not identify it. Fear of death? Homesickness for Erets Israel? Each time hope springs afresh in my heart I lose my tranquillity. Several times I sealed my fate with that of my coreligionists

---

[5] For attribution of the delay to political and other complications between the Lithuanians and the Soviets see 'Ven vet dos litvishe militer araynmarshirn keyn Vilnius', *Di idishe shtime* (Kovno) (18 Oct. 1939), 7; 'Anshlus fun Vilner gebit tsu Lite fartseygert zikh', *Haynt ba-tog* (Riga) (25 Oct. 1939), 1; 'Rushishe militer nokh alts in Vilne', *Forverts* (New York) (23 Oct. 1939), 1. According to one hypothesis, the Russians were reluctant to aouse Byelorussian anger prior to the convening of the Byelorussian National Assembly in Białystok on 28 Oct. 1939. See N. P. Vakar, *Belorussia* (Cambridge, 1956). 159 n. 13. According to the Lithuanian commandant's memoirs, the repeated Soviet delays in allowing the Lithuanian army to enter the Vilna region created such tension that he was prepared to give the order to proceed to Vilna on 27 Oct. 1939 at 11 a.m. without Soviet permission. At the last moment this permission was granted. See S. Rastikis, *Kovose del Lietuvos* (Los Angeles, 1956), 638–9.

in the diaspora. I felt little fear. I had decided to share in whatever fate has in store for them. For lack of an alternative, I was prepared for the worst. I was calm.

The very suggestion of a way out was a ray of light in the darkness. The possibility gives me no rest. In my thoughts I imagine the moment of meeting. I am immersed in a world of illusion. The return to reality is accompanied by great sorrow. Reality is extremely dangerous, but the retreat to dreamland is no less so. The best method is to prepare for the worst . . . not to ignore reality, but to display equanimity in the face of good and evil. Only a heart of stone can safely negotiate these upheavals. Blood is now as common as water. Both must be treated with equal indifference. The tears of wives and mothers must sound like the ticking of a clock in your ears, while the thunder of artillery and aerial bombardment should be perceived as a swallow's song. *Absolute indifference is the best defence against the present course of events.*[6]

INITIAL REACTIONS

Following two weeks of German air raids and Polish anti-aircraft fire, a tense calm descended on Vilna.[7] But rumours were rife; some raised the spectre of a German invasion of Vilna with its intolerable consequences for the entire population. At this juncture, the Polish authorities were preparing to resist, or if necessary to retreat to neutral Lithuania, following the example of high-ranking Polish officers and others.

On 18 September the echoes of artillery fire in the city intensified. It subsequently became clear that this was the Polish forces' resistance to the Red Army, clashes which claimed Jewish lives as well.[8] But Vilna's residents remained in the dark. Many hid in cellars, while a minority stood watch at the courtyard gates or stayed outdoors out of simple curiosity. As a visitor from Palestine wrote in his diary on this doubt-filled night: 'By all accounts, it is the Soviets! But it may be the Germans. This doubt is sevenfold more difficult.'[9]

---

[6] Excerpt from Gershon Adiv's diary (emphasis original), 24. Gershon Adiv (Adelson), a member of Kibbutz Ruhama (formerly 'Amal'), was in his native city of Vilna on official business at this juncture and kept a diary in Hebrew over the six-month period until his return to Erets Israel. The author thanks Mr Adiv for making his diary available for study and citation.

[7] Despite reports in the Jewish press regarding hundreds of Jewish fatalities in Vilna while Jews were attending synagogue on Rosh Hashanah (*Hatsofeh*, 27 Sept. 1939), in fact only two high-rise buildings in a poor area of Subocz Street sustained direct hits. According to the director of the Jewish hospital, Dr Sedlis, ten of the fifty casualties brought to the hospital later died: *Di idishe shtime* (2 Oct. 1939), 2.

[8] Shmuel Skurkowicz, a young Jew, was killed in skirmishes near his home at Nowogrodzka 6. The teacher, Yankl As, who had returned to Vilna from the Polish front and had been redrafted, also died in a clash with the Red Army: Sima and Nahum Skurkowicz's testimony, Oral History Division [OHD], the Institute of Contemporary Jewry, Hebrew University, Jerusalem, p. 1. According to Soviet sources (*Izvestiya*) 3,000 prisoners were taken in the battle for Vilna, including 600 officers (cited in the descriptive essay 'Vi azoy di royte armey hot bazetst Vilnius', *Di idishe shtime* (26 Sept. 1939), 3).

[9] Adiv diary (18 Sept. 1939), 24.

Jews of Vilna under Soviet Rule, 1939

The Red Army entered Vilna early on the morning of Tuesday, 19 September 1939, to an enthusiastic welcome by Vilna's Jewish residents, in sharp contrast to the Polish population's reserve and even hostility. Particular ardour was displayed by leftist groups and their youthful members, who converged on the Red Army tank columns bearing sincere greetings and flowers. But even non-leftist elements felt a sense of relief; the danger of attack by the Polish population, especially by recently released criminal elements, had been averted. In the words of an eyewitness to the Soviet entry to Vilna:

A great weight has been lifted from the population's hearts . . . It is not easy to describe the emotions that overwhelmed me upon seeing a Russian tank in the street opposite our gate manned by smiling young men with red stars on their caps. The crowd gathered round the stationary vehicles; someone shouted 'Long live the Soviet Regime', and everyone cheered . . . Few non-Jews could be discerned in the crowd. It was mostly Jews who publicly displayed their enthusiasm. This aroused the anger of the Poles somewhat . . . The Jews were openly jubilant. Russians were preferable to Germans. This opinion was also shared by those to whom the Russian saviour could bring no benefit . . . but at least they would not suffer as Jews. At the very worst, they would get jobs . . . Many did not stop to analyse the changes inherent in their [the Soviet] accession to power. Many of our brethren will have to forfeit lifelong habits and luxuries . . . But who engages in such analysis in these times?! With the German threat hanging over our heads, everyone greeted the Russians as if they were the Messiah . . .

Tensions in the city lessened immediately. The street lamps have been lit, blackout curtains no longer hide the windows. People stroll in the streets freely. Crowds gather round each Russian soldier . . . The Russian soldiers give people rides on tanks and buses to the city outskirts. This makes an excellent impression. They certainly know how to win over the masses.[10]

Indeed, the feeling that 'if Russia had not conquered Vilna, the Germans would have arrived a few days later'[11] left its imprint on the Jewish attitude towards the Red Army and Soviet rule. Although this motif naturally received less overt expression in the intervening period, it never entirely disappeared, and as we shall have occasion to see, it became a tangible factor influencing Jewish migratory patterns.

Leftist Jewish circles continued to celebrate openly by holding mass meetings, concerts, and festive parties outdoors or in public halls. Among the youth in particular, the new regime aroused hopes for the acquisition of knowledge or for career advancement, especially in the arts and literature. The general feeling was 'Now we can study and advance ourselves', implying the elimination of previous inhibitory factors.[12]

---

[10] Ibid. (19 Oct. 1939), 25, 28. For a description of picking flowers (with the roots) and flinging them at Soviet troops see Elijahu Yonas' testimony, OHD, p. 3.

[11] Adiv diary (20 Oct. 1939), 29.

[12] One such individual was Rachel Skidelski, who became a well-known actress in the Moscow

The Jewish public at large continued to benefit from the courteous behaviour of the Red Army troops who filled the streets. Apparently their effort to maintain a positive image was deliberate.[13] Contacts between Jews and Russian soldiers had a special impact, as described by an eyewitness:

I see the Red Army publicly explaining and disseminating its ideology. This massive military power is like no other. Its members are civilized (I will not discuss the nature of their education, but the difference between a Russian and a Polish soldier is immediately evident . . .). It is somewhat amusing to see a rank-and-file soldier with no special knowledge or talents trying to explain to his audience that in his country everything is good and beautiful, that the [Soviet] ideology will prevail worldwide . . . They dress alike . . . both officers and the rank and file wear the same uniforms . . . The soldiers feel at ease; they wander through the city unarmed. They make frenzied purchases of watches . . . They are on every corner and in every courtyard, ready to converse freely with all, and enter any home if invited.

Once when I arrived home for lunch, I found a Russian Jewish soldier enthusiastically holding forth about Russia, Minsk, the Red Army, etc. in Lithuanian Yiddish. All the tenants gathered and began to ask questions. I found the lad's patience in replying to these queries amazing . . . The most typical was that of the oldest member of the group. He enquired about the lot of the elderly in the USSR . . .

One can also witness dramatic scenes: a Vilna-born Soviet Jewish soldier asked about a sister he had not seen for twenty-five years. As usual, a crowd of curiosity-seekers had gathered round the soldier, especially since he was Jewish. One bystander immediately recognized the object of the soldier's enquiry, since she resided in his courtyard. Straight away he ran to fetch her. This happened on Wielka Street . . . Hundreds witnessed their joy. I saw them embrace—an elderly Jewess and a Red soldier in a grey coat with a helmet on his head . . . How many siblings, friends, and acquaintances are currently being reunited in Vilna?

I heard that a week prior to the Soviet takeover of Vilna a landlord evicted a poor Jewish family. The family lived on the street for a week. When the Russians entered, this case was brought to a Soviet commissar's attention. The commissar informed the landlord that unless this family was installed in an apartment within the hour, the landlord would be executed without trial. Having no alternative, the landlord was forced to evacuate several rooms in his own apartment for this family . . . While I cannot vouch for this story's veracity, the currency of such tales among the masses is a positive sign. It indicates that the Soviets are being accepted as guardians and protectors of the poor. Such tales bring people closer to the new regime.[14]

This anecdotal narrative, which is substantiated by other sources, sheds light

Yiddish Theatre: Sima Skurkowicz's testimony, OHD, p. 2. Hirsh Glik, who subsequently achieved fame as the composer of the Jewish Partisans' Song, left Vilna for Minsk at this time in order to obtain guidance in his literary career: Abraham Verses' testimony, OHD, pp. 10–11.

[13] This impression was confirmed by a visiting Polish professor from Paris. He conjectured in the presence of a *New York Times* reporter that the Red Army units stationed in Vilna were probably drawn from élite units, as they made an unusually good impression: *Forverts* (25 Oct. 1939), 1.

[14] Adiv diary (20–1 Oct. 1939), 30–3.

on the initial impact of Soviet rule on daily life in the public and private domain. Naturally, the Soviet occupation effected significant changes in the political, economic, cultural, and communicative fabric of life in Vilna as well. The changes in these spheres, along with the Jewish community's dominant concern for the physical safety of its members, comprise the focus of the following sections of this paper.

THE POLITICAL SPHERE: ACCEPTANCE BY THE LEFT AND REJECTION BY THE RIGHT

Initial Soviet preparations for civilian rule in Vilna were largely based on the assumption that, as in neighbouring areas, Vilna and its environs would shortly be annexed to the Soviet Byelorussian Republic. As a result of this assumption, Byelorussian elements received disproportionate representation in the few civilian openings; two Byelorussians were appointed to the provisional administration headed by the Russian Zelyanin.[15] Byelorussian was also the preferred language (after Russian) for wall posters and official placards. Similarly, while the local press was banned, a civilian Byelorussian-language newspaper was briefly permitted to appear.[16]

In contrast, not one of the four Yiddish dailies was allowed to go to press. Even a pro-Soviet stance did not guarantee permission to publish. On the day of the Soviet entry into Vilna the pro-Soviet *Vilner tog* [Vilna daily], edited by the writer and philologist Zalman Rejzen, sported a headline reading 'Jewish Vilna Gives Festive Welcome to Red Army'. Its leading articles reflected a similar spirit. Thousands of copies were sold that day. But while the next edition was in press

---

[15] The full complement of the members of the Provisional Administration formed on 20 Sept. included Col. M. Zelyanin. Col. Petrov, Adam Klepatenko (Klepacek), a teacher, and Karp Paulouski, a worker: *Di idishe shtime* (27 Sept. 1939), 11. According to another source, the first two were Russians and the other two Byelorussians: see Vakar, *Belorussia*, 260 n. 13. Moreover, according to this source, the Byelorussian leader in the former Polish areas, Luckevic, was appointed technical adviser (ibid. 157). Indeed, the rumour that Vilna would become the capital of Greater Belarus was not unfounded: see Adiv diary (9 Oct. 1939), 70. Even the summary of Molotov's policy speech regarding eastern Poland that was dropped from Soviet aircraft was in Byelorussian: see 'Vi azoy hot di royte armey tsum 3-ten mol farnumen Vilnius', *Di idishe shtime* (25 Sept. 1939), 5. Another contemporary source identified the head of the Provisional Administration as Krasov, who presided over the preparations for the forthcoming elections, aided by 300 volunteers: *Vilne di shtim fun di arbetndike* (Minsk) (10 Oct. 1939), 2.

[16] The Byelorussian-language newspaper that served as the municipal administration's mouthpiece, *Vilenskaya Pravda*, appeared from 22 Sept. to 12 Oct. 1939. According to an anti-Soviet and antisemitic Lithuanian report, published with the encouragement of the Nazi conquerors, the newspaper's editor was Yosel Moseyevich Openheim. See Rapolas Mackonis, 'Bolseviku teroras vos izengus i Vilniu', *Lietuviu archyvas* (Vilna, 1943), iii. 183. At the same time a Red Army newspaper, *Boevoe znamya*, was printed in the plant of the local Russian paper, *Russkoe slovo*, that had been shut down.

Soviet military police broke into the printing plant, confiscated the edition, and prohibited the paper's future publication. Justification for this act was subsequently provided in the form of the claim that 'in the USSR no private persons or societies are allowed to publish newspapers'.[17] Vilna's Jewish population found this a bitter pill to swallow; the expectations that the Soviet authorities would allow the progressive *Vilner tog* to continue publication, perhaps under a new name, were dashed. The leftist writer Szmerke Kaczergiński described the Jewish public's extreme disappointment:

Some tried to console themselves with the conviction that in the absence of *Vilner tog* a different newspaper would soon appear to serve the large Jewish population. They waited patiently. So did the journalists of the other Yiddish papers, *Tsayt*, *Ovnt-kurier*, and *Vilner radio*, that had all ceased publication with the appearance of the Soviets . . . The typesetters waited, as did the Jewish readers . . . A week passed, then two. A Polish paper began to appear, a Russian paper, but a Yiddish paper—not yet. The Jews were upset. How was this possible? The Jewish Communists and their sympathizers took it the hardest. For [the Soviets] had promised . . . that the change in regime from Polish to Soviet would bring the true flowering of Jewish culture in its wake.[18]

Despite the Soviet banning of the Yiddish press, many Jews continued to regard the regime in a positive light, drawing encouragement from the significant Jewish presence in the Workers' Guard and from the fact that young Jews wore red armbands and carried arms. Shortly prior to the Soviet occupation, Jewish youth comprised a significant portion of the armed civilian militia in various quarters of Vilna; the new regime's Workers' Guard continued and enhanced an already existing phenomenon. Not only did Jews guard installations and public places, they also discharged other tasks, including implementation of the regime's economic policies.[19] Jewish influence in the Workers' Guard (which manned the former Polish police precincts or commissariats) was not a consequence of numbers alone, but also resulted from their prominence in middle- and top-level

---

[17] S. Kaczergiński, *Tsvishn hamer un serp* (Paris, 1949), 15.

[18] Ibid. 16. According to a different account, the paper's Bundist employees objected to the headline welcoming the Soviet army. This disagreement ended in physical violence between Bundist and Communist workers. 'Two days later, the Communists appeared with an order from the local administration transferring the paper into their hands . . . but the new editors did not enjoy the new regime's patronage for long.' The paper was shut down at the end of the first week of Soviet occupation. See Haya Lazar, 'Kitvei-et ve'itonim yomiyim yehudiyim beVilna', in *Itonut yehudit shehayetah* (Tel Aviv, 1973), 251. For the Soviet regime's refusal to allow publication of a Lithuanian-language newspaper see *Lietuviu archyvas*, iii. 180.

[19] Forty-four-year-old Leib Shmercowicz, an activist with Agroid (an organization that supported Jewish settlement in Birobidzhan), was assigned to guard shops and warehouses detailed for impoundment. Like other members of the Workers' Guard, he wore a red armband: Sima Skurkowicz's testimony, OHD, p. 1.

administration.[20] For example, Jacob Rivkind held the position of deputy commanding officer.[21]

The Workers' Guard and the provisional administration, however, were only minor cogs in the apparatus of the Soviet regime. Although this was ostensibly only a military regime, it later became evident that branches of the Soviet political and security forces were active in the Vilna region. Externally the Soviet regime adopted a policy of 'smile and lay down the law', but the policy was accompanied by an unequivocal assertiveness that demanded respect. The order for all citizens and former Polish troops to disarm within twenty-four hours illustrates this approach. As described by an eyewitness: 'They disarm in such a friendly fashion that the defeated soldiers smile despite their sadness.'[22] Yet the same person saw fit to comment that 'the Russians are forcefully restoring order to the city'.[23]

Concurrent with the steps taken by the regime to impose order and ensure the safety of its troops, branches of the Soviet secret police began to operate in Vilna,[24] increasing tension among the anti-Soviet elements of the Jewish population. None the less, the danger from the Soviet regime was viewed as the lesser of two evils, in comparison with their probable fate under German sovereignty. Still, Jews felt increasingly uneasy,[25] as exemplified by the following

---

[20] According to Dr Shlomo Katz, who served in the Workers' Guard, at least 80% of the guards were Jewish, and a significant number held administrative positions (Berl Rabinowicz and others). For confirmatory evidence of the large number of Jews (in the hundreds) in the Workers' Guard see the following OHD testimonies: Nahum Skurkowicz, p. 3; Hayyim Gordon, p. 2; Elijahu Yonas, B, p. 8. For a similar evaluation see also Adiv diary (23 Sept. 1939), 38; (14 Oct. 1939), 81. Cf. *Lietuviu archyvas*, iii. 183–5.

[21] Jacob Rivkind (b. 1910, Riga) came to Vilna during the First World War and completed his university studies there. He served as a member of the YIVO staff and joined the Communist Party in 1932. He held administrative posts in Vilna and Warsaw. Following the 1939 Soviet exit from Vilna, Rivkind moved to Białystok, where he worked for the municipal bureau of statistics and as a teacher in a local school until the Nazi invasion. See *Mazoji lietuviskoji tarybine enciklopedija* (Vilna, 1973), iii. 93.

[22] Adiv diary (19 Sept. 1939), 25. In a different source we read: ' "Here comrade, your rifle," they called to the Poles, "and now return home"': 'Vilnius in di ershte teg nokhn onkum fun di Rusn', *Di idishe shtime* (27 Sept. 1939), 6.

[23] Adiv diary (20 Sept. 1939), 31.

[24] The first Soviet ordinance, issued on 20 Sept. 1939, included the following provision: (1) a nightly curfew from 10 p.m. to 6 a.m.; (2) obligatory registration of Polish officers; (3) an order to disarm within 24 hours 'Vi azoy hot di royte armey tsum 3-ten mol farnumen Vilnius', 5. A day earlier, at 10 a.m., ten NKVD operatives had taken over the local office of the political police with the aid of the municipal militia (ibid.). For the economic measures taken by the Soviets in order to facilitate purchases by Red Army personnel see the following section of this paper.

[25] For a description of the fears of Vilna Bundist leaders Anna Rosental and Jacob Zheleznikov (who were subsequently arrested) during the early hours of the Soviet occupation see Yonas testimony, B, OHB, pp. 1–2, 5. *Forverts* (20 Oct. 1939), 1, reported that Bund members in Vilna had gone into hiding. On the Bund leadership's refusal to accept the suggestion of flight to Lithuania see Y.A., 'Mit 35 Yor Tsurik', *Unzer tsayt*, 2 (1975), 28. Another source reported that a Bund delegation headed by 73-year-old Anna Rosental reported to NKVD headquarters and handed over a list

pithy epigram: 'Our death sentence has been commuted to life imprisonment.'[26]

The rich and variegated political activity that had characterized Vilna was seriously affected by the Soviet occupation. Although not officially banned, organizations and political groups were subjected to thorough investigation by the Soviet authorities. According to a report written within the first two weeks of Soviet occupation:

The commissar for social activities in Vilna informed the representatives of all organizations that had registered with him that they could continue their activities. They [the Soviets] had had no opportunity to determine the character of each individual organization. They still could not tell the difference between the 'Anti-Tuberculosis League' and 'Hashomer hatsa'ir'.

This informant further noted that 'two days ago the Zionist Federation House was closed, without direct orders from above. It has now been reopened, and is apparently awaiting the day of judgement.'[27] It is also noteworthy that during this period a Minsk soccer team contacted the Vilna Maccabi team regarding the possibility of a match.[28]

Not all political movements experienced a curtailment of activity. The arrival in Vilna of important organizational leaders from Warsaw and elsewhere infused new life into certain political movements, e.g. Hashomer hatsa'ir. Upon his arrival in Vilna from besieged Warsaw after eight days of wandering, Josef Shamir (Diament), a member of the movement's steering committee, called a meeting of the movement's Vilna cell. Its purpose was to 'take stock and discuss the situation created by the Soviet conquest'. On the agenda were fundamental questions, including the projected fate of the Polish Jewish community and the future of Hashomer hatsa'ir, as well as the *yishuv* in Palestine and the future functioning of the movement. Naturally, the question arose of steps to be taken by each individual member at this critical moment. The final resolution adopted was that 'we must wait, and that all means, both legal and illegal, must be employed to enable people to reach Erets Israel'. As a visitor from Palestine observed: 'It is not clear how these lads can achieve this. One thing is certain—the revolution has not detached them from their youthful aspiration—the rebirth of the Jewish nation in its chosen land.'[29]

---

of names and addresses of other committee members and the leadership. The next day the delegation members and scores of Bund activists were arrested: P. Schwartz, *Dos iz geven der onhoyb* (New York, 1943), 330–1; cf. n. 39 below.

[26] Some sources ascribe this epigram to Miriam Rejzen (wife of Zalman Rejzen, editor of the *Tog*), who was later arrested: see Michael Astor, *Geshikhte fun Frayland lige* (Buenos Aires and New York, 1967), i. 448. Others ascribe it to the well-known Vilna rabbi Hayyim Ozer Grodzeński, or others: see Yisrael Kaplan's testimony, A, OHD, p. 27. In any event, the saying was known in Luck: see 'Min hadin veheshbon shel Dr. M. Kleinbaum (Sneh)', in *Sho'at yehudei Polin* (Jerusalem, 1940), 34. [27] Adiv diary (4 Oct. 1939), 62. [28] Yatziv's testimony, OHD, p. 4.
[29] Adiv diary (21 Sept. 1939), 32.

Public as well as politically based educational activity continued, but on a reduced scale or covertly. Local organizational activity did not cease entirely, however, partly as a result of the Soviet authorities' call for all organizations and federations to 'report to a special commissar for investigation and legalization'.[30] While the investigative aspect was of concern to the Soviets, the various organizations were more interested in achieving legalization. It was apparently in line with this policy that Michael Astor (Chernikhov), head of Shperber, the youth division of the Jewish territorialist league, was summoned by the Soviet authorities. In their investigation the Soviets made enquiries regarding Shperber's attitude toward Jewish resettlement in Birobidzhan. Astor's reply, that the organization was defunct (in accordance with the decision to make do with 'maintaining a small clandestine core group of trustworthy members until the situation improves'),[31] did not satisfy the investigator, and he was requested to consult with his fellow members and return the next day with an authorized reply. Meeting secretly, Astor and his closest associates affirmed their previously determined policy, and Astor formally notified the commissar that the organization was no longer active.[32] To his surprise, the commissar made overtures, implying that Shperber could obtain official recognition by abandoning its Utopian outlook and adopting a more pro-Soviet ideological orientation. More importantly, the Soviets wished to use Shperber's organizational know-how to promote their project of settling indigent Jews from west Belarus and the western Ukraine in Birobidzhan. As a first step, the Soviets proposed that either Astor or a delegation of three chosen by the membership (at a meeting for which the Soviet authorities were willing to allocate a hall) should undertake an educational tour of Birobidzhan. To Soviet disappointment, the unexpected proposal was emphatically rejected.[33] The arrest two days later, on 1 October, of Astor and his father, attorney Josef Chernikhov—veteran journalist, Territorialist, and Folkist activist, renowned for his brave defence of accused Communists before Polish tribunals—shocked Jewish Vilna.[34] No less traumatic was the arrest of the *Vilner tog*'s editor, Zalman Rejzen, whose pro-Soviet editorial policy was common knowledge. Both Chernikhov and Rejzen were leading figures in the Yiddish

---

[30] Ibid. (29 Sept. 1939), 52.   [31] Astor, *Geshikhte*, 449.   [32] Ibid. 451–2.

[33] To this day Astor (ibid.) is still uncertain whether the Soviet proposal was intended as a provocation or was a sincere offer. A report published in the *Jewish Chronicle* (27 Sept. 1939) to the effect that Radio Kiev had issued an appeal to Galician Jews to settle in Birobidzhan is unsubstantiated. Astor's refusal to accept the Soviet proposal was consonant with his policy of having no dealings with either the NKVD or the Soviet regime.

[34] Kaczgerpiński, *Tsuvishn hamer un serp*, 17. Chernikhov's son, Michael Astor, who was arrested with his father, saw no connection between their arrest and his rejection of the Soviet proposal. In his view the arrests were the result of 'accusations made by the local Communists and toadies of the new regime': Astor, *Geshikhte*, 450. Persistent rumours attributed Chernikhov's arrest, among other reasons, to the publication and widespread distribution of his book *In revtribunal: Zikhroynes fun a farteydiker* (Vilna, 1932): Sima Skurkowicz testimony, OHD, p. 4; cf. Yonas testimony, B, OHD, p. 14. On the circumstances of Chernikhov's death see n. 39 below.

Kultur Farband (YKUF: Yiddish Cultural Association), founded at the World Conference in Paris in 1937 with the active participation of Jewish Communists. They were also members of the YIVO executive.

However, as in other Soviet-controlled areas of eastern Poland, it was Bundists who were the main target of the sweeping arrests in Vilna. Almost the entire local Bundist committee, along with several leading activists, was arrested: Anna Rosental (a founding member), attorney Josef Teitl, Jacob Zheleznikov, Josef Aharonowicz (deputy head of the municipal council), and Leibl Weinstein. Other prominent public figures who were detained included trade unionist Hayyim Walt, the teacher Haskel Potshenko, and Aaron Tsintsinatus, editor of the Zionist daily *Tsayt* and active member of Po'alei Tsion Right, as well as the owners of the Elektrit factory, Nahman Levin and Zechariah Chwoles, and the banker Zachs.[35]

The mass arrests included hundreds[36] of residents of Vilna and the nearby areas and affected a broad range of individuals of differing nationality, political affiliation, and social status. Notwithstanding Soviet attempts to proceed covertly, the detentions rapidly became public knowledge. But neither the protests of the local populace, including its pro-Soviet elements, nor worldwide objections,[37] nor even direct appeals to the Soviet authorities,[38] succeeded in securing the prisoners' release. Upon the Soviet evacuation of Vilna, the prisoners were transferred to jails in west Belarus, Białystok, Wilejka, and elsewhere. Some, like Chernikhov, died while being evacuated after the German invasion of the USSR;[39] others, such as Rejzen and Nahman Levin, perished while incarcerated under harsh conditions in the USSR. Only a few, including Tsintsinatus and Astor, managed to survive.

---

[35] Other individuals detained according to the Yiddish press included Max Tsheslo, Mendl Widuczański, Dr Avram Tsimbler, Dr Friedman, Y. Zhofer: see 'Vilner aktualitetn', *Di idishe shtime* (5 Nov. 1939), 3. Apparently, Communists suspected of Trotskyite deviations were subject to arrest. When the wife of the prominent gynaecologist Dr Jakubovski appealed to the Soviets for his release, she was informed that his detention was not a punishment; rather, they were in need of a competent physician. On the arrest and deportation of a former Hashomer Hatsa'ir member named Himmelfarber see Leib Koriski testimony, OHD, p. 6.

[36] According to later reports filed by M. Orzech, 226 individuals were deported to the USSR: see *Forverts* (8 Nov. 1939), 1. Other sources cite figures as high as 1,800: see Astor, *Geshikhte*, 450.

[37] An initial incomplete report of the arrests filed by M. Orzech appeared on the front page of *Forverts* (19 Oct. 1939). More detailed reports, written in a muted undertone of anger and full of appeals for the unconditional release of the innocent victims, appeared in the weeks that followed.

[38] The daily enquiries of Mrs Rejzen and Mrs Chernikhov at NKVD headquarters regarding their husbands' fate remained unanswered: see Kaczergiński, *Tsvishn hamer un serp*, 18. Moreover, Mrs Chernikhov herself was arrested, ostensibly for her own safety (ibid.).

[39] Reliable sources report that Chernikhov was shot somewhere between Minsk and Borisov by guards supervising the evacuation on foot of prisoners from the Wilejka prison to the USSR. Apparently he was too exhausted to keep up; he was 59 years old at the time of his death: Astor, *Geshikhte*, 451. This report was confirmed by an eyewitness, S. Katz, a political prisoner who marched in the same group. Salman Rejzen probably met a similar fate. Although included in a

THE SOCIO-ECONOMIC SPHERE: THE STRUGGLE FOR SUBSISTENCE

Vilna's already precarious economic position deteriorated further with the outbreak of war: food, including bread, and heating-fuel were in short supply, and the few local industries, including the Elektrit factory and the printing-presses, were virtually shut down. Unemployment naturally rose as a result. When the Soviets entered Vilna, orders were issued requiring all residents to return to their jobs, and authorizing the reopening of shops, businesses, and factories. The exchange rate for the zloty was set at one Russian rouble.[40] On the one hand, this step enhanced the already considerable purchasing power of the Red Army, whose troops descended on the shops, indiscriminately purchasing goods without bargaining. This in turn led to further shortages of goods and inflated prices. Not surprisingly, shops and warehouses were quickly emptied, and signs reading 'Closed owing to the lack of goods' were posted in shop windows.[41] While wealthier Vilna residents were able to stockpile food and fuel, the poorer classes began to suffer privation and hunger. Queues became a feature of daily life in Vilna, as may be seen from the following description:

Every Vilna resident spends most of his day waiting in line . . . Each and every Jew has but a single goal, to transform cash into commodities. This is not easy by any means. It requires standing in line for hours outside each shop until gaining entry, and even then there is no opportunity for choice, as goods are scarce and prices extremely high . . . The food supply is being rapidly depleted . . . One must brace oneself to acquire a little butter and some eggs. The queue for these items is enormous. Thousands wait from dawn for the 250 grams per person distributed weekly. It is pointless to join the queue at 6 a.m., for by that time thousands wait at the door.[42]

There were already individuals who could not afford to purchase even the few commodities still available, mainly those who now found themselves unemployed. Some turned to the Jewish community or to trade unions for assistance. The printers' union, for example, organized the distribution of meat along

---

sealed transport of political prisoners bound for the east on 10 Oct. 1941, he was among the few individuals who did not arrive at the final destination. During a halt at Polotsk, the most dangerous 'enemies of the [proletarian] regime' were removed and shot, including Rejzen: see Lazar, *Itonut*, 251. Mr Joseph Herman, a political prisoner held in the Cherven' jail (formerly the Igumen monastery), recounted that he shared a cell (No. 8) with Bundist activists Zheleznikov, Aharonowicz, and Teitl, and that Anna Rosental was held in a nearby cell. On 28 Apr. they were taken from their cells, along with Vilna's mayor Maliszewski, the deputy district governor Rakowski, and the Vilna PPS heads, and never returned. For further details of Herman's memoirs see *Unzer tsayt*, 2 (1975), 28–9.

[40] Vi azoy hot di royte armey'.
[41] 'Letste grusen fun Vilnius', *Di idishe shtime* (1 Oct. 1939), 6.
[42] Adiv diary (25 Sept. 1939), 41.

with other provisions.[43] While even in ordinary times many Vilna Jews had led a precarious existence, changing jobs as circumstances dictated, they now found themselves swept up in a new kind of intense economic activity, that proceeded uninterrupted even on the Jewish festivals with the Soviet regime's tacit agreement:

Although today is a festival, the streets are filled with vendors hawking their wares. This is a new and recent phenomenon. Up to now the Polish police limited street peddling; now no one does. The streets are filled with a variety of petty traders—a youth selling pencils, a woman selling notebooks, a third sweets, a fourth apples, a young boy selling thin paper for rolling cigarettes. His entire stock is worth no more than twenty groszy, but this boy loudly proclaims his wares . . . Women sell leather gloves; the Red soldiers gladly purchase gloves of any kind. Everything and anything is traded; every unemployed Jew tries his hand at commerce . . . He buys goods he has no need for . . . This simply illustrates how our Jewish brothers survive. Many hawk their wares in broken Russian, creating a deplorable impression. The trade in the Durkhhoyf [a group of courtyards providing passage from the Jewish quarter] and near the Halles [a large covered market on Zawalna Street] includes the sale of all and sundry goods. One vendor displays two left shoes, another a rag. Many offer their army uniforms for sale.[44]

Despite the Soviet regime's general toleration of this *ad hoc* economic activity, it did not hesitate to impose the full weight of the law upon merchants or small shopkeepers who closed their businesses for fear that they would find themselves saddled with worthless money and no goods. It was not without reason that a contemporary observer remarked: 'Along with their shops, these people's lives have been emptied of meaning . . . they have become apathetic.'[45] The Soviets intervened more forcefully in the industrial and wholesale sectors of the economy. Some major stores, like that of S. Yankelevitz, were closed.

The following anecdote illustrates a typical episode in the contemporary 'international' Jewish trade:

A Russian officer purchased enough cloth for several suits at a price of 50 roubles a metre, which had previously cost only 12 zloty. One of the sales clerks, a well-known joker named Moishele Chibok, turned to him and said: 'Tovarich [comrade], why do you enrich the bourgeoisie? After all, you could simply confiscate the goods, as is the practice of all conquering armies.' 'No matter,' replied the officer, 'let them play with paper.' Upon the officer's exit, one of the owners commented: 'Look at him! With this paper I'll buy *tsenerlakh* [gold roubles from the time of Tsar Nicholas] and with them I can purchase not only

---

[43] Leib Koriski's testimony, OHD, p. 5 (Koriski was secretary of the printers' union'. The regime also began to register the unemployed, so as to secure either jobs or assistance for them. Certain documents were obligatory—it was easier to become unemployed than to obtain official certification that one was in this condition: Adiv diary (5 Oct. 1939), 64.

[44] Adiv diary (5 Oct. 1939), 64–5. Cf. A. Verses testimony, OHD, p. 8.

[45] Adiv diary (3 Oct. 1939), 60. Cf. ibid. (18 Oct. 1939), 60.

bread, but a fat duck. Nobody, but nobody, can deprive me of that!' To which his colleague the retailer retorted, 'Maybe they cannot take the *tsenerlakh* from us, but they can take us from them [exile us to Siberia].'⁴⁶

In addition to the radio factory that was dismantled and transported to Minsk in early October, following the agreement to turn the city over to the Lithuanians, various commodities, heavy machinery and equipment, and even 'radiators, hospital beds, mattresses, etc.'⁴⁷ found their way to the Soviet Union. In most of the remaining factories work came to a standstill. According to one newspaper report, 'Day and night the workers sit in the cold and damp without food, and guard their former places of employment. The same holds true for factories that employ women. They [the women] endure cold and hunger while taking turns watching the equipment.'⁴⁸

In isolated instances goods were impounded from Jewish businesses: 'They impounded one thousand skins from Solomon the merchant and paid in zloty at the usual price'; 'From Yudke's factory the Russians took twenty carloads of plywood and in exchange paid the workers a month's salary, although they had been idle. Yudke is constantly seeking work but can find none.' The conclusion: 'At present only trade is feasible. Finding a job is wellnigh impossible. Anyone with [mercantile] talents can make a great deal of money.'⁴⁹

Many Vilna Jews arrived at this conclusion simultaneously. From a practical viewpoint, the requisite skills were mobility, a good business sense, and the willingness to spend time away from home. The essence of remunerative activity was the importation of goods from west Belarus to starving Vilna. 'In this manner, Jews found a livelihood,' a contemporary observer noted, going on to cite an additional facilitating factor: 'The trains are so crowded that it is possible to travel without a ticket. The ticket collector cannot pass from coach to coach.' He described this type of economic venture in detail.

A Jew travels from Vilna to Molodechno or Grodno, bringing back salt, butter, and sausage, goods which are plentiful there. Butter that sells for 8 zloty a kilo in the small town sells here for 20 zloty. The same is true of other commodities. Many travel to Białystok and return with dry goods. In that city they pay 30 zloty a metre for cloth worth 8 zloty, later selling it in Vilna for 70 zloty. Many earn a living in this fashion.⁵⁰

While Vilna Jews struggled for subsistence, the Jews of neighbouring Lithuania were engaged in raising funds and collecting commodities for transfer to Vilna upon the opening of the border.⁵¹

---

⁴⁶ M. Balberyszki, *Shtarker fun ayzn* (Tel Aviv, 1971), 71.
⁴⁷ 'Min hadin veheshbon', 39. Cf. *Foreign Relations of the United States: The Soviet Union, 1933–1939* (Washington, DC, 1952), 972–4, 979.
⁴⁸ 'Vos m'zet voz m'hert haynt in Vilnius', *Di idishe shtime* (22 Oct. 1939), 5.
⁴⁹ Adiv diary (18 Oct. 1939), 96.   ⁵⁰ Ibid. (23 Oct. 1939), 109.
⁵¹ On Lithuanian Jewish efforts to aid Vilna see *Di idishe shtime* (16 Oct. 1939), 7.

THE CULTURAL SPHERE: SUPERFICIAL NORMALITY

During the first days of the Soviet occupation, when the assumption that Vilna would become the capital of Soviet Belarus still prevailed, the Soviet authorities made considerable efforts to restore a semblance of 'business as usual'. Three days following the Soviet entry into Vilna, a Soviet source described the situation thus:

The city is reorganizing. Signs of the brief skirmishes remain only on the outskirts—destroyed and overturned cars, broken crates, uprooted paving-stones, and ditches. In the centre of town there are no signs of war. Public transportation was restored today, schools have opened, and pupils have returned to class. Libraries are functioning as usual. The cinemas are full, and the first performance of the Vilna Operetta is scheduled for tomorrow.[52]

These remarks are but a superficial reflection of the existing reality. Those institutions, factories, and social organizations that renewed their activity did not return to their previous level of operations. Social life was displaced from the home and café to the street and queue.[53] The cinemas were indeed crowded, but a significant portion of the audience was comprised of soldiers, refugees, and the unemployed, who frequented the cinema for lack of any better alternative. It is not surprising that cinemas opened their doors at 11.30 a.m. Even the films themselves differed in nature from those previously screened. Most were Soviet-produced and addressed the topics of revolution, the Russian civil war, and the Communist Party.[54]

As indicated in the above quotation, schools did reopen, but with a high rate of absenteeism among teachers and pupils. Hebrew schools continued to function despite rumours that Hebrew would not be on the list of approved languages of instruction.[55] In addition, the Soviets took direct steps to ban religious instruction in all schools. Although this ban represented the full extent of their direct intervention in religious life, the Soviet presence itself had a negative effect on traditional observance, as may be seen from the following report:

I am unable to recall any other *Sukkot* festival in Vilna without a single *sukka*. It is ill-advised to build *sukkot* when the red flag flutters. The Soviets are an anti-religious symbol in Jewish eyes . . . In conversations with the Reds they [the Jews] do not refrain from questioning them regarding their attitude towards religion. The reply is that each indi-

---

[52] *Pravda* (23 Sept. 1939); cited from *Tarbyu valdzios atkurimas lietuvoje* (Vilna, 1965), 38.

[53] Adiv diary (18 Oct. 1939), 94.

[54] Among the films shown during the final week of the Soviet occupation were *Tsirk* [Circus], *Peter the Great*, *Chapayev* (a Soviet hero), and *Party Card*: Adiv diary (24 Oct. 1939), 104. A critique of the films shown during the first week of the Soviet occupation (*Border Patrol* and *Musical Comedy*) is found ibid. (25 Sept. 1939), 43.

[55] Ibid. (4 Oct. 1939), 62. For the rationale behind the cancellation of religious instruction in schools as enunciated by the Commissar for Education and Culture, I. Klimov, at a Vilna teachers' meeting see *Lietuviu archyvas*, 181.

vidual is free to do what he feels imperative, but [they add], 'I have crossed the border, seen forests, rivers, roads, people, houses. I travelled for an entire week and saw everything but your God . . .' This is their most persuasive argument. In their view this contention can sway even the most religious person. They no longer take harsh measures to suppress religion. The older generation is allowed to die with its faith intact. The younger generation is estranged from religion in any case.[56]

That year even the usually joyous festival of Simchat Torah celebrations were muted. Although the ritual *hakafot* (ceremonial processions) were held in the synagogues, an observer who visited the magnificent Khor synagogue on the festival even commented that the 'discrepancy between what is taking place inside and outside' had never been sharper.[57] In many synagogues festive spirits were further dampened by the presence of *yeshivah* students and communal officials, who, having fled to Vilna from German- or Soviet-held territories, were now lodged in the synagogues.

Vilna's residents also suffered isolation from reliable information about current events, the direct result of the ban on publication of all Yiddish newspapers.[58] The issues of the Minsk Yiddish paper *Oktyaber* brought to Vilna often arrived late and failed to meet the Jewish public's need for up-to-date information. In any case, discerning readers criticized *Oktyaber*, noting that 'one issue resembles the next; each sings the praises of a great man. The paper does not report events accurately; moreover, it omits mention of many things, and this is its major failing.'[59] Essentially, none of the newspapers available, neither the local Byelorussian paper nor the Russian military's mouthpiece, printed adequate information on the European or global scene.

Radio broadcasts provided a more reliable and accurate source of information, and in one newspaper report Vilna's residents were depicted as spending their time incessantly clustered around the radio.[60] Each group contained individuals conversant with German, French, English, or Russian. Among the foreign stations, the British broadcasts were considered particularly trustworthy, but the number of listeners was limited by the language barrier. There were even individuals who succeeded in monitoring the 'Voice of Jerusalem'.[61]

In view of the restricted availability of accurate media coverage, it is not surprising that rumours were rampant during this uncertain period.[62] From mid-

---

[56] Adiv diary (28 Sept. 1939), 48.
[57] Ibid. (5 Oct. 1939), 65.
[58] See above; also nn. 17–18.
[59] Adiv diary (25 Sept. 1939), 43.
[60] 'Vi zet oys vilne erev dem araynmarsh fun litvishn militer?', *Haynt* (18 Oct. 1939), 1.
[61] Adiv diary (20 Sept. 1939), 29; (4 Oct. 1939), 63; (12 Oct. 1939), 78; (22 Oct. 1939), 100.
[62] Some of these dealt with exclusively Jewish matters and were associated with Ze'ev Jabotinsky. 'He made peace with the Histadrut and together they organized an armed uprising against the British and founded a Jewish kingdom in Palestine': Adiv diary (3 Oct. 1939), 61. A different version ran as follows: 'Weizmann has become President, and Jabotinsky Minister of War and the Navy . . . they made peace with the Arabs and together forced the British out of the Holy Land': ibid. (9 Oct. 1939), 70.

October the stories centred upon the projected Lithuanian takeover of Vilna, which had been delayed. Various explanations were proffered for the delay: 'French and British threats regarding the breach of neutrality'; or 'the Lithuanians will gain entry only when the Red Army has completed its purges of the city'. There were reported sightings of the Lithuanian army on the city outskirts. The Lithuanians were also the butt of jokes.[63] Yet the Jews took steps to prepare for the new regime by studying Lithuanian, and Russian primers of Lithuanian were in demand.[64] Upon verification of the imminence of the Lithuanian takeover, public manifestations of Soviet dress and manners, e.g. the use of *tovarich* as a form of address, declined.[65]

The news of the impending Lithuanian takeover stimulated the hopes of Jewish intellectuals that YIVO, the Jewish Scientific Organization, which had experienced hardship under the Soviet regime, would be able to continue functioning in Vilna.[66] Throughout this period, owing to the absence of its top leadership, YIVO functioned only on a limited scale.[67]

REDIRECTIONAL MIGRATION: TO VILNA AND BEYOND

Following the Soviet takeover, Vilna became a magnet for Jewish migration. The first to reach the city were Jews from Vilna who had fought with the Polish forces on the German front. Some belonged to units disbanded and disarmed by the Soviet forces; others had disarmed voluntarily[68] or had escaped German captivity.[69] With the exception of several former officers, who were arrested,[70] the

---

[63] Ibid. (13 Oct. 1939), 81. The following joke was current among Jews: upon being asked to prepare his tanks for entry into Vilna, the Lithuanian commandant enquired: 'How many shall I prepare? Two or all three?' In a humorous spirit Jews began to transform their surnames by adding Lithuanian endings—Koriski became Koriskitis, Adelson became Adelsonaitis, Burstein Bursteinas, etc.: Adiv diary (11 Oct. 1939), 75.

[64] 'Vi zet oys vilne', 1. A Jewish resident of Vilna purchased a Russian primer of Lithuanian published in 1906 for lack of anything more recent: Adiv diary (20 Oct. 1939), 99.

[65] Attorney Josef Chernikhov, known for his dapper appearance, so radically altered his dress as to arouse comment: see Yonas testimony, B, OHD, p. 13.

[66] According to later testimony, on 20 Sept. a proposal that YIVO be transferred to the United States was put forward, but withdrawn following the Soviet withdrawal: Z. Kalmanovich, 'YIVO banayt zayn tetikayt in vilne', *Di idishe shtime* (13 Nov. 1939), 5. None the less, YIVO correspondents and publishers were requested to forward routine post to YIVO's New York branch at 425 Lafayette Street: *Forverts* (2 Oct. 1939), 5.

[67] YIVO's main leader, Dr Weinreich, was on a lecture tour in Sweden and the United States; Zelig Kalmanovich, a Lithuanian citizen, fled to that country; Zalman Rejzen and Joseph Chernikhov were placed under arrest.

[68] Moshe Solz's testimony, OHD, pp. 9–10.

[69] Meir Dworzecki's testimony, OHD, pp. 8–9; Baruch Yankilev, Yad Vashem Archive 1190/31, pp. 16–19.

[70] The officers arrested and deported to Soviet camps (Ustashkov, Starobyelsk, Katowice) on their return to Vilna included Dr Misha Levin, Dr A. Romm, Dr S. Slowes, Y. Shapiro, and

Red Army did not interfere with the returning soldiers. Those unable to prove that they had been officially registered residents of Vilna, however, did encounter difficulties even in the initial stage of the Soviet occupation. The constant threat of expulsion to neighbouring towns hung over these individuals. The task of checking a resident's legal status rested with each courtyard's concierge, among others.[71]

Despite these restrictions, from late September a steadily increasing stream of Polish refugees arrived, particularly from the areas of Poland which the Germans had subjugated. Some hailed from Vilna originally, or had family ties there. A refugee who left Łódź on 6 September, making his way to Vilna via Warsaw, Kovel, Luninents, Baranovichi, and Lida, described his homecoming thus:

We reached Vilna on Friday night, but as the curfew was still in effect we had to spend the night in the [terminal's] first-class lounge. The railway station was overflowing with people, and finding a seat was no mean feat. Towards morning we were released ... On 30 September I reached my mother and sisters at my [childhood] home, 50 Wielka Street. Surprise was mingled with bitter tears. I was treated as if I had returned from the afterlife ... After a fourteen-year interval as a resident of Łódź, I was again in my parental home, where I had spent a significant portion of my life, my childhood and youth.[72]

The massive influx of refugees from all over Poland continued, especially following the announcement of impending Lithuanian rule in Vilna. For all practical purposes, the Romanian border was closed, leaving Vilna, or neutral Lithuania, as the only feasible means of escape from occupied Poland. Jews correctly surmised that from Vilna it would be easier to reach other parts of the world. Members and leaders of pioneering youth movements and their kibbutzim (training collectives) gathered in the city, steadfast in their determination to reach Palestine by any means. Local Vilna kibbutzim, such as Shachariya at 37 Subocz Street, served as initial absorption centres for some of the 400 *halutsim* (pioneers)[73] who reached Vilna during this period. Among the movements represented in Vilna we find Hashomer Hatsa'ir, Dror, and Hechaluts Hamizrachi. Important Zionist leaders who reached the city during this period included Dr Moshe Kleinbaum (Sneh) of the General Zionists and Zerach Warhaftig of Hapo'el Hamizrachi.[74]

others: Dr Misha Levin testimony, OHD, pp. 14–19. See also Salomon W. Slowes, *Katyn: 1940* [Hebrew] (Tel Aviv, 1987).

[71] 'Letse grusn fun vilnius', *Di idishe shtime* (1 Oct. 1939), 6.
[72] Balberyszski, *Shtarker fun ayzn*, 69.
[73] Letter from the Hechaluts representative in Lithuania, Shlomo Goldstein, to the United Kibbutz Movement's secretary: *Tseror mikhtavim: Dror–Hehaluts Hatsa'ir* (Ein Harod) (8 Mar. 1940).
[74] In the article 'Grusn fun vilnius [Greetings from Vilna]' the following Zionist leaders are mentioned: Dr M. Kleinbaum (chairman of the Zionist Federation's Central Committee); Dr M. Hindes (JNF chairman) and his family; Shmuel Rosenhak (director of Tarbut in Poland); Rafael Schaeffer

Despite their quite natural suspicion of the Soviet regime, Bundist leaders and activists also took refuge in Vilna, although some were careful to keep their presence hidden.[75] Prominent Polish Jewish journalists and literati also converged on the city,[76] accompanied by factory owners, bankers, and eminent businessmen from Warsaw, Łódź, and elsewhere. Conspicuous in the streets of Vilna were the students and faculty from the *yeshivot* of Mir, Kaminets, Baranovichi, Kletsk, and Ostrog (Wołyń), whose numbers totalled more than a thousand.[77] As the majority had no relatives or acquaintances in Vilna, their lot was a difficult one. '[They are] dirty, dress in rags, and sleep on synagogue benches.'[78] Having family or friends in Vilna was no guarantee of comfort, for

at present a guest places a heavy burden on every household, which is struggling to make ends meet in any event . . . The refugees are the worst off . . . A refugee who is not familiar with the city can wait in line all day and come away with nothing. The insolent and the ruffians request permission from the crowd to get bread without waiting, which is usually granted.[79]

With the approach of the deadline for their evacuation of Vilna, Soviet involvement in the city's affairs decreased. As a result of Soviet unconcern, in the final period of the occupation the number of refugees in Vilna swelled to 20,000, of whom 12,000 were Jews.[80] Not surprisingly, during this interim period the already neglected city was afflicted by a sharp increase in severe social, moral, and health problems. Foreign correspondents filed reports on the difficult conditions in Vilna:

Vilna is congested with refugees and its population suffers hunger and privation; economic life has come to a halt and many Jews wander the streets begging for a piece of bread to break their fast . . . Another result of the influx of refugees is a severe housing

---

(head of the Palestinian office) and his family; attorney Reuven Nochimovski and his family; Alter Klarman and his brother Joseph; Shmuel Bernholtz and his family; Benjamin Tomkevicz (*Hatehiyah* chairman); Dr Moshe Zeidman and his family; Dr Mondlik. All of the above wished 'to inform their friends and relatives that they are alive and well in Vilna. The Palestinian press is asked to reprint this announcement': *Di idishe shtime* (31 Oct. 1939), 8. On the arrival of Revisionist leaders Spector, G. Schofman, and Dr S. Zeidenman see *Forverts* (19 Oct. 1939), 10. See also Zorach Warhaftig testimony, A, OHD, pp. 3–4.

[75] *Forverts* (30 Oct. 1939), 1.

[76] Ibid. Among the journalists and writers were Z. Segalowich, N. Prilutski (of *Moment*), Neiman, S. Yeushzon (Justman), Kleinbaum, B. Zingher (*Haynt*), Kroy, L. Shpizman (*Unzer vort*), Shefner, Halter, Flakser (*Folkstsaytung*), L. Kahan (*Ekspres*), as well as Y. Rapaport, Pinhas Shwarz, D. Neimark, Dr Gliksman, Mandelboim, and Kuzcen. See 'Shreklikeh lage fun di idishe plitim in vilne', *Di idishe shtime* (23 Oct. 1939), 3.

[77] 'Shvere ekonomishe lage fun di vilner idn', ibid. (30 Oct. 1939), 2.

[78] Adiv diary (17 Oct. 1939), 92. [79] Ibid. (18 Oct. 1939), p. 94.

[80] 'Soviet militer nokh alts in vilne', *Forverts* (1 Nov. 1939), 1. Other sources cite larger numbers, e.g. '20,000 refugees from various parts of Poland now find themselves in Vilna': *Haynt* (31 Oct. 1939), 1.

shortage. Farmers refuse to accept payment for food in any currency other than Lithuanian; there are long queues in front of the bakeries, but these refuse to accept Polish or Soviet money.[81]

Other reports cited the eruption of bloody riots in the western section of the city, a series of epidemics, and a spate of robberies.[82]

The Soviet authorities ostensibly restricted egress from Vilna, at least during the initial period of their rule. Residents of the city or refugees seeking to relocate had to secure the necessary documents and passes from a special bureau. Some foreign nationals, including Palestinian Jews, sought permission to return to their native lands, but received nothing but polite vague promises and a bureaucratic run-around in response. The signing of the agreement turning Vilna over to Lithuania forestalled the need to formulate an official Soviet policy concerning these foreign nationals.[83] Appeals to the Latvian consul on this matter brought no practical results either. On the other hand, the Soviet authorities readily granted exit visas to those seeking to relocate in eastern Poland, to return to their places of employment, or to be reunited with their families.[84] While some individuals wanted to leave Vilna for fear of being reported to the authorities or persecuted for their political views,[85] ideological-political or economic reasons motivated a far greater number to relocate voluntarily in Soviet-controlled areas.

The relocation of the Elektrit radio factory in Minsk, Belarus, is a case in point. The factory workers were offered the option of relocating with their families. This invitation was issued in early October,[86] prior to the signing of the official agreement transferring the Vilna region to Lithuania, but rumours of the possibility were current even earlier, and 'Jews began to weigh which option was

---

[81] 'Vilne iz ibergepakt', *Forverts* (31 Oct. 1939), 1.

[82] See 'Hunger riotes tifus in vilne', *Forverts* (25 Oct. 1939), 1; 'Many shot and injured in Vilna as starving residents break into food stores': *Forverts* (26 Oct. 1939), 1. Cf. Adiv diary (25 Sept. 1939), 43.

[83] According to Zelyanin, who headed the Provisional Administration, two letters were sent to Moscow requesting instructions regarding foreign nationals: Adiv diary (10 Oct. 1939), 73. By mid-October all enquiries were answered thus: 'They will no longer deal with us and refer us to the official Lithuanian agencies that will enter Vilna shortly' (ibid. (18 Oct. 1939), 98).

[84] A factory worker employed in Lwów was allowed to leave Vilna: Pumpianski testimony, OHD, pp. 2–3.

[85] Five young educated Jews (including Elijahu Yonas, Hayyim Munitz, and Moshe Bloch) secretly left Vilna in an attempt to reach Scandinavia through Latvia. As they were unable to cross the Latvian border, they chose to remain in the Polish town of Druya that now belonged to Belarus: Elijahu Yonas testimony, A, OHD, p. 2; id. B, OHD, p. 21.

[86] The official explanation tendered was: '(1) It is not worthwhile for them [the regime] to run the factory in its present condition; (2) it needs expansion, which necessitates substantial investment in property and machinery; (3) Vilna is not a suitable site, first because it is distant from the sources of raw materials, and second, because it is near the border and is liable to suffer attack and bombardment ... in order to reopen the factory, it must be transferred to a secure location': Adiv diary (9 Oct. 1939), 70. Cf. Abraham Verses testimony, OHD, pp. 11–15.

more advantageous—to remain under Soviet or Lithuanian rule.'[87] In any event, the opportunity to relocate with the factory in the USSR met with an enthusiastic Jewish response, enhanced by the Soviet pledge to provide transportation and other forms of assistance. The number of willing Jewish candidates was relatively high, particularly in view of the fact that skilled labourers, 'not . . . simple workers',[88] were in demand. Of the forty families making up the two groups of emigrants that left for Minsk on 11 and 12 October, only a minority, five or six, were Polish;[89] the remainder were Jewish. Upon their arrival in Minsk, the Elektrit workers were housed in six large buildings,[90] and dormitories, special shops, and other services were provided. Some individuals were even afforded the opportunity to pursue academic studies.

This exodus was widely discussed in Vilna; moreover, it sparked a chain reaction, setting off waves of immigration, mainly by young Jews from the lower classes and leftist circles. In the latter half of October, shortly before the expected entry of the Lithuanian army, the exodus assumed mass proportions with the apparent sanction of the Soviet authorities, who now speedily issued permits 'to all and sundry'.[91] While some emigrants, particularly members of the Workers' Guard, were motivated to relocate by their pro-Soviet ideology, others chose to leave Vilna in order to escape the reputedly antisemitic Lithuanian regime. Similarly, many of the unemployed considered that they had a better chance of improving their economic lot in the Soviet zone than in a small Lithuanian state. 'They claim that conditions in Lithuania are not the best, and that there is antisemitism,' stated an unemployed typesetter considering emigration. 'Individuals who once belonged to the proletarian wing of the Zionist organization, not to say leftist circles, believe that the Soviets can provide an answer to the Jewish question, in the cultural sphere as well. Also, there is no unemployment in Russia.'[92]

---

[87] Adiv diary (9 Oct. 1939), 70.

[88] Ibid. (11 Oct. 1930), 76. According to one source, 'special connections were needed to join the Elektrit workers': Sima Skurkowicz's testimony, OHD, p. 4.

[89] The statistics are derived form the oral testimony of the factory's office manager, Mr Baruch Zhislin. Cf. Yatziv testimony, OHD, p. 2; Sonia R. Rindzunsky's testimony, OHD, pp. 5–6.

[90] Most of the buildings were located near the railway station. The engineering staff lived at 1 Novomoskovskovo, and the remainder at 77 Dolgobratska and 133 Sovetska: Yatziv testimony, OHD, p. 15.

[91] Adiv diary (15 Oct. 1939), 85. The scale of the exodus can be assessed from the fact that according to the union secretary's estimations 30–40% of the members of the printworkers' union were absent. Of the committee, only three individuals remained: Koriski's testimony, OHD, p. 8; Adiv diary (14 Oct. 1939), 82. Cf. Joel Engelstern's testimony (manuscript).

[92] Loriski's testimony, OHD, p. 7. For the factors influencing Koriski's decision on whether to stay in Vilna or emigrate see Adiv diary (12 Oct 1939), 78–9; (21 Oct.), 99. On a *yeshivah* student from Troki who left for the USSR to study veterinary medicine see Yeshayahu Levin's testimony, A, OHD, pp. 1–2.

Dramatic scenes accompanied this mass departure, leaving a discernible effect on those remaining in Vilna:

It is difficult to approach the [railway] station's enclosure. Thousands wait there day and night. Time is short—in a day or two the borders will be sealed. Everyone views it as a matter of life or death . . . Hellish scenes occur. People are suffocated in the scuffle to board the train. Thousands storm a train which can accommodate hundreds only. One must wait days for the train to arrive.

The buses are very full. Once I saw a bus go by . . . filled to capacity. Passengers stand in a crush. On the roof are piles of baggage; a man sits on top. This is typical—to decide to make a long trip on top of the baggage in the freezing cold is an act of desperation . . .

The exodus affects those who neither desire nor are able to travel; it also contributes to a sense of panic that disturbs those remaining in the city. New rumours continually circulate—so and so has left; oh, he left ages ago; X is intending to leave while Y is vacillating; yet another individual who had decided to leave has now changed his mind. Tension and nervousness prevail . . .

Many refugees leave their belongings behind, or sell them for a pittance. A completely furnished well-kept apartment can be purchased for 2,000 roubles.[93] In the absence of a buyer, belongings are distributed among friends and relatives. Bitter tears are shed by the owner who must part with the possessions so assiduously collected and cared for . . . each cup or decorative item that she will never see again is kissed. The belongings cannot be transferred. The trains carry no luggage because the luggage-cars are used for passengers . . .

I have never before witnessed such a migration. Sons bid farewell to parents, husbands to wives; families scatter.[94]

In his testimony one young Jew, a former member of the Workers' Guard who left Vilna for Belarus, stressed the aid tendered by the Soviet authorities:

Prior to departure we received clothing from the warehouses of the Polish Division as well as Polish currency: transportation by motor vehicle was provided and we were allowed to cross the border as a group . . . Thus I reached Stara Wilejka, a district capital. I stayed there [in Belarus] for between one and one and a half months; then I was sent to Disna on a course.[95]

While there was some southward movement toward Białystok, Baranovichi, and even Lwów,[96] the majority turned east, taking the shortest route to the Soviet border. Generally denied permission to cross the former Soviet border, some

---

[93] At that time 1 kg. of butter cost 20 zloty (or roubles), a duck 30, a metre of plain cloth 150: 'Vos m'zet voz m'hert haynt in Vilnius', 5.

[94] Adiv diary (14 Oct. 1939), 81–2.

[95] Hayyim Gordon testimony, OHD, pp. 3–4. Gordon was drafted into the Red Army, participated in the initial battles against Germany, and was taken prisoner. He escaped to Italy, where he joined an anti-Fascist partisan unit. At the end of the war end he returned to the USSR and was arrested: ibid., pp. 5–32.

[96] See Yatziv's testimony, OHD, pp. 6–7; Pumpiański's testimony, OHD, pp. 3–4; Moshe Rabinovitz's (Blitt) testimony, OHD, pp. 2, 5–6.

fugitives remained in the small towns of west Belarus, where Sovietization had just begun.[97] Yet this area was not necessarily a safe haven. During the process of obtaining the required documents, some refugees were classified according to Article 38: that is, they were barred from residing within a certain distance from the border.[98] These individuals were forced to relocate, and many returned to Vilna after suffering great hardship. One who managed to reach Vilna before war broke out described his experiences and the rationale for his return:

Our group, which arrived together, was very well received. We were simply unprepared for such a reception, so well were we received. We were given beds, pillows, and blankets—all our necessities. On the other hand, we suffered from the mad dash to the 'soup kitchen' for meals, and from queuing up for everything, like butter and sugar. We were not accustomed to that at home.[99]

Although the majority of the Vilna residents emigrating to Soviet-held areas belonged to either leftist or pro-Soviet circles, they were joined by others whose ideologies were unacceptable to the Soviet regime—members of the Freeland League, for example.[100] Ironically, at times the latter received better treatment than Vilna residents belonging to the Communist Party, who ran the risk of being accused of Trotskyite deviations.[101]

The official Soviet withdrawal from Vilna did not halt the mass exodus. Rather, following the anti-Jewish riots that erupted with the Lithuanian army's

---

[97] Communist trade-union activist Itzik Wittenberg, who later headed the Faraynikte Partizaner Organisatsye (FPO: United Partisan Organization) in the Vilna ghetto, was among the Vilna residents who ended up in the town of Dukszty: Sima Skurkowicz's testimony, OHD, p. 4.

[98] Yonas's testimony, A, OHD, p. 3; Yatziv's testimony, OHD, p. 5; Tsilah Hanin-Dworkin's testimony, OHD, p. 1.

[99] Shemaia Rudnicki's testimony, OHD, p. 3. According to Rudnicki, the refrain of the Warsaw refugees, 'Ikh vil tsurik aheym', was adopted by fugitives from Vilna in Belarus: ibid., p. 2. Cf. Hanin-Dworkin's testimony, OHD, p. 1.

[100] Members of Shperber who left Vilna at this time included the writers Leizer Wolf, Moshe Blitt, and Nahman Baranchuk: Astor, *Geshikhte*, 453. Blitt and Wolf had left earlier for Białystok and later reached Moscow and other locations in the USSR. Blitt was drafted into the Red Army when the war broke out. Wolf died in Uzbekistan in 1943; his book *Di broyne bestie* appeared immediately following his death: see Moshe Rabinovitz's (Blitt) testimony, OHD, pp. 1–7; cf. Astor, *Geshikhte*, 456, and Leizer Wolf, *Lider* (New York, 1956), 20. Other writers who left Vilna at the same time were Shimsohn Cohen, Peretz Miroński, and Shmerke (Kaczergiński?). Fugitive artists included Moshe Libovski, Ber Zalkind, and A. Bialogurski: *Di idishe shtime* (31 Oct. 1939), 3.

[101] Like their Polish colleagues, many Communist activists in Vilna were accused of Trotskyite deviations, as I was personally informed by Dr Shlomo Katz (n. 20 above). He approached the NKVD commander in Vilna (Petrov?) and asked him to investigate whether it was true that he was being denounced as a Trotskyite in leftist circles. The commander brushed him off. Upon Katz's departure for Wilejka with the stream of refugees, he again approached the NKVD, leaving his forwarding address in Lwów. Several months later Katz was arrested there, and imprisoned on charges of Trotskyite deviations. A Jewish Communist named Gordon, a law clerk, who had been released from jail and given permission to emigrate to the USSR, was arrested there: Lipkind's testimony, A, OHD, p. 6; see also Yonas's testimony, OHD, p. 19.

entry on 28 October, it intensified. The Lithuanians took no steps to stem the outward tide; on the contrary, they even waived the permit requirement. This tide of emigration continued until 11 November 1939, when the Soviets unilaterally sealed the border. By that date at least three thousand individuals had left Vilna.[102]

A NIGHTMARE BECOMES REALITY: THE UNDERMINING OF INTERNAL SECURITY

In mid-September, prior to the Soviet takeover of Vilna, tensions ran high among the city's Polish population. In contrast, the Byelorussians were calm, apparently pleased that their brothers from the other side of the border were approaching the city. In desperation, the Poles made preparations for a last-ditch stand, recruiting civilians for trench-digging and other defensive measures. Incidents of anti-Jewish violence accompanied these preparations. The Jews of Vilna correctly assessed their vulnerability to attack (based on past experiences during the intervals between regimes), especially in view of the general release of common criminals from prison. As in the past, Jews began to fortify their courtyard gates. In the words of an eyewitness:

The following scene is permanently engraved in my memory. It is late at night, but in the Jewish quarter broken gates are rapidly being repaired. In other locations barricades are being erected within them [the gates]. All sorts of objects are simply piled up inside the gate so that the expected vandals—an age-old source of disturbance—cannot gain access to the courtyard.[103]

In this instance, Jewish fears did not materialize. Various factors, including the deliberate dissemination of rumours regarding a crushing defeat ostensibly suffered by the Germans near Warsaw and of the outbreak of rebellion in Germany,[104] radically transformed the atmosphere. While the Poles kissed in public, the Jews heaved a sigh of relief. Vilna had escaped a pogrom. None the less, Jews regarded it as self-evident that were the Soviets to withdraw from Vilna at that moment, not one Jew in the entire city would survive. Wholesale slaughter would take place.[105]

[102] Y. Zhofer, 'Vilner aktualiteten', *Di idishe shtime* (5 Nov. 1939), 3. For similar estimates, as well as for figures reaching 4,000–5,000, cf. H. Gordon testimony, OHD, p. 2: Rudnicki testimony, OHD, p. 2.

[103] Adiv diary (23 Sept. 1939), 38.

[104] According to one source, this information appeared in a special edition of a Polish-language newspaper and had a calming effect: 'Vi azoy di alte historishe shtot vilne iz farnumen gevorn fun sovetishn militer', *Haynt ba-Tog* (20 Sept. 1939), 4. A different source attributed the dissemination of this surprising announcement to the Polish mayor of the city. It was spread publicly by loudspeaker, 'since the Vilna radio station has been destroyed': Adiv diary (28 Sept. 1939), 50.

[105] Adiv diary (28 Sept. 1939), 50.

On the surface, a state of law and order prevailed. Seemingly, even the Poles had come to terms with the new state of affairs and with the fact that they could no longer freely harass Vilna's Jewish population. The Jews were inclined to believe that the 'atmosphere is totally changed; it's easier to breathe—the air is no longer poisoned by antisemitic fumes'.[106] This hope was reinforced by indications of the desired change: 'A Jewish boy stands on Ostra Brama with a rifle over his shoulder directing traffic.'[107] A long-standing Jewish sense of injustice was rectified by the fact that Jews now dared to cross the Ostra Brama,[108] a Catholic holy site, without removing their hats. None the less, the atmosphere was not entirely free of Polish resentment and threats.[109]

Repeated claims voiced by former Polish army officers and Polish citizens that 'the Jews brought the Bolsheviks' were accompanied by threats of 'terrible slaughter as in Petlyura's day'.[110] Not surprisingly, this fostered the conviction among Jews that 'should the Russians leave Vilna, all the Jews will accompany them'.[111] Consequently, the announcement of the imminent transfer of Vilna to Lithuanian hands was received with shock, arousing fears for Jewish safety. 'Why are you deserting us?' Jews enquired of Red Army troops and commissars stationed in Vilna. This enquiry reflected the profound Jewish fear of the Lithuanians, assessed as having 'one characteristic in common with the Poles—hatred of Jews'.[112] Already apprehensive, the Jews fell prey to rumour and conjecture, each worse than the last. As they feared that the 'Poles intended to join the Lithuanians in establishing law and order in the city', the local conclusion was that 'a sizeable Soviet force must remain, otherwise the Lithuanians themselves may not be able to control the potentially explosive situation upon the Soviet troops' withdrawal'.[113] Although the strong Jewish presence in the Workers' Guard should have promoted a sense of security among the population at large and among the Jews in particular, internal antagonism between national groups within the Guard aggravated tensions instead.[114] Still, the existence of this quasi-military organization with its high proportion of Jewish members and officers did

---

[106] Adiv diary (20 Sept. 1939), 31.   [107] Ibid. (28 Sept. 1939), 50.
[108] Ostra Brama is a gate in the Vilna wall with a 16th-cent. shrine to the Madonna. Passers-by were obliged to acknowledge the site's sanctity by removing their hats.
[109] A young Jewish girl was attacked verbally and cursed by Polish women while she was picking flowers in a public park for the Red Army troops: Sima Skurkowicz's testimony, OHD, p. 4.
[110] 'Min hadin veheshbon', 45.   [111] Adiv diary (11 Oct. 1939), 75.
[112] Ibid. 74.   [113] Ibid. (14 Oct. 1939), 81.
[114] The following incident, which occurred in a Polish police commissariat, illustrates these nationalistic tensions. 'Two members of the Workers' Guard were arrested for a known offence. The detainees were Polish and were arrested by Jews, also members of the Guard. Their Polish colleagues came to the commissariat for redress. Apparently the debate was stormy. Words were transformed into deeds. There were exchanges of gunfire which continued until soldiers arrived, putting an end to the scandal': Adiv diary (14 Oct. 1939), 84. Adiv commented: 'Clearly the composition of the guards is not ideal. There is racial antagonism here, etc. Among its members there may be elements who are not only distant from the proletarian movement, but antithetical to it' (ibid.).

contribute somewhat to a greater feeling of security among Jews. Thus its disbanding on 19 October and the departure of some of its members from Vilna fostered the impression among the city's residents that 'Vilna was left with no defence'. Although a small Soviet force remained, its soldiers were preoccupied with tasks of evacuation, disinfection, and the like, not with keeping the peace.[115]

Vilna's Jewish population also regarded with trepidation the increased presence of the more dissipated elements among the former Polish troops, who wandered about Vilna starving and in rags. A contemporary newspaper article expressed the thought weighing upon the minds of Vilna's residents: 'What are the aims of this mass, and what is to be done?'[116] Apparently these ex-soldiers, along with released criminals and other dubious elements, were responsible for a wave of robberies in outlying districts of the city.[117] As a result, some Jews in suburban areas sought to relocate in the centre. Moreover, in response to the unsettled situation, guard duty by tenants was reinstituted in most houses.

The difficult economic situation led to inflammatory accusations by Poles that the Jews had 'hidden all the foodstuffs, therefore the Polish people suffer starvation'. However, among Jews the general impression was that 'for the time being, the Poles must restrain themselves from harming their hated enemy, the Jews, as the presence of the Red Army hampers them'.[118]

Rumours of an impending pogrom by a large group of Polish partisans immediately following the Soviet exit were deliberately spread in mid-October.[119] The Jewish reaction was twofold. On the one hand, the mass exodus already described intensified. On the other, some Jews found comfort in the supposition that a certain number of Soviet soldiers 'will remain to keep order'.[120] Other Jews put their faith in a reputed version of a Radio Lithuania report announcing that 'a civil militia, composed of Jews, Lithuanians, and Byelorussians, to the exclusion of Poles' would be formed.

Tense expectation combined with curiosity and trepidation characterized the state of the Jewish population when the spearhead of the Lithuanian military and police (accompanied by clerks, journalists, etc.) entered Vilna on Saturday, 28 October. The Jews' worst fears were realized: three to four days of intermittent rioting followed, in the course of which large numbers of Jews were assaulted and injured. According to a report filed by the correspondent of the American Yiddish daily *Forverts* [Onward], Maurycy Orzech (a Bundist activist covering the Lithuanian army's entry into Vilna), 'antisemitic outbursts began on

---

[115] 'Vos m'zet voz m'hert haynt in Vilnius', 5. Cf. Adiv diary (21 Oct 1939), 99.
[116] 'Voz m'zet voz m'hert haynt in Vilnius', 5.
[117] Adiv diary (24 Oct. 1939), 105. See also n. 82 above.
[118] Adiv diary (23 Oct. 1939), 102.
[119] 'Vi zet oys vilne erev dem araynmarsh fun litvishn militer?' *Haynt ba-Tog* (18 Oct. 1939), 4.
[120] Adiv diary (18 Oct. 1939), 93. Cf. 'Rusishe militer nokh alts in Vilne', *Forverts* (22 Oct. 1939), 1.

Saturday, even prior to the Soviet transfer of the city to Lithuanian armed forces. A young Jew named Faivl Magun was killed and a number of Jews were injured. Upon the Lithuanian army's arrival in Vilna on Sunday, there was a further outbreak.'[121] The same reporter summarized the aftermath of four days of rioting in a separate article:

Two hundred Jewish casualties were brought to hospitals in Vilna. Two hundred Jewish shops located on Trocka, Sadowa, Rudnicka, Zawalna, Straszuna, Niemiecka, and Wielka were looted by Endeks. Endek rioters held anti-Jewish demonstrations and riots in various towns in the Vilna region. In Wilejka and Landworowa the hooligans assaulted Jews and looted Jewish shops. One Jewish fatality and scores of injuries were reported. In the streets one sees many Jews with bandaged heads.[122]

Strict censorship prevented details of the disturbances from reaching Lithuania and nearby Latvia.[123] Naturally, accounts of the actions of Lithuanian or Soviet authorities during the riots were also censored. Reports by foreign correspondents and by eyewitnesses convey the distinct impression that the Lithuanian authorities were far from neutral. In fact, the opposite appears to be true—that they openly aided and abetted the rioters. An almost contemporary report by attorney S. Seidenman pinpointed the national identity of the perpetrators as well as the ostensible pretext for their actions:

The Polish militia started the pogrom. The agreed sign for identification was white socks. They were the ones who initiated the pogrom. Upon the approach of the Lithuanian police, these youths stated that they were seeking the organizers of the pro-Bolshevik demonstration.[124] The police became confused. Twenty-three Jews were seriously injured. Two Jews suffered fatal injuries—the first was pushed off a veranda, and the second was found stabbed.[125]

Another account, written soon after the events by Dr Moshe Kleinbaum (Sneh), chairman of the Zionist organization in Poland, provides further details:

That day the price of bread rose in Vilna. The residents stood in the streets in a queue near the grocery shops. Among them were demagogues who incited the masses with their comments of the new state of affairs, noting that a zloty that had been equivalent to a rouble was now worth only one-fifth of a litas! With these and similar remarks, they called for a demonstration opposite the town hall. The demonstrators called for a reduction in the price of bread. Cries of 'Let's go back to Russia' were also heard. As the police were

---

[121] 'Poylishe khuliganes pogromirn idn in vilne', *Forverts* (2 Nov. 1939), 1.

[122] Ibid. (3 Nov. 1939), 1.

[123] For example, the articles in *Di idishe shtime* covering the disturbances in Vilna were censored. The censored sections were published by Leyzer Ran, *Ash fun yerushalayim de-lite* (New York, 1959), 227–78. On the censorship see Ari Glazman, 'Dokument fun blutiken tog', *Di idishe shtime* (25 June 1940), 6.

[124] On 21 Oct. 15–20 youths had attempted to hold a pro-Communist demonstration. This insignificant demonstration was one of the pretexts for the pogrom.

[125] *Sho'at yehudei Polin* (Jerusalem, 1940), i. 45.

dispersing the demonstrators, someone tore a Lithuanian flag. The police were at a loss what to do and began striking bystanders indiscriminately. Suddenly youths began to hit Jews, calling out to the police that these Jews were Communists, whereupon the police joined in the assault. From my window I saw three Polish youths chasing a Jewish youth. The Jew fled through a courtyard gate. The police arrived and assisted in extricating him, and then they arrested him. Jewish *shetadlanim* [lobbyists] appealed to the Lithuanian authorities, but were not well received. The pogrom, which lasted a day, had a 'mixed' Polish–Russian nature. Pillows and feather-beds were torn and emptied into the streets, people were pushed from verandas, and so on. During the pogrom, the Jews did not defend themselves,[126] nor did they have the option. On the day after the pogrom the Jews asked to be accepted into the ranks of the civil guard, but their request was denied.[127]

It appears from this narrative, as well as from other sources,[128] that random or staged pretexts were employed to instigate anti-Jewish riots: the rise in bread prices, the additional devaluation of the zloty, an aborted (real or staged) pro-Communist demonstration. In addition, the Lithuanian authorities apparently wished to 'teach the Jews a lesson' for their pro-Soviet sympathies and at the same time allow the Polish population to let off steam by indulging its hatred of Jews, albeit under a certain measure of control.

Important Jewish personalities who had come to Vilna on organizational business as well as to encourage and assist the Jews of Vilna were not immune from attack during these riots. A number of these figures were staying at the Italia Hotel: Reuven Rubinstein, chief editor of *Di idishe shtime* [The Jewish voice]; attorney Jakub Goldberg, head of the Jewish Veterans' Organization; Dr Benjamin Bludz, head of ORT; and several journalists, including Y. Zhofer. Two

---

[126] Cf. Lipkind's testimony, A, OHD, p. 4. Other sources cite instances of organized Jewish resistance. According to one witness, a group of Polish *halutsim* were enlisted for Jewish self-defence 'at the request of the Zionist movement and of the Labour Zionist Party headquarters': Zvi Netzer testimony, OHD, p. 2; cf. Hillel Zeidel, *Adam be mivhan* (Tel Aviv, 1971), 24. The Polish *halutsim*'s answer to the call for Jewish resistance was enthusiastically endorsed by Mordecai Anielewicz, the Warsaw Ha'shomer Hatsa'ir activist who later led the uprising in the Warsaw ghetto. He proposed that they reject the Lithuanian offer of arms and come to the defence of Jews 'even with our bare hands, or with whatever we can pick up': *Sefer Hashomer Hatsa'ir* (Merhavia, 1956), i. 442. Another source cites an appeal made to Jewish workers and to the general public, calling upon them 'to take to the streets in defence of life, property, and the honour of Vilna's Jewish population. For this purpose, self-defence must be immediately organized in the courtyards': Ran, *Ash fun yerushalayim de-lite*, 291; cf. also Dworzecki's testimony, A, OHD, p. 10. Undoubtedly, the majority of these sources reflect preparations for self-defence made in response to the expectation of trouble on 10 Nov., the anniversary of the death of the Polish student Waclawski, who had been killed by Jews in self-defence several years earlier.

[127] *Sho'at yehudei Polin*, i. 39.

[128] See the relevant portions of the chapter 'Di general probe fun ponar' in Ran, *Ash fun yerushalayim de-lite*, 267–301, containing documentation and journalistic reports regarding the disturbances; see also Balberyszski, *Shtarker fun ayzn*, 74–5: Prof. Marian Mushkat's testimony, OHD, pp. 8–9, 48–9; Adiv diary (2 Nov. 1939), 118–19.

of the group attempted to repulse the rioters who tried to break in, one with his fists and the other with a pistol.[129]

Naturally, the Lithuanian Jewish leadership's response was to issue an immediate appeal to the Lithuanian authorities to quash the disturbances. A telling argument, if not the decisive one, was the forceful warning by Dr Jacob Wygodzki, acknowledged head of the official Vilna Jewish community, a Zionist leader and former deputy to the Polish Sejm, that 'the Soviet army is nearby, and if the Lithuanians cannot bring the situation under control, I will be forced to turn to the Russians to restore law and order'.[130] Several sources report the re-entry of some thirty-five Soviet tanks.[131] In any event, the Lithuanian authorities took active steps to restore order to Vilna.[132] This relative peace was of limited duration, however.

CONCLUSION

The six-week Soviet occupation of Vilna in September–October 1939 was marked by changes and processes that profoundly affected the lives of the city's Jewish residents. This period can be seen as a microcosm of the fateful events about to engulf Vilna and other Jewish communities in the course of their Sovietization, a process already taking place in areas of eastern Poland and which

---

[129] Reuven Rubinstein's testimony, B, OHD, pp. 11–12; Binyamin Bludz's testimony, A, OHD, pp. 31–2; cf. coverage by the confiscated edition of *Di idishe shtime* (n. 123 above) in Ran, *Ash fun yerushalayim de-lite*, 297.

[130] Dr Wygodski's warning was communicated to Mr Rubinstein by telephone. Rubinstein then repeated the contents of the call to Dr Bludz, who was also present. Subsequently, Mr Rubinstein conveyed this message to the Lithuanian authorities: Bludz's testimony, A, OHD, pp. 12–13. Cf. Ran, *Ash fun yerushalayim de-lite*, 291; Balberyszski, *Shtarker fun ayzn*, 74.

[131] *Forverts* (2 Nov. 1939), 1; *Amerikaner* (10 Nov. 1939); Ran, *Ash fun yerushalayim de-lite*, 292, 301. The latter two sources attribute the restoration of law and order largely, if not totally, to the return of Soviet units to Vilna. A different source provides a more plausible explanation: 'Immediately following the riots, a delegation approached the Russian authorities in the city. Although they were given a gracious reception, they [the Soviets] stated that it was not within their power to extend any aid, since the terms of the treaty forbade any intervention in Lithuanian internal affairs. The only advice they offered the delegation was to meet the rioters armed with axes': Adiv diary (2 Nov, 1939), 118. According to yet another source, the Soviet commandant cited his inability to intervene in internal Lithuanian affairs. Upon receiving a second appeal from the Jews, he sent tanks to Vilna in accordance with instructions received from Moscow in the interim: see I. Kowalski, *A Secret Press in Nazi Europe* (New York, 1969), 30–1.

[132] The official announcement made by the Lithuanian news agency Elta read as follows: 'Clashes occurred yesterday in Vilna between groups of fanatical Polish youths and Jews. The police immediately restored order. Several people were arrested and certain rioters will be brought to trial ... Quiet now prevails in Vilna and district', Ran, *Ash fun jerushalayim de-lite*, 292 (translation from Y. Arad, *Ghetto in Flames: The Struggle and Destruction of the Jews of Vilna in the Holocaust* (Jerusalem, 1980), 12). Four of the perpetrators of the anti-Jewish riots were tried and sentenced to between two months and six years in jail upon the Soviet army's return to Lithuania. For details see 'Der ershter groyser protses vegn di blutike geshenishn in vilne', *Vilner togblat* (21 June 1940), 5.

would affect the Baltic States and areas of Romania in the near future (1940–1). The brief Soviet occupation of Vilna highlights fundamental aspects of the eventual Soviet annexation of two million Jews.

Among the noteworthy motifs later played out in other areas, we must cite first of all the initial enthusiastic welcome given to Soviet troops by the Jewish masses. Various elements among the Jewish population identified with the new regime's aims and attempted to become integrated in its administrative apparatus, a course made possible by the regime's openness. Second, Vilna became a magnet drawing refugees from near and far, but the community experienced difficulty with their absorption. The middle and lower classes were rapidly pauperized, and in order to survive, Jews engaged in black-market trade and smuggling, activities that sooner or later were bound to evoke confrontation with the regime. Moreover, Vilna's Jews found themselves isolated from both world Jewry and the outside world. The traditional leadership was unequipped to cope with the waves of arrests and expulsions, and the atmosphere of terror. Cultural and political activities were suppressed; at the same time, clandestine activity emerged. Thirdly, Jews felt the threat of physical danger. The local population's hostility was clearly evident and increasing. Escalating fears for physical safety caused Jews to become increasingly dependent on the administrative authorities for protection. The massive influx of Jews to Vilna was governed by hopes of reaching the West in general, or Palestine in particular. The flight from Vilna to other Soviet-controlled areas in order to avoid persecution by hostile regimes reached mass proportions. These fugitives were granted asylum in accordance with Soviet national needs.

Although it was very short-lived, the Soviet occupation of Vilna served as a prelude to the future fate of Jews in Soviet-held areas. Further study may clarify whether, and to what extent, Vilna's Jews had absorbed the lessons of the brief Soviet regime upon its reinstatement in June 1940.

The Polish Underground and the Extermination of the Jews

SHMUEL KRAKOWSKI

DESPITE the fifty years which have elapsed since the end of the Second World War, historians still have a long way to go before they can be seen to have provided a full and objective representation of the intricate problems connected with the relations between the Polish underground and the Jewish population during the most tragic period in its history, the moment of its near total annihilation. A large number of archival documents on this subject remain inaccessible to many researchers. First and foremost this applies to much of the official documentation of the Office of the Government Delegate for the Homeland and the Home Army, which until recently was kept in the Archive of the Central Committee of the Polish United Workers' Party. Polish historiography has given extensive coverage to only one of many aspects of the Polish underground's attitude towards the Jews—the help which they were given—and it has greatly exaggerated the scope of that aid. The subject of Jewish–Polish relations, including the attitude of the Polish underground towards the Jews during the Nazi occupation, still evokes strong emotions, and, in the face of political pressures, that has made a factual analysis of this complicated problem extremely difficult.

The primary factor which determined the character of the relations between Poles and Jews was the totally different treatment meted out by the Germans to the two groups. German terror directed at the Polish population was extremely cruel from the very start. The Polish nation found itself in the most difficult situation to have arisen in all its history. However, the terror used against the Jewish population was, from the very beginning of the occupation, infinitely more brutal and was directed towards all Jews, without exception. Special anti-Jewish orders, compulsory marks of identification, a ban on the use of public transport, confiscation of property (including all goods produced), incessant labour round-ups in the city streets, systematic humiliations, and bullying—all this destroyed the social and economic life of the Jewish population. There followed additional calamities in the form of imprisonment in ghettos and finally total extermination.

The deliberate setting up of Jews as the target of a specific campaign of terror, which was a consequence of Nazi ideological convictions, resulted in turn in a difference between the Jewish and Polish reactions to the Red Army's advance into

Poland's eastern territories. Most Poles considered both Nazi Germany and the Soviet Union equally as invaders, and they did not see any real difference in the repression introduced by one or the other of Polish society. The majority of Poles had no understanding of the exceptional nature of the tragedy which had befallen the Jewish population.

The measures against Jewish society introduced by the Soviet authorities in the occupied Polish territories were no less serious than those against the Poles. Nearly all the Jewish cultural, religious, and social institutions were abolished; Hebrew teaching was banned and Jewish libraries and sports clubs closed down. It goes without saying that all Jewish political parties and organizations, like their Polish counterparts, were also made illegal. What followed was an immediate pauperization of the poorer and even the middle Jewish bourgeoisie, not to mention confiscations of property from the richer sections of Jewish society. But this repression, however cruel, was nothing in comparison with what the Jewish population experienced from the very first day of German occupation. This is why when the Jews were faced with a choice between Germans and Russians, they could not conceal their joy in those towns which were invaded by the Red Army rather than the Wehrmacht.

As it turned out, the Jews who suffered the most terrible treatment by the Soviet authorities—those who were dragged from their homes in the middle of the night and transported to the country in sealed carriages—were the ones who, as a result, managed to escape German extermination. Thus, ironically, this cruel and inhuman repression was an instrument of salvation for these Jews. Polish Jews who lived through the nightmare of Soviet camps could only keep silent on their return to Poland once they had spoken to others who had survived German occupation, because their suffering turned out to be insignificant in comparison with the tortures experienced by the latter. It seems that only very few people were capable of understanding the depth of the Jewish tragedy during the Second World War.

Up to the time of the mass deportations to extermination camps, there were practically no significant contacts between the Polish underground and Jewish society, or even the Jewish underground. The Polish underground concentrated its efforts on creating appropriate structures and on building an underground armed force which would play a prominent part in determining the fate of Poland the moment the German occupation collapsed. But the Jewish population, locked up in the ghettos and dying of starvation *en masse*, was facing different problems. It must be remembered that starvation claimed 85,000 victims (18 per cent) in the Warsaw ghetto and 43,000 victims (22 per cent) in the Łódź ghetto. At that time the main problem facing Jewish society and representatives of the Jewish community and its underground was the need to take every possible measure to reduce the catastrophic mortality rate, which was threatening to wipe out the Jewish community altogether.

Very few examples of real co-operation between the Polish underground and Jewish elements survive from that period. However, the Jewish question was discussed in the underground press and in the political statements of various Polish underground organizations. News of the repressions against the Jewish population and the tragic situation in the ghettos was regularly sent by the Polish underground to the Polish government-in-exile in London. This information became the main source of news about the plight of the Polish Jews which was being sent to the free world.

However, the programmes which formed part of the declarations made by Polish underground political elements did not generally include any attempt to take into account the real circumstances in which the Jews found themselves, but contained instead planned or proposed policies regarding the Jews to be implemented after Poland became liberated from German occupation. These ideas were not accommodated to the changed situation, but were simply a continuation of ideological programmes formulated by these political groups before the war. The Socialist and democratic organizations advocated full equality for Jews in the future liberated Poland. But the majority of political groups in the Polish underground proclaimed more or less radical anti-Jewish programmes, demanding forcible Jewish emigration after the liberation of Poland, and some political elements even proposed that Jews should continue to live in the ghettos after the German invaders had been repulsed.

Thus, for example, the underground newspaper *Naród* [Nation], an organ of the organization Unia of the Stronnictwo Pracy (Labour Party), which attracted the Catholic élite, published an article with the unambiguous title 'Jews Must Emigrate' on 20 January 1942. This text expatiated at great length upon the necessity of organizing a compulsory programme of Jewish emigration accompanied by dispossession, after the liberation of Poland. This was only one of many similar pieces which were being published in the Polish underground press.

Many pronouncements from the Polish underground expressed deep outrage and spoke out in protest against what the Germans were doing. At the same time they emphasized the impossibility of opposing the genocidal policies of the Germans. The most authoritative of these is the following statement by the Kierownictwo Walki Cyznnej (Leadership of Civil Warfare), published in the main underground organ of the Armia Krajowa (Home Army), *Biuletyn informacyjny* (17 September 1942):

Along with the tragedy which Polish society is having to endure—having been decimated by the enemy for nearly a year now—Jews are being brutally butchered in our land. This mass murder has no precedent in the history of the world, and all other atrocities known to history pale alongside it. Babies, children, youths, adults, the old, cripples, invalids, men, women, Jewish Catholics, and Jews practising the Mosaic faith are murdered in cold blood, poisoned by gas, buried alive, thrown out of windows, from high-rise buildings; they have to endure agonies before their death, the hell of homelessness, and the anguish of their cynical ill treatment by the executioners. The number of victims killed in this way has passed a million and is growing with every passing day.

Not being able to resist it actively, the Leadership of Civil Warfare protests in the name of the entire Polish nation at the crime being perpetrated against the Jews. All Polish political and social groups join in this protest. As in the case of Polish victims, responsibility for this crime will be laid at the door of the executioners and their accomplices.

But it remains true that many of the declarations denouncing Nazi genocide contained an element of antisemitism. So, for example, a leaflet entitled *Protest*, produced by Zofia Kossak-Szczucka in the name of the Front Odrodzenia Polski (Front for Polish Resurrection) in August 1942, simultaneously incorporates a protest against German genocide and antisemitic propaganda:

One has no right to remain passive when crimes are being committed. Whoever keeps silent in the face of murder becomes the murderer's accomplice. He acquiesces who does not condemn.

For this reason we, the Polish Catholics, are speaking out. But our feelings towards the Jews have not changed. We still consider them to be political, economic, and ideological enemies of Poland.

A striking example of this ambivalent attitude of some of the Polish underground groups is an article which appeared in *Naród* on 15 August 1942, entitled 'The Slaughter of Jews'. Here are some extracts:

At the moment, from behind the ghetto walls we can hear the unearthly moans and screams of the Jews who are being murdered. Ruthless cunning is falling victim to a ruthless brutal power, and there is no cross visible on this battlefield, as these scenes go back to pre-Christian times.

If this continues in the same manner, then it will not be long before Warsaw will be saying farewell to the last Jew. If it were possible to conduct a funeral, the reaction to it would be interesting to see. Would sorrow follow in the wake of the coffin, or weeping, or perhaps joy?

In one of our previous decrees we urged you to be kind, but today we are faced with the following question. For hundreds of years an alien, malevolent entity has inhabited our northern suburb—malevolent and alien from the point of view of our interests, as well as our psyche and our hearts. So let us not strike false attitudes of the sort adopted by professional mourners at funerals—let us be serious and honest.

We pity the individual Jew, the human being, and as far as possible, should he be lost or trying to hide, we shall extend a helping hand. We must condemn those who denounce them. It is our duty to demand from those who allow themselves to sneer and mock that they show dignity and respect in the face of death. But we are not going to pretend to be grief-stricken about a vanishing nation which, after all, was never close to our hearts.

It is obvious that this text contains many details which are based on primitive lies, on inhumane and disgusting diatribes against the Jews. But it also urges the extending of a helping hand to any individual Jew who is lost or in hiding—and that, after all, implies risking one's own life. Are we not dealing here with a peculiar contradiction, not uncommon at that time—the wish to salve one's human conscience while yet remaining steeped in a hackneyed ideology which includes pathological antisemitism as one of its tenets? It would be difficult to deny that this contradiction was widespread among certain sectors of the Polish underground. The attitude is clearly demonstrated by the report sent to the Polish government-in-exile in London in August 1943 by Roman Knoll, director of the Commission of Foreign Affairs attached to the Delegates' Office of the government-in-exile. The document outlines basic plans relating to the Jewish population:

Among all our other national problems, there is also the Jewish question. Formerly this seemed to us to be a purely internal matter. In reality it has always been an international issue, and has influenced our foreign relations. We realize that this will be the case to an even greater extent after the end of this war in which international Jewry officially belongs to one of the fighting factions. The mass murders of Jews in Poland carried out by the Germans will alleviate the Jewish problem for us, but it will not remove it altogether.... However, because of the monstrous persecution which European Jews have been subjected to, world public opinion is bound to be even more sympathetic towards their plight and will make an even greater effort to look after their interests. At the moment, Christian compassion for the agony of the Jews dominates our country, but apart from all this . . . it remains true, whatever the nature of the current temporary psychological reaction that the eventual return of Jews to their jobs and workshops, even in greatly reduced numbers, is completely out of the question. The non-Jewish population has filled the places vacated by the Jews in towns and cities throughout Poland, and this has brought about fundamental changes which have a final quality about them.

A mass return of the Jews would be regarded by the people not as a restitution, but as an invasion against which it would defend itself, even by physical means. In short, it would certainly be a tragic situation from the political point of view if at the time we were having our borders redrawn, our credits secured, new alliances and federations negotiated, Poland were to be pilloried by world opinion as a country where militant antisemitism was still being practised. Then all elements hostile to us would take advantage of this moment to bring about our ruin and to deprive us of the hard-won fruits of victory. The government is doing the right thing in reassuring world opinion that there will be no antisemitism in Poland, but this can only happen if the Jews who survive the pogrom make no attempt to return *en masse* to Polish towns and cities.

The weakly disguised antisemitic tone and lack of any sense of political reality revealed by the author of the above passage need no comment. Yet Roman Knoll held a very responsible position in the organs of underground Poland.

The intensification of the deportation of Jews to extermination camps during 1942 brought about three specific circumstances: mass escapes from many ghettos in the hope of finding a hiding-place in nearby woods or shelter among the Polish population; the formation of Jewish partisan groups; and attempts to organize armed resistance in some of the ghettos.

The attitude of the Polish underground towards Jews under these circumstances was extremely varied. The Polish underground press was full of exhortations to give help to the fugitives and to those seeking shelter, but at the same time wickedly savage anti-Jewish utterances were commonplace. Here I give only a few diametrically opposed instances by way of example. *Prawda* [Truth], a periodical of the Front for Polish Resurrection, published an article entitled 'The Prophecies Are Coming True' in May 1942, which contained the following passage:

The problem of demoralization and barbarity which the slaughter of Jews has inflicted on us is becoming a burning issue. It is not only Latvians, Volksdeutsche, and Ukrainians who are being used to perform these monstrous executions. In many places the local population volunteers to take part in these massacres. One must try to keep such ignominious actions in check by every available means. One must bring it home to people that they will earn the name of hired assassins; they must be condemned in the underground press; one must exhort people to boycott the butchers and to promise severe sentences for the murderers once Poland is free.

In March 1943 the same periodical published the following in an article entitled 'In the Name of the Polish Republic':

We are also referring to the Jews. The plight of these people is inciting blackmail. We have already expressed our attitude towards the Jewish community. Today, we wish emphatically to underline that we are witnessing the most despicable form of rapacity which is feeding on their calamity. There can be no justification for this. No antisemitism can change the fact that the blackmailer is a scoundrel.

I now cite two typical commentaries from the underground press which take the opposite view, selected from a large number of similar examples. *Szaniec* [The rampart], the organ of Obóz Narodowo-Radykalny (the National Radical Camp), published the following passage on 31 January 1942:

Jews were, are, and will be against us, always and everywhere. . . . And now the question arises of how Poles are to treat the Jews. . . . We, and certainly at least 90 per cent of Poles, have only one answer to this question: like enemies. . . . The basic mistake which both previous Polish constitutions had in common was to give equal rights to all its citizens, which also included national minorities. The only right and effective, authentic, and non-cowardly solution to the problem is to grant political rights to no one but Poles.

On 15 April 1942 the same periodical published an article entitled 'The Problem of the Nursing Home', which included the following:

There are nations which are degenerate and sick, on which one must keep a tight hold so as not to cause disaster to civilization. These include, first and foremost, Jews, Germans, and Muscovites.

We have had to fight the Jews and the Muscovites, but the Germans are liquidating them much better and more effectively than anyone else could hope to do, particularly us.

There is no need to dwell at length on the Jews—we know them only too well. There is not much hope of their joining the ranks of nations of good will until they totally cleanse by fire 'the eternal revolutionary Jew' and fertilize the sterile and fallow realm of the Jewish soul with the ashes.

It is scarcely necessary to provide evidence that the perpetuation of such vicious antisemitic propaganda at the time of the German extermination of the Jews did nothing to promote the creation of an atmosphere conducive to extending help to those Jews who had escaped from ghettos or concentration camps.

The attitude of the Polish underground to the Jewish partisans was no less complicated. As a rule, the Home Army did not accept or strive to absorb any Jewish partisan groups or detachments. Only an insignificant number of Jewish individuals, probably no more than a few hundred, were accepted into the Home Army's ranks. The one exception was Wołyń, where a close co-operation between Jewish partisan detachments and Home Army detachments was achieved in the face of the common threat from Ukrainian nationalists. Home Army outposts in the threatened villages were happy to see co-operation with Jewish partisans and were able to strengthen the defences of the Polish villages in this way, while the Jewish partisan groups, in turn, gained support in the Polish villages in their struggle against their common enemy, who was murdering large numbers of Jews as well as Poles.

However, in the remaining parts of occupied Poland things were very different. The particular situation in which the Jewish groups and detachments found themselves did not find any degree of understanding among the leadership of the Home Army. In the numerous documents of the Home Army and the Delegatura Rządu na Kraj (Office of the Government Delegate for the Homeland) Jewish partisans were described as 'bandits': it is regrettable that the term used was the very one employed by the Germans to characterize all partisan detachments without exception. The Narodowe Siły Zbrojne (National Armed Forces) had a decidedly hostile attitude towards the Jewish partisans.

Numerous Jewish documents also testify to the malevolent attitude of some of the Home Army detachments, to the armed clashes between Jewish partisans and these detachments, and to the many murders of Jewish partisans and of Jews hiding in the forests or villages. What is more, some of these documents also attest to the hostility of those elements towards Poles who helped the Jews.

The attitude of the Gwardia Ludowa (People's Guard) towards members of the Jewish partisan groups was quite different. The planned establishment of the Polska Partia Robotnicza (Polish Workers' Party) for the purpose of an immediate armed struggle with the German invader, on the largest possible scale, was a positive development for the Jewish partisans in that some Jewish detachments found support and assistance from the People's Guard, without which they would not have been able to hold their ground for any length of time. A number of Jewish partisan detachments in the Lublin and Kielce regions subordinated themselves to the People's Guard leadership in order to obtain weapons and support in some of the villages which sided with the Guard. For the same reasons, particularly near Nowogródek and Vilna, many Jewish partisans subordinated themselves to the leadership of the Soviet partisan groups.

Where such subordination took place—whether to the People's Guard or to the Soviet leadership—it was not ideological considerations which played the main role, but rather the lack of any alternative. Those who decided to subordinate themselves to the People's Guard in the territories of the former General Gouvernement, or to the Soviet leaders in the eastern regions, were far removed from Communist ideology: they included men like Jechiel Grynszpan, leader of the largest partisan unit in the General Gouvernement region, operating in the Parczew forest, or Tuwia Bielski, leader of the largest Jewish partisan group active in the Naliboki forest. The propaganda of the Polish Workers' Party constantly asserted that the reason for the Jewish disaster was their passivity. As it turned out, this party's propaganda apparatus, in striving to achieve the goals it had set itself, inadvertently promoted anti-Jewish prejudice. For example, on 15 January 1943 *Trybuna wolności* [Tribune of freedom] the party's organ, published an article entitled 'Once Again they are Urging Calm', criticizing the position the Home Army had taken when it warned against premature resistance:

Immediately a comparison with the slaughter of Jews comes to mind. The very role now being adopted by our 'moderate elements' was played by the Jewish community to the very end. Their activists urged their followers until the end not to provoke trouble, even when it became common knowledge that the Germans had sentenced every one of them to death. This is why we now understand very well how such meaningless appeasement can work in the oppressor's favour.

The height of demagoguery was reached by *Trybuna wolności* when, in commemoration of the first anniversary of the uprising in the Warsaw ghetto, it published an article entitled 'The Defence of the Warsaw Ghetto' in its issue of 1 May 1944. This included the following passage:

The reason that the Jews lost the campaign of April 1943 was that they fought it in conditions of total isolation, were obliged to face the modern power of the Nazi war machine on their own, and, finally, had already been morally and politically defeated in the summer of 1942, when it may still have been possible to thwart the plans of the Nazi criminals with some decisive action.

The scope of Polish assistance to the Jewish underground organizations which were planning armed action in the ghettos is complicated and has not been fully clarified. Nearly all these organizations made strenuous efforts to obtain help from the Polish underground in the form of weapons. Many Jewish documents describe how these efforts ended in fiasco and how the level of help was infinitesimal in comparison with the options available to the Polish underground and the Home Army in particular, in which the greatest hopes had been placed. On the other hand, however, it is obvious that without the Home Army's help the uprising in the Warsaw ghetto could never have taken place.

By the autumn of 1942 the main wave of Jewish deportations to extermination camps was completed. By the end of that year the Germans had murdered the overwhelming majority of Polish Jews, and practically all the ghettos within the territories of occupied Poland had been liquidated. Only a few hundred thousand Jews remained alive in the few dramatically reduced ghettos, in a number of hardlabour and concentration camps, and in hiding.

But this Jewish tragedy, unprecedented in human history, did not stem the flow of antisemitic demagogic rhetoric emanating from the political battleground of the different groups and factions of the Polish underground. I limit myself here to only two out of the all too numerous examples. On 27 May 1944 the organ of Stronnictwo Narodowe (the National Party), *Warszawski głos narodowy* [Warsaw national voice], included an article entitled 'Mikołajczyk on the Subject of Polish Toleration', which criticized the premier of the Polish government-in-exile, Stanisław Mikołajczyk, for making a speech which included the following statement:

Looking into the future I can assure everyone that the Government of the Polish Republic, according to its constitution and its proclamation of 24 February 1942, steadfastly stands by its pledge to respect the rights and freedom of all loyal citizens of the Republic, regardless of any differences based on nationality, religion, or race.

The periodicals' response to this declaration was as follows:

Mr Mikołajczyk only forgot to add that this toleration towards Jews, dissidents, and Germans has cost the Polish people an entire sea of blood spilt in defending itself, as well as the impoverishment of large sections of society, and that, as a rule—or at least more often than not—these different minorities and religious groups simply betrayed the Polish cause or consciously acted as its internal enemies.

Another of the National Party's publications, *Narodowa agencja prasowa* [National press agency], wrote in its edition of 28 June 1944:

We appeal to all who love their free and happy homeland and who do not wish to become Jewish slaves to join against the Jewish offensive which is supported by the Left in the guise of Freemasonry, the Polish Socialist Party, and the handful of people who at the moment are in charge of the Peasants' Party. One principle alone must reign: that only the Polish nation can be masters in Poland.

Antisemitic rhetoric was also used during the early postwar years. It was used by certain political groups opposed to the new regime in Poland and by various factions attempting to increase their political influence in the ruling party. During 1945–6 this led to the murder of several hundred politically uncommitted Jews, the culminating-point being the pogrom in Kielce on 4 July 1946, when forty-two people were murdered. As a result of these events the majority of Jews left Poland, both those who had survived German occupation in the camps or by hiding and those who had survived the war in the Soviet Union. The year 1956 marked the beginning of the widespread use of antisemitic demagoguery as a weapon in the political struggles occurring within the ruling Communist Party, and this phase reached its culmination during 1967-8, when an official antisemitic campaign was set in motion by the government.

It only remains to consider to what extent the antisemitism adopted by the Communists had its foundations in the antisemitic traditions of nationalist tendencies. The bankrupt regime was attempting to maintain its influence on society, and resorted to nationalist demagoguery. The authors of this campaign did not give much thought to the moral implications of these manoeuvres against the background of Jewish extermination.

In underlining negative aspects of the attitudes of certain elements within the Polish underground toward Jews during the period of their annihilation—a matter which has been largely passed over in silence in Poland—and in shedding light on the practice of antisemitic demagoguery for the purpose of achieving certain illusory political goals, I do not deny the existence of positive phenomena, especially the help given to Jews by Poles who risked their lives to do so. But it seems to me that such cases—e.g. the activities of Żegota (the Council for Aid to Jews) or the help given to the insurgents of the Warsaw ghetto—have had a deceptively wide coverage in Polish literature. The important thing is to be able to locate and establish the actual framework of these positive actions. After all, the help given to Jews was neither as universal nor conceived on as wide a scale as Polish historiography would have us believe. Our aim is to be honest and courageous in approaching the negative phenomena by removing the whitewash from the historical writing, and thus to try and determine the true scale of the help which was given to Jews during the Holocaust.

The Jewish Underground and the Polish Underground

TERESA PREKEROWA

POLISH-JEWISH relations tend to be treated in a one-sided way, from the standpoint of Poles and their attitude towards the Jews, so that the converse relationship—the attitude of the Jews towards the Poles—has been neglected. This one-sided approach to the question was introduced into the historical literature by Emanuel Ringelblum when in 1944, in his unfinished 'Polish–Jewish Relations', he concerned himself exclusively with the extent of friendship or hostility shown by the Poles.[1] No one was prepared to depart from this precedent, and this is how the problem has continued to be approached in the intervening fifty years, both in Jewish and in Polish literature.

In Poland various other factors influenced the adherence to this traditional approach: the main ones were the language barrier, which made it impossible for many historians to take advantage of relevant sources, and censorship, an even more insurmountable obstacle. There were certainly other causes besides. The fact that Jewish historiography has kept silent on the subject is something for Jewish historians to explain.

In 'The Polish Underground and the Extermination of the Jews', included in the present volume, Shmuel Krakowski is perfectly justified in his decision not to concentrate on the question of Jewish attitudes. The main subject of his article is the antisemitism which found expression in the Polish underground press and equally in the dearth of concrete help from the Home Army and the People's Guard for the ghetto fighters and fugitives. Krakowski has assembled in telling fashion a number of quotations from articles published between 1942 and 1944. These texts are known to Polish historians involved in research into the period of German occupation, and many (if not all) have already been published, primarily in monographs and professional journals, though never in such a concentrated form. It is precisely this concentration which intensifies their expressive power.

---

[1] See Emanuel Ringelblum, *Polish–Jewish Relations during the Second World War* [translation of *Stosunki polsko-żydowskie w czasie drugiej wojny światowej*], ed. J. Kermish and Sh. Krakowski (Jerusalem, 1972; repr. Evanston, Ill., 1992).

Krakowski does mention, albeit briefly, the problem of Jewish involvement in Polish affairs. He approaches it in the following way. Originally, the sole reason for the positive sentiments of many Jews towards the Red Army which had invaded eastern Poland was their fear of Nazi Germany. Later, in Nazi-occupied Poland, contacts with the Polish radical Left amounted to a tactical move, occasioned by the need to find assistance in view of the lack of help from the Home Army. The Jewish underground which was active in the Vilna and Byelorussian regions subordinated itself to the Soviet powers for the same reasons. These contentions seem to me so incompatible with the sources and documentation known to me that I feel obliged to write a few remarks by way of dissent.

Can the behaviour of the Jews at the beginning of the Soviet occupation really be fully explained by their fear of the Germans? Krakowski cites a number of German anti-Jewish decrees which testify to the terror from which the Red Army liberated the Jewish population and which makes their joy and gratitude readily comprehensible. However, on 17 September 1939 the Jews could not have predicted that the Germans were going to announce these decrees. Compulsory marks of identification were introduced in September, but only in Kraków: the general decree concerning them was announced by Governor Frank only on 23 November. The banning of Jews from travel by train was introduced from January 1940 onwards. The confiscation of Jewish (and indeed Polish) property in September applied only to refugees from the territories which were incorporated into the Reich; this was implemented more widely in the course of the following months in the General Gouvernement region. In the middle of September no one could foresee the tragic fate that awaited the Jews. People knew about the *Reichskristallnacht* of November 1938 and about the restriction of Jewish rights in Germany, but these events aroused anxiety rather than panic. That is why many Jews who had escaped eastwards from western Poland before the German advance became disillusioned with the Soviet regime and tried before long to return to the territories of the General Gouvernement.

It appears, then, that it was not fear of the Germans which was the chief reason for the joyous welcome extended to the invading Red Army. The more plausible view, which is now widely accepted, is that an important factor was the level of anti-Polish feelings, the result of the bad relations which had existed during the preceding period, especially the 1930s, which witnessed the negative Jewish policies of the leaders of the Second Republic, antisemitic declarations by the various political parties, and the excesses of the nationalistic thugs. Grudges and resentments produced a situation where among certain sections of the Jewish community the absence of any sense of solidarity with the Polish nation and identification with the Polish state was being demonstratively expressed.

It must also be emphasized that in many diaries, particularly those of young people, there are frequent expressions of spontaneous joy. This mood has no rational basis. 'Today is the happiest day of my life! We showered the approaching tanks with flowers,' wrote one young girl from Stanisławów in her diary.²

These factors induced the Jews, who knew the local scene well and were often in open conflict with non-Jewish segments of the population, to co-operate with the new administration and its apparatus of repression. The Soviets were not disappointed. Many Jews searched out and helped to arrest Polish officers, top pre-war officials, and representatives of the intellectual élite, which was hostile to the USSR. Aleksander Smolar summarizes the situation correctly:

> In no other European country during the war did such a dramatic clash occur between Jewish interests and attitudes and those of the population among which they lived as during the Soviet occupation of 1939–41. In other countries the Jews may have had conflicts of interest with certain sections of the society they lived in (e.g. collaborators), but these took place under conditions of solidarity and partnership with the rest of society. By contrast, in eastern Poland Jews themselves were perceived as collaborators. This should be remembered when one attempts to have an honest discussion about mutual relations.³

The fact that at the same time Jewish cultural, religious, and social institutions—just like the Polish ones—were being liquidated, and that Jews were also part of the mass deportations of the population of eastern Poland, did not really alter this situation.

But was it solely Jewish behaviour in eastern Poland which was responsible for fixing the stereotype of the Jew-Communist to such an extent that it produced a high level of distrust within the London camp? Could it be that Jewish co-operation with the Communist faction of the Polish underground and the Soviet partisans amounted to nothing more than a tactical move?

It should be noted that in the underground political struggle which was in progress throughout the years of occupation in Poland Communists were opposed not merely for their vision of the future structure of the Polish state. The London government-in-exile was totally indifferent to any social or economic views proclaimed by the Polska Partia Robotnicza (Polish Workers' Party), but the party's links with the USSR and the fact that 'they were Moscow's flunkies' evoked animosity or even hostility among the exiled leaders. The only pro-Soviet attitude in the Polish underground was to be found among the Communists. This was not quite the case in the Jewish underground—a fact which played an important role.

Many students of the history of the Second World War have used the Polish underground press as a primary source, while hardly anyone has taken advantage of its Jewish counterpart. Yet the answers to many of the questions raised here are to be found precisely in these periodicals. Unfortunately, the number of surviving copies is not very great. The vast majority of the titles (about 90 per

---

² Archiwum Żydowskiego Instytutu Historycznego, 302/267.
³ Aleksander Smolar, 'Tabu i niewinność', *Aneks*, 41–2 (1986), 89–133, at 98.

cent) appeared in the Warsaw ghetto and were published largely by the Bund (fourteen publications) and by Po'alei Tsion Left and Hashomer Hatsa'ir, a youth organization of similar political orientation (altogether ten publications). These organizations had the largest influence on the Jewish community, and not only in Warsaw.

The Bund's leaders accepted that Poland was the homeland of Polish Jews, and their attitude to the war and occupation was similar to that of the London underground. Even when they criticized various factions of this organization, they saw the need for co-operation and kept up contacts with the Socialist groups (the right-wing Polska Partia Socjalistyczna—Wolność, Równość, Niepodległość (Polish Socialist Party—Freedom, Equality, and Independence), and the left-wing Polskie Socjaliści (Polish Socialists).

However, the Zionists, and particularly the Zionist youth, had quite a different approach to all these matters. Their main goal was the creation of their own independent state in Palestine. This primary objective shaped their entire worldview. During the early period of the occupation, in attempting to analyse the meaning of the continuing war in many of their publications, left-wing Zionist organizations described it as a struggle between two capitalisms: the hungry one (German) and the satiated one (Western, especially English).[4]

Neged hazerem, a newspaper published by Hashomer Hatsa'ir and edited by, *inter alios*, Mordechai Anielewicz, expressed the opinion that 'in this war neither side is more or less guilty', because 'the responsibility for declaring the war belongs to *all* imperialist powers, regardless of which one of them made the first move in the war'.[5] The only just state which had a care for the interests of the Jewish working class was thought to be the USSR. In addition, according to Hashomer Hatsa'ir, 'the Soviet–German pact of August 1939 was a wise and justified move'.[6] It allowed the Soviet Union to realize its fundamental goals, which were 'strict neutrality and complete preparation for a struggle with the entire capitalist world, weakened by the war and its consequences'.[7] The Zionists had no doubts about the imminence of such a struggle: 'The moment is near, when the Red Army with the help of the broad masses of workers and peasants will begin its historic march . . . Jewish working masses consider this prospect to be their sole realistic hope for national and social liberation.'[8]

In the light of such an appraisal of the Second World War, there was no room for any clear evaluation of the situation in which Poland found itself, and so the Zionist press passed over this subject in silence. Even events on the 'Aryan' side were given only passing mention. The Vilna, Podole, and Wołyń regions were

---

[4] The attitude of Zionist parties toward England was decidedly negative because of the mandate it held in Palestine.

[5] *Neged hazerem*, 2 (Feb. 1941), 28 (emphasis original).

[6] Ibid. 6 (July 1941), 22.   [7] Ibid. 4 (May 1941), 32.

[8] *Proletarisher gedank* [published by Po'alei Tsion Left], 2 (Apr. 1941).

described as the 'Soviet lands', and even the term 'former Polish territory' was sometimes used.

In June 1941 this situation changed fundamentally. According to Zionist activists, at that time the Jewish people finally discovered where their essential self-interest in this war actually lay. 'Among the Jews who, almost to a man, counted on a Soviet victory, the outbreak of war was greeted with great hopes,' wrote Governor Ludwig Fischer. 'Many Jews began to don red ties ostentatiously in order to manifest their sympathies for the Soviet Union.'[9] This time their joy was quite understandable.

Despite early Soviet failures, the Zionists did not lose faith in the power of their great ally. The greatest confidence and youthful enthusiasm were expressed by Hashomer Hatsa'ir's publication *Jutrznia* [Dawn]:

On the ruins of Fascist barbarism the liberated people of Europe, under the direction of the Soviet Union, will found a truly free European federation—a federation of free nations within the framework of the Socialist Union of Soviets.[10] A victory for England or for the United States would result in bourgeois democracy in Europe . . . As long as capitalism continues to exist, the Jewish tragedy cannot end . . . and it is only the Soviet Union which is capable of bringing about the destruction of capitalism. This is the direction, the only direction, on which the gaze of all those Jewish masses locked up in the ghettos should be fixed.[11]

Under the banner of victory for the Union of Soviets and a full liberation in Soviet Palestine, Jewish masses will join the battle for a better and more radiant future.[12]

In a lengthy article entitled 'Brothers in Arms' the editors of *Jutrznia* turned their attention to the Poles for the first time. Reminding them of all the harm which the people in the ghettos had suffered at the hands of informers, Polish police, and rich smugglers who were preying on the isolated and interned Jewish population, they declared that 'at the present time the Jewish and Polish nations are united by the most essential common objective . . . [Jews] must concentrate their hopes on a Soviet victory and on a settlement of the Jewish masses in Soviet Palestine', and that only 'a Soviet victory and a free Soviet Poland within the framework of the Soviet Union can ensure the realization of Polish goals'.[13]

The term 'Soviet Palestine' recurs like a refrain in nearly all the editions of *Jutrznia*. Two years later Emanuel Ringelblum described this group of young Zionists in the following way:

Hashomer took a pro-Soviet stance, and it believed in the victory of the Soviet Union and its heroic army. The only party among the Jewish community which had identical political convictions was the left-wing Po'alei Tsion. Following this political line, Hashomer activists, together with some others, were organizing partisan groups and making close

---

[9] *Raporty Ludwiga Fischera, gubernatora dystryktu warszawskiego 1939–44* (Warsaw, 1987), 339.
[10] *Jutrznia* (14 Feb. 1942), 5.   [11] Ibid. (21 Feb. 1942), 1.
[12] Ibid. (21 Mar. 1942), 1.   [13] Ibid. (8 Mar. 1942), 1.

contacts with the Polish Workers' Party. They were generally ready to do anything to bring about a victory for the Soviet Union and its heroic Red Army.[14]

Communist influence in the Warsaw ghetto was also considerable. Before the Polish Workers' Party, groups such as Stowarzyszenie Przyjaciół ZSRR (Society of Friendship for the USSR) and organizations called Sierp i Młot (Hammer and Sickle), Robotniczo-Chłopska Organizacja Bojowa (Workers' and Peasants' Fighting Squad), and others were active there. At the beginning of March 1942 all of these were incorporated in the local district committee of the Polish Workers' Party. Only a few months later the ghetto district had acquired nearly 500 members for this party, while in the middle of 1942 it had only 400 members in the entire city of Warsaw.[15]

The strongest and most resilient Communist Party grouping was organized in the Łódź ghetto. It was called the Antyfaszystowska Organizacja (Anti-Fascist Organization) and, with a membership of 1,000–1,500, it represented the largest political party in this tightly sealed ghetto.[16] Many places had smaller active Communist groups. In general, they maintained contacts with pertinent Polish groups, including (from 1942) the Polish Workers' Party. In a number of cities Jews belonged to Polish Workers' Party cells on the Polish side.

Thus, one can find both Communists and members of other pro-Soviet groups in all ghettos among the organizers of armed resistance and later among its participants, frequently at a managerial level. Following an initiative from some Jewish Communists, the first combat squad, called the Blok Antyfaszystowski (Anti-Fascist Bloc), was organized in Warsaw in 1942. It remained active for a short time only, but it managed to blaze a trail for the Żydowska Organizacja Bojowa (ŻOB: Jewish Fighting Organization) established on 28 July of the same year by three youth organizations—Hashomer Hatsa'ir, Dror, and Akiva—while the great deportation of the population of the Warsaw ghetto was in progress. When in December 1942 the Jewish underground organizational structure of the ŻOB was established, it actually comprised twenty-two groups, four of which were created by Hashomer Hatsa'ir, four by the Communists, and one by Po'alei Tsion Left. Representatives of all these organizations, along with representatives of the Bund, Dror, and the Socialist Zionists, made up the command of the ŻOB.

The groups involved in armed resistance in other ghettos were similarly structured. In Białystok the commander was Mordechai Tennenbaum-Tamaroff

---

[14] Emanuel Ringelblum, *Kronika getta warszawskiego, wrzesień 1939–styczeń 1943* (Warsaw, 1983), 498.
[15] R. Nazarewicz, 'PPR wobec powstania w getcie', in *Za wolność i lud* (3 Feb. 1978); B. Hillebrandt and J. Jakubowski, *Warszawska Organizacja PPR 1942–1948* (Warsaw, 1978), 74.
[16] For reminiscences of witnesses and articles about the Łódź ghetto see S. Krakowski, 'Organizacja Antyfaszystowska . . . w getcie łódzkim' (2 parts), *Biuletyn Żydowskiego Instytutu Historycznego*, 52 (1964), 54 (1965).

(Dror) and his deputy was the Communist Daniel Moszkowicz. Young Communists and members of Hashomer Hatsa'ir made up a large part of the so-called Bloc A, and they formed part of the first groups of fighters who left the ghetto and went into the forest to begin their armed struggle there.

The first and highly respected commander of the Faraynikte Partizaner Organisatsye (FPO: United Partisan Organization) in Vilna was Itzik Wittenberg, a Communist activist from pre-war days. After his death in a Gestapo prison, which was most likely suicide, the command was taken over by Abba Kovner, a member of Hashomer Hatsa'ir.

Among the leadership of the Kraków combat organization, whose commander was Heszek Bauminger from Hashomer Hatsa'ir, any contacts with non-Jews, including those with the Polish Workers' Party, were made by the Communist Gela Mize, formerly a member of the Party under Soviet occupation in Lwów. Co-operation between Jewish fighters and the Polish Workers' Party and People's Guard was generally successful, though not without occasional tensions. The Polish Workers' Party supplied them with revolvers and hand-grenades, and provided the combatants with shelter in the homes of their members on the Aryan side of the city. Some acts of sabotage and assassination outside the ghetto were carried out in collaboration with members of the Polish Workers' Party. Within the People's Guard there were mixed groups which included members of the Polish Workers' Party and Hashomer Hatsa'ir.[17]

Thus, there was no shortage either of Communists or of members of other pro-Soviet parties within the leadership of the Jewish resistance. But this does not give validity to the stereotyped perception according to which every Jew was a Communist. First of all, the Jewish underground included only a very small section of the Jewish population—no more than 1 per cent even in large centres—and the combat organizations comprised only a fraction of that number. (Similarly, the Polish underground, which had far greater opportunities and was developed on a much larger scale, included only a small percentage of the population.) In addition, the underground parties, both Jewish and Polish, included the most politicized activists, who held the most clear-cut and extreme views: their attitude was not representative of the community as a whole, whose main concern was focused on daily concerns—how to survive and where to get the money to buy food for their starving families.

In any case, the underground itself cannot be described in blanket terms. Even within the Zionist bloc there were less radical parties, such as the Socialist Zionists, as well as youth groups like Dror and Akiva and far-right Zionist Revisionists with their youth organization Betar, creators of Żydowski Związek Wojskowy (the Jewish Army Union). Outside of this bloc, the Bund exercised substantial and, in some districts, preponderant influence.

[17] See e.g. A. L. Bauminger, *The Fighter in the Kraków Ghetto* (Jerusalem, 1986); A. Bieberstein, *Zagłada Żydów w Krakowie* (Kraków, 1985).

Nevertheless, although they did not express the views of the entire Jewish underground, parties sympathetic to the Soviet Union did play a major, if not a leading, role. Their natural ally was the Polish Workers' Party, not the London camp; this is the reason for the strong links with the former, mentioned above. The basis for this relationship was founded not just in ideological considerations, but also in the enjoyment of mutual benefits. On the one hand, Jews were able to find support outside the ghetto (as a rule, there was no antisemitism among members of the Polish Workers' Party), and were supplied with weapons or given help in obtaining them elsewhere. On the other, the Polish Workers' Party and the People's Guard, which had limited support among the Polish population, were able to extend their influence, increase their numbers, and secure wider co-operation from the intelligentsia: Jews in fact commanded many divisions of the People's Guard. Their common goal was to aid the Soviet Army by acts of sabotage behind the German front. Participation in the armed actions of the People's Guard gave the Jews a chance to wreak revenge on the Germans for the dire poverty of the ghettos and the horrors of the extermination camps.

However, the People's Guard had very few weapons at its disposal and was not able to give many away, something which soon led to disillusionment among the Jewish organizations; this was one of the reasons for the disintegration of the Anti-Fascist Bloc in Warsaw. Thus, when in the summer of 1942 the Jewish Fighting Organization was being formed, it was decided to make contact with the central organization of the London underground—i.e. with representatives of the government-in-exile and the Home Army—while at the same time maintaining co-operation with the various cells of the Polish Workers' Party, often at the top levels of command; this was now in effect a conspiracy within a conspiracy.

The establishment of such contacts and realization of the anticipated benefits were slow to take place. The Home Army's attitude to the Jewish underground was undoubtedly characterized by distrust. In the eyes of its commanders, the Jewish pro-Soviet left-wing groups prejudiced the whole armed underground in the ghettos. Their convictions seemed all the more justified since they were confirmed by reports of Jewish behaviour in the territories occupied by the Soviet Union in 1939–41; they were also bolstered by the all too common antisemitic attitudes found within the underground army.

The attitude to individual Jews was better, especially when they were introduced to the Home Army by persons of trust. Hundreds of Jews were admitted to various divisions, some of them passing for Aryans. In Warsaw both Jews and persons of Jewish background who considered themselves to be Poles worked in the chief headquarters of the Home Army and even fought in such élite corps as Kedyw Collegium A,[18] without attempting to hide their identity, and enjoyed friendly relations with their Polish colleagues. On the other hand, during the

---

[18] 'Kedyw' was the code-name of a special division of the Home Army, the best in equipment and training, which took orders directly from the C-in-C. 'Collegium A' was one section of Kedyw.

Warsaw uprising of 1944 Jewish volunteers were obliged to fight in the People's Army since their attempts to join the ranks of the Home Army were completely blocked.

Some of the negotiations over requests for weapons between the local Jewish groups and the leadership of the Home Army in Vilna and Białystok testify to the fact that mutual contacts proved very complicated in the provinces as well. In response to one such request the leadership of the Vilna District Home Army addressed the following preliminary questions to the FPO: (1) Is the FPO a Communist organization? (2) Whom will they support should the Russians return and a Polish–Soviet armed conflict over Vilna break out? These questions indicate a great degree of mistrust. The conviction that Vilna was a Polish city was a sign of patriotism not only within the Home Army, but among the mass of ordinary people. The FPO should have understood this, but in fact it maintained its stand and replied that it was perfectly true that it had some Communist members, though they were by no means a dominant force within its ranks; and as to the question concerning Vilna, this was not a matter which required an immediate decision and the FPO would approach it in due course.[19] As might have been expected, after such a response the request for weapons was turned down.

The Home Army underground in Białystok had similar doubts. A copy of Tennenbaum-Tamaroff's letter of July 1943 to the Kierownictwo Walki Cywilnej (Directorate of Civil Combat) in this district has survived.[20] In it he mentions that in response to his request for weapons, in his capacity as the chairman of the Żydowski Komitet Narodowy (Jewish National Committee), he had received

a reply whose content can be summarized more or less as follows: 'We are very sorry, but we ourselves have a very limited amount of weapons at our disposal and there are many takers. We know that your attitude to Germans is the same as ours, but, unfortunately there still remains the question of the Soviets.'

I would attempt to prove to you if I had time, and if the circumstances were different, that every single organization represented in the Jewish National Committee has without exception been dismantled and persecuted in the Soviet Union; their leaders have been sent to Siberia, and former members have not exactly been trusted by the authorities.

Thus, Tennenbaun-Tamaroff did not present his organization's attitude towards the USSR in a definite manner. The equivocation was all the more striking as the enthusiastic paragraphs quoted above from *Jutrznia* (p. 152) were published in the spring of 1942, nearly a year after the last persecutions and exiles to Siberia. At that time the Zionist Left described these actions by the authorities as 'slip-ups' and 'errors' on the part of the occupying administration. They did protest against them, but were not prevented by them from continuing to believe

---

[19] Abba Kovner's account appears in Yitzhak Arad, *Ghetto in Flames* (Jerusalem, 1980).

[20] Yad Vashem Archive M/11/10. Tennenbaum-Tamaroff is using an incorrect term. By summer 1943 the Kierownictwo Walki Cywilnej had become a part of the Home Army, and its name was changed to Kierownictwo Walki Podziemnej (Directorate of Underground Combat).

in the good will of the Soviet Union and its future role in the creation of a 'Soviet Palestine'.

In spite of Dr Krakowski's arguments, then, the Home Army had good reason to think that a part of the Jewish resistance movement was linked with the enemy Communist camp, and this is a view, as has already been mentioned, that was widely held. Nevertheless, during the period of the extermination of the population of the ghettos and attempts by the Jewish resistance movement at armed self-defence, Sikorski gave instructions to render assistance to the Jews, and in the summer of 1943 Grot-Rowecki issued an order to provide help at any place where 'an armed struggle between Jews and Germans might erupt'.[21] However, it appears that in this respect the Białystok and Vilna regional commands of the Home Army conducted an independent policy of their own. Their decisions were frequently based only on the political orientation of the Jewish fighting organizations, without taking into account the dramatic situation in which the young fighters found themselves. In their struggle the Jews had the right to assistance and support from the underground government. Tennenbaum-Tamaroff was perfectly justified in writing the following:

A willing Pole can serve his Country in another way: he can wait for the coming of the day of the order from the government of the Republic. We cannot wait. Every day brings with it the possibility of being taken to the place of execution. *We have to act immediately.*

Dear Sirs! This is not the time for making political 'overtures'. We are appealing to you, the representatives of Free Poland and citizens of the Republic. Two hundred hand-grenades and several score revolvers will not bring closer the day of your rebirth. But they may decide when the last day of the second-biggest ghetto in Poland is to be. Another possibility is to involve our people in active combat in this area.

We await your decision.[22]

But they waited in vain. Nowhere in Poland outside of Warsaw did the Home Army undertake to support acts of resistance by the people in the ghettos, whether on a small or on a larger scale. Sometimes it really was not in a position to do so, since it could not reach them. Sometimes, however, access was possible, but the Home Army did not make use of it.

The history of Polish–Jewish relations (these double-sided ones) certainly lacks quite a few pages, among which are perhaps the most precious ones of all, the day-by-day chronicle of events during 1939–45. This is all the more reason for us to read what we do have very carefully, omitting nothing.

[21] Cf. the telegram from 'Lawina' (code-name of Tadeusz Bór-Komorowski) to the Polish government-in-exile, no. 382 in Studium Polski Podziemnej (Archives of the Polish Underground), London.

[22] Letter to the leadership of Civil Combat, Yad Vashem Archive M/11/10 (emphasis original).

The Pogrom in Kielce on 4 July 1946

STANISŁAW MEDUCKI

ON 4 July 1946 there was a pogrom against the Jews in Kielce. This tragedy was especially poignant in that those who were murdered had just survived the Holocaust, and that there had been a long history of relatively good relations between the Polish and Jewish populations in the city.

The history of Jewish settlement in Kielce begins relatively late: they arrived only after the Tsar's emancipation decree of 24 June–5 July 1862, which removed the earlier prohibitions on Jews settling there. Because Kielce had been a bishop's seat, Jews had been forbidden to reside there on a permanent basis. They could, however, engage in activities on market days and during fairs. Moreover, the restrictions against settlement were not strictly enforced: in 1841 six Jewish families, amounting to thirty-two individuals, were recorded among the inhabitants.[1]

The decree removing restrictions did not immediately alter ingrained habits: at first local Jews preferred to continue to live in nearby Chęciny and commute to Kielce. The Jewish influx began only after 1866, and twenty years later Jews constituted 28 per cent of the city's inhabitants. One visible sign of Jewish economic and social advancement was the synagogue erected in 1902.[2]

With the defeat of those favouring a partitioned Poland and the return of Polish independence, Jews constituted a third of the population of Kielce. Data from the 1921 general census show that out of the city's 41,346 inhabitants, 15,530 were Jews (37.6 per cent). At the time of the next census in 1931 Jews made up 31.05 per cent of the population. Their traditional occupations were crafts, especially leather and clothing, and trade. There was significant variety in the material status of Jews: a few were owners of large industrial or trade enterprises, while some made their living from occasional jobs, independent contracting, or as small shopkeepers or owners of stalls. In 1938 six of the twelve owners

---

[1] K. Urbański, 'Stosunek bogatego mieszczaństwa do prób osadnictwa żydowskiego w Kielcach 1833–1863', *Biuletyn Żydowskiego Instytutu Historycznego w Polsce*, 1–2 (1985), 11. At that time the population of Kielce was approximately 4,500.

[2] J. Pazdur, *Dzieje Kielc 1864–1939* (Wrocław, 1971), 49.

of factories with the largest turnover and profit were Jews; but most firms were small, with little capital and low profits. Small traders were especially well represented: in 1926 as many as 2,100 permanent places of trade existed in Kielce, (60 per cent in Jewish ownership). There were fifty-five restaurants and eating-houses, and one greengrocer for every fifty-two inhabitants.[3] Such scattered trade had a weak economic base and provided the majority of tradespeople with only a poor livelihood.[4]

The same was true for the crafts. Jewish craftsmen were poor, and between 85 and 90 per cent worked alone, employing no journeymen, for in spite of low prices there was little demand for their products. In 1930 an independent shoemaker-contractor who worked sixteen hours a day earned up to 20 zloty a week, enough for a hand-to-mouth existence; moreover, contractors were not entitled to any form of social security.[5] The city and surrounding area were very poor and competition was fierce, with tradesmen vying for every customer. It seems that Jewish tradesmen and craftsmen were able to lower their production costs more than Poles could, and were willing to accept smaller profits; they also served their clients more politely. This gave rise to antisemitic sentiment among the Poles, who employed an old slogan from before the First World War: *Swój do swego i po swoje* ('A countryman goes to a fellow countryman to buy what's made in the country').

There were also Jews in the professional classes, including people who worked in offices or schools. There were physicians, lawyers, engineers, and teachers, many of them well respected in Kielce. Considering the size of the city, the number of Jewish professionals and office workers was substantial—about 250 people.

During the Second Republic there was noticeable progress in the assimilation of the Jews, but most remained within their national culture, which was very different from its Polish counterpart, in both form and content. There survives much evidence of Jewish participation in Polish culture,[6] yet despite some interest among Jews in their neighbours' customs, and many professional contacts between Poles and Jews, socialization between the two communities was rare.[7]

Jews actively participated in the political life of the city. They had many social, educational, cultural, sports, and professional institutions, and there was also a Jewish press. Most of these initiatives, however, were ephemeral, which was also true of similar activities undertaken by Poles. There was a mosaic of Jewish

[3] Ibid. 256.
[4] A. Massalski and S. Meducki, *Kielce w latach okupacji hitlerowskiej 1939–1945* (Wrocław, 1986), 99, 100.
[5] K. Urbański, *Społeczność żydowska w Kielcach* (Kielce, 1989), 22.
[6] M. Meducka, 'Żydowskie instytucje kulturalne w Kielcach 1918–1939', *Biuletyn Żydowskiego Instytutu Historycznego w Polsce*, 1–2 (1984), 63.
[7] A. Birnhak, 'Koniec pięknej epoki', *Przemiany*, 11 (1987), 12.

parties and political groups from the left to the extreme right. They organized demonstrations and meetings, and compiled their own lists for local and parliamentary elections. Sometimes these groups formed alliances during an election or if there was a need to obtain a particular decision in the city council, and sometimes they fought fiercely against one another.

Relations between the Polish and Jewish populations were generally good. Some friction occurred, but any manifestation of active antisemitic conduct was immediately checked by the authorities. According to a directive of 1931, the police were instructed that 'all anti-Jewish incidents must be dealt with most resolutely'.[8] In Kielce this order was enforced. In March 1938 six people accused of throwing foul rags into shops owned by Jews were tried. A year and a half later the police arrested four secondary-school students on a similar charge. Despite several attempts, the antisemitic organization Liga Zielonej Wstążki (League of the Green Riband) did not succeed in establishing a group there. Cases of harassment of Jews were becoming more sporadic, and when they did occur they were condemned by a growing number of Poles. On 12 August 1937 a picket organized by a group of nationalistic youths in front of Jewish shops was dispersed; the event was described in *Naye Folkstsaytung*, a Jewish newspaper.[9] Citizens of Kielce devoted much attention to the actions of the German Reich's government against the Jews. In 1938, when the Nazi authorities expelled Polish Jews from Germany, a group in Kielce immediately started collecting donations to help support them.

The shadow of impending war and the need to defend Polish independence aroused patriotic sentiments. These were expressed in donations to the Fundusz Obrony Narodowej (FON: Fund for National Defence) and the Liga Obrony Powietrznej i Przeciwgazowej (League of Air and Anti-gas Defence). Jews as well as Poles contributed, from small amounts donated by students to two hundred waggon-loads of lime contributed to FON by Stanisław Zagajski, the owner of the Wietrznia factory, who came from a well-known and respected Jewish family in Kielce. There were also more personal gifts: Chana and Josek Jakubowski donated their gold wedding-rings to FON. When the Kielce physicians collected 1,000 zloty to supplement the army, Jewish doctors matched the amount with a donation of their own.[10] Jews established a special committee to organize the fund-raising with the participation of people respected not just by Jews, but by all of Kielce: Dr Mojżesz Pelc, Anna Moszkowicz, Guta Kaufmann, and Sara Lichtenstein. The committee was chaired by Sara Rapoport, the rabbi's wife.[11]

Despite this generosity and the heroic struggle by the soldiers of the Polish

---

[8] Quoted from Urbański, *Społeczność*, 33.
[9] Ibid. 34.
[10] Massalski and Meducki, *Kielce w latach*, 10, 11.
[11] K. Urbański, 'Społeczeństwo żydowskie w Kielcach w latach 1862–1939', *Rocznik Muzeum Narodowego w Kielcach*, 15 (1989), 176.

army, attacks from both Germany and the Soviet Union could not be repulsed. Although many inhabitants of Kielce, including Jews, had been mobilized and took part in the defence, the war was lost. One of the defenders, a physician named Juda Flaszen with the rank of reserve captain, was captured by the Soviets and murdered in Katyń.

A small number of Jews escaped before the German army entered the city. Some of them went via Soviet labour camps to General Władysław Anders's army, or later to the troops of General Zygmunt Berling. The far-sighted ones tried to reach the West through Hungary and Romania. The rest fell foul of the discriminatory regulations of German occupational law and were later subjected to extermination. The cultural distinctness of the Jews, strengthened by their religious unity, made it easier for the Germans to isolate them in ghettos. The one in Kielce was established in April 1941. Within its borders there were about 500 houses, which could, according to official estimates, accommodate up to 15,000 people. Some 25,000 were in fact crowded into its confines,[12] comprising Jews from Kielce and the surrounding area as well as some who had been resettled from the Łódź and Poznań regions; about 1,000 Jews were transported from Vienna. From 20 to 24 August 1942 Jews were taken to the extermination camp in Treblinka. According to the estimates by Adam Rutkowski, approximately 500 people escaped from the ghetto and found shelter in the forest or with Poles.[13] The citizens of Kielce also helped many Jews.

On 15 January 1945 the German army was ousted from Kielce by the Red Army. According to data from the city registration office, on 1 June 1945 there were 53,560 inhabitants in Kielce, including only 212 Jews.[14] At the end of 1945, in the entire province of Kielce there were forty-five centres of Jewish population with approximately 2,000 people.[15] In Kielce itself Jews occupied a large building at 7 Planty Street. All Jewish social and religious institutions had their offices there, including the Wojewódzki i Miejski Komitet Żydow w Polsce (Provincial and City Committee of Jews in Poland). There was also a kitchen serving free meals that was maintained with the help of an American charity organization, and in addition some private apartments. Most of the 150/80 people living there came from outside Kielce. Jews stayed there temporarily, waiting for news of relatives, considering whether they should stay in Poland permanently or move on, and—if they had decided to stay—looking for employment. About a dozen Jewish families, some survivors of the Holocaust, lived in other parts of the city. Members of the families Kahane, Rozenkranc, and Zagajski returned to

[12] Massalski and Meducki, *Kielce w latach*, 58–67.
[13] A. Rutkowski, 'Martyrologia, walka i zagłada ludności żydowskiej w dystrykcie radomskim podczas okupacji hiterowskiej', *Biuletyn Żydowskiego Instytutu Historycznego w Polsce*, 15–16 (1955).
[14] *Dziennik Powszechny* (27 July 1945).
[15] Archiwum Żydowskiego Instytutu Historycznego w Polsce i Zespół. Centralny Komitet Żydów w Polsce, Wydział Ewidencji i Statystyki, file 569.

Kielce. Their factories were returned to them and they were allowed to resume production.[16]

Jews did not have difficulty regaining their property if it had not been destroyed by the Germans. The decree of 6 May 1945 concerning abandoned and deserted property stated that abandoned property was to be returned to the owner regardless of who currently possessed it. If the owner was dead, all members of the immediate family were entitled to inherit, including children out of wedlock, as well as brothers, sisters, and spouses. Property could be inherited even if the marriage was not legally recognized or was a common-law union. The decree stated that where there was litigation over the return of property, a hearing must be held no later than twenty-one days after submission of an appropriate request. Jews regained their property smoothly and efficiently; 99 per cent of cases were settled within the prescribed time.[17] The property in question included houses, building plots, craft workshops, and factories; usually they were claimed by heirs because the original owner had died. In most cases kinship and the right of inheritance were established through testimonies of Polish witnesses who had known the Jewish family before the war. They testified without any need for coercion and without prejudice.

Ironically, coexisting with compassion and friendship for particular families or individuals, there was hostility against the Jewish community as a whole.[18] Antisemitism emerged in many forms after the liberation. In part this may have been the result of a policy that helped create the idea that Jews had a privileged position in central institutions of the state—the security apparatus, the militia, and the army—as well as in the lower levels of state administration. Jews were identified with Stalinist authority and were for that reason unwanted.[19] Popular sympathies lay with the structures of the underground state created during the occupation by the Polish government in exile. Officers and soldiers who had returned from the Soviet Union, as well as repatriates, brought with them an

---

[16] Urbański, *Społeczność żydowska w Kielcach*, 39.

[17] K. Urbański, 'Z problematyki żydowskiej w Kieleckiem w latach 1945–1946', in F. Kiryka (ed.), *Żydzi w Małopolsce: Studia z dziejów osadnictwa i życia społecznego* (Przemyśl, 1991), 347, 348.

[18] On antisemitic feelings in the Kielce region in Feb. 1946 see 'Sprawozdanie z działalności Referatu dla Spraw Pomocy Ludności Żydowskiej przy Prezydium Rady Ministrów Rządu Tymczasowego RP', Archiwum Akt Nowych (Warsaw) [AAN] Zespoł: Ministerstwo Pracy i Opieki Społecznej, sygn. 335, 65–6. Antisemitic hostility continued even later: AAN, Zespoł. PPR, sygn. 295/vii-228, 8, 'Protokół z odprawy sekretarzy KW PPR (Kraków, Łódź, Katowice, Kielce, Dolny Śląsk)'; sygn. 295/ix-19, 19, 'Protokół z poszerzonego plenum KW PPR w Kielcach w dniu 10 września 1945 r.'

[19] On preferential treatment accorded to Jews in filling important positions see A. Sandauer (an eminent writer, literary critic, and scholar of Jewish origin), 'O sytuacji pisarza polskiego pochodzenia żydowskiego w XX wieku', *Życie literackie*, 50 (13 Dec. 1981), 5. A similar view was expressed by Edward Gierek, former first secretary of the central committee of the PZPR, in an interview with J. Rolicki (see Rolicki, *Edward Gierek, Przerwana dekada* (Warsaw, 1990), 48, 49.

aversion to the new political system, which was moulded on the Soviet model. A significant group hated Bolshevism, considering it to be a Jewish creation. This hatred stemmed from the policy of the Soviet authorities, such as exile to Siberia, slavery in work camps, hunger, and the violent suppression of any objections to the infringement of elementary human rights.

The new authority, installed with the help of the Red Army, employed against its opponents the methods acquired from its NKVD teachers, who supervised the administration through a network of 'advisers' and 'specialists'. In the security offices and the militia there were 'Soviet advisers' at each level. Many command and political positions in the Polish army were filled by Russians, including the command of Kielce's Second Infantry Division.

Organizations that opposed the Communist power and Soviet domination in Poland recorded every mistake and every instance of incompetence, inefficiency, or corruption. Such facts were immediately generalized. Jews were a frequent target in these attacks, since the nation identified them with Soviet authority.[20]

Hopes that life would improve now that the German invader was gone were not fulfilled. The economic burden was only slightly eased, which was why the relative well-being of Jews was so resented. Not only did Jews receive help from foreign institutions and Jewish organizations, they were also supported by Polish authorities. Moreover, because the majority sold their recovered property and planned to leave for Western countries, the financial position of the remaining Jews improved.[21]

This may have been why Jews were so often the victims of attacks by common thieves. The underlying cause of widespread criminality was the German brutalization of occupied Poland. The everyday threat to life and limb, the difficulties of earning a living, the pauperization of the entire society, ubiquitous cases of theft (sometimes treated as patriotic deeds)—all of this diminished sensitivity to the pain and suffering of others and weakened the constraining power of morality. From this brutalization it was only a small step to widespread lawlessness, and some people took this step.[22]

The documents of the Ministry of Public Administration recorded 117 assaults against Jews in March 1945 alone: thirty-five people were attacked in the Warsaw region, thirty-three in the Lublin region, twenty-three in the Rzeszów region, twenty-one in the Białystok region, and five in the Kielce region. In the course of

[20] On 4 Aug. 1945 an underground armed unit stormed the Kielce prison; at the same time leaflets entitled *Polacy* were distributed in the city claiming that 'The present government is not a government of national unity . . . at the helm there are Jews and servants of Russia to whom Stalin gives orders concerning all matters' (copy in a private collection).

[21] The Italian ambassador wrote about this in his diplomatic reports: E. Reale, *Raporty, Polska, 1945–1946* (Warsaw, 1991), 241.

[22] The pro-London Underground fought decisively against abuses of this type. To that end special services were established within the underground system of justice: see L. Gondek, *Polska Karząca 1939–1945* (Warsaw, 1988).

these assaults 108 people lost their lives and nine were injured. Both individuals and whole families were the object of attacks; women and children were killed as well as men. During the next five months, from April to August 1945, there were thirty more recorded assaults against Jewish families, eleven of them robberies. It was also recorded that one assault was provoked by the demand to return property lost during the occupation, two others resulted from attempts to repossess farms, and another two were efforts to regain a house. The Germans expelled the original owners of the houses and farms and gave them to Poles. In the thirty assaults eighty-one Jews lost their lives, fifteen were injured, and five were abducted.[23] As in March, the greatest number of assaults were recorded in the Białystok, Lublin, Warsaw, and Rzeszów regions. Events of a similar kind also took place around Łódź, Kielce, and Pomorze, but on a lesser scale. Official statistics cannot begin to give a full picture of the postwar reality. Many of the murders and robberies, let alone the beatings, were impossible for the weak state apparatus to deal with. Moreover, a significant part of Polish society was hostile to this apparatus.

There was also a group of people who were receptive to the antisemitic propaganda of the Germans during the occupation. The right-wing groups used antisemitic slogans in their political struggle against the left. Jew, Communist, paid lackey of Russia, Stalin's orderly: these became common synonyms. This propaganda was more widespread in the final period of the occupation, when the Germans tried to incite Poles to make common cause with them against the approaching Red Army. Such was the atmosphere that sustained the rapidly spreading rumours of Jewish ritual murder of children. Only ignorant people could have believed such nonsense. Thus it is fully understandable that most of those arrested in Kielce were poorly educated, even illiterates.

A few days before the pogrom the atmosphere in the city was tense; at the beginning of July 1946 there was an increase in antisemitic acts in the areas of Częstochowa, Radom, and Kielce. There are indications that these were instigated from outside the areas. Similarly, on 4 July rumours about the murder of Christian children appeared not only in Kielce, but also in Kalisz, where it was said that a Ukrainian had killed a boy and that Jews had drunk his blood. In Kalisz a crowd had begun to gather, but a resolute stance by respected citizens prevented a riot.[24] In Częstochowa the city authorities and the clergy also managed to react in time. Nor would the pogrom have happened in Kielce had the militia not provoked actions against Jews. It is difficult to find any other explanation for the conduct of the militia officers, who not only arrested a man whom a boy identified as his abductor, but also dispatched a patrol to search for the corpses of allegedly murdered children. While walking with the boy to the cellar where he

---

[23] AAN, Zespół. Ministerstwo Administracji Publicznej, sygn. 786, 22, 23.
[24] K. Kersten, *Polacy, Żydzi, Komunizm: Anatomia półprawd 1939–1968* (Warsaw, 1992), 122, 123.

claimed to have been held, the militia men spoke loudly about their destination and intended course of action. In this way they made rumour sound like truth, and fanned the crowd's emotions. When the militia patrol arrived there were about fifty people gathered in front of the house in question, inhabited by Jews. Although they were excited, they did not do anything; but half an hour later, when the crowd had swelled to about 150, people started gathering stones.

The commander of the security office called the army only when the house had already been surrounded by the crowd.[25] Some of the soldiers, together with the militia, entered the building and demanded that the Jews surrender their firearms, even though they had the appropriate permits for them. While these were being collected and the building was being searched, the first shot was fired. That acted as the signal for violence. In the two waves of the pogrom forty-two Jews were killed. The results of the autopsies reveal that along with injuries inflicted with blunt and heavy objects (the main cause of death), fourteen people suffered bullet wounds and six others had bayonet wounds. Among the injured, five had been shot and two had bayonet wounds, including one woman who was eight months pregnant, who had her stomach pierced by a bayonet.[26] It was only at 2 p.m., over 4½ hours after it had begun to gather, that the crowd was dispersed by shots fired into the air.

The events in Kielce were explained in a variety of ways by the authorities. Officially, they claimed that the pogrom was a plot by reactionary and anti-Communist powers, mainly Narodowe Siły Zbrojne (NSZ: National Armed Forces) and supporters of the *émigré* General Władysław Anders, who, after losing the referendum, wanted to cause civil war in Poland.[27] The political foes of the Polska Partia Robotnicza (PPR: Polish Workers' Party) thought that the event had been engineered by the head of the Wojewódzkie Urząd Bezpieczeństwa Publicznego (WUBP: Provincial Office of Public Security), who had acted with the knowledge and permission of higher authorities. The pogrom was supposed to make Polish society repugnant in the eyes of Western democracies and draw attention away from the fact that the results of the referendum had

---

[25] Those summoned were soldiers from a unit of the Corps of the Internal Army (Korpus Wojsk Wewnętrznych), 4th regiment, 2nd division of infantry, and gendarmes.

[26] Wojewódzkie Archiwum w Kielcach, Zespół: Wojskowy Sąd Rejonowy, file 520, I, 207–77, 280–336.

[27] This was the tone of the declaration of Polska Agencja Prasowa (PAP: Polish Press Agency) published on 5 June 1946 in all of the Polish press. The Warsaw speech of 6 July by Władysław Gomułka, general secretary of the PPR, given at the meeting of PPR and PPS activists, was similar. On the same day Edward Osóbka Morawski, prime minister in the Provisional Government of National Unity, gave a press interview in which he condemned 'reactionary forces' which 'because of their hatred for democracy stained themselves with the blood of innocent people'. The problem was similarly portrayed in part of the Polonia press in the United States: see A. Kwapiszewski, *Asymilacja i konflikt: Z problematyki stosunków etnicznych w Stanach Zjednoczonych Ameryki* (Kraków, 1984), 202.

been fabricated.[28] Some even believed that the first secretary of the Kielce regional committee of the PPR was one of the instigators.[29] These views arose from a suspicion that the PPR had orchestrated the events because of its poor showing at the polls and in order to discredit the Polskie Stronnictwo Ludowe (PSL: Polish Peasants' Party). If the PSL were to lose credibility, it would be deprived of Western help, and thus the PPR would gain support.[30] This would be analogous to the situation in Hungary, where anti-Jewish riots were used to strengthen the position of the Communist Party at the expense of the centrist farmers' alliance.

Increasingly, the belief that the events in Kielce were inspired by the NKVD has gained credence. It is the Soviet Union that would have benefited from the incident: if Poland were to become odious in the eyes of the West, this would weaken protests against the occupation. Moreover, a pogrom would force Jews to emigrate to Palestine, and it would be easy to infiltrate military instructors into the emigrating population: the Soviet Union had a broad political agenda linked to the establishment of the Jewish state. Mikhail Aleksandrowich Dyomin, a high-ranking Soviet intelligence officer and an expert in Jewish matters, was said to have come to Kielce to prepare the pogrom.[31] There were also claims that the Zionists needed the pogrom in order to raise the level of insecurity among Jews and thus persuade them to leave Poland for Palestine, where they would become a 'thundering majority'.[32] This would also put pressure on Great Britain to increase the Jewish immigration quota to Palestine, a move that was strongly resisted in Polish intellectual circles. In Jewish communities outside Poland, especially in France and the United States, the predominant feeling was that the pogrom was a result of extreme antisemitism within the Polish population.[33]

The authorities tried to lay part of the responsibility for the bloody events on the Kielce diocese and Bishop Czesław Kaczmarek personally. This was nonsense, because at the time of the pogrom the bishop had left Kielce owing to ill

---

[28] See Krystyna Kersten, 'Kielce—4 lipiec 1946 r.', *Tygodnik 'Solidarność'*, 36 (4 Dec. 1981), 8.

[29] A. Albert, *Najnowsza historia Polski*, iii. (Warsaw, 1986), 40; A. Blis-Lane, *Widziałem Polskę zdradzoną* (Warsaw, 1984), 133.

[30] R. Buczek, *Na przełomie dziejów: Polskie Stronnictwo Ludowe w latach 1945–1947* (Toronto, 1983), 195.

[31] W. Kalicki, 'Zabić Żyda!', *Gazeta świąteczna*, 156 (7–8 July 1990), 10.

[32] J. Orlicki, *Z dziejów stosunków polsko-żydowskich 1918–1949* (Szczecin, 1983), 256–61. The polemic is continued in J. Tomaszewski, 'Kwestia sumienia', *Polityka*, 1 (7 Jan. 1984); K. Koźniewski, 'Moim zdaniem', *Tu i teraz*, 10 (7 Mar. 1984); J. G. Kamiński, 'Nie wierzyć dziewiątce', ibid.; H. Piasecki, 'Klucz czy wytrych do historii stosunków polsko-żydowskich', *Biuletyn Żydowskiego Instytutu Historycznego w Polsce*, 3–4 (1984); M. Fuks, 'Przykre polemiki', ibid.

[33] This is the evaluation given by M. Hillel, *Le Massacre des survivants en Pologne après l'Holocauste, 1945–1947* (Paris, 1985), 256–81. See also the reviews by the Revd. D. Olszewski, 'Polski antysemityzm w czasie okupacji i po wojnie', *Znaki czasu*, 7 (1987), 85–95; J. Wijaczka, 'O kieleckim pogromie po francusku', *Przemiany*, 7 (1987).

health. Furthermore, the patrolling army and security officers did not allow priests near the scene.[34]

The arrests began that same evening. People were sometimes taken completely at random, including some who had not been present at the pogrom at all. For example, the entire Bartosiński family was arrested, including young children. All the neighbours of the Błaszcyzyks, without exception, were also arrested. It was enough to be pointed out by an officer or security agent. Confessions were obtained through torture and beatings. Requests by those arrested to interrogate specific witnesses were rejected. The Soviet advisers working for the militia and security forces were not interrogated, however, despite demands by the accused officers themselves. Moreover, there are no extant records of interrogation of soldiers or army officers. Although some were later brought to trial, they were mostly acquitted or received very light sentences, and the documents were destroyed. The trials of civilians were marred by numerous procedural faults, and failed to accord the accused their due rights. Requests to hear defence witnesses were rejected. There was also a lack of clear proof of guilt in some cases.

Speaking at the common meeting of the PPR and the Polska Partia Socjalistyczna (PPS: Polish Socialist Party), Władysław Gomułka, general secretary of the PPR and deputy prime minister, declared that those guilty of the Kielce pogrom would be tried by summary courts and given death sentences. In this way the good name of Poland would be cleared.[35]

The Kielce trial, which started on 9 July, was largely political. It followed the pattern of Soviet trials of the 1930s, and turned into a drama performed before a carefully selected audience. The press and the Polska Kronika Filmowa (State Film Chronicle) reported the proceedings. Those who appeared in the courtroom—judges, prosecutors, witnesses, and the accused—all had their parts prepared in advance. The defendants, physically and psychologically broken, admitted their guilt, and the confessions were considered to be the crowning proof. Those who did not confess were sentenced on the basis of testimony by witnesses, who were often security officers. Testimony from a fellow defendant was regarded as sufficient proof, even though in one case the co-defendant was mentally retarded and had been threatened and beaten during the investigation. In all the trials, particularly that before the Supreme Army Court, the truth was covered up. If the accused, their lawyers, or witnesses tried to tell the court about the role of the militia and the army during the pogrom, they were ruled out of order. The Polish National Council prepared a special decree to combat racism and antisemitism which included severe punishments. It was never put into effect although it was actually made ready for signature.

The conduct of the trial still leaves many questions unanswered. Why were the

---

[34] The Revd. J. Sledzianowski, *Ksiądz Czesław Kaczmarek biskup kielecki 1945–1963* (Kielce, 1991), 102–16.

[35] *Głos ludu*, 185 (7 July 1946), 5.

Russian advisers, who were officers of the NKVD working in the Polish security forces and the militia, never interrogated? Why was the case removed from the civilian prosecutor? Why did the judge residing at the Kielce trial interrupt anyone mentioning the role of the army? Why did the representatives of the central committee of the PPR, who had flown specially to Kielce, stand quietly in the crowd without reacting to the events? Why were recruits from the Security Office School not used to disperse the crowd? Why did General Franciszek Jóźwiak, commander-in-chief of the militia, not provide a clear brief concerning the tasks of the militia, instead of simply instructing the militia's regional commander to come to terms with the regional chief of the Urząd Bezpieczeństwa (UB: Office of Public Security)? Why did the soldiers receive no explanation of what they were expected to do at Planty Street? Why was no unified command sent to put down the pogrom? Why was Colonel Stanisław Kupsza, commander of the Second Infantry Division, who was a Russian in Polish uniform, never interrogated? Why was there no attempt to establish who had started the shooting? Why were Jews disarmed even though they had legitimate firearms permits? Why did the militia contingent which had been sent to conduct a search tell everyone on their way about the kidnapping of a child by Jews? Finally, if it was known that the boy had been lying, why was Kalman Singer, the man accused by the boy, arrested, and why was the real situation not explained to the people who had gathered? Who gave the signal to the workers to leave the Ludwików ironworks in order to 'wreak vengeance' on the Jews? Why were none of the workers put on trial despite their active participation in the pogrom? Why did the silence of the security guards, the army, and the militia during the pogrom help them in their future careers?[36] The questions are many, and they will remain unanswered until the operational documents of the UB, the militia, the military intelligence, and perhaps even the Soviet KGB are opened.

[36] Władysław Sobczyński, after being acquitted by the Wojskowy Sąd Rejonowy (Regional Military Court) in Warsaw (16 Dec. 1946), was promoted to deputy chief and then to chief of the Informacja (Counterintelligence) of the Korpus Bezpieczeństwa Wewnętrznego (Corps of Internal Security). Then he held the position of director of the Biuro Paszportów Zagranicznych (Passport Office). He was a senior councillor in the Department Kadr Ministerstwa Obrony Narodowej (Department of Cadres in the Defence Ministry), and finally a military attaché in Bulgaria.

Kazimierz Gwiazdowicz, who was also acquitted, was sent to a Party school to complete his education. Later he worked as director of the Agricultural Programme in the Polish radio service. In 1964 he became the Polish representative to the UN International Commission in Laos; he died while taking a swim in the River Mekong.

Major Kazimierz Konieczny, deputy commander of the 2nd Warsaw Infantry Division for Political Affairs, was transferred to an equivalent position in the prestigious 1st Infantry Division, then he worked in the Museum of the Polish Army in Warsaw, first as deputy director and finally as director.

Captain Bronisław Bednarz was soon promoted to the rank of brigadier general. He was the youngest general in postwar Poland.

The first secretary of the PPR regional committee, Józef Kalinowski (Romuald Iwanicki) was transferred to an equivalent position in Rzeszów and then to Lublin. In the period 1953–67 he was the secretary of the Front Jedności Narodu (Front of the Unity of the Nation).

The trial of the twelve inhabitants of Kielce before the Supreme Military Court was a farce. The sentence was decided outside the courtroom and the execution squad had arrived in Kielce even before it had been proclaimed. For many years a fog of secrecy surrounded events in Kielce; all information on the subject was withheld. The net of prohibitions gradually broke, articles appeared in the press, books were published, and a film was made.

The pogrom created hostility towards the Poles in the Jewish communities and Western democracies. It was especially bad for the citizens of Kielce. It erased all remembrance of the long-standing warmth of Polish–Jewish relations and of help given to Jews by Poles during the Nazi occupation. In some sense it also undermined the organized actions of the underground in Poland to rescue Jews. For too long has the Kielce pogrom been a stone on the grave of Polish–Jewish relations; it is time to move it aside by an examination of all the documents.

Only the regional commander of the militia, Wiktor Kuźnicki (Paweł Szkleniarz), was sentenced to one year in prison, primarily because of his manifest reserve towards the UB and the Russians. He died shortly after his early release from prison.

Antisemitism in Poland in 1956

PAWEŁ MACHCEWICZ

ANTISEMITISM was one of the problems that surfaced in Poland in 1956, along with the crisis of authority and the Stalinist system. Many link the emergence of this anti-Jewish sentiment to the struggle within the Polska Zjednoczona Partia Robotnicza (PZPR: Polish United Workers' Party), i.e. the conflict between the more hard-line 'Natolin' and more liberal 'Puławy' factions. This is the position of both Witold Jedlicki, author of the essay 'Chamy i Żydy [The Boors and the Kikes]', one of the most influential and popular portrayals of the October period, and Michał Chęciński, whose book *Poland, Communism, Nationalism, Antisemitism*, published in 1982, attempted a comprehensive portrayal of antisemitism in postwar Poland.[1] Krystyna Kersten, in her recent book on Polish–Jewish relations, also stressed the primarily instrumental character of the antisemitism of 1956: 'The Jewish question, somewhat mythologized and mainly artificial, became a spectacular weapon in the struggle of competing party factions.'[2]

Both Jedlicki and Chęciński believed that the antisemitism of 1956 was largely 'imposed from above' in an orchestrated way. It was 'thrown at' the public by the Natolin group, which used it to achieve its own political goals: to gain social support and a new political-ideological base to replace the lack of support for Communist ideology, obvious even to the most dogmatic believers; to relieve and neutralize the disappointment and growing frustration that threatened to turn against the existing system and the governing group; and finally to discredit the more liberal and reform-orientated Puławy group by presenting them to the masses as 'the Jews'. The most public events supporting this line of reasoning were the addresses of Wiktor Kłosiewicz at the sixth plenary session of the central committee of PZPR, and of Zenon Nowak at the seventh one. Kłosiewicz's objection to the candidacy of Roman Zambrowski, proposed as a member of the central committee's secretariat, was that 'the nation would receive such an appointment unfavourably'—a remark which, in view of the candidate's Jewish parentage, was interpreted as an antisemitic statement. At the seventh plenary

[1] W. Jedlicki, *Klub Krzywego Koła* (Paris, 1963); M. Chęciński, *Poland: Communism, Nationalism, Antisemitism* (New York, 1982).
[2] K. Kersten, *Polacy, Żydzi, Komunizm: Anatomia półprawd* (Warsaw, 1992), 159.

session Nowak raised the issue of over-representation of people of Jewish origin in key positions of authority. This caused an uproar, with objections from many delegates, and was interpreted as a call for a 'nationally orientated regulation of cadres'.[3]

Chęciński believed that the antisemitism of the Natolin could not be explained as a uniquely Polish phenomenon: 'It was mainly a diversion inspired by the Soviets aimed to better establish their power in Poland . . . The Soviet authority constantly flooded Poland with waves of antisemitism.'[4] Anti-Sovietism, which could endanger the basic interests of the Kremlin, was to be replaced by the much safer antisemitism. Advanced by Natolin as a weapon in the political struggle and a socio-technical tool, antisemitism was also used by the Puławy group, which dismissed opponents within the party as fanatical antisemites, reactionaries, and representatives of the worst tradition of Polish obscurantism. 'In moulding public opinion, the Puławy has managed . . . a very shrewd twist,' Jedlicki wrote. 'They used the Jewish problem to erase the much more uncomfortable problem of personal responsibility for excesses during the Stalinist period. If someone raised that question, he was immediately labelled as an antisemite.'[5] The shrewdness of the Puławy group, as portrayed by Jedlicki, went even further: 'In order to deprive their opponents once and for all of the opportunity to play on antisemitism', the Puławy gave the Jews, or Poles of Jewish origin, the freedom to leave Poland, an opportunity that thousands of people have subsequently taken advantage of. So the antisemitism of 1956 was perceived as a grand provocation and a grand manipulation. 'The antisemitic propaganda of Natolin was not well received in the country,' Chęciński wrote. 'It is noteworthy how little influence . . . it had on the disposition of the whole society. In that entire period, there was not a single genuine case of spontaneous anti-Jewish action.'[6]

This approach to the antisemitism of 1956 is so one-dimensional, however, that it does not reflect the reality of the situation. Without rejecting the view that antisemitism was used as a weapon in the current of political struggle, perhaps exaggerated by the press, it is still difficult to deny that in 1956 anti-Jewish sentiments in many circles of society were an indisputable fact. They were not new on the Polish landscape; in 1945–6 there were even some cases of open acts of aggression and pogroms, such as those in Rzeszów, Kraków, Tarnów, and Rabka, with the worst in Kielce.[7] From 1948 to 1955 any independent expression or open

---

[3] Z. Rykowski and W. Władyka, *Polska próba: Październik '56* (Kraków, 1989), 125, 210–11.
[4] Chęciński, *Poland: Communism*, 131.
[5] Jedlicki, *Klub Krzywego Koła*, 31.   [6] Chęciński, *Poland: Communism*, 106–7.
[7] These anti-Jewish incidents were usually based on vague rumours (in Rzeszów, for example, Jews had been accused of murdering Christian children). The most serious at this time, apart from the pogrom in Kielce in 1946, was the one in Kraków, when several Jews were killed by a mob on 11–12 Aug. 1945. See Kersten, *Polacy, Żydzi*, 110–13.

manifestation of social emotion was extremely limited, indeed practically impossible. National resentments disappeared from the surface of social life, but this did not mean that they ceased to exist. When the Stalinist vice started to relax its grip, what was hidden began to come to light.

Reports by branches of the Urząd Bezpieczeństwa (UB: Security Office) indicate that cases of antisemitic statements increased in April and May 1956, along with the progressive 'thaw' in which criticism of the authorities and the system surfaced. Jews were held responsible for the errors and crimes of the previous period. In April a UB informer reported that his source, an electrical engineer, claimed that 'In Poland . . . Jews have deeply penetrated political and social life by occupying the key posts, and have brought to politics their worst traditional qualities.'[8] The agent 'Szczęsny', working for the Poznań Wojewódzki Urząd Bezpieczeństwa Publicznego (WUBP: Provincial Office of Public Security), reported at the beginning of May 1956: 'Statements directed against Jews are appearing in comments about the recent events. It is said that there is substantial Jewish participation in political and economic life . . . that the Państwowa Komisja Planowania Gospodarczego [State Commission of Economic Planning] is a Jewish institution, and that the Delikatesy store-chain is a Jewish co-operative.'[9]

The Bydgoszcz and Poznán provincial (*wojewódzkie*) committees of PZPR observed that information about Jakub Berman's resignation from the Biuro Polityczne (Party Political Bureau) and the government at the beginning of May 1956 caused an increase in antisemitic feelings among the intelligentsia and the workers: 'Some state straightforwardly that "because of Berman too many Jews have come to power, and now this will change".' In Poznań people said, 'It's good Berman was removed—one Jew less in the central committee and the government.' Among the employees of the Poznań Zarząd Zieleni Miejskich (Direction of the City Gardens) the following was recorded: 'We don't trust Jews, they shouldn't hold such important positions in the party and government.'[10]

The increased wave of antisemitic sentiments often found expression in ordinary interpersonal relations. At the beginning of June a Jewish woman from Łódź wrote in a letter to *Trybuna ludu* [Tribune of the people]:

What do the Jews want to leave for? . . . The biggest problem is antisemitism. We constantly face it at every step . . . My ten-year-old daughter often comes back from the TPD[11] school crying. She says that she won't go to school any more. Children pick on her.

---

[8] The Biuro Ewidencji i Archiwum Urzędu Ochrony Państwa (UOP: Bureau of Records and Archives of the Office of the Protection of the State), 17/ix/100, 2 (unpaginated).   [9] Ibid.

[10] Archiwum Akt Nowych, Oddział VI [AAN VI], b. Centralne Archiwum KC PZPR (Archives of the Recent Acts, Div. VI, formerly Central Archives of the Central Committee of the PZPR), 237/VII-3835 (unpaginated).

[11] Towarzystwo Przyjaciół Dzieci (Society of the Friends of Children).

They constantly call her 'Kike'. Once, a girl from her class chased her through the street all the way to our home, yelling, 'Kike, you don't go to religion class!' There are dozens of incidents like this. My child comes home broken-hearted. Once she said: 'Mummy, we should leave, there is no place for us here.' Then she asked: 'Why was I born Jewish?'[12]

'One of my neighbours constantly harassed my children because of their Jewish origin,' wrote a Russian woman whose husband was a Jew:

> It went as far as putting leaflets in the entrance to our house and several other places calling one Polish woman who was friendly to our children a Jewish children's caretaker . . . I often hear children address my son. 'You Jew' instead of by his name . . . Recently my older son came home saying that some children had tried to force him to cross himself, and he only barely escaped . . . Statements openly hostile to Jews can be heard more and more often. One often hears the words: 'Enough! Your rule has ended!'[13]

Information about incidents of an anti-Jewish nature came from many places in Poland. In Łódź on the night of 14–15 May 1956 unknown perpetrators broke into the synagogue at Rewolucji 1905 Street. They stole boxes of candles and threw prayer-books on the floor. On 9 June in Wrocław twenty-two leaflets saying 'Down with the Jews!' were thrown in Kościuszko Street.[14] In Łódź, on Nowowiejska Street, 'A Polish child and a Jewish child got into a fight, and the mother of the Polish one roused a rabble by yelling that Jewish children beat up Polish children and nobody cared.'[15] In Bytom two miners from the Dymitrow mine severely beat two men who 'were talking among themselves in Yiddish in the back yard'.[16] Incidents in which Jews suffered also occurred at Wałbrzych, Bytom, Dzierżoniów, and Legnica.[17]

On the other hand, it is not always easy to determine whether particular incidents were purely antisemitic or were rather disturbances that just happened to affect Poles of Jewish origin. In addition, it is never certain to what extent a particular event was spontaneous or consciously provoked. For example, who can judge what the real intention was of those who desecrated the Łódź synagogue?

The press wrote extensively, often in an alarmist manner, about the danger of antisemitism. Among the responses were letters from readers that show the background to anti-Jewish resentment, as well as the stereotypes existing in ordinary thought. The articles 'Antysemityzm—pięć tez nienowych i przestroga [Antisemitism—Five Not Quite New Theses and a Warning]' by Leszek Kołakowski and 'Okrutne dzieci i sprawy dorosłych [Cruel Children and Problems of Adults]' by Jerzy Broszkiewicz provoked the strongest reaction.[18] There were references to these essays in a letter sent to Edward Ochab signed 'Party Comrade':

---

[12] AAN VI 237/VII-18, 177–8.
[13] Ibid. 184–6.
[14] UOP, 195/1, folder C, 93.
[15] AAN VI 237/VII-3835 (unpaginated).
[16] Ibid. VII-3843, 66.
[17] Rykowski and Władyka, *Polska próba*, 160.
[18] *Po prostu* 22 (1956) and *Przegląd Kulturalny*, 23 (1956) respectively.

Antisemitism in Poland is growing on the basis of observations of jews[19] and their behaviour . . . jews hold almost all executive positions in commerce, and among jews for their part the tendency to take over those positions where non-jews still remain is continuing . . . poles ask themselves why jews are assigned to almost all executive positions, while the percentage of jews living in Poland does not reflect the proportion of jewish to polish executives. Where are jewish miners or ironworkers, jewish comrades of polish labourers; where are jewish farm workers, etc.? Can't polish office and factory workers see who in Delikatesy is buying up imported groceries like oranges, lemons, and cocoa? Can't the same polish citizens see who in Gallux is buying furs, leather coats, luxurious clothing from abroad, and Belgian fabrics, and in the Jubiler shops gold, precious stones, and gold watches priced 10,000–11,000 apiece? It is even stranger that poles sometimes hold equal positions with jews but still cannot afford these luxury goods. Can't children in school see that the jews in their class are better dressed and bring delicacies for breakfast, while workers' children bring plain bread—at best with lard—and wear shoes with holes . . . jews were and are a state within the state; their . . . superior authority is 'Kahal': whether someone belongs to the party or not, he must submit to Kahal. Kahal doesn't care about the interest of the People's Poland . . . Is the situation in our commerce good? No, just the opposite, it is very bad. It is bad because most of the posts are filled by jews. We have to admit that a jew is a fair salesman, but he is not an organizer of work; the more jews that work in a commercial enterprise, the greater the disarray. It is obvious that the greater the disarray in a business, the easier it is to catch a fish in muddy water; and then those who have caught the fish—jews—are not accountable for this; the over-trustful poles in lower positions take the responsibility. That's where the income flowing into the pockets of jews is from, with which goods are bought in the various branches of Delikatesy, Gallux, and Jubiler. Doesn't this generate antisemitism, since the poles who work with jewish executives and directors see their thieving, but don't dare to oppose them, for the latter are usually members of the party and any struggle against them is doomed to fail? Aren't such Jews within the party undermining its authority? Didn't Mr Światło, Mr Berman, and the other jews with Polish names repay People's Poland with treachery? . . . Poles fought against Nazism everywhere in this country and abroad, and we followed the idea of the independent fatherland, and Polish blood was readily spilt for this idea, and nobody has won this independence for us but ourselves. And what about jews? They either wailed in ghettos or gave each other away to protect themselves— instead of organizing themselves in armed resistance against Nazism. They surrendered the gold won through the exploitation of a Polish worker and farmer, helping Hitler in this way with the war . . . In Poland these jews form a privileged caste; a Polish worker, farmer, or office worker sees and feels it, and rebels against it . . . Privileged castes must not be allowed, and then there won't be antisemitism. I think that the aversion towards jews which is found in society originated and grew because of the dishonest behaviour of the jews themselves.[20]

Even more emphatic in presenting his views was the anonymous author of a letter sent to the central committee:

---

[19] The use of lower- or upper-case letters for ethnic designation follows the Polish original here (and in all quotations below). [20] AAN VI 237/xxv-18, 168–72.

It is a long time since we have read an essay written with as much audacity . . . as Leszek Kołakowski's 'Antisemitism'.

The writer then went on to elucidate the reasons for antisemitic sentiments in the country, following the pattern of Kołakowski's text by enumerating them:

I—the first cause is that you are among us at all. II—Once you are here you should be quiet, but only cultured people act in such a manner. III—You extend your presence in high positions into all areas of economic, social, and cultural life. IV—You attempt to deal with things unfamiliar to you, because you think that you know everything. V—From your high positions you have spoilt many good things that were started without your help. VI—Anyone purposely committing sabotage would not have done more harm than what you have done in all your 'wisdom'. VII—There is so much hatred towards *goyim* among you that you can barely conceal it, and it erupts on any occasion, this hatred clearly shines through in the essay 'The Antisemites'. . . . VIII—You know nothing but ingratitude for favours and benefits granted to you. IX—The injuries you have inflicted on Poles are innumerable, and you are mendacious at every step. X—Let us part from you without regret; go to your country and establish your happiness there. What makes the blood boil most of all is the attitude shown towards the problems since the 20th Congress.[21] There were Jews who stated at open sessions of POPs[22] that there were injuries, that many people had suffered who had no guilt, and that many people had unjustly left this world. You were the ones who stated this because until recently you were in the UB and were well informed. Articles in the press lead to provocation or to the unleashing of even heavier Jewish pressure against our nation. In the name of antisemitism you will again oust our brothers. Whoever leaves his job with this label won't be able to join any institution, for you have links among yourselves better than the Freemasons of whom we have heard so much. You provoke hatred against yourselves by your arrogance, conceit, and the vulgar way you point to your own superiority. You think that you are chosen to rule the world, that that is your goal, and that it is yours to conquer. You took important positions in all areas of national life, from which ridiculous positions fell.[23] We had such Bermans, and unfortunately we still do, in every branch and in every central office. Continuous reorganization was undertaken in order to make it impossible to establish responsibility. A Jew carried out ridiculous policies that made one institution bankrupt, and after a year he transferred to yet another important executive position with a car, high salary, and a Catholic maid at home. You always were exploiters; whether capitalists or bankers or ordinary usurers, the Jews drew profits from the nation, they drew blood from our hard toil. You even draw it today, only in a more hypocritical and sly manner. These 40,000 Jews that remain here have brought all the disorder to Poland.[24]

The anti-Jewish resentment apparent in the statements quoted above fit into one of the basic patterns of pre-war or traditional Polish antisemitism, which was

---

[21] Of the party (Feb. 1956).   [22] Podstawowa Organizacja Partyjna (Fundamental Party Cell).
[23] 'W każdej dziedzinie życia narodowego pozajmowaliście pozycje ważne, z których padały pozycje bzdurne.' In this sentence the faulty structure of the Polish original is preserved. The author probably wished to say that Jews occupied important positions, in which they took ridiculous decisions.   [24] AAN VI 237/xxv-18, 198–200.

based on the belief that Jews were over-represented in all areas considered to be financially and professionally advantageous, that Poles suffered from Jewish exploitation, and that there was a general conspiracy of all Jews, who supported each other and took joint care of their own interests. It is noteworthy that in both letters the essence of the arguments against the Jews is identical with the theses included in Zenon Nowak's speech at the seventh plenary session of the central committee. The antisemitism of Natolin was not an isolated phenomenon artificially devised by one faction of the ruling élite. It undoubtedly had real social roots; it reflected and gave voice to the thoughts and resentments present in broad circles of society, even if it is not possible to determine their range with any precision.

In 1956 antisemitism became a real social problem, at least in the eyes of a substantial part of the press, which warned against it and condemned it not only as a morally hideous attitude, but also as one that served the interests of the 'reaction' (to use the vocabulary of that time). 'If at any time even the slightest shadow of antisemitism creeps near the doors of our houses, be careful! The rabble is around the corner, and the counter-revolution is showing its fangs,' concluded a famous article by Leszek Kołakowski. Some of the party cells also condemned the antisemitism that spread through the country. Members of the POP of the Polish Writers' Union wrote in their proclamation of 8 June 1956:

The tender spot in the party's educational attempt to broaden national horizons is the problem of antisemitism and racism. The opportunistic method of 'combating' antisemitism by avoiding 'provocation' of the antisemites has not been sufficiently strongly opposed by the party leadership. In the higher levels of the party and the state there were statements about 'the apparatus being polluted by nationally alien elements'. All of this is a clear violation of the principles of Marxism, and reeks of gloomy obscurantism . . . We consider it unacceptable to tolerate antisemitism in any guise.[25]

The POP of the philosophy department at Warsaw University issued a special resolution on antisemitism which included such statements as 'members of the party do not always take a strong stand against antisemitic trends. This passivity *vis-à-vis* obscurantism is apparent, for example, in the expression of opinions advising regulation of party hierarchy according to a "racial" key . . . We consider it necessary to employ all means of informed action in the struggle against antisemitism.'[26]

There also took place—initially in the Wrocław region—meetings of 'party activists of Jewish origin', who protested against widespread antisemitism. At a meeting in Świdnica, the following opinions were expressed:

A fish begins to rot at its head. Antisemitism originates in the central committee. Comrade Nowak said that the party apparatus is full of Kikes [*zażydzony*]. You do not want to have antisemitism in Świdnica, yet there is antisemitism in the central committee

[25] AAN VI 237/VII-153, 91.   [26] Ibid. v-295, 98.

... Even in the times of the Sanacja,[27] antisemitic disturbances were punished pro forma, but not now.... The party does not oppose antisemitism ... The party is afraid to lose popularity.

On the other hand, at the meetings of Jewish activists there were also voices claiming that the authorities were deliberately amplifying the problem of antisemitism in order to encourage Polish Jews to emigrate. The question was asked: 'Why does the press publicize news about antisemitic riots without reporting how the perpetrators were punished? This only provides the Jewish nationalists with more arguments.' It was stated at a meeting in Dzierżoniów: 'For over ten years there wasn't a single word about the state of Israel, and now we hear on the radio about the splendid life there.'[28]

Although antisemitism was certainly not marginal or negligible, it would also be a mistake to say that it was a dominant characteristic of popular thought in 1956. It is highly significant that during the Poznań upheaval antisemitic slogans were completely absent: not a single outcry against the Jews is recorded.[29] This is notable because popular feelings were given free reign on the streets of Poznań, and the temper of the crowd reached fever pitch during the crisis of 1956. Antisemitism was equally absent from the nationwide wave of commentaries on events in Poznań. Since the disruption served to release nationalistic emotions, the lack of antisemitic comments is significant.

The standard explanation—spread by rumours and commentaries—for the violent clashes in Poznań was that a Russian woman was shooting at the crowd from the security offices: only in one instance (recorded by the UB) was she stated to be a Jewess (with the additional charge that she had killed eight children).[30]

[27] The last period of Independent Poland before the Second World War, when antisemitism was relatively widespread.

[28] AAN VI 237/vii-3843, 64–5. The sudden emergence of praise for Israel was also brought up by the president of the main board of the Zarząd Główny Towarzystwa Społeczno-Kulturalnego Żydów w Polsce (TSKŻ: Social-Cultural Society of Jews in Poland), Grzegorz Smolar. In a letter of 8 Aug. 1956 to Edward Ochab he wrote: 'The lack of an official statement about the true intentions and limitations of our emigration policy contributed significantly towards the desperation to emigrate among the Jewish population. Such feelings existed even among the party members and among former members of the KPP [Komunistyczna Partia Polska, the pre-war Communist Party of Poland], who openly claimed that "The government and the party are interested in the mass emigration of Jews from Poland." A substantial proportion of the Jewish party members are convinced that the current emigration practice ... is an attempt to get rid of the Jewish question' (AAN VI 237/xiv-100, 7).

[29] The Poznań upheaval of 28–9 June 1956 was a popular revolt against the Communist regime. It began as a workers' protest but very quickly resulted in violent clashes between crowds and the army, and in attacks by the people against Party and UB buildings. Nearly 100 people died in the two days of fighting.

[30] In Białystok an employee of the Medical Academy, supposedly an eyewitness of the events in Poznań, said that 'workers had organized a march with children at the head, and a Jewess from the UB killed eight children with a pistol, starting the events' (AAN VI 237/vii-384, 6). One of the few incidents with antisemitic overtones happened at the Kędzierzyn railway station. On 30 July a

It can also be assumed that the increase in antisemitic feelings occurred in tandem with the worsening political situation in the autumn of 1956. The party reports, as well as those of the security authorities, recorded antisemitic statements and actions in the course of the many meetings and demonstrations in October and November throughout Poland.

In Łódź there was a demand during a workers' meeting in the Zakłady Bakelitowe plastics factory 'to take influential positions away from all Jews, exile them to Israel, and let Poles take their places. There were deliberations about why Jews were better off than Poles, and how Jewish women managed to live without working—there were some who even had servants.'[31]

The removal of citizens of Jewish origin from office was demanded at a meeting in Lublin, where several thousand participants gathered. Similar statements were heard at a student meeting in Lublin a few days earlier, where one speaker said: 'Students don't support racial discrimination, but they oppose the fact that a majority of important positions are occupied by Jews.'[32]

During a demonstration in Gdańsk harbour the slogan 'Down with the Jews in all offices; the worst Pole is better than a Jew in office' was used.[33] In private conversation employees of the Związek Izb Rzemieślniczych (Union of Craftsmen's Chambers) said that 'the members of the Party Political Bureau . . . Gomułka, Ochab, and others, are of Jewish origin . . . changes are inspired by those of "Jewish descent" . . . to protect their privileges'.[34] In Legnica, some employees of the co-operative named after the Rosenbergs moved to change its name 'because the Rosenbergs were Jews'; however, the majority of the workers rejected this motion.[35]

The PZPR members in the main board of the Social-Cultural Society of Jews in Poland warned the Political Bureau about laying off Poles of Jewish origin, in a letter of 20 November 1956:

We receive information from many cities:—Bielawa, Wałbrzych, Łódź, Szczecin, and others—that with the wave of personnel changes Jews are laid off *only because of their nationality*. In the Szczecin shipyard Mr Szapiro, who held the position of director of education and ran the Ruch news-stand,[36] was laid off. The chairman of the Factory

---

drunken railway worker was arrested after he had assailed a policeman with the statement. 'I am curious to know why there wasn't a Poznań in Kędzierzyn'; then he raised his hand and started to yell 'Azoty [a large chemical plant in Kędzierzyn] there you are not; how much do you earn there?' After being taken to the police station, he shouted that he 'wanted Poland like it was under President Mościcki, when a Jew was paid half a grosz for an egg, and he didn't like the way it was now because Cyrankiewicz was a Jew; it should have happened in the rest of Poland the same way as in Poznań, and maybe it would have been better' (UOP, 171/2, 186).

[31] AAN VI 237/VII-3843, 177.
[32] UOP, 17/IX/99, f. 6. (unpaginated).   [33] AAN VI 237/VII-3843, 109.
[34] UOP, 17/IX/99, f. 6. (unpaginated). Władysław Gomułka was elected first secretary of the PZPR in Oct. 1956.   [35] AAN VI 237/VII-3861, 82.
[36] Ruch was the state-controlled newspaper distribution network.

Council . . . told him: 'Berman was removed and so was Minc; we have to remove somebody too.' In Wałbrzych Chana Osińska was removed from her job with the explanation: 'the workers don't want a stranger to deal with their files and they are demanding a native Pole . . . Nobody in Wałbrzych wants to employ her . . . The people who were laid off are not being helped to find new employment by the Local Councils or the party committees.'[37]

We can assume that one of the groups most amenable to antisemitic sentiment was comprised of the PZPR activists (although their attitudes may seem more striking in part because of their prominent positions). Reports from the Rzeszów region during the first half of December stressed that strong antisemitic sentiments had emerged at the local conventions of the PZPR in Gorlice, Leżajsk, and Brzozów.

In Leżajsk and Brzozów there were demands to expose the comrades of Jewish origin who are members of the central committee or hold positions in the apparatus of the central committee; also in the Foreign Ministry and the Państwowa Komisja Planu Gospodarczego [State Commission for Economic Planning] . . . In these cases there was little opposition. For example, in Gorlice nobody protested against the antisemitic statements.[38]

Urszula Kozierowska, an envoy of the Warsaw Komitet Wojewódzki Polskiej Zjednoczonej Partii Robotniczej (KW PZPR: Regional Committee of the Party), who visited Sokołów Podlaski, gives an even more vivid account. She wrote:

On 30 November I was at the local [*powiatowy*] committee in Sokołów Podlaski. From my conversations with the staff of the committee I learnt about strong antisemitic feelings in the area. The comrades mentioned, among other things, the fact that they were often confronted with the statement that apart from two Poles there were only Jews in the present Political Bureau. Similar feelings are also noticeable among the staff of the committee itself. They agreed with these feelings, adding that the Jews had taken over the press and radio. They also claim that the press is now fulfilling a subversive role—it acts against the party apparatus. The articles being published were causing disregard and a lack of respect for the party apparatus in the area. The comrades think that the press has finished off the Poles, Kłosiewicz, and Nowak. Because there has to be justice, now it is time to dispose of the Jews. The POP of the local committee in Sokołów Podlaski adopted a resolution demanding that Berman, Minc, and Zambrowski be reprimanded.[39]

Antisemitic feelings were most intense in Lower Silesia, in areas where the Jewish population was dense. Nationalistic emotions were further aggravated by the presence of numerous units of the Soviet army that were quartered there,

---

[37] AAN (materials of the Political Bureau), package 15, no. 60, file 59, 41–2.
[38] AAN VI 237/VII-3843, 195.
[39] AAN (materials of the Political Bureau), package 15, no. 60, file 59, 25. Jakub Berman, Hilary Minc, and Roman Zambrowski were members of the Political Bureau who were of Jewish origin.

groups of German-speaking indigenous inhabitants, Ukrainians (relocated there from south-eastern Poland during the Wisła resettlement of 1947), and even Greeks (refugees from the civil war). Party reports described harassment and even the sacking of Jews and Greeks, instances of slander, and even the encouragement of pogroms.[40] The author of a letter to *Trybuna ludu* wrote: 'In Wrocław Jews don't walk the streets after 7 p.m.'[41]

It was in this area that the most serious anti-Jewish incidents occurred. The Wrocław UB reported that on 23 October, during a tumultuous street demonstration,

A group of hoodlums entered a restaurant on Poniatowski Street and demanded money from citizens of Jewish nationality . . . one of them . . . on the street started to shout slogans about beating the Jews. Some fifteen people gathered around him, and they beat up two citizens of Jewish nationality who were passing by. The next day four Jews were beaten near another restaurant.[42]

Jewish activists from Dzierżoniów (where the Jewish population made up 10 per cent of all inhabitants) requested help from the authorities in Warsaw. In a letter addressed to the central committee they wrote:

In recent months there have been 40 incidents in which Jews have been slandered or beaten that have gone unpunished. We assert that the regional and local authorities are not reacting appropriately to these cases and to our complaints. The most upsetting events took place on 27 October, when in a single day there were four beatings; this happened in the period after the seventh plenary session.[43]

A letter from the TSKŻ struck an equally alarmed tone:

In Bielawa on 13 November a teacher of the TPD school beat a ten-year-old pupil so badly that she bled . . . they told her that her place was not here, but in Palestine. When her mother came to complain, [the teacher] chased her away shouting 'Kike!' at her. In Wałbrzych hoodlums repeatedly overturned a stand in Słowacki Street run by a citizen of Jewish nationality. On the 16th of this month anti-Jewish slogans were written on the stand . . . In Ząbkowice, someone by the name of Matuszewski beat up a Jewish child . . . Despite the physician's examination and a report that included statements by Polish children, the attorney closed the case, claiming lack of evidence.[44]

Antisemitic statements appeared during the election campaign too. According to reports, there were anti-Jewish remarks in many candidates' speeches. In the Olsztyn region a candidate of Zjednoczone Stronnictwo Ludowe (ZSL: United Peasants' Party) said at the electoral meetings that in the Ministry of Agriculture 'there are those who should have been in Israel long ago, and I wish them a good trip'.[45] In several places there were attempts to discredit candidates by presenting

---

[40] AAN VI 237/VII-3843, 82.
[41] Ibid. XXV-20, 149.
[42] UOP, 17/IX/99, f. 6 (unpaginated).
[43] AAN VI 337/XXV-20, 100.
[44] AAN (materials of the Political Bureau), package 15, no. 60, file 59.
[45] AAN VI 237/VII-2726, 14.

them as Jews. We can assume that sometimes the electorate was sympathetic to this. A listener from Poznań wrote to the Polish Radio Service:

Despite entire pages in newspapers describing the activities of the proposed candidates, I don't in fact know for whom I will vote, because nothing is being said about their parentage . . . As for myself, I have a problem with certain social spheres and nationalities. I wouldn't like to vote for some landowner or Jew. The former I know about from books and from the not so distant past, the latter from their belligerency at a time when we want peace, and from my mother's stories of their supposed 'great honesty' . . . What I want to know is whether I can publicly ask a candidate at a meeting about his origin, and, if I don't get concrete data about his origin, whether I can refuse to vote for him.[46]

Many leaflets giving warnings against the Jewish danger appeared in various locations. Anti-Jewish statements were used in the internal party struggle: accusations of having Jewish origin were generally directed towards activists of the Puławy group. It seems that the Catholic Church was most concerned with this aspect of antisemitism. Prime Minister Józef Cyrankiewicz, in his talks with Primate Stefan Wyszyński on 14 January 1957 (during the final phase of the election campaign), stressed the threat posed by widespread antisemitic sentiment. The reaction of Cardinal Wyszyński was hostile, according to his biographer Andrzej Micewski, who expresses the cardinal's views as follows: 'Since it was an exclusively internal phenomenon within the party, tied to the struggle of the factions, the primate stressed that the press action concerning this problem harmed the image of Poland in the West.'[47]

The increased antisemitism was accompanied by an acceleration in the emigration of Jews from Poland. The main board of the TSKŻ dramatically drew attention to this in a letter of November 1956 to the Political Bureau:

In many towns there is an increase in the number of anonymous letters to Jews demanding that they leave for Palestine; if they do not, the authors of these letters threaten them with retaliation. As a result, there is a panic among the Jewish population, which in some cases is even stronger than it was in 1946. Its expression is the mass registration for emigration to Israel. At present, the majority of the Jewish population in Poland (workers, craftsmen, office workers) are registered for emigration. Among them there is a substantial number of party members, and even of old activists of the Communist Party of Poland.[48]

In 1956–7 about 40,000 Jews (or Poles of Jewish origin) left Poland. Approximately half of these were repatriates from the Soviet Union who were in Poland only temporarily. According to the estimates of the secretariat of the central committee in August 1956, the Jewish population living in Poland amounted to 50,000. After the wave of emigration there remained between 25,000 and

---

[46] Ibid. xxv-21, 31.
[47] A. Micewski, *Kardynał Wyszyński, Prymas i mąż stanu* (Paris, 1982), 166.
[48] AAN (materials of the Political Bureau), package 15, no. 60, file 59, 42.

30,000.⁴⁹ But it is important not to overstate the link between antisemitism, which in 1956 was undoubtedly stronger than in preceding years, and the mass emigration of the Jewish population. We need to remember that from 1951 onwards there were only limited opportunities to leave Poland. It was not until 1955 that this became a realistic option, and it was possible on a mass scale only in 1956.⁵⁰ It is likely that a considerable number of those leaving were taking advantage of the new opportunity to fulfil wishes they had entertained for many years, especially since the facility might only be temporary. There is no way to measure what part of the Jewish population left because it could not deal with the antisemitism, and what part was simply fulfilling a desire to leave the People's Republic of Poland and settle in Israel or somewhere outside the Communist world. Probably there was a combination of the two motives, even within the mind of a single individual. This does not change the fact that there were certainly Poles of Jewish origin who had not considered leaving until they encountered antisemitism. Sometimes the hostility came from a completely unexpected quarter—e.g. the party in which they had placed their hopes of creating a society free from racial discrimination. However, the majority of the Jewish population that had left the USSR had probably always looked on Poland as no more than a stop on the way, and were thus not influenced by the matter of Polish antisemitism.

The antisemitism of 1956 can be considered from three perspectives. In the first instance it was a political ploy on the part of the Natolin group, which used antisemitic slogans to increase its power, discredit and eliminate its opponents, and muster social support.

Secondly, there existed real antisemitism among a large number of members of the party apparatus and its activists. These were among the most consistent and influential promoters of such feelings. It is difficult to pinpoint the exact reasons for this. Perhaps it was an act of self-defence on the part of those who had experienced great social advancement in the previous decade, rising from the bottom of the social ladder to positions of power and privilege. Facing a deep and serious crisis that threatened their positions, and often their entire world-view, they were receptive to explanations pointing to an easily recognizable source of evil. Bearing in mind the scope of antisemitism in 1956, we should not be surprised by the slogans that Moczar's group used in its struggle for power in the

---

⁴⁹ Kersten, *Polacy, Żydzi*, 160; A. Skrzypek, 'O drugiej repatriacji Polaków z ZSRR (1954–1959)', *Kwartalnik historyczny*, 4 (1991), 67–74; AAN VI, 237/XIV-100, 2.

⁵⁰ Chęciński, *Poland, Communism*, 128. According to the Central Committee of PZPR secretariat's evaluation from the end of Aug. 1956, a significant number of those who elected to emigrate from Poland were people who had attempted to leave before: 'Recently persons applying for emigration are frequently people who had already submitted an application in 1949–50; in Wrocław, for example, these comprise 50 per cent of the total' (AAN VI 237/XIV-100, 3).

1960s.⁵¹ What the Natolin group failed to achieve in 1956—the removal of the political conflict and the struggle for power to the plane of 'nationalistic regulation' and the replacement of many of the party cadres through the use of antisemitic slogans—the 'partisans' did achieve twelve years later.

The third element in the antisemitism of 1956 was a grass-roots sentiment that came from deeper layers of the social mentality. It reflected traditional antisemitic motifs transposed to the reality of the People's Poland. These fed on the stereotype of the Jewish web encompassing all influential and lucrative positions, and the image of 'Jewish Communism' (żydokomuna).

It is not always possible to differentiate between the three dimensions of antisemitism, to distinguish grass-roots and spontaneous antisemitism from that which was manipulated or orchestrated politically. In certain spheres the three types would come together, strengthening and feeding on one another.

The antisemitism of 1956 was undoubtedly a genuine political and social problem. It is impossible, however, to assess precisely its range, spread, and varying manifestations within different social groups. It was a painful and very obvious episode, one that was exacerbated for political purposes. In such a situation it is easy to perceive the antisemitism of the period as a mass occurrence, one which played a central role in common thoughts and emotions. But that would be to exaggerate its importance. The antisemitism that seemed to erupt with such violence in 1956 can also be seen as part of a broader phenomenon, the general release of collective imagination following the Stalinist strait-jacket that brought anti-Sovietism and anti-Communism to the surface, along with anti-Jewish resentment. Anti-Soviet and anti-Communist feelings led to mass social mobilization; antisemitism, however, did not have a significant impact. The efforts of the Natolin group to encourage the political mechanisms feeding on antisemitism were in vain. While antisemitism played a significant role among the Poles in 1956, it remained an isolated phenomenon without any noticeable impact on the main course of events. In 1968 the movement would be much more widespread and have much deeper consequences.

[51] Gen. Mieczysław Moczar was a very influential Minister of the Interior who headed a nationalist faction in the party which made an unsuccessful bid for power in 1968, engaging in a nationwide antisemitic compaign.

PART II

New Views

Dov of Bolechów: A Diarist of the Council of Four Lands in the Eighteenth Century

ISRAEL BARTAL

THE COUNCIL OF FOUR LANDS (Va'ad Arba Aratsot) was convened in the 1580s and lasted until 1764, when it was dissolved by a decision of the Convocational Sejm. The first known document which with all certainty originates from the deliberations of the Sejm of the Four Lands and deals with the decisions it took was drawn up in 1581. The last surviving document, however, dates from the years after 1764 and deals with discussions on the ways of paying Jewish community dues, which were owed to the Liquidation Commission for the Council's debts. No original documents from the period of nearly 200 years between these two dates have survived, with the exception of three pages from the Council minutes. The existing gaps in the record were a stimulus to try to reconstruct it at least partially. The fundamental work by Professor Israel Halpern of Jerusalem is the result of a search lasting many years.[1] Using various sources from both within and outside the Jewish community, Halpern re-created a credible version of the texts of resolutions by the Council of Four Lands. His work was not conclusive; further searches by other scholars have shown that a fair number of new documents could be added to Halpern's text. I have recently been taking part in work on the publication of a new edition of the Va'ad resolutions, corrected on the basis of Professor Halpern's notes and supplemented by new documents supplied by colleagues in Israel and abroad.

The picture of the Council of Four Lands which emerges from these diverse sources differs considerably from that presented in nineteenth-century literature. The Council was generally described at that time (and it was assumed that this was also the case earlier) as fulfilling national and religious functions—a view that had little in common with the considerably more prosaic reality. However, this view became particularly well established in historiography, and has in fact been maintained up to the present. Most Jewish historians view the Council of

[1] I. Halpern, *Pinkas Va'ad Arba Aratsot/Acta Congressus Generalis Judaeorum Regni Poloniae* [*1580–1764*] (Jerusalem, 1945).

Four Lands anachronistically, from the point of view of those processes which led to the development of a feeling of modern national awareness, something which grew during the nineteenth century and in the first decades of the twentieth. For them the Va'ad was a 'model' institution, providing the most suitable pattern for the autonomous administration of the Jewish community through institutions set up in a changing social and political situation. Thus, both Shimon Dubnow and Majer Bałaban clearly overestimated the significance of the Sejm of the Four Lands in the Republic.

The famous memoirs of the wine merchant from Bolechów, Dov Ber, written at the turn of the eighteenth and nineteenth centuries, are testimony to the severe crisis which affected Jewish autonomous institutions in the last years of the Polish–Lithuanian Commonwealth. This text has gone through various vicissitudes. During the First World War it turned up in London and was then published by Mark Wischnitzer in several languages. In this essay I cite the English edition of 1922, although it needs to be used with caution, continually comparing the text with the Hebrew original. Dov Ber's reminiscences provide us with a great deal of information about the autonomous Jewish institutions at various levels, starting with the local communities and ending with the Council of Four Lands. The text is characterized by its concentration on the deeds of its author. Dov Ber describes, above all, his own activities, attributing to himself great services in his work for his local community. In the 1920s the scholar A. N. Frank questioned the reliability of the memoir.[2] He argued that a person could not be trusted who concentrates on his own, not entirely honest, activities in his local community and in the Council of Four Lands. I do not agree with this view, since I have established from contemporary documents that Dov Ber confirms many facts found in sources now available but not accessible to scholars until recently. The memoirs have not survived in their entirety, and the excerpts which have come down to us do of course deal with relations between the community in Bolechów and the Council of Four Lands. They reveal a discrepancy between the way everyday reality is described and the manner in which the Council and other autonomous Jewish institutions are idealized by the author. Describing the dissolution of the Council of Four Lands, Dov Ber refers to this event as a great misfortune, even a catastrophe, placing the main blame on the Poles. He even goes so far as to say that all the misfortunes which befell Poland during this time were the outcome of their dissolution of the Va'ad. Yet he reveals his true attitude to the Council when he describes the manner in which tax issues were arranged. Here his assessment is sober, even marked by criticism. To take a particular case, fires were an all too frequent occurrence in the Jewish communities in the eighteenth century. As a result of a fire in Bolechów in 1759, which our diarist describes, the elders of the community undertook steps

---

[2] A. N. Frank, 'Zikhronot R. Dov meBolekhov', *Hatekufah*, 20 (5683), 521–5.

designed to free the community from the obligation to pay taxes for several years. For this purpose a list of the damage caused by the fire was drawn up; Dov Ber claims credit for this. Three copies were made of the list: the first was sent to the office collecting taxes on wine, the second reached the Council of Four Lands with a request to defer the community's taxes, and the third was sent to Countess Lubomirska, the owner of Bolechów.

Here are some excerpts from Dov Ber's memoirs on the steps taken:

The second copy of the list [of the damages] was sent to Brody to the local Jewish authorities and to the Council of Four Lands. We also gave them letters written in the correct style and in the holy language describing the story of the ruin of our community and the great losses incurred as a result of theft and fire.[3]

The reply which conceded that 'Certain reductions will be granted to you',[4] did not fulfil the expectations of the Bolechów community. If we bear in mind the fact that the Council of Four Lands accepted responsibility for the unpaid debts of individual communities, both the failure of the Bolechów inhabitants in their attempts to get full tax relief and the deferment on the payment of their debts are understandable.

The approaches made to Countess Lubomirska also failed to yield results. It was only as a result of lengthy interventions that the Bolechów community was able to obtain reductions in its payments, which were made in the end by the Va'ad. In addition, it demanded to be reimbursed for the costs incurred. However, in order to obtain the maximum reduction possible, Dov Ber and other members of the community went to a meeting of the Council of Four Lands and obtained a deferment of the deadline for payments still due, and also a further reduction.

This story might seem unedifying to those who have an idealized picture of the functions of Jewish autonomous institutions in the eighteenth century. Yet if we compare this case with surviving documents dealing with the internal dependence of the Jewish community, the relations between Poles and Jews, and the economic connections linking them, the picture presented seems to be accurate.

Who in fact was Dov Ber? When we read his memoirs, we see a person who never became a member of the Jewish élite in spite of the fact that he tried by various means to build up the prestige of his family. There is no shortage of cases in the text where the author attempts to demonstrate to the reader the importance of his family. He devotes much space to his brother, who took part in the debates of the Council of Four Lands (he was one of those present at the last session in 1764). However, in spite of all appearances, Dov Ber continued to be an upstart, who on the one hand tried to make a career in the community institu-

---

[3] *The Memoirs of Ber of Bolechów (1723–1805)*, trans. with introduction by M. Vishnitzer (London, 1922), 103; *Zikhronot R. Dov MeBolekhov (5483–5565)* (Berlin, 1922), 62.

[4] *Memoirs*, 103; *Zikhronot*, 62.

tions, but on the other was continually snubbed by members of the élite. He speaks about the members of the community in a negative manner, describing them as a group of ungrateful individuals, incapable of appreciating what he had done for the good of the community. The fate of his family is a good illustration of the problem of the social and financial rise of people who did not belong to the circle of the traditional community élite.

Dov Ber's memoirs describe the weakness of the Va'ad, which in the eighteenth century was to become ever more apparent. As is known, one of the main reasons why this institution was created was to divide the tax burdens between individual communities. We have seen by the example of Bolechów with what great reluctance these taxes were paid. This problem became more acute with the impoverishment of the Jewish community. What is more, as Dov Ber writes, although it was the duty of a community to pay its debts, whenever they managed to avoid doing so its members were proud of the fact. Yet in spite of this attitude of the members to the Va'ad, Dov Ber saw its dissolution as a catastrophe, speaking of its demise as 'the destroyed pride of Israel'.[5] The decline in importance and eventual liquidation of the Council of Four Lands was also a testimony to the deterioration of the hitherto good relations between the Polish and Jewish communities. Although the Council of Four Lands in the first half of the eighteenth century was no longer the force it had once been, its existence remained a positive factor from the point of view of Jewish interests. However, the crisis of the institution became increasingly apparent. Internal Jewish social transformations, which were based to a large degree on the loosening of traditional bonds and structures in the communities, had a progressively deleterious influence on its functioning. This process went forward fairly quickly, contributing to a decline in the significance of the Council. An example of this is provided by the small community in Bolechów, which could allow itself to treat the instructions of the Va'ad with a certain disregard. Attention should also be drawn to another aspect of the crisis of Jewish autonomy, namely the rivalry between individual communities. One example—even if it had been going on for many years—was the competition between the communities of Lwów and Brody. By utilizing those tensions, the authorities of the Republic were able to secure the election of suitable people to the regional bodies of Jewish local government. We can also find confirmation of this fact in Dov Ber's memoirs. By taking advantage of the various local conflicts, an increase in the independence of the individual communities could be brought about. Such a situation occurred precisely in Bolechów.

The decline in the importance of the Council of Four Lands in the eighteenth century was the basic reason for the growth in the independence of individual communities. The Va'ad crisis was in part a result of a basic weakness in the

[5] *Memoirs*, 142; *Zikhronot*, 87.

structure of that institution, which in fact had already been evident when the Council started to function at the beginning of the sixteenth century. Moreover, at this time it is possible to discern a change in the nobility's attitude towards the Jews. The effectiveness of the Va'ad's power to intervene also declined, as, for example, in matters concerning complaints about ritual murders.

In conclusion, it should be emphasized that regardless of the extent to which Dov Ber was at pains to express his admiration for the Council of Four Lands, at the same time he wrote quite openly about the way in which its decisions were evaded and ignored. I believe that this contradiction can be explained by analysing the deeply embedded difficulty experienced by the Jews of eastern Europe at that time in grasping and assessing phenomena from the sphere of ideology and religion as against those of everyday life, which they were able to assess in a completely pragmatic manner.

A Peaceable Community at Work
The *Chevrah* of Nasielsk

ROSS KESSEL

CENTRAL to the development of an ethic for a pluralist society lies the notion of a peaceable community, one that renounces force as a means of resolving conflicts: a notion whose implications for society in general, and for medicine in particular, have been worked out most elegantly in recent times by H. Tristram Engelhardt.[1] Recognition that a society is pluralist involves acknowledgement of the fact that individuals will be unable to agree on a set of values—on how a good life ought to be lived. Furthermore, such recognition obliges us to acknowledge that each of us will be unable to find good reasons to force our own view of the good life upon others. Having no deity in common, we shall be unable to resolve our differences by appeal to revelation, and sharing no common set of premisses, we shall be unable to do so by appeal to rational argument. Without such common ground, each of us will be obliged to accept that the views of rightness and wrongness held by others are as worthy of consideration as our own; that others have as much right to live in peace as we do; and that the resolution of our differences can only be achieved through negotiation, agreement, and compromise. A pluralist society claiming to be ruled by moral standards will be obliged to abjure force as a way of settling disputes among its members.

What sanctions can such a community call upon against someone who rejects the renunciation of force? Clearly they are not those of law or religion, for morality cannot of itself imprison or execute, curse or damn. Nor are they those of social convention or of professional mores. However, what morality can do is to demonstrate that certain kinds of actions are incompatible with continued membership in the moral community, and that those who undertake such actions reject the very fabric of the peaceable community and thereby lose all claim to such a community's protections. They become outlawed. The following example shows the power of such a sanction at work.

The eighteenth- and nineteenth-century Jewish communities of central and

---

[1] H. Tristram Engelhardt, Jr., *The Foundations of Bioethics*, 2nd edn. (Oxford, 1995), esp. pp. 67–74, 105–11.

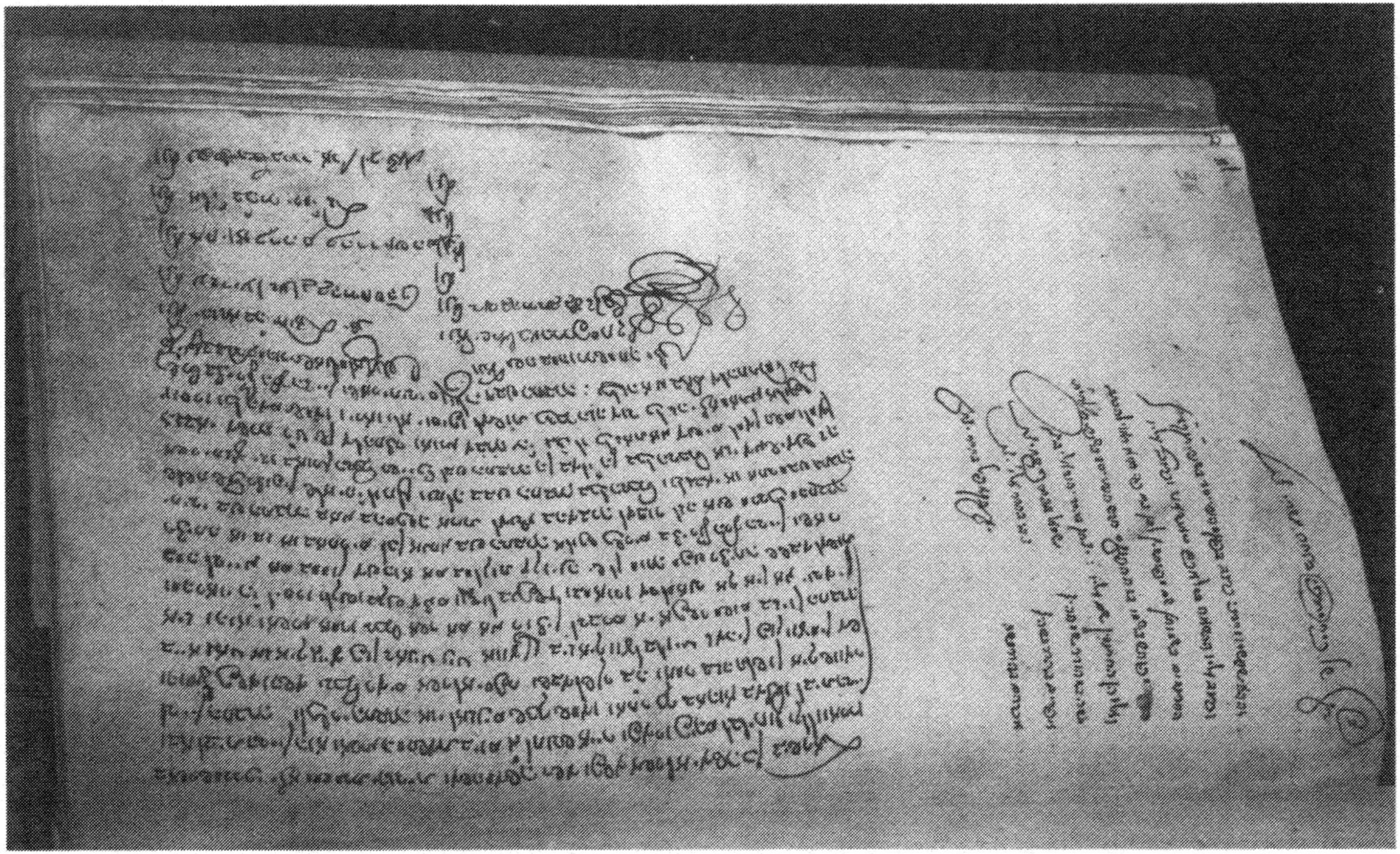

Fig. 1. Mordecai's page from the 'Chronicle of the Association of Tailors, Furriers, and Jewellers in Nasielsk, Poland: 1778–1841' (see n. 2).

eastern Europe existed as enclaves within an often hostile Christian state. Nominally subject to the laws of the land, they were often loath to call in the local civil power to resolve their disputes. And yet the community's own court had very little authority over those who refused to subject themselves to its rulings. Such was the situation faced by the members of the Jewish trade association (*chevrah*) in the Polish settlement of Nasielsk in about the year 1780. The following entry in the association's minute-book (*pinkas*) makes plain what happened.[2]

This person whose name is Mordecai was written about in the previous minute-book, but we deem it worthy to rewrite his name in this new minute-book which was started in 1758, and these are his sponsors: [*The names of his ten original sponsors are then given.*]

Because Mordecai went with his wife Judith and committed an evil act reprehensible among the people, he and his wife came before the court on the third day of the month of Iyar [*sic*]. There they blasphemed and cursed and used their mouths wildly against the Association, and woe it was to the ears that had to listen to them! On a later day he himself came to the court and continued to blaspheme in words that cannot be repeated. Then he said [*in Yiddish*]: 'I swear by God that I will not leave this place until I draw blood from one of you.' He and his wife said strongly that if they wanted to throw them out, it was impossible because to do so would shame the Association. If they wanted to fine them they could because [*text unclear*] he was rich.

We are afraid that Mordecai is a violent person and capable of murder. Therefore we, the officers of the Association, with other members, and with the members of the court, have agreed to remove the man Mordecai from the Association for three consecutive years because he did things that make it impossible to have a portion of this Brotherhood. Any member of the Association who supports him in that time shall be fined. And all of this we have done for the sake of God and that the whole community shall hear, see, and fear and will no longer conduct themselves in such a manner. All this comes from us the officers of the Association, all of which we sign.[3]

[2] 'Chronicle of the Association of Tailors, Furriers, and Jewellers in Nasielsk, Poland: 1778–1841', Jewish Historical Institute, Warsaw. The Chronicle has been microfilmed under the auspices of Dr Herbert C. Zafren, Director of Libraries, Hebrew Union College, Cincinnati, Ohio.

[3] I am grateful to Ms Cissy Grossman, guest curator, 'Fragments of Greatness Rediscovered: A Loan Exhibition from Poland' (1983), for providing this translation. The words in square brackets have been supplied by the present author.

Zionist Pioneering Youth Movements in Poland and their Attitude to Erets Israel during the Holocaust

DINA PORAT

AN understanding of the attitude of the Zionist pioneering youth movements to the Land of Israel (Erets Israel), the centre and embodiment of their ideals, is essential to the appreciation of a much larger issue—the relations between the diaspora and the Yishuv (the Hebrew Zionist community in Palestine during the early 1920s to the late 1940s, under the British Mandate), and between Zionists and the Jewish people at large. It is all the more so during the Holocaust, the most difficult and controversial moment in these relations.

Despite its importance and implications, this issue has hardly been investigated, for two reasons. The first is the general difficulty of assessing and weighing attitudes and relations involving both national aspirations and individual dreams, phenomena that belong to an intangible sphere where the life and death of thousands of youngsters were determined. Moreover, the issue is of the utmost political and ideological significance in the post-Holocaust Yishuv and in the Jewish state, so that perhaps—and paradoxically—it has been avoided for so long precisely because of its importance.

The nature of the sources also poses difficulties. The source material is very small in quantity. It includes diaries written in Europe by members of the youth movements, during the events or very close to them; letters they sent to Erets Yisrael; and the press they published clandestinely. The latter survived the war in greater volume than the letters, and the letters in greater volume than the diaries. Yet the sum total of surviving material is but a fraction of the rich corpus of published and private writing originally produced. Moreover, the picture must necessarily remain incomplete: the output of certain movements has hardly survived, most members of other organizations have perished. The available material is thus random, and no reflection of the number of members or relative importance of the various movements.

The contents of the sources also raise problems. Does the press, the public expression of the movements' views, reflect the same attitude as private writings such as letters and diaries? Do the sources reflect differences in the attitudes of the various movements to Erets Israel, and possible changes in such differences, arising from the war and the Holocaust?

Moreover, despite the special ties created between these movements and their counterparts in Palestine in the interwar period, the survivors living in Israel today have hardly referred to the issue that played such a central role in their lives. Many of their memoirs and testimonies contain no reference to it at all, and some still maintain deliberate silence in interviews and public utterances. A researcher must also take into consideration the passage of time, the encounter with reality in Palestine and later in Israel, and their impact on the content of the references which are made. Conscious of such difficulties, we shall nevertheless endeavour to examine these youth movements, their pre-war ties with and attitudes to Palestine, and the vicissitudes of the ties and attitudes during the two main parts of the war and the Holocaust.

There were six main Jewish pioneering youth movements in Poland. Four belonged to the Hechaluts Centre (Centre of the Pioneer): Hashomer Hatsa'ir, Dror–Hechaluts, Gordonia, and Akiva. A larger organization, called the Pioneering Co-ordination (Hako'ordinatsiah Hachalutzit), included these four, and also Hano'ar Hatsioni and Hechaluts Hamizrachi. These movements educated their members towards 'self-fulfilment' (*hagshamah atsmit*), which meant cultivating the land and living a communal life in kibbutzim in Zion.[1]

For the following study three diaries were chosen that reflect the character of their authors both as individuals and as members of political movements: the diary of Gusta Davidson of Akiva; that of Chaika Klinger of Hashomer Hatsa'ir; and that of Mordechai Tennenbaum-Tamaroff, of Dror–Hechaluts.[2]

[1] Hashomer Hatsa'ir (the Young Guard), the centre of which was in Warsaw, was a Zionist Socialist pioneering movement which advocated life in a kibbutz. Affiliated to Hakibbutz Ha'artsi (the National Kibbutz) in Palestine, it was the most left-wing of these six movements, with a pro-Soviet ideology.

Dror–Hechaluts (Freedom–the Pioneer) was a Socialist working-class movement, active all over Poland. It was affiliated to Po'alei Tsion ZS (Zionist Socialist Workers) and to Hakibbutz Hameuchad (the United Kibbutz) in Palestine.

Gordonia (named after A. D. Gordon, an ideologist advocating a return to nature and a programme of productive work), was a moderate Social Democratic movement, favouring life in a *kevutsah* (a larger form of collective settlement than a kibbutz), and belonged to the World Union of Mapai, the main party in Palestine.

Akiva, whose main centre was Kraków, was a non-Socialist moderately religious movement, affiliated to the moderate wing of the General Zionists (A) in Poland.

Hanoa'ar Hatsi'oni (the Zionist Youth) was affiliated to the Ha'oved Hatsioni (the Zionist Worker) in Palestine and to the radical wing of the General Zionists (B) in Poland.

Hechaluts Hamizrachi (the Eastern Pioneer, so named because Zion is in the east) was affiliated to the Religious Zionist Party, Hamizrachi.

[2] Gusta Davidson, *Yomana shel Ustina* (Tel Aviv, 1953); Chaika Klinger, *Miyoman bageto* (Merchavia, 1959); Mordechai Tennenbaum-Tamaroff, *Dapim min hadelikah*, 2nd edn., ed. Bronka Klibansky and Zvi Shner (Jerusalem, 1984). It should be emphasized that only the last of these was written in the midst of events (covering just January and February 1943, unfortunately); the other two are a sort of a summary, written very close to the events.

Regrettably, hardly any others survive. Use was also made of the surviving press of Gordonia, Hano'ar Hatsioni, and Akiva,[3] and of many letters written and sent to Palestine by members of all movements,[4] including one each by Yitzhak Zuckerman (Antek) and Zivia Lubetkin, Mordechai Tennenbaum-Tamaroff, and Frumka Płotnicka, leaders respectively of the revolts in Warsaw, Białystok, and Będzin, summarizing the situation of Polish Jewry and its youth movements as observed at the moment of writing.

The Zionist pioneering youth movements in Poland had about 100,000 members on the eve of the Second World War.[5] They constituted important centres of activity for a large and well-organized public, living a very intensive life, involving seminaries, *hakhsharot* (centres of training for collective life in Palestine), summer camps, year-round activity in the urban areas, extensive press and publications, and so on. The life of a member centred around these activities and around his comrades.

Erets Israel played a unique and pivotal role in this framework. It is no exaggeration to say that the Zionist youth, while living physically in Poland, had their spiritual home in Erets Israel. They studied, and some of them even wrote and spoke, Hebrew; they celebrated festivals and memorial days in the way in which they were celebrated in Erets Israel; they read the Hebrew press and kept abreast of the life of the Yishuv; they felt personally attached to the leaders of the movements and parties they were affiliated to, and believed that their current existence was but a preparation for another life.[6] 'Every piece of information is a treasure, an encouragement, an exhilarating part of a wonderful heroic saga, starting in the Bilu'im, continuing in Hashomer, Tel Hai, Hulda, and reaching Hanita . . . The golden chain of heroism will go on. We will carry it on!'[7] Such expressions and others in the same vein idealized the internal strife and failures of the Yishuv, whose population numbered 470,000 on the eve of the Second World War and was ruled by the British Mandatory government.

---

[3] *Hechaluts halochem*, organ of the Akiva underground movement in Kraków, Aug.–Oct. 1943 (Bet lohamei hageta'ot and Hakibbutz Hameuchad, 1984); *Itonut hamahteret hayehudit beWarsha* (Jerusalem, vols. i and ii 1949, vol. iii, ed. Yoseph Kermish, 1984); *Itonut Gordonia bemahteret geto Warsha* (Hulda, 1966).

[4] However, I have not found any letters sent by members of Hechaluts Hamizrachi to Palestine during the war, except for those printed in *Hatsofeh*, the Mizrachi daily.

[5] This is the estimation of the centres for research into youth movements in Yad Tabenkin and Givat Haviva, Israel. See also *Itonut hamahteret*, i. 50 in the introduction; Shalom Cholavski, 'On the Lost Jewish Youth', *Yalkut moreshet*, 43–4 (Aug. 1987), 143–8 at 145; Rivka Perlis, *Tenuot hanoar hehalutsiot bePolin hakevushah* (Bet lohamei hageta'ot, 1987), 18, 457.

[6] It should be emphasized that Erets Israel was a source of inspiration and hope for many who were outside the youth movements. See Yehoshua Eivshitz, *Erets Yisrael kegorem mashpia bagetaot uvemahanot harikuz* (Kiriyat Ata, 1973).

[7] *Unzere yedies*, 87 (Mar. 1939), quoted in Tennenbaum-Tamaroff, *Dapim min hadelikah*, 195); this newspaper ('Our Information') was published by Dror. The writer refers to people and places that became symbols of the building and safe-keeping of Palestine.

Indeed, it was immigration from Poland, including the influx of pioneers, that brought to Palestine most of its newcomers between the two world wars. The pioneering immigration would probably have assumed much larger dimensions had the British Mandatory government allowed it, and had the Arab riots of 1936–9 not resulted in further restrictions.[8] Those members of youth movements who remained in Poland—temporarily, as they hoped—felt virtually responsible for the fate of the small Yishuv, and bound to develop and defend it even from their great distance. When news reached Europe about the 'White Paper' published by the Mandatory government in May 1939, limiting immigration to Palestine to 75,000 in five years, and prohibiting the purchase of land by Jews in most areas of the country, it stimulated the members of the youth movements to declare a state of emergency that 'impels us to victory . . . the White Paper must be abolished . . . all Jewish youth must be recruited to support the country and the land'.[9]

The immigration of pioneers strengthened the already close ties between Poland and Palestine on the eve of the war. Through intensive correspondence, visits, and the dispatch of parcels, very active contacts were maintained between parties and movements, as well as at the personal level. With the outbreak of war, when Polish Jews were gradually forced into the ghettos, the direct ties with Palestine had to be replaced by indirect ones. A few thousand refugees did reach Palestine in 1940, including some members of youth movements, but their numbers dwindled, and by the end of that year immigration from the General Gouvernement stopped altogether. Moreover, emissaries from Palestine left Poland at the outbreak of the war; the last emissary returned home in mid-1940.[10]

Correspondence continued for a while between Palestine and Vilna, then the capital of independent Lithuania, where thousands of Jewish refugees gathered, including 2,000 members of the various youth movements; these served as mediators between Nazi-occupied Poland and Palestine. Some of them managed to reach Palestine and bring more news, but in June 1940 Lithuania was annexed by the Soviet Union and these contacts were severed. Communication was maintained until the end of the war between Poland and Geneva, so that there was contact with representatives of the Yishuv, such as Nathan Schwalb, representative of the four Hechaluts Centre movements, and for a short time in 1940 also through Mordechai Orenstein (later Oren), of Hashomer Hatsa'ir. Mail was transferred from Geneva to London and thence to Palestine.

---

[8] According to Melech Neustadt, *Shenat hashmadah* (Tel Aviv, 1944), 23, 40% of all immigrants to Palestine up to the end of 1943 came from Poland. See also Binyamin Gil, *Dapei aliyah* (Jerusalem, 1950).

[9] See Tennenbaum-Tamaroff, *Dapim min hadelikah*, 201.

[10] See, e.g. *Al masuot Polin* (Merchavia, 1940; *Biyemei Shoah* (testimonies of Hechaluts emissaries) (Ein Harod, 1940); also Yechiam Weitz, 'The Return of the Hakibbutz Hameuchad Emissaries from Europe, 1939–1941', in Anita Shapira (ed.), *Ha'apalah* (Tel Aviv, 1990), 108–23.

By the end of 1942, when the Yishuv rescue delegation was established in Istanbul, mail was sent there from Geneva, and then on to Palestine (and in the reverse direction). Thus, representatives of the movements in Erets Israel who were stationed in Istanbul could maintain indirect contact with their comrades in Poland. But at that late stage, when the process of extermination that started in Poland in the spring of 1942 was already in full swing, members and leaders of the youth movements were compelled to change their locations constantly. The exchange of mail was hardly possible, and was gradually replaced during 1943 by the use of gentile emissaries, who could reach Poland from Geneva via Slovakia, or from Istanbul via Hungary. Naturally, contact through emissaries was more frequent with closer places such as Zagłebie in south-eastern Poland, sparse with the central parts of the General Gouvernement, and non-existent with the areas across the Bug.

THE YOUTH MOVEMENTS' ATTITUDE TOWARDS ERETS ISRAEL FROM THE BEGINNING OF THE WAR TO 1942

The different categories of source material for the period 1940–1 deal with different issues: the letters and diaries refer to the ties with Palestine, the changes which these ties underwent during the war, and the aid sent from Palestine; whereas the press refers to the general and theoretical problems of the present and, even more so, of the future.

The letters reflect the feelings of loneliness, even of orphanhood, that the writers felt with the outbreak of the war and the return of the emissaries who had been sent from Erets Israel. These feelings are clearly and sharply expressed, as is the craving for more contacts, for a warmer response, for many letters—all far more important to them than the material support. They rejoice with each letter and are grateful for every parcel, but at the same time they do not shy away from expressing anger, disappointment, and amazement at the paucity of letters and parcels reaching them.

'We beg you, with all possible insistence: do not stop writing to us . . . lest our faith, the only one left for us in these dark days, be extinguished';[11] 'remember all those that are here';[12] 'remember, dear friends, and understand that our existence and the movement's depend mostly on you';[13] 'you tend to be silent—what is the meaning of your silence?'[14] 'We saw newspapers [from Palestine], and wondered

[11] A letter from 'Sh.S.' (full name unknown) in Vilna, dated 10 June 1940, in *Ha'oved hatsioni*, 3/7 (10 June 1940).
[12] Ibid. 3/9 (10 July 1940) (unsigned).
[13] *Sefer Hashomer Hatsa'ir*, ed. Levi Drov and Israel Rosenzweig, i (Bet lohamei hageta'ot, 1956), 458.
[14] Abraham Givelber to Zvi Rozenstein, 5 May 1940, in the Histradut (Workers' Union) archives, file 372/1.

at their tranquil spirit.'[15] These are quotations from letters written in 1940 by members of five different movements, an indication that all felt the same way about this issue.

Letters from 1941 and the first half of 1942 are similar. 'I received all the letters dated March and April, and all parcels. Please accept our heartfelt thanks.' 'We received your parcels this week, and they helped us very very much.' 'Through your dispatches I was able to give important help to many relatives [i.e., members of the same movement].' One even says: 'With the same certainty that we know you all remember us, know that we fulfil our duties here . . . there is no need for more words.'[16] And yet, sometimes within the very same letters, one can find contrasting sentiments. 'You must know that this help is not at all sufficient for constructive work.' 'I allow myself to tell you that you and others must help us as soon as possible.' 'Z.[17] complains about your silence and lack of support: there is no way we can go on like this!' 'Why don't you write to me?!' 'Gevalt! Where is your help? What on earth has happened to you?' 'I will never forget and never forgive you.'[18]

These ambivalent feelings are reminiscent of those one might find in love letters: strong dependency and great joy, alongside deep anger and the fear of being deserted or losing contact. The letters express the intimate personal attachment felt by the leadership and senior members of the youth movements, who spent years in *hakhsharot* and engaged in political activity in Poland, towards the leadership and friends in Palestine.

During the first two and a half years of the war the letters express the certainty that more support in the form of parcels and written material could have found its way to occupied Poland, once the channels of communication had been established. This is why, in the course of time, a distinction came to be made in the letters between the singular 'you' addressed to Schwalb in Geneva and the plural 'you' addressed to colleagues in Palestine. Schwalb, the main contact for Hechaluts Centre and its four youth movements during the war, sent thousands of letters and hundreds of parcels, and constantly received the warmest thanks for his care in maintaining the contact; whereas letters to Palestine (though transmitted through Schwalb) claim that the comrades there could and should have done a lot more. With the passage of time and the increase of hunger and distress,

---

[15] A letter from Hechaluts Hamizrachi in Vilna, printed in *Hatsofeh* (5 Jan. 1940).

[16] From Opoczno, 21 Mar. 1941; from Warsaw, 30 Mar. 1941; from Będzin, 29 Oct. 1941; and from Hrubishow, 14 Jan. 1942. Further similar statements can be found in letters from Warsaw, 6 Apr. 1941; from Częstochowa, 6 Jan. 1942; from Parczow, 15 Feb. 1942; from Kraków, 27 Apr. 1942; from Lublin, 3 June 1942 in *Mikhtavim min hagetaot*, ed. Beracha Chabas (Tel Aviv, 1943), 7–40.

[17] Zivia Lubetkin, a central leader of Dror–Hechalutz, and later of the ghetto uprising in Warsaw.

[18] Letters from Warsaw and from Lublin, 30 Mar. 1941; from Grochów, 11 May 1941; from Będzin, 10 June 1941; from Upper Silesia, 6 Oct. 1941; from Warsaw, 19 Oct. 1941, all in *Mikhtavim min hagetaot*, pp. 9–18. See also Tosia Altman's letter to Mordechai Orenstein of 29 Mar. 1940, in *Sefer Hashomer Hatsa'ir*, i. 486.

the demand for real practical help—for food—became a matter of life and death, of existence itself: the parcels were sold to keep the members alive and maintain the movements' activities.

The atmosphere in the ghettos during those two years was one of hope: *Uberlebn*, 'surviving [the Germans]'. There was a burning desire to have revenge by hanging on till the end of the war—surely not so far off—inspired, for the most part, by the prospect of the day of victory in spite of the terrible conditions. This hope was the basis for the youth movements' activity at that time, and provided the stamina to reorganize the young members and continue as they had done before the war. Paradoxically, the movements flourished, and the membership was never greater than in 1940 and 1941. Erets Israel was still—even more than before—at centre stage, serving as a focus for dreams and activities. The work for Keren Hakayemet (the National Fund established in order to purchase and reclaim lands in Palestine) was more intensive than before the war, and so was the wish to emigrate to Palestine.

When the front lines drew nearer to Palestine, concern in Warsaw about the safety of the Yishuv rose to extreme levels. When Tel Aviv was lightly bombarded by the Italian fleet in 1940 and then again in 1941, anxious letters were sent from Nazi-occupied Poland. When the danger was over, they were replaced by letters of relief and happiness, for 'the homeland is healthy'.[19] This is understandable; less so is the appearance in a Gordonia newspaper of August 1941 of an article detailing the *rapprochement* between Jews and Arabs, the creation of new settlements, and the increase in the wealth of the Histadrut (the workers union), which had reached the sum of £5 million.[20] The death rate in Warsaw at this time had reached thousands a month, yet there is no hint in the newspaper of any comparison between the situation in Warsaw and that in Palestine; there is only an expression of joy and satisfaction at the growth and development of the Yishuv.

As another example of this attitude, in September 1941 Eliezer Geller, chief editor of the Gordonia press and its main leader, advocated regular purchase of the Keren Hakayemet stamps, and wrote in opposition to 'the use of these funds for relief [in Warsaw]. They should be kept intact until the day comes when they will be transferred to the right hands.'[21] One would have to achieve a very high degree of 'love of Zion', as the Zionist expression goes, to show such devotion in such a place at such a time. But we must still consider the question of whether it was only the press organs of the movements that continued the old pre-war line, while private letters gave expression to the painful and problematic relations with Palestine that developed during the war. Would Geler have written the same words in a letter to the Gordonia leadership in Erets Israel?

---

[19] e.g. *Mikhtavim min hagetaot*, 35, 39.
[20] *Itonut Gordonia*, 254, quoted from *Oisdoyer* ('Perseverance'), 4 (25 Aug. 1941).
[21] Ibid. 26, from *Słowo Młodych* (6–7 Sept. 1941).

The letters and diaries discussed not only the levels of response and support received in Poland, but also the possibilities of emigration. The horrors of the war and the Nazi occupation strengthened the wish to 'make *aliyah*' (emigrate to Erets Israel), not only as a means of realizing ideals, but also as an escape from the terrible situation in the ghettos. Requests for the necessary certificates, finance, and formal arrangements occupy a prominent position in the letters sent by pioneers from Vilna during 1940, on their own behalf and on behalf of friends in occupied Poland. These appeals remained almost totally unanswered, for two reasons. First, the number of certificates made available by the Mandatory government was negligible in comparison with the demands that reached Palestine from all European countries after the outbreak of the war. Secondly, the veteran activists of the various Zionist parties in Vilna and Warsaw, including those whose contribution to the Zionist cause had been slight, were also desperate for immigration certificates, and their claim met with a better response. 'The first steps of the Erets Israel committee [in Vilna] were to try and obtain a suitable number of certificates for party activists,' the committee's report frankly admitted.[22] 'We especially supported Zionist activists of all parties,' wrote the Joint Committee for the Help of Polish Refugees in Tel Aviv.[23]

Members of all youth movements were quick to notice this state of affairs, and to react with bitterness and deep disappointment: 'Indeed, all of us together do not have the same ability to cry out and send cables as any one of the activists, let alone all of them put together'.[24] A list of candidates for immigration to Erets Yisrael, compiled in 1940 by Chaim Barlas, director of the Jewish Agency Immigration Department, did not include 'even one out of all the members of Frumka's family[25] . . . the reasons are not clear to us, yet the intention to avoid helping the pioneers is clear enough . . . there is no way we'll agree to such treatment.'[26] The frustration is expressed most openly in a private diary: 'And if I ever reach Palestine . . . even then disappointment and terrible embitterment will not fade away . . . because I received no letter or information, had no contact, and felt that none cared . . . (while they . . . had everything, even certificates) . . . I feel shame for you, comrades in Erets Israel.'[27]

---

[22] Histadrut archive, file 372/1.

[23] A letter to the Revisionist party in Tel Aviv, dated 2 Dec. 1940, in the Jabotinski archive, Rescue file. See also Apolinary Hartglas, 'Rikuz manhigei yahadut Polin be'Erets Yisrael', *Davar* (8 Jan. 1941).

[24] An unsigned letter of 29 June 1940, in the Histadrut archive, file 372/1.

[25] Of the Dror–Hechaluts movements of which Frumka Płotnicka, later a leader of the revolt of Będzin, was a central leader. (The revolt of Będzin started with the final liquidation of the ghetto on 1 Aug. 1943: on that day members of the youth movements, led by five commanders, fought with arms from a number of bunkers.)

[26] Letter from Abraham Givelber to Eliyahu Dobkin, a co-director of the Jewish Agency's Immigration Department, dated 15 Mar. 1940, in the Histadrut archive, file 372/3.

[27] *Dapim min hadelikah*, 26 Jan. 1943 (writing retrospectively).

At that time the press of the movements dealt with other issues. Until the great deportation to Treblinka in the summer of 1942, the press, especially the Warsaw publications, was a means to propagate news, to educate the youth, and to represent the movements among the general Jewish public. The writers analysed the current situation and expressed their views about the future in a theoretical and sophisticated manner, evidence of their long years of ideological disputes and extensive reading in both literature and political science. The issues covered were Zionist aspirations for the post war period; the future of the Jewish people; the attitude towards the Soviet Union; and policies that the Yishuv should adopt during the war. On one matter there was no dispute among the movements: every page of their publications is imbued with the axiom of 'love of Zion'. Yet the movements differed and disputed among themselves regarding the correct answers to political questions.

Akiva took the view that enrolment in the British army, involving dispatch 'to far away battlefields', was 'a preventative measure' for the British, because a young Yishuv member away from Palestine would not be able to influence the event unfolding there. 'It is unwise to strain relations at an inopportune moment and to kindle fires hard to extinguish;[28] but at the same time the strength of Jewish youth, whose only task is to defend the building of Palestine, should not be wasted.' The goal was clear: 'The war that brought about the destruction of the Jewish people should bring about, as fair compensation [!], a Jewish Palestine.' The means were clear as well: careful relations with Britain, a moderate level of recruitment to the British army, participation in the universal struggle—but first and foremost, safeguarding the country of the Jews.[29]

Gordonia differed: reliance on Britain was the correct attitude, whether in wartime or in peace. It was therefore necessary to place all power and resources at Britain's disposal. In this way, when the war ended, the appropriate political reward would be obtained.

Hashomer Hatsa'ir had a quite different view, one that stemmed from its identification with the Soviet Union: 'The Jewish people must refrain from participating in this world collision, must maintain independent political views, must not shed its blood in foreign battlefields.' In any case, the British colonial empire had weakened and would soon be replaced by the Red Army and the long-awaited Socialist revolution. The Yishuv should therefore not interfere in this capitalist and imperialist war; its duty was to remain neutral. Thus, joint Jewish action in occupied Europe as a whole, even within the framework of the Zionist parties, was not the most urgent item on the agenda, but rather the realization of Socialism and the establishment of a Soviet regime in the Jewish communities of

---

[28] In other words, refusal to join the British army might disrupt relations with the British authorities.

[29] Hechaluts halochem, 238–40.

Europe and Palestine. Then the Soviet Union would recognize Zionism, and all would end well.[30]

This is not the place to follow the changes in Hashomer Hatsa'ir's attitude to the Soviet Union after the Ribbentrop–Molotov pact and after the German invasion of the Soviet Union. However, the end result was that Zionist ideology outweighed identification with the Soviet Union, and, regardless of its Socialist and pro-Soviet views, Hashomer Hatsa'ir drew closer to the other Zionist youth movements and supported the Jewish communities in their distress.

This is why *Hechaluts halochem*, the Akiva publication in Kraków, was able to publish the following retrospective summary in the summer of 1943:

The pioneering youth, divided into quite a number of political tendencies . . . from the extreme left through the moderates to the General Zionists, was nevertheless completely united on the premiss of personal Zionist self-fulfilment . . . when self-fulfilment was discussed all differences of opinion and attitude were forgotten . . . the distrust felt by the youth movements towards the political parties was all too well known . . . there was no such distrust among the movements themselves . . . not even after the most extreme differences of opinion.[31]

The process of *rapprochement* between the movements, especially on the part of Hashomer Hatsa'ir, was not thoroughly discussed between the members in Europe and their leadership in Palestine, where partisan disputes raged. A matter of such importance could not be an issue for discussion via irregular mail between continents in time of war, and except for a warning from the Hashomer Hatsa'ir leader Meir Ya'ari, of Kibbutz Merchaviah, not to draw too close to the other movements, and a quick apology from his disciples in Vilna—'we never thought of a full union'—there are no traces of the matter in the surviving correspondence: it was raised again, along similar lines, after the liberation, when the European movements wanted to unite fully and the leaders from Palestine prevented it.[32]

One may conclude, then, that during the first two and a half years of the war, when the movements—and the Jewish public as a whole—still hoped to survive the Nazi occupation, Erets Israel continued to be the focus of their education and their hopes for a personal and collective future. Yet the material they wrote expressed a craving for more tangible contacts, as well as disappointment and sharp criticism.

---

[30] *The Underground Gordonia Press*, 260. For a similar characterization see *Neged hazerem* (the Hashomer Hatsa'ir organ in Warsaw), 5/16 (24 Sept. 1941), repr. in *Itonut hamaḥteret*. i. 276.

[31] *Hechaluts halochem*, 96.

[32] Perlis, *Tenuot hanoar heḥalutsiot*, 79. See also Anita Shapira, *Visions in Conflict* (Tel Aviv, 1988), 325–54.

FROM MID-1942 TO THE UPRISINGS IN THE GHETTOS

In the spring of 1942, when the Germans started to evacuate the ghettos and send their inmates to the death camps, a new period opened for the youth movements. The hesitations and difficulties in coming to terms with the information about the systematic extermination—news which reached them from Vilna at the beginning of 1942—were gradually overcome. The idea of self-defence and revolt started to crystallize, and the movements began the transition towards becoming a fighting armed underground that could replace the elder leadership of the ghettos. These deep internal processes changed the movements and were bound to alter their attitude to Palestine as well.

The basic attitude towards Erets Israel as an ideal did not change. 'The dream of Ein Harod and Mishmar Ha'emek'[33] was still their dream. Yet, under such terrible circumstances, the distance between the youth movements and this dream kept growing. Their immediate aim was no longer emigration to Palestine, nor could it be. Once they realized the real intent of the German treatment of Jews in occupied Europe, and once they made the decision to revolt, the only conclusion left for them was to stay in Europe and to stop looking for ways to emigrate. Moreover, care for the younger members, whose number kept diminishing, was no longer a top priority. Instead, their identification with the general Jewish tragedy intensified, and other aims came to dominate: self-defence, remaining with the communities, maintaining the honour of the Jewish people. These goals could only deepen the growing gulf between the movements and Palestine. Life there and tomorrow was replaced by fighting here and now.

This profound change, which took place slowly and painfully through a long process of inner deliberation and exchange of conflicting opinions, is reflected in all the sources—diaries, letters, and press—of the period. Its beginnings can be traced as early as 1941: 'The educational work is already worthless. It is so difficult to describe the kibbutz. It is all so far away, so intangible, so unreal,'[34] wrote Chaika Klinger of Hashomer Hatsa'ir in Będzin in her diary, some time after June 1941. Tosia Altman, a member of the Hashomer Hatsa'ir leadership in Warsaw, wrote to close friends in Palestine in no uncertain terms: 'I hardly ever think about you and about Erets Israel . . . we feel that you have deserted us.'[35] In mid-1942 Frumka Płotnicka wrote about the emissaries who had returned to Palestine at the outbreak of the war: 'I am so sorry they have no idea what our life here is like.'[36] So, despite the correspondence that still went on, and despite the still close ties,

---

[33] Central kibbutzim of Dror–Hechaluts and of Hashomer Hatsa'ir, serving as symbols of inspiration and leadership in their respective movements.   [34] *Miyoman bageto* 61, (no exact date).

[35] In her letter of 23 July 1941 to Adam Rand, a member of the Hashomer Hatsa'ir executive, who had been in Palestine since 1940. My thanks are due to my student Ziva Shalev, whose MA thesis on Tosia Altman unearthed this letter.

[36] A letter of 5 June 1942 from Częstochowa, quoted in *Mikhtavim min hagetaot*, 32.

their feeling was that those in Palestine did not grasp what was going on in Poland, what a ghetto was really like, and what spiritual resources were needed in order to carry on the daily public work. They realized that this work was consuming all their time and energy, that it engulfed all their being and became their only reality, so that no room was left for thoughts of Palestine. 'Erets Israel drifts further and further away from us,' wrote Chaika Klinger simply.[37]

Palestine was replaced as the centre of awareness by a sense of identification and by contact with the dying communities. In the most desperate and angry of her letters Tosia Altman vents 'the bitterness accumulated inside me against you and your friends, who forgot me with such total forgetfulness', and cries out against the death of the Jewish people: 'Israel is dying before my very eyes . . . and he is my best friend.'[38] These words are perhaps the best characterization of the process that the movements were undergoing: it was the people of Israel and its communities that became their best friend.

The change determined a new definition of goals:

We are still part of the Jewish pioneering movement that builds Palestine for the Jewish people. But our field of struggle is here, on the ruins of Polish Jewry. To avenge their blood, to express our vital need to gain freedom, and to be prepared to sacrifice our lives for that freedom—this is our immediate goal. It was dictated by the Jewish reality.[39]

Shimshon Dranger, editor of *Hechaluts halochem*, the Akiva organ in Kraków, repeated this concept time and again. Another goal was defined by Mordechai Tennenbaum-Tamaroff at the end of a fierce discussion of the remaining options: 'Most important of all is not to diminish the image and pride of the movement until the last minute';[40] and later: 'We achieved our goal, we resisted with arms . . . because we refused to be led like sheep to the slaughter; we did not want history to say that the Jews of Poland died a miserable death.'[41]

The new definition of goals excluded emigration to Palestine, for which they had struggled so much. They had opportunities to cross the border, 'but we did not want to use this way because it did not offer a practical passage to Palestine, and because we refused even to consider an escape simply in order to save ourselves'.[42] So it was in Warsaw, Kraków, and Będzin, and in other ghettos: 'Z[ivia] would not hear a word about ties with Avrem!'.[43] Tosia 'married Haganah', i.e. committed herself to self-defence. In April 1943, when the revolt in Warsaw started, Zivia and Tosia 'were too busy to have time for their own rescue'.[44]

---

[37] *Miyoman bageto*, 147.   [38] *Mikhtavim min hagetaot*, 41–3.
[39] These are the words of Shimshon Dranger written in Oct. 1943: *Hechaluts halochem*, 65, 97, 180.
[40] A debate among the members of Kibbutz Tel Chai (which belonged to Dror) in Białystok, Feb. 1943, quoted in *Dapim min hadelikah*, 84.
[41] *Hechaluts halochem*, 42.   [42] Ibid. 97.
[43] A leader of her movement, then in Palestine.
[44] A letter dated 6 Apr. 1943, quoted in *Mikhtavim min hagetaot*, 50–1.

Leaders of the movements refused to save themselves and tried instead to rescue their disciples by sending them, when possible, to Slovakia and Hungary.

In Będzin, the closest point to Slovakia, plans were conceived to rescue members of the youth movements, older leaders, and public figures by means of various passports, predominantly South American, which Schwalb was trying to send to them, and by exchange with Germans residing outside the Reich. This is why in Będzin the deliberations and hesitations regarding the decision to revolt took longer than in other places. Zivia Lubetkin tried several times to force Frumka Płotnicka, who in 1943 was one of the central leaders of the youth movements in Będzin, to leave with a passport sent from Switzerland, for 'Who could tell our story better than Frumka?'[45] In most of her letters Frumka refused, though in others she did request a passport. Her letters to Switzerland, and others from Będzin, taken together, indicate that the possible contradiction between rescue, even of a few, and uprising was repeatedly discussed there during 1943.

It seems that the leadership in Będzin finally agreed to accept passports only as a protection against the deportations and in order, at best, to send a small delegation to the free world so as not to be forgotten by history once they had all been killed in combat. It also seems that most of the members of youth movements in Będzin reached a decision that excluded personal rescue and favoured fighting.[46] Letters were sent to Schwalb, 'who does not understand us' or the idea of the revolt,[47] to explain that 'marriage with Miss Haganah is soon to be expected'.[48] In August 1943, when the final liquidation of the ghetto was drawing near and with it the supposed moment for the revolt, Frumka sent back the messenger who came for her from Istanbul on behalf of the emissaries of the Yishuv, and stayed with the community and her friends so that they could die together. 'I lived with my brothers, and with them I will die,' she told the messenger.[49]

Letters arriving from Palestine at this stage—the summer of 1943—were completely out of touch with the reality of ghettos in Poland. Upon receiving a letter from comrades in Palestine, members of the youth movement could still write 'I cried with joy and pain',[50] or 'we cried with happiness . . . and realized that God has not yet totally forsaken us',[51] and so on. They were still happy to read that the Yishuv was building and creating, but the contrast at that stage was too terrible even for the most devoted lovers of Zion. 'Letters reached us telling of a new settlement, a new kibbutz. They sometimes came in the middle of the

---

[45] *Miyoman bageto*, 89.

[46] See Ruth Zariz, 'Attempts of Rescue and Revolt: The Attitude of the "Dror" Youth Movement in Będzin to the Use of Foreign Passports as a Means of Rescue', *Yad Vashem Studies*, 20 (1990) 143–62.

[47] *Miyoman bageto*, 90. [48] Perlis, *Tenuot hanoar hehalutsiot*, 272.

[49] Venia Pomerantz at a Mapai Centre meeting, 24 Aug. 1943; Labour Party archive.

[50] A letter dated 7 June, 1943, quoted in *Mikhtavim min hagetaot*, 50.

[51] Neustadt, *Shenat hashmadah*, 5.

horrors of the deportation'[52]—as if they came from another planet, as if they were written inconsiderately and insensitively. 'Gerushinski' ('Mr Deportation') visited the ghettos frequently, yet 'only Bendori is still refusing to understand that'.[53] 'A.' from Warsaw 'has a heart full of bitterness about you and Olamovitch [free-world Jewry], and will not write to you any more', for 'their impression is that ... they were forsaken and forgotten'.[54]

Another prevailing feeling was that 'in Palestine they did not understand our idea'[55]—namely, the idea of the revolt and of co-operation among the various movements for this purpose. The youth movements in Europe did not consider revolt and co-operation to be in any sense a deviation from the original Zionist ideas, but felt obliged to explain their position. 'At the same time [i.e. while preparing the revolts together] we did not forget our Zionist ideas even for one moment';[56] on the contrary, it was their duty to stay with the communities precisely because they were Zionist pioneers. Their leaders in Palestine had not understood their situation before, nor did they grasp their sacrifice at the time of the revolt; they were still perplexed at the process of *rapprochement* among the movements, which was a logical and natural outcome of the circumstances dictated by the Nazis. Understanding of these issues came at a later stage in Palestine.[57]

The discrepancy acquired clear and blunt expression at the time of the revolts. 'Why should we know Hebrew? Won't we know how to die without it?'[58] All questions were as nothing compared with the eternal ones of 'life and death'.[59] In a debate during which a member claimed that death was not a foregone conclusion and that they should still try to save themselves with a view to reaching Palestine in the future, 'their ever dear and sacred ideal', Dolek Liebskind, a leader of the Kraków underground, answered: 'No! We owe our brothers in Palestine the honourable death of pioneers, and nothing else. There is no bond of life between them and ourselves any more'.[60]

The very decision to rebel and the unique stature of the leaders of the revolts were to a great extent the result of education within the movements, and the Zionist idea at its centre, between the two world wars. Of course, this was not the only factor: others included the desire for revenge; the feelings of solidarity and mutual responsibility, which intensified with the loss of the members' families; and the uncompromising ideals of romantic youth (most of them were 16–23

---

[52] *Miyoman bageto*, 147.
[53] A letter dated 27 Mar. 1943, quoted in *Mikhtavim min hagetaot*, 50. Pinchas Bendori was a former emissary to Europe, then in Palestine.   [54] Ibid., and a letter dated Feb. 1943, ibid. 48–9.
[55] Chaika Klinger reporting to the Histadrut executive, 15 Mar. 1944: the Histadrut archive.
[56] *Hechaluts halochem*, 97.
[57] See Dina Porat, *The Blue and the Yellow Stars of David; The Zionist Leadership in Palestine and the Holocaust, 1939–1945* (Cambridge, Mass., and London, 1990), 239–45.
[58] *Miyoman bageto*, 61.   [59] *Dapim min hadelikah* (1st Hebrew edn., Jerusalem, 1948), 171.
[60] *Yomana shel Ustina*, 130.

years old). But above all these contributory factors, first and foremost stood their membership of the various movements and a deep commitment to their education, to the image of their movement, to the Zionism that fostered the ideal of a new positive and creative Jew, to the example set by Palestine, and consideration of 'what they will say about us' there.

Yet the decision to rebel was reached strictly by the members themselves, and was not the result of deliberations between them and their leaders in Palestine.

How would it have looked, if they,[61] who were living safely in Palestine, had cabled, for instance, an order to 'fight until the last person' or any other instruction of the sort . . . only those who were there could and should have decided . . . we embarked upon self-defence and revolt, knowing there was no chance for salvation, without any instructions from our leaders in Palestine—indeed, without their knowledge—but we were confident that we were acting according to the best tenets of our pioneering tradition and education . . . the movements in Palestine lived in another world, and if they did not manage to send us help, they certainly could not order us 'to die bravely'.

It was Ruzka Korchak, a member of the Vilna underground, who thus reconsidered, years later, a cable sent by Ya'ari and Tabenkin after the Warsaw ghetto revolt, asking the leadership to save themselves.[62]

In the second half of 1943 three letters were sent to Palestine from Warsaw, Białystok, and Będzin respectively. Yitzhak Zuckerman and Zivia Lubetkin, Mordechai Tennenbaum-Tamaroff, and Frumka Płotnicka and her comrades-in-arms each wrote eulogies of Polish Jewry and its youth movement, unaware of the letters by the others. All three are devoted mainly to description of the ghettos, the deportations, and the movements' decision to revolt following the mass murders. Palestine is mentioned in each of them only fleetingly. Tennenbaum-Tamaroff ended his letter with the exhortation: 'Friends, it is a great honour for a movement to have raised such people [as the members in Poland] . . . Do not ever forget them!'[63] Frumka and her friends opened: 'After a prolonged period of expectation we received only today, with enormous joy, your emissary and your letter. Unfortunately, he came a little too late. For years we have dreamt about an opportunity to tell you of our life and struggle.' And they ended: 'Do as much as you can. I doubt if you could still help us, because we face our last days . . . Lamentably, our hope of seeing our homeland will not materialize. We send you heartfelt regards . . . we have no more strength and patience to write to you about everything . . . we greet you from the bottom of our hearts.'[64] Zivia and Antek wrote: 'We know that you would have done everything to save us. And we also

---

[61] Ya'ari and Tabenkin, leaders of Hashomer Hatsa'ir and Dror–Hechalutz.
[62] Quoted from Ruzka Korchak's letter of 16 Feb. 1987 to Eliyahu Stern of the Ghetto Fighters' House following the passing away of Meir Ya'ari, a copy of which she sent to me.
[63] This was written in Apr. 1943; see *Dapim min hadelikah*, 93–111.
[64] Written in July 1943; see *Mikhtavim min hagetaot*, 56–8.

know you were powerless. It will be easier for us to die knowing that a free world will rise, and believing that Erets Israel will be a homeland for the Jewish people.'[65]

These few sentences reflect in a nutshell, though in an inexplicit fashion, the complex of feelings and attitudes of the youth movements towards the Yishuv: Tennenbaum-Tamaroff's fears that they would all die and be forgotten; Frumka's irony over the emissary and letter arriving 'a little too late'; and the contradiction in Zivia and Antek's words—'We know that you would have done everything', with the implied query 'Why in fact was not everything done, even by a powerless Yishuv?'; the adieu to life, in the certainty of imminent death; and in the last analysis the disappointment at the Yishuv's inappropriate response. Yet the farewell is still imbued with faith in Zionism and in the Yishuv, with warm wishes and greetings.

Why did they not write explicitly? Was it only because the moment before the curtain falls is not the right time for settling accounts? If so, why did the survivors not speak out or write when they came to Palestine after the war? 'During the deportations we used to make up lists of "those we would hang in Palestine" when we came there,' said Antek Zuckerman in his memoirs, 'because it was a one-sided affair'; even after the liberation, the National Committee in Lublin, of which he was a member, waited for months for someone from Palestine to show up, and when no one did, Antek went southward to Italy to meet the Jewish Brigade. Still, he did not hang anyone there, and he stipulated that his long memoirs, in which he raised the subject shortly and sharply (the Yishuv's reaction 'will not be forgiven!'), would be published only after his death.[66] Nor did others give vent to accusations upon reaching Palestine, or later.

There are, perhaps, four possible explanations for this silence. First, most of the survivors from the youth movements were plunged directly into the difficult reality of the War of Independence, and into the struggle for the survival of the state during its first harsh years. That was not the right time for a settling of accounts, but rather for participation in the general effort. Indeed, most of the earliest memoirs of survivors from the youth movements were written towards the middle of the 1950s, and still with very little reference to this issue, as if it were being postponed for a more suitable time.

Secondly, when they came to Palestine and met the leaders to whom they had been writing from so far away, they found it hard to blame them, realizing their personal stature, their deep concern for the youth movements in Europe, and their commitment to the movements' ideals.[67] They realized that these leaders,

---

[65] Written in Nov. 1943; text in Melech Neustadt, *Hurban vamered shel yehudei Warsha* (Tel Aviv, 1947), 151–3.

[66] Yitzhak Zuckerman (Antek), *Sheva hashanim hahen 1939–1946* (Bet lohamei hageta'ot, 1990), 224, 516–21.

[67] This was stated by Zuckerman during the recording of his memoirs (see n. 66), as Yoske Rabinovitch, who recorded them, told me on 26 July 1987.

whom they had admired and considered omnipotent, were in fact heading a small and weak Yishuv; and that 'there was a Mussa Dag' here too.[68]

Thirdly, they were bound to reach an understanding of 'the psychological gap', as Zuckerman defined it, between the sane and normal world of Palestine during the war and the impossible and unprecedented world of occupied Europe. As a result, each side, the Yishuv and the survivors, had completely different concepts of life and death, of heroism and defeat, of the limits of human endurance, of the possible and the impossible.

And finally, those who had lived, and almost died, by the light of their ideals could not go on living without them. To have destroyed even some of them publicly, opening a nationally and politically sensitive, perhaps endless, debate, would have made their lives in Israel impossible, and most of them could not live anywhere else. The dream filled their lives to such an extent that it could not have been forsaken.

---

[68] Zuckerman, *Sheva hashanim hahen*, 516–17. 'Mussa Dag' refers to a place where Armenians resisted the Turkish genocide in the First World War.

Resistance through Education: Polish Zionist Youth Movements in Warsaw, 1939–1941

ERICA NADELHAFT

THE pioneering Zionist youth movements in Warsaw played a decisive role in the organization and implementation of the ghetto's armed revolt against the Germans. Members of movements such as Dror, Hashomer Hatsa'ir, and Gordonia were the driving force behind the active and passive resistance of Warsaw's remaining Jews. The resistance led by these young leaders was not, however, fortuitous. It was rather the result of the continuous development and maturation of the youth movements during the previous years.

The period between the outbreak of the Second World War and the fall of 1941, when the first rumours of mass murder reached Warsaw, was an important time for the youth movements. Unable to foresee the coming extermination of the Jews, youth leaders first attempted to foster the values and goals of the movements by means of traditional activities. As time progressed, the reality of life under Nazi rule forced them to redirect their energies into new activities that better fulfilled the needs of both their members and, eventually, the general population. Despite these changes, however, the values and principles held by the youth movements remained the same, enabling them to adapt and go on to lead Warsaw's Jews in revolt.

The education of youth played a crucial role in this process. Always central to the youth movements' activities, education became essential not only as a means to continue and ensure the movements' existence, but as a value in itself. The movements' leaders became increasingly aware of the importance of education and intellectual activity as a means to withstand the degradation of life under Nazi rule. Education was a form of defiant resistance to Nazi aggression and the demoralization of ghetto life. Responding to changing circumstances, the movements broadened their educational activity as their understanding of the need for resistance grew. With time, it became clear to the leaders that education was a tool that could actively prepare members for the future and sustain the movements

The research for this paper was partly funded by a grant from the Tauber Institute for the Study of European Jewry at Brandeis University.

and their ideologies. 'We must not quietly witness decisions and events,' wrote one member of Hashomer Hatsa'ir, 'we must not sit, watch, and wait for redemption. We must understand, predict, and prepare for the future.'[1] Through their discussions and analyses of both the present and the future, members of the movements defied the German occupiers and expressed their faith in themselves and the continuation of their organization.

In the decades prior to the outbreak of war, the practical and ideological education of members of youth movements revolved around the ideals of Erets Israel and the creation of a new and just society in the Jewish homeland. Movements such as Dror, Hashomer Hatsa'ir, Gordonia, Hanoar Hatsioni, and Akiva, while differing in approach, all stressed the centrality of Erets Israel and the importance of *aliyah*. Their energies were directed towards the future: members viewed their activities in the diaspora as a preliminary stage leading to the realization of their goals in Erets Israel, an Erets Israel of their own creation. They believed in an ideology that 'superseded their youth and was to give them purpose in their future lives'.[2]

Hechaluts, the umbrella organization that absorbed the graduates of various youth movements as well as unaffiliated older youths, provided members with practical training for *aliyah* to Erets Israel, developing the kibbutz-training camp as a particular means to this end. Members were instructed in agricultural occupations and other related trades. Within this framework the movement attempted to create a new type of person, one who would incorporate Socialist and collectivist ideals and play a leading role in the development of a model society.

Despite the ideological differences between the movements, there were many similarities in their educational methods, which were based on those developed by Hashomer Hatsa'ir. In addition to participating in educational activities, members also took part in national organizations. Summer camps for all age levels were held, as were general meetings for older members on the practical application of the movements' ideologies. Training seminars for counsellors were also held. All the movements published newspapers and guides for members and counsellors, which were distributed to all the branches.

When war broke out between Germany and Poland on 1 September 1939, the youth movements were not immune to the general fear and chaos. The speed of the German advance came as a complete surprise. By the fifth day of the war it was clear to the leaders of the movements that they could not maintain connections between Warsaw and outlying branches and kibbutzim, and that any centrally organized activity was fast becoming impossible.

Before making any decision, leaders first considered the plight of the emissaries

---

[1] *El al*, 2 (June 1941), in Yosef Kermish (ed.), *Itonut hamaḥteret hayehudit bigeto Varsha*, ii [Feb.–June 1941] (Jerusalem, 1979), 461.

[2] Israel Gutman, 'The Youth Movements in Eastern Europe as an Alternative Leadership', *Holocaust and Genocide Studies*, 3/1 (1988), 70.

from Erets Israel in Poland at that time. After lengthy discussions at an emergency meeting on 5 September, leaders of Dror and Hechaluts decided that the Palestinian emissaries must leave Poland as soon as possible,[3] and passed this information to other movements. This was not an easy decision either for the youth movements or their emissaries. Some of the latter wondered whether they had a moral obligation to stay, especially in view of the fact that contact with Erets Israel and with other branches of the movements in Poland had been virtually severed. But the local leaders prevailed and the emissaries left.

Before the war the Palestine emissaries had actively determined the movements' ideological line, and 'were essential in determining their internal dynamics as well as policy regarding external events'.[4] Their departure left the Polish youth leaders on their own for the first time. This new reality 'changed the status of the leadership of each of the youth movements, by making it into an independent and self-reliant body, one forced to find its way in a complicated situation, to determine and answer all questions and problems on its own.'[5]

That it was the local youth leaders themselves who decided on the emissaries' departure was important in itself. When the outbreak of war severed contact with the homeland, those actually in Poland had to decide their fate. The Polish leaders who took this decision, even when faced with the hesitation of some emissaries, showed that they had begun to take responsibility for their movements and were prepared to continue their activity in Poland independently of direction from Palestine.

Within a day or two after the counsellors from Erets Israel had departed, movement leaders had themselves to abandon their plans to remain in Warsaw and flee eastward. It was not until the Germans threatened a particular area and the numbers of local refugees increased, however, that members left their branches and training kibbutzim. Some returned to their homes and families; others joined the general exodus eastward.

Members of the youth movements were not the only ones to flee: Jewish community and party leaders also left for the east. Thus, 'the traditional parties and the public institutions that had represented and guided the Polish Jewish community between the two World Wars were left without contact with party headquarters abroad and without any guiding forces within the country itself', and the community was left leaderless.[6]

Although many of the movements' leaders had initially fled to the east in the hope of establishing a base for activities there, they did not allow the branches in

[3] Rivka Perlis, *Tenuot hanoar hehalutsiot bePolin hakevushah* (Bet lohamei hageta'ot, 1987), 44.

[4] Gutman, 'The Youth Movements in Eastern Europe', 70.

[5] Israel Gutman, 'Tenuot hano'ar kemanhigut hilufit bemizrah Eiropah', in Y. Kohavi (ed.), *Tenuot hano'ar hatsiyoniot besho'ah* (Bet lohamei hageta'ot, 1989), 234.

[6] Israel Gutman, 'Youth Movements in the Underground and the Ghetto Revolts', in *Jewish Resistance during the Holocaust: Proceedings of the Conference on Manifestations of Jewish Resistance, Jerusalem, April 7–11, 1968* (Jerusalem, 1971), 261. Among those who left both during the war and in the first months following the German occupation were recognized leaders of Zionist groups such

the west to remain without guidance. The executives of the movements, concentrated in Vilna and the Soviet-occupied territories, quickly decided to send a number of leaders back to the German territories. They hoped to ensure the continuation of their respective movements in all areas, including those now under German occupation. This was not an easy decision for them; in fact, it was extremely courageous, as it meant leaving areas where they were less likely to be persecuted as Jews, and from where there was a chance of emigrating to other countries, including Palestine. The importance of this decision was heightened by the fact that the youth movements were the only organizations to send members back; leaders of other Jewish political, religious, and community institutions virtually abandoned the Jewish communities that remained in the west. Leaders of these groups tried instead to reach Erets Israel, the free world, or the interior of the Soviet Union.

The conditions under which the youth movements now operated in German-occupied Poland were vastly different from any they had known before. Although the explicit Nazi extermination of the Jewish people did not begin until 1941, the Germans pursued a policy which deliberately weakened and impoverished the Jews. By the autumn of 1940 most of the Jews under German control were crowded together in ghettos; disease and starvation were rampant, and the death rate soared.

Despite the intolerable conditions under which they were forced to live and operate, the youth movements reorganized and carried on as best they could. Following their initial disarray and subsequent reorganization, movement leaders attempted to continue former educational and ideological activities. Although youngsters responded with enthusiasm to the leaders' attempts to reorganize the various Warsaw branches, the actual process was not easy. Conditions were difficult: gatherings had to be held in at least semi-underground conditions, and meeting-places were scarce. The closure of the ghetto exacerbated the situation, as contact with branches outside of Warsaw became increasingly difficult and dangerous. However, the youth movements were aided by the Germans' obvious lack of interest in the political activity of the Jews at this time. Having isolated the Jews from the surrounding population and established supervision of their economic activities, the Germans 'viewed Jewish spiritual or ideological involvement as inconsequential, as long as it was limited to the confines of the ghetto and could not influence the outside world'.[7]

The young age of those who reorganized and directed the movements' activity must be emphasized. The older leaders were only in their mid-twenties, others considerably younger. No longer under the direction of the Palestine branches of their respective movements, which had guided activities before the

as Moshe Kleinbaum [Moshe Sneh], Dr Zerach Warhaftig, and Apolinary Hartglas; Bund leaders Victor Alter, Henryk Erlich, and Abraham Mendelsohn; the leading spiritual leaders of Orthodox Jewry; and the activists of the radical left.

[7] Israel Gutman, *The Jews of Warsaw* (Bloomington, Ind., 1982), 133.

war, the young Polish leaders skilfully and courageously took responsibility for themselves and their movements.

Within the various groups (*gedudim*), intensive educational and ideological activity was organized, including lectures and group projects on a number of topics. Both traditional subjects and new topics occasioned by the war were studied and discussed. These included topics such as the sociology of the Jews, Fascism, problems specific to the individual movements, Erets Israel, the establishment of the Soviet Union and its subsequent development, different currents within Polish Jewry and a solution for the Jewish problem in Europe, the French Revolution, the labour movement, Hebrew, Haim Nahman Bialik (the unofficial national Hebrew poet), the history of the struggle for human freedom, the war, and the current situation in the ghetto. The variety even of this selective list is impressive. The devotion of the youngsters, and in particular their counsellors, to intellectual activity and critical analysis of the past, present, and future is evident. Counsellors were aware of their charges' lack of knowledge in certain areas, and tried to direct activities to fill the gap. Leaders of the Hashomer Hatsa'ir group Ma'anit felt that 'the *gedud* was not knowledgeable enough concerning the ideological problems of the Shomerian movement', and therefore decided 'to open a new lecture series that would firmly establish and deepen' their knowledge and outlook.[8]

Members participated actively in lectures and discussions. Those belonging to Ma'anit were instructed to prepare individually for each lecture, and to record their impressions and ideas on paper. In a discussion held by the Mishmeret group on the Russian–German war, 'close to 90 per cent of the *gedud*'s members expressed an opinion'.[9] On another occasion, discussions within various Mishmeret groups were described as 'lively' and 'providing much food for thought'.[10] This group also organized courses to provide education at the sixth level of primary school and the first level of high school.

Lectures and discussions were not the only means by which educational activities were carried out. Individual subgroups (*kevutsot*—the primary organizational groups of the movement) worked on specific projects and prepared reports and presentations for the others. The *kevutsot* organized in Mishmeret were involved in a project entitled 'A Journey through Erets Israel', in which a variety of aspects of life in Palestine were studied. At the end of the project a celebratory evening for the entire *gedud* was held, in which each group represented a city or village in Erets Israel. The group members appeared with placards and in characteristic costume. There appeared Jewish and Arab labourers, a *chaluts*, (pioneer), a member of the intelligentsia, and many others.

[8] *El al*, 3 (Aug. 1941), in Yosef Kermish (ed.), *Itonut hamaḥteret hayehudit beVarsha*, iii [July–Oct. 1941] (Jerusalem, 1984), 199. All translations are mine unless otherwise noted.
[9] *El al*, 2 (June 1941), ibid. ii. 480; *El al*, 3 (Aug. 1941), ibid. iii. 198.
[10] *El al*, 2 (June 1941), ibid. ii. 480.

Reading was an important educational tool for both old and young within the movements. Hashomer Hatsa'ir organized libraries for its members. There were at least two of these, one for the scouting level and one for the entire Warsaw branch. In April 1941 *El al* (the newspaper of the Hashomer Hatsa'ir scouts) reported that 'the branch library was open regularly', and that a Yiddish section would open in the near future. The following month, *Neged hazerem*, Hashomer Hatsa'ir's publication for older members, mentioned that preparations for opening both a Yiddish and a Hebrew section in the branch library were under way. According to a later article, the two sections had approximately one thousand books between them.[11] In the summer of 1941 a campaign by the scouting levels collected approximately 250 books for their library, although reports of the total number of books vary.[12] Other movements probably had libraries also.

As in the past, knowledge of Erets Israel remained central to the youth movements' educational activities. The sense of connection with Palestine was vital to their self-definition and identity. Wartime conditions, however, had disrupted the physical contact with Palestine; it was unstable, irregular, and often non-existent. The younger groups, as the leaders recognized, were in particular danger of 'losing the emotional connection with Erets Israel'. In response, leaders realized that they needed to develop educational programmes which would provide new members with a basic knowledge of the country and reinforce and deepen that of older members. 'In order to preserve the connection of the young generation with Palestine,' declared a *Neged hazerem* article, 'we must include within our work programmes conversations, illustrations, and stories about Erets Israel.' The article expressed the fear that 'the ideal of Erets Israel would cease to be the one and only goal of the movement'. To this end, counsellors decided that the older levels should concentrate on the problems of the country, while the movement would continue to emphasize that 'the only possible future' for members was on kibbutz in Palestine.[13]

In addition to the Erets Israel project, virtually all the *gedudim* carried out other similar group projects. Campaigns for Keren Kayemet LeYisrael (the Jewish National Fund) were also held. This activity was considered to be of particular value to the younger levels. 'For this level', wrote a member of Gordonia, 'the Keren Kayemet was the first stage in the realization of pioneering goals.' The scouts' education would be incomplete, he stressed, if it consisted only of discussions about the fund.[14] A more practical educational activity was vital to the

[11] *El al*, 1 (Apr. 1941), ibid. 251; *Neged hazerem*, 4 (May 1941), ibid. 361; *El al*, 2 (June 1941), ibid. 481.

[12] *El al*, 3 (Aug. 1941), ibid. iii. 199. The total number of books following the collection campaign is given in the August issue of *El al* as 400. An earlier issue of the paper (June 1941) had claimed that the library had approximately 500 books prior to the campaign. The reason for this numerical discrepancy is unclear.

[13] *Neged hazerem*, 4 (May 1941), ibid. ii. 347.

[14] *Słowo młodych*, 6–7 (Sept. 1941), ibid. iii. 351.

development of their Zionist understanding. Despite the poverty of many of the members, the scouts were obliged to campaign for and donate regularly to the fund. Hashomer Hatsa'ir and Dror also campaigned for the Keren Kayemet.

While the youth movements continued a great many of their traditional educational methods and activities, the conditions of life under German occupation demanded that they re-evaluate and in fact change their policies in a number of areas. The movements responded to these conditions with flexibility, ingenuity, and great sensitivity. Both local and national meetings of counsellors and leaders were held to consider changes. The innovations in the educational process demonstrated the movements' ability to react constructively to the current situation while continuing to foster the values, traditions, and goals of their past. This successful expression of traditional values by both traditional and newly developed means taught the youth movements that it was possible to preserve their identity while adapting to a vastly altered situation.

In order to adjust to current conditions, which made the meeting of large groups impossible, and still maintain the intensive educational activity of the past, the movements reordered their internal structures. While the traditional framework was left in place, the relative importance of its parts was changed. Whereas prior to the war the *gedud* was considered to be the primary educational group, the emphasis, especially within the younger levels, was now shifted to the smaller *kevutsah*. This group became 'the basic educational tool . . . which even during the war and in the ghetto has preserved its special nature as educator'.[15]

The time that a member was to remain in the *kevutsot* and *pelugot* was also lengthened, mainly so as to allow older members to remain in the movement for longer periods, as they were frequently unable to find employment upon graduation. The number of members of each *kevutsah* was thus increased to approximately fifteen, 'enriching the group's internal life, without affecting its organizational nature'. Similar changes were introduced in the *pelugot*.[16]

The traditional image and role of counsellors within the movements also changed. The counsellors not only continued to direct the majority of the activities which had been in place before the war, but now managed to deal with a completely new situation and its effect upon the youngsters. As a result of the decline in the educational level of many members, brought about by the lack of formal education in the ghetto, they were forced to devote more time to basic educational work. Elementary instruction was often given together with—and on occasion superseded—ideological instruction.

The counsellor more than ever served as a role model for the youngsters. 'The counsellor must be a model of personal behaviour,' wrote Eliezer Geller of Gordonia, 'in direct contrast to the surrounding environment.'[17] The counsellor,

[15] *Neged hazerem*, 5 (July 1941), ibid. 43.   [16] Ibid.
[17] *Słowo młodych*, 6–7 (Sept. 1941), ibid.351.

by offering the youth an alternative society filled with idealism, learning, and mutual aid and respect, was to stand in opposition to the deterioration of life in the ghetto and the general decline in moral values.

A decisive change in the education programmes of the youth movements was occasioned by the difficult material conditions in which virtually all members found themselves. In response to the devastating situation, and in opposition to past policies, the movements were forced to incorporate social-welfare programmes into their regular branch activities. While the step was viewed as necessary, it was none the less taken with reservations. Activists within the movements realized that although the provision of aid by the branches obviously relieved the material distress of the youngsters, it could also have a negative psychological and ideological impact on the recipient. As leaders of strongly ideological movements, they took precautions to ensure that the welfare enterprise would be carried out in a way that would correspond with and illustrate the goals and values of the movements.

To this end, Hashomer Hatsa'ir developed the *shituf* enterprise, which was instituted in a number of *gedudim*. Members of the group contributed as much as they could to a joint fund, and received in return the supplies which they needed. On other occasions a member with greater resources would invite a poorer member, usually a refugee, for a meal. This seemingly innocent traditional act of charity was a new custom for the youth movements. 'The accepted rule during normal times' for the movements had been to draw 'a sharp dividing line between the spheres of movement and home.'[18] 'We began with a type of work that was foreign to us,' wrote one member of Hashomer Hatsa'ir, 'and made it work.'[19]

An article in the Gordonia newspaper *Słowo młodych* proposed that aid be distributed by lottery, 'finding some way in which, through "a strange combination of events", the needy member would win.' The author emphasized that the methods used would need to be altered at frequent intervals. A weekly contribution by *gedud* members, the author believed, would not be sufficient for the enterprise's needs. Rather, 'performances, parties, and other occasions should be periodically organized by all members of the younger groups together' in order to obtain the necessary funds.[20]

Despite their hesitations, the leaders generally viewed the programmes of social aid within the movements in a positive light. They realized that this help was vital to many of the members, and frequently to their families as well. Its usefulness as an educational activity was also appreciated. Properly handled, leaders felt, welfare projects could be utilized as a form of social education. Through the development of an activity foreign to their traditional programme, they attempted to satisfy not only material needs, but educational and ideological ones as well.

[18] Gutman, *The Jews of Warsaw*, 135–6.
[19] *Sefer Hashomer Hatsa'ir*, i (Bet lohamei hageta'ot, 1956), 491.
[20] *Słowo młodych*, 6–7 (Sept. 1941), in Kermish (ed.), *Itonut hamaḥteret*, iii. 350.

With the disappearance of summer camps and other forms of social training for the younger levels, 'the lack of possibilities for social education has been seriously felt, and the self-help enterprise continues to be the only form of training in this area, and must be valued for this reason', wrote one Gordonia member. 'It gives us opportunities to connect our present education with a long tradition of education before the war. It will fill the gap that has been created and give our work a feeling of continuation, despite all the changes that have taken place.'[21]

The devastating conditions of life under German rule affected the movements in another area as well. As a result of the poverty, hunger, and demoralization rampant in the ghetto, and the lack of legal education for the youth, it was clear to the leaders that the educational, and therefore ideological, level of young members had declined. This issue was of particular concern to them, since ideology was the foundation of the pioneering movements, and members were expected to absorb and implement the beliefs of their respective movements. Young members, counsellors feared, deprived of their childhood and forced to engage in the struggle for food and survival, were losing those qualities stressed by the movements, and were coming increasingly to resemble the remainder of the population. The desperate conditions, wrote Eliezer Geller, have 'caused the younger members to get old before their time'. This was due, in part, to 'the lack of space, of green grass, of fields, rivers, and forests . . . it is not only the bodies of the youth that are in decline; the same thing is happening to their souls.'[22]

Leaders and counsellors recognized the importance of halting this decline within their ranks. Educational activity, both general and ideological, was intensified, and changes in style were experimented with as they sought to adapt to new conditions. To increase the understanding of the movement's ideology, a member of Hashomer Hatsa'ir declared in the spring of 1941 that the movement must 'frequently focus the content of our work on the social sciences and ideological problems, and must demand of members independent reading on the subject'. Members were to be encouraged to study the 'Shomerian newspapers published both during and before the war'. Education within the movement needed to be 'intensive' and to 'encompass all realms of members' lives and interests'.[23]

A number of ways to fight the apathy and depression that were believed to be widespread among members were suggested. Counsellors were asked to use games, songs, lively discussions, and other forms of entertainment to stimulate the youngsters' interest. While songs and games were not always appropriate to the subject-matter being taught, as a member of Gordonia pointed out, the counsellor must remember that the child was upset and in a weakened state, and that 'dry instruction without this entertainment would not bring the desired

---

[21] Kermish (ed.), *Itonut hamahteret*, iii. 350.   [22] Ibid. 347.
[23] *Neged hatserem*, 4 (May 1941), ibid. ii. 347.

results'.²⁴ The work itself should be 'varied and rich in basic feelings and emotions'. Youngsters' interest in reading was to be stimulated, and, above all, counsellors were encouraged to 'carry on in spite of failures'.²⁵

As part of their activity, the movements also organized a variety of underground conventions and seminars. Some of these were designed specifically for group leaders, while others were more general gatherings with a broader range of participants. It was not just Warsaw members who participated in these seminars; *chalutsim* from throughout German-occupied Poland travelled to the capital illicitly in order to take part. The organization of these gatherings was a daring enterprise, as meetings of this sort were forbidden by the Nazi occupiers. Not only were Jews forbidden to travel by train, they were also debarred from changing their place of residence. Emissaries from the movements, usually women, brought information about the seminars to other groups and helped participants travel to Warsaw. These gatherings helped to reinforce the tenuous connection between the various branches of the movements and gave the participants the feeling of belonging to a greater whole.

The first underground seminar was held by Dror in June and July 1940. It lasted an entire month, and approximately 'thirty-one members from twenty places participated. The total number of hours of work was 252.' Its main purpose was to train new counsellors for work within the movement. Lectures were given by such public figures as Eliezer Bloch, Stepha Wilchowsky, Yosef Sak, Yitzhak Katznelson, Janusz Korczak, Emmanuel Ringelblum, and others. A second gathering met in the autumn, this time for members of the various training farms, of whom approximately 200 participated. The final national seminar convened in December 1941–January 1942, attended by forty-two participants from eight cities.²⁶

The first Dror seminar originally aroused the opposition of some public organizations, whose leaders claimed that illegal activity of this sort would endanger other Jews in the ghetto. Leaders of the movements were aware of this, and at first hesitated, unsure whether to adapt themselves to Nazi laws or to break them in spite of the risk involved. Eventually the first seminar took place, and proved to be one of the first important steps in the line of daring illegal activity. It is significant that, for the first time, the youth movements overrode the hesitation of older, more established public figures and pursued the course that they believed to be right. Indeed, a number of those who had at first opposed the idea eventually participated in the seminar themselves.

Hashomer Hatsa'ir held its first large gathering in the spring of 1940. The

---

[24] *Słowo młodych*, 6–7 (Sept. 1941), ibid. iii. 349.
[25] *Neged hazerem*, 4 (May 1941), ibid. ii. 346; *Słowo młodych*, 6–7 (Sept. 1941), ibid. iii. 347.
[26] *Dror*, 3 (July–Aug. 1940), in Yosef Kermish (ed.), *Itonut hamahteret hayehudit beVarsha*, i [May 1940–Jan. 1941] (Jerusalem, 1979), 43; Rivka Perlis, *Tenuot hanoar hehalutsiot bePolin hakevushah* (Israel, 1987), 113 (giving 45 members from 23 branches).

lecturers included Shmuel Breslev, Yosef Kaplan, and Mordechai Anielewicz. This seminar was soon followed by a second meeting of the entire Warsaw branch. In addition to the attending graduates of the movement, some 600 members reportedly took part.[27] At the end of May 1941 the movement organized an 'ideological council' meeting of leaders and graduates. The gathering lasted for six days, and between 110 and 120 members took part in the discussions. The third and final large gathering organized by Hashomer Hatsa'ir was a leadership seminar held in December 1941–January 1942. It lasted almost six weeks, and over forty-five members took part.[28]

Gordonia and Akiva ran similar events. Gordonia held a convention lasting three weeks at the end of 1940. The thirty-odd participants met every evening, six times a week, between 6.00 and 8.00 p.m.[29] In the spring of 1940 Shimek Drenger and Gusta Davidson of Akiva arrived from Kraków to run an ideological seminar for the older members of the Warsaw Akiva branch; approximately fifty members took part. The seminar lasted for five days, with 'lectures from morning until late in the evening'.[30]

A wide variety of subjects were covered, though obviously not all of them are known today. The activities and organizational methods of the movements during the war were discussed, as was the Jewish economy under the Nazis and the political situation both of the world at large and of the Jewish people in particular. At the second Dror seminar, for example, the following subjects were among those discussed: 'The Jewish workers' movement in Erets Israel and in the world in general; solutions to the Jewish question; the economy and demography of the Jewish people; Jewish history and information on Erets Israel; Hebrew literature; problems of Socialism.'[31] In contrast to discussions before the war, the youth movements also began to consider and study the Bible and martyrdom in Jewish history, and to relate these topics to contemporary issues. While the youth movements continued to discuss issues that were important to them in pre-war days, they were also increasingly concerned with understanding the current situation of European Jewry.

Leaders used the gatherings to review and evaluate their particular movement's current activities and direction, and to plan for the future. 'It was necessary', declared an article in the Hashomer Hatsa'ir newspaper *Iton hatenuah*, 'to take stock of achievements and failures, to evalute the situation of the movement, and to determine the future direction of its activity.'[32]

---

[27] Yitzhak Zuckerman and Moshe Basok (eds.), *Sefer milhamot hageta'ot: Bein hahomot, bemahanot, uveya'arot* (Israel, 1954), 31–2.

[28] Ibid. 32; *Sefer Hashomer Hatsa'ir*, 494. The 'ideological council' gathering lasted for six days, with 110–20 members participating in the discussions.

[29] Zuckerman and Basok (eds.), *Sefer milhamot hageta'ot*, 21.   [30] Ibid. 34.

[31] *Dror*, 5 (Jan.–Feb. 1941), in Kermish (ed.), *Itonut hamahteret*, i. 378.

[32] *Iton hatenuah* (Dec. 1940–Jan. 1941), ibid. 303.

The seminars had a strong emotional impact on members. In addition to the practical results of decisions taken and problems solved, the gatherings served to strengthen members' feelings of belonging to a larger movement, one which went beyond their individual selves and united them in a greater whole. Following the first gathering of Hashomer Hatsa'ir, one member wrote that 'now . . . one of the major deficiencies of the movement has been taken care of: the lack of awareness of a broad and developed movement, whole and united'. From this standpoint, he continued, the gathering was important not only because of the quality of the lectures and discussions, but 'because of the personal meeting of all the participants, of the greetings of peace that were received from dozens of branches. All realized that the movement had overcome hardships . . . and had preserved its belief in its direction and nature.'[33]

The seminars and gatherings created for members an alternative, if temporary, world, distinct and separate from the pain of ghetto life. Outside these meetings was a world filled with hostility and threats; inside were young people debating 'how to preserve the humanity of the Jews despite the degeneration of ghetto life'.[34] Shmuel Breslev of Hashomer Hatsa'ir described a session of the 1941 seminar for senior members:

Only fifteen minutes are allocated to each speaker. Thoughts are therefore expressed in short sentences—the ideas alone, with no extra words . . . The pencil writes agitatedly, in abbreviation . . . The discussions continue from morning until evening. Outside is the world of the ghetto. Noise and suffocation. In vain the noise of the ghetto tries to enter . . . no one will listen. Here beats a different rhythm. Another world.[35]

It appears, however, that some questioned the legitimacy of such intellectual gatherings. At the meeting of Dror in October 1940 Yitzhak Zuckerman put forward some of the arguments of those who questioned the movement's right to immerse itself in its own world at a time of national tragedy:

The street is enmeshed in disaster and agony; the street is full of horror. Does this meeting, with its visions of the future, have any meaning for the gray daily life in the street? Might it not be that these visions are nothing but weakness, an escape from this life into the mind? Perhaps someone thinks that we should not have convened today, since our thinking will not in any way determine anything and our talking will not change the order of the world.[36]

Zuckerman answered his own questions, declaring that the importance of the gathering lay in the attempt of members to analyse present events and plan for the future. By thinking, discussing, and questioning, the movement resisted the

---

[33] Ibid. 303–4.   [34] Zivia Lubetkin, *Beyamei kilayon vamered* (Israel, 1979), 42.

[35] *El al*, 2 (June 1941), in Kermish (ed.), *Itonut hamahteret* i. 469.

[36] *Dror*, 4 (Oct. 1940), ibid. 103–4; translation taken from Leni Yahil, 'The Warsaw Underground Press: A Case Study in the Reaction to Antisemitism', in Jehuda Reinharz (ed.), *Living with Antisemitism: Modern Jewish Responses* (Hanover, NH, and London, 1987), 413–42, at 420.

degeneration of life under Nazi occupation, and expressed its continuing faith in its ideology and future:

> We who know the strength of the avant-garde, however, who are aware of the meaning of pioneering, we understand the impact of our discussions . . . The force behind our considerations will show itself and become meaningful as the driving force of ideas pierces the walls that keep tomorrow from our sight.[37]

The seminars were thus an integral part of all the educational and intellectual activities carried out by the movements.

The youth movements also published a variety of underground newspapers. They were issued, with increasing frequency, until the start of the mass deportations from Warsaw on 22 July 1942.[38] From the start, these journals were an important form of education and resistance. Their very appearance constituted opposition to the sterile and degenerate life the Germans had planned for the Jews of the ghetto. With the passage of time, the youth movements' newspapers also led the call for active, as well as passive, resistance to the Nazis.

The journals were originally directed only towards members of their respective movements, preserving the traditional format and content of past youth-movement publications. They included ideological and political articles, short literary pieces, book reviews, profiles of famous personalities, and summaries of events in Erets Israel and within the movements in Poland. Many of the newspapers opened with or included an editorial or article on a particular subject, usually dealing with current events, that the editor wished to emphasize. While the editorials followed the particular convictions and beliefs of the individual movements, they were all expressions of the movements' attempts to understand and analyse the current situation. Despite their ideological differences, virtually all expressed the desire 'not only to hold out . . . but to preserve their human dignity and to wrestle, at the same time, with the intellectual clarification of their beliefs . . . There is one axiom they all share: in the end, Hitler will be defeated, and afterwards a better world will rise out of the destruction he perpetrated.'[39]

In time, however, the youth movements' newspapers moved away from their special format to a broader one, more responsive to the needs and questions of the

---

[37] *Dror*, 4 (Oct. 1940), in Kermish (ed.), *Itonut hamaḥteret*, i. 104; translation from Yahil, 'The Warsaw Underground Press', 420.

[38] While virtually all the political organizations in the Warsaw ghetto published in the underground press, the youth movements distinguished themselves in the number and frequency of their publications. In the spring of 1940 Dror began to publish its Yiddish-language newspaper *Dror*. *Neged hazerem*, of Hashomer Hatsa'ir, appeared in the first half of the same year. Hashomer Hatsa'ir ultimately brought out eight different publications, while Dror published three. The Gordonia newspaper, *Słowo młodych*, first appeared in Nov. 1940. All in all, at least two-thirds of Warsaw's underground publications (excluding those of the Bund) were published by the youth movements and youth divisions of the parties.

[39] Yahil, 'The Warsaw Underground Press', 415.

general public. By the end of 1941 much space was devoted to discussion of the war and its essence, the position of the Jewish people in the German-occupied territories, and evaluation of the policy of the Soviet Union in the light of the Molotov–Ribbentrop pact. While the information reported was generally accurate, the movements' standard, dogmatic positions often made it difficult for them to 'arrive at realistic appraisals of the war, Nazi antisemitism and its objectives, and other essential subjects'.[40]

The papers also dealt with daily life in the ghetto, although news of this sort did not dominate. In response to the devastating situation which they described, the movements used their publications to encourage their readers to withstand the pressures and demoralization of ghetto life. 'All try to free their readers from those destructive influences, to lift them out of their incessant struggle to keep life going, to demonstrate the truth of the biblical saying that "man doth not live by bread alone".'[41]

The members of the youth movements were well aware of the importance of the underground press as a means of resisting the deteriorating conditions of ghetto life. In addition to publishing the standard newspapers, the movements also brought out a number of other works. A few guidebooks for counsellors were issued, such as *Lamadrikh*, by Dror. Dror also published, in the summer of 1940, an exceptional booklet entitled *Suffering and Heroism in the Jewish Past in the Light of the Present*. In this book Dror, like other movements in their publications, 'tried to show the strength of the people, to spread belief, and to train young hearts to stand firm when the critical hour arrives'.[42]

The movements tried to continue the practical and vocational education of their members as well as their intellectual development. Early in 1940 they attempted to re-establish the agricultural training camps that had played an important role in their pre-war educational activities. Prior to the Nazi invasion the movements had devoted much of their energy and resources to both agricultural, and, in particular, urban communes, in preparation for their eventual settlement in Erets Israel. Belief in the values of collective living and manual labour, and the desire to create a new and better way of life, were fundamental to the ideologies of the pioneering youth movements. Thus, continued concrete expression of these ideals, even in a form adapted to wartime conditions, was a vital part of the movements' self-definition and understanding. The wartime kibbutzim offered not only a hope of physical survival, but also of spiritual and ideological survival. 'Only in the kibbutzim, and thanks to them, was it possible to preserve the pioneering and humane image of the movement.'[43]

Of the agricultural kibbutzim of the past, only one, Grochów, was successfully

[40] Gutman, *The Jews of Warsaw*, 152.
[41] Yahil, 'The Warsaw Underground Press', 429.
[42] *Peyn un gvurah in dem yiddishn over in likht fun der gegnvort*, in *Itonut hamahteret*, i. 44.
[43] Yitzhak Zuckerman, *Perakim min ha'izavon* (Bet lohamei hageta'ot, 1982), 47.

re-established. Originally a joint venture by all the movements, it eventually became the sole province of Dror. In spite of the difficulties and disagreements involved, the re-establishment of Grochów was a vital achievement for all the youth movements. The farm was a source of pride for all, a symbol of their continuation and growth under German rule. 'Grochów was a symbol for the movement,' wrote Zivia Lubetkin. 'In the first weeks of Grochów's founding, the information spread throughout Poland, to even the most remote areas: Grochów exists! It shows that the movement exists, Hechaluts exists!'[44]

All the movements attempted to establish training farms: Dror in Czerniaków, Hashomer Hatsa'ir in Częstochowa, Gordonia in Opoczno and other areas, and Hanoar Hatsioni in Czestoniew.[45] Seasonal labour also offered the movements another means by which to provide members with practical training, and the organized youth were quick to take advantage of those opportunities.

The number of Dror members who took part in these activities was greater than the number of participants from other movements. Even before the war, members of Dror had played a greater role in Hechaluts training kibbutzim. To a larger extent than with the others, agricultural training was an important educational tool within Dror, and was high on the movement's list of priorities. With the outbreak of the war, Dror invested much energy in the establishment of various forms of training camps, while Hashomer Hatsa'ir, for example, devoted more effort to the organization of activities within the area branches, and gave educational activity priority over the founding of training farms.[46]

The youth movements also founded urban communes and workshops as a means of educating members in the values of communal living and social interaction. These communes not only provided for the material needs of members, but also offered spiritual comfort and strength. In the urban kibbutz one heard 'a word of living Hebrew, a new Erets Israel song, or a lecture on a literary, scientific, or public topic'.[47] In the evenings, discussions on the ideological and political direction of the movements often took place. 'On occasion discussions would arise on the events of the period in which we were living, and on the responsibilities that had been imposed upon us.' News from illegal radio broadcasts was shared and discussed.[48]

---

[44] Lubetkin, *Beyamei kilayon vamered*, 40. On the establishment of Grochów, see Sarah Segal and Arieh Pialkow (eds.), *Beshadmot Grohov* (Bet lohamei hageta'ot, 1976).

[45] On the founding of the kibbutzim see Mordechai Tennenbaum-Tamaroff, *Dapim min hadelikah*, 2nd edn., ed. Bronka Klibansky and Zvi Shner (Jerusalem, 1984); Gutman, *The Jews of Warsaw*, 139–41; and Zuckerman and Basok (eds.), *Sefer milhamot hageta'ot*.

[46] A document of the central Dror leadership stated that from the beginning of the occupation until May 1942 approximately 1,000 members of Dror (from the entire General Gouvernement) passed through training camps in one form or another; of this number, over 350 were from the Warsaw branch. (Quoted in Perlis, *Tenuot hanoar hehalutsiot*, 123.)

[47] *Sheviv* (Dec. 1940), in Kermish (ed.), *Itonut-hamahteret*, 256–7.

[48] Zuckerman, *Perakim min ha'izavon*, 50, 52.

While the movements were unable to recreate exactly the kibbutzim and communes of the past, their continuous evaluation of current problems and changes allowed them to create similar, albeit different, establishments which responded to the demands of the new situation in which they found themselves. Perhaps most important of all was the fact that life in the kibbutz allowed for the continued expression and teaching of the youth movements' traditional ideologies and values. Despite wartime conditions, within the kibbutz the movements were able to organize their members in a way which allowed them to live their lives in a manner that all believed in, on principles of equality and sharing. There was a feeling of solidarity, of not being alone, and a chance to 'talk freely and get rid of one's feelings of depression'.[49] Members supported and encouraged one another. They managed to create an atmosphere of freedom, and to uphold the values of honour and dignity, in direct opposition to the environment that surrounded them. 'We were able to create in our farms a communal, humane experience', wrote Zivia Lubetkin, 'that was founded on mutual aid, equality, and social relationships that were completely different from those in the ghetto. When I was able to get away from the ghetto either to Czerniaków or Grochów, I felt as if I had come to another world.'[50]

At least as important as the seminars and activities within the movements themselves were the more general systematic and ideological activities that they undertook in the ghetto. Before the outbreak of the war, the general education of all sectors of Jewish youth was not a real concern of the Zionist youth movements. Attention was concentrated, rather, on the ideological, political, and practical education and preparation of their own members. These activities usually took place in addition to a youth's general schooling.

With the onset of German occupation, however, any form of organized education was forbidden. All young Jews, of both elementary- and secondary-school age, were left without the framework and direction previously provided by community schools and organizations. Not until September 1941, when the Germans allowed (for only one year) the teaching of the first four or five primary grades, was any sort of organized education permitted in the Warsaw ghetto. Some older youths, for whom education remained illegal, studied clandestinely in small groups (*kompletim*) set up by both private individuals and public organizations. Members of the youth movements participated in this enterprise as both teachers and students. The movements, however, were not satisfied with these limited, albeit important, activities, which were able to reach only a small portion of the young people in the ghetto. Aware that the ghetto lacked the necessary leadership and organization to tackle the problem fully, and believing that they were now responsible for much of Jewish youth, the movements expanded their activities to include a number of new, more general, educational programmes.

[49] Gutman, 'Youth Movements in the Underground', 265.
[50] Lubetkin, *Beyamei kilayon vamered*, 40.

Drawing from their own rich educational experiences, the movements devoted time and energy to the various 'children's corners' and youth groups organized in several houses and by a number of political parties. Members worked as counsellors for the older youths, and as nursery-school teachers for younger groups. At the request of many parents, they watched over children while the adults were away. They sang, played, and exercised with the children 'in the few open spaces belonging to destroyed houses'[51] that remained in the ghetto. Dror ran a special course in which twenty-five girls were trained for this work.

These counsellors were popular with the various institutions, and their assistance was frequently requested. Three girls worked at the orphanage on Gęsia Street, teaching the children 'first of all Hebrew and the history of the Jewish people'. At the children's house on Miła Street the girls taught the children Yiddish, Hebrew, history, and 'national ideas', and organized days when the children would be fed in various homes.[52] At the gardens to which they took the children to play, the youngsters were able to 'forget for a few hours the terrible crowding at home, the fights . . . the lack of air to breathe, and the hunger'.[53]

One of the most outstanding achievements in the field of education was the establishment of the Dror gymnasium (secondary school). The decision to undertake this task was taken at a meeting of the central leadership in June 1940, and the school itself opened in August. Two main factors prompted this step: 'the neglect which members believed this area suffered, and the desire to improve the educational level of the movement, which even in the past had suffered from a lack of intellectual strength'.[54]

Dror originally established the school solely for its own members, desiring 'to teach them both general and Jewish subjects'. With the passage of time, however, the framework was broadened and the gymnasium came to include non-members as well. Eventually, the school numbered some 120 students and thirteen teachers, including Yitzhak Katznelson. Classes began with the fourth year of primary school and continued through the second year of the lyceum (high school). The lower grades studied for 18–20 hours per week, the upper levels 32–4 hours. In addition to the regular humanities programme, students were taught Hebrew, Yiddish, Bible studies, singing, art, and Jewish history for 10–11 hours each week. French and German were also taught; in the second year of the school's existence, however, German was replaced with English.[55]

Working conditions for both teachers and students were difficult. There were no permanent classrooms, benches, books, or learning materials. Groups of five

---

[51] Zuckerman and Basok (eds.), *Sefer milhamot hageta'ot*, 18–19.
[52] Ibid.   [53] Tennenbaum-Tamaroff, *Dapim min hadelikah*, 98.
[54] Perlis, *Tenuot hanoar hehalutsiot*, 131.
[55] Zuckerman and Basok (eds.) *Sefer milhamot hageta'ot*, 24; Lubetkin, *Beyamei kilayon vamered*, 49, and Yosef Korniansky, *Beshlihut hahalutsim* (Bet lohamei hageta'ot, 1979), 61.

or six students were forced to move from apartment to apartment in search of a place to study. Often they studied in one-room apartments 'with the whole family crowded in'. Students and teachers alike suffered from poverty and hunger. None the less, they persevered in their studies. 'Hungry, with legs swollen from the cold, the teachers would instruct the students, who, like themselves, were also hungry and bloated.'[56] Through the gymnasium, Dror was in fact able to reach more young people than those actually participating in the classes. Students who attended passed on their knowledge to friends who were unable to come.[57]

The educational and intellectual development of Jewish youth, members believed, was a crucial form of defence for the entire community. They feared that a decline in this area among young Jews would be catastrophic for the Jewish people as a whole. 'The nation will not recover from its fall if our youth are flawed and degenerate,' wrote a member of Hashomer Hatsa'ir, 'and only we, the children aged 13–18, will be the ones to lead the Jewish masses to a different future, a better future.'[58] The integrity of Jewish youth, leaders felt, must be preserved for the future, when they would be faced with the task of rebuilding their shattered people.

Continuing to educate the young in spite of Nazi prohibitions was thus a form of resistance for the youth movements. They believed that in order to safeguard both the physical and the spiritual existence of Jewish youth they must continue to be active intellectually and culturally. Both the underground publications and the discussions that took place in various seminars and gatherings expressed the movements' acute perception and awareness of Nazi policy in this area. They realized that the Nazis' attack on education was a deliberate attempt to destroy the Jewish people from within, and they acted purposefully and forcefully to counter the blow. The movements understood that only by continuing their analytical and intellectual activity, in conjunction with other enterprises, could they hope to remain intact in spirit, as well as in body. 'We must overcome our feelings of hopelessness,' wrote one Dror member in October 1940. 'It is not worthwhile to be diverted by false delusions; rather, we must utilize objective analysis in order to arrive at the conclusion that there is no basis for our despair.'[59]

An article in an issue of *Płomienie* in September 1940 illustrated this awareness and is worth quoting at length. 'They [the Nazis] have forbidden us schools, literature, and libraries,' the writer declared. 'Why? They have forbidden us private education—and for what reason? Perhaps because of suspicion and fear of what could grow out of our thinking, our thoughts.' In opposition to the Germans, he continued,

Must not Jewish youth begin to resist with thinking, with ideas? We must think. We must

---

[56] Lubetkin, *Beyamei kilayon vamered*, 49.   [57] Ibid.
[58] Quoted in Gutman, 'Youth Movements in the Underground', 264.
[59] *Dror*, 4 (Oct. 1940), in Kermish (ed.), *Itonut hamahteret*, i.111.

not surrender to reality, must not lose hope and belief.... We must study! We must form opinions and precisely analyse historical events.... If we rely on thought, the rest will come.... Thought has always been the most dangerous weapon and greatest enemy of oppression. Thought—that is the slogan which will serve as a beacon to Jewish youth.... Thought—our slogan and our goal.[60]

It is fitting to close with a quote from the introduction to the Dror publication on Jewish martyrdom which reflected the reasoning behind these and all other activities of the movements. It professed Dror belief not only in the need and ability of Jewish youth to overcome the terrible circumstances, but also the movement's faith in all of mankind. 'Despite all this,' the introduction began, 'we, the Jews, and in particular our youth, must overcome our bitterness and revulsion. ... we will be able to overcome the depression of our souls and will not lose hope. ... truly man is good at heart.'[61] These words are a testimony to the continuing faith, not only of Dror, but of all the youth movements, in themselves, their people, and the ultimate victory of mankind in its long and painful struggle for freedom and justice.

All of the activities of the youth movements, from the beginning of the war until the end of 1941, were a form of defiance of and resistance to the Nazi occupiers and the horrors of ghetto life. During these years the movements were still confident that the troubled times would pass. They concentrated their energies, therefore, not only on the struggle for life, but also on the preservation of the spiritual and ideological image of Jewish youth. They developed new activities with which to prepare for the future while remembering and utilizing the traditions and lessons of their own and the Jewish people's rich past.

With the German invasion of the Soviet Union, the situation of Europe's Jews changed dramatically, though few were able to foresee the impending Holocaust. The youth movements' sensitivity to current events, and their continual attempts to understand Nazi aims, helped them to interpret Nazi plans for extermination at a relatively early date, near the start of the gassings at Chełmno (which began in December 1941) and the mass murders at Pona (October–December 1941). It was their constant intellectual activity, together with their awareness of and sensitivity to both current and past Jewish suffering, that enabled the youth movements to overcome the psychological and cognitive barriers that stood in the way of the Jewish masses, and to grasp the true meaning of the overall German plan of extermination. This exceptional, and indeed courageous, comprehension was first expressed by Abba Kovner in Vilna on the night of 31 December 1941. The virtually intuitive understanding of the nature of the Jewish tragedy, coupled with the movements' high moral standards and

[60] *Płomienie* (Sept. 1940), ibid. 91.   [61] *Peyn un gvurah* (July–Aug. 1940), ibid. 46.

commitment to the Jewish people, led to their ultimate change in direction and the decision to resist the Nazis with arms.

Though some leaders later expressed regret that the movements had not begun preparation for armed resistance earlier, the activities of the first years of the war were crucial ones for the *chalutsim*. Through their educational programmes, cultural events, social-welfare programmes, and other activities, the youth movements were able to preserve their vitality and strength despite the overpowering demoralization and deterioration of ghetto life. Their ability to enclose themselves in their own spiritual world, to cling stubbornly to values and norms of behaviour in spite of all, and their refusal to acknowledge moral decay gave them the strength and determination to survive under Nazi rule. Members remained compassionate, loyal, and, above all, human. It was because of this determined and courageous effort that, when the time for armed resistance came, there existed a united, organized, and morally responsible body of young people willing to make a stand.

The Second Competition of Scholarly Works on Polish Jewish Themes

ALINA CAŁA

IN 1992 the Polish–Israeli Friendship Society and the Jewish Historical Institute in Warsaw organized the second competition of master's theses on Polish Jewish and Israeli subjects, this time also including doctoral theses; not many of the latter were submitted, although, according to available information, many more have been defended than were entered in the competition. Whereas 40 theses were submitted to the first competition in 1990, in 1992 there were 67 and the level was higher, which forced the jury to evaluate them in stages: 35 master's and 5 doctoral theses reached the second stage, and 12 master's and 5 doctoral theses reached the final stage. The choice of winners was extremely difficult. The jury was composed of Dr Alina Cała, the Jewish Historical Institute (ŻIH), Warsaw, (chairman); Eleonora Bergman, MA, ŻIH; Prof. Stanisław Frybes, Department of Polish Philology, Warsaw University; Prof. Jakub Goldberg, Department of History, Hebrew University of Jerusalem; Prof. Daniel Grinberg, ŻIH; Jan Jagielski, MA, ŻIH; Prof. Aleksandra Jasińska-Kania, Institute of Sociology, Warsaw University; Prof. Aleksander Lewin, Institute of Pedagogical Research of the Polish Academy of Sciences; Prof. Irena Maciejewska, Institute of Polish Philology, Warsaw University; Prof. Jerzy Malinowski, Arts Institute of the Polish Academy of Sciences; Prof. Szymon Rudnicki, Department of History, Warsaw University; Prof. Franciszek Ryszka, Department of Journalism and Social Studies, Warsaw University; and Prof. Jerzy Tomaszewski, Department of History, Warsaw University. It was decided to award two equal first, second, and third prizes, one special award, and five distinctions in the master's category, and three prizes and two distinctions in the doctoral category.

The awards reflect the level of the competition. They were funded by the Israeli Embassy in Poland, the Ministry of Foreign Affairs, the Ministry of Culture and Arts, the Mayor of Warsaw, the Polish Committee for UNESCO Affairs, the Stefan Batory Foundation, the 'Shalom' Foundation for the Promotion of Polish Jewish Culture, the Polish Council of Christians and Jews, and the Socio-Cultural Society of Jews in Poland.

The first prize in the doctoral category went to EUGENIA PROKOP-JANIEC's thesis, entitled 'Polish Jewish Literature between the Two World Wars', defended in 1990 at the Institute of Polish Philology, Jagiellonian University, under the direction of Prof. HENRYK MARKIEWICZ. The author of this dissertation in the field of literary criticism dealt with a little-known and neglected subject, the creation of literature in the Polish language by Jews, and brought back to our knowledge many valuable works by authors from the two decades between the two world wars, who had created their own literary environment, brimming with vitality (and manifestos). It was a bridge between the cultures of the two peoples and allowed Polish literature access to some important western European works, including those of Kafka. It also strongly influenced the opinions of the Jewish intelligentsia, stimulating their national consciousness. This thesis was also awarded a prize by the Jan Karski Foundation, New York.

The second prize went to the dissertation by GABRIELA ZALEWSKA, entitled 'The Jewish Population of Warsaw in the Period between the Two World Wars', defended in 1989, at the Historical Institute of the Polska Akademia Nauk (PAN: Polish Academy of Sciences), under the direction of Prof. JANUSZ ŻARNOWSKI. This is a piece of research which will be of great value for the history of Warsaw; it deals in detail with the demographic and professional structure of the Jewish population in the city and its economic activities and history during the Second Republic. Continuing the work of such historians as Jakub Szacki or Emanuel Ringelblum, and using modern methodology, it adds significantly to our knowledge about the largest concentration of Jews in Europe.

The third prize went to the doctoral thesis by MAŁGORZATA MELCHIOR, entitled 'The Social Identity of the Individual', defended in 1990 at the Institute of Sociology, Warsaw University, under the direction of Prof. HANNA ŚWIDA-ZIEMBA. On the basis of in-depth interviews with people of Jewish origin born after the Second World War, the author tries to recreate their differing attitudes to their Jewish roots, and the influence of these attitudes on self-identification.

The first of the two prizes in the master's category went to BOGDAN KWIATEK for his thesis entitled 'The Will as the Source of Life in *Fons Vitae*, by Salomon ibn Gabirol', defended in 1992 at the Department of Philosophy, the Catholic University in Lublin, under the direction of Fr. Prof. STANISŁAW WIELGUŚ. This dissertation deals with the philosophical and theological aspects of the works of a medieval Jewish philosopher from Spain, whose thought has influenced the renewal of Christian theology.

The second of the two first prizes went to MARCIN WODZIŃSKI for his thesis entitled '*Tsadik* Graves in Poland', defended in 1991 at the Institute of Polish Philology, University of Wrocław, under the direction of Prof. JERZY WOROŃCZAK. The author of this dissertation has undertaken the task of analysing Hebrew inscriptions on ancient and modern tombstones of Hasidic leaders from fifty locations, such as Bobowa, Nowy Sącz, Leżajsk, Lublin, and Przysucha. The thesis uses a linguistic approach and the methods of cultural anthropology to analyse the extent and popularity of the cults of different *tsadikim* among contemporary Hasidism.

The first of the two second prizes went to JOLANTA ŻYNDUL for her thesis entitled 'Anti-Jewish Disturbances in Poland, 1935–1937', defended in 1990 at the Department of History, Warsaw University, under the direction of Prof. MARCIN KULA. With a cool eye, the author has analysed the intensity, geographic distribution, and internal structure of anti-Jewish incidents provoked by Polish Nationalists in the period after the death of Piłsudski (1935–7). This shocking account contributes to our understanding of the mechanisms and tendencies whose outcome was felt in later times.

The second of the two second prizes went to JAROSŁAW MATŁOKA for his thesis entitled 'Julian Stryjkowski's *Voices in the Dark, Austeria, The Dream of Azriel, The Newcomer from Narbonne, Echo*', defended in 1991, at the Institute of Polish Philology, Adam Mickiewicz University, Poznań, under the direction of Prof. MARIA ADAMCZYK. This is a literary analysis of texts from the most important works of a contemporary Jewish writer living in Poland and writing in Polish. A weakness of this thesis is the rendering of Stryjkowski's works as fables, seen from the point of view of Catholic ethical theories, which results in oversimplification of some important parts of the author's writings (the problem of Jewish identification) and also in a certain 'Catholic-centricity', which does not seem, to me personally, to be appropriate.

The first of the two third prizes went to EWA KOŹMIŃSKA for her thesis entitled 'Polish Jewish Wartime Accounting: The Challenges of the Holocaust. An Analysis of Letters to the Editor of *Tygodnik powszechny* Sent in Reply to the Błoński–Siła-Nowicki Discussion', defended in 1992 at the Institute of Sociology, Warsaw University, under the direction of Dr PAWEŁ ŚPIEWAK. This is a very interesting sociological analysis on the subject of the attitude of Poles towards the Holocaust. These letters were provoked by the article by Prof. Jan Błoński entitled 'The Poor Poles look at the Ghetto', published in the Catholic paper *Tygodnik powszechny* in 1987, and Władysław Siła-Nowicki's response, entitled 'In Reply to J. Błoński'.

The second of the two third prizes went to DOROTA KRAWCZYŃSKA for her thesis entitled 'Henryk Grynberg: Witness and Artist', defended in 1991 at the Polish Department, Warsaw University, under the direction of Prof. MARIA JANION. The thesis analyses the writings on the Holocaust of this Polish-speaking Jewish writer living in the United States, placing them against the backdrop of a philosophical discussion about the causes and consequences of this unprecedented crime.

In the category of master's theses the special Warsaw Mayor's Prize went to DANUTA GIBAS for her thesis entitled 'Ida Kamińska, Director and Actress in the Jewish Theatre in Poland (1946–1968): An Analysis of her Artistic Activity on the Basis of Selected Performances', defended in 1991 at the Institute of Polish

Philology, Jagiellonian University, under the direction of Associate Prof. KAZIMIERZ NOWACKI.

Those receiving distinctions for their doctoral theses were WOJCIECH JAWORSKI, for his thesis entitled 'The Jewish Population in the Province of Silesia, 1922–1939', defended in 1991 at the Department of History, Warsaw University, under the direction of Prof. JERZY HOLZER; and JÓZEF WRÓBEL, for his thesis entitled 'Jewish Themes in Polish Prose, 1939–1987', at the Institute of Polish Philology, Jagiellonian University, under the direction of Prof. HENRYK MARKIEWICZ.

Distinctions for their master's theses were awarded to the following:

1. The dissertation of SYLWIA BEIER-ŻYLAR, entitled 'The Attitude of Polish Catholics to the Idea and Reality of the State of Israel, on the Basis of Articles in *Przegląd powszechny*, 1884–1953', defended in 1989 at the Department of Theology, the Academy of Catholic Theology, under the direction of Fr. Prof. WALDEMAR CHROSTOWSKI.

2. The dissertation of IZABELA GLADYSZ, entitled 'The Socio-Cultural Life of Lublin Jews, 1918–1939', defended in 1991 at the Historical Institute, Maria Curie-Skłodowska University in Lublin, under the direction of Prof. JÓZEF MARSZALEK.

3. The dissertation of BOŻENA GŁOWACZ, entitled 'Julian Stryjkowski's *Austeria*: An Attempt at a Monograph', defended in 1991 at the Department of Polish Philology, Jagiellonian University, under the direction of Prof. WŁODZIMIERZ MACIĄG.

4. The dissertation of BEATA SABLIK, entitled 'Judaica in Bielsko Biała: Save its Remnants from Oblivion, and Use it in Local Cultural Activity', defended in 1991 at the Institute of Pedagogy, Jagiellonian University, under the direction of Prof. JERZY SAMEK.

5. The dissertation of HANNA WĘGRZYNEK, entitled 'The History of Jews in Przemyśl, to 1559', defended in 1984 at the Department of History, Warsaw University, under the direction of Prof. HENRYK SAMSONOWICZ.

The level and number of submissions indicate, to the satisfaction of the organizers of the competition, that the theme of Jewish history has become part of the regular university curriculum, in spite of what are still substantial difficulties. One of these is a lack of sufficient scholarly support, caused by the hiatus in the process of research. One must remember that many historical syntheses which are used for studying the history of Polish Jews came into existence before the war and are, for the most part, outdated. The majority of their authors were murdered by the Nazis. One constantly comes across new works which, from a methodological point of view, start from completely mistaken assumptions, e.g. a study of the activities of Zionists and Agudas Yisroel in Łódz which was based exclusively on Polish sources, and antisemitic ones at that. Another, and very significant, barrier is the lack of knowledge of the Yiddish and Hebrew languages, indispensable not only to the study of primary sources but also for an appreciation of the latest publications in Israel. Here, most of the theses left much to be desired: only Marcin Wodziński, winner of one of the first prizes in the master's category, revealed a knowledge of Hebrew in his analysis of inscriptions on the tombstones of leaders of the Hasidic movement.

However, many centres of learning include in their scientific interests the Jewish theme, thanks to which there are more and more interesting studies about local Jewish history. Apart from the Interdisciplinary Centre for the Study of the History and Culture of Polish Jews, Jagiellonian University, Kraków, research of this type was undertaken by the Department of History, Mikołaj Kopernik University, Toruń, and the Historical Institute, Adam Mickiewicz University, Poznań. One can observe a certain lack of works relating to the history of Jews in pre-partition Poland. Perhaps the coming years will bring results and, in this field, historical interest. At the same time, many other disciplines are taking up the Jewish theme, from literature to psychology. Works relating to the analysis of the religio-philosophical legacy of Jews is regularly undertaken by the Warsaw Academy of Catholic Theology, as by the Catholic University of Lublin. More and more supervisors encourage their students to undertake this theme. Some have already 'released' to the world several alumni who have written on the Jewish theme. Prof. JERZY WOROŃCZAK of the Institute of Polish Philology at Wrocław University was honoured with a prize from the Polish Committee on UNESCO Affairs in recognition of his enthusiasm in propagating the Polish Jewish theme among students.

It may be of interest to present a list of all the works submitted to the first and second competitions; supervisors are given at the end of each entry. All of the dissertations have been placed in the Jewish Historical Institute archives in Warsaw.

MASTER'S THESES SUBMITTED TO THE FIRST COMPETITION (1991)

BAŻAŃSKI, EDWIN, 'The Jewish Theatre in Poland after the Second World War.' The Higher Theatre School in Kraków. *Associate Prof. Józef Keler.*

BERENDT, GRZEGORZ, 'The Situation of the Jewish Population in the Free City of Gdańsk, 1933–1939' (distinction). Gdańsk University. *Prof. Stanisław Mikosa.*

BERGMAN, OLAF, 'The Jewish Issue on the Pages of *Kurier Poznański*, 1918–1926.' Department of History, Adam Mickiewicz University, Poznań. *Associate Prof. Przemysław Hauser.*

BERUS, ELIZABETH, 'Everyday Life in the Warsaw Ghetto.' Historical Institute, Warsaw University. *Associate Prof. Tomasz Nałęcz.*

BIAŁAS, BARBARA, 'The Social Basis for Anti-semitism in Poland after 1945.' Institute of Sociology, Warsaw University. *Prof. Jan Malanowski.*

BIEGANOWSKA-LIPMAN, EWA, 'Henryk Grynberg: A Poet after the Holocaust.' Institute of Polish Literature and Culture, Silesian University. *Prof. Jerzy Paszek.*

BOGUSZ, MONIKA, 'The Vision of a New Jewish Society in Palestine, in the Light of the Daily *Nasz Przegląd*, 1923–1935' (distinction). Historical Institute, Warsaw University. *Prof. Marcin Kula.*

BORZYCH, JACEK, 'The Situation of the Jewish Population in the Free City of Gdańsk, 1933–1939.' Department of Journalism and Political Sciences, Warsaw University. *Prof. Jerzy Tomaszewski.*

BRONIEWICZ, LUCJAN, '*Jutrzenka*: *A Weekly for Polish Israelites* (1861–1863) as an Instrument for the Assimilation of Jews in the Kingdom of Poland.' Historical Institute at the Mikołaj Kopernik University in Toruń. *Associate Prof. Sławomir Kalemba.*

DUSZYŃSKI, LESZEK, 'Jewish Themes in the Literary Works of Wilhelm Feldman.' Department of Polish, Wrocław University. *Prof. L. Tatarowski.*

GAŁAS, MICHAŁ, 'The Evolution of Messianic Ideas in Judaism, in the Workings of Gershom Scholem' (distinction). The Institute of Religious Studies, Jagiellonian University. *Associate Prof. Jerzy Ochman.*

GASEK-ARDELLI, ELŻBIETA, 'The Stereotype of the Jew in the Eyes of Polish Society.' The Institute of Sociology, Warsaw University. *Prof. Edward Ciupak.*

JAROSZKIEWICZ-DĄBROWA, BEATA 'A New Kind of Anti-semitism on the Territories of the Kingdom of Poland at the End of the Nineteenth Century.' Institute of Sociology, Warsaw University. *Prof. Jerzy J. Wiatr.*

JĘDRYCHOWSKA, HALINA, 'Jewish Heroes in *The Manor* and *The Legacy*, by Isaak Bashevis Singer, and their own Identity.' Department of Polish Philology, Wrocław University. *Associate Prof. Jerzy Jastrzębski.*

JÓŹWIAK, EWA, 'The Essence of the Relationship between Jewish and Christian Israel in Catholic Theological Thinking after the Second Vatican Synod.' Department of Theology, Academy of Catholic Theology in Warsaw. *Associate Prof. Fr. Michał Czajkowski.*

KARCZYŃSKA, MIROSŁAWA, '*Kurier Poznański* on the Jewish Question in Poland, 1933–1935.' Historical Institute, Adam Mickiewicz University, Poznań. *Associate Prof. Przemysław Hauser.*

KAŚKOW, ROBERT, 'A Comparison of Polish and Jewish Biblical Proverbs' (distinction). Department of Polish Philology, Wrocław University. *Prof. Jerzy Worończak.*

KOPÓWKA, EDWARD, 'The Political and Cultural Life of Jews in Siedlce, 1918–1939.' Department of Pedagogy and Culture at the Higher School of Agriculture and Pedagogy, Siedlce. *Dr Bolesław Gerlach.*

KUBERCZYK, TOMASZ, 'Purim Plays: A Monograph.' Department of Ethnology and Cultural Anthropology, Warsaw University. *Associate Prof. Anna Zadrożyńska.*

KUNC, ANNA, 'The Literary Content of *Nasz Głos*: A Supplement to *Folks-shtime*, 1957–1969.' Department of Polish Philology at Wrocław University. *Prof. Jerzy Worończak.*

LESZCZYŃSKA, EWA, 'Poznań Synagogues, in the Light of the History of the Town's

Jewish Community' (2nd prize). Department of History, Poznań University. *Prof. Konstanty Kalinowski.*

LEWALSKI, KRZYSZTOF, 'The Conversion of Jews in the Polish Kingdom, 1866–1914.' Department of Human Studies, the Catholic University in Lublin. *Associate Prof. Hanna Dylągowa.*

LIKOWSKA, EWA, 'The Problem of Being a Jew in the Diaspora, in the Light of Selected Works from World Literature.' Department of Polish Philology, Warsaw University (Białystok campus). *Dr Elżbieta Feliksiak.*

LUBLIŃSKI, RYSZARD, 'The Organization and Functioning of a Kibbutz' (distinction). Department of Law and Business Administration, Maria Curie-Skłodowska University, Lublin. *Prof. Roman Tokarczyk.*

MADEYSKA-PILCHOWA, ANNA, '*The Dybbuk* by Sh. Ansky: An Attempt at a Monograph' (special award from the 'Shalom' Foundation for the Promotion of Polish Jewish Culture). The Institute of Polish Philology, Jagiellonian University. *Associate Prof. Marta Fik.*

MŁODOŻENIAK, DARIUSZ, 'The Jewish Resistance Movement on Polish Territory, 1939–1943.' Department of Law and Business Administration, Wrocław University. *Associate Prof. Franciszek Połomski.*

MUSZYŃSKA, DANUTA, 'The New Jewish Cemetery in Łódź.' National Higher School of Art, Poznań.

MYĆKO, JOANNA, 'The Polish Origin of Heroes in the Works of I. B. Singer.' Department of Humanities, Warsaw University (Białystok Campus). *Prof. Helena Karwacka.*

PARADZIŃSKA, RENATA, 'The Care of Jewish Children in Warsaw and its Environs, 1918–1939' (distinction). Department of Pedagogy, Warsaw University. *Prof. Józef Miąso.*

REWIS, PAWEŁ, 'The Legal Status of Jews on Polish Territory on the Eve of Regaining Independence: The First Efforts at New Solutions.' Department of Law and Business Administration, Warsaw University. *Assoc. Prof. Jerzy Senkowski.*

RUSEK, MARZENA, 'The Emigration of the Jewish Population, 1945–1948, with Special Emphasis on the Śląsk-Dąbrowski Province.' Department of Social Studies, Śląsk University. *Prof. Andrzej Werblan.*

RYMSZA-LEOCIAK, MARZANNA, 'The Mode of Communication in Jewish Children's Diaries from the Nazi Occupation of Poland.' Department of Polish Philology, Warsaw University. *Associate Prof. Zofia Mitosek.*

SARNOWSKI, LESZEK, 'A Look at the Polish Jewish Street, from the Window of *Nasz Przegląd*.' Historical Institute, Gdańsk University. *Prof. R. Wapiński.*

SELLIN, JAROSŁAW, 'The Jewish Question in Poland during the Four-year Sejm.' Historical Institute, Gdańsk University. *Prof. Stanisław Gierszewski.*

SIERDZIŃSKA, HANNA, 'The Adoption of the Nuremberg Laws and its Reflection in the Polish Press, 1935–1936.' Department of History, Mikołaj Kopernik University, Toruń. *Prof. Harold Grünberg.*

SKRZYPCZAK, ALINA, 'Jews in Łańcut.' Historical Institute at the Higher School of Pedagogy, Rzeszów. *Associate Prof. Józef Półćwiartek.*

SZAYNOK, BOŻENA, 'The Jewish Pogrom in Kielce, 4 July 1946.' (1st prize). Historical Institute, Wrocław University. *Prof. Wojciech Wrzesiński.*

TOŁCZYK, DARIUSZ, 'The Image of Jews in Polish Novels, as Compared with the Image of Poland and Poles in Jewish Novels, at the Turn of the Nineteenth Century' (3rd prize). Institute of Polish Literature, Warsaw University. *Prof. Stanisław Frybes.*

WOLFRAM-ZAKRZEWSKA, AGNIESZKA, 'The Jewish Question in Polish Literature in the Second Half of the Nineteenth Century.' Institute of Sociology, Warsaw University. *Associate Prof. Ewa Nowicka.*

ŻUREK, JANUSZ, 'The "Jewish Question" in the Polish Press, 1987–1989.' Institute of Political Sciences and Journalism, Silesian University. *Associate Prof. Jerzy Mikułowski-Pomorski.*

MASTER'S THESES SUBMITTED TO THE SECOND COMPETITION (1992)

ADAMOWICZ, KATARZYNA, 'An Assessment of the Quality of Life in Israel' (1991). The Academy of Economics, Poznań. *Prof. Janusz Piasny.*

BARAŃSKA, BEATA, 'West German–Israeli Relations, 1949–1991' (1992). Institute of International Affairs, Warsaw University. *Prof. Edward Halizak.*

BASIURA, EWA, 'The World of Jewish Spirituality and its Individual Family and Community Dimensions in Selected Fiction by I. B. Singer' (1992). Jagiellonian University. *Prof. J. Bedell.*

BEIER-ŻYLAK, SYLWIA, 'The Attitude of Polish Catholics to the Idea and Reality of the State of Israel, on the Basis of Articles in *Przegląd powszechny*, 1884–1953' (1989). Department of Theology, the Academy of Catholic Theology. *Prof. W. Chrostowski.*

BĘCAL, PIOTR, 'The Social, Religious and Political Life of Jews in Krasnostaw County during the Twenty Years Between the Two World Wars' (1991). Historical Institute, Marie Curie-Skłodowska University in Lublin. *Prof. Z. Mańkowski.*

BIEGALA, MIROSŁAW, 'Jews in the Pages of *Siewcy prawdy*' (1992). Department of Theology, Catholic University of Lublin. *Prof. Zygmunt Zieliński.*

BORKOWSKA, INGA, 'Death, Burial, Mourning and the Cemetery in Ashkenazi Jewish Culture' (1991). Department of Historical and Pedagogical Sciences, Wrocław University. *Prof. F. Rosiński.*

BOROWSKA, MONIKA, 'Two Generations of Polish Intelligentsia *vis-à-vis* the Jews: Attitudes, Stereotypes, and Prejudices' (1992). Department of Economy and Sociology, Łódź University. *Prof. B. Sułkowski.*

BUDLEWSKI, LUCJAN, 'Jews in Ciechanowiec in the Eighteenth and Nineteenth Centuries' (1992). Historical Institute, Warsaw University (Białystok Campus). *Prof. A. Dobroński.*

CHWASTEK, TATIANA, 'Synagogues of Małopolska from the End of the Sixteenth to the Beginning of the Nineteenth Century' (1991). Arts Department, Mikołaj Kopernik University, Toruń. *Dr Szczęsny Skibiński.*

DEWOR, FR. GRZEGORZ, 'The Religious Meaning of Jewish Holidays and Contemporary Celebrations in the Jewish Congregation of Katowice' (1991). Higher Spiritual Seminary in Katowice, Papal Theological Academy, Kraków. *Fr. Dr J. Górski.*

DOBRUCKA, MAŁGORZATA, 'Jewish Tradition in the Painting of Jewish Painters in

Poland in the Period between the Two World Wars' (1991). University of Silesia (Cieszyń Campus). *Dr J. Olbrycht.*

DOMAGALSKA, MAŁGORZATA, 'Jews in A. Nowaczyński's "Ofensywa—myśl narodowa 1929–1934", *Prosto z mostu* 1938–1939' (1991). Department of Polish Philology, Łódź University. *Prof. W. Puś.*

GAWOR, MARTA, 'The Image of the Jew in the Consciousness of the Inhabitants of Tarnów' (1991/2). Institute of Sociology, Jagiellonian University. *Prof. A. Paluch.*

GĄSIOROWSKI, STEFAN, 'Jewish Autonomy in the Korona in the Sixteenth and the First Half of the Seventeenth Century' (1991). Department of History, Jagiellonian University. *Prof. J. Gierowski.*

GIBAS, DANUTA, 'Ida Kamińska, Director and Actress in the Jewish Theatre in Poland (1946–1968): An Analysis of her Artistic Activity on the Basis of Selected Performances' (1991). Institute of Polish Philology, Jagiellonian University. *Associate Prof. Kazimierz Nowacki.*

GLADYSZ, IZABELA, 'The Socio-Cultural Life of Lublin Jews, 1918–1939' (1991). Historical Institute, Marie Curie-Skłodowska University in Lublin. *Prof. Józef Marszałek.*

GŁODEK, MARIA, 'The Parallels between Polish Literature and Jewish Literature, on the Basis of Selected Works of Icchak Lejbusz Perec' (1991). Polish Department, Warsaw University. *Prof. St. Frybes.*

GŁOWACZ, BOŻENA, 'Julian Stryjkowski's *Austeria*: An Attempt at a Monograph' (1991). Department of Polish Philology, Jagiellonian University. *Prof. Włodzimierz Maciąg.*

GÓRSKA, BEATA, 'Jews as a Separate Social and Religious Group in Poland in the Twenty Years between the Two World Wars' (1991). Institute of Sociology, Adam Mickiewicz University, Poznań. *Prof. J. Leoński.*

GRUSZYŃSKA, ZOFIA, 'Intolerance towards Judaism in a Local Urban Community', Higher School of Agriculture and Pedagogy in Siedlce. *Prof. Tadeusz Pilch.*

HANTKIEWICZ, ROBERT, 'The Attitude of the Poznań National Democrats towards the Jewish Minority in 1938–1939' (1992). Department of History, Poznań University. *Prof. Zbigniew Dworecki.*

HARTMAN, BARBARA, 'The UNO and the Emergence of the State of Israel' (1992). Department of Social Studies, Catholic University of Lublin. *Fr. Prof. Joachim Kundziela.*

JANKOWIAK, IWONA, 'The Attitude of *Słowo pomorskie* to the Jewish Question in 1935–1939'. An Attempt to Create a Bibliography' (1992). Institute of Library Sciences, Mikołaj Kopernik University in Toruń. *Prof. St. Kalembka.*

JANUSZKIEWICZ, JADWIGA, 'The Assimilation of Jews on Polish Territory, based on the Life and Output of W. Feldman' (1992). Department of Humanities, Mikołaj Kopernik University, Toruń. *Prof. A. Hutnikiewicz.*

JASIŃSKA, BARBARA, ' "I am a Jew": The Dynamics of Having an Ethnic Identity' (1990). Department of Ethnology, Warsaw University. *Dr A. Zadrożyńska.*

JURZYSTA, ALEKSANDRA, 'The Remains of Jewish Material Culture in the Territory of the Kielce Province' (1991). Institute of Political Geography, Łódź University. *Dr. W. Michalski.*

KACZMARZYK, MAŁGORZATA, 'The Characteristic Stereotype—Polish and Foreign—of the Jewish National Group in the Eyes of Poles'. Department of Social Studies, Catholic University of Lublin. *Prof. A. Biela.*

KISLER, JOLANTA, 'The Jewish World, in the Novels of the Galician Trilogy by J. Stryjkowski' (1990). Institute of Polish Philology, Gdańsk University. *Prof. R. Karwacki.*

KLEJDYSZ, NATALIA, 'The Stereotype of the Jew in the Press of Wielkopolska in the Period between the Two World Wars' (1992). Institute of Political Science, Adam Mickiewicz University, Poznań. *Associate Prof. J. Sobczak.*

KORZECKA, MAŁGORZATA, 'Jewish Orphanages in Legnica, 1945–1948' (1992). Department of Historical Studies and Pedagogy, Wrocław University. *Dr Czesław Kozak.*

KORZENIAK, BEATA, 'The Cultural Life of Jews in Poland, 1945–1968' (1991). Historical Institute, Jagiellonian University. *Associate Prof. A. Pańkiewicz.*

KOZIOŁ, KATARZYNA, 'Wiktor Alter: Ideologue and Leader of the Bund' (1992). Department of Humanities, Higher School of Pedagogy, Kraków. *Prof. Michał Śliwa.*

KOŹMIŃSKA, EWA, 'Polish Jewish Wartime Accounting: The Challenges of the Holocaust. An Analysis of Letters to the Editor of *Tygodnik powszechny* Sent in Reply to the Błoński–Siła-Nowicki Discussion' (1992). Institute of Sociology, Warsaw University. *Dr Paweł Śpiewak.*

KRAKOWIAN, DARIUSZ, 'Nationalistic Jewish Political Groups in Łódź, 1930–1939' (1991). Historical Institute, Łódź University. *Prof. B. Wachowska.*

KRAWCZYŃSKA, DOROTA, 'Henryk Grynberg: Witness and Artist' (1991). Polish Department, Warsaw University. *Prof. Maria Janion.*

KRÓL, LUCYNA, 'Selected Issues from the Culture of Polish Jews and their Reflection in Written Works in the Polish Language of the Nineteenth and Twentieth Centuries' (1991). Department of Historical Philosophy, Jagiellonian University. *Prof. Olga Mulkiewicz Goldberg.*

KRÓL, SYLWIA, 'The Directions and Forms of Reception in Poland of Tourists from Israel in the Context of the Touristic Needs of Jews' (1991). Department of Tourism, Academy of Sport, Kraków. *Dr B. Walas.*

KUŚ, EWA, 'Zionism: An Outline of its Doctrine to the Beginning of the Twentieth Century' (1991). Department of Law and Business Administration, Wrocław University. *Prof. K. Jońca.*

KWIATEK, BOGDAN, 'The Will as the Source of Life in the *Fons Vitae*, by Salomon ibn Gabirol' (1992). Department of Philosophy, Catholic University of Lublin. *Fr. Prof. Stanisław Wielgus.*

MALSKI, JAKUB, 'The Doctrine of Political Zionism of Theodore Herzl' (1992). Department of Law and Business Administration, Wrocław University. *Prof. K. Jońca.*

MARDEWSKI, ADAM, 'Jews in Toruń between the Two World Wars' (1992). Institute of History and Archives, Mikołaj Kopernik University in Toruń. *Prof. M. Wojciechowski.*

MATŁOKA, JAROSŁAW, 'Julian Stryjkowski's *Voices in the Dark, Austeria, The Dream of Azriel, The Newcomer from Narbonne, Echo*' (1991). Institute of Polish Philology, Adam Mickiewicz University, Poznań. *Prof. Maria Adamczyk.*

MAZURKIEWICZ, PIOTR, 'The World According to Szolem Alejchem's *The History of Tevya the Milkman*' (1991). Higher Upper School of Pedagogy, Zielona Góra. *Dr Cz. Dutko.*

MICHALCZUK, MARIOLA, 'Selected Issues in the Evaluation and Appraisal of the "Jewish Problem" (e.g. by Students of WSP in Opole)' (1992). Department of Historical Philosophy, Higher School of Pedagogy, Opole. *Dr I. Gniazdowska.*

MURCZKIEWICZ, PRZEMYSŁAW, 'Polish–Jewish Relations during the Second World War on the Basis of Archival Material Relating to Polish Territory from the Archives of Yad Vashem in Jerusalem' (1992). Department of Church History, Catholic University of Lublin. *Fr. Prof. Z. Zieliński.*

NIECIKOWSKA-PLOTEK, OLGA, 'The Jewish Question in the World-view of Maria Dąbrowska' (1991). Polish Department, Warsaw University. *Prof. Tadeusz Drewnowski.*

ORONOWICZ, KRZYSZTOF, 'Po'alei Tsion Left in Poland after the Second World War' (1992). Department of Social Studies, Wrocław University. *Associate Prof. J. Albin.*

PÓŁGROSZEK, AGATA, 'The Polish–Jewish Conflict in the Pages of the *Gwiazda Niedzielna*, 1937–1938' (1991). Department of Pedagogy, Jagiellonian University. *Prof. F. Adamski and Dr B. Urban.*

SABLIK, BEATA, 'Judaica in Bielsko Biała: Save its Remnants from Oblivion and Use it in Local Cultural Activity' (1991). Institute of Pedagogy, Jagiellonian University. *Prof. Jerzy Samek.*

SADOWSKA, JOANNA, 'A Profile of a Jewish Politician in the Second Polish Republic (Yitzhak Grünbaum)' (1991). Historical Institute, Warsaw University. *Prof. A. Garlicki.*

SAMSONOWSKA, KRYSTYNA, 'An Outline of the Functioning of a Jewish Community in Kraków in 1918–1939' (1991). Historical Institute, Jagiellonian University. *Assoc. Prof. Michał Pułaski.*

STANDY-NOWAKOSKA, ANETA, '*Aficianados* of Jewish Culture in Poznań: A Monograph on the Polish–Jewish Society in Poznań' (1991). Department of Social Studies, Adam Mickiewicz University, Poznań. *Prof. St. Kozyra-Kowalski.*

SZENWALD, BEATA, 'The Jewish Self-Portrait, on the Basis of an Analysis of Jewish Humour' (1991). Institute of Sociology, Adam Mickiewicz University, Poznań. *Prof. J. Leoński.*

WASIEWICZ, MAGDALENA, 'The Jewish Question in the Polish Language Press in the Period between the Two World Wars, on the Basis of the Newspaper *Rozwój*' (1991). Department of Philosophy and History, Łódź University. *Dr Ryszard Rosin.*

WĘGRZYNEK, HANNA, 'The History of Jews in Przemyśl, to 1559' (1984). Department of History, Warsaw University. *Prof. Henryk Samsonowicz.*

WODZIŃSKI, MARCIN, '*Tsadik* Graves in Poland' (1991), Institute of Polish Philology, Wrocław University. *Prof. Jerzy Worończak.*

WREŚNIEWSKA, MAŁGORZATA, 'Elements of Cultural Auto-stereotyping in the Creativity of Polish Writers of Jewish Origin' (1991). Institute of Philosophy, Higher School of Pedagogy in Kraków. *Dr Tadeusz Budrewicz.*

ZATYKA, JACEK, 'The Jewish Population in Śląsk Opolski, with Particular Reference to the Nineteenth and Twentieth Centuries' (1990). Department of Philosophy and History, Higher School of Pedagogy in Opole. *Dr W. Lesiuk.*

ZĘBIK, DOROTA, 'Care of the Jewish Child in Częstochowa Province in 1939–1945' (1991). Higher School of Pedagogy, Częstochowa. *Dr Zb. Grzędzielski.*

ŻYNDUL, JOLANTA, 'Anti-Jewish Disturbances in Poland, 1935–1937' (1990). Department of History, Warsaw University. *Prof. Marcin Kula.*

DOCTORAL THESES SUBMITTED TO THE SECOND COMPETITION (1992)

JAWORSKI, WOJCIECH, 'The Jewish Population in the Province of Silesia, 1922–1939' (1991). Department of History, Warsaw University. *Prof. Jerzy Holzer.*

MELCHIOR, MAŁGORZATA, 'The Social Identity of the Individual' (1990). Department of Sociology, Warsaw University. *Prof. Hanna Świda-Ziemba.*

PROKOP-JANIEC, EUGENIA, 'Polish Jewish Literature between the Two World Wars' (1990). Institute of Polish Philology, Jagiellonian University. *Prof. Henryk Markiewicz.*

WIŚNIEWSKI, PIOTR, 'Missions to Convert Jews: The Barbikan Mission in Białystok' (1989). Historical Institute, Warsaw University (Białystok Campus). *Associate Prof. A. Dobroński.*

WRÓBEL, JÓZEF, 'Jewish Themes in Polish Prose, 1939–1987' (1988). Institute of Polish Philology, Jagiellonian University. *Prof. Henryk Markiewicz.*

ZALEWSKA, GABRIELA, 'The Jewish Population in Warsaw in the Period between the Two World Wars' (1989). Historical Institute, Polish Academy of Sciences. *Prof. Janusz Żarnowski.*

PART III

Reviews

REVIEW ESSAYS

History, Drama, and Healing
On the Television Play *A i B* by Harvey Sarner

DAVID ENGEL

The poet and the historian differ not by writing in verse or in prose.... The true difference is that one relates what has happened, the other what may happen. Poetry, therefore, is a more philosophical and a higher thing than history; for poetry tends to express the universal, history the particular. By the universal I mean how a person of a certain type will on occasion speak or act, according to the law of probability or necessity; and it is this universality at which poetry aims in the names she attaches to the personages.

ARISTOTLE, *Poetics*, ch. 9

When I see scholars wrestling with the dust of ancient books and writings in order to resurrect the heroes of history in their true form, in the belief that they are sacrificing their eyesight for the sake of 'historical truth', I say to myself, 'How these learned men go on and on about the importance of their discoveries, and yet they do not deign to observe the simple fact that not every archaeological truth is a historical truth!' Historical truth is really nothing more than that which reveals the forces at work in human social life. Anything of notable effect upon life is a tangible historical force, and its reality is a historical truth, even if by itself it is nothing more than a figment of the imagination.... And so, when I read the story of the Exodus from Egypt on the first night of Passover, in which the figure of Moses the son of Amram ... hovers before me and elevates me to a higher world, in that moment I pay no heed to all those doubts and questions with which the Gentile scholars have beset us about whether there really was such a man as Moses who lived and worked as our people believes he did.... Instead I brush all of them aside with a single curt reply: The primordial Moses, whose reality and essence you seek to clarify, is of no interest to anyone save scholars like yourselves. We, on the other hand, have a different Moses, our own Moses, whose image has been fixed in the heart of our people for generations.... And even if you could prove with absolute certainty that Moses the man never existed ... you would take nothing away at all from the historical reality of the ideal Moses.

AHAD HAAM, 'Moshe' (1904)

Translated from the English by Wojciech A. Wierzewski; produced by Stefan Szlachtycz; starring Piotr Fronczewski, Henryk Talar, and Teresa Budzisz-Krzyżanowska.

As an academic historian who has emphasized *ad nauseam* that he strives to report the results of his research without conscious reference to their implications for any current concerns of the general public, I find myself called upon from time to time by sceptical laymen to defend the social utility of my craft. Usually my reply includes, among other things, some assertion to the effect that societies committed to weighing present options in the light of past experience and to employing past experience as a guide for present action (and most Western societies do indeed profess to be so committed) ought to have available as accurate a description as possible of that experience, so that their deliberations may be informed to the greatest extent possible by fact rather than by fantasy. The historian's primary function, I explain, is to provide such descriptions; and in order to maximize the probability that his descriptions will indeed be as accurate as possible, he dare not take into account how he supposes any particular public might wish or need to perceive the past in formulating them.

I confess that that response often does not prove terribly satisfying. Recently, for instance, I was challenged by a graduate student of literature who complained that the historian's insistence upon accuracy of detail generally results in the evocation of an ostensible reality at once so dry and so full of qualification as to render it useless as a guide or inspiration for any action whatsoever. Strict accuracy, the student remonstrated, lacks any significant social motive power; hence, those who have made the investigation of the past their life's work would perform a far greater public service by combing the experience of previous generations for stories that could be formed into socially useful myths. In so far as such myths promote behaviour leading towards a desirable social goal, she contended, they ought to be regarded as embodying a greater measure of historical truth than accounts of the past that sacrifice clear moral vision in the name of factual precision; by implication she argued that if historians' devotion to fact renders them temperamentally incapable of constructive myth-making, they ought to relinquish their claim to primacy as narrators of the past in favour of poets and dramatic artists.

Of course, this student was not the first to wave such a red rag in a historian's face, as the two quotations with which I have introduced these remarks will attest. Nor, most likely, is she alone in her suspicion that the historical profession brings society at most a dubious benefit. Indeed, after viewing the recent Polish Television production of Harvey Sarner's drama *A i B*, I suspect that she and the author of this fantasy of what might have been would find themselves nodding avid agreement at each other were another playwright to bring them together for the sort of meeting that Sarner has conjured up for two great myth-generating figures of the recent past.

A i B presents an imaginary discussion between Lieutenant-General Władysław Anders, commander of the Polish exile army established in the Soviet Union in August 1941, who after the Second World War became a towering symbol of resistance to the Communist domination of his country, and Menahem Begin, a former soldier in Anders's army who, upon removing the Polish uniform in late 1943, assumed command of a Jewish underground force in British-held Palestine and was eventually chosen the sixth prime minister of the State of Israel. The parley is set in the Polish general's London hotel room, overlooking Trafalgar Square, on 8 May 1946, in full view of the grand parade held that day to mark the first anniversary of the Allied victory over Nazi Germany. Begin, the underground renegade, has sought out his former commander for reasons that are, by his own admission, not clear even to him; perhaps, he explains, he wishes merely to look into the face of the Polish leader towards whom, as the dialogue quickly reveals, he bears considerable ire. Anders, for his part, shows no reticence in setting forth his many complaints about what he perceives as insufficient loyalty demonstrated by Polish Jews towards a country and a people that, in his words, offered them a haven during the centuries when no other country would tolerate them. And yet, as the two thrust and parry at each other over glass after glass of cognac poured liberally from the general's decanter, they come to realize that their situations are similar: both are exiles, without a homeland, outlaws in the eyes of the ruling authorities in the countries they are determined to free, prepared to offer the ultimate sacrifice for the one cause that matters to each of them—their respective peoples' independence. Anders draws his faith in the ultimate triumph of his mission in part from parables taken from the history of Palestine and the Jews, while Begin—who quotes verses from Mickiewicz that Anders does not recognize—at one point actually finds it appropriate to invite the general to join the Jewish fight against the British (a proposition that the Pole graciously declines). What is more, in the course of their brutally frank, no-holds-barred discussion—assisted by a sort of one-woman Greek chorus whose periodic interjections of moral and historical commentary move both the principals and the audience towards resolution—the two come to understand, and perhaps even grudgingly to accept, the responses offered by each adversary to the other's charge. They part with a newly found respect for one another, as the chorus muses over what might have been if only such a conversation had actually taken place.

Of course, such things never happened. In May 1946 Menahem Begin was actually occupying an apartment on Yehoshua Bin Nun Street in Tel Aviv, disguised as an Orthodox rabbi named Yisrael Sassever, in order to hide from a British Mandatory authority that had put a price on his head; the thought that he would have abandoned his masquerade and travelled to the British capital merely to steal a glance up close at the face of a Polish general is preposterous. Moreover, the piece is rife with anachronisms: the two principals discuss the Kielce pogrom (which did not happen until two months after this fictional meeting is supposed to have taken place) and the death of General Leopold Okulicki (which occurred the following December), and they refer occasionally to a place called

Israel, even though in May 1946 even the most zealous advocates of immediate Jewish statehood in Palestine had not thought of such a name for their future country. But then such details evidently did not matter to the author of this drama. Indeed, at the outset the chorus informs us that 'it is a hundred times more important to understand history than to know it', whatever that means. It seems that for Harvey Sarner 'understanding history' implies, after Aristotle, grasping the possibilities inherent in a past situation, even if it is known that such possibilities never materialized in fact. Sarner has grasped that it is possible to relate the history of Polish–Jewish relations during the Second World War, or at least significant aspects of that history, in such a way as to promote Polish–Jewish *rapprochement* in place of the antagonism that other versions of that history have so often engendered. What the author has set forth in his play is a historical text that both sides can accept proudly, one that not only preserves a positive self-image for both Poles and Jews but that impels both groups towards empathy for one another. And if, in order to present that text, it is necessary to concoct a fantasy that ignores a few fine points of chronology, so be it.

Now I am all in favour of improving current relations between Poles and Jews. I question, however, whether the sort of historical 'imagineering' in which Harvey Sarner has engaged in *A i B* is a suitable way to pursue that goal. The problem is that the proposed new text itself, and not merely the dramatic framework in which Sarner has presented it, does violence not only to the actual sequence of the historical events that comprise it but to the essential character of those events as revealed in their extant documentary traces. As it turns out, the version of the past set forth in this drama—a version that is supposed to lead to mutual understanding and respect—is actually based upon a series of interpretations of action and motivation that at best lack substantial documentary foundation and at worst are demonstrably false. Accepting it requires, therefore, a willing suspension of disbelief not merely for the play's duration but at all times when confronting the actual historical record; it implies continual readiness either to live knowingly in accordance with an illusion or to deny the existence of a conflicting historical record altogether.

Consider, for example, the play's treatment of the manner in which Begin terminated his service with General Anders's forces. On three occasions the audience is informed emphatically that, in contrast to many other Jewish soldiers, the future prime minister did not desert the Polish army but received a proper discharge. To be sure, it is true that throughout his life Begin insisted that he had refused to follow the example of many of his Jewish comrades, even for the exalted purpose of assuming command of a great armed struggle against the occupiers of his country, because in his eyes desertion, even from an army not one's own, was dishonourable, and no deserter was fit to lead a war of national liberation. Unfortunately, the facts of the situation are nowhere nearly so cut and dried. As I have detailed in my recent book *Facing a Holocaust*, Begin was not actually discharged from the Polish army; he was merely granted leave of absence for a period of one year, with the proviso that during that time he participate in a Polish-sponsored delegation of Zionist Revisionists to the United States that had been charged with the task of conducting pro-Polish, anti-Soviet propaganda. Moreover, the formation of such a delegation and Begin's service in it had both been proposed to the Polish authorities in Palestine by a group of Begin's political allies, who were seeking a way to engineer his release from the ranks. His supporters have freely acknowledged that Begin never had any intention of living up to the terms of his leave but intended immediately to assume command of the underground Irgun Tseva'i Le'umi (Jewish National Military Organization). There are documents that suggest that the Polish military leadership attempted to recall Begin to active service once it became clear that the propaganda delegation was not about to materialize and that when he failed to report they regarded him as a deserter. These documents are not conclusive; indeed, there are many aspects of the episode of Begin's detachment from the Polish ranks that still require clarification. But even from what is known definitely at present it is clear that the story does not chime with the image of a man steadfastly loyal to his Polish military oath, animated fundamentally by an acute sense of honour, that the play categorically presents.

Or take the drama's explication of Anders's attitude towards those Jews who did desert his forces. The chorus, in her role as moral arbiter, suggests that the general did not take action to return Jewish deserters to the ranks or to punish them because he was an idealist, and he understood and appreciated the Jews' loyalty to their own national cause. She even counsels that Jewish historians ought to be thankful to the Polish general, who contributed half a division of trained armed soldiers to the future Israeli army. One can only wonder where the author might have come across such a notion. Anders himself explained in his memoirs, published in 1949, that he 'did not permit the pursuit of the deserters' because he had 'determined not to apply strictly with respect to the national minorities the laws regarding universal compulsory military service for Polish citizens residing abroad' and because he 'did not want to have soldiers under his command who did not want to fight'. He indicated further that he had 'warned the British authorities that they might have difficulties with such a large number of Jewish deserters', and he noted proudly that he 'was not mistaken, for . . . at the head of the terrorist action in Palestine stood a deserter from the second army corps, a corporal of the fifth infantry division, Begin'. Those are hardly the words of someone who had been so moved by the Jews' national ardour that he was prepared willingly to suffer the loss of trained troops so that they might acquire the military means to realize their two-thousand-year hope. Moreover— again as documented in *Facing a Holocaust*—it is simply not the case that Anders did not permit the pursuit of Jewish deserters and opposed their punishment; in the event, Polish military police conducted at least two raids upon Palestinian kibbutzim suspected of harbouring fugitives from the Polish forces, and Anders himself advocated severe reprisals against the deserters' families, including revoking their Polish citizenship. If in the end deserters were not pursued with greater vigour, the reason lay far less with Anders's personal attitude towards them than with the fact that the desertions took place within an extremely complex political context in which the overriding Polish interest was to call as little attention to the Jewish soldiers' defection as possible. Finally, no evidence has been adduced so far in support of the play's suggestion that the Jews who deserted the Polish forces eventually made a significant contribution to the military struggle to establish a Jewish state; not nearly enough is known at this point about the individual deserters and their subsequent fates to justify such speculation.

I could go on at length in the same vein about the imaginary nature of the play's presentation of other episodes, including the proposal of some of Begin's Revisionist colleagues to establish a Jewish legion as part of Anders's army, the supposed prescience of Begin's mentor, Vladimir Jabotinsky, regarding the fate of Polish Jewry in the 1930s, and the Kielce pogrom; but the point has been made. I do not mean to say that I believe Harvey Sarner to have sacrificed accuracy deliberately in all cases in the service of better understanding between Poles and Jews; I should prefer to think that he was simply not aware of much of the historical record. The question is rather what people committed to the cause of better understanding ought to do in the light of the historical record once it is exposed. Are they to chide those who have exposed it for their lack of social responsibility or concern? Are they to echo the words of the turn-of-the-century Jewish intellectual Ahad Haam with regard to the relation between the historical and the ideal Moses and assert that no matter what historians may eventually discover about Anders, Begin, or any of the key figures and episodes in past Polish–Jewish relations, those discoveries will be of no importance to anyone save scholars unless they conform to a preformed picture of those relations whose source is in the collective hearts of the Polish and Jewish peoples? Or are they simply to claim that the dramatist's concern with what might have been is so much nobler and higher than the historian's preoccupation with what has been in fact that it endows him with absolute licence to ignore the historical record altogether?

Indeed, in the final analysis does it really matter that Anders and Begin were not exactly as Harvey Sarner has portrayed them in his drama? It seems to me that it matters precisely to the extent that Poles and Jews today regard the past as significant in determining how they ought to relate to each other in the present. There is, I think, something fundamentally contradictory, and perhaps even a bit disingenuous, in arguing on the one hand that current Polish–Jewish relations ought legitimately to be affected by what has transpired between the two groups in previous generations, and on the other that the nature of previous encounters between the two groups in ultimately whatever we today wish it to have been. For if the past is to count it must be a real past, one as faithful to the historical record as historians are able to provide; to argue otherwise—to posit the primacy of a mythic past—is actually in the final analysis tantamount to conceding that the past really does not count at all. And is it not more honest, and thus potentially more therapeutic, to insist that if Poles and Jews are to make peace today they must do so *in spite of* a past that has often been marked by conflict than to imagine a new past of mutual respect through common struggles that can lead the two peoples to *rapprochement because of* it? The study of history and the promulgation of its results may not always promote healing directly, but they can protect against the sort of illusion that militates against the formation of stable, healthy relationships in the long run.

Does this mean that dramatists cannot contribute to the healing process? Of course not. But if they are to do so they must remain faithful to the canons of dramatic art, just as historians must remain faithful to the canons of their craft if they are to perform any positive social function. Ultimately it is in this regard that Harvey Sarner's play has missed the mark. In his determination to create a new historical text Sarner has, like a historian, confined his discussion largely to the realm of the particular: his two principals are not just any Pole and Jew but two specific individuals, and the exchange between them concerns not situations of general significance but definite actual events, of which Sarner purports to present not merely a useful but also a true account. Indeed, it is important, given Sarner's aim, that they be so; it aids the acceptance of his new text by Poles and Jews today that it has been formulated, as it were, by two of their leaders, who have given it their seal of approval. The chorus, adding her voice of authority to the discussion, also serves this purpose. But by doing so Sarner has in effect relinquished his claim to universality, which is the source of the dramatist's licence to invent in the first place. The actions of Anders and Begin are matters of record, but Sarner is not faithful to it; hence, what Aristotle termed 'the law of probability or necessity' would probably preclude their coming to terms on the basis of a formula that mangles that record to the extent that Sarner's does. Matters might have been different, however, had Sarner created two truly universal characters—say, an unnamed Pole and Polish Jew who happen to find themselves standing next to each other at the victory parade and set to talking about their respective experiences during the war, before, and after, or their respective notions of honour, loyalty, exile, and defeat—to bear his message, for the past invented for them could not be subject to challenge on the grounds of inaccuracy. Any resolution achieved between such characters would, of course, lack the imprimatur of history that Sarner has sought; but if Sarner wishes to achieve that imprimatur he is obligated to operate as a historian, not as a dramatist.

I shall not speculate about what sort of a resolution two such characters might achieve, for I am a historian, qualified to relate only what has happened, not what may happen. I should be interested to see, however, what a dramatist who chooses to develop such a scenario does with it.

Inside, Outside: Interpreting Jewish Difference

SYLVIA BARACK FISHMAN

DURING the summer of 1925 the illustrious American thermodynamicist Percy Bridgeman, chairman of Harvard University's physics department, wrote to Britain's most distinguished physicist, the New Zealander Professor Ernest Rutherford, strongly urging employment for his brilliant young protégé, J. Robert Oppenheimer: 'As appears from his name, Oppenheimer is a Jew, but entirely without the usual qualifications of his race. He is a tall, well set-up young man, with a rather engaging diffidence of manner, and I think you need have no hesitation whatever for any reason of this sort in considering his application.'[1] Bridgeman reveals by implication what the 'usual' defects of the Jewish 'race' might be considered to be: Oppenheimer is atypical because he is not short, physically awkward, unattractive, or aggressive.

Assumptions about Jewish faults 'of this sort' were ubiquitous among the intelligentsia and élite classes of nineteenth-century London and Vienna. During the first decades of the twentieth century negative images of Jews were prevalent in the United States as well; Bridgeman's statement was made during the heyday of antisemitic quotas in most American universities. While discriminatory quotas have largely disappeared in the United States, portrayals of Jews in contemporary Western literature, cinema, and the media indicate that negative images of the 'usual' Jew still flourish. Jews are still often pictured as being physically smaller or lacking in prowess, loud, over-emotional, and aggressive.[2]

Negative images of Jews were propagated publicly by non-Jews for hundreds of years. Yet today, more often than not, American Jewish writers, film-makers, and television personalities are responsible for portraying characters whose peculiarities of physique and personality make them recognizable as Jews to large and diverse audiences. One common element in such contemporary portrayals of

---

[1] Robert Oppenheimer, *Letters and Recollections*, ed. Alice Kimball Smith and Charles Weiner (Cambridge, Mass., and London, 1980), 77.

[2] Examples of this phenomenon change from season to season. In 1994 American television reveals such instances of this type as Dr Joel Fleishman in *Northern Exposure*, producer Miles Silverberg in *Murphy Brown*, and Franny Fine in *The Nanny*.

Jews has been a sense of marginality based on a profound discomfort with their own physical being, and especially with their erotic impulses. The characters created by novelist Philip Roth, film-maker Woody Allen, and comics Jackie Mason and Richard Lewis convey vivid impressions of themselves as being different—and often unpleasantly so—from the non-Jews around them.

The definitive novelistic articulation of Jewish difference and marginality in mid-twentieth-century America came out of the mind and mouth of Roth's Alexander Portnoy, who, as an adolescent, noticed his nose growing at an alarming rate into distinctively Jewish proportions. Suffering in Jewish Newark, Portnoy wanted to obliterate the ethnic nature of his nose, despite the fact that his mother said it would give him 'character'.

But who wants character? I want Thereal McCoy! In her blue parka and her red earmuffs and her big white mittens—Miss America, on blades. With her mistletoe and her plum pudding (whatever that might be), and her one-family house with a banister and a staircase, and parents who are tranquil and patient and dignified, and also a brother Billy who knows how to take motors apart and says 'Much obliged,' and isn't afraid of anything physical . . . this amazing creature—to whom no one has ever said, 'Shah,' or 'I only hope your children will do the same to you someday!'[3]

While affluent and assimilated American Jews today have acquired such mainstream accoutrements as one-family houses with banisters, contemporary American fiction and film suggest that Jews have not yet attained 'tranquil, patient, and dignified' parents who avoid oppressing their children with guilt. Nor have they attained, according to the same cultural evidence, the unselfconscious physical confidence of non-Jews, those ice-skating and car-fixing 'real McCoys'. Two powerful and fascinating recent books by David Biale and Sander Gilman[4] suggest that images which symbolize the physical marginality of Jews derive from diverse sources within Christianity proper and within Christianized secular/scientific and Jewish literary traditions.

David Biale's *Eros and the Jews* traces the often unacknowledged dialectic of ambivalence towards erotic desire and sexual activity which has surfaced repeatedly in rabbinic writing, and which informs modern secular Jewish literature as well. Sander Gilman's *The Jew's Body* documents diverse and persistent prejudicial beliefs regarding Jewish bodies which appear in Christian writings from the gospels and early Church fathers through modern scholarly and secularized popular writing.

Together, these books shed much light on the stubborn sense of discomfort which both Jews and non-Jews experience when regarding the physical Jew. As

---

[3] Philip Roth, *Portnoy's Complaint* (1969; repr. New York, 1971), 170.
[4] David Baile, *Eros and the Jews: From Biblical Israel to Contemporary America* (New York: Basic Books, 1992), 319; and Sander Gilman, *The Jew's Body* (New York: Routledge, 1991), 303.

Biale illustrates, the most valiant of males, according to Jewish tradition, is the man who can control his sexual impulses. An elaborate complex of rabbinic law and tradition was built up over the centuries to enhance this valorized self-control. Gilman reveals that the interpretation of Jewish self-control by the Greeks, the authors of the gospels, and a succession of Church fathers and clerics was profoundly different from the vantage-point within the Jewish community. Non-Jewish observers often believed that Jewish males had been feminized; to many non-Jews the circumcision of the Jewish male symbolized phallic weakness, the antithesis of manhood. Some suggested that the sexual drive of Jewish males was rendered unwholesome, had a criminal colouring, or, at the very least, had been diverted into avarice.

Given the compelling and suggestive thesis and execution of each of these books, one basic shared flaw is especially egregious. As each author states from the outset, the books focus primarily on the writings of male élites about Jewish men. Each author, to his credit, finds it necessary to explain his book's almost exlusively male focus: Biale because extant Judaic literature about sexuality was composed by men, and Jewish notions about sexuality were viewed through male eyes; Gilman because gentile fear and hatred of the sexual Jew were aimed almost exclusively at male Jews. How curious, then, that the titles of each book indicate that the whole of the Jewish people will be discussed. In Biale's and Gilman's titles the understood meaning of the word 'Jew' is 'Jewish male'. The modifier 'male' is invisibly present: it is unnecessary to state the masculinity of the subject, because the male is the defining or normative Jew. This is, of course, a tendency which has pervaded, and continues to do so, various fields of scholarly thinking about Jews. Numerous histories and ethnographies, ostensibly about Jewish communities, have focused almost exclusively on men. In literature as well, Judaic images and motifs usually evoke the masculine experience.

In one telling recent example a literature professor describes a confrontation following the presentation of a paper on American Jewish writers at the annual meeting of the Modern Language Association of America:

This male professor kept insisting that circumcision was the universal symbol of the Jew. I kept trying to convince him that it's only universal for half the Jewish people—that Jewish women can only relate to circumcision vicariously. And he acted as though I was crazy. He just kept repeating the same thing again and again. Circumcision is the universal symbol of the Jew.[5]

Noting the minimal presence of women in Biale's and Gilman's books is not a mere matter of feminist pieties. It is not only that in the last decade of the twentieth century books about images of 'Jews' should aim for a balanced discussion of the varieties of gendered imagery and the responses they evoke. Rather,

---

[5] Cited in Sylvia Barack Fishman, *A Breath of Life: Feminism in the American Jewish Community* (New York, 1993), 123.

disappointment arises from an awareness of how much might be added by an exploration of the images of Jewish females and the impact which such images have had on women.

Perceptions of Jewish distinctiveness have often varied by gender, and attending to these variations makes for a more subtle and interesting analysis. Gilman devotes many pages to tracing the aetiology of images of the ugly, murderous Jewish male; one wonders what insights he might offer on the history of the Jewish *femme fatale*. One thinks, for example, of the image, common in medieval English blood-libel ballads, of the dark, seductive 'Jewess' luring Christian children to their macabre doom at the hands of hideous Jewish men. On another note, Biale has some perceptive comments about images of women in the twenty-one pages he devotes to sexual stereotypes in American Jewish culture. One can only speculate on what he might have produced by devoting this kind of attention to images of women in rabbinic literature, the ways in which *halakhah* translated attitudes towards women into prescriptive laws for female behaviour, and the impact which such laws had on the lives of women in Jewish societies—much as he does with images, laws, and societal impact when he deals with men. As both books stand now, each is a lively analysis of the symbolic portrayal of one gender; they point the way towards a larger project to be undertaken by scholars in the future. Building on the foundation offered by Biale and Gilman, forthcoming works can offer nuanced explorations of the ways in which attitudes towards sexuality have shaped the cultures and societies in which Jewish men and women lived.

The belief that Jewish men are essentially different from other men extends back to the narrative in Genesis describing the covenant between God and Abraham, and the distinctiveness of Abraham's progeny has been symbolized, from biblical times onward, by the act of circumcision. However, that unmistakable 'mark in the flesh' of the Jewish male has had one set of meanings within Israelite and Jewish societies, and quite another set of meanings for the non-Jewish communities in which Jews resided.

The outlines of what are popularly considered mainstream Jewish attitudes towards sexuality are ably reviewed in Biale's narrative. Within the ethos of biblical and then rabbinic Judaism, as it developed through the Mishnah, the Talmud, rabbinic commentaries, and *responsa* literature, and in the literature of specialized philosophies such as the kabbalist movement and its accompanying ethical prescriptions, circumcision was often depicted as representing self-control and devout discipline. Judaic writings described the circumcised male Jew as a member of a nation of priests, chosen by God to live according to complex prescriptions which putatively encouraged holiness in daily life. This holiness was to be accomplished through a relentless process of taming sexuality and other powerful, irrational impulses. By following a myriad of laws, and through them domesticating his own 'evil impulses', the Jewish male conquered himself and, in a kind of circular cause-and-effect relationship, was freed to serve God and follow his laws.

The Hebrew Bible saw not only moral but also political dangers in unregulated sexuality; sexual activity outside permitted parameters might lead to idolatry or to cultural dissolution. Nevertheless, Biale notes, although biblical texts fluctuate in their definitions of appropriate boundaries, 'sexuality within proper boundaries was not a problem'. Indeed, in the Hebrew Bible matrimonial love was considered sanctified as part of the orderly universe of disciplined human behaviour, and also because it was perceived to imitate and reflect the relationship between God and the Jewish people. Body and soul were not viewed as separate and oppositional entities; biblical references to soul and spirit indicate the immanent, although divinely provided, vivifying force within physical beings. Later, however, Biale argues, 'influenced by Hellenistic and Roman notions of sexuality, Jewish culture of late antiquity was forced to struggle with negative attitudes towards Eros, even within marriage'. These struggles led to a profound ambivalence towards physical sensation, especially of a sexual nature, and to the occasional ascendancy of tendencies towards 'sexual renunciation and asceticism'.

Ambivalent, and sometimes directly oppositional, views of sexuality go back at least to Talmudic times, Biale demonstrates. Talmudic discussions often echo positive biblical attitudes towards sexuality. Some rabbis approvingly describe the attempts of women to make themselves attractive to their husbands; these writers urge men not to disregard these signs and disappoint their wives, and they prescribe the husband's obligation to provide his wife with *onah*, sexual pleasure, at regular intervals. However, other Talmudic discussions display attitudes of repugnance towards sexual activity, reminding men that they emerged from a 'smelly drop' of semen and that women are 'vessels filled with excrement' whose mouths (a euphemism) 'are filled with blood'.

Biale explores the evolution of approaches to the physical being and sexuality in Jewish cultures which often became more, rather than less, sexually repressive as the centuries passed. In the process, some rabbinic writing also tended towards increasingly gynophobic, and sometimes overtly misogynistic, attitudes. Biale proposes a pattern of geographical differences placing more tolerant, pro-sexuality attitudes among the Ashkenazic European rabbinate, with more ascetic values developing among the Sephardic rabbinate:

In the centuries after the Talmudic period, different medieval Jewish cultures would take up these opposing strands of rabbinic ambivalence. Where the northern European elite was to emphasize the more affirmative view of sexuality, the Jewish philosophers of the Mediterranean, under the impact of Greek philosophy, would opt for a more radical asceticism than had ever existed in rabbinic thought. (p. 59)

During medieval and early modern times, the Ashkenazic rabbinic ethos aimed to enhance the affectionate bonds within legitimate marriage, because it regarded such marriages as the most effective bulwark against the extramarital temptations which aroused anxiety in European communities. According to Biale, the hegemony of Jewish marriage was threatened by opportunities for adultery or for sexual relationships with non-Jews. In order to combat those possibilities, Jewish legal and anecdotal literature was tolerant of both male and female needs for sexual satisfaction, and encouraged married couples to enjoy mutually pleasurable erotic interaction. While the primary consideration in sexual activity during the most fertile time of a woman's reproductive cycle was the impregnation of the wife with (preferably male) progeny, mutual pleasure was the primary—and enthusiastically sanctioned—consideration at all other times when the laws of family purity allowed the Jewish wife to her husband, and for non-fertile women as well.

In contrast to the Ashkenazic rabbinate, which was during the medieval period largely insulated from the intellectual currents prevalent in the Christian societies of their host countries, the Jews of southern France and Spain had close interactions with and were very much influenced by their Muslim and Christian neighbours, Biale suggests. Contemporary Western Jews often idealize the intellectual and artistic productivity of the 'Golden Age' of Spanish Jewry, in which rabbinic leaders were also known to be physicians or to write exquisite erotic poetry. However, this interaction with non-Jewish culture did not work towards the liberalization of rabbinic attitudes, Biale argues. Instead, the twelfth- and thirteenth-century Sephardic religious élite were often intellectually at war with themselves. The very fact that Jews—including the rabbinic élite—participated in Spanish culture created its own rabbinic backlash.

While they were intimately familiar with and sometimes contributed to non-Jewish philosophy, literature, and sciences, the Sephardic rabbinic élites were frequently horrified by the libertinism they observed. Not only the masses of ordinary people, who might be expected to succumb to opportunities for freer sexual mores, but even the most affluent and well-educated classes within Jewish and non-Jewish communities displayed the effects of the prevailing culture. Some Sephardic rabbis responded to this challenge by valorizing marital love and the monogamous female sexuality which could potentially protect men against extramarital affairs. Other rabbis, however, condemned female sexuality—and females in general—for distracting and seducing men from higher goals.

One reaction to the pervasive sensuality of Spanish culture was to reject the senses and elevate the intellect. The authors of the Bible and the Talmud did not dichotomize human nature into body and spirit; terms such as 'soul' and 'spirit' found in the Hebrew Bible refer to the divinely provided animating principle which vitalizes all living creatures. In contrast, Biale argues, Sephardic rabbinic luminaries such as Abraham Ibn Ezra (1092–1167), Moses Maimonides (1135–1204), and Moses Nachmanides (1194–1270), influenced by 'Neoplatonic and then Aristotelian ideas as translated and transmitted by Arabic authors', depicted a 'sharp duality between spirit and matter' in their own religious writings.

Maimonides mistrusted the physical senses, which he saw as leading men into vicious behaviour; he was repelled by 'the sense of touch in particular'. Indeed, Maimonides wrote, the mutual goals of circumcision and monogamy were to dull male sexual desire and satisfaction, 'to bring about a decrease in sexual intercourse and a weakening of the organ in question, so that this activity be diminished and the organ be in as quiet a state as possible' (*Guide to the Perplexed*, 3: 8, p. 609). Although Maimonides ruled that men might participate in whatever sexual acts were mutually pleasurable to husband and wife, he urged that scholars avoid all but the most basic sexual interaction. Ibn Ezra divided the soul into three parts, the rational element being the highest, fully developed only in philosophers. Sexual intercourse, likewise, Ibn Ezra divided into three types, and suggested that the highest and most preferred type of intercourse should be undertaken by philosophical men without any feelings of desire, only for purposes of procreation. Nachmanides, seemingly unconcerned with the Talmudic injunction that every husband owes his wife connubial pleasure, *onah*, warned: 'Know that sexual intercourse is a matter alien and detestable to the Torah with the exemption of that which propagates the species, and anything connected to it that does not lead to procreation is forbidden' (commentary on Leviticus 18: 10).

The Sephardic rabbinic élite thus differed from the Ashkenazic élite in their delegitimization of marital erotic desire. In contrast, some Sephardic rabbis proposed a purely spiritual vision of desire; this Sephardic condemnation of carnal feelings and activities was articulated in terms which glorified asceticism and spirituality in highly erotic language. The terminology for rejection of the sensual was drawn from the sensual realm.

This tendency to reject the physical while extolling the spiritual in the most physical of terms was extensively and creatively expanded within the writings of the kabbalist movement in Safed and in Spain. Within texts such as the Zohar or the Book of Splendour, written by Moses de León at the end of the thirteenth century, the entire universe is described as being animated by masculine and feminine divine principles. Human men who aspired to holiness were encouraged to be 'sexual eunuchs' throughout the week, devoting themselves to spiritual and scholarly tasks; when they united sexually with their wives on Sabbath eve, both husband and wife were urged to think of spiritual matters, so that their union would serve a theurgic function, sympathetically bringing together male and female emanations of godhead.

The kabbalist emphasis on sacred theurgic activity liberated neither men nor women. Men were vigorously warned within the Zohar not to indulge in sexual activity except with their wives; sexual activity with wives was to take place only at the prescribed time and while the partners were thinking correct thoughts. Male masturbation was seen as a sin beyond atonement, equivalent to the killing of one's own sons. Nocturnal emissions were a plague, which might indicate that demonesses had visited one in the night. And sleeping with a Christian woman was a crime against the Judaic covenant and against God. As Biale summarizes, 'by "inserting the sign of the covenant [that is one's circumcised penis] into a foreign domain," one damages . . . God's symbolic penis'.

Within the Zohar's world-view, women shared with the female divine emanation volatile qualities, comprised of 'the Great Mother and the Devouring Goddess, the nurturing power of fertility and the violent demoness of destruction', Biale writes. Nevertheless, he points out, women could be educated by their husbands concerning the proper attitude during sexual intercourse, so that they too could become partners in holy behaviour. Thus, despite the fact that the Zohar contains much material relating to women, including the concept of female attributes of godhead, anxiety about female sexuality and the impact of women on men attained a negative vividness within the kabbalist movement arguably unmatched in earlier rabbinic literature.

When the Jews were exiled from Spain in 1492, the ideas promulgated by Sephardic rabbinic scholars spread throughout Holland, Germany, and Poland. Asceticism and sexual renunciation became common attributes in many writings, especially those which focused on Jewish ethical behaviour. One of the chief proponents of the Jewish ethicist literature, which prescribed punitive penances for sexual infringements, was Joseph Karo (1488–1575), best known as the author of the *Shulḥan arukh*, later regarded as the most authoritative code of Jewish law. In his code-book Karo condemned any male pleasure as sinful, and posited that the Talmudic prescriptions for providing one's wife with *onah* indicated the maximum, rather than the minimum, suggested frequency of cohabitation.

For a brief time the Hasidic movement, founded by the Baal Shem Tov (d. 1760), reunited soul and body through doctrines which urged joy rather than self-mortification. According to Biale's sources, the early Hasidic masters taught that 'every mitzvah or act of holiness starts with thoughts of physical pleasure'. However, such positive attitudes towards carnal impulses and enjoyment were soon subsumed into ascetic reactions by the Baal Shem Tov's disciples and followers, and the spread of Hasidism became the vehicle for the further spread of ascetic traditions. A rather striking example of ascetic attitudes is found in the writings of one of the most idiosyncratic and eccentric—but often quoted—Hasidic masters, Rabbi Nahman of Bratslav (1772–1810), who commented: 'Copulation is difficult for the true *tsadik*. Not only does he have no desire for it at all, but he experiences real suffering in the act, suffering which is like that which the infant undergoes when he is circumcised' (*Shivḥei haRan*, sec. 17, p. 20).

Although Biale is always careful to distinguish between the pronouncements and theories of rabbinic élites and the actual lives of the Jewish masses, with the spread of Hasidic lifestyles and values attitudes and behaviour towards women were affected in very concrete ways. The primary emotional loyalty of the masses of Hasidic men was devoted to the dynasties of their spiritual charismatic leaders, the rebbes. Many a Jewish woman was left alone with her children to fend for herself while Hasidic husbands spent weeks or months soaking up holy words and melodies in the rebbes' courts.

The near abandonment of wives and children by Hasidic men sparked an outraged backlash from the anti-Hasidic, mitnagdic rabbinic movement. Some critics even asserted that Hasidic courts were hypocritical hotbeds of illicit sexual behaviour, but such mitnagdic accusations seem to have stemmed primarily from acute discomfort at the florid, eroticized language for spiritual interaction which Hasidism had inherited from the kabbalist movement. Ironically, as Biale points out, although the rabbinic *mitnagdim* did not eroticize the study of the Torah with explicitly sexualized language, they also urged the brightest of their young men to leave families and spend months in the rabbinical seminaries or *yeshivot*. Time not devoted to study of the Torah was regarded as a 'waste', and the demands of family life were often perceived as competing with the higher calling of sacred scholarship.

During the nineteenth century, early in western Europe and later in eastern Europe, the Jewish Enlightenment, or Haskalah, liberated Jewish intellectuals from strict adherence to traditional Jewish lifestyles. Enlightenment writers, the *maskilim*, criticized traditional Jewish societies, both Hasidic and mitnagdic, for their practice of early marriage, for their refusal to educate young men for useful professions in the wider world, and for the unfair economic and emotional burdens which were placed on Jewish women and children. The *maskilim* at first championed the reinstatement of spontaneity and sensuality as the appropriate well-springs of romantic and marital attachments. However, for complicated reasons, many of the *maskilim* found it difficult to sustain long-standing relationships with women, and often their affection for women was powerfully intermixed with resentment; they found their true friendships with Jewish male colleagues instead. The celebrated Hebrew literary figure Abraham Mapu, for example, wrote to his brother in 1861: 'Yes, the love of women is strong, but as its price it takes the souls of husbands. . . . Not so is brotherhood, whose candle will never be extinguished' (p. 158).

Theoretically, the *maskilim*'s critique of traditional Jewish behaviour was based on egalitarian values, which the Haskalah shared with other Utopian movements of the time. However, as Biale's summary indicates, the vision of the *maskilim* did not really empower the masses, but rather shifted power to a new set of élites: 'power would be shared between the enlightened state and enlightened, acculturated intellectuals like themselves . . . secular learning would take the place of rabbinic learning, just as modern leaders would take the place of rabbis' (p. 150). Secularized Hebraic and Yiddishist intellectualism had replaced the study of rabbinic texts as the primary sacred activity, but basic cultural patterns were retained. To an extent that many of them perhaps never admitted, the male leaders of the Jewish Enlightenment were the inheritors of a system in which men bonded intellectually and emotionally with other men, and women remained eroticized outsiders.

Biale's discussion of 'Eros and the Enlightenment' brings his ambitious survey into the historical period which is the primary focus of Gilman's entire work. At this point, the two books provide complex and evocative contextualization for each other. As both Biale and Gilman illustrate, with the emancipation and the secularization of European life, gentile distrust of Jews did not dissipate; secularized gentile intellectuals were often just as suspicious of their secularized Jewish neighbours as their devout Christian grandfathers had been of pious Jewish forebears.

For Jewish intellectuals who expected the emancipation to gain them free entry into gentile society, the continuing and even exacerbated hatred and suspicion of Jews was a source of unremitting pain. Some Jewish intellectuals felt that they had been duped: they had been asked to forfeit their Jewish individuality in return for complete intellectual and political acceptance within their host cultures. For the sake of such acceptance, they had championed the values of Western humanism. When true acceptance was not forthcoming, some Jewish intellectuals rejected what they now saw as alien values. As Biale puts it, 'love and erotic fulfillment seemed doomed', and 'many turned their hopes to the new nationalism' (p. 175). Other prominent Jewish thinkers, as Gilman points out in his discussion, internalized negative attitudes towards the bodies of their co-religionists and attempted to categorize and ameliorate their infirmities, in ever more vigorous efforts towards true acceptance.

During the nineteenth century the Jewish body and its functions were widely regarded with profound distrust. Xenophobic attitudes towards Jews continued to find expression in the notion that the bodies and bodily functions of Jewish males were diseased. Gilman focuses on a succession of intellectuals and scientists who obsessively discussed their conviction that the Jewish male body was diseased and was the source of contagion and calamity throughout gentile society. He demonstrates the pervasiveness—and the ancient aetiology—of viciously negative attitudes toward the bodies and minds of Jewish men.

For example, Gilman provides profuse examples of a widespread nineteenth-century belief among physicians and scientists that Jews had pathologically misshapen feet and recognizably defective gaits. Some believed that Jewish feet were innately diseased by virtue of Jewish religious practices or through the genetic effects of generations of intermarriage; others felt that Jews, as the ultimate urban dwellers, somatized and concentrated the diseases of urban existence within their bodies. The appearance and usefulness of Jewish feet were ruined because they were deprived of fresh air and exercise. These Jewish 'pathognomonic' feet marked Jewish males as unfit for military service and even for full citizenship. Gilman places the origin of such notions within the medieval idea that Jews had cloven hoofs, by virtue of their relationship with the evil and their status as Christ-killers, a belief which goes back at least to a statement in Robert Burton's *Anatomy of Melancholy*, that the Jew's 'pace' as well as his 'voice . . . gesture and looks' bespeak his demonically degraded condition.[6] Similarly, the putatively distinctive shape of the Jewish nose was variously seen as indicating the genetic similarity between—and inferiority of—Jews and Blacks, or the supposed prevalence of syphilis within the Jewish community, or most benignly, as in a treatise of 1848 by George Jabet called *Notes on Noses*, 'considerable Shrewdness in worldly matters; a deep insight into character, and facility of turning that insight into profitable account'.

Jewish feet and Jewish noses were regarded with disgust not for themselves alone, but because they could be seen as euphemisms for or as symbolic of the circumcised Jewish phallus, Gilman suggests. Circumcision was considered a 'perversion', an 'unnatural practice', and a 'mutilation of the genitals'. Reviewing the ubiquitous disgust with which Christian intellectuals regarded circumcision, Gilman focuses on such authors as the physician and anthropologist Paolo Mantegazza (1831–1901), whose widely read three-volume study of the physiology, hygiene, and anthropology of love contained the following polemic: 'Cease mutilating yourselves: cease imprinting upon your flesh an odious brand . . . until you do this, you cannot pretend to be our equal.'

Circumcision also had symbolic meaning, and was not only vilified for itself but for the role which some felt it played in the Jewish purveyance of disease. Armand-Louis-Joseph Béraud repeats in his dissertation of 1897 the commonly held belief that Jews needed to circumcise their males because otherwise the filthiness of their habits and dwellings would encourage the spread of syphilis. Indeed, Gilman points out that Jews were often held responsible for the spread of syphilis—just as they were once held responsible for the plague.

The measurably lower rate of venereal disease in Jewish communities might have posed a challenge for some who saw Jews as the transmitters of syphilis, but this problem was resolved through the theory that the disease behaved differently in the Jewish body and in the gentile body. While gentiles manifested syphilis with a well-known spectrum of physical afflictions, among Jews syphilis was thought to cause dark, dull complexions, large, ugly hooked noses, flat feet and limping, and, most commonly, hysterical behaviour. According to this theory, the 'typical' Jewish appearance and personality was, by definition, the appearance and personality of disease.

Notions of Jewish inferiority extended to perceptions of Jews as a criminal class, Gilman demonstrates. Because of the lower-class neighbourhoods in which

---

[6] Robert Burton, *The Anatomy of Melancholy*, ed. Holbrook Jackson (New York, 1977), 211–12.

many poor Jews lived, Jews as a group were perceived as having a close relationship with pariah groups generally feared and despised by the Victorian bourgeoisie, such as lepers, syphilitics, prostitutes, and Blacks. According to contemporaneous 'scientific' theories, Jewish men, like prostitutes, tended towards a criminal mentality because they had an eroticized, unnatural attachment to money. Circumcised Jewish males did not have a normative relationship with women. Instead, both popular and 'scientific' belief proposed, Jews loved money because their libidos as well as their phalluses were mutilated.

Moreover, Jews were perceived as having both a natural affinity to and a natural antipathy against prostitutes, the attraction–repulsion of two pariah groups for each other. Symbolic of this belief, Jack the Ripper, who terrified London by slaughtering and eviscerating a series of prostitutes, was assumed by many, including law-enforcement officials, to be a Jew from the East End of London. This Jewish murderer was sometimes perceived as performing a ritual slaughter of the prostitutes, an idea which of course goes back to the ritual-blood libels of medieval times. In addition, as Gilman notes, the idea that Jews had a 'sexual relationship to capital' has its roots in the role which Jews performed as 'usurers' during historical periods when their occupational possibilities were severely limited.

Non-Jews defined the Jewish male as a mutilated creature, and those secularized Jews who interacted with them often absorbed the negative definition. Gilman provides a powerful analysis of contemporaneous Jewish antisemitism. He compellingly illustrates the ways in which Jewish intellectuals—including some of the most famous minds of their age—internalized antisemitic images of the Jewish body. The German Jewish political theorist Moses Hess, for example, notes in *Rome and Jerusalem* that

> even baptism cannot redeem the German Jew from the nightmare of German Jew-hatred. The Germans hate less the religion of the Jews than their race, less their peculiar beliefs than their peculiar noses. . . . Jewish noses cannot be reformed, nor can black, curly, Jewish hair be turned through baptism or combing into smooth hair. The Jewish race is a primal one, which had reproduced itself in its integrity despite climactic influences. . . . The Jewish type is indestructible.[7]

The 'black-yellow' skin of fellow Jews was seen by Enlightenment Jewish physician Elcan Isaac Wolf as a sign of Jewish disease.

Not only were the skin, hair, feet, noses, bodily odours, and, most fundamentally, penises of Jewish males considered to be afflicted, but their patterns of thought and speech were regarded as repugnant as well. No matter how assimilated the Jew, no matter how diligently he strove to sound as refined and elegant as the gentiles around him, Jewish distortions of European languages would

---

[7] Moses Hess, *Rom und Jerusalem* (1808; English trans. London, 1864), 11; cited by Gilman, p. 179.

always betray him. The Jew was an irredeemable *Mischling*, mixing up the pure languages of Aryan Europe with his ugly accent and foreign words. Perhaps most damning, once born a Jew, a man could never be an original thinker. Baptism could not save a writer or artist or musician from the curse of Jewish shallowness and derivativeness. The biological inferiority of Jewish-born writers such as Heine emerged even after conversion to Christianity, according to this theory, and his writings were perceived by some critics to be fundamentally trivial or unoriginal. Creative Jews merely produced artificial structures which perched on top of the genuine creativity of Christian artists.

Gilman exposes a fabric of secularized antisemitism which wove together the putative physical, intellectual, and spiritual failings of the Jewish man. According to these widespread prejudices, the Jewish man could not think or create as well as the non-Jewish man. His intellectual and creative deficiencies were linked to his physical inadequacies. His nose and hair and skin were unattractive. He could not walk or run or march as well as Christian men. Moreover, he seemed to be afraid of virile behaviour; he shied away from robust sexuality and from physical competitions such as contact sports or war games. As symbolized by his circumcised penis, the Jewish man was inferior, body and soul.

The antisemitism which pervaded the interpretative framework of many non-Jewish thinkers led to tragic misunderstandings; however, the discomfort with physical prowess, with militarism, and with untrammelled sexuality which non-Jews sensed in Jewish culture was not imagined. In addition to the centuries of oppression which had deprived Jews of opportunities for agrarian lifestyles and regular exercise, Jewish societies were often suspicious of unregulated physicality. Rabbinic law, growing out of distinctive value-systems, aimed at creating and maintaining differences between Jewish men and putatively less disciplined males. Rabbinic culture was profoundly fearful of humanity's powerful, irrational impulses. Men were encouraged to distance themselves from, rather than to indulge in, many forms of behaviour which were perceived as the essence of manhood in other cultures. Before the emancipation, in traditional Jewish societies, types of behaviour idealized by militaristic or 'macho' cultures were regarded as failures of manliness rather than its apotheosis. Within Jewish literary myth, when the Jews needed a violent defender to battle against the antisemitic violence which threatened them, they resorted to the creation of a *golem*, a mindless hulk, a creature external to the Jewish community although committed to serve its needs. Indeed, not until the rise of Zionism did large groups of Jews make physical strength and skills a societal goal. And even in the case of Zionism, as Biale suggests, doctrine, if not practice, often rechannelled erotic energies into the patriotic effort of building a new land.

Jewish laws and rituals were designed to discipline men and give them control over those aspects of themselves which the rabbis feared might, in their uncontrolled form, be destructive to a stable and holy society. Trying to protect the males who were the designated citizens of its universe, rabbinic dialogue often anxiously regarded women as a class of beings whose sexual presence might, like alcohol or anger, weaken or breach the barriers which male self-control had built around its own irrational impulses. According to one Hasidic master, if a man had a sexual fantasy, the woman about whom he dreamt had fantasized about him first and had planted the idea in his head. Role divisions by gender and barriers between the sexes were reinforced. The Jewish laws created by rabbinic élites effectively fenced women off from public Judaism, in order to protect Jewish men from their own passions.

In patterns at once very different and very similar, many non-Jews attempted to isolate Jewish men so that their putative sexual perversity might not infect society. Some non-Jewish men regarded Jewish men as though they comprised a separate gender-role classification. Jews in turn-of-the-century Vienna and London often internalized these antisemitic images, which denied Jewish men true equality through a system of sexual stratification. Battling against these exclusions, and in order to enhance their own access to and acculturation into the Christian societies around them, Jewish intellectuals tried to identify and isolate Jewish sources of internal contagion.

The secularized Jewish intellectuals described by Gilman tried to cure their own social ills by devising yet another system of sexual stratification. They 'discovered' that Jewish women had all of the defects commonly ascribed to Jewish men. Women were thought to be emotionally hysterical and physically weak. Women were described as regarding their own bodies as deformed, because their genitalia might be thought to resemble a castration. Women were believed to have paranoid fantasies of abuse, and to be jealous of men's bodies, physical strength, and intellectual creativity. Some social scientists accused women of trying to compensate for their inferior status and inadequacies by using their sexuality to control men. Just as Jewish men were accused of being shallow and unoriginal thinkers, Jewish analysts helped to spread the belief that women, while possessing the capacity for repetitious tasks, or an intuitive or instinctive grasp of non-intellectual issues, had little capacity for original thinking or sustained intellectual activity.

Secular Jewish intellectuals and rabbinic thinkers were, of course, far from alone in their anti-female attitudes. On the contrary, the disdain of some prominent gentile intellectuals for women far surpassed anything that had been imagined even in the most ascetic rabbinic writings. Rabbinic mistrust of women seldom approached the systemic disgust expressed by some prominent nineteenth-century gentile philosophers: Schopenhauer, for example, saw the female species as the wide-hipped, mindless instrument of the blind animal will of the procreative force. Perhaps partially because rabbinic Judaism viewed procreation as a commandment and a gift from God, resentment of women's roles in the procreative process seldom took the same dark shape in the rabbinic imagination as it did among the secular intelligentsia. Moreover, while rabbinic leaders from medieval times onward were deeply concerned about the disturbing powers of the erotic passions, they did not use these anxieties as an excuse to strip women of their spiritual human dimensions. Indeed, both Maimonides and Nachmanides rule that women have an innate need to pray at least once and possibly three times a day; they argue only over the biblical bases for this prescription.

All this having been said, the terrible irony remains that while the non-Jewish world derided the Jewish male for his lack of masculinity, in two very different spheres both rabbinic Jewish leaders and secularized Jewish male intellectuals strove valiantly to emphasize the 'innate' differences between themselves and Jewish women. By cataloguing the ways in which women were supposedly and essentially inferior to men, secularized Jewish thinkers tried to differentiate themselves, creating a redeeming aura of manliness. Among Jewish men, neither religious leaders nor agnostic intellectuals perceived the analogies between the destructive calumnies perpetrated upon them by non-Jews and the attributes which they themselves ascribed to the females among them. A comment by Dr Jean Baker Miller in *Toward a New Psychology of Women* might be applied with equal effectiveness to the position of the nineteenth-century Jew in interaction with non-Jewish society: 'If women step beyond the bounds of the realms assigned for them, they cannot help but confront and challenge men. But even in their traditional roles, women, by their very existence, confront and challenge men because they have been made the embodiment of the dominant culture's unsolved problems.'[8]

Discomfort with Jewish particularism, symbolized by perceived and imagined differences between Jewish and non-Jewish bodies, goes back hundreds of years in Christian thought. The asymmetrical, sexually structured stratification suggested by antisemitic non-Jewish scientists in the nineteenth and early twentieth centuries continues to influence external perceptions of Jews—and the way some Jews see themselves. Jewish men and Jewish women in the diaspora still suffer from the legacy of these delegitimizing images, imposed from inside and outside the Jewish community. In the popular Western media today, Jewish women are often identified by their non-Western 'flaws': large noses, kinky hair, dark complexions, and vulgar patterns of speech and thought. Jewish men are often the authors of these portrayals. At the same time, the media include images of the over-anxious, physically inept Jewish male, who displays many of the defects of mind and character with which Jewish men and all women were once erroneously assumed to be afflicted.

Thus, even today, cultural evidence reveals that substantial numbers of Western Jews feel simultaneously inside and outside of the non-Jewish societies in which they live and work. Similarly, despite the changes effected by feminism,

---

[8] Jean Baker Miller, *Toward a New Psychology of Women*, 2nd edn. (Boston, 1986), 58.

some Jewish women continue to feel inside and outside of both Jewish communal and religious environments and American societal norms. Jewish men and women have yet to arrive at the condition of personal integration in which they look at themselves and see the incarnation of mental and physical well-being. It remains for other books to explore the extent to which Jewish men and women can recognize and accept themselves without recognizing and accepting each other.

BOOK REVIEWS

ALFRED EBENBAUER AND KLAUS ZATLOUKAL (EDS.)
Die Juden in ihrer mittelalterlichen Umwelt
(Vienna and Cologne: Böhlau, 1991); pp. 320 (14 pp. illustrations, 4 maps)

This volume contains the lectures delivered at a symposium of the Faculty of Humanities at Vienna University on the fiftieth anniversary of the Anschluß. It includes twenty articles: ten on historical topics, five on Germanic philology, two on the Yiddish language, and three on art history. They are arranged alphabetically and not by subject, but this review is arranged in the latter manner. Articles are written in German, except where otherwise noted.

Two very prominent experts in Jewish history, whose loss we have since had to mourn, initiate the series of historical contributions: Bernhard Blumenkranz of Paris and Frantřišek Graus of Basle. The former (pp. 17–26) deals with distorted and incorrect descriptions of historical facts: the role of Archbishop Agobard of Lyons, the ineradicable misunderstanding of Pertz concerning (*Villa*) *Iudeis* in Richer of St Rémy as 'Jewish physicians', the alleged participation of Jews in the slave trade conducted by the Verdun merchants, and Jews as smallholders in early medieval Burgundy. Graus (pp. 53–66) again addresses fundamental problems, objecting to the construction of a continuous history of the Jewish people as a 'nation in the diaspora' by 'nationalizing the past in a modernistic way'. For him the history of the Jews cannot be mastered either by limiting it to the reactions of the other inhabitants of the regions in which they lived or by idealizing it in a naïve and apologetic way. In contradistinction to this approach Graus points to the possibilities of a new medieval discipline that proceeds by analysing the results of socio-historical research, by seeking to grasp the mentality of past cultures, and by trying to complete the fragmentary picture by comparison with the fate of other marginalized and persecuted groups as well. For Graus the disintegration of social and economic structures as well as the claim to exclusiveness made by both major religions necessarily resulted in mutual delimitation and exclusion. However, the intensity of productive Jewish–Christian coexistence, which functioned rather well during long periods of time, should not be underestimated. Modern antisemitism, unlike medieval anti-Judaism, rested on the new ideological foundation of racism.

Apart from those two all-embracing themes, other authors concentrate on certain geographical regions or on special topics. Alfred Haverkamp of Trier (pp. 67–90) describes the legal order, conditions, and change of Jewish settlement in the region of the archdiocese of Trier on the Moselle and middle Rhine. Ewald Kislinger of Vienna (pp. 105–12) deals with Jewish craftsmen as producers of silk and purple clothes, weavers, dyers, tanners, and glaziers in Byzantium. Ariel Toaff of Ramat Gan (pp. 275–80, English) points out that in Italy it was only in the fifteenth century that the wearing of the Jewish badge was made compulsory, and even then this order was only partially enforced. Klaus Lohrman of St Pölten (pp. 113–30) sums up the policy concerning the Jews in Austria until their expulsion in 1420. At that time the expulsion orders of Albert V were no longer opposed by the nobility, because the latter's indebtedness to the Jews tightened its bonds to the sovereign and, in turn, reduced the sovereign's interest in the Jews. Marcus J. Wenninger of Klagenfurt (pp. 281–300) compares Christian and Jewish moneylenders. The former included, besides Lombards and Cahorsins, members of the nobility, monasteries, and townspeople. It seems that during the second half of the fourteenth century it was only in certain regions that the Jews were the most important group of creditors for the Austrian nobility. With the increase of Jewish pawnbroking, however, peasants and poorer townspeople constituted the majority of debtors. The ban on interest, being incompatible with economic necessities, was evaded in many ways.

Finally, Rudolf Palme of Innsbruck (pp. 183–204) deals with the social and legal history of Tyrolese Jews and touches upon many questions: pawnbroking, territorial law, the position of the Church, the ritual-murder libels of Ursula of Lienz, Simon of Trent, and Andrew (Anderl) of Rinn. However, the author's extensive use of unprinted sources and a vast bibliography only add to the impression that he has handled too much and too little at the same time. In the end Palme arrives at some questionable judgements—for example, that humanism prepared the ground for the spreading of blood libels in the fifteenth century, and that the continuance of the cult of Anderl of Rinn was encouraged by right-wing extremists from Germany. As if Austria were lacking in such people!

Among the historical contributions there are also two treatises on Christian–Jewish interaction. Kurt Schubert of Vienna (pp. 223–50) reprints an article formerly published in *Kairos* (vol. 19, 1977) on Christian–Jewish disputes in the twelfth and thirteenth centuries. The confrontation of anti-Judaic polemics by Peter the Venerable and by the converts Nicholas Donin and Pablo Christiani on the one hand with the corresponding anti-Christian polemics by Josef Kimchi (twelfth century) and in the *Nizzahon vetus* of a German Jew (thirteenth–fourteenth centuries) on the other is very informative. This controversy is complemented by Kurt Smolak of Vienna (pp. 261–74) with his study of the convert Petrus Alfonsi as mediator between Arabic-Oriental wisdom and Latin-Christian tradition. Petrus enriched this tradition not only by the use of exempla in moral preaching but also by employing the genre of the entertaining novelette—which, however, was not to reach its peak until the heyday of vernacular literature.

The Germanic contributions begin with Winfried Frey of Frankfurt a.M. (pp. 35–52), who gives a rich survey of the image of the Jew in medieval German literature. He begins with sermon literature by Berthold of Regensburg and then describes examples of verse poetry and passion plays up until the sixteenth century. Lydia Miklautsch of Vienna (pp. 173–82) explains in detail the legend of St Sylvestre in its version by Konrad of Würzburg. Franz M. Ebl of Vienna (pp. 27–34) deals with the representation of Anderl of Rinn's passion in baroque sermons of the eighteenth century. Wernfried Hofmeister of Graz (pp. 91–104) offers perhaps the earliest Middle High German version of the *Jüdel* legend in a New High German translation that, in contrast to former versions, portrays the conduct of the father—but not of the Jewish community—in a positive way and ends on a conciliatory note (from the Christian point of view), with baptism. Edith Wenzel of Aachen (pp. 307–31) traces parallels between Luther's late treatises against the Jews and the verse poems by Hans Folz and Heinrich von Hesler. In her comparison between rather different developments she makes Luther here adapt the 'scheme of argumentation of the old Church, whose images and models were formed in vernacular literature'. However, Christian institutions as well as individuals on different levels have always argued in very different ways, and there never existed a uniform conception or even faith of 'the Church' except in theory.

The Yiddish question is presented first by Jakob Allerhand of Vienna (pp. 11–16), who understands the Jewish German dialect (Yiddish) in its later use and development in eastern Europe as the expression of a Jewish national culture. The Enlightenment scholar Moses Mendelssohn, however, rejected it as the language of the ghetto, and the *maskilim* of the nineteenth century wanted to replace it with Hebrew as the genuine national language. The late Bettina Simon of Berlin (pp. 251–60) argues persuasively that from a linguistic point of view modern Yiddish, which is rooted in eastern Europe, is an individual language, while the original language of the Jews in Germany ('West Yiddish') has to be regarded as a specific variant of German.

Last but not least, the contents of the volume are complemented by contributions in art history. Thérèse Metzger of Strasburg (pp. 151–72), writing in French, with 41 illustrations, publishes an inventory, complete with frequency statistics and stylistic analysis of the illuminations in Sephardi and Ashkenazi Bible manuscripts from the thirteenth century onwards. In the course of this tradition there also developed a custom of illuminating the Passover Haggadah, particularly in Spain during the fourteenth century. Although the canons of illustration followed a Jewish orientation, they always showed the influence of Christian iconography. Mendel Metzger of Strasburg (pp. 131–50), writing in English, with 17 illustrations, deals in particular with the development of illumination in Jewish books in the thirteenth and fourteenth centuries in Italy. In northern regions it was largely influenced by Ashkenazi iconography. Finally, Ursula

Schubert of Vienna (pp. 206–22) presents a thorough description of a sixteenth-century illuminated Bible with 123 pen-and-ink drawings (Cod. 1164 of the Jewish Historical Institute, Warsaw) rendering the wood-engravings of another illuminated Hebrew Bible. Schubert attributes these wood-engravings to the Venetian painter and medal-engraver Moses dal Castellazzo and tries to show similarities between this iconography and that of Ashkenazi and Sephardi Bibles and Passover *haggadot,* as well as Christian illuminated Bibles.

All in all, the contributors to the Vienna Symposium of 1988 have produced a very informative volume of generally high quality, one which will contribute not a little to our knowledge of Jewish–Christian relations in the Middle Ages.

FRIEDRICH LOTTER

RIVKA SCHATZ-UFFENHEIMER
Hasidism as Mysticism: Quietistic Elements in Eighteenth Century Hasidic Thought
translated from the Hebrew by Jonathan Chipman.
(Princeton, NJ: Princeton University Press and Jerusalem: Magnes Press, 1993);
pp. 398

This English edition of Rivka Schatz-Uffenheimer's classic work *Haḥasidut Kemistika* contains some completely new material as well as supplements to the original text, and is bound to be of interest not only to scholars of Hasidism but to every student of religious thought in general. With the great erudition for which the distinguished author was renowned (alas, she died soon after the book was published), she provides a fresh understanding of what the early Hasidic thinkers were trying to achieve or better—since, as she shows, their emphasis was on quietism—were trying not to achieve. This study, employing the tools of both phenomenology and comparative religion, exposes the one-sidedness of those scholars and popular writers who dwell on the activist and social elements in Hasidic life and thought to the virtual exclusion of the mystical and quietistic elements by which the masters themselves, at least in the school of the Maggid of Mesirech, set great store.

Quietism is that attitude in religious thought in which the worshipper sees himself as a passive instrument in the hands of God. The Hasidim, as Orthodox Jews, could not and did not ignore the active life represented by the performance of the precepts. Judaism has rightly been defined as the religion of *doing* the will of God. For all that, considerable tension can be observed in early Hasidic writings between the need to be up and doing for the sake of God and the equally compulsive need to sit back and let God take over, so to speak. For instance, to recite the prayers three times a day was as much an obligation for the Hasidim as it was for all Jews, but since the majority of the standard prayers are petitionary, the very act of praying tended to frustrate the Hasidic ideal of *bitul hayesh*, 'annihilation of selfhood'—the losing of the self in God. The usual response was that the true Hasid should pray for his needs to be satisfied for the sake of the Shekhinah (divine presence), in which there is a lack whenever humans are in distress. The more subtle thinkers were aware of the danger of self-delusion; the Hasid could easily imagine that he was praying for the Shekhinah's lack to be satisfied when indirectly he was really calling attention to his own needs. The daring idea was put forward that the Shekhinah is present in the psyche of the Hasid, so that his prayer for the Shekhinah constitutes a psychological attempt to reach the divine spark inherent in the Jewish soul, thus making even petitionary prayer a contemplative exercise. The Talmudic saying (*Berakhot* 7a) that 'the Holy One, blessed be he, prays to himself' (that his mercy should prevail over his justice) is given the astonishing, quietistic turn that whenever the true contemplative prays it is really an instance of God communicating with himself. In some of the early Hasidic texts there emerges an attitude of relative indifference to the betterment of the world in the Messianic age, the contemplative being far more concerned with the *unio mystica* in the here and now. Here again it is not that the Hasidic masters did not believe in the Messianic hope. It was rather that, as Scholem puts it, there was a neutralization of Messianism.

In connection with the study of the Torah, the Hasidic ideal of *devekut*, attachment to God in the mind at all times, came into conflict with the precept of studying the Torah. As the *mitnagdim* pointed out, how is it possible to study the involved, extremely complicated Halakhic texts, so essential a feature of study of the Torah, if the mind is directed towards God instead of towards the difficult problems discussed in these texts? Christian quietists are quoted who dealt with similar problems from the standpoint of their own faith.

The author is not to be faulted for confining her study to Hasidism in the eighteenth century. But it would have been useful to explore how the ideas she has culled from the early texts were used or abandoned or softened in later Hasidic thought. There is hardly anything on quietism in medieval Jewish thought, except for references to Bahya. There might have been, for instance, a reference to Saadiah's discussion of the subject (*Emunot vede'ot* x. 15) and to the influence of Sufism on Bahya and others in connection with this whole question.

There are a number of typographical and other errors in the book. The concept of annihilation is correctly transcribed as *'ayin* in the heading to chapter 2 (p. 67) but incorrectly as *'iyun* on the next page. Throughout, the infelicitous 'brought' is used for 'quoted'. Even on the jacket blurb 'borrowed form Kabbalah' appears instead of 'borrowed from'. R. Zevi Hirsch of Zhidachov was not a disciple of the Maggid (p. 226); he was a boy of 9 when the Maggid died. He was rather a disciple of the Seer of Lublin, himself a disciple of the Maggid. The quote from the *Tosafot* in Rosh Hashanah is correctly given at p. 219 n. 12 as 16b but incorrectly at p. 227 n. 27 as 17b—especially odd since the latter note gives a cross-reference to the former. Mordecai Wilensky's *Ḥasidim umitnagdim* (Jerusalem, 1970) is referred to (p. 20), but one misses quotation of the reference in Wilensky (ii. 33) to the Mitnagedic polemic, strictly relevant to the whole thesis, according to which the worship of the Hasidim resembled that of the Quakers (*sic*).

LOUIS JACOBS

JADWIGA MAURER
'*Z matki obcej . . .*'; *Szkic o powiązaniach Mickiewicza ze światem Żydów*

(London: Polska Fundacja Kulturalna, 1990); pp. 141

For many historical, and therefore socio-psychological, reasons, Poland has hundreds of statues of her beloved writers but a modern biography of none. We needed our great poets to serve us as teachers and prophets, to be our national heroes and role models, to represent rather than to reveal. Thus, one of the functions of Polish literary scholars was to create and preserve legends of the geniuses' lives, cleansed of any aspects considered controversial or inappropriate. Needless to say, the task kept them very busy, since 'shrinology' is a tough field anywhere—witness the struggles of the defenders of the Freud Archives—and the inhabitants of the Polish Hall of Fame, for all their great virtues, are a pretty unruly crowd. And as greatness almost by definition implies controversy, the best and most important require particular vigilance against the approaches of the truth-seekers, the blasphemers. Not surprisingly, then, the biggest of all Polish literary monuments, Adam Mickiewicz, has been guarded by generations of the mightiest scholarly troops, steering the readers away from his darker, disturbing features. In his preface to Mickiewicz's *Collected Works*, published in 1929, Tadeusz Żeleński (Boy) wrote: 'He was for a whole century our national banner. All parties were therefore trying to fly it from their flagpoles. He has been twisted, trimmed, read with the intention of finding only what was sought. Mickiewicz, we can say, never belonged—could not belong—to the "normal" history of literature.'

Seventy years, and several new or restored flagpoles later, Professor Jadwiga Maurer of Kansas University proves with her excellently researched study of what she calls Mickiewicz's affiliations with the Jewish world that little has changed since Boy's outcry. In the introductory chapter of her short but dense book she points to the three areas which have traditionally daunted Mickiewicz scholars: adulterous relations, the leading role in Andrzej Towiański's sect Koło Boże (God's Circle), and, above all, the interest in Jews and Judaism. The ban on Mickiewicz's love affairs, first lifted by Boy, has been entirely removed in the last decades, as no one seemed offended any more. The same applies, up to a point, to Mickiewicz's involvement with Towiański, quite thoroughly examined in several recent publications, which conclude that in joining Koło Boże Mickiewicz was the victim of delusions, depression, and manipulations. But the point which remains untouched in any of these analyses is Towianism's major preoccupation—recognized and scorned by the contemporary Polish *émigré* circles— with the idea of a reconciliation between Judaism and Christianity. For that was the reason why Mickiewicz co-founded the Koło and stayed on there for ten years! Conversely, that is also the reason why the word 'Judaism' is barely mentioned in the entire Polish literature, old and new, on the Towiański–Mickiewicz sect. The subject, all too apparently, belongs to the themes which Maurer says are 'of the lowest category; long killed and buried' (p. 12).

Of course, the major theme, and the root cause of all this deaf-and-dumbness, is the persistently denied rumour about the Jewish origins of Mickiewicz's mother. I doubt if such rumours concerning the national bard would have been welcome in any other nineteenth-century European country (e.g. that Cervantes was a *marrano*), and the fact that Mickiewicz often spoke of himself as a Lithuanian already bothered the more fervent nationalists—at a time, we must remember, when Poland kept fighting for her lost political freedom, and was continually rising and falling. Mickiewicz's first biographer, his son Władysław, a French citizen tutored in his youth by Armand Lévy (Mickiewicz's close friend, who, apparently under the poet's influence, reclaimed his Jewish roots), was under significant pressure from Polish academic circles to conceal and even destroy documents containing information about matters 'inappropriate', particularly concerning his father's marital problems and the Jewish affiliations. Promptly recognizing a somewhat dull Władysław as an original culprit, Professor Maurer indicts the more recent generations of scholars on several counts, ranging from outright dishonesty, in not telling what they knew, to cowardly and sloppy research.

If the entire issue were limited to a few clues about the ethnicity of the poet's mother, coming from the area that for centuries had been a melting-pot of nationalities, creeds, and social strata, the case could indeed remain buried in academic footnotes. But quite clearly—and Maurer is the first scholar to make this clarification point by point—in addition to birth, the Jewish connection had also marked Mickiewicz's marriage and the circumstances of his death. The strongest, and so far the least mentioned, evidence of Mickiewicz's personal tie with the Jewish predicament appears in the story of his marriage. Maurer's research into this subject strikes the reader of her book as quite rudimentary; Celina Szymanowska's Jewish-Frankist background (Frankists were a group of several hundred Polish Jews of the eighteenth century who, while converted to Catholicism, preserved their sense of Jewish identity) was known to everybody at the time and, with a very few exceptions, the poet's choice had been accepted with remarkable tolerance. All that Maurer needed to do in order to bring forth this shelved bundle of historical facts was to put together easily available information about Celina's prominent direct ancestors and about the surprisingly short and decisive courtship, which puzzled Mickiewicz's friends. Why did the famous bard, adored by women, take for his wife a comely girl whom he had not seen since she was a child, but had traced and summoned to Paris using a network of seemingly distant acquaintances from the Frankist circles? After reviewing all the hypothetical answers, none more substantial than the 'mystery of the heart' cliché, Maurer does not even have to spell out the conclusion: Mickiewicz married Celina because she was Jewish.

In the remaining fifteen years of his life Mickiewicz abandoned his lyre—like the Jew Jankiel in *Pan Tadeusz*—and, also like Jankiel and Father Robak, devoted his energies to the cause which combined two objectives, Poland's independence and a universal spiritual revival. All his pronouncements and actions during that period—in Koło Boże, at the lectern of the Collège de France, and finally in Constantinople, where shortly before his sudden death from a mysterious ailment he organized the Jewish Legion to fight side by side with the Polish troops in the Crimean war—contained one common determinator: his faith in the Messianic destiny of the Polish–Jewish union and in the new Judaeo-Christian religion. Here again Maurer is at her best providing documents, carefully considered clues, and the connecting commentary on the final developments in Mickiewicz's life as they reflected his pro-Jewish passion, so thoroughly dismissed by the official Mickiewiczology. Writing in a lively, jargon-free style which gives credence to her workmanlike, stick-to-the-facts method, Professor Maurer addresses her book to the general Polish reader rather than to the academic establishment. Her last paragraph, appealing to the readers to 'use common sense and to refuse to be duped', is a gentle reminder of Mickiewicz's famous apostrophe in the Epilogue to *Pan Tadeusz*, to the effect that his poetry is intended for 'simple people'.

And accordingly, her ground-breaking and in all respects scholarly and rigorous work met with—guess what?—the time-honoured conspiracy of silence. There were no more, in over three years since the publication, than three (mostly laudatory) reviews in the Polish press, none at all in any of the specialist periodicals by a professional critic or scholar. The credit for a solitary exception to this cowardly rule belongs to the *Polish Review* (a quarterly published by the Polish Institute of Arts and Science of America), where (in vol. 38/1 (1992), 121) a young Slavist, Roman Koropeckyj, both disapproves of Maurer's 'righteous indignation' and admits that 'Maurer's singular achievement in these essays has been to raise questions and possibilities that should never have been nor no longer can be "buried in the cemeteries of Mickiewicz scholarship"'. Still, he doubts whether such revised perceptions of Mickiewicz's life could influence the understanding of his poetry, its mythical system of meanings and images so deeply ingrained by inheritance in the Polish consciousness.

I disagree. Firstly, Mickiewicz is a historical figure, and therefore the facts of his life need to be established as truthfully as possible. Secondly, if reading is—or should be—an individual effort at discovery of the text's meaning, we must be able to confront, to confirm or to challenge, the established interpretative formulae, otherwise we will be performing a ritual rather than going through a process of understanding. Myths obscure reality, including the reality of works of art. And myths about Mickiewicz's life were as instrumental in obscuring some of the inherent meanings in his poetry as their revision may be in helping readers to widen and redirect the focus, at which point, together or apart, we may experience anew the shudder of recognition. For the attentive readers of Professor Maurer's brave essays, not only will Jankiel regain his remarkable position of artist-turned-prophet, lost to the stereotype of a good old Jew among other secondary local types of Soplicowo, but *Dziady* too may reveal some fascinating and completely overlooked meanings, especially in the so-called mystical scenes of Part III. And so on.

Thirdly, for a great number of Polish readers who share with Mickiewicz the complex emotions resulting from their somewhat 'alien' backgrounds, Maurer's '*Z matki obcej . . .*' is the belated and most welcome gift of reasserted truth: that yes, one of the greatest Poles, and a devout Christian, never forgot that he was also a Jew. In what sense? For a large part of his life he himself struggled with the question, and it is up to the individual reader to decide to what extent that lonely struggle informed his immortal verses—sometimes at the least expected moments, and quite lightheartedly. Here we are, for example, in book VIII of *Pan Tadeusz*, looking at the stars:

> And, waiting for a rider, David's Car
> Turns its long shaft towards the northern star.
> The older Lithuanians rightly know,
> That people wrongly call the chariot so.
> It is the Angel's Car, in which once rode
> Proud Lucifer that time he challenged God,
> Speeding full gallop on the Milky Way,
> Till Michael overthrew him. Since that day
> The ruined car among the stars lies strewed,
> Nor will the Archangel let it be renewed.

But how many Archangels does it take to renew Adam's Car?

JOANNA ROSTROPOWICZ CLARK

WŁADYSŁAW T. BARTOSZEWSKI AND
ANTONY POLONSKY (EDS.)
The Jews in Warsaw: A History
(Oxford and Cambridge, Mass.: Basil Blackwell Ltd., 1991); pp. vi + 392

For Jews Warsaw after the Second World War constitutes something of a ghost town, with scarcely a thousand persons surviving the horrific events which transpired between 1939 and 1945. Warsaw, 'the mother city of Israel', is, however, far from being a historical wasteland. This collection of essays bears witness to that once teeming life of Warsaw's Jewry, whose vicissitudes, as well as some of their remarkable achievements, are recorded in this volume.

Although most of the pieces have already been published in the present journal, this is not a random collection. A strict editorial hand has ensured that between them the previously published and the new essays leave virtually no chronological gap from the eighteenth to the twentieth century. If there are any remaining interstices, a fifty-page introduction by the editors fills them neatly with a lucid overview of the history of the Jews in Warsaw from the fifteenth through to the mid-twentieth century.

The essays vary in scope. Some authors pan over a broad historical period, e.g. Stefan Kieniewicz in his perceptive examination of how each of the partitioning powers from 1795 to 1861 impinged on Jewish life; others focus on micro-histories of particular events or institutions, e.g. Marian Marek Drozdowski in his description of events under King Stanisław August, or Artur Eisenbach in his study of Jews in Warsaw at the end of the eighteenth century. Some essays rely on published material, others, such as Krystyna Zienkowska's deft probe of the anti-Jewish riots of 1790, utilize archival material. To round off the narratives and analyses, there are two historiographical essays: Israel Gutman on Emanuel Ringelblum, an underground activist historian, and Robert Moses Shapiro on Jacob Shatzky, a historian of Warsaw Jewry.

This book will clearly be invaluable to all students of Judaica. Cultural historians will find particular interest in Alexander Guterman's chapter on the origins of the Great Synagogue, Kieniewicz's description of assimilated Jews in the nineteenth century, and Chone Shmeruk's suggestive sketch of Yiddish literary enterprises in Warsaw. From many of the essays one gains a sense of the great variety of Jews who lived in Warsaw: the Hasidim (who formed a majority by the late nineteenth century), the *misnagdim*, the *maskilim*, Litvaks, Polonized Jews, Germanized Jews, Russified Jews, Frankists, and other converts. Politically, Jews were just as heterogeneous, ranging from Zionists to Bundists, from Social Democrats to conservative bankers.

Several of the authors, including Kieniewicz and Piotr Wróbel, concentrate on how both Polish and Russian policies affected living patterns, work opportunities, and the quality of life for Jews. Paradoxically, it was the Tsarist regime which emancipated Polish Jews and afforded them (and Poles in general) economic opportunities. In the end, however, Tsarist attitudes brought repression, pogroms, and exposure to local antisemitism upon Jews in Warsaw.

I would recommend this book to all urban historians of whatever period or region, not only for comparative purposes, but also for some of the methodologies used: for example, Stephen D. Corrsin's use of census materials for his demographic profile of the Jewish population in the city in the nineteenth century and the contribution by Edward D. Wynot, Jr., for the twentieth. Urban historians will also find useful material in the discussions by Peter J. Martyn and by Wróbel of the physical growth of the city, its neighbourhoods, and patterns of Jewish residency and employment.

The book is enhanced by 14 plates (leaving one eager for even more of these vivid scenes of daily life), 7 maps in Martyn's essay, and tables in several of the chapters. Fortunately, there is also an index, but it could have been more detailed. For example, if one is looking for material on pogroms, there are no entries 'pogrom', 'violence', or 'riot'. Almost inevitably, there are a few minor typographical slips, e.g. on pp. 23, 25, 193, and 233. One, however, is so jarring that it should be mentioned: Polish losses during the Second World War are stated on p. 2 to have 'amounted to over 250,000 million'; at least the exaggeration is so great that the figure is easily recognized as an error. There are also some unavoidable overlaps and repetitions as each author surveys the subject before launching into his or her essay.

As one would also expect, not all the authors are in agreement over their interpretation of events or even statistics. Corrsin, for example, while admitting that the data are unreliable, seems to think that fertility was less among Jews than among Catholics (p. 216), whereas Wróbel believes the opposite to be true (p. 255).

In succinct form the reader will gain from this volume much knowledge of many aspects of the Jewish experience in Warsaw over the centuries. In a more general way, anyone concerned with contemporary problems of ethnic and religious minorities fighting for survival within militantly nationalistic communities would profit from pondering over these excellent essays.

The first sentence of the introduction to the book will serve as a suitable conclusion to this review. It cites Isaac Bashevis Singer's character Hadassah in *The Family Moskat*: 'Warsaw, dear city of mine, how sad I am!' Although not all the authors of this volume are Jewish, there appears to be a general feeling among historians writing here that in many ways the city, despite all the hardships they endured, was dear to the Jews. In fact, during the 1861 Polish uprising against Russia Rabbi Ber Meisels affirmed, 'And we too feel that we are Poles, and we love the Polish land as you do' (p. 166). Bartoszewski's essay on 'Martyrdom and

Struggle' confirms what is evident on nearly every page of this important book: that 'sad' is too pale a term for what Jews in Warsaw have suffered over the centuries, whether at the hands of Polish burghers, Tsarist rulers, the Kaiser's occupation forces, Stalin's army, or, ultimately, from the Nazi Holocaust.

PATRICIA HERLIHY

MARIA KLAŃSKA
Problemfeld Galizien in deutschsprachiger Prosa 1846–1914
(Vienna and Cologne: Böhlau, 1991); pp. 231

This German version/second edition of a 1985 'Habilitationsschrift' at the University of Kraków (published originally in an edition of only 150 copies) is undoubtedly a valuable contribution in that it demarginalizes a narrative world that appeared to be irretrievably lost to the canon of 'German' literature of that period. The author presents a representative triad of authors. There is Karl Emil Franzos, whose village stories were immensely popular during this period, like those of his counterpart in mainstream German literature, Berthold Auerbach. A second writer is Leopold von Sacher-Masoch of Freudian and Deleuzian fame (*Sacher-Masoch: An Interpretation together with the Entire Text of* Venus in Furs, 1967; English edn. 1971). Hans Weber-Lutkow (Hans Pokorny), a third author, is today largely forgotten. Many lesser authors are also introduced.

The book is clearly structured and composed. Since large parts of it are conventional history of literature, this facilitates back-checking when reading through new territory. After an introduction listing major methodological considerations, the first main chapter discusses the national-political dynamics leading to literary reflections in the works of Sacher-Masoch and Franzos. A second chapter addresses the issue of how the three above-mentioned authors viewed the social conflicts emerging from a number of changes and significant historical episodes (e.g. the gradual granting to Jews of equal civil rights under the Habsburg monarchy). The third chapter is basically a survey of literature that deals with assimilation and non-assimilation within the period mentioned in the title. In this reviewer's opinion, the principal merit of the study lies in its descriptive width and its embedding of this feature within historical-factual parameters. There are, however, also limitations when one looks for more profound insights along the lines of the history of mentalities; and there are shortcomings when it comes to literary analysis. Thus, for example, when the author surveys recent research on *Heimatliteratur*, or regional literature, in the introduction, Norbert Mecklenburg's seminal study of 1982 is briefly discussed (pp. 19 ff., although not mentioned in the register of names at the end of the book), but the rest of the monograph bears practically no evidence of his important and valuable set of criteria for the genre. The role model for any *Kulturbilder* in German, the *Culturgeschichtliche Novellen* of 1856 by the German ethnologist W. Riehl—best sellers in their time—is not even mentioned when the author is dealing with a corpus of tales that mostly fall under this heading.

The need to set a historical framework is obvious. But should not the 'high' literature portraits of Galician Jewry that were written and published after 1914, but almost always dealt with a past reaching far back before that year, also have been included—if not explicitly, then at least by way of a prospective outlook? One example would be Alfred Döblin's *Reise in Polen* (1924–5, recently translated by Joachim Neugroschel as *Journey to Poland*, 1990); Döblin was researching his collective past on commission from the famous Fischer publishing house and the *Vossische Zeitung* (cf. the first sentence of the chapter on 'Lemberg' (Lwów), where he explicitly refers to 'South Galicia'). There are also extensive references to Galician Jews in the works of novelist Joseph Roth (d. 1939). Klańska does, however, mention (pp. 217–18) that this type of analysis will form the subject of her next research project. Another slight reservation is the author's exclusion of minor modern 'low-literature' authors who did use some of the stories and tales as stripped-down or recycled anecdotes for the reading public after the Second World War. See my monograph (Bonn, 1980), on Mosche Ya'akov Ben-gavriel, an Austrian–Israeli writer who enjoyed moderate success with such 'transplanted' stories in the 1950s and 1960s in German-speaking countries.

Chapters 3.1 (on Christian–Jewish coexistence) and 3.2 (the push for assimilation by Franzos) list an impressive number of themes and motifs surrounding this type of social cohabitation. Itta Shedletzky's 'Some Observations on the Popular Zeitroman in Jewish Weeklies in Germany 1870–1900' (*Canadian Review of Comparative Literature*, 9/3 (1982)) might have been helpful in providing a context for the wider problem of this social constellation. When briefly discussing what is considered to be Franzos's main work, his 'Entwicklungsroman' *Der Pojaz* (1905), Klańska approaches it in a slightly myopic way as primarily a 'portrait of Galician Jewish petty bourgeois', omitting to mention that a model for this type of novel was obviously Goethe's *Wilhelm Meister*.

But our most serious reservation concerns the author's reliance on outdated viewpoints regarding 'the Jewish question' from literary texts that are hard to accept after 1933. For example, when discussing Sacher-Masoch's famous novella *Der Juden-Raphael*, a story containing incidents of supercilious condescension towards all social classes of Jews, she talks about 'typische Züge eines gemäßigten Antisemitismus' (p. 193) that should be seen as silly slips in taste ('Albernheiten'). Or when discussing Franzos's *Der Shylock von Barnow* (p. 170), a horrific tragedy of religious blindness, Klańska simply treats it as falling into a set of established motifs concerning the author's view of the problems of assimilation (without including in her brief interpretation the figure of a Jewish doctor who embodies unresolved issues of assimilation).

This book is rich in information, but its analysis is limited.

JOSEF SCHMIDT

ISRAEL OPPENHEIM
Tenuat Hehaluts bePolin, 1929–1939
(Beer-Sheva: Hamerkaz Lemoreshet Ben-Gurion and Hotsa'at Hasefarim shel Universitat Ben-Gurion baNegev, 1993); pp. 673

Jacob Rader Marcus, the doyen of American Jewish history, is credited with the statement 'I would trade in all my theories for one new fact.' No doubt historian Israel Oppenheim would concur with this viewpoint. Indeed, Oppenheim's *Tenuat Hehaluts bePolin, 1929–1939* is a magisterial compilation of data concerning the Polish Socialist Zionist youth movement known as Hechaluts [the Pioneer]. This 673-page Hebrew tome, the second volume of a continuing study, focuses on the early and middle 1930s, when Hechaluts enjoyed its greatest success. The author meticulously documents the cultural, ideological, and political development of that segment of Polish Jewish youth for whom Hechaluts offered a meaningful response to the adversity and uncertainty of the interwar period.

Oppenheim, the undisputed expert on Hechaluts, bases his study on a rich storehouse of hitherto neglected primary sources preserved in the Central Zionist Archives, the Beit Lohamei Hageta'ot Archives, the Kibbutz Hameuhad Archives, the Hashomer Hatsa'ir Archives, the Lavon Labour Institute Archives, the Moreshet Ben-Gurion Archives, the Israel Labour Party Archives, and the Jewish National Library. David Engel's assertion that 'there is probably no newspaper, pamphlet, handbill, or collection of unpublished material having some bearing on this subject that [Oppenheim] has not examined' is probably correct: see Engel's review of Oppenheim's *The Struggle of Jewish Youth for Productivization: The Zionist Youth Movement in Poland* in *AJS Review*, 17/1 (Spring 1992), 129. I hasten to add, however, that Oppenheim's encyclopaedic grasp apparently exceeds his analytic reach. For despite *Tenuat Hehaluts bePolin*'s many worthy features—particularly the detailed narrative accounts of the *senifei hechaluts* [local pioneering chapters], *kibbutzei hakhsharah* [training farms], the influence of Palestinian *shelihim* [emissaries], and relations with the Histadrut [General Federation of Jewish Workers in Palestine]—the work is marred by the lack of a clear and cogent methodological framework.

At the heart of this volume is Oppenheim's keen, virtually exclusive, interest in Hechaluts. Although the study painstakingly illustrates the ascendance of Hechaluts in the 1930s, it pays scant attention to the revolution which took place in Polish Jewish politics as a whole. That the country's economic misery, growing right-wing extremism, and increasingly virulent antisemitic climate had a profound impact on Polish Jewry is assumed but not sufficiently demonstrated by the author. Nor is Hechaluts analysed within the context of the generation of secular, Polonized Jewish youth who grew to maturity in independent Poland and were especially shaken by the country's deteriorating social, economic, and political environment. Against this general background, Oppenheim posits, many Jewish young people turned to Zionism—notably Hechaluts—as an avenue of hope and escape. Oppenheim contributes significantly to the scholarly enquiry into east European Jewry by documenting the youth movement's impressive growth in this period, but he fails to investigate *why* Hechaluts was the movement of preference.

In a similar vein, the author's examination of Polish Jewish youth culture glosses over the appeal of right-wing and religious Zionism. Especially glaring is his neglect of the Betar youth movement. In at least two respects, the countervailing Betar Zionists were akin to Hechaluts. First, they opposed the seemingly respectable General Zionists' preoccupation with local politics, accusing the latter of apologetic and timid leadership in the face of rising anti-Jewish discrimination. Second, they too advocated a radical Palestinocentric solution to the Jewish predicament in eastern Europe. Unlike the would-be *chalutsim* [pioneers], however, Betar members shunned Socialism and despised left-wing Jewish ideologies, which they considered delusory, Utopian, and élitist. Rather, Betar glorified the concept of military preparedness and viewed mass Jewish emigration to Palestine as the only means of solving the Jewish problem completely. In their zealous opposition to Hechaluts, Betar members sharpened their self-ascribed collective identity; the movement also assumed many of the trappings of Polish Fascism. Undoubtedly, there is much to be learnt from a comparison of Hechaluts and Betar. It is disappointing, therefore, to find that Oppenheim only sporadically examines Betar, on fourteen separate pages.

The author's penchant for descriptive history is also apparent in the complete omission of an adequate conclusion. After leading the reader through 477 pages of narrative, Oppenheim concludes his investigation of Hechaluts by adding yet another 50-page chapter detailing the movement's status on the eve of Hitler's invasion of Poland. In short, I suggest that this poorly edited book should have been approximately half its present length, and would have benefited enormously from a solid introduction and conclusion whose primary emphases were analytic.

Finally, a word must be said about the author's transparent filiopietistic agenda. As a product of the generation and world he describes, Oppenheim seeks to preserve the memory of the east European pioneering youths who played a leading role in the creation of Israel's pre-state infrastructure. This is a worthy effort in itself, but one which unfortunately interferes with Oppenheim's scholarship. As a result, whatever insights that one may glean from the volume—and there are many—must be carefully considered within the confines of this partisan historiographic tradition. Knowing this, we can better understand and appreciate Oppenheim's vast study—a chronicle which is essentially a subtle apologetic as well as a unique source of information. In all, despite its flaws, *Tenuat Heḥaluts bePolin* represents a Herculean scholarly effort. Oppenheim has bequeathed to future students of this topic an extremely useful and important research tool that cannot be ignored.

MARK A. RAIDER

The Letters of Martin Buber: A Life of Dialogue

EDITED BY

NAHUM N. GLATZER AND PAUL MENDES-FLOHR

TRANSLATED BY

RICHARD AND CLARA WINSTON, AND HARRY ZOHN

(New York: Schocken Books, 1991); pp. xiii + 722

The Letters of Martin Buber is an important and extremely well executed text, based upon the three-volume German edition of 1975. It includes a fine 62-page biographical sketch by Grete Schaeder that reviews the major persons and developments in Buber's life, extensive notes to the individual letters of Buber and his correspondents by Mendes-Flohr, a descriptive list of correspondents, photographs, and an index. In all, the editors provide all the requisite resources to enable the reader to plumb the depths of this valuable cache.

What might we hope to find in turning to the letters of a man who is famous for his philosophic writings about the redemptive quality of relationship? We might hope to encounter exchanges that are not mere correspondence, to uncover insights into the ways in which individuals struggle together with matters of ultimate concern. The letters do not only succeed in providing such moments and insights, but they also corroborate Buber's understanding that the most elevated events of 'the between' are transient. The letters attest to what Ernst Simon described as Buber's 'sense of "responsibility for the word"' (p. xii). However, in the light of the heavy volume of daily correspondence Buber faced, one must admire his honest admission that he is surprised when a 'real letter' issues from his pen (p. 288).

Paradoxically, the text gives evidence of Buber's ambivalence concerning the writing of letters. In addition to being demanding work, Buber and many of those who corresponded with him believed that writing was an inadequate substitute for speaking face to face (p. 269). In the letters there are an impressive number of allusions to how powerful such personal encounters with him really were (p. 606). Letters were also problematic for Buber because, even in the context of a dialogue, he valued most highly the silent exchange of glances between persons (p. 288; see also his essay 'Dialogue').

The letters vividly illuminate the most important relationships in his life, those with his wife Paula Winkler, Florens Christian Rang, Gustav Landauer, Franz Rosenzweig, and Ernst Simon. All of these were begun before Buber was 40, and they played decisive roles in the development of his life and thought. With the early deaths of Rang, Landauer, and Rosenzweig, Buber experienced grave personal and intellectual losses.

Buber first met Paula in 1899, and Schaeder's description of her as 'a woman who was his equal, indeed his superior, in poetic talent and articulateness' (p. 10) and of the deeply emotive, almost lyrical quality of their relationship seems accurate.

The letters between Buber and Rosenzweig, as Schaeder notes, are unrivalled in terms of their intensity and intellectual challenge. Here are 'real letters', fittingly, the most personal and philosophic of the collection. Each of these men was drawn out by the other, through exchanges on various subjects, including the Psalms, the Bible, magic and religion, revelation and the law, as well as everyday affairs and responsibilities.

Unlike many of the other letters in the volume, this fascinating and engaging interchange between the 'reverential *apikores* [atheist]' Buber and the 'homecomer' Rosenzweig (p. 271) requires careful attention. Complex ideas are often concisely communicated, and Rosenzweig's extended metaphors are intricately spun out. Although many of the letters have been published elsewhere, the editors were right to include them here. They reveal the substance of the relationship that Rosenzweig once described in terms of 'two entangled skeins of yarn' (p. 286).

It is impressive how Buber's friendships stood fast, or better, developed by way of criticism. Among many examples are Landauer's censure of the 'war Buber' for his romantic enthusiasm that ignored the horrible brutalities of the First World War (pp. 188 ff.), Buber's criticisms of the *Star of Redemption*'s treatment of religious persons who are neither Jews nor Christians (p. 275), Rosenzweig's famous two-page critique of the first part of *I and Thou*—'in the I-It, you give the I-Thou a cripple for an antagonist' (p. 278)—and Rang's objections to Buber's book that also insist on a much larger role for the category of creation (p. 284).

Additionally, the letters are of considerable interest as pointers to the life of one who was involved in significant historical events and corresponded with many famous and important individuals. They portray the early years of the Zionist movement, the impact of the First World War on some intellectual circles, the rise of the Nazis, Buber's life in Palestine and the State of Israel, and his abiding commitment to adult education and to humanitarian causes. It is exciting to peruse the correspondence with such persons as Herzl, Kafka, Walter Benjamin, Agnon, Weitzman, Scholem, Ernst Simon, Max Brod, S. H. Bergman, Walter Kaufmann, Hesse, Schweitzer, Einstein, Gandhi, Eleanor Roosevelt, Dag Hammarskjold, and others besides. The development of the rift between Buber and Herzl is striking, and the letters from Benjamin about Kafka cast light on these important but complex thinkers.

The topic of Buber's belated immigration to Palestine and his reception there is a prominent feature in Schaeder's introduction (pp. 5–6) and in the correspondence itself. The letters reveal some of the personal, intellectual, and vocational reasons that caused him to remain in Germany much longer than many of his admirers and friends had hoped. In some of the more poignant reflections in the collection, he speaks of himself as a 'border guard' (p. 336) and as someone who is neither lonely nor surprised at being unpopular in Israel (p. 590).

What do we learn from the letters? We experience a man's life with others in history. There is not much in terms of philosophical additions and clarifications, nor of what Simon called his 'private life' (p. xi). A query about Buber's early childhood elicited the reply 'I do not even want to explain myself to myself' (p. 572), which could have been anticipated by anyone who has looked at his 'Autobiographical [?] Fragments'. Yet, if these be lacunae, they serve to corroborate the character of the letters of a man who valued dialogue over either exposition or soliloquy.

Perhaps the greatest boon provided by the letters is the reflections on meaning. The question of the meaning of a particular life, and consequently of what we call life, is addressed sometimes obliquely and sometimes directly throughout this volume. Buber attained to important personal and historical accomplishments, but also experienced failures and losses. The letters give profound testimony to his belief that, although it may be acutely elusive, there is meaning. As though addressing the absent author, Buber writes to Max Brod, who has just sent him a copy of the posthumously published *The Castle*:

> Certainly, that's the way it is; the meaningless has been installed as the executor of meaning, and that is what we have to deal with here, to the very last moment. But as we concern ourselves with it and suffer the entanglements of concrete absurdity, do we not again and again, whether we admit it or not, become aware, in cruel sanctification, of the meaning that proves to be totally uncongenial to us and yet is something that faces us and penetrates all that effluvium and at the last, right moment reaches and occupies the innermost chambers of our heart? (p. 348)

MICHAEL OPPENHEIM

ALEXANDER BEIDER
A Dictionary of Jewish Surnames from the Russian Empire

(Teaneck, NJ: Avotaynu, 1993); pp. xxiii + 760

The book under review is a very impressive publication that will be welcomed by students of east European Jewish linguistics, history, and genealogy. The fact that the author is a 31-year-old computer-systems analyst and not a professionally trained linguist or historian makes his achievement all the more remarkable. The major accomplishment of the book is the compilation of approximately 50,000 names borne by Jews in the former Tsarist Russian Empire with geographical and etymological notes. Preceding the dictionary are a hundred pages consisting of an introduction to Jewish onomastic research and four chapters entitled 'History of Jewish Names in Eastern Europe', 'Types of Jewish Surnames', 'Jewish Surnames and Surnames of Other European Peoples', and 'Linguistic Aspects of Jewish Surnames'. There are also three appendices (on hyphenated surnames, the most common Jewish surnames in the Russian Empire at the beginning of the twentieth century, and the must common in the Soviet Union) and nineteen tables on various topics of linguistic structure and the geographical distribution of surnames. The bibliography on Slavonic and non-Slavonic Jewish surnames is reasonably comprehensive;[1] a map of major Jewish settlements in the Pale of Settlement is also provided.

With this book, Beider has raised the quality of east European Jewish onomastics by several notches. But while genealogists will welcome this comprehensive listing of names borne by Russian Jews, the utility of the list is occasionally marred by linguistically unsound comments and by arbitrary geographical characterizations.

Students of genealogy will be anxious to have geographical information on Jewish surnames, but what is the value of Beider's information? The author did well to take his data from before 1917, since after that date the accelerated mobility of the Jews within the Pale of Settlement (e.g. from rural to urban centres) and the mass migration to cities in the RSFSR make it extremely difficult to plot the original geographical contours of the names. Had Beider relied on Soviet data, there would have been gross inaccuracies: major cities which could have served as magnets for Jewish settlement, such as Kiev, Minsk, and Odessa, are in

---

[1] Additional references can be found in R. Singerman, *Jewish and Hebrew Onomastics: A Bibliography* (New York and London, 1977); add *Akty, izdavaemye Vilenskoj Komissiej dlja razbora drevnix aktov* (39 vols.; Vilna, 1865–1915); I. Šiper, 'Der onhejb fun "lošn aškenaz" in der balajxtung fun onomatiše kveln', *Jidiše filologje*, 1/2–3 (1924), 101–12; M. Altbauer, 'Od typu metronomicznego do "pajdonomicznego"', *Onomastika*, 4 (1958), 355–64.

fact less informative than small towns. Yet what can we learn from an account which states that *Fajn* is found in Kovno (Kaunas), but related *Fajner* in far-off Odessa?[2] Could this really be the entire domain of these names? Sibilant confusion (confusion of *s* and *š*, *z* and *ž*, etc.) in Jewish surnames is another case in point. We know that this feature was characteristic of dialects of Byelorussian (Lithuanian) Yiddish, Byelorussian, and the Mazowsze dialect of Polish.[3] Beider mentions these facts (p. 73), expressing surprise that there are examples of the confusion in names from the Ukraine, e.g. *Tkackij* (Elysavethrad [his 'Elisavetgrad']/Soviet Kirovohrad) < -*čk*-;[4] but he does not attempt to explain this unexpected development. I suppose that either Byelorussian Jews with these names migrated to the Ukraine or that there were indigenous Jews in the Ukrainian lands whose speech (Yiddish?, Ukrainian?, Turkic?) once (but no longer) had the feature of sibilant confusion. Migration is the simplest explanation, but the stereotyped Ukrainian speech of Jews in Ukrainian plays of the seventeenth and eighteenth centuries reveals this feature, and occasionally even Yiddish Slavisms exhibiting this phenomenon are found in unexpected locales (for example, standard Yiddish *holupces* 'stuffed cabbage' < Ukrainian *holupci* surfaces in Kraków and to the east of the city as *holupčes*).[5] Hence, there may have been a local precedent for sibilant confusion among Ukrainian Jews at an earlier historical period.[6]

There is probably no point in giving geographical detail with surnames based on Yiddish *pejsex* (< Hebrew *pesax* 'Passover'), since the holiday term apparently first became a masculine anthroponym in Ukrainian Khazar Jewish circles in the tenth century, and from there spread throughout the Slavonic and east German (i.e. Sorbian) lands.[7] Hence, geographical data on a variety of Slavonic suffixes in Jewish surnames (see e.g. table 2.5, showing the distribution of -*in* in different *gubernias*, and pp. 35, 37, 43), while interesting, may ultimately be of limited value. Were names such a reliable index of early dialect borders and isoglosses, dialectologists would use them more often.

It is imperative in a work of this kind to exploit the findings of Yiddish and

[2] I do not follow Beider's system of romanizing non-Latin alphabets since it deviates from international practice and is unnecessarily weighted in favour of English. For example, Beider's use of *ch* for Slavonic *č* will cause confusion to non-English readers.

[3] See U. Weinreich, '*Sábesdiker losn* in Yiddish: A Problem of Linguistic Affinity', *Slavic Word*, 1 (1952), 360–77.

[4] Given the perennial changes in place-names in the former USSR, it would have been helpful to provide new and old names, and certainly in their newly reconstituted Byelorussian, Ukrainian, and Baltic forms. Here I use the current Byelorussian and Ukrainian place-names.

[5] See the as yet largely unpublished *Language and Culture Atlas of Ashkenazic Jewry*, ed. M. I. Herzog *et al.*, housed at Columbia University, questionnaire No. 122 030. Might this fact suggest a south-westward migration of Yiddish speakers from the Byelorussian lands?

[6] See Wexler, *Explorations in Judeo-Slavic Linguistics* (Leiden, 1987), 192 ff., and 'Judeo-Slavic Frontispieces of Late 18th and 19th-century Books and the Authentication of "Stereotyped" Judeo-Slavic Speech', *Welt der Slaven*, 39/2 (1994), 201–30.

[7] See Wexler, *Explorations in Judeo-Slavic Linguistics*, 75–6.

Slavonic linguistics. For example, in Yiddish dialects the term for 'to make meat ritually pure' comes from a variety of sources: *trejbern* < Judaeo-Sorbian *poršn* < Judaeo-Romance *menaker zajn, menakern* < Hebrew. According to Beranek,[8] the first variant is typical of Polish and Eastern Slavonic Yiddish, but his data are rather imprecise. Beider's data may enable us to make more specific recommendations regarding the geography of the Slavonic and Hebrew terms. He notes that surnames based on the Hebrew agent noun 'person who makes meet ritually pure' occur in three variants: *Menaker* (Vilna, Vynnycja) ~ *Monaker* (Volodymyr Volyns'kyj) ~ *Manaker* (Belarus). Beider also gives the surnames *Trejb(man)* (Pinsk), *Trejbač* (Białystok, Bielsk, Dubno), *Trejber* (Rivne, Odessa), *Trejberman* (Novhorod, Ostrih), *Trejbič* (Soroki, Luck, Mohyliv-Podil'sk), and *Trejbic* (Klimavici—with sibilant confusion), *Trejbučan* (Kišinev), and *Trajberman* (Izjaslav, formerly Zaslav). The listings are also important to the linguist in that they expand the corpus of derived forms from the root *trejbern*.

Beider suggests that few Slavs converted to Judaism (p. xiii). This is a surprising statement, given the evidence that such conversion was widespread in the west Slavonic lands (including originally Sorbian eastern Germany), at least up to the twelfth century.[9] How else can we explain the plethora of Slavonic names among the Russian Jews, which are not derived from indigenous place-names? Note also the name *Canaan* given to Slav converts to Judaism, since this was the term used in 'medieval Ashkenazic Hebrew for the Slavs—an allusion to the Bible, where the Canaanites were slaves, this being the status of Slavs in many parts of western Europe in the early Middle Ages.[10] Perhaps the Jewish surname *Kozak*, literally 'Cossack', was also originally the name of a convert to Judaism. Beider's discussion of differences between Jewish and Christian names (pp. 61–2) is good; unfortunately, he provides no explanation for how these differences might have developed.

In this connection, Beider's data on the relative frequency of Slavonic names among Jews in the different regions of the Russian Empire are extremely important. It is a pity that he does not give a breakdown between Ukrainian, Byelorussian, and Russian names, and that the proportion of Germanic and Hebrew names are not similarly plotted. The fact that the Jews use fewer Slavonic suffixes in their names than the Slavs do suggests that Slavonic was not the original language of the Jews at the time that these Jewish surnames were created (p. 31). Beider's data mirror those of Yiddish, where the number of borrowed Slavonic suffixes is also far less than the actual number available in the donor languages.

More discussion about the relative chronology of all the surnames with a Slavonic component in use among the Jews would have been welcome. Beider

---

[8] F. J. Beranek, *Westjiddischer Sprachatlas* (Marburg, 1965), map 93.
[9] See details in Wexler, *The Ashkenazic Jews: A Slavo-Turkic People in Search of a Jewish Identity* (Columbia, Oh., 1993), ch. 6.
[10] See Wexler, *Explorations in Judeo-Slavic Linguistics*, 5, 169.

occasionally gives historical attestation for Jewish names of Germanic origin in western and central Europe. It is possible to add historical information on some of the Slavonic names as well. For example, the *Belaruski arxiw*, 3 (Minsk, 1930), reprints documents containing Jewish names in the Byelorussian lands, some of which are still in use today, e.g. *Danilovič* (1510), *Dlugač* (1565), *Jaximovič*, *Mošeevič*, and *Markovič* (1579) (see Nos. 14, 22, and 26 respectively); conversely, some historical documents contain names not attested today, e.g. *Smerlevič* (1565—though Beider cites a related form) and *Ilič* (1579) (see ibid., Nos. 22 and 26). A considerable corpus of Jewish names can also be extracted from the *Akty, izdavaemye Vilenskoj Komissiej dlja razbora drevnix aktov*. See also the discussion of *Pejsaxovič* above.

A rough clue to the relative chronology of a name is often provided by its phonetic form. For example, in the earliest period of Yiddish–Polish contact, Yiddish speakers replaced Polish *rz* [š, ž] in words borrowed from Polish by *r*, e.g. Yiddish *breg* 'river bank' < Polish *brzeg*; only later did Yiddish speakers, especially in the central part of the country, integrate Polish *rz* according to the shortest phonetic path, i.e. by *š* and *ž*, which had always been available in Yiddish.[11] Beider has a number of names which appear with both variants—*š*/*ž* and *r*. Can we assume that *r*-variants are oldest?

The surname *Aškenuz* is surprising because *u* in a Hebrew word suggests the vowel diacritic *qamac* (yet this should have been spelt with *patax*), which should yield *a* in Yiddish (of course, the more common variant *Aškenazi* also exists). We could assume incorrect vocalization, or that an original *a* became *o* according to the rule affecting all instances of *a* in Yiddish from whatever source (e.g. Byelorussian *sad* 'orchard' > Yiddish *sod*). If the latter explanation is correct, then the variant of the name with *-nuz* might be older than that with *-az*.

Beider assumes that Hebrew names are older than their translation equivalents and that names related to *levi* and *kohen* were actually borne by the descendants of these biblical functions (see pp. 18–19 and his commentary on *Rappe* and *Ettinger*). Yet many Hebrew names are known to have been coined as secondary translations of non-Hebrew names: thus *Kaplan* is probably older than *Kohen*; compare Romance *Bondi* as the prototype of Hebrew *Jomtov*. As to *Levin*, even Beider seems to doubt the exclusively Hebrew origin (see his introduction). I suspect that a name like *Levin* probably originates in the Slavonic root for 'left (-handed)'—such a surname is common in many Slavonic communities—which among Jews, sometimes later underwent 'Hebraization' to the similar-sounding Hebrew *levi*.[12] It is thus unnecessary to assume that *Levin* exists among non-Jews because Jews with this name once converted to Christianity; compare the non-Jewish figure with this name in Tolstoy's *Anna Karenina*.

Beider often overstates the case for a Russian origin for all variants of a Jewish

---

[11] For details see Wexler, *Explorations in Judeo–Slavic Linguistics*, 176–80.
[12] Details in Wexler, *The Ashkenazic Jews*, 209.

surname. It is unclear why he should prefer Russian when Byelorussian and Ukrainian are more obvious sources. For example, he derives *Bondar* from Russian, but Ukrainian *bondar* 'cooper' seems more plausible since the name is used by Ukrainians and Ukrainian Jews; *Bondarenko* 'cooper's son' is not glossed. The surname *Xolodivker* should be described as a Ukrainian place-name (though Russified forms also exist). We are told that *Dolgij* comes from Russian, but the variant *Dlugač*, with its distinctive Polish form, is not so identified. Beider notes that Polish surnames are rare in the eastern Slavonic lands (this is an important clue to the relative chronology of the Russian Jewish names); Beider should have identified them as Polish in the dictionary (genealogists and historians would welcome this information); see e.g. *Glembockij* (though Beider does give the underlying Polish place-name, *Głąboczek*). Beider might have added that Yiddish frequently replaces Polish *a* coming before a consonant (pronounced [o] + a nasal consonant) by *e* + a nasal consonant (see Yiddish *demb* 'oak-tree' < Polish *dąb*, pl. *dęby*).[13] A name like *Mondry* (~ Polish *mądry* 'wise') breaks this rule, and thus should probably be considered a relatively recent name reflecting the shortest phonetic path between Yiddish and Polish; see also discussion of Polish *rz* above.

Similarly, German and Yiddish are not always properly distinguished, though Beider gives a useful summary of German and Yiddish phonetic features (p. 68). On p. 41 Beider speaks of a 'German Umlaut' in Yiddish names, but Umlaut is also characteristic of Yiddish (e.g. Yiddish *Glezer* (= 'glazier') vs. German *Glaser*). *Ferber* (= 'dyer') is correctly defined as German, but *Farbar* is not defined as Yiddish. *Feferkorn* cannot be 'German' (German would be *Pfefferkorn*). Finally, many names are not defined by language, e.g. Yiddish *Frejda/Frejde*. Beider suggests that Yiddish is a highly fused language: 'An important feature that distinguishes Yiddish from other languages is the merging of elements from different languages' (p. 69). A glance at east German onomastics would reveal a similar fusion of German and Sorbian elements.

The characterization of Judaeo-Slavonic is inadequate (pp. 4–5, 8–9, 31). The writings of the sixteenth-century author Katz are not the only evidence that Jews in a number of east Slavonic lands were monolingual speakers of (Judaized) Slavonic.[14] Would the relatively high percentage of Slavonic surnames in Navahrudak be an indication of an earlier Slavonic-speaking Jewish community there? It is unclear why Beider needs to derive all Slavonic surnames from Polish and east Slavonic place-names and roots, when the contact of Jews with Sorbs

---

[13] See Wexler, *Explorations in Judeo-Slavic Linguistics*, 173. The Eastern Slavonic cognate *dub* is rare in Yiddish (it is found in scattered locales of Belarus) and is rarer still in the Ukraine, according to the *Language and Culture Atlas of Ashkenazic Jewry*, questionnaire No. 102 090. Beider cites the surname *Dub* in some parts of the Ukraine, mainly in the east. Would the Yiddish data suggest that the surname might have been current in Belarus as well?

[14] See Wexler, *Explorations in Judeo-Slavic Linguistics*.

and Czechs lasted for several centuries.[15] For example, while the surname *Nemec*, literally 'German', could be derived from Russian (Beider's choice), it could just as well be from Polish or even Sorbian.[16] Beider derives the name *Moločnyj* (and variants) from 'milk'. Such a derivation is plausible, given the Russian surname *Moločnikov/Mološnikov* (= 'milkman'),[17] but I wonder if the Jewish surname was not a reworking of an earlier from based on Czech Yiddish *meloč(e)* '(junior) member of a burial society', a word rarely attested in Ukrainian Yiddish;[18] the unintelligibility of the name might have prompted convergence with the similar-sounding Russian surname.

It would be interesting to know if all synonymous names have similar geographical contours, e.g. *Nemec ~ Aškenazi* 'German (Jew)' (see the discussion of *Menaker* etc., above). Some remains of Judaeo-Slavonic pronunciations of Hebrew names might be: *Kagan* (vs. Yiddish *Kojgen*); *Xanukov*; *Baxur* (in Belarus and the Ukraine; Beider, p. 115) vs. *Boxur, Buxarec*.

A serious problem confronting a dictionary of this sort is how to distinguish between names borne exclusively by Jews and those borne by both Jews and non-Jews. Beider might have provided this information where known: for example, *Dzjuba* is the name of a well-known Ukrainian non-Jewish dissident (Ivan Dzjuba). Not all of Beider's names are construed by Russians as 'Jewish' names; otherwise, why would Lev Davidovič Bronštejn have assumed the 'Russian' name of *Trotskij* (which Beider seems to regard as 'Jewish': p. 61)? Note also the name *Levin* discussed above. Moreover, some of the derivations seem arbitrary. How does Beider decide when a surname should be derived from a place-name or from a proper noun? For example, he derives *Dzjuba* from a place-name, but why not from the same word meaning 'pock-marked' or 'long-beaked'? *Dzjubannyj* he derives from the Ukrainian 'pock-marked', probably because there is no corresponding place-name available.

There are occasional errors in citation, which is to be expected in a work of such intricacy. For example, Beider derives the name *Ljubošic* from the village of Ljubiščycy in the Slonim district, but the Byelorussian village is located in the Ivačevicy district of the Brėst voblasc'; Beider says that *Veliž* and *Nevel'* are Russian towns (p. xxii) when they are, in fact, Byelorussian; Brėst (sometimes also given in its pre-Soviet form Brest-Litovsk) is located in Belarus, but in a Ukrainian-speaking area. Beider writes that *Šneer* 'is derived from' Latin *senior* (p. 1), but a more precise term would be 'replaces' or 'is a reinterpretation of'

---

[15] See Wexler, 'Yiddish—the Fifteenth Slavic Language: A Study in Partial Language Shift from Judeo-Sorbian to German', *International Journal of the Sociology of Language*, 91 (1991), 1–150, 215–25; *The Ashkenazic Jews*.

[16] On the use of this term among west German Jews in the 14th cent. see Wexler, *Explorations in Judeo-Slavic Linguistics*, 160.

[17] See B. O. Unbegaun, *Russian Surnames* (Oxford, 1972), 113.

[18] For geographical details and other variants see the *Language and Culture Atlas of Ashkenazic Jewry*, questionnaire No. 182 034.

(assuming that *Šneer* is Hebrew for 'two' + 'light'); but why Latin if the earliest Jewish anthroponymic use of the root does not occur until the fifteenth century in the Iberian peninsula? Finally, the glossary of linguistic terms is very imprecise (see in particular the definitions of 'Loez', 'affricates', 'diphthong', 'etyma', 'palatalization'). Why are *Cvajgbejn* and *-bojm* (p. xiv) 'phonetic' variants if the first means 'branch + bone' and the second 'branch + tree'?

With more precise linguistic and geographical notes (which should be added to any future editions, along with any references that exist on individual names, most of which can be found in the very onomastic literature that Beider lists), the value of this dictionary for onomastic and genealogical research would increase considerably. But even in its present form, Beider's *magnum opus* provides much food for thought and constitutes an indispensable starting-point for all future research in east European Jewish names. For this he deserves our heartiest congratulations.

PAUL WEXLER

ALICE L. ECKARDT (ED.)
Burning Memory: Times of Testing and Reckoning

(Holocaust Series; Oxford: Pergamon Press, 1993); pp. xi + 340

For more than twenty years the Annual Scholars' Conference on the German Church Struggle and the Holocaust, meeting in different parts of the United States, has provided one of the main opportunities for discussion and dialogue between Jewish and Christian scholars concerned with the legacy of these events in today's world. More recently, some of the findings of the conferences have been printed, put out by a variety of publishers under some sufficiently unifying title. But since there is now a plenitude of such anthologies, such as those issued by the Simon Wiesenthal Center or the Millersville Annuals, the reader interested in any particular subject, such as Polish–Jewish relations, needs to maintain a careful system of cross-reference; otherwise individually valuable contributions can easily get lost.

This particular collection of articles, edited by Alice Eckardt, is part of the continuing debate about how the events of the Holocaust can be remembered, or more appropriately made relevant to younger generations. Surviving participants, whose numbers are now necessarily diminishing, are joined by professional scholars, mainly historians and theologians, in depicting both the necessity and the difficulty of recalling the tragedies of fifty years ago. Particularly notable are the personal testimonies of three survivors, all young girls at the time. Frieda Aaron from Poland, who was incarcerated in three concentration camps, recalls how the spiritual resilience of the Jewish prisoners was both an enabling and an ennobling factor in challenging the dehumanizing brutality of the ghettos and camps. Renate Bethge, living in middle-class Berlin, was forced to face the fact that her father and three uncles, one of them being Dietrich Bonhoeffer, were murdered as traitors by the Gestapo, and describes how she has subsequently taken up the cause of making Germans come to terms with their guilt. Nechama Tec survived by disguising herself as a Catholic, and was protected by a family of poor Polish labourers, a fact which has led her to write notable books about the compassion and altruism shown to some Jews despite all the dangers.

Such compassion, Ms Tec believes, was an individual, even unpredictable, response, and often came from people classified in Poland as socially marginal. Lawrence Baron, in discussing the Dutch dimension of Jewish rescue, in a manner similar to Mordecai Paldiel's comparison of Dutch and Polish efforts to save Jewish children, points to the Christian motivation of many rescuers, while Susan Zucotti attributes similar responses in Italy to the long history of tolerance and the absence of antisemitic traditions.

But these responses were exceptional. In far too many countries, as is by now well known, lack of sympathy for Hitler's victims led to the failure to rescue even the few who could have escaped. The timidity of the German Christians was matched by the obstructiveness of foreign governments, such as that of Australia, which is here described by Paul Bartrop, or by the indifference of American public opinion, against which Reinhold Niebuhr waged a lone campaign. In this volume neither churches nor governments match up to the heroism displayed by individual rescuers of Jews.

In the aftermath, the necessity of facing up to the facts affected not only Germans. The convenient amnesia which led prominent figures like the former president of Austria, Kurt Waldheim, to 'forget' his part in the Nazi crimes is here succinctly analysed by Richard Rubenstein. Eberhard Bethge outlines his continuing efforts to overcome his fellow Germans' desire to forget the past, as well as his splendid resolve to forge a new relationship between Christians and Jews. Ilona Irwin-Zarecka gives a thoughtful analysis of the difficulties encountered in undertaking the same endeavour in Poland. One of the more original contributions is written by Gabriella Tyrnauer, who describes the mass murder of the gypsies, a group whose fate has long been overlooked by historians. 'The silence on the gypsies', she claims, 'remains intact.' Not entirely, for the new museum in Washington does include them, following a long and passionate debate in the US Holocaust Memorial Council.

Most of these essays are drawn from larger works by their respective authors, and thus serve as appetizers for the more substantial books mentioned in the footnotes. As such they are useful summaries of the present state of the debate, not merely about how the past should be remembered, but also about how the evil forces of antisemitism and intolerance are to be combated today.

JOHN S. CONWAY

RUTA SAKOWSKA
Ludzie z dzielnicy zamkniętej: Z dziejów Żydów w Warszawie w latach okupacji hitlerowskiej (październik 1939 – marzec 1943)

2nd edn., corrected and expanded (Warsaw: PWN, 1993); pp. 274

The first edition of this book, published in 1975, was limited to 2,000 copies, which disappeared with lightning speed. Evidence of its popularity is the none too edifying fact that all copies were stolen both from the library of the University of Warsaw and from the Jewish Historical Institute. For this reason alone the reissue of this weighty volume is a laudable initiative by the publisher.

Ludzie z dzielnicy zamkniętej is the first work in the Polish language which describes life in the Warsaw ghetto based on documents of the underground archives of the ghetto, named, after its founder, the Ringelblum Archives. The author attempted to engage polemically with the most popular stereotypes, as much those prevalent among Poles as those which Jews often hold with reference to their own history. One of these is the conviction of the passivity of the Jewish population in the face of annihilation. This characteristic was supposedly never challenged until the resistance of 'a handful of heroes, fighting for human dignity'. Such statements, suggesting a lack of dignity in those who missed taking an active part in the fight, appear even today, repeated *ad infinitum* in the press coverage of the fiftieth anniversary of the Warsaw Uprising. That is why I heartily recommend this book to all journalists and ask them not to repeat this thoughtless slogan in the future.

Stressing the strength of the civilian opposition in the ghettos, as well as its close connection with the conspiracy movement, the author calls attention to their mutual connection and co-operation, thanks to which social aid in the ghetto was conducted as much out in the open, through the work of institutions connected with the Judenrat, as in conspiracy in the form of voluntary, spontaneous activity by, for example, home committees, as well as through the organized activity of political organizations which arose in the underground but, simultaneously co-operated closely with the Judenrat. Various forms of civilian resistance, analysed in depth by the author, created an informal council in the ghetto; its existence and multifarious activity made possible an easy transformation into armed resistance.

An example of such interconnections is the Warsaw Ghetto Archives, created by Emanuel Ringelblum. The archives were a covert, conspiratorial institution, and yet one which was established under the Judenrat while its creator and some of his workers were employed there. At the same time, Ringelblum belonged to the conspiratorial leadership of the Po'alei Tsion Left. He thus operated both openly and conspiratorially; it was he who prepared the reports on the conditions of life in the ghetto for the Polish underground leaders, as well as reports on the Holocaust for the London government-in-exile. He also took part in clandestine sessions of the Żydowska Organizacja Bojow (ŻOB: Jewish Fighting Organization), where the uprising was prepared.

With these facts in mind, the matter of a moral critique of the activity of the Judenrat in the Warsaw ghetto becomes a complicated business. On the one hand, it was without doubt a creation called into being by Hitlerites with the aim of facilitating the administration of the ghetto, so as to lift from the shoulders of the invader the burden of ruling a community of 300,000 people. Though the servile administrative function of the Judenrat in the process of liquidation was undoubtedly ignominious, this institution was nevertheless part of the self-help effort thanks to which the ghetto did not succumb to a process of 'suicidal' self-destruction from hunger and sickness. The insurgents did, however, have legitimate accusations to level against Czerniakow: his inability to effect an even distribution of the costs of that self-help, the existence of fortunes amassed through speculation adjacent to extreme poverty, and his refusal to consider a mandatory contribution from the wealthiest.

In the latest version of her book Ruta Sakowska places greater emphasis on demonstrating the interconnectedness of the forms of civilian resistance on both sides of the wall. Owing to the discovery of new archival materials, it was possible to undertake a comparative study between the Ringelblum Archives and documentation of the Bureau of Information and Propaganda of the Headquarters of the Home Army; the results of this analysis throw new light on the correlation between the Polish and Jewish civil resistance. It is a pity, however, that the author did not expand on that issue by discussing the problem, including its darker aspects, of Polish–Jewish relations during the occupation. But the omission is understandable, since that subject remains under-researched and poorly documented, and tends to arouse reckless emotions.

Our historiography continues to devote too little attention to the history of Jews as an integral part of Polish history. The popular version, widely circulated and taught in schools, speaks of the Jewish population as if it inhabited the opposite end of the world. Even in history textbooks now in use, the Holocaust is a separate chapter, superficially summarizing the fate of Jews during the occupation and completely detached from the detailed description of the fate of Poles. The history of the ghetto presented by Ruta Sakowska is a fragment of Polish history. The subject, represented in this way, gains a perspective through which the Polish reader may perceive his own history in a new and intriguing manner. In translation, this book would also be a revelation for the non-Polish reader, as I do not know of any other work whose author reflects so deeply on the fate, feelings, and thoughts of ordinary people experiencing the death of their own family and nation. It is in fact odd that hitherto no publisher outside Poland has been interested in translating the work. I would encourage it: it would truly be worthwhile.

ALINA CAŁA

IWONA IRWIN-ZARECKA
Neutralizing Memory: The Jew in Contemporary Poland
(New Brunswick, NJ, and Oxford: Transaction Publishers, 1989); pp. xiii + 207

It is not easy to review a book towards whose creation, at the risk of sounding immodest, I made a contribution, spending many hours in discussion with its author, who in her turn praises my work (though some inaccuracies can be found in her accolades). It may not be possible to maintain an appropriate level of objectivity, even more so because this review will be enthusiastic. I would very much like the book to be translated and published in Poland.

I shall begin with a few corrections of inaccuracies regarding my own work. On p. 162 the author describes my experience in uncovering the bloody history of postwar Polish–Jewish relations. I conducted my first ethnographic research in 1975 (not 1974 as stated), and at that time I heard from the inhabitants of Leżajsk of the murder by a group of partisans (Polish or Ukrainian, of unknown political orientation, led by a certain 'Wołyniak') of about fifteen Jewish repatriates, who had arrived in the town under the protection of the Red Army. I knew then of the Kielce pogrom, and that it was not the only incident of that type after the war. When I continued my research in 1984, my questionnaire included questions about the postwar fate of surviving Jews. The results were shocking: in the area surrounding the town of Przeworsk, in south-eastern Poland, Jews were murdered after the war in nearly every town. This fact, not sufficiently documented by historians, reaches the consciousness of Poles with difficulty, which is not so strange. I felt, however, and still do, that above all, Poles should hear this truth; this is why I wished to publish the results of my research first in Poland and not abroad—not because I feared that it would be misunderstood. The publication of my work in Poland was not, however, easy to achieve at that time: it would not have passed the censors before 1989. That is why I decided to publish an English version through the Center for Research on the History and Culture of Polish Jews at the Hebrew University of Jerusalem; unfortunately, this has yet to appear in print.

Iwona Irwin-Zarecka has covered almost every topic which should be discussed in the area of Polish–Jewish relations after the Second World War. Her work is more of an essay than involved authoritative research, but it is a very in-depth synthesis of the subject. The author, who was raised in Poland, knows Poland's postwar history but also displays a fine understanding of the political systems and social phenomena of the country. This is much more than the historian or sociologist usually has at his or her disposal, so often depending solely on documents and written sources and lacking direct contact with the country being researched.

The book is composed of six chapters which systematically develop the subject. The first, 'Poland: Past in Present Tense', is devoted to a description of the situation in Poland in the years of martial law, as well as the implications of the past in the present. It is a very deep analysis of the political situation then existing, the moods of society, and the national consciousness of Poles, especially of the Polish intelligentsia. When Iwona Irwin-Zarecka came to us, the times were interesting: the brief period of Solidarity's legal functioning changed the social and national consciousness of many Poles; it also altered the way they perceived their own past. The multicultural Second Republic began to be viewed as an idealized example of pluralism, and not as the prison of exploited lower classes we had been taught about in school. For all that it was a naïve image, it nevertheless boosted democratic goals and strengthened the will to create an open, civic society. Martial law was a defeat of that idealization, the undoing of the vision of a free and democratic society. It was then that a process of rebirth began for the traditional Polish right, together with the demons of antisemitism and nationalism; this process was discreetly aided by the Polish primate, Cardinal Glemp. From as early as the mid-1980s, the Church stopped being the oasis of freedom and independence for *all* Poles, believers and atheists, Catholics and Protestants; it was becoming increasingly clear that the Church was following its own, distinct political agenda, not always in agreement with the expectations of the democratic opposition.

The Jewish theme became one of the central elements in these changes of political consciousness. Again, as at several points in the past, Jews, or the so-called 'Jewish problem', became a ball which several groups tossed to and fro in an attempt to prove their point. It is to this phenomenon—the presence (in their very absence) of Jews in current politics, the transformation of consciousness, and political manipulations—that chapters 2–4 are dedicated: 'Poland's Jews—A Memory Void', 'The Breaking of Silence', and 'Memory Work'. It is a very detailed and exhaustive analysis, written interestingly, and sometimes revelatory even for me, who observed all of this 'from the inside'. I disagree with only one of the suggestions advanced here, implying that the Jewish heritage of some of the leading democratic activists had an essential influence on the shaping of an internal, Solidarity opposition; rather, anyone who held a leading place in politics was 'suspected' of a hidden Jewish heritage in the 'whispered' propaganda of virtually the entire emerging right, which materialized in all its strength during the presidential elections of 1991.

Chapters 5 and 6, 'Challenges to Memory Work' and 'Neutralizing Memory', are devoted to a critical elucidation of what brought in the 'discovery' of Jews by contemporary Poles. It is a very subtle analysis of all the positive and negative aspects of this changing phenomenon. The author differentiates a few types of 'memory'. First there was the idealized image of exotic Jews, dancing in their black gabardine and humming 'If I were a rich man'. (By way of paradigmatic aside, it is worth contemplating the reasons for the popularity of the film *Fiddler on the Roof*, which passed all expectations, uniting as it did the tastes of the most refined intellectuals with those of mass-media consumers. The above-mentioned song has entered Polish folklore and is often played at village weddings.)

Secondly, there was 'instrumental memory'—that is, the exploitation of the image of the Jew, as well as the vision of Polish–Jewish relations, for various reasons, beginning with political manipulation and ending with commercial benefits. Third comes the observation that immersion in the history of Polish–Jewish relations provides a chance to alter one's martyrological vision of the nation. This is the most valuable form of 'memory about Jews', though even this type could be treated instrumentally, serving solely to further the resolution of Polish problems. That is indeed how it happens to a great extent. This is a very difficult process: it is not known whether it will succeed in transforming the popular vision of the Poles' own history or in influencing a change in social attitudes and the Polish self-image, making Poles responsible for their own actions and able to foresee the results thereof. It is a process of litigation between Poles and their own tradition so as to create a better, more modern society. It is unclear whether the process will end in success, especially since the government has decreed, as a countervailing image, the propagation of a Polish Catholic model in pre-schools, public schools, and the mass media.

On the other hand, a discussion has begun on the history of Polish–Jewish relations, pre-war antisemitism, attitudes during the occupation, and postwar pogroms. The history of Jews has become a part of Polish events, an indispensable subject for their study, one to be researched in a cool and objective fashion. Not only is the Jewish Historical Institute occupied with this matter: it is also being pursued in at least five other centres in Warsaw, Kraków, Toruń, Poznań, and Wrocław. Many new academic works have appeared, and in the last two years over sixty master's theses have been written on the subject. Courses in the Yiddish and Hebrew languages are very popular among students, and Jewish or Israeli literature constantly produces best sellers among the reading public.

There is a further side to this phenomenon: the rebirth of the Jewish community in Poland. Apart from the group described by Iwona Irwin-Zarecka, there is also a Związek Studentów-Żydów (Union of Jewish Students). Young Jews study Judaism and attend synagogue; they have their own rabbi. They argue with their parents, who wish to see only a religious group in the Jewish community; and also with their grandparents, who do not understand at all and prophesy evil—'You will see what this democracy brings.'

It brings different things. In the last four years almost all of the extant Jewish cemeteries have been desecrated, the Warsaw cemetery three times. A rabbi and a 70-year-old worker of the Jewish Congregation were assaulted. Windows in the Jewish Historical Institute have been broken twice; in the synagogue it has happened so often that they have installed bullet-proof glass. Then there are the anti-Jewish graffiti on the walls of many cities. In Poland at least six antisemitic parties function legally, in spite of the fact that propagating antisemitism is prohibited. Until now it has been possible to bring only a single prosecution, against the leader of the Neo-Fascist Party; that trial lasted over three years and the sentence was derisory. Although the tension of antisemitism is, as in all of Europe, gradually decreasing, in Poland and Slovakia, two Catholic countries, there is relatively more than elsewhere.

ALINA CAŁA

STANISŁAW MEDUCKI AND ZENON WRONA (EDS.)
Antyżydowskie wydarzenia kieleckie, 4 lipca 1946 Dokumenty i materiały

(Kielce: Kieleckie Towarzystwo Naukowe, 1992); pp. 399

This book constitutes the first of three planned volumes of documents regarding the Kielce pogrom. According to the editors, the others will include documents of state and Church authorities, political parties, opinions, commentaries, and reports (vol. ii) and material from planned academic conferences devoted to the Kielce pogrom (vol. iii). The most important documents, the editors state, are those from the three trials which are included in the first volume. These materials come from the State Archive in Kielce and the Central Archive of the Ministry of Internal Affairs in Warsaw. The documents are presented in the chronological order of the trials, and are taken from the proceedings of July, November, and December 1946. In addition to these, the first volume includes protocols from the interrogations of witnesses and suspects, as well as indictments and the protocols of cases and verdicts. Documents from the July trial have been supplemented by both the medical and the court examinations of pogrom victims, and by the protocol regarding the execution of nine Poles sentenced in July 1946. In his introduction Stanisław Meducki presents a history of the Jews in Kielce from the nineteenth century to the 1946 pogrom. In addition, the work includes a calendar of the tragedy prepared by Zenon Wrona, covering the period July to

December 1946. Also included are maps of Kielce city centre, the neighbourhood of Planty Street, and other Kielce districts, as well as photographs.

There is much to disagree with in the brief history of Kielce Jewry in the introduction, especially those sections devoted to the period after 1945. Meducki's statement that 'Jews did not have problems regaining their property if it had not been plundered by Germans' conflicts with documents of the Ministerstwo Administracji Publicznej (MAP: Ministry of Public Administration) regarding this region. In the month of June alone, according to MAP, thirteen Jews were murdered in the county of Kielce, ten of whom were involved in disputes over Jewish property.

Meducki's characterization of postwar antisemitism is also questionable. The (correct) statement that the wider context of anti-Jewish behaviour was a multilayered phenomenon is supported by a single example of preferential hiring, which according to the editors corroborates their opinion concerning the privileged position of Jews. The work and publications of researchers who have written about this subject—Krystyna Kersten, Israel Gutman, Abel Kainer—have been ignored; the editors have based their analysis solely on the literary outline of Sandauer and the memoirs of Edward Gierek. One cannot agree that the rumour of ritual murder was accepted only by people 'of low intellectual level'. Documents such as those from the British embassy, reports from the meetings of Bishop Wyszyński, and many other reports and memoirs show that these rumours were believed by some Church dignitaries and by representatives of state and party authorities. The introduction also provides a simplified and often inaccurate picture of the history of the Jews in Kielce. It is important to remember that the issue under examination very often carries with it emotions and personal prejudice; that is why its presentation requires the utmost fairness.

In contrast to the introduction, the chronology provides a thorough presentation of the most important events in connection with the Kielce pogrom. Prepared by Zenon Wrona, the chronology not only describes the incidents leading up to the pogrom but also reconstructs its course, the behaviour of the administrative, party and Church authorities, and the actions of the police, security forces, and army. This section also details the aftermath of the pogrom, giving a full picture of all relevant events. It is necessary, however, to point out that the contents of the proclamation concerning the pogrom issued jointly by all the political parties of 4 July 1946, which is referred to in the chronology, were changed without the agreement of the signatories, and published in this altered version. The defence lawyers acting for those accused of participating in the pogrom in the first trial were asked to compose their request for a pardon before the verdict was announced and not, as Wrona states, immediately after the verdict. Further, Stanisław Radkiewicz did not attend the funeral of the pogrom victims on 8 July 1946.

The documents in this book provide much detailed information. The numerous reports, interrogation protocols, and depositions well reflect the atmosphere of the events in Kielce. They show both the collective behaviour of the crowd and that of individuals. However, the huge body of facts presented to the reader contains many ambiguities, with often contradictory information. The presentation of the documents leads to a chaotic picture of the events of 4 July 1946. For example, descriptions of the beginning of the pogrom accompany each successive trial.

The documents would have been more effective if they had been grouped together by category. Some of the depositions have very little to do with the accused, and serve only as a tool in the reconstruction of events. The reports in this selection should, in my opinion, be used only in this context. The arrangement of the documents is such that descriptions of the events and arguments for indictment or for a particular verdict are repeated.

The editors have not included any documents regarding the trials of 25–6 September, 10 October, and 3 December 1946, during which policemen and soldiers were prosecuted. Other unjustifiable omissions, in my view, include the absence of documents from November 1946, Szymkiewicz's case, the trials of Marian Antonkiewicz and Franciszek Furman, and the protocols of the interrogations of Kuźnicki and Gwiazdowicz from the trial of March 1947, which brought out new elements in the Kielce events. These are important materials because they show the haphazard presentation and untrustworthiness of the prosecution's witnesses. The book also lacks information about the amnesty for the majority of those accused in November 1946 and an additional trial of three of those accused at that time (Stepnik, Zagórski and Sedek, prosecuted in March 1947).

The documents which were selected could have been used to present information about the events of 4 July 1946 in a more thorough manner. The reconstruction of the Kielce pogrom could have been clearly based on all existing documents. The reader would then have been thoroughly acquainted with the issues surrounding the events in Kielce, including the fact that some questions remain unanswered.

BOŻENA SZAYNOK

Bibliography of Polish–Jewish Studies 1993

The bibliography is arranged according to the framework listed on p. 306.
Readers should note related headings.
All titles are given in their original languages.

REFERENCE WORKS 307

FESTSCHRIFTEN AND COLLECTED STUDIES 307

LITERATURE, LINGUISTICS, AND THE ARTS 307
Belles-lettres 307
(*See also* HISTORY: 1939–1945: *Belles-lettres*)
Literary Studies and Criticism 308
Linguistics 308
Visual Arts 308
Painting and Sculpture 309
Film and Photography 309
Ceremonial Art 309

HISTORY 309
Documents and Sources 309
Biographies 309
Historiography 310
General Works 310
To 1648 310
1648–1795 310
1795–1918 311
1918–1939 311
1939–1945: The Second World War and the Holocaust 312
General Works 312
Reference Works 312
Special Studies 312
Photographic Records 313
Memoirs 313
Belles-lettres, *Visual Arts, and Literary Studies* 315
1945–present 316
Regional and Community Monographs; Memorial Books 316
Emigration 317
Cultural History 317
Polish–Jewish Relations 317

SOCIAL SCIENCES 317
Political Studies: Parties and Movements 317
Women's Studies 317

JUDAISM AND OTHER RELIGIONS 317
Religious Thought 317
Kabbala 318
Hasidism 318
Relations between Judaism and Christianity 318

REFERENCE WORKS

GALAS, MICHAŁ, and PILARCZYK, KRZYSZTOF (eds.), *Judaika wydane w Polsce: Druki zwarte i niesamoistne, materiały do bibliografii 1990* (Studia Polono-Judaica: Series Bibliographica, 2; Kraków: Uniwersytet Jagielloński, Zakład Historii i Kultury Żydów w Polsce, 1993); pp. 232. ISBN 8323307458.

GATES-COON, REBECCA, *Eastern European Bibliography* (Metuchen, NJ: Scarecrow Press, 1993); pp. ix + 175. ISBN 0810827751.

MAGOCSI, PAUL ROBERT, *Historical Atlas of East Central Europe*, Cartographic design by Geoffrey J. Mathews (Seattle and London: University of Washington Press; in Canada University of Toronto Press, 1993); pp. xiv + 218. ISBN 0802006078.

MUSZYŃSKA, KATARZYNA (ed.), *Bibliographies of Polish Judaica: International Symposium, Cracow, 5th–7th July, 1988, Proceedings* [Studia Polono-Judaica: Series Librorum Congressus, 1; Kraków: Jagiellonian University, Research Center of Jewish History and Culture in Poland, 1993); pp. 231. ISBN 8323306222.

VINOGRAD, YESHAYAHU, *Thesaurus of the Hebrew Book: Listing of Books Printed in Hebrew Letters since the Beginning of Hebrew Printing circa 1469 through 1863*, pt. 2. *Places of Print* (Jerusalem: The Institute for Computerized Bibliography, 1993); pp. 702.

WUNDER, MEIR, *Elef Margoliot* [*Biographies and Genealogical Charts of More than a Thousand Ancestors of Our Family, a Lineage of Jewish Leaders from Ancient Times until our Father, Rabbi Israel Arie Margulies*] (Jerusalem: Hamakhon lehanstaḥat yahadut Galitsia, 1993); pp. c. 800.

FESTSCHRIFTEN AND COLLECTED STUDIES

BARTAL, YISRAEL, MENDELSOHN, EZRA, and TURNIANSKY, CHAVA (eds.), *Studies in Jewish Culture in Honour of Chone Shmeruk* (Jerusalem: Zalman Shazar Center for Jewish History, 1993); pp. 118 (English) + 428 (Hebrew). ISBN 9652270830.

POLONSKY, ANTONY (ed.), *From Shtetl to Socialism: Studies from Polin* (London and Washington: The Littman Library of Jewish Civilization for the Institute for Polish–Jewish Studies, Oxford, 1993); pp. xxxiii + 581. ISBN 1874774145.

—— BASISTA JAKUB, and LINK-LENCZOWSKI, ANDRZEJ (eds.), *The Jews in Old Poland 1000–1795* (London and New York: I. B. Tauris & Co. Ltd. in association with the Institute for Polish–Jewish Studies, Oxford, 1993); pp. 361. ISBN 1850433429.

LITERATURE, LINGUISTICS, AND THE ARTS

Belles-lettres (see also HISTORY: 1939–1945: *Belles-lettres*)

BAUM, ANNA, *A Chance Encounter and Other Stories of Polish Jewry*, illustrated by Leah Taylor (Toronto: Childe Thursday, c.1993); pp. 159. ISBN 0920459331.

GRYNBERG, HENRYK, *Dziedzictwo* (London: Aneks, 1993); pp. 90. ISBN 0906601983.

LÖW, RYSZARD, *Pod znakiem starych foliantów: Cztery szkice o sprawach żydowskich i książkowych* (Kraków: Towarzystwo Autorów i Wydawców Prac Naukowych, Universitas, 1993); pp. 83. ISBN 8370521983.

Singer, Isaac Bashevis, *Certyfikat*, trans. Elżbieta Petrajtis-O'Neill (Gdańsk: Marabut, 1993); pp. 222. ISBN 8385883029.
Szereszewska, H., *Krzyż i Mezuza* (Warsaw: Czyt., 1993); pp. 554. ISBN 8307022142.
Weissbrem, Israel, *The World of Israel Weissbrem: Between the Times and the Lottery and the Inheritance*, trans. Alan Crown (Boulder, Colo.: Westview Press, 1993); pp. 171. ISBN 0813316316.

Literary Studies and Criticism

Aberbach, David, *Realism, Caricature and Bias. The Fiction of Mendele Mocher Sefarim* (London: The Littman Library of Jewish Civilization, 1993); pp. 131. ISBN 1874774080.
Baumgarten, Jean, *Introduction à la littérature yiddish ancienne* (Paris: Éditions du Cerf, 1993); pp. 530. ISBN 07620829.
Kac, Daniel, *Na Krawędzi Życia: Mojsze Kulbak, żydowski poeta, prozaik, dramaturg, 1896–1937* (Warsaw, 1993); pp. 129. ISBN 83000041.
Kantor, Tadeusz, *A Journey through Other Spaces: Essays and Manifestos, 1944–1990* (Berkeley, Los Angeles, and London: University of California Press, 1993); pp. xxi + 430. ISBN 0520084233.
Shmeruk, C., and Turniansky, C., *Di yidishe literatur in 19tn yahrhundert: Zamlung fun yidisher literatur farshung un kritik in Ratn-Farband* (Jerusalem: Magnes Press, 1993); pp. 595. ISBN 9652238287.
Singer, Icchok Baszewis, *Felietony, Eseje, Wywiady*, trans. Tomasz Kuberczyk, introd. Chone Shmeruk (Warsaw: Sagittarius, 1993); pp. 214. ISBN 8386078006.

Linguistics

Frakes, Jerold C. (ed.), *Max Weinreichs Geschichte der jiddischen Sprachforschung* (Alpharetta GA: Scholars Press, 1993); pp. xxv + 326. ISBN 1555408168.
Harshav, Benjamin, *Language in Time of Revolution* (Berkeley, Los Angeles, and London: University of California Press, 1993), pp. xii + 234. ISBN 0520079582.
Moskovich, W., Shvarzband, S., and Alekseev, A. (eds.), *Jews and Slavs*, vol. 1 (Jerusalem and St Petersburg, 1993); pp. 358. ISBN 5020281794.
Simon, Bettina, *Jiddische Sprachgeschichte: Versuch einer neuen Grundlegung* (Frankfurt a.M.: Jüdischer Verlag, 1993); pp. 231. ISBN 3633540776.
Wexler, Paul, *The Ashkenazic Jews: A Slavo-Turkic People in Search of a Jewish Identity* (Columbus, Oh.: Slavica Publishers, 1993); pp. x + 306. ISBN 0893572411.

Visual Arts

Masterpieces of Jewish Art: A Pictorial Series of Treasures in the Commonwealth of Independent States, vol. i. *Bronze*, ed. A. Kantsedikas (Moscow: Image, n.d.), pp. 320, ISBN 586044012X; vol. ii. *Artists from Vitebsk: Yehuda Pen and his Pupils*, ed. G. Kasovsky (Moscow: Image, n.d.), 151 ill. = pp. 75, ISBN 5860440359; vol. iii. *Silver*, ed. A. Kantsedikas, Y. Volkovinskaya, and T. Romanovskaya (Moscow: Image, n.d.), pp. 383, ISBN 5860440561; vol. iv. *Jewish Tombstones in Ukraine and Moldova*, ed. D. Goberman (Moscow: Image, 1993), pp. 54 + 263 photos, ISBN 5860440197; vol. v. *Wooden Synagogues*, ed. Z. Yargina (Moscow: Image, n.d.), pp. 368, ISBN 5860440219.

MOORE, CLARE, *The Visual Dimension: Aspects of Jewish Art* (Boulder, Colo.: Westview Press, 1993); pp. 184, 8 colour plates, 136 b/w photos. ISBN 081331259.

Painting and Sculpture

LIPSZYC, WISNA, *Album Żydowski* (Warsaw: PWN, 1993); 120 plates. ISBN 8301111070.

ROSTWOROWSKI, MAREK, *Żydzi w Polsce: Obraz i słowo* (Warsaw: Wydawnictwo Interpress, 1993); pp. 347, 460 ill. ISBN 8322326300.

Film and Photography

KRAJEWSKA, MONIKA, *A Tribe of Stones: Jewish Cemeteries in Poland* (Warsaw: PWN, 1993); pp. 244. ISBN 830111231X.

Ceremonial Art

MARTYN, EWA (ed.), *Judaica ze zbiorów Muzeum Narodowego w Warszawie* (Warsaw: Muzeum Narodowe, 1993); pp. 311. ISBN 8371000081.

SEIPEL, WILFRIED (ed.), *Thora und Krone: Kultgeräte der jüdischen Diaspora in der Ukraine* (Vienna: Kunsthistorisches Museum, 1993); pp. 259. ISBN 3900325308.

HISTORY

Documents and Sources

BEAUPLAN, G. Le VASSEUR, SIEUR DE, *A Description of Ukraine*, introd., trans., and notes by Andrew B. Pernal and Dennis F. Essar (Cambridge, Mass.: Harvard Ukrainian Research Center, 1993); pp. cxiii + 242. ISBN 091645844X.

BEN-YEHUDA, ELIEZER, *A Dream Come True*, trans. T. Muraoka, ed. George Mandel (Boulder, Colo.: Westview Press, 1993); pp. 131. ISBN 0813316723.

DAVID, ABRAHAM (ed.), *A Hebrew Chronicle from Prague, c. 1615*, trans. Leon J. Weinberger with Dena Ordan (Tuscaloosa: University of Alabama Press, 1993); pp. x + 106. ISBN 0817305963.

FIJAŁKOWSKI, PAWEŁ *Dzieje Żydów w Polsce: Wybór Tekstów Źródłowych XI–XVIII wieku* (Warsaw: Żydowski Instytut Historyczny, 1993); pp. 124. ISBN 8385888004.

GOLDSHTEIN, ROMAN IL'ICH, *Materialy k istorii evreev Ukrainy* (Dnipropetrovsk: Dnipro, 1993); pp. 95. ISBN 5770737093.

LAZUTKA, STANISLOVAS, and GUDAVICHIUS, EDWARDAS, *Privilege to Jews Granted by Vytautas the Great in 1388* (Moscow and Jerusalem: Jewish University in Moscow, 1993); pp. 119 (English, Russian). ISBN 9654210045.

ŻEBROWSKI, RAFAŁ *Dzieje Żydów w Polsce: Wybór Tekstów Źródłowych 1918–1939* (Warsaw: Żydowski Instytut Historyczny, 1993); pp. 142. ISBN 8385888012.

Biographies

WUNDER, MEIR, *Elef Margoliot [Biographies and Genealogical Charts of More than a Thousand Ancestors of Our Family, a Lineage of Jewish Leaders from Ancient Times until our Father, Rabbi Israel Arie Margulies]* (Jerusalem: Hamakhon lehanstahat yahadut galitsia, 1993); pp. c. 800.

ZAWADZKI, W. H., *A Man of Honour: Adam Czartoryski as a Statesman of Russia and Poland 1795–1831* (Oxford: Clarendon Press, 1993), pp. xvii + 374. ISBN 0198203039.

Historiography

MICHAEL, REUVEN, *Haketivah hahistorit hayehudit: MehaRenesans ad ha'et hahadashah* (Jerusalem: Mossad Bialik, 1993); pp. 554. ISBN 965342601X.

MUSZYŃSKA, KATARZYNA (ed.), *Bibliographies of Polish Judaica: International Symposium, Cracow, 5th–7th July, 1988, Proceedings* (Studia Polono-Judaica: Series Librorum Congressus, 1; Kraków: Jagiellonian University, Research Center of Jewish History and Culture in Poland, 1993); pp. 231. ISBN 8323306222.

General Works

BAUMGARTEN, JEAN, ERTEL, RACHEL, NIBORSKI, ITZHOK, and WIEVIORKA, ANNETTE (eds.), *Mille ans de cultures ashkénazes* (Paris: Liana Levi, 1993); pp. 659. ISBN 2867461081.

BIBÓ, ISTVÁN, *Kwestia żydowska* (Warsaw: Niezależna Oficyna Wydawnicza, 1993); pp. 160. ISBN 8370540597. [First published as *Zsidókerdes Magyarországon 1944 után*.]

ERB, RAINER (ed.), *Die Legende vom Ritualmord: Zur Geschichte der Blutbeschuldigung gegen Juden* (Berlin: Metropol, 1993); pp. 296. ISBN 392689315X.

Slaviane i ikh sosedi: Evreiskoe naselenie tsentral'noi, vostochnoi i iugovostochnoi Evropy: srednie veka—nachalo novogo vremeni: sbornik tezisov XII Chtenii pamiati V. D. Koroliuka (Moscow: RAN, 1993); pp. 109. ISBN 5201007589.

La Société juive à travers l'histoire, ed. Shmuel Trigano (Paris: Librairie Arthème Fayard, 1992–3), vol. i. *La Fabrique du peuple*, pp. 779, ISBN 221302155; vol. ii. *Les Liens de L'Alliance*, pp. 632, ISBN 2213028087; vol. iii. *Le Passage d'Israel*, pp. 594, ISBN 2213030531; vol. iv. *Le Peuple-monde*, pp. 791, ISBN 2213030616.

ŻEBROWSKI, RAFAŁ, *Dzieje Żydów w Polsce: Kalendarium* (Warsaw: Żydowski Instytut Historyczny, 1993); pp. 181. ISBN 8385888020.

To 1648

CHYNCZEWSKA-HENNEL, TERESA, *Rzeczpospolita XVII wieku w oczach cudzoziemców* (Warsaw: Ossolineum, 1993); pp. 253. ISBN 830404I073.

KŁOCZOWSKI, JERZY, *La Pologne dans l'église médiévale* (Aldershot and Brookfield, Vt.: Variorum Publishing, 1993); pp. 336. ISBN 0860783596.

MICHALSKI, SERGIUSZ, *The Reformation and the Visual Arts: The Protestant Image Question in Western and Eastern Europe* (New York: Routledge, Chapman & Hall, 1993); pp. 232. ISBN 0415065127.

SEDLAR, JEAN W., *East Central Europe in the Middle Ages, 1000–1500* (Seattle: University of Washington Press, 1993); pp. 552. ISBN 0295972904.

1648–1795

FROST, ROBERT, *After the Deluge: Poland and Lithuania and the Second Northern War, 1655–1660* (Cambridge: Cambridge University Press, 1993); pp. xxiv + 211. ISBN 0521420083.

KATZ, JACOB, *Tradition and Crisis: Jewish Society at the End of the Middle Ages*, 2nd edn., trans., bibliographical appendix, and afterword by Bernard Dov Cooperman (New York: NYU Press, 1993); pp. 416. ISBN 0814746373.

1795–1918

ETKES, EMANUEL, *Rabbi Israel Salanter and the Mussar Movement* (Philadelphia: Jewish Publication Society of America, 1993); pp. 400. ISBN 0827604386.

GUTERMAN, ALEXANDER, *Mihitbolelut lele'umiyut: Perakim betoledot beit hakeneset hagadol: Hasinagogah beVarsha, 1806–1943* (Jerusalem: Karmel, 1993); pp. 174. ISBN 9654070464.

HARSHAV, BENJAMIN, *Language in Time of Revolution* (Berkeley, Los Angeles, and London: University of California Press, 1993); pp. xii + 234. ISBN 0520079582.

KOCKA, JURGEN, and MITCHELL, ALLAN (eds.), *Bourgeois Society in 19th Century Europe* (Oxford and Providence: Berg, 1993); pp. xi + 468. ISBN 0854966765.

LOWENSTEIN, STEVEN M., *The Berlin Jewish Community: Enlightenment, Family and Crisis 1770–1830* (New York and Oxford: Oxford University Press, 1993); pp. 288. ISBN 0195083261.

MILLER, PHILIP E., *Karaite Separatism in Nineteenth-century Russia* (Cincinnati: Hebrew Union College Press, 1993); pp. xix + 252. ISBN 878204156.

OPALSKI, MAGDALENA, and BARTAL, ISRAEL, *Poles and Jews: A Failed Brotherhood* (Hanover NH, and London: New England University Press, 1993); pp. xi + 191. ISBN 0874516013.

STRAUSS, HERBERT ARTHUR (ed.), *Hostages of Modernization. Studies on Modern Antisemitism, 1870–1933/9*, vol. iii/2. *Austria, Hungary, Poland, Russia* (Berlin and New York: Walter de Gruyter, 1993); pp. 749. ISBN 3110137151.

1918–1939

BLANKE, RICHARD, *Orphans of Versailles: The German Minority in Western Poland, 1918–1939* (Lexington, Ky.: University of Kentucky Press, 1993); pp. xii + 316. ISBN 0813118034.

ELICHAI, YOSEF, *Tenu'at haMizrahi bePolin haKongresa'it, 1916–1927* (Tel Aviv: Moreshet, 1993); pp. 237.

MENDELSOHN, EZRA, *On Modern Jewish Politics* (New York and Oxford: Oxford University Press, 1993); pp. 192. ISBN 0195038649.

OPPENHEIM, ISRAEL, *Tenu'at Hehaluts bePolin, 1929–1939* (Kiryat Sedeh Boker: Hamerkaz Lemoreshet Ben-Gurion and Hotsa'at Hasefarim shel Universitat Ben-Gurion baNegev, 1993); pp. 673. ISBN 9653426109.

PAWLINA-MEDUCKA, MARTA, *Kultura Żydów Województwa Kieleckiego (1918–1939)* (Kielce: Kieleckie Towarzystwo Naukowe, 1993); pp. 221. ISBN 839008046x.

WEINBAUM, LAURENCE, *A Marriage of Convenience: The New Zionist Organization and the Polish Government* (New York and Boulder, Colo.: East European Monographs, 1993); pp. xiii + 295. ISBN 0880332662.

ŻEBROWSKI, RAFAŁ *Dzieje Żydów w Polsce; Wybór tekstów źródłowych 1918–1939* (Warsaw: Żydowski Instytut Historyczny, 1993); pp. 142. ISBN 8385888012.

—— and BORZYMIŃSKA, Z., *Po-Lin: Kultura Żydów Polskich w XX wieku* (Warsaw: Amarant, 1993); pp. 368. ISBN 83000032.

1939–1945: The Second World War and the Holocaust

General Works

ECKARDT, ALICE L. (ed.), *Burning Memory: Times of Testing and Reckoning* (Holocaust Series, Oxford; New York: Pergamon Press, 1993); pp. xi + 340. ISBN 0080419313.

FASCHING, DARRELL J., *The Ethical Challenges of Auschwitz and Hiroshima: Apocalypse or Utopia?* (Albany: SUNY Press, 1993); pp. xvi + 366. ISBN 0791413764.

FRIEDLANDER, SAUL, *Memory, History and the Extermination of the Jews of Europe* (Bloomington; Ind.: Indiana University Press, 1993); pp. xiv + 142. ISBN 0253324831.

Reference Works

EDELHEIT, ABRAHAM J., and EDELHEIT, HERSCHEL, *Bibliography on Holocaust Literature: Supplement*, vol. ii (Boulder, Colo.: Westview Press, 1993); pp. 564. ISBN 0813314127.

—— ——*History of the Holocaust: A Handbook and Dictionary* (Boulder, Colo.: Westview Press, 1993); pp. 550. ISBN 0813314119.

Special Studies

BARTOSZEWSKI, WŁADYSŁAW, and EDELMAN, MAREK, *Żydzi Warszawy 1939–1943* (Lublin: Towarzystwo Naukowe KUL, 1993); pp. 201. ISBN 8385291458. [The essays first appeared in W. Bartoszewski, *Los Żydów Warszawy 1939–1943* (London, 1983), and M. Edelman, *Getto walczy* (London, 1983).]

BLADY-SZWAJGER, ADINA, *Die Erinnerung verläßt mich nie: Das Kinderkrankenhaus im Warschauer Ghetto und der jüdische Widerstand* (Munich: List Verlag, 1993); pp. 216. ISBN 347177178.

DOBROSZYCKI, LUCJAN, and GUROCK, JEFFREY S., *The Holocaust in the Soviet Union: Studies and Sources on the Destruction of the Jews in the Nazi-occupied Territories of the USSR, 1941–1945* (Armonk, NY: M. E. Sharpe, 1993); pp. xii + 260. ISBN 1563241730.

ENGEL, DAVID, *Facing a Holocaust: The Polish Government-in-exile and the Jews, 1943–1945* (Chapel Hill: University of North Carolina Press, 1993); pp. x + 317. ISBN 0807820695.

FRIEDMAN, TUVYA, *Es gibt keinen jüdischen Wohnbezirk in Warschau mehr: 50 Jahre nach dem Aufstand des Warschauer Ghettos, Dokumentensammlung* (Haifa: Institute of Documentation in Israel for the Investigation of Nazi War Crimes, 1993); pp. 119 (also Hebrew text).

GORDON, HARRY, *In the Shadow of Death: The Holocaust in Lithuania* (Lexington, Ky.: The University Press of Kentucky, 1993); pp. xv + 174. ISBN 0813117674.

GRYNBERG, MICHAŁ (ed.), *Księga sprawiedliwych* (Warsaw: PWN, 1993); pp. 766. ISBN 8301111860.

KATZMANN, FRITZ, and FRIEDMAN, TUVYA (eds.), *Bericht des SS- und Polizeiführers über die Vernichtung der Juden Galiziens: Dokumentensammlung* (Haifa: Institute of Documentation in Israel for the Investigation of Nazi War Crimes, 1993).

NAJBERG, LEON, *Ostatni powstańcy getta* (Warsaw: ŻIH, 1993), pp. 160. ISBN 83000103.

PELED (MARGOLIN), YAEL, *Krakuv hayehudit, 1939–1943: Amidah, mahteret ma'avak* (Tel Aviv: Beit Lohamei Hageta'ot, 1993); pp. 360. ISBN 9653940236.

POHL, DIETER, *Von der 'Judenpolitik' zum Judenmord: Der Distrikt Lublin des Generalgouvernements, 1939–1944* (Frankfurt a.M.: Peter Lang, 1993); pp. 208. ISBN 3631457162.

PRZEDPELSKI, JAN, *Żydzi płoccy: Dzieje i martyrologia 1939–1945* (Płock: Fraza, 1993); pp. 211. ISBN 8390060914.

RITTNER, CAROL, and ROTH, JOHN K., *Different Voices: Women and the Holocaust* (New York: Paragon House, 1993); pp. xiv + 435. ISBN 1557785031.

ROSENBAUM, ALAN S., *Prosecuting Nazi War Criminals* (Boulder, Colo.: Westview Press, 1993); pp. 144. ISBN 0813383579.

SAKOWSKA, RUTA, *Ludzie z dzielnicy zamkniętej: Z dziejów Żydów w Warszawie w latach okupacji hitlerowskiej (październik 1939–marzec 1943)*, 2nd edn., corrected and expanded (Warsaw: PWN, 1993), pp. 274. ISBN 8301111146.

STEIN, ANDRÉ, *Hidden Children: Forgotten Survivors of the Holocaust* (New York and Toronto: Viking Press, 1993); pp. xi + 273. ISBN 067084518 3.

TEC, NECHAMA, *Defiance: The Bielski Partisans. The Story of the Largest Armed Rescue of Jews by Jews during World War II* (Oxford and New York: Oxford University Press, 1993); pp. xiii + 276. ISBN 0195075951.

WEITZMAN, MARK, LANDES, DANIEL, and KLEIN, ADAIRE (eds.), *Dignity and Defiance: The Confrontation of Life and Death in the Warsaw Ghetto* (Los Angeles: Simon Wiesenthal Center, 1993); pp. iv + 117. ISBN 0943058155.

WIEHN, ERHARD ROY, *Ghetto Warschau: Aufstand und Vernichtung 1943* (Konstanz: Hartung-Gorre, 1993); pp. 302. ISBN 3891916264.

YOUNG, JAMES E., *The Texture of Memory: Holocaust Memorials and Meaning in Europe, Israel and America* (New Haven: Yale University Press, 1993); pp. 384. ISBN 030005835.

Photographic Records

Auschwitz: A History in Photographs, compiled and edited by Teresa Świebocka; English edn. prepared by Jonathan Webber and Connie Wilsack (Bloomington and Indianapolis: Indiana University Press, Warsaw: Książka i Wiedza 1993); pp. 292, 20 colour 290 b/w photographs. ISBN 0253355818 and (KiW) 8305126439.

GEORG, WILLI, *In the Warsaw Ghetto, Summer 1941*, with passages from Warsaw Ghetto diaries compiled with an afterword by Rafael F. Scharf (New York: Aperture, 1993); pp. 112. ISBN 0893815268.

Memoirs

BODEK, HELENA, *Jak tropione zwierzęta* (Kraków: Wydawn. Literackie, 1993); pp. 154. ISBN 8308025056.

CARGAS, HARRY JAMES (ed.), *Voices from the Holocaust* (Lexington, Ky.: University Press of Kentucky, 1993); pp. xix + 164. ISBN 0813118026.

DIMANT, ITA, *A Diary of the Holocaust* (Brooklyn: I. Diamant, 1993); pp. 50.

EIBESHITZ, JOSHUA, and EIBESHITZ, ANNA, *Women in the Holocaust: A Collection of Testimonies* (Brooklyn: Remember, 1993); pp. xvii + 247. ISBN 0932351441.

GEFEN, ABBA, *Defying the Holocaust: A Diplomat's Report*, ed. Nathan Kravetz (San Bernardino, Calif.: Borgo Press, 1993); pp. 248.

GERSTENFELD-MALTIEL, JACOB, *My Private War: One Man's Struggle to Survive the Soviets and the Nazis* (London: Vallentine Mitchell, 1993); pp. xxii + 313. ISBN 0853032602.

GRYNBERG, HENRYK, *Pamiętnik Marii Koper* (Kraków: Znak, 1993); pp. 103. ISBN 8370063225.

GRYNBERG, MICHAŁ (ed.), *Pamiętniki z getta warszawskiego: Fragmenty i regesty*, 2nd edn., corrected and expanded (Warsaw: PWN, 1993); pp. 464. ISBN 8301110554.

HABBERMAN, NATALIA, *Ne'urai she'avdu*, trans. Eldad Zaltsman (Tel Aviv: Sa'ar, 1993); pp. 224.

HALTER, MAREK, *La Mémoire inquiète: Il y a cinquante ans le ghetto de Varsovie* (Paris: R. Laffont, 1993); pp. 79. ISBN 2221076672.

HERTSSHTARK, ZUSHA, *Dam vedem'a begeto lodz* (Jerusalem: Mossad Harav Kuk, 1993); pp. 288.

IWASZKIEWICZ, JOANNA, *Wtedy kwitły forsycje* (Warsaw: bis, 1993); pp. 256. ISBN 8385144188.

KAJTOCHOWA, ANNA, *Tamten brzeg* (Kraków: Oficyna Wydawnicza Krakowskiego, Klubu Artystyczno-Literackiego, 1993); pp. 225. ISBN 8385816054.

KARCZYŃSKA, ALICJA, *Obok piekła: Wspomnienia z okupacji niemieckiej w Warszawie* (Gdańsk: Marpress, 1993); pp. 132. ISBN 8385349162.

KAZIMIRSKI, ANN, *Witness to Horror* (Montreal: Devonshire Press, 1993); pp. ii + 152. ISBN 0969734204.

KENIGSBERG, HAYYIM SHLOMOH, *Sefer in fayyer un in vasser: Mayn iberleben un dukh makhen in di tsvayte velts krig* (Brooklyn: H. Kenigsberg, 1993); pp. 358.

KLUKOWSKI, ZYGMUNT, *Diary from the Years of Occupation, 1939-1944* (Urbana, Ill.: University of Illinois Press, 1993); pp. xx + 371. ISBN 0252019601.

KSHEPITSKY, TIRTSA, *On a Tightrope*, ed. and trans. Walter and Gudette Shapira (Petach Tikva: Lilach, 1993); pp. 128.

LAUFER, YOSEF, with TAL, HAYYIM, *Kehayat hasadeh: Lisrod bisedot Ukrainah* (Tel Aviv: Misrad Ha-Bitahon, 1993); pp. 128. ISBN 965050690X.

LEVENSTEIN, MEIR, *Du sollst sterben und nicht leben!* (Münster: LIT, 1993); pp. xvi + 133. ISBN 3894736631.

LEWI-KUROWSKA, MARIA, *Pamięc pozostanie* (Warsaw: Myśl, 1993); pp. 126. ISBN 8385233563.

LIEBLICH, RUTHKA, *Ruthka: A Diary of War*, ed. and trans. Joshua and Anna Eibeshitz (Brooklyn: Remember, 1993); pp. xxix + 129. ISBN 0932351425.

MALTZ, MOSHE, *Years of Horror—Glimpse of Hope: The Diary of a Family in Hiding*, trans. Gertrude Hirschler (New York: Shengold, 1993); pp. 173. ISBN 0884001687.

PERECHODNIK, CALEL, *Czy ja jestem morderca?*, ed. Paweł Shapiro (Warsaw: Karta, 1993); pp. 272. ISBN 8390067617.

RAN-CHARNYI, ZHANNA, *Neveroiatnaia pravda* (Vilna: Svyturys, 1993); pp. 208.

REISS, HENRYK, *Z deszczu pod rynnę: Wspomnienia polskiego Żyda* (Warsaw: Polonia, 1993); pp. 263. ISBN 8370211666.

RINGELBLUM, EMMANUEL, *Ketavim miyemei milḥamah*, ed. I. Gutman, Y. Kermish, and Y. Shaham (Jerusalem: Yad Vashem, Beit Lohamei Hageta'ot, 1993). vol. i, pp. 476, ISBN 9653080229; vol. ii, pp. 391, ISBN 9653080210.

ROSEN, SARA, *My Lost World: A Survivor's Tale* (London: Vallentine Mitchell, 1993); pp. vii + 299. ISBN 0853032602.

ROSENBERG, BLANCA, *To Tell at Last: Survival under False Identity, 1941–1945* (Urbana, Ill.: University of Illinois Press, 1993); pp. xv + 178. ISBN 0252019989.

ROTEM, SIMCHA, *'Kazik': Wspomnienia bojowca ŻOB* (Warsaw: PWN, 1993); pp. 162. ISBN 8301111984.

SCHWARTZ, SHIFRAH, *Zikhronot* (Tel Aviv: S. Schwartz, 1993); pp. 160. ISBN 9654180464.

SCHWARZ, RENÉE FODOR, *Symphony of the Heart* (New York: Shengold, 1993); pp. 107. ISBN 0884001695.

ŚLIWOWSKA, WIKTORIA (ed.), *Dzieci Holocaustu Mówią*, with afterword by Jerzy Ficowski (Warsaw: Nakładem Stowarzyszenia Dzieci Holocaustu w Polsce, 1993); pp. 291.

SOŁOMIAN-LOC, FANNY, *Getto i gwiazdy* (Warsaw: Czytelnik, 1993); pp. 220. ISBN 8307020379.

TOLL, NELLY S., *Behind the Secret Window: A Memoir of a Hidden Childhood during World War Two* (New York: Dial Books, 1993); pp. xiii + 161. ISBN 0803713622.

TSIPORI-DYER, IRENA, *Dapim shenitslu me'esh*, trans. Ami Shaffir (Tel Aviv: Hakibbutz hame'uhad, Beit lohamei hageta'ot, 1993); pp. 96. ISBN 9653940163.

TUKEL, SEYMOUR, *The Unquenched Brand*, as told to Jane D. Turner (n.p., 1993); pp. 133.

WERDYGER, DUVID, *Songs of Hope*, as told to Avraham Finkel (New York and Jerusalem: CIS, 1993); pp. 330. ISBN 1560622261.

WERMUTH, HENRY, *Breathe Deeply, My Son* (London: Vallentine and Mitchell, 1993); pp. 232. ISBN 0853032467.

WIDAWSKI, CELINA, *The Sun Will Shine Tomorrow* (Hawthorn, Australia: Essien, 1993); pp. viii + 120. ISBN 0949873446.

ZUCKERMAN, YITZHAK, *A Surplus of Memory: Chronicle of the Warsaw Ghetto Uprising*, trans. and ed. Barbara Harshav (Berkeley: University of California Press, 1993); pp. xviii + 702. ISBN 0520078411.

Belles-lettres, *Visual Arts, and Literary Studies*

AMISHAI-MAISELS, ZIVA (ed.), *Depiction and Interpretation: The Influence of the Holocaust on the Visual Arts* (New York and Oxford: Pergamon Press, 1993); pp. xxxiii + 567, 560 illustrations, 100 in colour. ISBN 0080406564.

GLATSTEIN, JACOB, *I Keep Recalling: The Holocaust Poems of Jacob Glatstein*, trans. Barnett Zumoff (Hoboken, NJ: Ktav Publishing House, 1993); pp. xi + 289. ISBN 0881254290.

KRALL, HANNA, *Taniec na cudzym weselu* (Warsaw: Polska Oficyna Wydawnicza BGW, 1993); pp. 173. ISBN 8370664733.

TEICHMAN, MILTON, and LEDER, SHARON (eds.), *Truth and Lamentation: Stories and Poems on the Holocaust* (Urbana, Ill.: University of Illinois Press, 1993); pp. 526. ISBN 0252020286.

1945–Present

ADELSON, JOZEF, et al., *Najnowsze dzieje Żydów w Polsce w zarysie (do 1950 roku)*, ed. Jerzy Tomaszewski (Warsaw: PWN, 1993); pp. 498. ISBN 8301110708.

BERNHARD, MICHAEL H., *The Origins of Democratization in Poland: Workers, Intellectuals and Oppositional Politics 1976–1980* (New York: Columbia University Press, 1993); pp. xv + 298. ISBN 023108093X.

ENGELKING, BARBARA, *Na łące popiołów ocaleni z Holocaustu* (Warsaw: Cykłady, 1993); pp. 223. ISBN 8390059223.

FOWKES, BEN, *The Rise and Fall of Communism in Eastern Europe* (New York: St Martin's Press, 1993); pp. 234. ISBN 0312041494.

GOLDKORN, YOSEF, *Aliyato venefilato shel ha'iton hayehudi harishon bePolin: 'Das Naye Lebn'* (Tel Aviv: Tel Aviv University Press, 1993); pp. ix + 47.

HOFFMAN, EVA, *Exit into History: A Journey through the New Eastern Europe* (New York: Viking Press, 1993); pp. 410. ISBN 0670836494.

MICHNIK, ADAM, *The Church and the Left*, ed. and trans. David Ost (Chicago: University of Chicago Press, 1993); pp. xvii + 301. ISBN 0226524248.

ROTHSCHILD, JOSEPH, *Return to Diversity: A Political History of East Central Europe since World War II*, 2nd edn. (Oxford and New York: Oxford University Press, 1993); pp. 320. ISBN 0195073819.

SACK, JOHN, *An Eye for an Eye* (New York: Basic Books, 1993); pp. xii + 252. ISBN 0465042147.

Special Topics

Regional and Community Monographs; Memorial Books

CZAJECKA, BOGUSŁAWA, *Archiwum Związku żydowskich stowarzyszeń humanitarnych B'nei B'rith w Krakowie (1892–1938): Zarys dziejów związku, historia zespołu i inwentarz* (Kraków: Jagiellonian University, Research Center of Jewish History and Culture in Poland, 1993); pp. 149. ISBN 8322307075.

FELDENKRAIZ-GRINBAL, EVA, DEROR, LEVI, and RAV, YOSEF (eds.), *Et ezkerah: Sefer kehilat Tsuzmir [Sandomierz]* (Tel Aviv: Irgun yotsei Tsuzmir beYisrael and Moreshet bet edut al shem Mordekhai Anielewicz, 1993); pp. 586. In Hebrew, Yiddish, and English.

KARPINOWITZ, AVRAHAM, *Vilne, mayn Vilne* (Tel Aviv: Y. L. Peretz, 1993); pp. iii + 165.

MARKUS-KARBLANIK, EDA, *Kelme: Ets karot* (Tel Aviv, 1993); pp. vii + 215.

MATLOVSKI, SHIMON (ed.), *Sefer yizkor lekehilat Lokatsch* (Jerusalem: S. Matlovski, 1993); pp. 98. In Hebrew, Yiddish, and English.

MINCZELES, HENRI, *Vilna–Wilno–Vilnius: La Jérusalem de Lituanie* (Paris: La Decouverte, 1993); pp. 485. ISBN 2707121827.

MÓRAWSKI, KAROL, *Kartki z dziejów Żydów Warszawskich* (Warsaw: KIW, 1993); pp. 180. ISBN 8305126358.

PAWLINA-MEDUCKA, MARTA, *Kultura Żydów Województwa Kieleckiego (1918–1939)* (Kielce: Kieleckie Towarzystwo Naukowe, 1993); pp. 221. ISBN 839008046x.

Present in Our Midst: Polish Jews in the Political, Economic, Social, Scientific and Cultural Life of Warsaw (Warsaw: Historical Museum of Warsaw, 1993); pp. 127.

SZCZEPAŃSKI, JANUSZ, *Dzieje Społeczności żydowskiej powiatów Pułtusk i Maków Mazowiecki* (Warsaw: Pułtuskie Towarzystwo Społeczno-Kulturalne, 1993); pp. 192. ISBN 8385345027.

URBAŃSKI, KRZYSZTOF, *Kieleccy Żydzi* (Kraków: Pracownia Konserwacji Zabytków w Kielcach, 1993); pp. 279.

Emigration

BETTELHEIM, PETER, and LEY, MICHAEL (eds.), *Ist jetzt hier die 'wahre Heimat'?: Ostjüdische Einwanderung nach Wien* (Vienna: Picus, 1993); pp. 155. ISBN 3854522460.

Cultural History

ETKES, EMANUEL, *Rabbi Israel Salanter and the Mussar Movement* (Philadelphia: Jewish Publication Society of America, 1993); pp. 400. ISBN 0827604386.

FEINER, SHMUEL (ed.), *MeHaskalah lohemet leHaskalah meshameret: Mivhar mekitvei Ra"Shl Fuenn* (Jerusalem: Merkaz Dinur, 1993); pp. 208.

HARSHAV, BENJAMIN, *Language in Time of Revolution* (Berkeley, Los Angeles, and London: University of California Press, 1993); pp. xii + 234. ISBN 0520079582.

Polish–Jewish Relations

ALFASSI, YITSCHAK, *Zakhor nizkor: Polin haharavah umasa'ot benei no'ar bePolin* (Petach Tikvah: Yad Peninah veShimon Yehuda le'ahavat hatorah ha'am veha'arets, 1993); pp. 248.

SOCIAL SCIENCES

Political Studies: Parties and Movements

AVNER, YOSSI (ed.), *Amalim umahapkhanim: Tenu'at hapo'alim hayehudit* (Tel Aviv: Beit hatefutsot, 1993); pp. 135. ISBN 9654250012.

WEINBAUM, LAURENCE, *A Marriage of Convenience: The New Zionist Organization and the Polish Government* (New York and Boulder, Colo.: East European Monographs, 1993); pp. xiii + 295. ISBN 0880332662.

Women's Studies

SHEPHERD, NAOMI, *A Price below Rubies: Jewish Women as Rebels and Radicals* (Cambridge, Mass.: Harvard University Press, 1993); pp. xii + 336. ISBN 067470410X.

JUDAISM AND OTHER RELIGIONS

SIEMIEŃSKI, M., *Księga Świąt i Obyczajów Żydowskich* (Warsaw: Interpress, 1993); pp. 89. ISBN 8322326378.

Religious Thought

ELBAUM, YA'AKOV, *Teshuvat halev vekabalat yisurim: Iyunim beshitot hateshuvah shel hakhmei Ashkenaz uPolin* (Jerusalem: Magnes Press, 1993); pp. ix + 262. ISBN 9652238120.

SHEINBERGER, AVRAHAM (ed.), *Sefer kav hayashar hashalem*, by Zevi Hirsch Koidonover (Jerusalem, 1993).

Kabbala

ALFASSI, YITSCHAK, *Me'orot me'olam hakabalah vehahasidut* (Jerusalem?: Daat Yosef, 1993?); pp. 574.

AVIVI, YOSEF, *Kabalat Hagra* (Sidrat sefarim al haGR"A, ed. Y. Wynograd, 1; vol. 1; Jerusalem: Makhon kerem ha-gr"a, 1993); pp. 152.

HILLEL, MOSHE, *Ba'alei shem: Hitpashtut torat hakabalah be'eiropah* (Jerusalem: Makhon benei yisaskhar, 1993); pp. iv + 384.

NIGAL, GEDALYAH, *Ba'al Shem lema'asar olam: Goralo hatragi shel harav Hirsh Fränkel* (Ramat Gan, Israel: Bar Ilan University, 1993); pp. 22 (Hebrew) + 45 (German). ISBN 9654070553.

Hasidism

LEVIN, SHALOM D., *Sifriyat Lubavitch: Sekirat toledoteihah al pi mikhtavim, te'udot vezikhronot* (Brooklyn: Kehot Publication Society, 1993); pp. 11 (English) + 226 (Hebrew). ISBN 0826653375.

SCHATZ UFFENHEIMER, RIVKA, *Hasidism as Mysticism: Quietistic Elements in Eighteenth Century Hasidic Thought*, trans. Jonathan Chipman (Princeton, NJ: Princeton University Press and Hebrew University, Jerusalem: Magnes Press, 1993); pp. 398. ISBN 0691032238.

STERN, YOSEF, *The Three Festivals: Ideas and Insights of the Sfas Emes* (Brooklyn: Mesorah Publications, 1993); pp. 462. ISBN 0899064299.

Relations between Judaism and Christianity

MUSSNER, FRANZ, *Traktat o Żydach*, trans. Joanna Kruczyńska, ed. Waldemar Chrostowski (Warsaw: Akademia Teologii Katolickiej, 1993); pp. 429. ISBN 8370720137.

WAHLE, HEDWIG, *Wspólne Dziedzictwo: Judaizm i chrześcijaństwo w kontekście dziejów zbawienia*, trans. and ed. Zofia Kowalska (Tarnów: Biblos, 1993); pp. 239. ISBN 8385380124.

Notes on Contributors

ISRAEL BARTAL is Professor of Modern Jewish History at the Hebrew University and Director of the Center for Research on the History and Culture of Polish Jews. He is the editor of the second, revised edition of the minute-book of the Council of Four Lands (Jerusalem, 1990) and co-author (with Magdalena Opalski) of *Poles and Jews: A Failed Brotherhood* (Hanover, NH, and London, 1993). He is the author of several monographs and articles on Eastern European Jewish history and on the history of the pre-Zionist Jewish community in Palestine. He is a member of the Editorial Committee of *Polin*.

DANIEL BLATMAN is a lecturer at the Institute for Contemporary Jewry of the Hebrew University of Jerusalem and is a research fellow at the International Institute of Holocaust Studies at Yad Vashem. He has written widely on the topic of the Jews in Poland during the Holocaust. His book about the activities of the Jewish Labour Bund during the Holocaust is about to be published by Yad Vashem.

ALINA CAŁA is an assistant at the Jewish Historical Institute in Warsaw. She is the author of *Wizerunek Żyda w polskiej kulturze ludowej* [The image of the Jew in Polish peasant culture] (Warsaw, 1987) and *Asymilacja Żydów w Królestwie Polskim (1864–1897): Postawy, Konflikty, Stereotypy*. [The assimilation of the Jews in the Kingdom of Poland (1864–1897): Attitudes, conflicts, stereotypes] (Warsaw, 1989). At present, she is one of the organizers of a project to assess the strength and nature of antisemitism in Poland today.

STEPHEN D. CORRSIN is professor and chief of Research and Access Services in the Brooklyn College Library, City University of New York. His Ph.D. (History) is from the University of Michigan, Ann Arbor. He is the author of *Warsaw before the First World War: Poles and Jews in the Third City of the Russian Empire* (Boulder, Colo., 1989) and numerous articles in the history of eastern Europe, as well as librarianship and bibliography.

DAVID ENGEL is Professor of Modern Jewish History at New York University and co-editor of the journal *Gal-Ed: On the History of Polish Jewry*. He is the author of *In the Shadow of Auschwitz: The Polish Government-in-exile and the Jews, 1939–1942* (Chapel Hill, 1987) and *Facing a Holocaust: The Polish Government-in-exile and the Jews, 1943–1945* (Chapel Hill, 1993). At present he is working on a study of the Jewish community in Poland after the Second World War.

SYLVIA BARACK FISHMAN is Assistant Professor of Contemporary Jewish Life in the Near Eastern and Judaic Studies Department and Senior Research

Associate in the Cohen Center for Modern Jewish Studies, both at Brandeis University. She has written *A Breath of Life: Feminism in the American Jewish Community* and *Follow my Footsteps: Changing Images of Women in American Jewish Fiction*, and was co-editor of *Changing Jewish Life: Service Delivery and Planning in the 1990s*. She is the author of numerous articles on American Jewish literature and sociology.

ROSS KESSEL was professor and head of the medical humanities programme at the University of Maryland, Baltimore. He now lives in England.

SHMUEL KRAKOWSKI was born in Poland and educated at the Hebrew University. He is senior adviser (formerly director) of the Yad Vashem Archives. He is the author of *The War of the Doomed: Jewish Armed Resistance in Poland 1942–1944* (New York, 1984) and, with Yisrael Gutman, *Unequal Victims: Poles and Jews during World War Two* (New York, 1986).

DOV LEVIN is a survivor of the Kovno ghetto and also fought as a partisan during the Second World War. He emigrated to Palestine in 1945 and is currently a researcher both at the Institute of Contemporary Jewry at the Hebrew University, where he is director of the Institute's Oral History Division, and at Yad Vashem. He has published many books and articles on Baltic Jewry during and after the Second World War, including *Fighting Back: Lithuanian Jewish Armed Resistance to the Nazis*, (New York, 1985), which was awarded the Yitzhak Sadeh Prize, and *Baltic Jewry under the Soviets* (Jerusalem, 1994).

PAWEŁ MACHCEWICZ studied history at the University of Warsaw and is an assistant professor in the Institute of Political Studies in Warsaw. He is the author of *Polski rok 1956* [The Polish year 1956] (Warsaw, 1993), an analysis of public opinion, collective behaviour, and mass movements based on newly available archival sources.

STANISŁAW MEDUCKI was born in Kielce and studied history at the Polish Academy of Sciences and the Adam Mickiewicz University in Poznań. He has written widely on economic history and the politics of the Second World War and postwar period. He is director of the Department of Economic History at the Świętokrzyska Polytechnic.

ERICA NADELHAFT received an MA in Holocaust Studies from the Institute of Contemporary Jewry at the Hebrew University. She is currently completing a Ph.D. in the Department of Near Eastern and Judaic Studies at Brandeis University. The title of her dissertation is 'The Jewish Community of Piotrków Trybunalski, 1939–1945'.

RICHARD PIPES is Baird Professor of History at Harvard University. His most recent books are *The Russian Revolution* (New York, 1990) and *Russia under the*

Bolshevik Regime (New York, 1994). He is currently working on a historical survey of the relationship between property and freedom.

DINA PORAT is senior lecturer in the Department of Jewish History and head of the Project for the Study of Antisemitism at Tel Aviv University. She is the author of *The Blue and the Yellow Stars of David: The Zionist Leadership in Palestine and the Holocaust, 1939–1945* (Cambridge, Mass., 1991), and editor of the original Hebrew version (Tel Aviv, 1988) of Avraham Tory's *Surviving the Holocaust: The Kovno Ghetto Diary* (Cambridge, Mass., 1991), edited with an introduction by Martin Gilbert, historical and textual notes by Dina Porat. She is a member of the Scientific Committee and of the Board of the Yad Vashem International Center for Holocaust Research.

TERESA PREKEROWA graduated as a historian at Warsaw University and worked for many years in various publishing-houses. She is the author of *Konspiracyjna Rada Pomocy Żydom w Warszawie 1942–1945* [The Underground Council for Aid to Jews in Warsaw 1942–1945] (Warsaw, 1982), *Zarys dziejów Żydów w Polsce w latach 1939–1945* [An outline of the history of the Jews in Poland 1939–1945] (Warsaw, 1992), and many articles on Polish Jewish themes.

MICHAŁ ŚLIWA is a professor of political science at the Pedagogical Academy in Kraków. His main interest is the history of political theory in the nineteenth and twentieth centuries. Among his books are *Teoria polityczna Mieczysława Niedziałkowskiego* [The Political Theory of Mieczysław Niedziałkowski] (Kraków, 1980), *Feliks Perl: Biografia* [Feliks Perl: A Biography] (Warsaw, 1989), and *Polska teoria polityczna w pierwszej połowie dwudziestego wieku* [Polish political theory in the first half of the twentieth century] (Kraków, 1993).

JANUSZ SUJECKI is completing a doctorate at the Historical Institute of the University of Warsaw on the PPS-Proletariat.

BARBARA WACHOWSKA is Professor of History at the Historical Institute of Łódź. She is director of the section dealing with recent Polish history. Her scholarly interests lie in the history of Poland between 1918 and 1939, in particular the history of the workers' movement in Łódź and its region.

Notes on Translators

JACEK KOLĄTAJ, freelance translator, Kraków, translated Janusz Sujecki, 'The Relation of the Polish Socialist Party: Proletariat to the Bund and the Jewish Question, 1900–1906'.

ERICA NADELHAFT, doctoral student, Brandeis University, translated Daniel Blatman, 'The Bund in Poland, 1935–1939', and Alina Cała, 'The Second Competition of Scholarly Works on Polish Jewish Themes'.

DENA ORDAN, freelance translator, Jerusalem, translated Dov Levin, 'The Jews of Vilna under Soviet Rule, 19 September–28 October 1939'.

ANNAMARIA ORLA-BUKOWSKA, doctoral student, Jagiellonian University, Kraków, translated Alina Cała, 'Jewish Socialists in the Kingdom of Poland', and Michał Śliwa, 'The Jewish Problem in Polish Socialist Thought'.

THERESA PROUT, freelance translator, Somerset, England, translated Shmuel Krakowski, 'The Polish Underground and the Extermination of the Jews', and Teresa Prekerowa, 'The Jewish Underground and the Polish Underground'.

JOSHUA ZIMMERMAN, doctoral student, Brandeis University, translated Barbara Wachowska, 'Łódź Remained Red: Elections to the City Council of 27 September 1936'.

GWIDO ZLATKES, doctoral student, Brandeis University, translated Stanisław Meducki, 'The Jewish Pogrom in Kielce on 4 June 1946', and Paweł Machcewicz, 'Antisemitism in Poland in 1956'.

Glossary

Agudas Yisroel (Ashkenazi pronunciation; *Agudat Yisrael* in modern Hebrew pronunciation) The principal political party of religiously Orthodox Jews in Poland. Founded in 1916, under the influence of German Orthodoxy, it had the backing of the Gerer Rebbe, leader of the largest Hasidic group in the **Congress Kingdom**. It was very hostile to Jewish radicalism and fought the Jewish Socialist parties, especially the **Bund**. It supported a daily Yiddish paper, *Der Tog*, and a network of private religious schools.

Bund (Yiddish: 'Algemayner yidisher arbayter bund') General Jewish Workers' Alliance. A Jewish Socialist party, founded in 1897. It joined the Russian Social Democratic Labour Party, but seceded from it when its programme of national autonomy was not accepted. In independent Poland it adopted a leftist anti-Communist posture and from the 1930s co-operated increasingly closely with the Polish Socialist Party (PPS).

Chadecja (Polish: Partia Chrześcijańsko-Demokratyczna). The Christian Democratic Party. In interwar Poland its main area of support was Upper Silesia. Its adherents were referred to as 'Chadecy', sing. 'Chadek'.

chaluts See *ḥaluts*

Commonwealth (Polish: *Rzeczpospolita*) The term *Rzeczpospolita* is derived from the Latin *res publica*. It is sometimes translated as 'commonwealth' and sometimes as 'republic', often in the form 'Noblemen's Republic' (*Rzeczpospolita szlachecka*). After the Union of Lublin in 1569 it was used officially in the form *Rzeczpospolita Obójga Narodów* (Commonwealth of the Two Nations) to designate the new form of state which had arisen. In historical literature, this term is often rendered as 'The Polish–Lithuanian Commonwealth'.

Congress Kingdom (otherwise Kingdom of Poland) A constitutional kingdom created at the Congress of Vienna (1814–15), with the Tsar of Russia as hereditary monarch. After 1831 it declined to an administrative unit of the Russian Empire in all but name. After 1864 it lost the remaining vestiges of the autonomy it had been granted at Vienna and was now officially referred to as *Privislansky kray* (Vistula territory).

Council of Four Lands The principal body through which the Jews governed themselves autonomously in the Polish–Lithuanian Commonwealth (*see* **Commonwealth**). The actual number of lands represented in the council increased in the course of the life of the body (from the late sixteenth century to 1764). Made up of delegates from the local kahals and regions, the Council generally met twice a year and was responsible for negotiating with the Royal Treasury the level of Jewish taxation and for levying taxes on the Jewish communities. In addition, it passed laws and statutes on internal, educational, and economic matters and other general concerns of Jewish life. A separate but similar body existed in the Grand Duchy of Lithuania.

curia In the elections to the third and fourth **Dumas** elections were indirect, and different sections of the electorate elected representatives to a curia which was responsible for selecting the representative to the parliament.

Duma The parliament with restricted but still significant powers established in the Tsarist Empire after the revolution of 1905.

Endecja Popular name for the Polish National Democratic Party, a right-wing party which had its origins in the 1890s. Its principal ideologue was Roman Dmowski, who advocated a Polish version of the integral nationalism which became popular in Europe at the turn of the nineteenth century. The Endecja advanced the slogan 'Poland for the Poles' and called for the exclusion of the Jews from Polish political and economic life. Its adherents were called 'Endeks'. See **Obóz Wielkiej Polskiej**.

Folkism A Jewish political ideology which favoured a non-territioral form of Jewish autonomy in the diaspora, in terms of which the Jews would control their own educational and social institutions, which would be financed through special taxes levied on the Jewish community. Though not hostile to Hebrew, the Folkist party argued that Yiddish was the national language of Polish Jews. The Folkists' main ideologue was the Nestor of East European Jewish historians, Shimon Dubnow. Their main spokesman in Poland was Noah Prilucki.

gedud (Hebrew) Literally, a small group formed specifically for the purpose of defending an objective, often a military one. Commonly used to refer to the basic unit of a Zionist youth movement.

General Gouvernement An administrative-territorial unit created in Poland during the Nazi occupation from some of the territory seized by Germany after the Polish defeat. The GG was established on 26 October 1939 and first comprised four districts: Kraków, Lublin, Warsaw, and Radom. Its capital was the town of Kraków and its administration was headed by Hans Frank. After the Nazi invasion of the Soviet Union, an additional province, Galicia, made up of parts of the pre-war Polish provinces of Lwów, Stanisławów, and Tarnopol, was added to the GG. On the territory of the GG the Germans pursued, from early 1942, a policy of mass murder of the Jewish population and reduced the Christian Poles to slaves with no rights, who were to provide a reservoir of labour for the Third Reich.

government-in-exile After the German defeat of Poland in 1939, a government was established made up of the less compromised elements of the **Sanacja** regime and representatives of the democratic opposition and headed by General Sikorski. This government made its headquarters in Angers and after the fall of France it moved to London. It attempted to represent the Polish cause, but was abandoned by the Western powers at the Yalta Conference in February 1945, when it was decided that the pro-Communist government established in Poland by Stalin should be recognized on condition that it broaden its ranks by the addition of democratic politicians from Poland and the West and hold free elections. In practice, neither condition was fulfilled in any meaningful way.

gubernia A province of the Tsarist Empire.

haggadah, pl. *haggadot* (Hebrew) The liturgy for the Passover Seder.

Glossary

ḥaluts, pl. **ḥalutsim** (Hebrew: lit. 'pioneer') A person who joined a kibbutz in Palestine. (Sometimes also used to refer to a member of a youth movement who intended to do so.)

halakhah (Hebrew, lit. 'the way') A word used to describe the rules of Jewish religious observance.

Hashomer Hatsa'ir (Hebrew, lit. 'The Young Guard') A pioneering Zionist youth movement.

Hasidism A Jewish revivalist movement with charismatic leadership which grew up in the eighteenth-century Polish–Lithuanian Commonwealth. The Hasidim (from *hasid* (Hebrew) 'a righteous man') sought direct communion with God by various means, including singing and dancing. Originally opposed by the rabbinic establishment in Poland, who described themselves as *misnagdim* (lit. 'opposers', i.e. of Hasidism), the movement soon became particularly strong in central Poland (the **Congress Kingdom**), southern Poland (**Małopolska** or Galicia), and Ukraine. See *tsadik*.

Haskalah (Hebrew: lit. 'education', but used in the sense of 'Enlightenment') A rationalistic movement which emerged in the Jewish world under the impact of the European Enlightenment in the second half of the eighteenth century. It first became important in Germany and soon spread to the rest of European Jewry, first in the west and then, more slowly, in the east. The *maskilim* (proponents of Haskalah) sought to reduce Jewish separateness from the nations among whom they lived and to increase their knowledge of the secular world. In eastern Europe it opposed **Hasidism** and what it regarded as the relics of Jewish fanaticism and superstition.

Hechaluts (Hebrew: lit. 'The Pioneer') The body which co-ordinated the activities of the various Labour Zionist youth movements.

Histadrut The labour-dominated trade-union confederation in the **Yishuv**.

Hitachdut (Hebrew: lit. 'brotherhood') A non-Marxist labour Zionist party.

January Insurrection The ill-fated Polish insurrection against the Tsarist monarchy which began in January 1863. After its defeat, the Russian government embarked on a determined effort to Russify not only the **Kresy** but also the **Congress Kingdom**.

kahal, **kehillah** (Yiddish: *kehile*) (Hebrew: lit. 'congregation') The lowest level of the Jewish autonomous institutions in the Polish–Lithuanian Commonwealth. Above the local *kehillot* were regional bodies, and above these a central body, the **Va'ad Arba Aratsot (Council of Four Lands)** for the Kingdom of Poland (Korona) and the Va'ad Lita (Council of Lithuania) for the Grand Duchy of Lithuania. The **Va'ad Arba Aratsot** was abolished by the Polish authorities in 1764, but autonomous institutions continued to operate legally until 1844 and in practice for many years after this date in those parts of the Polish–Lithuanian Commonwealth directly annexed by the Tsarist empire, and longer in the **Congress Kingdom** and the remaining parts of Poland. In interwar Poland the legal status of the *kehillot* was regulated by statute in October 1927 and March 1930. This legislation gave them control over many aspects of Jewish communal life with both religious and social functions. All adherents of the 'Mosaic faith' were required to belong to a *kehillah*, and one could not withdraw except through baptism.

kevutsah (Hebrew: lit. 'group')   Often a small group within a Zionist youth movement; also a communal agricultural settlement in Palestine.

Kingdom of Poland   *See* **Congress Kingdom**.

Kresy   The eastern provinces of Poland between the two world wars. Today parts of Lithuania, Belarus, and Ukraine.

Małopolska (Polish: lit. 'lesser Poland')   Southern Poland, the area around Kraków. Also referred to under the Habsburgs as Galicia.

maskil, pl. *maskilim* (Hebrew)   Followers of the **Haskalah**.

mitnaged (*misnagid*) pl. *mitnagdim* (Hebrew: lit. 'opposer')   The rabbinic opponents of **Hasidism**.

Mizrachi   The party of religious Zionists.

Narodnaya Volya   *See* **Narodnik**.

Narodnik, pl. **Narodniki** (Russian: populist, supporter of the people—*narod*)   One of the young radical members of the Russian intelligentsia who, in the 1870s, attempted, for the most part unsuccessfully, to carry their doctrines for the political and social transformation of the Tsarist system to the villages in the hope of winning the support of the recently emancipated peasantry. When this failed, a part of the group established the organization Zemlya i Volya [Land and Liberty], which attempted to achieve its aims by revolutionary means. One section of this organization took the name **Narodnaya Volya** [the People's Will] and made it their goal to assassinate the Tsar Alexander II, which they achieved in March 1881. However, their conviction that this would lead to the collapse of the Tsarist regime proved incorrect and a new period of repression followed. Smaller offshoots of **Narodnaya Volya** continued to function in the 1880s. Because of his involvement in one of their plots against the life of the Tsar Alexander III, Lenin's elder brother was executed.

Obóz Wielkiej Polskiej (Polish: 'The Camp for a Greater Poland')   Extreme right-wing and pro-Fascist organization founded in December 1926 by Roman Dmowski because of his dissatisfaction at the weak reaction of the National Democratic Party (*see* **Endecja**) to the coup of May 1926 which brought Józef Piłsudski back to power.

pelugah (Hebrew: lit. 'group')   Often, a group within a Zionist youth movement.

Po'alei Tsion (Hebrew: lit. 'Workers of Zion')   A Labour Zionist organization. It split into a right and left wing. The right wing was much more interested in settlement in Erets Israel (Palestine), the left wing in establishing links with left-wing non-Zionist parties.

Proletariat (Polish)   The name given to a number of Socialist groupings in the **Congress Kingdom**. The First Proletariat, sometimes known as the 'Great Proletariat', was founded by Ludwik Waryński in November 1882. It called for the revolutionary overthrow of capitalism and for co-operation between the Polish and Russian workers' movements. It was discovered by the police in 1885 and four of its members were executed for terrorist activities. Waryński was imprisoned in the Shlüsselberg fortress outside St Petersburg, where he died. The Second, or 'Little', Proletariat was created to be the successor of the now defunct organization, and was

Glossary

headed by Marian Kasprzak and Ludwik Kulczycki. It organized a number of strikes and was active until 1893. The Third Proletariat, or Polska Partia Socjalistyczna—'Proletariat' [Polish Socialist Party—'Proletariat'], whose activities are described by Janusz Sujecki in this volume, was founded in 1900 as a result of a secession of a number of the members of the Polska Partia Socjalistyczna [PPS: Polish Socialist Party]. It was active until 1905.

Sanacja (from Latin *sanatio*: 'healing, restoration')   The popular name taken by the regime established by Józef Piłsudski after the coup of May 1926. It referred to Piłsudki's aim of restoring health to the political, social, and moral life of Poland.

Sejm   In pre-partition Poland, the central parliamentary institution of the **Commonwealth**, composed of a **Senate** and a Chamber of Deputies. Between 1918 and 1939, the lower house of the Polish parliament. From 1947, the sole legislative organ in the Polish People's Republic. After the end of Communist rule in 1989 a Senate was re-established alongside the Sejm.

Sejm of the Four Lands   *See* **Council of Four Lands**.

Senate   In pre-partition Poland, the upper house of the **Sejm**. After 1918, the upper house of the Polish parliament. Abolished by a referendum in 1947, it was re-established after the fall of Communism.

tsadik (Hebrew: lit. 'the just one' or 'a pious man')   A leader of a Hasidic sect (or community). Hasidim often credited their *tsadikim* or *rebbes* with miraculous powers and saw them as mediators between God and man.

Va'ad Arba Aratsot   Hebrew: **Council of Four Lands**.

voivode (Polish: *wojewoda*)   In pre-partition Poland, a provincial dignitary, who between the sixteenth and eighteenth centuries conducted the local dietine, led the *pospolite ruszenie*, the *levée-en-masse* of the *szlachta* in times of danger to the **Commonwealth**. In Poland after 1918, the appointed administrator of a **voivodship**.

voivodship (Polish: *województwo*)   In both pre-partition and interwar Poland, a province governed by a **voivode**. After 1944 voivodships were re-established, but not voivodes.

Yishuv (Hebrew: lit. 'settlement')   The Jewish community in Mandatory Palestine.

Index

A

Aaron, Frieda 295–6
Adam Mickiewicz University, and study of Jewish history 236
Adamczyk, Maria 234
Adiv (Adelson), Gershon 109–10, 111–12, 115, 120, 122–3, 127–9, 131, 132 n. 114, 136 n. 131
Agroid organization 114 n. 19
Agudas Yisroel 70 n. 38
   and the Bund 62, 71
   electoral successes 78, 79
   and municipal elections 1936 99
Agudat Hasotsialistim Haivriyim BeLondon (Jewish Socialist Union in London) 4–5
Aharonowicz, Josef 118
Akaemov, N. 52–4
Akiva youth movement 153, 154, 196–7
   and Erets Israel 203–4, 206, 213
   and resistance through education 222
Akselrod, Luba 9
Alekseev, Sergei 49 n. 4
Algajer, Karol 86
Algemayner Yidisher Arbeter Bund in Rusland un Poyln (General Jewish Labour Union in Russia and Poland), *see* Bund
aliyah, *see* emigration
Allerhand, Jakob 273
Alter, Viktor 29 n. 37, 68, 214 n. 6
   and emigration 66–7
   and Jewish proletariat 69–70
   and Joint Distribution Committee 76
   and municipal elections 1936 63, 99
   and Second International 59–60
Altman, Tosia 205–6
Anders, Władysław 161, 165, 248–54
Anielewicz, Mordecai 135 n. 126, 151, 222
antisemitism:
   and 1912 Duma elections 48, 54
   in 1946, incidents 164
   in 1956, incidents 173, 178, 179–80
   and the Bund 61, 65, 68–70, 80, 82
   compulsory identification of Jews 138, 149, 272
   and economic boycott 45, 50–1, 62
   and economic rivalry 16
   by intelligentsia 255

   in interwar Poland 58, 61–2, 64, 66–70, 73, 90, 98, 234, 285, 301
   in Kielce 159, 160, 162–6
   in Lithuania 128, 132
   and Polish underground 140–4, 146, 148, 155
   and Polish Workers' Party 155
   postwar 146–7, 170–83, 300–2, 303
   in Poznań 172, 177
   and PPS Proletariat 36
   and racism 271
   secular 266–9
   and Socialism xviii, xix–xx, 17, 18, 20–1, 23, 28, 30, 31, 64, 67, 70
   in Vilna 133–4
   see also Catholicism; pogroms; murder, ritual; nationalism, Polish; Natolin group
Antonkiewicz, Marian 304
Antyfaszystowska Organizacja (Anti-Fascist Organization) 153
Arabs, Palestinian 68–9, 198, 201
Arbeter Emigratsie Byuro 67 n. 33
Arbeter shtime (The workers' voice) 20
Argajer, Karol 96
Aristotle, *Poetics* 247, 250, 253
Armia Krajowa (Home Army) 140
   Bureau of Information and Propaganda 298
   and Jewish underground xxi, 144–6, 148–9, 155–7
Aronson, M. 4
As, Yankl 110 n. 8
Ashkenazi Judaism:
   Bible manuscripts 273–4
   and sexuality 59–61
assimilation:
   and the Bund 36
   and the intelligentsia 3–8, 11, 13, 24
   and Jewish Socialists 3, 7–8, 11, 24, 53
   in Kielce 159
   'natural' 37 n. 25
   and PPS Proletariat 35–7, 39, 44
   and Socialism 14, 15, 16–17, 19, 23, 25–6, 35, 37
Association of Jewish Trade Unions 76
Association of Łódź Merchants 99
Association of Textile Industry Manufacturers 99
Association of Trade Unions 95–6, 104
Association of Working Youth 'Union' 92

Astor, Michael (Chernikhov) 117, 118
Auerbach, Berthold 282
Austria, and Jewish Communists 56
Austrian partition, and Socialism 15, 18, 19–24, 40, 43
autonomy, Jewish:
  and the Bund 18, 21, 30, 69, 72, 81
  and Council of Four Lands 187–91
  and Minority Statute 26–7
  opposition to 25–7, 30
  and Polish Socialist Party 21–2, 28–31
  and PPS Proletariat 40–3
  religious 26–7
  as a right 12, 14

B
Baal Shem Tov 262
Babiański, Gen. 51
Badiorova, Olga 37
Bajer, Karol 86
Bałaban, Majer 188
Balberzycki, Mendel 99, 125
Baranchuk, Nahman 130 n. 100
Baranowski, Ignacy 50
Barczewski, Jan 95
Barlas, Chaim 202
Barlicki, Norbert 67, 105–6
Baron, Lawrence 296
Bartosiński family 167
Bartoszewski, Władysław T. 280–2
Bartrop, Paul 296
Bauer, Otto 18, 25, 29
Bauminger, Heszek 154
Bednarz, Bronisław 168 n. 36
Będzin, and youth movements 197, 206, 207, 209
Begin, Menahem 249–53
Beider, Alexander 289–95
Beier-Żylar, Sylwia 235
Beilawa, and antisemitism of 1956 178, 180
Beilis case 47, 48, 52
Bełdowski, Tadeusz 86
Ben-gavriel, Mosche Ya'akov 283
Bendori, Pinchas 208
Benjamin, Walter 288
Beranek, F. J. 291
Béraud, Armand-Louis-Joseph 265
Bereza Kartuska concentration camp 101
Bergman, Eleonora 232
Berling, Zygmunt 161
Berman, Jakub 172, 174, 175, 179
Bernholtz, Shmuel 125 n. 74
Betar youth organization 154, 285
Bethge, Eberhard 296
Bethge, Renate 296

Bezpartyjni Żydzi Religijni (Independent Religious Jews) 99
Bezpartyjny Blok Współpracy z Rządem (BBWR: Non-Party Bloc for Co-operation with the Government) 95–6
Biale, David 256–64, 267
Bialik, Haim Nahman 216
Bialogurski, A. 130 n. 100
Białystok:
  and Jewish underground 153–4, 156, 157, 197, 209
  pogrom of 1906 36
Bielski, Tuwia 145
Birnbaum, Zdisław 51
Birobidzhan, resettlement of Jews in 117
Bitner, Władysław 89
'Black Hundred' 46, 47
Blit, Lucjan 78
Blitt, Moshe 130 n. 100
Bloch, Eliezer 221
Bloch, Moshe 127 n. 85
Blok Antyfaszystowski (Anti-Fascist Bloc) 153, 155
Błoński, Jan 234
Bludz, Benjamin 135, 136 n. 130
Blumenkranz, Bernard 271
Bohuszewiczówna, Maria 6–7
Bolechów, and Council of Four Lands 188–90
Bolsheviks:
  and 1912 Duma elections 54 n. 12
  role of Jews xxi, 6, 55–7
  and working class 60
Bomash, Meyer 50
Bonhoeffer, Dietrich 296
Borski, Jan M. 29–30, 66
bourgeoisie, Jewish:
  and 1912 Duma elections 49–50
  and the Bund 17, 50, 71
  and Soviet Union 139
bourgeoisie, Polish, and anti-Jewish boycott 51
boycott, anti-Jewish 45, 50–1, 62
Breslev, Shmuel 222, 223
Bridgeman, Percy 255
Brimberg, Yosef 74 n. 47
Britain:
  and Jewish involvement in Russian revolution 55, 56 n. 2
  and Palestine 68, 166, 195, 197–8, 203, 249
Brod, Max 288
Broszkiewicz, Jerzy 173
Buber, Martin 286–8
Buesiewicz, Wacław 97
Bugaj, Stanisław 97
Bund and Class Trade Unions of Jewish Workers 99–100

Index

Bund (General Jewish Workers' Alliance) xx–xxi, 11–12
  defence organizations 65
  and Duma elections 1912 45, 49–50, 53
  Eighth Polish Congress 61 n. 10
  Fifth Congress 38, 59–60
  finances 71–8, 82, 100
  formation 15
  Fourth Congress 18, 34, 35, 40, 42
  and Jewish emigration 66–9
  and Jewish separatism 12, 18, 26, 30
  and Jewish underground 151, 153, 154
  and *kehillot* 62–3
  membership of 79
  and municipal elections: 1934 83; 1936 63–4, 78–81, 88, 90–1, 98, 99–102 1938–9 65, 78–81
  and nationalism 33, 37–9
  in Poland 1936–9 58–82
  and Polish Socialist Party xx, 12–13, 17–19, 26, 33–4, 39, 59–60, 62–6, 69–71, 80, 81–2, 99
  and Polish Socialist Party: Proletariat 32–44
  in Russia 38, 43, 59 n. 3
  and Sejm elections 1930 63 n. 21
  Sixth Congress 42 n. 46
  and Soviet control of Vilna 114 n. 18, 115 n. 25, 118, 126
  and unions 75–6
  in United States 71–2, 74–7
  welfare programmes 76, 82
  and workers' conditions 71–8
  youth movements 65, 78
  and Zionism 38–9, 61, 67–71
  and ZPSD 21
  see also Tsentralrat fun Yidishe Proffarraynen; Tsisho
Burton, Robert 265
Byelorussia:
  and Jewish surnames 290, 291, 293
  and Vilna 108, 113, 122, 129–30, 131
Bytom, and antisemitism of 1956 173

C

Camp of Great Poland 97
capitalism:
  and the Jewish question 15, 23
  and Jews 24, 56, 71, 203–4, 266
  and Second World War 151–2, 203–4
caste, Jews as 25
Catholic Cultural-Education Association 92
Catholicism:
  and emigration of Jews 140
  and Jewish literature 23
  and Nazi genocide 141
  and pogroms 166–7, 303
  and postwar antisemitism 181, 300–2
CeKaBe (lending societies) 72
censorship xvii, 5, 134, 148
Częstochowa, 205 n. 36
Chadecja, *see* Christian Democratic Party
change, social 10–11, 15
Chęciński, Michał xvii, 170–1
Chełmno, gassings 230
Chernikov, Josef 117–18, 124 n. 65
Chevrah of Nasielsk 192–4
Chodyński, Edmund 90
Christian Committee of Unified Łódź Voters 94, 100
Christian Democratic Party (Chadecja) 88, 92–5, 104
Christiani, Pablo 272
Christianity:
  and Holocaust 295
  and Judaism 272–3, 277–8
  and Socialism 4
  see also Catholicism
Chrostowski, Waldemar 235
Chudziński, Wiktor 86 n. 41
Churchill, Winston S. 56 n. 2
Chwoles, Zechariah 118
circumcision 257–9, 261, 265–7
Citizens' Economic Committee 94
citizenship, rights 58, 252, 265
class:
  and the Bund 70, 71
  and ethnicity 7, 12, 20
  and municipal elections 1936 89–90
  see also proletariat
Class Trade Unions of Jewish Workers 95, 98, 99–100, 101–5
Cohen, Shimsohn 130 n. 100
Comintern, and the Bund 59
Communism:
  and antisemitism of 1956 170–1, 181–3
  and Jewish history 4, 5
  and Jewish underground xxi, 144, 145, 153–7
  and Polish underground 150
  and role of Jews xvii–xviii, xx, xxi, 55–7, 145, 162–4
  and Zionism 203–4
  see also Polish Communist Party; Polska Partia Robotnicza
Communist International, *see* Socialist International
communities, Jewish, see *kehillot*
concentration camps 101, 144, 146, 295
  see also extermination camps
constitution, Polish:
  1921 27, 143
  1935 58, 83, 84, 143

contractors xix, 158-9
Council of Four Lands (Va'ad Arba Aratsot) 187-91
Council of Trade Unions 99-100
craftsmen, Jewish 10-11, 159
criminality:
    and image of Jews 257, 265-6
    postwar 163
Crowe, Sir Eyre 55-6
Cukierman, L. 4
Cwikliński, Jan 86 n. 41
Cyrankiewicz, Józef 181
Cyrański, Adam 92
Czechoslovakia, Jewish refugees from 76
Czerniakow, Adam 298
Czernik, Antoni 105
Częstochowa, ritual murder accusations 164

D
dal Castellazzo, Moses 274
Danecki, Władisław 89
Daszyński, Ignacy 19-20, 21
Davidson, Gusta 196, 222
Davidson, I. (Y. Davidsohn) 53
de Courtenay, Baudouin 51
de León, Moses 261
Delegatura Rządu na Kraj (Office of the Government Delegate for the Homeland) 138, 144
Dembiński, Jan 105
Dembo, Izaak 3
democratization, and nationalism 22, 23
Denikin, Anton Ivanovich 55, 56 n. 2
deportations, mass 139, 142-3, 146, 150, 153, 203, 207-10, 224
Der arbeter (The worker) 12, 17, 18, 20
Der yiddisher arbeter (The Jewish worker) 39
desertion, from Polish army 250-2
Deutsche Sozialistiche Arbeitspartei (DSAP: German Social Democratic Worker's Party) 64, 83
    and municipal elections 1936 88, 90-1, 99, 103
Deutscher Volksverband in Polen (German People's Union) 100, 101
Diamand, Herman 20-1
diaspora:
    and the Bund 67-8, 72
    and Yishuv 195, 213
discrimination:
    and the Bund 69, 72, 75
    and municipal elections 1936 97, 101
    opposition to 12
    and Russia 7, 16, 17
Dmowski, Roman 45, 48, 50, 51, 52 n. 10, 53
Döblin, Alfred 283

Do boju (To battle) 33
Domosławski, Kazimierz 26
Donin, Nicholas 272
Dov Ber of Bolechów 187-91
Dranger, Shimshon 206
Dratwa, Bolesław 105
Drenger, Shimek 222
Drobner, Bolesław 39
Dror (newspaper) 224 n. 38, 229
Dror-Hechaluts (Freedom-the Pioneer) 125, 153-4
    and Erets Israel 196, 213-14
    and kibbutzim 226
    and resistance through education 212, 218, 221-5, 228-30
Drozdowski, Marian Marek 280
Dubiński, David 75 n. 50
Dubnow, Simon 69 n. 36, 188
Dubois, Stanisław 67
Duma, elections 1912 xviii, 45-54
Dwugroszówka 50
Dyomin, Mikhail Aleksandrowich 166
Dzierżoniów, and antisemitism of 1956 180
Dzierżyński, Feliks 6 n. 12, 45-54

E
Ebenbauer, Alfred 271-4
Ebl, Franz M. 273
Eckardt, Alice L. 295-6
economy:
    Jewish exclusion from 58, 62, 72
    Jewish influence on 66, 69, 97
education:
    and the Bund 69, 71, 73-4, 75, 77-8
    religious 122
    and resistance 208-9, 212-31
    secular 73
    and workers' movements 10, 11, 75, 82
Eisenbach, Artur 280
elections:
    Duma 1912 45-54
    municipal: 1936 xviii, 61, 63-5, 83-106; 1938-9 65, 78-81
    Sejm: 1922 82; 1930 63 n. 21; 1935 78, 84
élites, Jewish 189-90
Ellenberg, Zygmunt 98-9
emancipation:
    and intellectuals 264
    of proletariat 3
    and Socialism xviii, 24
emigration, Jewish:
    and the Jewish problem 28-30, 58, 62, 65-9, 80, 140
    and postwar antisemitism 177, 181-2
    and Soviet Union 166

and Zionist youth movements 198, 201–2, 205–6, 213, 285
Endecja 45, 48, 52 n. 10
 and 1912 Duma elections 50
 and antisemitism 62, 66, 134
 and Bund 61
 and Jewish emigration 58, 65
 and Łódź municipal elections 63–5, 96
 and municipal elections 1934 83, 84, 86
Endeks, *see* Endecja
Engelhardt, H. Tristram 192
Engels, Friedrich 51
Erets Israel:
 aid to Jews in 72
 emissaries 198–9, 205, 207, 213–14, 284
 and Zionist youth movements 116, 151, 195–211, 213–14, 216–17, 225
 see also Palestine
Erlich, Henryk 61 n. 10, 69 n. 36, 214 n. 6
 and the Bund 59, 60 n. 6
 and emigration 67–8, 80
 and Joint Distribution Committee 72, 74
 and municipal elections: 1936 62, 99; 1938–9 79, 80, 81
extermination camps 139, 142–3, 146, 161, 205
 see also concentration camps

F
Faraynikte Partizaner Organisatsye (FPO: United Partisan Organization) 130 n. 97, 154, 156
Farbshtein, Geshel (Heschel) 53
Fascism, in Poland 58, 61, 64 n. 22, 67–8, 82, 98
Fascist Party, Italy, and Jews 56
federalism 38, 42, 43
Felsenhardt, Natan 6
Felsenhardt, Rozalia 6–7
Finkelstein, Abel 3
First World Congress of Zionists 15
Fischer, Ludwig 152
Flaszen, Juda 161
Folkists 99, 117
Folkstsaytung (People's newspaper) 61, 67, 69 n. 36, 77, 78–80
Folz, Hans 273
Forverts (Onward) 133–4
Frank, A. N. 188
Franzos, Karl Emil 282, 283–4
Freeland League 130
Frey, Winfried 273
Fronde, *see* National Democratic 'Secession'
Front Morges 104
Front Odrodzenia Polski (Front for Polish Resurrection) 141, 143
Frybes, Stanisław 232
Fuks, M. 79 n. 64

Fundusz Obrony Narodowej (FON: Fund for National Defence) 160
Furman, Franciszek 304

G
Gałązka, Wacław 84
Galicia:
 and the Bund 81
 and Jews 24
 in literature 282–4
Galician Social Democratic Party 19–21
Ganzke, Edward 100
Gąsiorowski, Marian Stanisław 86
Gazeta poranna (*Gazeta codzienne dwa grosze*) 50
Gdańsk, and antisemitism of 1956 178
Geller, Eliezer 201, 218, 220
General Gouvernement region 145, 149, 198–9
General Jewish Workers' Alliance:
 in Lithuania 32
 in Poland, *see* Bund
General Zionists 71, 78, 98, 99, 125, 204, 285
 see also Akiva youth movement
genocide, and Polish underground 138–47
Geral, R. Moshe Katz ix
German Communist Party 8
German Cultural-Economic Union 100
Germans, and municipal elections 1936 88, 90–1, 99, 100, 101–5
Germany:
 and Jewish Communists 56
 and Jews 138–47, 148–9, 295–6
 and Nazi–Soviet pact 108, 151, 204, 225
 and Poles 138–40
 see also Nazism
ghettos:
 death rates 139, 201, 215
 escape from 142–4
 Kielce 161
 Kraków 154
 Łódź 139, 153
 and Nazism 138, 139–44, 146, 148, 152, 157, 161, 215
 Warsaw 139, 145–6, 147, 151, 153, 201, 209, 297–9
 and youth movements 198, 201–2, 205–8, 215–31
Gibas, Danuta 234–5
Gierek, Edward 303
Giertych, Jędrzej 96–7
Giliński, Shlomo 73, 74 n. 47, 76
Gilman, Sander 256–8, 264–8
Giterman, Isaac 74 n. 48
Gladysz, Izabela 235
Glatzer, Nahum N. 286–8
Glemp, Cardinal Józef 300

Glik, Hirsh 111 n. 12
Gliksman, Jerzy 126 n. 76
Głos Bundu (Voice of the Bund) 39
Głowacz, Bożena 235
Godlewska, Eugenia 96
Goldberg, Jakub 135, 232
Goldflam, S. 52
Goldstein, Bernard 65
Goldwasser, Edwin 74 n. 48
Gomułka, Władysław 165 n. 27, 167, 178
Gordon, A. D. 196 n. 1
Gordon, Abraham 11
Gordon, Ester and Elżbieta 3
Gordon, Ewa 3
Gordon, Hayyim 129 n. 95
Gordonia youth movement:
  and Erets Israel 196–7, 201, 203, 213
  and resistance through education 212, 217, 218–22
  and training farms 226
  and welfare projects 219–20
Górewicz, G. 4
government-in-exile:
  and attitudes to Jews 140, 142, 146, 150, 163
  and Jewish underground 155, 298
Grabowski, Albin 86
Graus, František 271
Great Christian Bloc 92
Grendyszyński, Ludomir 51
Grinberg, Daniel 232
Grochów kibbutz 225–6
Grodzeński, R. Hayyim Ozer 116 n. 26
Grosser, Bronisław 49, 53
Grossman, Henryk 24
Grot-Rowecki, 157
Grünbaum, Yitzhak 68 n. 34, 79–80, 81
Grynberg, Henryk 234
Grynszpan, Jechiel 145
Grzegorzak, Leon 97, 105
Guterman, Alexander 280
Gutman, Israel 213, 214, 215, 225, 227, 280, 303
Gwardia Ludowa (People's Guard) 144–5, 148, 154–6
Gwiazdowicz, Kazimierz 168 n. 36, 304

H

Haam, Ahad 247, 252
Haecker, Emil 20
Ha'emet (The truth) 4–5, 6
Hakibbutz Ha'artsi (National Kibbutz) 196 n. 1
Hakibbutz Hameuchad (United Kibbutz) 196 n. 1
Hako'ordinatsiah Hachalutzit (Pioneering Co-ordination) 196
Halpern, Israel 187

Hamizrachi party 196 n. 1
Haneman, Jan 89–90
Hano'ar Hatsioni (Zionist Youth) 196–7, 213
  and training farms 226
Ha'oved Hatsioni (Zionist Worker) 196 n. 1
Hapo'el Hamizrachi 125
Harasz, Antoni 92
Hartglas, Apolinary 202 n. 23, 214 n. 6
Hashomer Hatsa'ir (Young Guard) 116, 125, 135 n. 126
  and Erets Israel 196, 198, 203–4, 205, 213
  and Jewish underground 151–4
  Ma'anit group 216
  newspapers: *El Al* 217; *Iton hatenuah* 222; *Jutrznia* (Dawn) 152, 156; *Neged hazerem* 151, 204 n. 30, 217, 218, 221, 224 n. 38
  and resistance through education 212, 213, 216–18, 219–20, 221–3, 229
  and *shituf* enterprise 219
  and training farms 226
Hasidism 5, 280
  and *kehillot* 62
  leaders, graves of 233–4, 236
  as mysticism 274–6
  and sexuality 262–3, 268
Haskalah 263–4, 280
Hauke-Nowak, Aleksander 85
Haverkamp, Alfred 271–2
Haynt (Today) 46, 47, 49
Hebrew:
  knowledge of 236
  right to use 12, 139
  and surnames 291–2, 294
  and Zionist youth movements 197, 208, 217
Hechaluts Centre (Centre of the Pioneer) 196, 198, 200
Hechaluts halochem 204, 206
Hechaluts Hamizrachi (Eastern Pioneer) 61, 78, 125
  and Erets Israel 196, 213–14
Heine, Heinrich 267
Held, Adolf 75, 78 n. 61
Helser, Heinrich von 273
Herberg, Will xix
Herman, Joseph 118 n. 38
Herszkowicz, Mojsze 98
Hertz, Y. Sh. 67 n. 33
Herzl, Theodore 288
Hess, Moses 266
Hindes, M. 125 n. 74
Histadrut (workers' union) 201, 284
historiography:
  and accuracy 247–54, 271, 279
  Jewish 148, 187–8, 235–6, 298, 301
Hitachdut 98

Hitler, Adolf 56
Hodes, Ludwig 78
Hofmeister, Wernfried 273
Holcgreber, Jan 86 n. 41
Holenderski, Lew 100
Holman, H. C. 55
Holocaust:
   Polish attitudes to 234, 298
   and Polish Socialist Party 15
   and Polish underground 138–47
   survivors 158, 161, 210, 295–6
   and Zionist youth movements 195–211, 215, 230
Holzer, Jerzy 235
Horowitz, Maksymilian (H. Walecki) 12, 23
Hungary:
   and anti-Jewish riots 166
   and Jewish Communists 56

I

identity, Jewish 33, 35, 36–7, 37 n. 25, 233, 234
independence, Polish xx, xxi, 16, 158, 160
   and the Bund 39–40
   and the Jewish question 26
intelligentsia, Jewish:
   and antisemitism 172, 266
   and assimilation 3–8, 11, 13, 24
   and the Jewish problem 7–10, 19
   and literature in Polish 233
   and the proletariat 9–10
   and sexuality 268–9
   and Socialism xviii, 3, 4–7, 18, 19, 21
intelligentsia, Polish:
   and Jews 7
   postwar 300
   and Soviet Union 150
Interdisciplinary Centre for the Study of the History and Culture of Polish Jews 236
International League of Socialist-Revolutionaries, Jewish Section 4
internationalism, and nationalism 16, 26
Irgun Tseva'i Le'umi 251
Irwin-Zarecka, Iwona 296, 299–302
Iskra (The spark) 33, 37, 38, 40
Iwanicki, Romuald (Józef Kalinowski) 168 n. 36
Izba Rzemieślnicza (Artisan Chamber) 94

J

Jabet, George 265
Jabotinsky, Vladimir 67, 252
Jabotinsky, Ze'ev 123 n. 62
Jackan, Samuel Jacob 47–8
Jacob, Jack xvii
Jagiellonian University, and study of Jewish history 236

Jagiełło, Eugeniusz 45, 49–50, 52 n. 10, 54
Jagielski, Jan 232
Jakubowski, Chana and Josek 160
Jan Karski Foundation 233
Janion, Maria 234
Janowski, Jan 94
Jasińska-Kania, Aleksandra 232
Jaworska, Maria 105
Jaworski, Wojciech 235
Jedlicki, Witold 170–1
Jewish Historical Institute 301–2
   thesis competition 232–43
Jewish Labour Committee, United States 72, 74–6, 78
Jewish Professional Unions 60
Jewish Socialist Union in London 4–5
Jewish Workers' Committee, United States 74
Jews:
   changes in Jewish society 10–11, 15
   as Duma delegates 48–50, 52–4
   extermination 138–47, 161
   general Jewish congress 70
   Litvak Jews 16, 17, 280
   and the Jewish problem 7–11, 14–31, 58, 142
   and nationhood 16–17, 18
   and Nazism 138
   Orthodox Jews: and flight from Germans 214 n. 6; and Socialism 7, 63, 81
Jeżierski, Stanisław 92
Jeziorowski, Kazimierz 39
Jochelson, W. 4
Jogiches, Leon (Jan Tyszka) 3, 8–10
Johnpoll, Bernard K. 81
Joint Distribution Committee 71, 72, 74, 75, 76–8
Jóźwiak, Franciszek 168
Judaeo-Communism (*Zydokomuna*) xviii, 2, 98, 183
Judenrat 297–8
Jungdeutscher Verband (Young German Union) 100

K

kabbalist movement, and sexuality 258, 261–2, 263
Kaczergiński, Szmerke 114
Kaczmarek, Czesław 166–7
Kafka, Franz 233, 288
Kahan, L. 126 n. 76
Kahane family 161–2
Kahn, Abraham 74
Kahn, Bernard 72, 74, 77
Kainer, Abel 303
Kalinowski, Józef (Romuald Iwanicki) 168 n. 36
Kalinowski, Mieczysław 86 n. 41
Kalisz, ritual murder accusations 164
Kalmanovich, Zelig 124 n. 67

Kaminer, Izaak 3, 4
Kamińska, Ida 234–5
Kapczyński, Wacław 97
Kaplan, Yosef 222
Katyn, murders 161
Katz, Shlomo 115 n. 20, 118 n. 39, 130 n. 101
Katznelson, Yitzhak 221, 228
Kaufmann, Guta 160
Kautsky, Karol 16–17, 25, 37
Kazhdan, Chaim-Shlomo 73, 77
kehillot 174
  and the Bund 62–3, 65, 71, 78–9
Kelles-Krauz, Kazimierz 22–3, 24, 34
Kempner, Rafa 105
Kempner, Stanisław 51
Keren Kayemet LeYisrael (Jewish National Fund) 201, 217–18
Kersten, Krystyna xvii, 170, 303
kibbutzim, and youth movements 196, 205, 213–14, 225–7
Kielce:
  ghetto 161
  Jewish settlement 158–9, 302
  pogrom 146–7, 158–67, 171, 249, 252, 299, 302–4
  and ritual murder accusations 164–5
Kieniewicz, Stefan 280
Kierownictwo Walki Cynnej (Leadership of Civil Warfare) 140–1
Kieszkowski, Feliks 92
Kiliński, Jan 92
Kingdom of Poland:
  and the Bund 19, 80
  and Jewish Socialists 3–16
  and PPS Proletariat 32–44
Kislinger, Ewald 272
Klańska, Maria 282–4
Klarman, Alter and Joseph 125 n. 74
Kleinbaum, Moshe (Sneh) 69 n. 36, 70, 125, 126 n. 76, 134–5, 214 n. 6
Klepatenko, Adam 113 n. 15
Klikar, Kurt Aleksander 98
Klimov, I. 122 n. 55
Klinger, Chaika 196, 205–6, 208
Kłosiewicz, Wiktor 170, 179
Knoll, Roman 142
Knor, Aleksander 105
Koc, Adam 65
Kołakowski, Leszek 173, 175, 176
Koło Boże (God's Circle) sect 277, 278
Komitet Wyborczy Zblokowanych Organizacji Kobiecych (Electoral Committee of the Unified Organization of Women) 93
Komunistyczna Partia Polska [KPP], *see* Polish Communist Party

Kon, Feliks 6, 7
Konieczny, Kazimierz 168 n. 36
Kopczyński, Stanisław 94
Korchak, Ruzka 209
Korczak, Janusz 221
Koropeckyj, Roman 278–9
Kosowski, Vladimir 59
Kossak-Szczucka, Zofia 141
Kovner, Abba 154, 230
Kowalski, Kazimierz 97
Kozakiewicz, Jan 20
Kozierowska, Urszula 179
Kożmińska, Ewa 234
Kraków:
  and Jewish underground 154, 206, 208
  postwar pogroms 171
Krawczyńska, Dorota 234
Kremer, Arkady 3, 10, 11
Kruczkowski, Bronisław 105
Krytyka (Critique) 22
Kuchar, Wacław xix
Kucharzewski, Jan 45, 48, 50, 52 n. 10, 53
Kula, Marcin 234
Kulczycki, Ludwik 32, 33–7, 39–44
Kulczyński, Stefan 92
'Kultur-Amt' (Cultural office) 100
'Kultur-Liga' (cultural associations) 100
Kun, Bela 56
Kupsza, Stanisław 168
Kurier codzienny (Daily courier) 12
Kurier polski (Polish courier) 51
Kuryluk, Władysław 94
Kuźnicki, Wiktor (Paweł Szkleniarz) 168 n. 36, 304
Kwiatek, Bogdan 233
Kwiatek, Józef (T. Wileński) 13, 14, 23
Kwieciński, F. 92

L

Labour Zionism, *see* Po'alei Tsion
Landauer, Gustav 289
language:
  and nationhood 25, 27, 37
  and nomination for election 85, 87, 98
  see also Hebrew; Yiddish
Latsis, M. I. 55
Lavrov, Piotr 4, 5, 6
Lednicki, Aleksander 51
Legnica, and antisemitism of 1956 178
Lendvai, Paul xvii
Lenin, V. I.:
  and the Bund 33
  and Communism 56
  and Jewish Marxists xx–xxi
  and Jewish nationhood 37–8

Leński, Julian 104
Leśniczak, Zygmunt 95
Leszczyński, Yosef (Y. Chmurner) 59, 73
Levin, Misha 124 n. 70
Levin, Nahman 118
Lévy, Armans 277
Lewandowski, Miron 86 n. 41
Lewicki, I. 95
Lewin, Aleksander 232
Lewin, Izaac 105
Lewinson, Anna 105
Lewis, Richard 256
Lewandowski, Andrzej 94
Lewsztajn, Juliusz 99
Liberman, Feszel 99
Libovski, Moshe 130 n. 100
Lichtenstein, Sara 160
Lichtensztain, Gerszon 99
Lieberman, Aron Samuel 3, 4–6
Lieberman, Herman 20
Liebskind, Dolek 208
Lifszyc, Yosef 78
Liga Obrony Powietrznej i Przeciwgazowej (League of Air and Anti-gas defence) 160
Liga Zielonej Wstążki (League of the Green Riband) 160
Limanowski, Bolesław 23
literature:
  contemporary 234
  history of 282–4
  and image of Jews 256
  Jewish, in Polish 233
  in Polish 233, 235
Lithuania:
  and control of Vilna 107–9, 110, 121, 124, 125, 127–8, 130–6
  and Council of Four Lands 187–91
  and Jewish assimilation 36
  and Jewish Socialists 3, 43
  and Russophilia 36
Łódź:
  and antisemitism of 1956 173, 178
  election 1934 83–4, 88
  election 1936 xviii, 61, 63–5, 83–106; Main Electoral Commission 86–7, 98, 100–1; and party blocs 89–101, 105; and Polish Communist Party 88–91, 94–5, 99, 102–6; and Polish Socialist Party 88–91, 94–6, 99–105; and political issues 101; results 102–5
  ghetto deaths 139
  Jewish Duma delegates 52
  population 85–6
  see also ghettos
Lohrman, Klaus 272

Lower Silesia, and antisemitism of 1956 179–80
Lubetkin, Zivia 197, 200, 206–7, 209–10, 223, 226–7
Lublin:
  and antisemitism of 1956 178
  Catholic University 236
Lubomirska, Countess 189
Luther, Martin 273
Luxemburg, Rosa 8, 9

M
Ma'anit youth group 216
Maciąg, Włodzimierz 235
Maciejewska, Irena 232
Magun, Faivl 134
Maimonides, Moses 260–1, 269
Malinowski, Jerzy 232
Mandecki, Józef 94
Mantegazza, Paolo 265
Manusievitch, Aleksandr 33
Mapu, Abraham 263
Marchlewski, Julian 6 n. 12, 12
Marcus, Joseph 79, 81
Mark, Bernard 33
Markiewicz, Henryk 233, 235
Marszalek, Józef 235
Martov-Tsederbaum, J. 3, 10
Martyn, Peter J. 281
Marx, Karl:
  and antisemitism xx
  and nationalism 16–17
Marxism:
  and the Bund 81
  and nationalism 20, 22, 30
Mason, Jackie 256
Matłoka, Jarosław 234
Maurer, Jadwiga 276–9
Mazeh, R. Jacob 57
Mecklenburg, Norbert 283
Mehring, Franz 17
Meir, David 75 n. 50
Melchior, Małgorzata 233
Meltzer, Emanuel 80
Mensheviks, and 1912 Duma elections 54 n. 12
Mendelsohn, Abraham 214 n. 6
Mendelsohn, Ezra xviii
Mendelson, Shlomo 73, 74, 76
Mendelson, Stanisław 13, 17, 50, 51
Mendelssohn, Moses 273
Mendes-Flohr, Paul 286–8
Merchants' Union 98
Messianism, and Socialism xix
Metzger, Mendel 273
Metzger, Thérèse 273
Micewski, Andrzej 181

Michalak, Zbigniew 97
Michels, Robert xviii
Mickiewicz, Adam 249, 276–9
Mickiewicz, Władysław 277
middle ages, and Jewish history 271–4
middle classes:
　Jewish xviii, 65, 69, 94, 98, 102, 105
　Polish 97–8
migration, and Soviet occupation of Vilna 124–31
Miklautsch, Lydia 273
Mikołaj Kopernik University, and study of Jewish history 236
Mikołajczyk, Stanisław 146
Mileski, Jan 86
militia, in Kielce 164–5, 167–8
Mill, Yosif-John 3, 11
Miller, Jean Baker 269
Milman, S. 90, 100, 105
Minc, Hilary 179
Mincberg, Lejb 99
Ministry of Culture and the Arts, Poland 232
Ministry of Foreign Affairs, Poland 232
Minorities' Bloc 81, 82
Miroński, Peretz 130 n. 100
Mishmeret youth group 216
mitnagdic movement 263, 275, 276, 280
Mize, Gela 154
Mizrachi 71, 98
Moczar, Gen. Mieczysław 182–3
Mogilnicki, Tadeusz 86
Moment 46
Morawski, Edward Osóbka 165 n. 27
Mościcki, President 178 n. 30
Moszkowicz, Anna 160
Moszkowicz, Daniel 154
Munitz, Hayyim 127 n. 85
murder, ritual:
　accusations 164–5, 168, 171 n. 7, 191, 266, 272, 303
　and Beilis case 47, 48, 52
Mużdżyński, Edward 105

N
Nahman of Bratslav 262
Najdus, Walentyna 33
Napieralski, Antoni 105
Naród (Nation) 140, 141
Narodnaya Volya (The People's Will) 4, 8–9
Narodowa agencja prasowa (National press agency) 146
Narodowa Partia Robotnicza-Prawica (NPR: National Workers' Party) 88, 92–3, 95, 104

Narodowe Siły Zbrojne (NSZ: National Armed Forces) 144, 165
Narodowe Stronnictwo Pracy (National Party of Labour) 92, 93
Narodowo-Chrześcijański Front Robotniczy (National Christian Workers' Front/National-Christian Labour Front) 93–5, 100, 104
Narodowy Związek Robotniczy-Kilińczycy (National Workers' Union) 92
Nasielsk, *chevrah* of 192–4
Natanson, Kazimierz 50, 53
'National Concentration' 48 n. 3, 52 n. 10
National Democratic party, *see* Endecja
National Democratic 'Secession' 45, 48, 50
National Textile Industry Union 99
nationalism, Jewish 13, 15–16, 18, 20–5
　and 1912 Duma elections 51
　and the Bund 33, 37–9, 43, 68, 70–1
　and postwar antisemitism 177
　and PPS Proletariat 35–7
　and SDKPiL 37
　and self-determination 35
　see also language; territory; Yiddish; Zionism
nationalism, Polish:
　and 1912 Duma elections 45
　and antisemitism 28, 147, 149, 160, 177, 179–80, 234
　and elections: 1934 83; 1936 103–5
　and Socialism 16, 28–9, 31, 60, 64, 67
nationalism, Ukrainian 144
Natolin group, and antisemitism of 1956 170–1, 176, 182–3
Nazism:
　and 'international Jewry' 55
　and Jewish support 56
　and support for Jews 160
　and underground movement xxi, 138–47
　see also extermination camps; Holocaust
Neimark, David-Leyb 72, 126 n. 76
Neustadt, Melech 198 n. 8
newspapers, *see* press
Niebuhr, Reinhold 296
Niedziałkowski, Mieczysław 27, 29, 102, 104
Niedzielski, Józef 105
Niezależna Socjalistyczna Partia Pracy (Independent Socialist Labour Party) 26
NKVD, and Kielce pogrom 163, 165–6, 168
Nochmovsky, Reuven 125 n. 74
Novogrudski, Emanuel 75, 77
Nowa gazeta [The new gazette] 51
Nowacki, Kazimierz 235
Nowak, Zenon 170–1, 176, 179
Naye Folkstsaytung (Jewish newspaper) 160
Nutkiewicz, Szlama 100

Index

O
Oberpolitseimeister, Warsaw 52–4
Obóz Narodowa-Radykalny (ONR: National Radical Camp) 97, 143
Obóz Zjednoczenia Narodowego (OZON: United National Camp) 65, 67, 70
obshchina, and Socialism 4
Obuchowicz, Antoni 86
Ochab, Edward 173–4, 177 n. 28, 178
Ochedalski, Henryk 86 n. 41
Office of the Government Delegate for the Homeland 138, 144
Oktyaber (Yiddish newspaper) 123
Okulicki, Leopold 249
Openheim, Yosel Moseyevich 113 n. 16
Oppenheim, Israel 284–6
Oppenheimer, Robert 255
Orenstein (Oren), Mordechai 198
Orzech, Maurycy 63, 74 n. 48, 118 nn. 36, 37, 133–4

P
Paderewski, Ignacy Jan 50
Paldiel, Mordecai 296
Pale of Settlement 10, 12, 57, 289
Palestine:
  and Begin 249
  emigration to 28, 66–9, 80, 125, 137, 166, 198
  partition 68
  and youth movements 195–211, 213–14, 216–17, 285
  and Zionism 67, 69, 151–2
  see also Erets Israel
Palme, Rudolf 272
Paris Convention of Socialists 12
Paris Peace Conference, Minority Statute 26
parliament, and minority representation 41–3
partisans, *see* underground movements
Pat, Yaakov 74, 75 n. 50, 77, 78 n. 61
Patora, Konstanty 105
patriotism, Jewish 30
Paulouski, Karp 113 n. 15
Pawlicki, Jan 105
Peel Commission 68
Pelc, Mojżesz 160
periodicals, Jewish Socialist 4–5
Perl, Feliks 13, 17, 18, 19, 25
Peters, Ia. Kh. 55
Petrażycki, Leon 51
Petrov, Col. 113 n. 15
Pfefer, Mojzesz 53
Piast 65
Piłsudski, Bronisław 9
Piłsudski, Józef xvii, xx, 3, 9, 28

and the Bund 13, 19
  death of 58, 61, 234
  and Polish Socialist Party 6 n. 12, 17
Pioneers, *see* youth movements
Piotrowski, Czesław 105
Płomienie (newspaper) 229–30
Płotnicka, Frumka 197, 202, 205, 207, 209–10
pluralism 192, 300
Po'alei Agudas Yisroel (Orthodox workers) 99
Po'alei Tsion xx, 26, 75, 78, 100, 152–3, 196 n. 1
  Left 62, 64, 69–70, 73, 98, 99, 151, 153, 156, 298
  Right 62, 71, 98, 100, 118
Podgórski, Zygmunt 97
Podliszewski, Abraham 49
pogroms 16, 20
  and 1912 Duma elections 48, 54
  and Beilis case 48
  in Kielce 146–7, 158–67, 171, 249, 252, 299, 302–4
  postwar 146–7, 158–67, 171, 180, 299, 301
  and PPS Proletariat 36
  in Przytyk 61–2
  and Russian revolution 55–6
  in Ukraine 57
  in Vilna 109, 133–5
  see also antisemitism
Poland:
  Russification 16
  Sovietization 107, 136–7
  tradition of Jewish settlement in ix–x
Półciennik, Stefan 96
Polish–Bolshevik war 6 n. 12
Polish Communist Party 60, 76, 81, 83
  and antisemitism 147, 177 n. 28
  and municipal elections 1936 88–91, 94–5, 99, 102–6
  and Soviet occupation of Vilna 117, 130
Polish Council of Christians and Jews 232
Polish Front of the Unemployed 100
Polish–Jewish relations:
  and 1912 Duma elections in Warsaw 45–54
  and aid to Jews 138, 141–7, 148, 155–7, 158, 160, 296
  and history 249–54
  in Kielce 158, 160–1, 169
  postwar 172–3, 299–302
  and Socialism xx, 13, 16, 21–4, 28
  and underground movements 138–47, 148–57, 250, 298
  see also antisemitism
Polish–Lithuanian Commonwealth, and Council of Four Lands 187–91
Polish National Council, and Kielce pogrom 167

Polish Socialist Party Left (PPS-Lewica) 19, 23–4
  and 1912 Duma elections 45–6, 49–50, 52, 53, 54 n. 12
Polish Socialist Party Opozycja (Opposition) 26
Polish Socialist Party (PPS) xviii, 6 n. 12
  and the Bund xx, 12–13, 17–19, 33–5, 39, 43, 59–60, 62–6, 69–71, 80, 81–2, 99
  Centralny Komitet Robotniczy (Central Workers' Committee) 34
  Fourth Congress 34–5
  and Jewish emigration 66
  and Jewish underground 151
  and Jews 12, 14–15, 17, 22–3, 26–9, 37, 45
  and Kielce pogrom 167
  Łodzianin 94
  and municipal elections: 1934 83; 1936 88–91, 94–6, 99–105
  Nineteenth Congress 27
  Okręgowy Komitet Robotniczy (District Workers' Committee) 90–1
  Sixth Convention 18, 23, 34
  Tenth Congress 26
  Twenty-fourth Congress 26, 29
Polish Socialist Party: Proletariat, and the Bund 32–44
Polish Socialist Party Revolution Faction (PPS Frakcja Rewolucyjna) 19, 24–5, 96, 104
  First Rally 26
politics:
  in interwar Poland 58–82
  in Kielce 159–60
  postwar 300–1
  and Yiddish press 46–8
Polonization, *see* assimilation
Polska Agencja Prasowa (Polish Press Agency) 165 n. 27
Polska Kronika Filmowa (State Film Chronicle) 167
Polska Organizacja Wojskowa (Polish Military Organization) 93
Polska Partia Robotnicza (Polish Workers' Party) 144, 145, 150, 153
  and Kielce pogrom 165–8
Polska Partia Socjalistyczna, *see* Polish Socialist Party (PPS)
Polska Partia Socjalno-Demokratyczna Galicji i Śląska (PPSD) 14, 17, 20–1
  Sekcja Żydowska (Jewish Section) 21–2
Polska Zjednoczona Partia Robotnicza (PZPR: Polish United Workers' Party) 138, 170–2, 176–82
  POPS (party cells) 175, 176, 179
Polski Komitet Wyborczy (Polish Electoral Committee) 96, 104

Polski Związek Obrońców Ojczyzny (Polish Union of Defenders of the Fatherland) 93
Polskie Socjaliści (Polish Socialists) 151
Polskie Stronnictwo Ludowe (PSL: Polish Peasants' Party) 166
Polskie Zjednoczenie Zawodowe (Polish Trade Association) 95
Ponar, mass murders 230
population:
  postwar Jewish 181–2
  Silesia 235
  Warsaw 233, 281
  of Yishuv 197
Portnoy, Yekutiel (Noah) 59, 75
Positivists, Polish 8
Potęga, Edward 94
Potshenko, Haskel 118
poverty:
  and emigration 30
  and ghettos 155, 218–20, 229
  of Jewish proletariat xix, 15, 71–2, 76, 97–8
  in Soviet-occupied Vilna 119
Poznań, antisemitism 172, 177
Poznański, Chaim Lejb 100
Pranaitis, Fr 48
Prawda (Truth) 143
press:
  and antisemitism of 1956 172–4, 176–7
  Hebrew 197
  Jewish underground 3, 150–3, 195
  and municipal elections 1936 94–5, 101
  Polish underground 140–1, 143, 146, 148
  Polish-language 51
  Yiddish 46–8, 49–50, 78–9, 113–14, 123
  and youth movements 201, 203–4, 217, 224–5
Prilutski, Noah 70, 126 n. 76
professions, Jews in 97, 159
Prokop-Janiec, Eugenta 232–3
Proletariat 33, 34, 35, 38, 42
proletariat:
  and the Bund 59, 62–5, 68–70, 71–8
  emancipation 3
  growth 11
  Jewish 6–8, 10–12, 15, 17–21, 24, 34–5, 41–3, 70
  and municipal elections 1936 89–90
  and nation 24
  and Polish independence 39–40
  Russian 10
  and Socialist activism xviii, 6–8, 10–11, 24, 95
  solidarity xvii, 16, 21, 23, 28–9, 89–90
  see also poverty
Proletariat organization 3, 6–7, 51
  II 8
  III, *see* Polish Socialist Party: Proletariat

Proletariusz (The proletarian) 33, 36, 44 n. 57
property:
  confiscation 138, 139, 149
  reclamation 161–2, 163–4, 303
Protocols of the Elders of Zion 55
Prussian partition, and the Jewish problem 15
Pruszkowski, Kazimierz ('Orczyk') 39
Przedświt (Dawn) 17, 18, 25
Przegląd codzienny (Daily review) 51
Przegląd powszechny 235
Przegląd Socjaldemokratyczny (Social Democratic review) 40
Puławy group, and antisemitism of 1956 170–1, 181
Puzyreński, Rachel and Fanny 3

Q
quietism, and Hasidism 274–6

R
racism, and antisemitism 271
Radical-Democratic Electoral Committee 100
Radkiewicz, Stanisław 303
Rafaelowicz, Chaim (Meir Wasser) 59, 60 n. 6
Rang, Florens Christian 287
Rapaport, Y. 126 n. 76
Rapoport, Charles 3, 9
Rapoport, Sara 160
Realists 51
Red Army:
  Jewish attitudes to 57, 138–9, 149–50, 299
  and Soviet control of Kielce 161–3
  and Soviet control of Vilna 107–9, 110–12, 119–20, 124, 125, 132
Red Cross Society 6
refugees:
  and the Bund 76, 77
  confiscation of property 149
  and Palestine 198
  and Soviet-occupied Vilna 109, 122, 125–30, 198
  in Warsaw 214, 219
Reichskristallnacht 149
Reis, Anshel 70
Rejzen, Miriam 116 n. 26, 118 n. 38
Rejzen, Zalman 113, 117–19, 124 n. 67
Remiszewski, Antoni 86 n. 41
resistance:
  civilian 143, 144–5, 153–7, 205–9, 297–9
  passive 145, 297
  through education 212–31
  see also underground movements
revolution 1905:
  and antisemitism 23 n. 20
  and the Bund 12, 37
  and PPS Proletariat 32
Reznikowska, Teresa 18, 137
Riehl, W. 283
rights, civic:
  and 1912 Duma elections 52–3
  and the Bund xx, 18–19, 69–70, 80
  and Łódź municipal elections 63
  and nationality 23, 27
Ringelblum Archives 297–8
Ringelblum, Emanuel 148, 152–3, 221, 233, 280
Rivkind, Jacob 115
Robotniczo-Chłopska Organizacja Bojowa (Workers' and Peasants' Fighting Squad) 153
Robotniczy Komitet Pomocy Uchodzcom z Niemiec (Workers' Committee for Aid to Refugees from Germany) 76, 77
Robotnik (The worker) 17, 28, 29
Romm, A. 124 n. 70
Rosenberg, Chil 89
Rosenhak, Shmuel 125 n. 74
Rosental, Anna 115 n. 25, 118
Rosiak, Paweł 89
Rosiiskaya Sotsial-Demokraticheskaya i Rabochaya Partia (RSDRP: Russian Social Democratic and Workers' Party) 32, 37, 44
Roth, Joseph 283
Roth, Philip 256
Rozenberg, Lajbuś 99
Rozenberg, Szaja 98–9
Rozenblatt, Jerzy 98
Rozenkranc family 161–2
Rozenzweig, Franz 289
Rubenstein, Richard 296
Rubinstein, Reuven 135, 136 n. 130
Rudnicki, Shemaia 130 n. 99
Rudnicki, Szymon 232
rumour:
  in Soviet-occupied Kielce 164–5, 171 n. 7, 303
  in Soviet-occupied Vilna 123–4, 127–8, 131–3
Ruppin, Arthur 68 n. 34
Russ, Benjamin 99
Russia:
  1912 Duma elections 45–54
  and the Bund 33, 38, 43, 59 n. 3
  civil war 57
  and Jewish Socialists 3, 12
  see also revolution 1905; social democracy; Soviet Union
Russian, and Jewish surnames 291–4
Russian partition, Socialism 10, 15, 17, 22
Russian revolution xx, 55–7
Russification 16, 17, 36
Rutherford, Ernest 255

Rutkowski, Adam 161
Ryszka, Franciszek 232

S
Sablik, Beata 235
Sacher-Masoch, Leopold von 282, 283
Sachs, F. 13
Sak, Yosef 221
Sakowska, Ruta 297–9
Samek, Jerzy 235
Samsonowicz, Henryk 235
Sanacja:
    and antisemitism 28, 61, 177
    disintegration 86
    and municipal elections 1936 89, 93–6, 102, 104–6
    and Sejm elections 1935 84
    and Stronnictwo Ludowe 65
Sandauer, Artur 303
Sandberg, Zofia 3
Sarner, Harvey, *A i B* 247–54
Schaeder, Grete 286, 287, 288
Schaeffer, Rafael 125 n. 74
Schatz, Jaff xvii
Schatz-Uffenheimer, Rivka 274–6
Schofman, G. 125 n. 74
Schopenhauer, Artur 268
Schubert, Kurt 272
Schubert, Ursula 273–4
Schwalb, Nathan 198, 200, 207
Secessionists 32, 33–4
Second International Congress (1891) 19, 37–8, 44
Second World War:
    and Jewish underground 148–57
    and Polish underground 138–47
    and Soviet occupation of Vilna 107–37
Segalowich, Z. 126 n. 76
Seidenman, S. 134
Seidler, Alfred 100
Sejm:
    elections: 1922 82; 1928 89; 1930 63 n. 21, 79; 1935 78, 84
    and Jewish delegates 70
separatism 12, 18, 24, 26, 30
Sephardic Judaism:
    Bible manuscripts 273–4
    and sexuality 259–62
Serwatka, Karol 100
sexuality:
    and image of Jews 256–64, 267–70
    and rabbinate 256, 258–63, 267–9
Shafran, Nahman (Natan) 76
'Shalom' Foundation for the Promotion of Polish Jewish Culture 232

Shamir, Josef (Diament) 116
Shapiro, Robert Moses 280
Shapiro, Y. 124 n. 70
Shatzky, Jacob 280
Shedletzky, Itta 283
Sherer, Emanuel 80
Shmercowicz, Leib 114 n. 19
Shmeruk, Chone 280
Shperber 117, 130 n. 100
Shpizan, L. 126 n. 76
Shwarz, Pinhas 126 n. 76
Shweitzer, David 72
Sierp i Młot (Hammer and Sickle) 153
Sikorski, Władysław 157
Siła-Nowicki, Władysław 234
Silesia, Jewish population 235
Simon, Ernst 286, 287, 288
Singer, Bernard 46–52
Singer, Isaac Bashevis 281
Singer, Kalman 168
Skidelski, Rachel 111 n. 12
Skif (Sotsialistisher Kinder Farband) 78
Składkowski, F. Sławoj 62
Skurkowicz, Shmuel 110 n. 8
slaughter, ritual 61, 71, 81
Słoniewski, Modest 86
Słonimski, Chaim Zelig 5
Slowes, S. 124 n. 70
Słowo młodych (Gordonia newspaper) 219–21, 224 n. 38
Smolak, Kurt 272
Smolar, Aleksander 150
Smolar, Grzegorz 177 n. 28
Sobczyński, Władysław 168 n. 36
social democracy:
    and 1912 Duma elections 45–6
    Austrian 18, 19–24, 40, 43
    in Germany 8, 64 n. 23
    Jewish 15–16
    Polish 14, 15–16, 26, 45–6
    in Russia 3, 10, 12, 19, 32, 44
    in Vilna 10
Social Democratic Party of Russia 12, 19
Socialism:
    and 1912 Duma elections 45–53
    and acculturation 7, 10
    and antisemitism xviii, xix–xx, 17, 18, 20–1, 28, 67–9, 70
    attractions for Jews xviii–xix
    Austrian 15
    European 60
    Jewish, *see* Bund
    and the Jewish question xvii, xix–xx, 7–11, 14–31, 32–44, 58, 66–7
    in Kingdom of Poland 3–13

and Piłsudski xvii, xx, 3, 9
and Polish nationalism 16, 67
and religious belief 8
and repression of Jews 140
and role of Jews xvii–xviii, 3–4, 12
Russian 15
see also Polish Socialist party; Polskie Socjaliści
Socialist Electoral Alliance 52 n. 10, 53
Socialist International 28
and Jews 56
Second 59–61
Socialist Party, Germany 60 n. 6
Socialist Zionists 153, 154, 196 n. 1
Socialists, and Jewish emigration 58
Socjaldemokracja Królestwa Polskiego i Litwy (SDKPiL: Social Democracy of the Kingdom of Poland and Lithuania):
and 1912 Duma elections 45, 49, 51–2, 54
Jewish involvement xx, 8, 12
and Jewish nationality 37, 40, 43, 44
and the Jewish problem 14, 19
Third Congress 37
Sokolow, Nahum 52–3
Sokołów Podlaski, and antisemitism of 1956 179
Sombart, Werner 56
Somin, Bettina 273
Soviet Union:
attitude of Jews towards 139, 145, 149, 151–7, 203
attitude of Poles towards 139, 149–50, 162–4
and control of Kielce 161–3, 166–7
and control of Vilna 107–37, 151–2, 198
and emigration of Jews to Palestine 166
emigration to 127–30, 137, 215
and Jewish surnames 289
labour camps 161, 163
and Nazi–Soviet pact 108, 151, 204, 225
and postwar antisemitism 170–1
repatriation from 181
Sozialistischer Jugenbund 100
Spartacus League 8
Spektor, Mordechaj 125 n. 74
Spiewak, Paweł 234
Sprawa robotnicza (The workers' cause) 8, 9
Stalin, Joseph, and Bund 59, 60 n. 6
starvation:
in ghettos 139, 154, 215, 220, 229
in Vilna 108–9, 119, 121, 126, 133
Stefan Batory Foundation 232
Steinlauf, M. 79 n. 64
Sternhell, Zeev 56 n. 4
Stolarek, Aleksandr 97

Stowarzyszenie Robotników Chrześcijańskich (SRCh: Association of Christian Workers) 91–2
Stowarzyszenie Zjednoczenie Zawodowe (Christian Trade Association) 91–2, 95
Stowarzyszenie Kobiece (Association of Women) 96
Stowarzyszenie Przyjaciół ZSRR (Society of Friendship for the USSR) 153
Straszewicz, Ludwik 51
strikes 49, 61–2, 63, 71, 84, 89
Stronnictwo Ludowe (SL: Peasants' Party) 65, 70
Stronnictwo Narodowe (National Party) 96–8, 101–3, 105, 146
Stronnictwo Pracy (Labour Party) 140
Stryjkowski, Julian 234, 235
suffrage, restrictions 85
surnames, Jewish 289–95
Świda-Ziemba, Hanna 233
Szacki, Jakub 233
Szaniec (The rampart) 143–4
Szawel, Szyfra 6
Szczerkowski, Antoni 90
Szereszewski, C. 4
Szewczyk, Artur 105
Szkleniarz, Paweł (Wiktor Kuźnicki) 168 n. 36
Sztajn, Fanny 6
Sztrauch, Zurech 105
Szulc, Henryk 97
Szwajdler, Franciszek 97
Szymanowska, Celina 278

T
Tabaczyński, Benjamin 74, 77
Tartakover, Arieh 70
taxation, and Council of Four Lands 188–90
Tec, Nechama 296
Teitl, Josef 118
Tennenbaum-Tamaroff, Mordechai 153–4, 156, 157, 196–7, 206, 209–10, 228
territory, and nationhood 25, 29, 30, 37, 40
terror:
against Jews 138–9, 149
against Poles 138
terrorism 34, 42, 101
theatre, Jewish 234–5
Toaff, Ariel 272
Tomaszewski, Jerzy 232
Tomczyk, Anna 92
Tomkevicz, Benjamin 125 n. 74
Torah, in Hasidism 263, 275
Towiański, Andrzej 277
transport, Jews banned from 138, 149, 221
Treblinka extermination camp 161, 203
Trop, Sarah 6

Tropper, Morris 74 n. 48
Trotsky, Leon 57
Trusiewicz, Stanisław 37
Trybuna ludu (Tribune of the people) 172–3, 180
Trybuna wolmości (Tribune of freedom) 145
tsadikim, graves 233–4, 236
Tsayt (Zionist daily) 118
Tsentralrat fun Yidishe Proffaraynen (Central Association of Jewish Trade Unions) 75
Tsherikover, A. 5
Tsheslo, Max 118 n. 35
Tsimbler, Avram 118 n. 35
Tsintsinatus, Aaron 118
Tsisho (Tsentrale Yidishe Shul Organizatsie) 71, 73, 74, 77
Tsukunft (Bund youth movement) 65, 78
Tułecki, Szymon 86 n. 41
Tygodnik powszechny 234
Tyrnauer, Gabriella 296
Tyszka, Jan, *see* Jogiches, Leon

U

ugoda (agreement) 82
Ukrainian, and Jewish surnames 290, 293–4
underground movements xxi
  Jewish 139, 143–6, 148–57, 208–9, 297–8
  Polish 138–47, 148, 150, 154, 163 n. 22, 169
  see also youth movements
unemployment:
  and municipal elections 1936 97, 100–1
  in Soviet-occupied Vilna 119, 122, 128
UNESCO, Polish Committee 232, 236
Unia Związków Zawodowych Pracowników Umysłowych (Association of Trade Unions of White-Collar Workers) 93, 95
Unified Jewish Front, Górna and Chojna Districts 98
Unified Zionist Bloc 98–9
Union of Petty Merchants 98
Union of Primary School Teachers 101
Union of the Russian People 49 n. 4
Union of Socialist Artisans 63
Union of State Zionists 98
Union of White-Collar Workers 93, 95
Union of Young Catholic 'Revivalists' 92
unions:
  and the Bund 75–6
  Jewish workers 69, 71, 77, 82, 98
  and municipal elections 1936 90–1, 93–5, 98–100, 101–5
  in Soviet-occupied Vilna 119
  in the United States 71–2, 74
United Jewish Electoral Bloc 98, 99, 105

United Jewish Social-Economic Front 99
United States:
  and the Bund 71–2, 74–5, 76–7
  Jewish workers' unions in 71–2, 74–5
Urząd Bezpieczeństwa (Office of Public Security) 165, 168, 172, 180

V

Va'ad Arba Aratsot, *see* Council of Four Lands
Veseille, Otton 86
Vienna Government Council 21–2
Viestnik Bundu (Herald of the Bund) 39
Vilna:
  and emergence of Socialism 3–4, 6, 8, 11–12, 17
  and Jewish social democrats 10
  and Jewish underground 154, 156, 157, 209
  and Palestine 198, 202
  and Soviet control xxi, 107–37, 151–2; bombing 108, 109–10; cultural sphere 122–4; economic sphere 119–21; first reactions 110–13, 149; and internal security 131–6; and Jewish migration 124–31; and newspapers 113–14, 123; Poles in 131–3, 135; political sphere 113–18; and relocation of Elektrit factory 108, 121, 127–8
  and youth movements 215
Vilner tog [Vila daily] 113–14, 117
violence, anti-Jewish 65–6, 131
  see also pogroms
Vize, Adolf 94
Vladek, Berl 75 n. 50
Vladimir Medem Sanatorium 73–4, 77
Vperiod (Forward) 4–5

W

Wachowicz, Henryk 90
Wadowski, Marian 96
Wałbrzych, and antisemitism of 1956 173, 178–9
Walczak, Adam 105
Waldheim, Kurt 296
Walecki, H. (Maksymilian Horowitz) 12, 23
Walt, Hayyim 118
Warhaftig, Zerach 125, 215 n. 6
Warsaw:
  1912 Duma elections 45–54
  Academy of Catholic Theology 236
  and anti-Jewish boycott 50–1
  Communists 153
  ghetto deaths 139, 201
  history 280–2
  kehillot elections 63
  Mayor 232, 234
  Oberpolitseimeister 52–4
  population 233, 281

Socialists 10, 12, 45, 48–9
uprising 145–6, 147, 156, 197, 206, 209, 212–31, 297
workers' curia 48–9, 54
and youth movements 206, 209, 212–31
see also ghetto
Warszawski głos narodowy (Warsaw national voice) 146
Waryński, Ludwik 51
Wasilewska, Sofia (Wanda) 67
Wasilewski, Leon 18, 25–6
Waszkiewicz, Franciszek 86 n. 41
Waszkiewicz, Ludwik 92, 93
Weber-Lutkow, Hans 282
Wegrzynek, Hanna 235
Weinreich, Uriel 124 n. 67
Weinstein, Leibl 118
Weizmann, Chaim 55–6, 123 n. 62
Wenninger, Marcus J. 272
Wenzel, Edith 273
Wiatr, Jerzy J. 37 n. 25
Wic, Władysław 43
Wilchowsky, S. 221
Widuczański, Mendl 118 n. 35
Wiedza (Knowledge) 51–2
Wielguś, Stanisław 233
Wierczak, Karol 96
Wileński, T. (J. Kwiatek) 13, 14, 23
Wilensky, Mordecai 276
Winchewski, Morys 4, 6
Winkler, Paula 287
Wischnitzer, Mark 188
Wiśniewski, Eugeniusz 86
Wistrich, Robert xvii
Wittenberg, Itzik 130 n. 97, 154
WIZO (Women's International Zionist Organization) 98
Wodziński, Marcin 233–4, 236
Wojewódzki i Miejski Komitet Żidow w Polsce (Provincial and City Committee of Jews in Poland) 161
Wojewódzki, Wacław 86 n. 41
Wojewódzkie Urząd Bezpieczeństwa Publicznego (Provincial Office of Public Security)
  Kielce 165
  Poznań 172
  Wrocław 180
Wojkowski, Franciszek 105
Wojskowy Sąd Rejonowy (Regional Military Court) 168 n. 36
Wolf, Elcan Isaac 266
Wolf, Leizer 130 n. 100
Wołyń, and Home Army 144
women:
  and images of Jews 257–8, 262
  and sexuality 258–64, 266, 268–70
  as Socialist activists 6–7
Workers' Guard, Vilna 108, 114–15, 128, 129, 132–3
working classes, *see* proletariat
World Jewish Congress 70
World Union of Mapai 196 n. 1
Worończak, Jerzy 233, 236
Wróbel, Józef 235
Wróbel, Piotr 280–1
Wróblewski, Wacław 49
Wrocław, and antisemitism of 1956 173, 180
Wrona, Zenon 302–4
Wygodski, Jacob 136
Wymysłowski, Michał 96
Wynot, Edward D. 281
Wysocki, Adam 86 n. 41
Wyszyński, Cardinal Stefan 181, 303

Y
Ya'ari, Meir 203, 209
Yankelevitz, S. 120
Yazborovskaya, Inessa 33
Yermolayeva, Rosaliya 33
yeshivot, Socialist view 5, 6
Yeushzon, S. 126 n. 76
Yiddish:
  and the German intelligentsia 11
  and Jewish Socialism 18, 20, 21–2, 35
  knowledge of 236
  and nationalism 22, 27, 36, 44
  newspapers 46–8, 49
  right to use 12, 23, 36, 37
  study 273
  and surnames 290–4
  and youth movements 217
Yidish Kultur Farband (YKUF: Yiddish Cultural Association) 117–18
Yidisher Arbayter Komitet (Jewish Labour Committee) 72, 74–6, 78
Yidisher Arbayter Farband in Varshe (Jewish Labour Union in Warsaw) 11
Yishuv, and youth movements 116, 195, 197–9, 201, 203, 207, 210–11
YIVO, and Soviet occupation of Vilna 118, 124
Yonas, Elijahu 127 n. 85
youth movements:
  emissaries from 198–9, 205, 207, 213–14, 284
  and Erets Israel 116, 151, 195–211, 213, 216–17, 225
  and *gedudim* 216, 217, 218, 219
  and *kevutsot* 216, 218
  and kibbutzim 196, 205, 213–14, 225–7
  and *pelugot* 218

youth movements (*cont.*):
  and resistance through education 208–9, 212–31
  source material on 195–7, 199–200, 284
  and welfare projects 219–20, 231

Z

Zagajski family 161–2
Zagajski, Stanisław 160
Zagłębie, and the Bund 80–1
Zaideman, Maurycy 53
Zaleska-Jankowska, Maria 13
Zalewska, Gabriela 233
Zalkind, Ber 130 n. 100
Zambrowski, Roman 170, 179
Zand, Chaja 90
Zaremba, Zygmunt 30
Żarnowski, Janusz 233
Zarząd Główny Towarzystwa Społeczno-Kulturnego Żydów w Polsce (TSKZ: Social Cultural Society of Jews in Poland) 177 n. 28, 178, 180–1, 232
Zatloukal, Klaus 271–4
Zdrojewski, Marian 86 n. 41
Zdziechowski, M. 91, 105
Zdziechowski, W. 99
Żegota (Council for Aid to Jews) 147
Zeidenman, S. 125 n. 74
Zeidman, Moshe 125 n. 74
Żeleński, Tadeusz (Boy) 276–7
Zelyanin, M. 113, 127 n. 83
Zerbe, Emil 90, 100
Zevi Hirsch of Zhidachov 275–6
Zheleznikov, Jacob 115 n. 25, 118
Zhitlovski, Chaim 75 n. 50
Zhofer, Y. 118 n. 35, 135
Zienkowska, Krystyna 280
Zionism:
  and the Bund 38–9, 61, 67–71
  First World Congress 15
  and German occupation 151–3
  and Jewish emigration 66–9, 80, 166
  and Jewish underground 153–4
  and municipal elections 1936 105; 1938–9 79, 80
  and physical strength 267
  Russian 57
  and Socialism 13, 17, 21, 51, 69
  Socialist 153, 154, 196 n. 1
  and Soviet occupation of Vilna 118, 125, 128
  and Soviet Union 203–4
  youth movements 151, 195–211, 212–31

Zionist-Revisionists 99, 125 n. 74, 154, 251–2
Zjednoczenie Zawodowe Polskie (Union of Polish Trades) 92
Zjednoczone Stronnictwo Ludowe (ZSL: United Peasants' Party) 180–1
Zjednoczony Komitet Mniejszości Narodowych (United Committee of National Minorities) 82
Zohar, and sexuality 261–2
Zuckerman, Yitzhak (Antek) 197, 209–11, 223–4
Zucotti, Susan 296
Zundelewicz, Aron 3, 4
Związek Izb Rzemieślniczych (Union of Craftsmen's Chambers) 178
Związek Legionistów Polskich (Union of Polish Legionaries) 93
Związek Nauczycielstwa Polskiego (Union of Polish Teachers) 93
Związek Posłów Narodowści Żydowskiej (Union of Delegates of Jewish Nationality) 27
Związek Rezerwistów (Union of Reservists) 93
Związek Rzemieślników Chrześcijań (Union of Christian Artisans) 94
Związek Studentów-Żydów (Union of Jewish Students) 301
Związek Zagraniczny Socjalistów Polskich (Union of Polish Socialists Abroad) 17, 18
Związek Zawodowy Pracowników Handlowych (Trade Union of Businessmen) 101
Związki Zawodowe 'Praca' (Trade Unions 'Work') 92, 95
Zwierzewicz, Ewaryst 97
Żydowska Organizacja Bojowa (ZOB: Jewish Fighting Organization) 153, 155, 298
Żydowska Organizacja Polskiej Partii Socjalistycznej (Jewish Organization of the PPS) 11, 19
Żydowska Partia Robotnicza (Jewish Workers' Party) 20
Żydowska Partia Socjalno-Demokratyczna (Jewish Social Democratic Party) 15, 21, 24
Żydowska Socjalna-Demokracja Galicji (Jewish Social Democracy of Galicia) 21
Żydowski Komitet Narodowy (Jewish National Committee) 156
Żydowski Związek Robotniczy w Warszawie 11
Żydowski Związek Wojskowsky (Jewish Army Union) 154
Żyndul, Jolanta 234

CPSIA information can be obtained
at www.ICGtesting.com
Printed in the USA
LVOW01s1801180117
521395LV00003B/94/P